UNITED NATIONS FORCES

FINN SEYERSTED

UNITED NATIONS FORCES
IN THE LAW OF PEACE AND WAR

A. W. SIJTHOFF – LEYDEN
1966

Library of Congress Catalog Card Number: 66-25084

Printed in the Netherlands

TO SÖLVI

ACKNOWLEDGEMENTS

The writer wishes to express his gratitude for valuable material and information provided throughout the preparation of this book by officials of the United Nations, including in particular Mr. C. Stavropoulos, Legal Counsel, Dr. Oscar Schachter, Director, General Legal Division, and Messrs. W. Cox and Blaine Sloan, Deputy Directors; by officials of the *Comité international de la Croix-Rouge*, including in particular, MM. Pictet and Pilloud, Directeur et Directeur-adjoint des Affaires générales; and by the libraries of the Norwegian Ministry for Foreign Affairs and the Norwegian Nobel Institute, as well as several libraries in Vienna. The writer also wishes to express his thanks for helpful material and information provided by Dr. Rémy Gorgé, Legal Adviser of UN-FICYP, former Legal Adviser of UNTSO, UNEF and ONUC; by MM. Saba and Lussier, Legal Adviser and Deputy Legal Adviser of UNESCO; by Lieutenant-Colonel Björn Egge, Royal Norwegian Army, formerly with ONUC; by Mr. Alf Monsen, General Advocate, Royal Norwegian Army; by Lieutenant-Colonel Arne Sörensen, Royal Norwegian Ministry of Defence; by Mr. Sverker Åström, Swedish Permanent Delegate to the United Nations, and Count Wachtmeister, Deputy Director, Royal Swedish Ministry for Foreign Affairs; by Ambassador von Numers, then Director, Legal Department, Finnish Ministry for Foreign Affairs; by Mr. Egil Amlie, Deputy Director and Mr. Per Ravne, Chief of Division, Royal Norwegian Ministry for Foreign Affairs; by Mr. Ole Bierring, Royal Danish Ministry for Foreign Affairs; by MM. Hans Blix, Kaj Sundberg and J. Wingstrand, Royal Swedish Ministry for Foreign Affairs; by Mr. G. F. Bruce of the Canadian Foreign Service; by the Norwegian Institute for International Affairs; and by the libraries of the *Palais des Nations* and the Peace Palace.

The Editors of the *British Year Book of International Law*, Sir Humphrey Waldock, and of the *Österreichische Zeitschrift für öffentliches Recht*, Professors Verdross and Zemanek, have kindly permitted the incorporation, with additions, into the present book, as Chapters I-IV, of articles by the present writer which appeared in their publications for 1961 and 1962, respectively.

The writer is also indebted to Professor François, Secretary-General of the Permanent Court of Arbitration, and to Sijthoff's Uitgeversmaatschappij N.V., for their assistance and work, respectively, in connexion with the publication of the book.

7

ACKNOWLEDGEMENTS

Typing, composition and checking have been efficiently done by a number of helpful assistants, including Miss E. Houdek, Miss M. Lindholm and Mrs. R. Macmillan.

The photo on the cover has been kindly supplied by the Royal Norwegian Army.

Above all, the writer wishes to thank his wife, Sölvi, without whose manifold assistance this book could never have been written.

All views expressed in the present book are the personal views of the writer and should not be attributed to the Norwegian Ministry for Foreign Affairs or to the International Atomic Energy Agency.

CONTENTS

Chapter I

CIVILIAN FORCES INDIVIDUALLY ENLISTED BY THE UNITED NATIONS

Chapter II

MILITARY FORCES COMPOSED OF NATIONAL CONTINGENTS: EXTENT OF UNITED NATIONS CONTROL

Chapter III

INTERNATIONAL REPRESENTATION OF AND RESPONSIBILITY FOR THE FORCE

Chapter IV

COMPETENCE TO ESTABLISH AND OPERATE FORCES AND TO PERFORM OTHER ACTS WITHOUT CONSTITUTIONAL PROVISIONS

Chapter V

APPLICATION OF THE LAWS OF WAR. GENERAL

Chapter VI

EXTENT OF APPLICABILITY OF THE LAWS OF WAR TO
ACTIONS AGAINST AN AGGRESSOR
DISCRIMINATION IN FAVOUR OF THE UNITED NATIONS?

Chapter VII

POSITION VIS-A-VIS NON-MEMBERS
IS RECOGNITION OF THE UNITED NATIONS REQUIRED?

Chapter VIII

THE CONVENTIONS ON WARFARE

Chapter IX

Annexes

ABBREVIATIONS

(chiefly used in footnote references)

AJIL	The American Journal of International Law
BYIL	The British Year Book of International Law
ECOSOC	The Economic and Social Council of the United Nations
GA	The General Assembly of the United Nations (Roman numeral indicates the number of the session)
ICJ	International Court of Justice
ONUC	Organisation des Nations Unies au Congo, also used for the United Nations Force in the Congo
OR	Official Records
Recueil des Cours	Académie de droit international (La Haye), Recueil des Cours
SC	The Security Council of the United Nations
UNEF	The United Nations Emergency Force in the Middle East
UNESCO	United Nations Educational, Scientific and Cultural Organization
UNFICYP	The United Nations Force in Cyprus
UNTS	United Nations Treaty Series

Earlier studies by the present writer are usually cited merely by a reference to the reviews in which they have been published:

BYIL, 1961: The British Year Book of International Law, XXXVII (1961) pp. 351–475 (United Nations Forces, Some Legal Problems)

Indian Journal of International Law, IV (1964) pp. 1–74 and 233-268 (International Personality of Intergovernmental Organizations)

International and Comparative Law Quarterly, XIV (1965) pp. 31-82 and 493-527 (Jurisdiction over Organs and Officials of States, the Holy See and Intergovernmental Organizations)

Nordisk Tidsskrift (for international Ret og Jus gentium) XXXIV (1964) pp. 1-112 (Objective International Personality of Intergovernmental Organizations)

Tidsskrift for rettsvitenskap (Oslo), 1945, pp. 113-138, and 1946, pp. 267-308 (Okkupantens 'rettigheter'—spesielt overfor offentlige tjenestemenn)

Zeitschrift für ausländisches öffentliches Recht und Völkerrecht, XXIV (1964) pp. 1-121 (Settlement of Internal Disputes of Intergovernmental Organizations by Internal and External Courts)

INTRODUCTION [1]

Since 1950 the United Nations has on a number of occasions (Korea, the Middle East, the Congo, West New Guinea and Cyprus) established a military Force for the purpose of combatting aggression or performing peace-keeping functions. This has brought home to the world, as never previously, both the importance and the diverse implications of international military action. In 1961 the British Commonwealth Prime Ministers' Conference proposed the establishment of a Force 'to prevent aggression and enforce observance of disarmament agreements'. The following year both the Soviet Union and the United States of America included provisions for a United Nations Force to fight aggression in the proposals which they submitted to the Disarmament Conference in Geneva. Two years later the Soviet Union submitted more detailed proposals for such a Force under the Security Council; under these the Force would not be composed of contingents provided by the permanent Members of the Council. Parallel with this, the Scandinavian and certain other countries in 1964 established permanent military units trained and ready for participation upon call in United Nations peace-

1. The following general literature may be cited: Mezerik: 'The United Nations Emergency Force', *International Review Service*, III (1957) No. 33; Scheuner: 'Eine internationale Sicherungsmacht im Dienste der Vereinten Nationen', *Zeitschrift für ausländisches öffentliches Recht und Völkerrecht*, XIX (1958) pp. 389–415; Kunzmann: 'Aktuelle Vorschläge für eine Friedenstruppe der Vereinten Nationen', *Europa-Archiv*, XII (1958) pp. 10811–26, Danish translation in excerpts in *Nordisk Tidsskrift for international Ret*, XXIX (1959) pp. 32–48; Schwarzenberger: 'Problems of a United Nations Force', *Current Legal Problems* (1959) pp. 247–68; 'Report of the Committee on the Charter of the United Nations on Problems of a United Nations Force' (with discussion) in the International Law Association's *Report of the Forty-Ninth Conference, Hamburg 1960*, pp. 96–152. For a more complete list, see *ibid, Forty-Eighth Conference, New York 1958*, pp. 627–8. A fairly complete list, not limited to legal literature, may be found in *Frydenberg: Peace-Keeping, Experience and Evaluation - The Oslo Papers* (Oslo 1964) pp. 333–9. More recent general legal publications include: *Clark and Sohn: World Peace through World Law, 2nd edition* (Cambridge, Mass., 1960) at pp. 314–34; *Weissberg:* The International Status of the United Nations (New York 1961) at pp. 78–140; Gamal el din *Attia: Les forces armées des Nations Unies en Corée et au Moyen-Orient* (Genève 1963); *Bowett: United Nations Forces, a Legal Study of United Nations Practice* (London 1964); and *Frydenberg, op. cit.*, pp. 211–312. Studies of special Forces or special legal aspects have been cited at the appropriate headings below. Some of the information related in Chapters I-II has been based upon the earlier studies listed above. It has only to a limited extent been possible to add footnote references to the more recent studies listed above.

keeping Forces.[2] These proposals and actions have lent further emphasis to the problems of United Nations Forces.

The present study is concerned with both combat and peace-keeping Forces, although in the chapters dealing with the laws of war the main emphasis naturally is on combat Forces. First each Force will be examined separately, from the point of view of facts, in order to establish notably its mandate, its system of command and its relationship to the Charter. Then the external legal problems relating to the Forces, i.e. their position under international law, will be examined in respect of United Nations Forces generally, concentrating upon problems which are not directly linked to the mandate of, or otherwise specific to any given United Nations Force[3] and which are not usually solved by express provisions in the relevant instruments. These problems include notably the international responsibility for and representation of the Force, the establishment of Forces in cases other than those specified in the Charter, the relationship to non-members and, especially, the application of the laws of war. The relationship to the host State, which is usually defined in detailed agreements concluded in each case,[4] as well as the internal legal problems relating to the Force and to the distribution of powers between the various organs of the United Nations will not be specially dealt with.[5]

In connection with particular problems of United Nations Forces, the study also takes up certain general problems of the laws of war and of the law of intergovernmental organizations which have not been sufficiently examined elsewhere. The former problems include that of discrimination between an aggressor and a defending State.[6] The latter problems include those of the capacity of the Organization to perform acts not specified in its constitution,[7] its capacity to become a party to multilateral conventions between States[8] and its capacity to exercise criminal jurisdiction.[9]

2. *Below*, Chapter II, 10.

3. In this respect reference is made to the studies which have been published on specific Forces, see above, note 1, and at each Force *below*, in Chapter II.

4. See Jean Salmon: 'L'accord O.N.U.-Congo (Léopoldville) du 27 Novembre 1961', *Revue générale de droit public*, 1964, pp. 60–109.

5. See, however, *below*, Chapter IV, 4(d).

6. Chapter VI, 2, pp. 222–269.

7. Chapter IV, 3.

8. Chapter VIII, 9.

9. Chapter VIII, 11.

CHAPTER I

CIVILIAN FORCES INDIVIDUALLY ENLISTED
BY THE UNITED NATIONS

Neither the United Nations nor any other intergovernmental organization is known to have ever established a genuine military force by direct international recruitment. The many important proposals for an international police force which were made during the period of the League of Nations were never seriously considered by the League;[1] and the proposal of Secretary-General Trygve Lie in 1948 for a United Nations Guard, composed of from 800 to several thousand uniformed, lightly armed men recruited by the Secretary-General as a unit of the Secretariat,[2] received no support from the Big Powers and had to be abandoned. His proposal of 1952, for a *United Nations Legion,* composed of volunteers but recruited and trained on a national basis, suffered the same fate. The three different examples of special non-fighting groups recruited by the United Nations which will now be examined do, however, furnish some material for a discussion of the legal position of an individually enlisted international military force.

1. UNITED NATIONS GUARD AND UNITED NATIONS FIELD SERVICE

The first example is the force of uniformed, unarmed United Nations Guards established at an early date for the purpose of maintaining order and security at headquarters (Headquarters Guard Force, Headquarters Security Service). These guards are recruited individually as members of the Secretariat. Again, in 1948 a special force of some fifty United Nations Guards was sent to Palestine to assist the military observers of the truces ordered by the Security Council. These, too, wore United

---

1. See citations in *Sohn: Cases and Materials on World Law* (Brooklyn 1950) pp. 852–3. Many proposals concerned an international force made up of national contingents; see, for example, the French proposals submitted to the Disarmament Conference 1932 (reproduced *ibid.,* pp. 845–9), under which the League would arrange for the command of the international police force and would be entitled to inspect its component elements.

2. A/656, *OR GA*, 3rd session, Part 2, Annexes, pp. 6 et seq.

Nations uniforms and were unarmed, and some of them lost their lives owing to military action by the opposing sides.[3]

Then in 1949 the General Assembly, by Resolution 297 (IV), authorized the establishment by the Secretary-General of a United Nations Field Service on the basis of a Secretariat proposal which had been considerably modified as compared to the original proposal for a United Nations Guard Force.[4] This force of 350 men, recruited individually as part of the Secretariat from among young and physically fit men 'with field experience', wear United Nations uniforms, but carry arms (side-arms) only in special cases. Their functions are entirely civilian and consist of providing technical services for missions (transportation, radio communications, security of members, premises, supplies and archives, maintenance of order during meetings) as well as doing guard duties at headquarters. The communist countries opposed the creation of the Field Service on the ground that it had 'the character of a military unit'. But the majority of the Special Committee which reported on the Secretariat proposal felt that the Field Service 'could not be considered as an armed force under Article 43 of the Charter, nor could it ever be used for enforcement purposes under Chapter VII'.[5] The Field Service has been employed with a number of United Nations missions in troubled areas, including Palestine, Kashmir and Korea.

2. MILITARY OBSERVERS

The second example, which concerns a rather different type of force, is the truce observation groups and the other military observation missions which the United Nations has employed in a number of troubled areas,[6]

3. The first—and indeed the first United Nations official to give his life—was Ole Helge Bakke, a Norwegian citizen. He was killed on 13 July 1948 by a shot fired by an Arab soldier (see the reports of the Secretary-General contained in documents A/674 [1948] and A/1347 [1949]).

4. See the modified proposal of the Secretary-General and the report of the Special Committee on a United Nations Guard in *OR GA*, 4th session, Suppl. No. 13. Extracts, and the text of the resolution, may be found in *Repertory of Practice of UN Organs*, V, pp. 266–8. The Secretary-General's report is also reproduced in *Sohn: Cases and Materials on World Law*, pp. 853–62. See also *Repertory of Practice of United Nations Organs*, at Article 101, especially Vol. V, p. 218.

5. *OR GA*, 3rd session, part 2, plenary meetings, Annexes, p. 10.

6. See in general, *Ereli: United Nations Supervision of Provisional Measures for the Cessation of Hostilities* (1956), unpublished thesis, Fletcher School of Law and Diplomacy, Medford, Mass., U.S.A.; and Mohn: 'Problems of Truce Supervision', *International Conciliation* (1952) No. 478.

including Palestine,[7] Kashmir,[8] Lebanon,[9] West New Guinea (Irian Barat) [10] and Yemen,[11] and which the League of Nations employed in Vilna in 1920-2.[12] The members of these groups (except sometimes for their commanders [13]) are not recruited as members of the Secretariat, but are seconded, on an individual and temporary basis, from the armies of Member States. They are normally volunteers, but are sometimes ordered by their national authorities to serve with the United Nations. They wear their own country's uniforms, with distinctive United Nations markings. They usually retain their salaries from their Governments, which are then reimbursed by the United Nations. In addition, the United Nations pays directly to the members certain allowances and, furthermore, provides facilities and assumes responsibility for total disability or death. The observers are instructed by and report to the United Nations. They are assisted by regular United Nations staff members (including members of the Field Service) who perform political, legal, administrative, communications and other functions of a civilian character.

7. The United Nations Truce Supervision Organization (UNTSO) was established by the United Nations Mediator for Palestine, under the authority of the Security Council's resolutions of 29 May and 15 July 1949, to observe the truces ordered by the Council. Article X of the Armistice Agreement concluded at Rhodes on 24 February 1949 between Israel and Egypt and the corresponding provisions of the armistice agreements concluded with the other Arab states authorized UNTSO to observe the armistices (*UNTS*, Vol. 42, pp. 251 et seq.). See Hurewitz: 'The United Nations Conciliation Commission for Palestine', *International Organization*, VII (1953) pp. 484–97; *International Review Service*, III (1957) No. 33, pp. 7–8; and the Reports of the United Nations Mediator.

8. The United Nations Military Observer Group in India and Pakistan was established by authority of the Security Council's Resolution of 21 April 1948 (par. 17) and was authorized to station observers where it deemed necessary by the cease-fire line agreement concluded on 27 July 1949 (S/1430, Annex 26). See Lourié: 'The UN Military Observer Group in India and Pakistan', *International Organization*, IX (1955) pp. 19–31.

9. The United Nations Observation Group in Lebanon (UNOGIL) was established by the Security Council's Resolution of 11 June 1958 and comprised 592 officers from 21 countries. See the reports of the Group in OR SC, 1958, pp. 3, 33, 34, 79, 127 and 156. For a general account, see the article by its Commander, Odd Bull: 'De Forenede Nasjoners Observatörgruppe i Libanon i 1958', *Norsk Militært Tidsskrift* (Oslo) 1959, pp. 543–70 and 618–642.

10. See OR GA, XVII, Annexes, A.i. 89, p. 5; *Annual Report of the Secretary-General 1962–63*, pp. 35–36; and *The United Nations in West New Guinea* (UN Sales No. 63. I. 35) pp. 6–7. These observers preceded and were distinct from the United Nations Security Force discussed *below*, Chapter II, 8.

11. See *Annual Report of the Secretary-General 1963–64*, p. 18 and *Introduction*, p. 8.

12. *Walters: A. History of the League of Nations* (Oxford 1952) I, pp. 107 and 141–2.

13. *International Organization*, IX (1955), pp. 21 and 24–25.

The functions of the observers are to *observe* military events, and to mediate and persuade when hostile actions or other violations of a truce occur. They do not themselves perform military operations; indeed, they carry arms for self-defence only or not at all. However, they frequently operate in the line of fire, equipped with vehicles or planes, and several of them have lost their lives owing to military action by the opposing sides.[14]

The military observation groups are established *ad hoc* in each case, but the General Assembly has established a permanent basis for them in the form of a United Nations Panel of Field Observers.[15]

3. THE FORCE CLEARING THE SUEZ CANAL

The third example arose out of the Suez war. Whereas the United Nations Field Service is concerned primarily with internal tasks, and the military observers' task in principle is to observe and report, the blocking of the Suez Canal in 1956 provided an opportunity to establish a temporary civilian force for the performance of an active, external operation, although of an entirely civilian nature, that is, the clearance of the Suez Canal. This task was undertaken—on the basis of General Assembly Resolution 1121 (XI) and an exchange of letters of 8 January 1957 between the United Nations and Egypt [16]—through contractual arrangements concluded by the United Nations Secretariat with private firms. The general plans for the operation were elaborated in consultation with, and approved by, Egypt, and were then implemented under the instructions, direction and control of the Secretary-General and his representative.

The men engaged in the operation, being entirely civilian employees of the private firms involved, did not wear uniforms, but enjoyed the status of United Nations personnel *vis-à-vis* Egypt. The ships employed flew the United Nations flag and enjoyed the status of United Nations property. In the exchange of letters between Egypt and the United Nations this was set out as follows:

> 'The undertaking would be regarded as a United Nations enterprise and its personnel would be under obligation to discharge their functions and regulate their conduct solely in the interests of the United Nations. In keeping with the United Nations responsibilities, the vessels would fly the flag of the United

14. The first victim was a French officer, de Labarrière, who was killed on 6 July 1948 in front of a Jewish barricade in Jerusalem.

15. Resolution 297 (IV), the same as established the United Nations Field Service; see *above*, under 1. Cf. also General Assembly Resolution 377 (V) B/6 (Uniting for Peace).

16. *UNTS*, Vol. 257, p. 75. These and other relevant documents are reprinted in E. Lauterpacht: *The Suez Canal Settlement* (London 1960) pp. 39 et seq.

Nations in place of their national flags. The property and persons engaged in the clearance operation (including the contractors, subcontractors and their personnel) would, in view of their United Nations character, be covered by the Convention on the Privileges and Immunities of the United Nations to which Egypt is a party, in so far as it may be applicable *mutatis mutandis*.'

MILITARY FORCES COMPOSED OF NATIONAL CONTINGENTS: EXTENT OF UNITED NATIONS CONTROL

In those cases where international organizations have required military forces for external operations—to prevent or repel aggression or to maintain order and security in a disputed or troubled area—such forces have been made up of contingents from national armies, placed at the disposal of the organization by the Governments concerned. Both the Covenant of the League and the Charter of the United Nations contain specific provisions for the creation of an international force of this kind to resist aggression. And both organizations have in fact established military forces by national contingents, although for other purposes and not in the manner prescribed in the constitutions. Only in one case—Korea—has an international force been set up against an aggressor.

It is proposed to summarize in turn the relevant constitutional provisions of the Covenant and the Charter and the facts regarding each force actually set up by the two organizations. Special regard will be paid to the control which the Organization exercises over the force, since this is crucial to the determination of the question who represents the force internationally.[1]

1. ARTICLE 16 OF THE LEAGUE OF NATIONS COVENANT

Under Article 16(1) and Article 17 of the Covenant of the League, a Member or non-member State which resorted to war in violation of the provisions of the Covenant should '*ipso facto* be deemed to have committed an act of aggression against all other Members of the League'. These undertook immediately to sever all economic and other intercourse with the State concerned and with its nationals (economic sanctions). The Covenant went on to provide, in Article 16(2), that 'it shall be the duty of the Council in such case to recommend to the several Governments concerned what effective military, naval or air force the Members of the League shall severally contribute to the armed forces to be used to protect the covenants of the League' (military sanctions).

---

1. *Below*, Chapter III. See also Sohn in *American Journal of International Law*, LII (1958) pp. 235–8.

The Members also undertook to 'take the necessary steps to afford passage through their territory to the forces of any of the Members of the League which are co-operating to protect the covenants of the League'.[2]

Thus the Covenant, as originally written, appears to have envisaged an *obligation* for all Members to apply economic sanctions and to permit the passage of troops, while there would be no clear obligation for all Members to take part in military sanctions.[3] The provision that an aggressor should, *ipso facto*, be deemed to have committed an act of war against all other Members was interpreted by the Second Assembly to mean—not that the unilateral action of the aggressor in itself was enough to bring about a state of war vis-à-vis the several Member States or vis-à-vis the League itself—but that each Member had a right to declare war and to take military action. Only those who chose to do this would juridically be at war with the aggressor. The League itself was only to declare war as a last resort.[4]

The system of the Covenant thus appears to have been based upon the concept of an 'old-fashioned' war of coalition, conducted by the several States taking part in the military sanctions,[5] although it was conceived that the League also as an entity could declare war.[6] The Covenant did not provide for any supreme military command of the League, but it did not, on the other hand, preclude the Organization from deciding to establish a unified League command, under whose direction and responsibility the Member States could voluntarily place their troops. Proposals were, indeed, made for pre-planning a force with a central staff, although these were never adopted. It would, however, serve no purpose to speculate further on this point, since the League never proceeded to the length of military action to repel aggression in accordance with

2. Cf. League of Nations, *Reports and Resolutions on the Subject of Article 16 of the Covenant* (Geneva 1927).

3. Cf. *Schücking and Wehberg: Die Satzung des Völkerbundes* (2nd edition, Berlin 1924), p. 632, and *Oppenheim, International Law*, II, § 52c.

4. Resolution of 4 October 1921; *Reports and Resolutions, op. cit.*, pp. 17 and 42. *Schücking and Wehberg, op. cit.*, pp. 621–2; cf. pp. 631–2.

5. In this sense *Goodrich and Hambro: Charter of the United Nations* (2nd edition, Boston 1949) p. 282; *Martin and Edwards: The Changing Charter* (London 1955) p. 17; Taubenfeld: 'International Armed Forces and the Rules of War', *American Journal of International Law*, XLV (1951) p. 672. The latter concludes that the League approach 'added nothing significant to the preexisting international law of war and consequently affords no direct precedent for the more integrated United Nations actions'. See also *Oppenheim, op cit.*, II, § 292c, who states that any State contributing military forces 'almost of necessity became a belligerent'.

6. *Schücking and Wehberg, loc. cit.; Oppenheim: op. cit.*, I, § 167c; *Fauchille: Traité de droit international public* (Paris 1922), I, p. 215. As correctly pointed out by Guggenheim, *Lehrbuch des Völkerrechts* (Basel 1951), II, p. 788, the League could not exercise a *jus belli* if it did not have a centralized direction of the enforcement action.

Article 16, despite the fact that on several occasions it had to take cognisance of aggression,[7] and that in one of these cases it went as far as to apply certain economic sanctions.

2. MILITARY FORCES ESTABLISHED BY THE LEAGUE OF NATIONS

On the other hand, the League of Nations did on a few occasions employ military forces to maintain order and security in disputed territories, but these forces were not established on the basis of Article 16 or of any other specific provision of the Covenant.

In 1920 a League force was planned for the purpose of occupying and maintaining order in the *Vilna* area during the plebiscite which it had been decided to hold there to determine whether it should become part of Lithuania or Poland. Nine European countries promised contingents (companies). The Force was to be placed under the command of a French officer, assisted by Staff officers. The *extra* costs incurred by the States providing contingents were to be reimbursed by the League, which, in turn, would be reimbursed by the parties to the dispute. But in the end, in view of the opposition of certain States, the Council had to abandon the idea of holding a plebiscite.[8]

In 1933-34 a League Commission administered for one year the *Leticia* area on the Upper Amazon, which was in dispute between Colombia and Peru. The Commission kept order by means of a few Colombian troops who were placed under its command. They wore armlets with the letters S.D.N. and were regarded as an international force.[9]

The first truly international military force was established a few months later, when the Council of the League, by resolutions of 8 and 11 December 1934, established an international force and placed it at the disposal and under the authority of the Governing Commission of the *Saar*, for the purpose of assisting it in maintaining order during the plebiscite in the Saar. The Force, 3,300 strong, was made up of large contingents from the British and Italian armies and smaller detach-

---

7. By Japan against China, by Italy against Ethiopia, by the Soviet Union against Finland. See the Assembly's resolutions of 24 February 1933, of 11 October 1935 and of 14 December 1939, respectively. The two latter resolutions also requested the Member States to assist the victim of agression.

8. Council decisions of 21 and 25 November 1920, *League of Nations Official Journal* (January-February 1921) pp. 5–6; *Walters, op. cit.*, I, pp. 109 and 141.

9. *Société des Nations, Journal officiel* (1933) pp. 502 et seq.; *Walters, op. cit.*, II, pp. 538–40. See also the 'First Report of the Commission for the Administration of the Territory of Leticia, 3 September 1933', *Société des Nations, Journal officiel* (1934) pp. 21–25.

ments from the Netherlands and Swedish armies, which these states had placed at the disposal of the League at its request. The Commander of the Force was designated by the British Government at the request of the Council's Committee on the Saar. Each contingent was independent as regards discipline and internal administration, but general orders were issued in regard to billeting, communications, military transport and furlough. The costs of the Force were borne by the fund for ple-biscite expenses and by the Governments of the Saar, France and Germany, and were not included in the budget of the League. The Force, its command and members enjoyed complete immunity from suit in local courts. The Force was to intervene at the request of the Governing Commission of the Saar or, in an emergency, on the initiative of its Commander.[10] However, it was never called upon to use its arms, its mere presence being sufficient to maintain order.[11]

3. ARTICLES 42 ET SEQ. OF THE CHARTER [12]

Article 42 and the immediately following articles of the Charter con-tain specific provisions concerning military measures against an aggressor if economic and other measures not involving the use of armed force are considered inadequate.

In the first place, Article 51 recognizes the inherent right of individ-ual or collective self-defence if an armed attack occurs. This means that the Charter, like Article 16(1) of the Covenant, recognizes the right of (but establishes no duty for) Member States acting individually to declare war upon the aggressor and to take military action against him 'until the Security Council has taken the measures necessary to maintain international peace and security'.

The other articles are concerned with such measures to be taken by the Security Council. Article 42 provides that the Security Council 'may take such action by air, sea or land forces as may be necessary to maintain or restore international peace or security', and adds that such action 'may include' operations by military forces of Member States. It thus leaves the way open for the Security Council to compose its forces either of national contingents contributed by Member States or by other methods, such as individual enlistment.[13]

10. *Ibid.*, pp. 1705–8, 1729–30, 1762–3 (with text of the main resolution) and 1840–2; cf. the information booklet on *The Saar Plebiscite*, published by the League's Information Section (Geneva 1935) pp. 18–21.

11. *Walters: op. cit.*, II, pp. 592–3, referring to an unpublished report of October 1935 by the Commander of the Force, Major-General Brind.

12. On the interpretation of these articles, see *Goodrich and Hambro: op. cit.*, and *Kelsen: The Law of the United Nations*, pp. 724 et seq., 744 et seq., and 766 et seq.

13. Cf. *below*, Chapter IV, 2(b) and 4(c) at note 145.

While the Charter contains no specific provisions on individual enlistment or other methods, it provides, in Articles 43-45, that Member States have a duty to make armed forces available to the Security Council, on its call and in accordance with special agreements to be concluded between the Council and the Member States concerning the 'numbers and types of forces, their degree of readiness and general location' (Article 43).

As pointed out by Kelsen, these agreements are not concerned with 'the question as to how the Security Council shall or may use the armed forces placed at its disposal by the member State'.[14] Indeed, with regard to the organization and operation of the force, it follows from Article 44 that it is the Security Council which makes the 'decisions' concerning the employment of the contingents of armed forces of Member States which these provide in fulfilment of the obligations assumed under Article 43. Article 45 provides that Members shall hold immediately available national air force contingents for 'combined international enforcement action', and the Council shall 'determine' the strength and degree of readiness of these contingents and 'plans for their combined action', within the limits laid down in the special agreements. Article 46 provides that the Security Council shall make 'plans for the application of armed force'. Finally, Article 47 provides that the Military Staff Committee—which is composed of the Chiefs of Staff of the permanent Members of the Security Council or their representatives—shall assist the Security Council in all these tasks, including 'the employment and command' of forces 'placed at the disposal' of the Council. The Committee shall be responsible, under the Security Council, for the 'strategic direction' of these forces. The question of tactical command was left for subsequent determination, after the Sponsoring Governments had explained at the San Francisco Conference that this could not be exercised by a committee and that it should be left to individuals to be decided upon later.[15] It does not appear from the terms of Article 43(2) that this and other problems relating to the distribution of powers between the Organization and the several States contributing forces are to be dealt with in the special agreements to be concluded by the Security Council with the members contributing forces. These matters were thus left for determination by the Security Council, upon the advice of the Military Staff Committee. In its report of 30 April 1947 on 'General Principles Governing the Organisation of the Armed Forces made available to the Security Council by Member Nations of the United Nations' the Military Staff Committee made certain unanimous recommendations in this respect,[16] which were provisionally approved by the Security

14. *Op. cit.*, p. 750; see, however, also pp. 751–2.
15. *Goodrich and Hambro: op. cit.*, p. 292; cf. Article 43 (3).
16. Report of the Military Staff Committee, *OR SC*, 1947, Special Suppl. No. 1.

Council at its 142nd and 143rd meetings on 18 and 20 June of that year.[17]

It follows from the articles which were thus agreed upon that the forces are to be composed of units which are normally maintained as components of national armed forces (Article 3). They are to be employed only by decision of the Security Council (Article 18), although two of the permanent members felt that exception should be made in case of self-defence and national emergency (Article 17). The forces are to remain under exclusive national command 'except when, having been made available to the Security Council, on its call, they will operate under its authority' (Article 36). When called upon for action under Article 42 of the Charter, 'they shall come under the control (French text: *autorité*) of the Security Council' (Article 37) and 'the Military Staff Committee shall be responsible, under the Security Council, for their strategic direction' (Article 38). On the question of command, agreement was reached only on the following provisions:

Article 39

The command of national contingents will be exercised by commanders appointed by the respective Member Nations. These contingents will retain their national character and will be subject at all times to the discipline and regulations in force in their own national armed forces.

Article 40

The commanders of national contingents will be entitled to communicate directly with the authorities of their own country on all matters.

There was also agreement that the Security Council might appoint a supreme or over-all commander or commanders (for different theatres of war), but no specific provision was adopted because of disagreement as to whether it would be appropriate to add that the Security Council should also have the authority to appoint commanders-in-chief of air, sea or land forces acting under the supreme commander or commanders (Article 41). Those resisting this addition did so because they felt that it was premature to make provisions for the chain of command until one knew the situation that might arise, and because they were in doubt as to whether the appointments should be made by the Security Council or by the supreme commander. They did not suggest that the appointment should be a national responsibility.

Replacements, supplies and transportation are a national responsibility (Article 29). Member States are also to retain their national sovereignty and their 'control and command over bases and other facilities placed at the disposal of the Security Council' (Article 27).

The provisions of the Charter clearly envisage that the national con-

17. Text as approved in *Repertory of Practice of UN Organs*, II, p. 396; and in Sohn: *Cases and Materials on World Law* (Brooklyn 1950) p. 834.

tingents shall be under much closer direction by the Organization than was envisaged by the Covenant. And so do the articles proposed by the Military Staff Committee and provisionally approved by the Security Council. The intention appears to be that the supreme direction of the military operations shall be exclusively in the hands of the United Nations and that the commanders of national contingents shall take their operational orders from the United Nations, not from their national Governments. It is true that the national commanders are to have a right to communicate with their national Governments 'on all matters'. However, this cannot mean that the commanders may refuse to carry out orders of the United Nations commander, but merely that they may ask their Governments to take the matter up with the United Nations or its supreme command.[18] And the Government itself has no *right* to demand a reversal of the order. It has even, rightly, been questioned whether, *in the special agreements* to be concluded under Article 43 of the Charter, the national Governments would be entitled to insist that their armed forces be used only within certain areas.[19] Indeed, it appears that with regard to *operational* and *external* relations, the supreme power of decision is intended to lie with the United Nations.[20] In the field of *internal* relations, including discipline and criminal jurisdiction, the power lies with the national Government.[21]

Unfortunately, the members of the Military Staff Committee and of the Security Council were unable to agree upon the composition and size of the force and certain other subjects. This prevented the Council from adopting finally the articles proposed by the Military Staff Committee, and the special agreements provided for in the Charter have therefore not been concluded.

4. THE FORCE IN KOREA

For this reason, when the war in *Korea* broke out in 1950,[22] the Security Council was unable to invoke the duty of Member States under Articles 43 et seq. to contribute national contingents. Nor was there time to

18. In Korea a similar system was adopted in the course of the United Nations action. The agreements concluded by the United States with the several United Nations Members contributing forces to that action expressly provided that orders of the United Nations Command were to be carried out as given and that 'in the event of disagreement with them, formal protest may be presented subsequently'. See *below*, p. 36. Cf. also *below*, p. 43.

19. *Goodrich and Hambro: op. cit.*, p. 294; *Kelsen: op. cit.*, pp. 751–2.

20. The terminology of Article 48 to which Kelsen (*op. cit.*, p. 763) draws attention cannot alter this conclusion. Article 48 is concerned with entirely different problems and the terminology incidentally employed should not be given too wide significance.

21. See also the discussion *below*, pp. 96–98.

22. On the role played by the United Nations in the Korean war, see *Korea and the*

establish a force by individual enlistment. So the Council, without referring to any article of the Charter, but apparently basing itself upon Article 39, *recommended* that Member States furnish assistance and, subsequently, made certain basic provisions for the command of contingents offered voluntarily by Member States pursuant to this recommendation. On the first day of the attack, 25 June 1950, the Council—by 9 votes to 0, with 1 abstention and one permanent member absent—adopted a resolution determining that the armed attack upon the Republic of Korea constituted a 'breach of the peace'. The resolution called for the immediate cessation of hostilities, for the withdrawal of troops and for a report from the United Nations Commission on Korea. It concluded by calling upon all Members to render every assistance to the United Nations in the execution of the resolution. Two days later the Council, noting that North Korea had not complied with the resolution, recommended—by 8 votes [23] to 1, with one abstention and one permanent member absent—that the Members 'furnish such assistance to the Republic of Korea as may be necessary to repel the armed attack and to restore international peace and security'. United States forces had at that time already intervened.

On 7 July 1950, after a number of other Members had sent combat units or had decided to do so, or had offered other assistance, the Security Council—by 7 votes to 0, with three abstentions and one permanent member being absent—adopted a third basic resolution. In this resolution the Council recommended that all Members providing military forces and other assistance should make these available to a unified command under the United States, which was requested to designate the commander of the forces and 'to provide the Council with reports on the course of action taken under the unified command'. The Unified Command was authorized at its discretion to use the United Nations flag 'concurrently with the flags of the various nations participating'. In introducing the draft resolution the representative of the United Kingdom observed that there was no need for further machinery at this stage, since the Council's functions were not operational but to co-ordinate the ef-

United Nations, UN publication, 1950, 1/8; the First Report of the Collective Measures Committee, *OR GA,* 4th session, Suppl. No. 13, pp. 45–48; Padelford: 'The United Nations and Korea', *International Organization,* V (1951) pp. 685–708; and Goodrich: 'Korea: Collective Measures against Aggression', *International Conciliation* (1953) No. 494. The factual information related in the following has been drawn partly from these publications, and partly from official United Nations documents including the *Annual Reports of the Secretary-General,* the *Reports of the Security Council,* and the *Repertory of Practice of UN Organs;* see also Frankenstein: *L'Organisation des Nations Unies devant le conflit coréen* (Paris 1952). On the constitutionality of the United Nations action, see *below,* Chapter IV.

23. One of these did not vote at the meeting because of lack of instructions, but informed the Council later of his affirmative vote.

forts of Members.[24] Finally, on 31 July 1950, the eve of the return of the Soviet Delegation to the Council, the Council adopted a resolution on international relief for the civilian population of Korea, also under the direction of the Unified Command ('the responsibilities being carried out by the Unified Command on behalf of the Security Council').[25]

This was the end of Security Council action, since on 1 August 1950 the representatives of the Soviet Union returned to the Council table, and unanimity between the permanent members was then no longer possible. All the Council could do thereafter—apart from discussing and rejecting draft resolutions—was to receive the reports on the military situation which the Unified Command submitted periodically through the United States Mission to the United Nations.[26]

From then on, and even before the matter had been taken off the Council's agenda on 31 January 1951, official United Nations action was taken by the General Assembly or its organs, but only on political issues, such as the question of the aims to be attained, alleged violations of the laws of war and neutrality,[27] administration of occupied North Korean Territory,[28] the Chinese intervention, the negotiation of an armistice and violations of the armistice agreement.[29] Military matters were, in accordance with the Security Council's resolution of 7 July and the British observations introducing it, left to the United States Government, as the Unified Command.

The first United States combat units in Korea were under General MacArthur's Far East Command in Tokyo. (General MacArthur was concurrently Commander-in-Chief, United States Army Forces, Pacific, and Supreme Commander for the Allied Powers in Japan.) The first British Commonwealth units were similarly placed under the operational control of the Far East Command. After the adoption by the Security Council of the resolution of 7 July, the President of the United States appointed General MacArthur as 'Commanding General of the military forces which the members of the United Nations place under the unified command of the United States'. The later recall of General MacArthur

24. OR SC, 1950, 476th meeting, p. 4, discussed fully *below* Chapter IV, 2(b) and 4(c), at note 145.

25. For an account of the discussion in the Security Council, with the texts of the resolutions, see *Report of the Security Council*, 1949–50, pp. 21–29, and *Korea and the United Nations*, UN publication, 1950 1/8.

26. The reports were published by the United States Department of State; see, for example, publication 4108, containing the *Eleventh Report*, dated 31 January 1951, and covering the period 1–15 December 1950.

27. Cf. *below*, Chapters III, 4 (b) and V, 2(a). In some cases these matters were discussed in the Security Council.

28. See *Attia: Les forces armées des Nations Unies en Corée et au Moyen-Orient* (Genève 1963) pp. 268–9.

29. Cf. *below*, pp. 104–5.

and appointment of a new commander was also made by the President, without consulting the United Nations.

On 25 July 1950 General MacArthur established the 'United Nations Command' with headquarters in Tokyo. This was practically indentical with the Far East Command and was composed exclusively of United States officers. Later, however, these were joined by a British Commonwealth Deputy Chief of Staff. The chain of command, and of reporting to the United Nations, was from the United Nations Command, through the Chief of Staff of the United States Army, to the Joint Chiefs of Staff, to the Secretary of Defence and finally to the President of the United States.

Fifteen Member States [30] in addition to the United States made combat units available to the United Nations Command and placed them under its orders. Other Members contributed medical units, ships, supplies, &c., which were equally placed under the United Nations Command.[31] The offers of combat units and other assistance were made to the Secretary-General, pursuant to his circular cables of 28 June and 14 July requesting assistance.[32] The Secretary-General transmitted the offers, through the United States Mission to the United Nations, to the United States Government, which then negotiated directly with the Member States concerned and which decided what offers should be accepted. Formal or informal agreements were then entered into between the United States and each contributing State.[33] The formal agreements were similar or identical in terms. The contingents were equipped and paid by their national Governments, but supplies were partly furnished by the United States, against payment from the Government contributing the contingent.[34]

The ground forces contributed by Members were incorporated as units into divisions of the United States Eighth Army and brought under the operational command of United States divisional officers, except that

30. Australia, Belgium, Colombia, Canada, Ethiopia, France, Greece, Luxemburg, the Philippines, the Netherlands, New Zealand, Thailand, Turkey, Union of South Africa, the United Kingdom.

31. Table of offers of assistance as of 23 April 1951 in *International Organization* V (1951) p. 659.

32. The Secretary-General also maintained a Personal Representative at the United Nations Command in Tokyo for the purpose of transmitting its requests for assistance to Member States and for performing general liaison functions.

33. Goodrich in *International Conciliation*, No. 494, p. 158.

34. See Article 1 of the agreements concluded with Norway, Sweden, the Netherlands and the Union of South Africa, respectively, concerning the participation in 'United Nations operations in Korea' of Norwegian and Swedish field hospitals and Netherlands and South African armed forces; *UNTS*, Vol. 140, p. 319; Vol. 148, p. 83; and Vol. 177, pp. 237, 245. The contributing States also paid for supplies from sources other than the United States; cf. Article 5 and the Agreement between the United States and the Republic of Korea of 28 July 1950, par. 5; *ibid.*, Vol. 140, p. 65.

after 27 July 1951 all units of the British Commonwealth were combined into one division of their own under the Eighth Army. Naval and air units of United Nations Members were similarly attached to the Seventh United States Fleet and to the Far Eastern Air Force, respectively. Each service was under a United States service commander. The senior military representative of each Member State contributing forces was accorded direct access to the United Nations Commander on 'matters of major policy affecting the operational capabilities of the forces concerned'. Likewise, the senior military representative in the theatre of each State contributing military forces was given the right of direct communication with his Government on administrative matters affecting the forces of his Government.[35] The agreements with the participating States provided, however, that 'all orders, directives, and policies of the Commander' issued to the unit 'or its personnel shall be accepted and carried out by them as given' and that 'in the event of disagreement with such orders, directives, or policies, formal protest may be presented subsequently'.[36]

The forces of the Republic of Korea were similarly at an early stage brought under United States command, and were incorporated into United States units, first as small groups and later as distinct divisions. Formal provision for the assignment to General MacArthur's command of all military forces of the Republic of Korea was made by an exchange of letters between him and the President of the Republic on 15—18 July 1950,[36a] before the formal establishment of the United Nations Command.

Some of the national contingents wore national uniforms, while others wore United States uniforms bearing their national insignia. The forces of Greece, the Netherlands and Thailand wore shoulder patches embodying the United Nations emblem, while the Canadians wore a shoulder patch that included the United Nations wreath around a maple leaf, and the French, a red, white and blue badge with the French abbreviation for United Nations. Of the United States forces, only the 2nd Logistical Command wore a shoulder patch that included part of the United Nations emblem—the wreath.[37]

The United States Government kept the other Member States contributing forces informed of the military developments—through weekly meetings with their diplomatic representatives in Washington (the Committee of Sixteen) and otherwise. But there was little or no real advance consultation on military matters, except in some cases where they had political implications. There is no indication that the Republic of Korea,

35. OR GA, 6th session, Suppl. No. 13, p. 46.
36. See Article 7 of the four first Agreements cited in note 34 *above*.
36a. Text in the *Department of State Bulletin*, XXIII (1950) p. 206, and (in full) in S/1626 (mimeographed only).
37. *United Nations Bulletin*, 11 (1951) p. 342.

which was not a member of the Committee of Sixteen, was consulted.[38]

The *General Assembly*, like the Security Council, did not interfere with purely military matters. However, it did on some occasions adopt resolutions on political, relief and other matters of wider scope.

Thus on 7 October 1950, when the North Koreans had been driven back to the 38th Parallel and the political question arose as to whether they should be pursued into North Korean territory, the General Assembly adopted a Resolution (376 [V]) recommending that 'all appropriate steps be taken to ensure conditions of stability throughout Korea' and that constituent acts be taken 'for the establishment of a unified, independent and democratic government'. This was interpreted by the United Nations Command, as a green light for crossing the parallel. The resolution, furthermore, established a new United Nations Commission for the Unification and Rehabilitation of Korea, and resolved that an Interim Committee of this Commission should consult with and advise the 'United Nations Unified Command' on the political and relief questions dealt with in the resolution.

By its Resolution 483 (V) of 12 December 1950 the General Assembly requested the Secretary-General to make arrangements with the Unified Command 'for the design and award, under such regulations as the Secretary-General shall prescribe, of a distinguishing ribbon or other insignia for personnel which has participated in Korea in the defence of the principles of the Charter of the United Nations'. This implied refutation of the view advanced by the representative of Poland that the Korean war was a concern of the United States and not of the United Nations and that the United Nations did not have the power to award decorations because it was not a State and because the power was not laid down in the Charter.[39] Later, by Resolution 699 (VII), the General Assembly, following anew the pattern of national armies,[40] declared 'to have "Died for the United Nations" all those who are killed in the course of an action or a mission on behalf of the Organization in connexion with the maintenance of international peace and security, the prevention or ending of hostilities, or the suppression of aggression.' In the preamble the personnel participating in Korea under the United Nations Command were mentioned expressly alongside members of other missions of the United Nations whose status as United Nations organs is usually not disputed. Indeed, although prompted by the war in

---

38. See Goodrich, in *International Conciliation*, No. 494, pp. 167–8; cf. pp. 175–6 and 181.

39. OR GA, 5th session, Sixth Committee, Summary Records, pp. 257–61. Cf. *below*, Chapter IV, 3(f) at note 105.

40. Cf. the French memorandum of 16 July 1952 explaining the proposal (A/2145, OR GA, 7th session, Annexes A.i.59).

Korea, this resolution was in general terms and was applicable also to other United Nations actions.

The political problems raised by the Chinese intervention gave the General Assembly occasion to intervene in several instances. In its Resolution 498 (V) of 1 February 1951,[41] the Assembly—by 44 votes to 7, with 9 abstentions—found the People's Republic of China to have 'engaged in aggression', affirmed 'the determination of the United Nations to continue its action in Korea to meet the aggression' and called for continued assistance to the United Nations action in Korea. The resolution also requested the members of the Collective Measures Committee [42] 'to consider additional measures to be employed to meet the aggression'. Such additional measures were adopted by General Assembly Resolution 500 (V) of 18 May 1951, which provided for an embargo on war materials.

The General Assembly earlier made an effort to secure a cease-fire by its Resolution 384 (V) of 14 December 1950 and by subsequent direct exchange of communications with the Government of the People's Republic of China.[43] However, this initiative led to nothing, and when *armistice* negotiations did start, on 10 July 1951, this was brought about by direct contact between the United Nations Command and the Commander on the opposing side.[44]

The armistice negotiations, which lasted nearly two years, were conducted by the United Nations Command under instructions which in the final analysis were given by the United States Government. Members with armed forces in Korea were kept informed, and the advice of some of them was taken into account to some extent. The Republic of Korea was represented by an officer in the armistice delegation of the United Nations Command, but there is no evidence that Korea had any real part in the directions or decisions.[45]

The United Nations was kept currently informed of the armistice negotiations by the Unified Command through the United States Mission to the United Nations. When a deadlock had arisen over the question of the repatriation of prisoners of war, the General Assembly, by its Resolution 610 (VII) of 3 December 1952, made certain proposals which laid the foundation for success at a later stage, and again communicated

41. Text in *International Organisation*, V (1951) p. 421.
42. *Below*, under 5.
43. See *Annual Report of the Secretary-General*, 1950–1, pp. 47–52; cf. the text of the first 'Report of the Committee of Three' of 2 January 1951 in *International Organization*, V (1951) pp. 233–5, and in OR GA, 5th session, Annexes, A.i.76, p. 6; and the text of the reply of the People's Republic of China of 17 January 1951, *ibid.*, p. 14. Cf. also General Assembly Resolution 498 (V), par. 7.
44. *Annual Report of the Secretary-General*, 1950–51, p. 54.
45. Goodrich in *International Conciliation*, No. 494, pp. 178–81.

directly with the Governments on the opposing side.[46] The communications, together with the related resolutions and reports, offer no clear indication as to whether the Assembly was acting as the supreme political organ of one party to the conflict, or as the universal organization for mediation and world peace, or both.[47]

On 11 April 1953 an agreement for the Repatriation of Sick and Injured Captured Personnel was signed at Panmunjom by a representative of the 'Korean People's Army and Chinese People's Volunteers Liaison Group' and a representative of the 'United Nations Command Liaison Group'. The agreement was taken note of by the General Assembly by its Resolution 705 (VII) of 18 April 1953. On 8 June 1953 an agreement was signed on the exchange of prisoners of war. Finally, on 27 July 1953, followed the signature of the Armistice Agreement 'between the Commander-in-Chief, United Nations Command, on the one hand, and the Supreme Commander of the Korean People's Army and the Commander of the Chinese People's Volunteers, on the other hand'. The United Nations Commander, General Clark, and another United States officer signed for the United Nations Command.[48]

The agreements were not submitted to the United Nations until they had been signed and entered into force. Then, pursuant to its Resolutions 507 (VI) of 5 February 1952 and 705 (VII) of 18 April 1953, the General Assembly met and adopted on 28 August 1953 a resolution (711 [VII]) noting with approval the Armistice Agreement which had been concluded. In another resolution of the same day (712 [VII]), the General Assembly saluted 'the heroic soldiers of the Republic Korea and of all those countries which sent armed forces to its assistance' and expressed its satisfaction that 'the first efforts pursuant to the call [49] of the United Nations to repel armed aggression by collective military measures have been successful', and 'its firm conviction that this proof of the effectiveness of collective security under the United Nations Charter will contribute to the maintenance of international peace and security'.

During the campaign, the various organs of the United Nations, the

46. *Annual Report of the Secretary-General*, 1952–53, p. 21, and A/2354.

47. See *Annual Report of the Secretary-General*, 1952–53, pp. 18–21, on the role played by the 'neutral' Members (India) in the elaboration of the resolution. See also Goodrich in *International Conciliation*, No. 494, p. 182, on the distinction which was made between those Members which had combat forces in Korea and those Members which were designated as 'neutrals'.

48. See *Vachter: The Story of the Korean Military Armistice Negotiations* (New York 1953) with text of the agreements. Text also in *OR SC*, 1953, Supplement for July-September p. 22.

49. This term (which coincides with that employed in Article 43 of the Charter) was adopted in lieu of 'under the auspices', as proposed originally. See *Annual Report of the Secretary-General*, 1953–54, pp. 8–10.

United States Government, the other participating Member Governments, and the United Nations Command at most stages fairly consistently used the denomination 'United Nations Command'.[50] Moreover, they most frequently referred to the forces as 'United Nations Forces'[51] and to the action as a 'United Nations action'[52] or as 'United Nations operations'.[53] However, they were also frequently referred to as forces or action of the Member States, with or without an additional phrase to indicate connexion with the United Nations.[54] The divergent terminology is illustrated in the preambles to the agreements concluded by the United States with the several Members contributing forces. In these, the United States Government was referred to as 'the executive agent of the *United Nations* Forces in Korea', while the Commander, in the same sentence, in keeping with the original presidential appointment of 8 July 1950, was referred to as 'the Commanding General of the Armed Forces *of the Member States* of the United Nations in Korea'.[55] The term 'on behalf of the Security Council' was also used occasionally.[56]

50. An early Soviet proposal to delete the mention of the 'United Nations Command' in the Security Council's Resolution of 10 November 1950 was rejected by the Council; *ibid.*, 1950–51, p. 24. The term 'United Nations Command' was used also by the Governments opposing the United Nations Force in addressing communications to it (*ibid.*, 1952–53, p. 14), as well as in the Armistice Agreement.

51. See, for example, the preambles of the agreements reproduced in *UNTS*, Vol. 140, p. 314; Vol. 148, p. 78; and Vol. 177, pp. 234 and 242. General Assembly Resolution 376 (*V*) used the term 'United Nations armed forces' and 'the United Nations Unified Command'.

52. This term was employed, for example, in the declaration of the President of the Security Council at the meeting on 7 July 1950 (*OR SC*, 1950, 476th meeting, p. 2) and by the Norwegian Government in proposing to the National Assembly the allocation of funds for placing a ship at the disposal of the Unified Command (*Stortingsproposisjon nr. 1, Tillegg nr. 21* [1951]). The Secretary-General, at his press conference on 14 July 1950, spoke of 'collective United Nations action' (*Korea and the United Nations*, p. 21).

53. See, for example, the titles of the agreements reproduced in *UNTS*, Vol. 140, p. 313; Vol. 148, p. 77; and Vol. 177, pp. 231 and 241.

54. When introducing the draft of the Security Council Resolution of 7 July 1950, the UK representative spoke of co-ordinating the assistance which it was recommended in the earlier Security Council Resolution that the members should furnish (*OR SC*, 1950, 476th meeting, p. 3). General Assembly Resolution 711 A (VII) spoke of 'collective military measures' 'pursuant to the call of the United Nations'. The Agreement with Korea of 28 July 1950 spoke of 'forces operating in Korea under the Unified Command of the Commanding General of the Armed Forces of Member States of the United Nations designated by the United States pursuant to the resolutions of the United Nations Security Council of June 25, 1950; June 27, 1950 and July 7, 1950' (*UNTS*, Vol. 140, p. 68).

55. Italics supplied.

56. The United Kingdom, prior to the Security Council's resolution of 7 July 1950, placed its naval forces in Japanese waters 'at the disposal of the United States authorities to operate on behalf of the Security Council in support of South Korea' (*OR SC*,

4. KOREA

The facts reviewed above leave little doubt that the United Nations Command had full operational direction and control over the national contingents. This was expressly provided in the agreements concluded with the Governments concerned, and was further emphasized by their integration in United States military units which were already under the United Nations Command. It is equally clear that the United Nations Command took its orders from the United States Government, as the Unified Command, and not from the United Nations, nor from the other States contributing forces or from any common organ (committee) of these. The United States Government, for its part, did not take orders from anybody, although it did consult and seek political guidance from the United Nations and from some of the States contributing forces. The United Nations did not interfere at all in the purely military aspects of the operations. And even in political matters it confined itself to making 'recommendations', although in fact these seem to have always been acted upon by the United States Government.

Nevertheless, it remains important that the parties involved on the United Nations side commonly spoke of the forces and the action in terms of United Nations forces and United Nations action, for this strongly suggests that they did not regard the action as a regular 'old-fashioned' coalition-war, but as a collective action within the framework of the United Nations.

5. THE UNITING FOR PEACE RESOLUTION [57]

The experience in Korea demonstrated the feasibility of United Nations action based upon the voluntary contribution of contingents by Member States pursuant to a recommendation by the Security Council. But it was felt that this had been made possible in the Korean war only by three accidental facts: (1) that a United Nations Commission was already present on the scene, (2) that forces of Member States which could be made quickly available were already present in the area, and (3) that one of the permanent members was absent from the Security Council. Since these facts might not repeat themselves in case of any further aggression, it was proposed that the *General Assembly* be put in a position to recommend collective measures and to draw upon national contingents made ready in advance. Accordingly, on 3 November 1950

1950, Suppl. for June, July and August, p. 28. Australia used similar terms (*ibid.*, p. 34). Other States offered assistance to aid 'the Republic of Korea', 'the United Nations', or 'United Nations efforts' (*ibid.*, and *Report of the Security Council*, 1949–50, pp. 26–27).

57. Cf. *Kelsen: Recent Trends in the Law of the United Nations*, pp. 953 et seq.; and Sohn in *American Journal of International Law*, LII (1958) pp. 233–4.

—three months after the return of the Soviet delegation to the Security Council and immediately before the Chinese intervention in Korea was officially reported—the General Assembly adopted, by 52 votes to 5 and with 2 abstentions, the 'Uniting for Peace' Resolution (377 A [V]), the relevant parts of which read:

The General Assembly, . . .

Reaffirming that the initiative in negotiating the agreements for armed forces provided for in Article 43 of the Charter belongs to the Security Council, and desiring to ensure that, pending the conclusion of such agreements, the United Nations has at its disposal means for maintaining international peace and security,

Conscious that failure of the Security Council to discharge its responsibilities on behalf of all the Member States . . . does not relieve Member States of their obligations or the United Nations of its responsibility under the Charter to maintain international peace and security,

Recognising in particular that such failure does not deprive the General Assembly of its rights or relieve it of its responsibilities under the Charter in regard to the maintenance of international peace and security,

Recognising that discharge by the General Assembly of its responsibilities in these respects calls for possibilities of observation which would ascertain the facts and expose aggressors; for the existence of armed forces which could be used collectively; and for the possibility of timely recommendation by the General Assembly to Members of the United Nations for collective action which, to be effective, should be prompt,

A

1. *Resolves* that if the Security Council, because of lack of unanimity of the permanent members, fails to exercise its primary responsibility for the maintenance of international peace and security . . . the General Assembly shall consider the matter immediately with a view to making appropriate recommendations to Members for collective measures, including in the case of a breach of the peace or act of aggression the use of armed force when necessary . . . ;

B

3. *Establishes* a Peace Observation Commission . . .

C

8. *Recommends* to the States Members of the United Nations that each Member maintain within its national armed forces elements so trained, organised and equipped that they could promptly be made available, in accordance with its constitutional processes, for services as a United Nations unit or units, upon recommendation by the Security Council or General Assembly, without prejudice to the use of such elements in exercise of the right of individual or collective self-defence recognised in Article 51 of the Charter; . . .

10. *Requests* the Secretary-General to appoint, with the approval of the Committee provided for in paragraph 11, a panel of military experts who could be made available, on request, to Member States wishing to obtain technical advice regarding the organisation, training, and equipment for prompt service as United Nations units of the elements referred to in paragraph 8;

D

11. *Establishes* a Collective Measures Committee . . . and directs the Committee . . . to study and make a report to the Security Council and the General Assembly . . . on methods, including those in section C of the present resolution, which might be used to maintain and strengthen international peace and security

in accordance with the Purposes and Principles of the Charter, taking account of collective self-defence and regional arrangements (Articles 51 and 52 of the Charter).

The Collective Measures Committee subsequently submitted three partly repetitive reports [58] to the General Assembly which took note of them and made certain recommendations to Member States, while directing the Committee to continue its studies.[59] In the first report (1951) the Committee discussed, *inter alia,* basic procedures and principles which could be applied 'to co-ordinate the efforts of States and to integrate national contingents promptly and effectively into a combined force acting on behalf of the United Nations'.[60] The Committee recommended that the United Nations should authorize a State or group of States to *'act on its behalf'* as *'executive military authority'* which should have 'full responsibility for the co-ordination and strategic direction and control of the United Nations forces, within the framework of the policies and objectives as expressed through such resolutions as the United Nations may adopt at any stage of the collective action'. The 'executive military authority' was to determine the needs for assistance and negotiate agreements directly with the victim State and with the several Member States concerning the contributions they might be willing to make. The Committee stated, furthermore:

> The executive military authority should be authorised to designate the Commander-in-Chief of the United Nations forces and to replace him. Where the executive military authority consists of a group of States, the Commander-in-Chief should be designated by mutual agreement. The Commander-in-Chief's authority should be defined by the executive military authority, and he should receive instructions from that authority.[61]

According to the Committee 'national contingents should be provided with their own commander and officers by the contributing State concerned'. But it added:

> Military contingents should come under the sole operational control of the United Nations Commander-in-Chief on their arrival in his theatre or theatres of operations. The senior military representative in the theatre of operations of each State contributing military forces should, however, have direct access to the United Nations Commander-in-Chief on national matters and matters of major policy affecting the operational capabilities of the forces concerned. He should also have the right to communicate directly with his government upon administrative matters affecting its forces.[62]

---

58. *OR GA,* 6th session, Suppl. No. 13; 7th session, Suppl. No. 17; 9th session, Annexes A.i. 19.
59. General Assembly Resolutions 503 A (VI), 703 (VII) and 809 (IX).
60. *OR GA,* 6th session, Suppl. No. 13, p. 24.
61. *Ibid.,* p. 26.
62. *Ibid.,* p. 28.

The Committee proposed, furthermore, that the 'executive military authority' should report regularly to the United Nations and that 'information provided by the Commander-in-Chief on operational developments should be transmitted to the United Nations through the executive military authority'.[63]

The measures proposed by the Committee for the 'identification of the United Nations character of operations' include the following:

> The body deciding upon or recommending military measures should provide that the forces serving under the executive military authority will be known as the United Nations Forces. The Commander-in-Chief should initiate and conduct all operations as Commander of the United Nations Forces, and should issue all orders, reports and instructions, and carry on all relationships, in the name of the United Nations Command. The Security Council or the General Assembly should authorise the use of the United Nations flag in the field, and the Commander-in-Chief should ensure that that flag, in addition to national flags, is used in United Nations operations. Arrangements should be made for the proper identification of personnel and property of the United Nations in the theatre of operations. Similarly, consideration should be given to providing a United Nations service medal for the forces engaged in future United Nations military action.[64]

It will be noted that all the above is a faithful reproduction of the system adopted in the Korean conflict, which was at that time still in its first year. In its second report (1952) the Committee reproduced and recommended for study certain proposals by the Secretary-General which go beyond the procedure adopted in Korea. The Secretary-General proposed that 'States whose resources would not permit of the contribution of self-contained combat or ancillary units as contemplated in paragraph 8 of the "Uniting for Peace" resolution ... could alone or jointly with other States similarly placed, organise in advance combatant or auxiliary units (such as labour or transport units) of a nature adequate for effective integration into a United Nations force.' In addition, individual volunteers might be enlisted and trained on a part-time basis on behalf of the United Nations through the existing national military establishments of States willing to do so. Such United Nations Volunteer Reserve units could be incorporated in national military reserve establishments as special United Nations reserve units or groups, and could, in case of need, be mobilized for service by the United Nations as part of a national force contributed by the State concerned or as a separate unit. In either case, the international character of the reserve component should be recognized and preserved. Co-operating States would be asked to meet the cost of recruiting, equipping and training the United Nations volunteer reservists as part of their over-all advance contribution to collective security under the United Nations.[65]

63. *Ibid.*, p. 30.
64. *Ibid.*, p. 28; cf. *above*, p. 37, on General Assembly Resolution 483 (V).
65. OR GA, 7th session, Suppl. No. 17, pp. 12–13.

The recommendations of the Collective Measures Committee, including the recommendation to the effect that the forces mobilized under the Uniting for Peace Resolution should be organized and commanded in essentially the same manner as the forces in Korea, were not made in categorical terms in the sense that they were presented as the only way in which the United Nations force could operate. Moreover, the recommendations were never adopted by the General Assembly, but merely taken note of. It is thus quite clear that they do not constitute any binding directives. Indeed, the Security Council and the General Assembly are free to organize the national contingents called for in paragraph 8 of the Uniting for Peace Resolution in any manner they see fit which does not contravene the United Nations Charter or the desires of the contributing States.[66]

Less than three months after its adoption, the General Assembly applied for the first time the Uniting for Peace Resolution, without specifically mentioning it, by extending the United Nations action against North Korea to be directed also against the intervening forces of the Central People's Government of the People's Republic of China.[67]

6. THE UNITED NATIONS EMERGENCY FORCE IN THE MIDDLE EAST [68]

The Uniting for Peace Resolution which had thus been applied without being specifically mentioned in extending the United Nations military

66. On this and another constitutional aspect see *below*, Chapter IV,4 (c), cf. 2 (c).

67. General Assembly Resolutions 498 (V) and 500 (V), reported *above*, under 4, p. 38.

68. The texts of the basic documents of legal importance are collected in *E. Lauterpacht: The United Nations Emergency Force* (London, 1960). Three of the basic documents may also be found in *UNTS*, Vol. 271, pp. 235–85. For an official summary of these and other facts of lasting importance, see 'Summary Study of the Experience Derived from the Establishment and Operation of the Force', *Report of the Secretary-General*, 9 October 1958, *OR GA*, 13th session, Annexes, A.i. 65, pp. 8–33. For unofficial descriptions and commentaries see, in addition to the general literature cited at the Introduction, *above*, p. 19: Goodrich and Rosner: 'The United Nations Emergency Force', *International Organization*, II (1957) pp. 413–30; Pearson: 'Force for U.N.', *Foreign Affairs*, XXXV (1956–7) pp. 395–404; Armstrong: 'The UN Experience in Gaza', *ibid.*, pp. 600–19; Maxwell Cohen: 'The United Nations Emergency Force: A Preliminary View', *International Journal*, XII (1957), pp. 109–27; *Frye: A United Nations Peace Force* (New York 1957); Spry 'Canada, the United Nations Emergency Force and the Commonwealth', *International Affairs*, XXXIII (1957) pp. 289–300; 'Report of Committee on Study of Legal Problems of the United Nations', *Proceedings of the American Society of International Law* (1957) pp. 205–29; *Stone: Aggression and World Order* (London 1958) pp. 184 et seq.; Chaumont: La situation juridique des États membres à l'égard de la force d'urgence des Nations Unies', *Annuaire français de droit international*, IV (1958) pp. 399–440; Martinez: 'La fuerza de emergencia de las Naciones Unidas', *Revista española de derecho internacional*, XIII (1960) pp. 83–147 and XIV (1961) pp. 55–96; and *Poirier: La Force internationale d'urgence* (Paris 1962).

action in Korea against the intervening Chinese forces was invoked, *eo nomine*, after the attack [69] upon Egypt [70] on 29 October 1956 by Israel and, later, by France and the United Kingdom. The Security Council, being unable to act because of French and United Kingdom negative votes, called an emergency special session of the General Assembly, as provided in the Uniting for Peace Resolution, 'in order to make appropriate recommendations'.[71] The Assembly adopted on 2 November 1956 Resolution 997 (ES-I) urging the parties to agree to an immediate cease-fire (par. 1) and promptly to 'withdraw all forces behind the armistice lines, to desist from raids across the armistice lines into neighbouring territory and to observe scrupulously the provisions of the armistice agreements' (par. 2). The resolution also urged, generally, that 'steps be taken to reopen the Suez Canal and restore secure freedom of navigation' (par. 4).

On the following day the Secretary-General reported to the Assembly that France and the United Kingdom had declared themselves willing to stop military action if, *inter alia*, both the Egyptian and the Israeli Governments agreed to accept a United Nations Force to keep the peace; and if the United Nations decided to constitute and maintain such a Force until an Arab-Israeli peace settlement was reached and until satisfactory arrangements had been agreed in regard to the Suez Canal, both agreements to be guaranteed by the United Nations.[72]

By Resolutions 998 (ES-I) of 4 November, 1000 (ES-I) of 5 November and 1001 (ES-I) of 7 November 1956 the General Assembly thereupon without a negative vote [73] established an emergency international United Nations Force—later referred to as the United Nations Emergency Force (UNEF). The purpose, organization, status, functioning and financing of the Force were defined (*a*) in the Assembly's resolutions of 5 and 7 November 1956, (*b*) in the Second and Final Report of the Secretary-General on the Plan for an Emergency International United Nations Force [74] approved by General Assembly Resolution 1001; (*c*)in a number of subsequent General Assembly resolutions;[75]

---

69. The United Nations did not formally qualify the invaders as aggressors, as it had done in Korea, see Chaumont in: *Annuaire français de droit international* (1958) p. 418, and *Chaumont: L'organisation des Nations Unies* (Paris 1959) p. 71.

70. The 'United Arab Republic' was established only after most of the events described in the following had taken place. 'Egypt' is therefore used consistently in the present text.

71. *Report of the Security Council*, 1956–57, pp. 37–38.

72. *OR GA*, 1st emergency special session, Annexes, A.i. 5, p. 3.

73. The votes were, respectively, 57–0–19, 57–0–19 and 64–0–12; *ibid.*, plenary meetings, pp. 71, 89 and 126.

74. *Ibid.*, Annexes, A.i. 5.

75. 1089 (XI), 1090 (XI), 1121 (XI), 1122 (XI), 1125 (XI), 1126 (XI), 1151 (XII); [1263 (XIII), 1337 (XIII), 1441 (XIV), 1442 (XIV), 1575 (XV)].

(*d*) in an 'Aide-memoire on the Basis for Presence and Functioning of UNEF in Egypt', approved by Egypt and the General Assembly in November 1956;[76] (*e*) in another agreement concluded by the Secretary-General with Egypt on 8 February 1957 concerning the status of UNEF in Egypt;[77] (*f*) in the 'Regulations for the United Nations Emergency Force' enacted by the Secretary-General on 20 February 1957;[78] and lastly, (*g*) in a letter dated 21 June 1957 from the Secretary-General to the States providing contingents. This letter of 21 June 1957 refers to or reproduces as annexes most of the documents cited above and constitutes, together with the replies of each 'participating' State, the basic agreements between these States and the United Nations.[79]

The purpose of the Force was not to fight an aggressor, as in Korea, but 'to secure and supervise the cessation of hostilities' agreed to by the parties 'in accordance with all the terms of General Assembly Resolution 997 (ES-I)'.[80] In accordance with the second operative paragraph of this resolution and in the light of subsequent developments, the Force has performed two principal tasks: first, it entered the areas occupied by the invading forces as these withdrew, to maintain quiet (it also performed temporarily certain administrative duties) and to turn the areas over to Egypt. Secondly, after the complete withdrawal of the invading troops, the Force has been stationed on the Egyptian side of the Egyptian-Israeli armistice demarcation line and the international border south of the Gaza strip, patrolling these lines in order to prevent incidents across them,[81] and apprehending infiltrators and turning them over to the local police.[82] Thus UNEF is 'more than an observer's corps, but in no way a military force temporarily controlling the territory in which it is stationed'.[83]

The Force is equipped with normal regimental weapons [84] and with means of transportation and reconnaissance—including motor vehicles

---

76. OR GA, 11th session, Annexes, A.i. 66, p. 9.

77. *Op. cit.*, p. 52; *UNTS*, Vol. 260, p. 61, and Vol. 271, p. 145.

78. *Ibid.*, Vol. 271, p. 169.

79. Text in *ibid.*, Vol. 271, pp. 135 (Finland), 187 (Sweden) and 223 (Norway); Vol. 274, pp. 47 (Canada), 61 (Denmark), 199 (Brazil) and 233 (India); and Vol. 277, p. 191 (Yugoslavia). Colombia and Indonesia did not reply to the Secretary-General's letter and subsequently withdrew their contingents (as did Finland). – The most recent version of the three basic documents (for Cyprus) is reprinted *below*, p. 427.

80. General Assembly Resolution 1000 (ES-I).

81. Secretary-General's Summary Study, OR GA, 13th session, Annexes, A.i. 65, pp. 15–16.

82. *Ibid.*, 12th session, Annexes, A.i. 65, p. 6.

83. Par. 12 of the Secretary-General's Second and Final Report, OR GA, 1st emergency special session, Annexes, A.i. 5, p. 21; cf. Secretary-General's Summary Study, pars. 15 and 77.

84. Secretary-General's Summary Study, *loc. cit.*, p. 13; cf. Status agreement with Egypt, par. 22.

and aircraft—but not with heavy arms. The troops have a right to fire in self-defence. They are never to take the initiative in the use of arms, but may respond with force to an armed attack upon them, including attempts to use force to make them withdraw from positions which they occupy under orders from the Commander.[85] It has been said that UNEF serves by being present and by acting as a plate-glass window—not capable of withstanding assault but nevertheless a lightly armed barrier that all see and tend to respect.[86]

As we have seen, in Korea the United Nations had entrusted to one of its Member States the task of organizing the Force and directing its operations, and the Collective Measures Committee had also recommended this system for military action under the Uniting for Peace Resolution. In the case of UNEF, however, the Organization chose itself to assume these functions.[87] The General Assembly appointed a *Commander* of the Force—as a regular United Nations official, responsible to the Organization and fully independent of the policies of any one nation—to organize the Force 'in consultation with the Secretary-General as regards size and composition'.[88] He was entrusted with full command authority and operational responsibility for the performance of the functions assigned to the Force by the United Nations and for the deployment and assignment of troops placed at the disposal of the Force, though he was to exercise this autority and responsibility 'in consultation with the Secretary-General'.[89] Several other matters—in the administrative, financial, political and legal field—were entrusted to the Secretary-General,[90] but the day-to-day administration was to be and is carried out by the Commander and his staff. The Secretary-General, in consultation with the Advisory Committee,[91] has issued Regulations for the Force; and the Commander of the Force has issued orders consistent therewith and subject to review by the Secretary-General.[92] As expressed by the Secretary-General, the Commander has 'the position of an international civil servant responsible for the discharge of his task to the Assembly, but administratively integrated with

85. Secretary-General's Summary Study, *loc. cit.*, pp. 17 and 31.

86. *International Review Service*, III (1957) No. 33, p. 19.

87. On the relationship of UNEF to the Uniting for Peace Resolution and the proposals of the Collective Measures Committee, see *below*, Chapter IV,2 (c), cf. *above*, under 5 *in fine*.

88. General Assembly Resolutions 1000 (ES-I) and 1001 (ES-I) par. 4; cf. Second and Final Report of the Secretary-General, par. 4 (*a*), and Secretary-General's Summary Study, par. 13.

89. UNEF Regulations 11 and 16.

90. UNEF Regulation 15; cf. General Assembly Resolutions 1000 (ES-I), par. 4 and 1001 (ES-I), par. 7.

91. See *below*, p. 50, at note 102.

92. UNEF Regulation 4.

the United Nations organisation and under instructions from the Secretary-General'.[93] This position 'combines leadership of the Force with the role of representative of the United Nations. Much the same qualities are called for in the Chief of Staff of UNTSO,[94] although the military observers in UNTSO do not form a military organization in the UNEF sense and their functions are quite different. Both operations, however, combine political and administrative with military functions.' [95]

It will be seen that the functions and powers of the Commander are closely interwoven with those of the Secretariat. This fact is also reflected in the composition of his staff. He was authorized to recruit the *military* members of his command from the observer corps of the United Nations Truce Supervision Organization for Palestine (UNTSO) and directly from various Member States.[96] In fact, they were recruited first from UNTSO and later from among the officers of national contingents.[97] The *civilian* staff of the Commander is, in the first place, made up of members of the United Nations Secretariat, detailed by the Secretary-General to serve with the Command. These include administrative, financial, procurement, political, legal, information and other officers, as well as the United Nations Field Service,[98] which performs technical services, notably with regard to external communications and security. Additional personnel are hired locally by the Commander under terms of employment prescribed by him.[99] Only the military members of the staff, together with the Commander and the members of national contingents, are technically considered 'members of the Force'.[100] Nor does this term include the members of the staff of the Secretary-General *at headquarters* who are concerned with the Force. In addition to his regular civilian staff, the Secretary-General had, initially, a senior military adviser and three officer assistants attached to his Executive Office as consultants, assisted by a group of military representatives from the countries providing contingents, sitting as an informal military advisory committee. When the operation had been

93. Secretary-General's Summary Study, par. 76; cf. pars. 84, 127 and 169.
94. *Above*, Chapter I, 2, note 7.
95. Secretary-General's Summary Study, par. 77.
96. General Assembly Resolution 1000 (ES-I).
97. Secretary-General's Summary Study, pars. 37 and 78.
98. *Above*, Chapter I, 1.
99. UNEF Regulation 19 (c); Status Agreement with Egypt, par. 37, cf. par. 24, and with Congo, par. 27. The latter goes further in specifying UN's independence of the host State in this respect. However, there can be no doubt that the local personnel of UNEF are also international officials, subject only to the authority of the United Nations in respect of their official functions and their relationship of employment cf. *below* Chapter IV, 3 (b).
100. UNEF Regulation 5 (d); see, however, Regulation 6, cf. Regulation 5 (b).

established, however, these arrangements were reduced.[101] The Secretary-General is, moreover, assisted in his task by an Advisory Committee, composed of himself as chairman and of representatives of five States providing contingents and two States which had offered to do so.[102]

The field forces are, as in Korea, supplied by various Member States in the form of relatively self-contained *national contingents*. This was necessary 'in order to avoid the loss of time and efficiency which is unavoidable when new units are set up through joining together small groups of different nationalities'.[103] As in Korea, the national contingents retain their identity and organizational unity, although the demands of service made upon the Force frequently require the deployment of elements of a contingent, whether companies or platoons, in separate sectors.[104] The contingents are commanded by their own officers. Those contingents which furnish units for more than one functional task designate a contingent commander, in addition to commanders for each functional activity. This contributes to clarification of responsibility in those matters affecting personnel which are subject to national authority.[105] Some of the contributing Governments also designate 'liaison officers' to represent their interests on the scene of operations and to serve as points of contact. These liaison officers, not being under the authority of the Commander, are not members of UNEF.[106]

The members of the Force, whether serving in national contingents or as part of the United Nations Command, wear their national uniforms with United Nations blue helmets, berets and desert caps and UNEF badges and insignia.[107] They also carry United Nations identity cards. The Force, whose functions are exclusively international,[108] flies the United Nations flag,[109] and its means of transportation and other equip-

101. Secretary-General's Summary Study, pars. 31 and 182.
102. General Assembly Resolution 1001 (ES-I), pars. 6–9.
103. Second and Final Report of the Secretary-General, par. 14. In this way it was possible to organize the Force with great speed. Indeed, the first national contingent was reported ready for dispatch on 5 November, the same day as the resolution deciding to set up the Force had been adopted, despite the fact that parliamentary approval had had to be obtained in advance (*ibid.*, Annex 5).
104. OR GA, 12th session Annexes, A.i. 65, p. 3.
105. Secretary-General's Summary Study, par. 80; cf. *below* under 6 (d)–(f).
106. *Ibid.*, par. 82. The Danish and Norwegian liaison officers also perform the disciplinary and other personnel functions usually vested in the contingent commander, since the regular companies of those two contingents have been joined together under a common battalion commander of alternating nationality.
107. UNEF Regulation 8; Secretary-General's Summary Study, par. 43.
108. UNEF Regulation 6.
109. UNEF Regulation 7; cf. Status Agreement with Egypt, par. 20, and with the Congo, par. 26.

ment bear a distinctive United Nations mark and licence.[110] The total size of the Force has ranged between 4,000 and 6,000 men, of which little more than half perform active patrolling duty and the rest form part of the supporting units and services, including administration, signals, engineering, supply, transport, workshop, ordnance, medical,[111] dental, postal, pay, provost and movement control.[112]

Military reconnaissance aircraft have been provided by the Royal Canadian Air Force. Air transport to the area of operations has been provided by the same air force, by the air forces of two 'non-participating' Member States and by a civilian airline.[113] Sea transport of troops and material has been performed by vessels chartered or owned by UNEF or made available by 'participating'[114] or other Governments. Some of these vessels have flown the United Nations flag, some their national flag and some both. In Egyptian ports all ships on UNEF assignments display the United Nations flag.[115]

The Force is a subsidiary organ of the United Nations and in particular of the General Assembly,[116] and it enjoys the status, privileges and immunities of the Organization in accordance with the Convention on the Privileges and Immunities of the United Nations. This applies also to the property, funds and assets of 'participating' Governments used in the host State.[117] The Commander and the staff detailed from the United Nations Secretariat to serve with him are entitled to privileges and immunities under the Convention as officials of the United Nations; the military members of the UNEF Command are entitled to privileges and immunities as experts on mission for the United Nations. Personnel recruited locally enjoy only immunity in respect of official acts as provided in § 18(a) of the Convention,[118] which is the most basic immunity of an international official. Members of national contingents are

110. UNEF Regulation 9; cf. Status Agreement with the Congo, par. 32.

111. The medical units were, for most of the time, provided by the Medical Corps of the Norwegian Army. An extensive report, with conclusions and recommendations for future Forces, has been published as a supplement to *Revue internationale des services de santé des armes de terre, de mer et de l'air* (Liège), XXXVI (1963) No. 5.

112. *OR GA*, 12 session, Annexes, A.i. 65, pp. 2–3.

113. Secretary-General's Summary Study, pars. 36 and 38.

114. This term, used by the Secretariat, is here used in quotation marks because it does not adequately reflect the fact that the action is under the direction and responsibility of the United Nations and that the States as such are not legally engaged; cf. *below*, pp. 118–9 and 126.

115. United Nations Conference on the Law of the Sea, Official Records, IV, p. 139.

116. UNEF Regulation 6; Status Agreement with Egypt, Introduction and par. 23.

117. UNEF Regulation 10; Status Agreement with Egypt, par. 23, and with the Congo, pars. 15–16.

118. UNEF Regulation 19; Status Agreement with Egypt, pars. 24–25, and with the Congo, par. 28.

not covered by the Convention on the Privileges and Immunities of the United Nations,[119] but are accorded largely corresponding privileges and immunities, including immunity in respect of official acts, in Egypt under the Status Agreement with that country.[120] All members of the Force are entitled to the legal protection of the United Nations as agents of the Organization.[121]

The character of the Force and the Division of functions and powers between the United Nations and the 'participating' States are, in most respects, defined in the UNEF Regulations, whose binding force for the national contingents was expressly recognized by the 'participating' States in paragraph 4 of their agreements with the United Nations, which reads:

> The Regulations referred to above affirm the international character of the Force as a subsidiary organ of the General Assembly and define the conditions of service for the members of the Force. National contingents provided for UNEF serve under these Regulations.

The Regulations are largely similar to those which were subsequently enacted for the United Nations Forces in the Congo and in Cyprus.

It follows from the Regulations that the Force, although composed of national contingents, is a genuine United Nations Force under the full control of the Organization as far as operational and external matters are concerned. The principal rights and functions retained by the Governments providing contingents (or officers for the UNEF Command) may be found in the following fields:

(a) Recruitment and composition

The recruitment of the individual members of national contingents is in the hands of the 'participating' Governments [122] which either place regular units of their army temporarily at the disposal of the United Nations or which recruit special volunteer units for service with the United Nations. However, the choice of the national units as such is in the hands of the United Nations, which thereby retains over-all authority for the composition of the Force. The Secretary-General and the Commander decide what States to ask for contingents and what offers to accept, and may, after adequate prior notification and consultation, request the withdrawal of a contingent already provided.[123] In so doing,

119. *Below*, p. 57.
120. Pars. 7–38, see especially pars. 11–12.
121. UNEF Regulation 30; cf. *below*, Chapter III,5(a).
122. Except that the commanders of national contingents can only be replaced in consultation between the UNEF Commander and the 'participating' Government (UNEF Regulation 12, as expressly restated in par. 9 of the agreements with 'participating' States) and that the UNEF Commander may make provisional emergency assignments.
123. Agreements with 'participating' States, *UNTS*, Vol. 271, par. 8.

they retain the necessary authority with regard to the size and overall composition of each contingent as well as with regard to achieving a balanced composition of the Force as a whole. In this way the United Nations has indeed been able to secure both an effective and a balanced Force, composed, on the one hand, of adequate numbers of regular patrolling units and of the various types of supporting units, and, on the other hand, of contingents from States in several regions of the world.[124]

Unlike the course followed in the case of Korea, the United Nations had deliberately excluded contingents and military staff officers from the permanent Members of the Security Council [125] and from States which, for geographical or other reasons, might have a special interest in the conflict.[126] Under this formula it has been possible to avoid contingents and staff officers from States whose neutrality might be questioned by the parties to the dispute, without at any point conceding to the parties a right of veto which could detract from the exclusive authority of the United Nations to decide upon the composition and constitution of the Force.[127]

(b) Withdrawal

A 'participating' Government has the right to withdraw its contingent after adequate prior notification.[128] This might provide it with an indirect way of exercising pressure upon the United Nations and the Commander in their decisions concerning the deployment of the contingent and the general operation of the Force. However, this danger is counterbalanced by the policy of the Secretary-General to avoid such differences in the size of national contingents as might lead to excessive dependence on any one State.[129] Only a group of 'participating' States acting jointly are therefore in a position to exercise pressure. And any influence they might thus exert upon the operation of the Force is, of

124 The Force included originally 4 (later 3) Scandinavian, 3 (later 2) American, 2 (later 1) Asiatic, and a Yugoslav, contingents, the Asiatic contingent being the largest and the Scandinavian contingents the smallest.

125. General Assembly Resolution 1000 (ES-I); Second and Final Report of the Secretary-General, par. 6, as approved by General Assembly Resolution 1001 (ES-I).

126. Secretary-General's Summary Study, pars. 16 and 44.

127. Second and Final Report of the Secretary-General, par. 6 i.f., as approved by General Assembly Resolution 1001 (ES-I); Secretary-General's Summary Study, pars. 16 and 161; International Organization, II (1957) p. 423; International Review Service, III (1937) No. 33, p. 13.

128. Agreements with 'participating' States, UNTS, Vol. 271, par. 8; cf. Secretary-General's Summary Study, par. 50.

129. Secretary-General's Summary Study, par. 17. On 31 July 1961 the largest national contingent (the Indian) numbered 1,251 men as compared to a total Force of 5,159. The other contingents numbered from 463 to 936 men (A/4857). Earlier figures may be found in OR GA, 12th session, Annexes, A.i. 65, p. 2; ibid., 13th session, Annexes A.i. 65, p. 5; ibid., 15th session, Annexes, A.i. 27, p. 14.

course, one of fact, not one of law. Only if the functions of the Force, as originally defined by the General Assembly, should be altered in such a manner as to go beyond the understanding upon which the contingents were originally provided, would the States providing the contingents have a legal right to intervene in that capacity, rather than through their membership of the General Assembly.[130]

(c) Command

It has already been pointed out that the national contingents retain their identity and organizational unity and are commanded by their national officers. However, the commanding officers of the national contingents (the contingent commander or the commanders of units operating separately) [131] in turn take their orders from the Commander and through him from the Secretary-General and the General Assembly. The UNEF Regulations explicitly provide that 'in the performance of their duties for the Force the members of the Force shall receive their instructions only from the Commander and the chain of command designated by him',[132] and that they shall discharge these duties and regulate their conduct with the interests of the United Nations only in view.[133] The contingent commanders are free to communicate with their home Governments on all matters affecting their units.[134] But this does not mean (any more than in Korea or under the proposals of the Military Staff Committee) [135] that the Government can instruct the contingent commander in matters falling under the authority of the UNEF Commander as long as he does not overstep this authority or otherwise violate the understanding on the basis of which the contingent was provided.

(d) Costs

The members of national contingents receive a daily overseas service allowance from the United Nations. Otherwise they receive their regular pay and allowances—as well as compensation for service-incurred death, injury or illness—from their Government according to the national re-

---

130. Cf. Chaumont in *Annuaire français de droit international* (1958) p. 434 and *below*, Chapter III, 2 (a).

131. Cf. Secretary-General's Summary Study, par. 80.

132. The acceptance of this principle by the 'participating' Governments from the outset is evidenced by the declaration of the Norwegian Minister of Defence to the press that the Norwegian UNEF contingent is fully under the command of the United Nations and the UNEF Commander, and that the Norwegian Ministry of Defence is kept informed through the United Nations (*Arbeiderbladet*, Oslo, 21 November 1956).

133. UNEF Regulations 6, 11, 12, 16 and 31; cf. *OR GA*, 12th session, Annexes, A.i. 65, p. 3.

134. Secretary-General's Summary Study, par. 79.

135. *Above*, pp. 36 and 43.

gulations.[136] The 'participating' Governments also provide certain equipment—now in principle confined to the personal equipment of the soldiers together with small arms and ammunition. Other equipment is procured and paid for by the United Nations even if, in special cases, it has been requisitioned from the 'participating' Governments.[137] The United Nations also pays all other costs of the Force, including food, quarters, welfare, transportation, communications services, and use of the Royal Canadian Air Force planes composing the UNEF squadron.[138] In addition the United Nations reimburses the 'participating' Governments for 'all extra and extraordinary costs' which they are 'obliged to incur in making the forces available for UNEF service'.[139] Under this formula the 'participating' States are entitled to receive reimbursement both for pay and allowances paid to members of the contingent [140] and for indemnities paid in respect of death, injury or illness as a result of service with UNEF,[141] as well as for destruction, loss or depreciation of equipment supplied by them.[142] The direct and reimbursement costs for the United Nations, totalling $ 15–20 million per year,[143] are borne in part by voluntary contributions and in part by assessment of Member States.[144] It may be said in conclusion that although the 'participating' States themselves had to carry part of the expenses during the first emergency period, the United Nations has since undertaken to pay or reimburse practically all the expenses of the Force. This means both that the United Nations has become financially independent of the 'participating' States and that it is easier to achieve a balanced geographical

136. UNEF Regulations 38—40.

137. Report of the Secretary-General of 13 September 1960, A/4486, pars. 67–70 (OR GA, XV, Annexes, A.i. 27) approved by General Assembly Resolution 1575 (XV).

138. For a more complete list, see the Secretary-General's Summary Study, loc. cit., p. 23; cf. the subsequent expansion in A/4486, cited in the preceding note.

139. Report of the Secretary-General, OR GA, 12th session, Annexes, A.i. 65, pp. 10–11, approved by General Assembly Resolution 1151 (XII).

140. The legal situation in this respect has not been clarified; see the Secretary-General's Summary Study, par. 118.

141. OR GA, 12th session, Annexes, A.i. 65, p. 11.

142. Report of the Secretary-General of 13 September 1960, A/4486, pars. 67–70 (OR GA, 15th session, Annexes, A.i. 27, approved by General Assembly Resolution 1575 (XV)).

143. The 1961 budget totalled $ 19 million, of which $ 11,250,000 were for direct United Nations costs and $ 7,750,000 for reimbursement to 'participating' Governments (General Assembly Resolution 1575 (XV), and OR GA, 15th session, Suppl. No. 5B). Later the budgets were reduced, down to $ 15 million for 1966.

144. General Assembly Resolutions 1089 (XI); 1151 (XII); 1337 (XIII); 1441 (XIV); 1575 (XV); 1732-3 (XVI); 1854 and 1864 (XVII); 1983 (XVIII); 2006 (XIX); 2115 (XX). On the political and financial crisis which developed from the assessment of all Members, see below, pp. 65 and 172.

composition of the Force with contingents from prosperous as well as less prosperous countries.

(e) Disciplinary action and criminal jurisdiction

The members of the Force remain subject to their national military rules and regulations without derogating from their responsibilities as members of the Force. They are, furthermore, under the criminal jurisdiction of their Governments, even in respect of acts performed in their capacity as members of the Force.[145] Disciplinary action in national contingents is therefore the responsibility of the contingent commander.[146] To confer such authority upon the UNEF Commander would probably require specific legislation in most 'participating' States.[147] Each contingent also has the power to arrest its own members.[148] Despite all these powers vested in 'participating' Governments and contingent commanders *vis-à-vis* individual members of the Force, the UNEF Commander has general responsibility for the good order of the Force. He receives reports on disciplinary action and may consult with the contingent commander and the Government concerned.[149] And the military police provided by him for the Force also has the power of arrest in so far as necessary to maintain order and discipline among members of the Force.[150] Furthermore, the powers of national Governments and contingent commanders are confined to the criminal and disciplinary fields. As shall be explained in another context, any international or civil responsibility *vis-à-vis* third parties injured by the acts of the members of the Force is vested in the United Nations, not in the 'participating' Governments.[151] Even if the injured State wishes to complain merely about failure to take disciplinary or criminal action, it must address itself to the United Nations—not to the 'participating' State.[152]

145. UNEF Regulation 34 and Status Agreement with Egypt, par. 11, as confirmed in the agreements with 'participating' States, pars. 5 and 7.

146. UNEF Regulation 13; confirmed in the agreements with 'participating' States, pars. 6–7. By a Norwegian decree of 23 November 1956 the company commanders of the Norwegian contingent were given the disciplinary powers normally vested in battalion commanders. The Norwegian liaison officer was named the highest local disciplinary authority. Appeal can always be made to the Commander of the Norwegian Army (*Norsk Lovtidend, 2nen avd.,* 1956, p. 739).

147. Secretary-General's Summary Study, par. 139. Cf. *below,* pp. 98 and 365 et seq.

148. UNEF Regulation 14 i.f.

149. UNEF Regulation 13. The Congo and Cyprus Regulations give the Commander wider powers, see *below,* p. 376, cf. pp. 398 and 439.

150. UNEF Regulation 14; cf. Status Agreement with Egypt, pars. 14 et seq., and with Congo, par. 12, both of which provide that the United Nations military police 'shall have the power of arrest over members of the Force' (S/5004).

151. *Below.* Chapter, III, 4 (a).

152. *Below,* Chapter III, 3 (a) *in fine.*

(f) Status, privileges and immunities of members of national contingents

It has already been pointed out that members of national contingents, unlike members of the UNEF staff, cannot claim privileges and immunities as United Nations officials or experts under the Convention on the Privileges and Immunities of the United Nations, but that they have been accorded, in the host country, rather similar privileges and immunities under the Status Agreement with Egypt. These include immunity in respect of official acts (par. 12 (*a*)) and complete immunity from criminal jurisdiction (par. 11). The inapplicability of the United Nations Convention in Egypt follows from an express provision in paragraph 25 of the Status Agreement.

Not even in other countries can members of national contingents claim privileges and immunities as officials or experts under the Convention on the Privileges and Immunities of the United Nations. This follows *a contrario* from the silence in this respect of UNEF Regulation 19, which must thus be assumed to limit the general provision for application of the Convention in Regulation 10, and from the fact that the United Nations has not designated the members of the national contingents as officials and included them in the relevants lists as prescribed in § 17 of the Convention. This leaves only Article 105 of the Charter, which, in view of its terms, may by of doubtful value in respect of agents of the Organization who are neither officials of the Organization nor representatives of Member States.[153] Consequently, should the Force be stationed or otherwise have to perform official functions in other countries, arrangements for privileges and immunities, including immunity in respect of official acts, would have to be made, either by agreements with these countries, or by extension of the provisions of the Convention on the Privileges and Immunities of the United Nations to members of national contingents. This the Organization could probably do unilaterally, by action under paragraph 17 of the Convention and by an appropriate amendment to UNEF Regulation 19.[154]

---

153. In fact the United Nations has claimed immunity from criminal jurisdiction for members of national contingents in third countries merely on the basis of UNEF. Regulation 34 (*a*), which reserves such jurisdiction for their home States. This is hardly tenable, since United Nations regulations, in the absence of special authority, cannot impose obligations upon Member States (see *below*, p. 158 and pp. 161–2), and since Article 105 of the Charter (like par. 18 of the Convention on Privileges and Immunities) normally could not cover unofficial acts.

154. The International Law Association's Committee on the United Nations Charter submits that the injunction in Article 100 of he Charter, preventing members of the Secretariat from accepting instructions from authorities external to the Organization, would appear to preclude acceptance as part of the UN staff of 'national contingents on the UNEF pattern with its division of control between the United Nations and the contributing States over members of the Force' (International Law Association, *Report*

However, in the 'participating' States most of the applicable privileges and immunities specified in §§ 18 and 22 of the Convention on the Privileges and Immunities of the United Nations would be out of harmony with the circumstances and Regulations referred to under (a)—(e) above.[155] Although it might have been possible to grant members of national contingents immunity from *civil* suit in respect of official acts even in their home country,[156] they could not be granted immunity from *criminal* jurisdiction in the country which has expressly undertaken to prosecute them.[157] And there is no reason why they should enjoy exemption from taxation on the pay and emoluments which they receive from their home State according to its normal regulations, i.e. on a gross basis. In fact, they are granted tax exemption only in respect of the daily allowance paid directly by the United Nations.[158] Thirdly, the 'participating' State, of course, cannot accord to members of its national contingent immunity from the national service obligation pursuant to which most of them have been placed at the disposal of the United Nations. But, as pointed out under (b), the 'participating' States have undertaken not to withdraw their contingents without adequate prior notification. The other privileges and immunities listed in §§ 18 and 22 concern only the countries in which the officials perform their United Nations duties. And, unlike many other categories of international officials, members of UNEF national contingents will never be called upon to act in an international capacity in their home countries.

of the Forty-ninth Conference, Hamburg 1960 p. 144). However, UNEF Regulation 31 explicity provides that 'in the performance of their duties for the Force the members of the Force shall receive their instructions only from the Commander and the chain of command designated by him'. And UNEF Regulation 6 provides that 'the members of the Force, although remaining in their national service, are, during the period of their assignment to the Force, international personnel under the authority of the UN'.

155. Cf. also UNEF Regulation 6 which provides that the members of the Force remain in their national service.

156. The procedures provided by the Secretary-General under UNEF Regulation 34 (d) for the settlement of such claims are presumably not intended to be exclusive; cf. Regulation 34 (b), which excludes the courts of the host State only. Cf. also Status Agreement with Egypt, pars. 12 and 38.

157. Agreements with 'participating' States (*UNTS*, Vol. 271), pars. 5–7; cf. UNEF Regulation 34 and Status Agreement with Egypt, par. 11. The military members of the UNEF staff have been accorded immunity in respect of official acts and immunity from arrest even in their home countries under UNEF Regulation 19 (a); cf. the Convention on Privileges and Immunities of the United Nations, § 22 (a) and (b). The UN will have to waive this immunity if their home State is called upon to prosecute them, unless UNEF Regulation 34 is considered as a general waiver.

158. *Above*, p. 54 and e.g. § 12 of the Finnish Law of 20 May 1964 on a Finnish Security Force. Norwegians serving more than one year with the Force are exempt from Norwegian municipal taxes, but not from *national* income tax on pay received *from their government*. Tax exemption and immunity in respect of official acts are granted in the host State; see Status Agreements with Egypt and Cyprus, pars. 10–12 and 26, and *below*, pp. 428 and 431.

It will be seen that the legal powers retained by the 'participating' States in respect of their contingents relate to *personnel matters*. In this connexion it is useful to recall that under UNEF Regulation 6 'the members of the Force, although remaining in their national service, are, during the period of their assignment to the Force, international personnel under the authority of the United Nations'.

The major practical and legal implications of the first provision, that they remain in their national service, are that their Government is responsible for providing their uniforms and for all questions of promotion and in large measure pays and equips them, that it exercises disciplinary and criminal authority over them, and that it does not have to grant them privileges and immunities in these or in other respects.

The second provision, that they are *international* personnel during the period of their assignment to the Force, implies, on the one hand, that they have the *duties* of international personnel. They are, through their own national officers, subject to instructions only from the Commander in the performance of their duties for the Force. And they must discharge these duties with the interests of the United Nations, not those of their own Government, in view. They must exercise the utmost discretion in regard to all matters relating to their functions.[159] This duty, too, is one vis-à-vis the United Nations and in theory seems to apply even against their own Government. On the other hand, although their 'internal' *rights*, in respect of pay, uniform, promotion, &c., are mainly rights vis-à-vis their Government, not vis-à-vis the United Nations, they enjoy, as far as external rights are concerned, basically the status of international personnel. They are entitled to immunity in respect of official acts and to other privileges and immunities similar to those of United Nations officials and experts in the country where they perform their functions. And they are entitled to the legal protection of the United Nations as agents of the Organization.

It will be noted that none of the legal powers retained by 'participating' States has any direct bearing upon the operation and functions of the Force within the mandate assigned to it by the General Assembly, or upon its relations to the parties to the conflict, to the host State, or to any other third parties. The command and operation of the Force and its external relations, including public information,[160] and the conclusion of agreements with other States providing contingents, with the parties to the dispute and the host Government,[161] as well as relations of members of national contingents when acting in their capacity of members of the Force, are clearly in the hands of the United Nations.

159. UNEF Regulation 32.
160. UNEF Regulation 28.
161. *Below*, Chapter III,3(a) *in initio*.

It may be said in conclusion that the United Nations, legally speaking, appears to have essentially the same operational and external powers in respect of UNEF,[162] as long as it exists, as a national government has in respect of its national army. The United Nations itself cannot, however, expand UNEF's functions beyond those originally assigned to it by the General Assembly with binding effect for the 'participating' (and host) States.

7. THE UNITED NATIONS FORCE IN THE CONGO [163]

Shortly after the accession to independence of the Republic of the Congo on 30 June 1960, some units of the Congolese forces mutinied against their Belgian officers and committed acts of violence against members of the European population, in particular Belgians. The Belgian Government, acting against the wish of the Congolese Government, sent troops in order to maintain or restore order. This gave rise to bitterness and panic among the African population and to a new flight of Europeans and the consequent breakdown of many public services and important economic enterprises.[164] In this situation the President and the Prime Minister of the Congo, by telegrams of 12 and 13 July 1960, requested the urgent dispatch of a United Nations Force composed of military units from neutral countries in order to protect Congolese territory against what they termed the Belgian 'act of aggression'.[165]

On 14 July the Security Council, at the request of the Secretary-General and without a dissenting vote, adopted a resolution calling upon Belgium to withdraw its troops and authorizing the Secretary-General

> to take the necessary steps, in consultation with the Government of the Republic of the Congo, to provide the Government with such military assistance, as may be necessary, until, through the efforts of the Congolese Government with the technical assistance of the United Nations, the national security forces may be able, in the opinion of the Government, to meet fully their tasks.[166]

The vote was 8-0-3. China, France and the United Kingdom abstained because they could not support Belgian troop withdrawal before the United Nations Force had taken over; they did, however, support the dispatch of the United Nations Force.[166a]

162. See also *below*, Chapter III,2(a).
163. See Schachter: 'Legal Aspects of the United Nations Action in the Congo', *AJIL*, LV (1961) pp. 1–28, and in *Annual Review of United Nations Affairs*, 1960–61, pp. 142–161.
164. *OR SC*, 1960, 873rd meeting, p. 12; S/4531, par. 5, *ibid.*, Suppl. for July-September, p. 177.
165. S/4382, *OR SC*, 1960, Suppl. for July-September, p. 11.
166. S/4387, *OR SC*, 1960, Suppl. for July-September, p. 16.
166a. *OR SC*, 1960, 873rd meeting, pp. 25–44.

As to the *mandate* of the Force, the Secretary-General, in requesting this authority, pointed out that the difficulties which had developed in the Congo were connected with 'the maintenance of order in the country and the protection of life', and he expressed the understanding that, if a United Nations Force was dispatched, Belgium would see its way to withdraw.[167] Some members of the Council spoke of the Belgian action as external aggression which the Security Council should take effective action to halt; others spoke of it in terms of a humanitarian intervention which must be continued until the United Nations Force could take over responsibility for internal security. The latter was also the thesis of the Belgian Government, which supported the dispatch of a United Nations force as proposed by the Secretary-General, and which declared itself willing to withdraw its forces when United Nations troops had arrived and were able to ensure the effective maintenance of order and the security of persons.[168] Taking such different views of the nature of the Belgian intervention, the members of the Security Council disagreed as to the timing of the withdrawal of Belgian forces.[169] However, the majority rejected an amendment calling for an *immediate* withdrawal,[170] and the withdrawal ultimately took place only as and when United Nations troops entered the various areas.[171]

Later, in the Security Council's Resolution of 24 November 1961, the relevant policies and purposes of the United Nations with respect to the Congo were restated, on the basis of other resolutions adopted in the meantime,[172] as follows:

> (*a*) To maintain the territorial integrity and the political independence of the Republic of the Congo;
> (*b*) To assist the Central Government of the Congo in the restoration and maintenance of law and order;
> (*c*) To prevent the occurrence of civil war in the Congo;
> (*d*) To secure the immediate withdrawal and evacuation from the Congo of all foreign military, para-military and advisory personnel not under the United Nations Command, and all mercenaries.[173]

167. *Ibid.*, pars. 19 and 27.
168. *Ibid.*, pars. 195–6.
169. *Ibid.*, pp. 43–44; cf. par. 224.
170. *Ibid.*, p. 41.
171. Cf. the Secretary-General's interpretation of the mandate in his first report, S/4389, OR SC, 1960, Suppl. for July-September, p. 17.
172. The successive development of the mandate, from the Secretary-General's initial statement to the Security Council on 13 July (OR SC, 1960, 873rd meeting, pp. 3–5) and his first report (S/4389, *ibid.*, Suppl. for July-September, p. 17), unanimously commended by Security Council Resolution of 22 July 1960, is reflected in General Assembly Resolution 1474 (ES-IV) pars. 2 and 6, Security Council Resolution of 21 February 1961, pars. 1–2, General Assembly Resolutions 1599 (XV) par. 2, and 1600 (XV) par. 3. Cf. also S/4531, pars. 7 and 20, OR SC, 1960 Suppl. for July-September, pp. 178 and 181.
173. S/5002, OR SC, 1961, Suppl. for October-December, p. 148.

In the Status Agreement, which had been negotiated immediately before and which was signed three days later, the purposes of the Force were merely described in a general way as 'maintaining public order, peace and security'.[174]

Despite its greater size and heavier tasks, the United Nations Force in the Congo was constituted on a much more modest *formal basis* than the UNEF. In view of the urgency of the matter and the difficulties involved in reaching agreement among its members, the Security Council did not lay down in its resolutions [175] even the basic principles on which the Force should be organized, as the General Assembly had done in the case of UNEF. The organization of the Force, including the appointment of its Supreme Commander, was thus left to the Secretary-General, who, however, made detailed reports to the Council. In September 1960, when the Security Council was unable to agree on what action to take after the split between President Kasa-Vubu and Prime Minister Lumumba, the matter was referred to the General Assembly under the Uniting for Peace Resolution.[176] However, the resolutions of the General Assembly did not concern themselves directly with the Force, except for the budgetary aspects.[177]

A basic agreement with the host country, on the lines of and pushing somewhat further than the 'Aide-Mémoire on the Basis for the Presence and Functioning of the UNEF in Egypt',[178] was concluded two weeks after the decision to establish the Force.[179] However, a detailed Status Agreement between the United Nations and the Congo—partly modelled upon the UNEF Status Agreement,[180] but covering also the civilian operations—was not concluded until 27 November 1961.[181] And Regulations for the Force—following closely, but not in all respects, those of UNEF—were formally enacted only in July 1963.[182] However, both

174. S/5004, OR SC, 1961, Suppl. for October-December, p. 151, par. 43 (a).

175. Resolutions of 14 July, 22 July, 9 August and 17 September 1960 and of 21 February and 24 November 1961 (S/4387, S/4405, S/4426, S/4526, all in OR SC, 1960, Suppl. for July-September, pp. 16, 34, 91, 174; S/4741, OR SC, 1961, Suppl. for January-March, p. 147; S/5002, OR SC, 1961, Suppl. for October-December, p. 148).

176. Security Council Resolution of 17 September 1960, S/4526, OR SC, 1960, Suppl. for July-September, p. 174.

177. Resolutions 1583 (XV), 1590 (XV), 1595 (XV), 1619 (XV) and 1633 (XV); see also Resolutions 1474 (ES-IV), 1599 (XV) and 1600 (XV) on certain operational matters. The other resolutions on the Congo (Resolutions 1498, 1592 and 1601) have no bearing on the Force.

178. OR GA, 11th session, Annexes, A.i. 66, p. 9.

179. S/4389/Add. 5, 29 July 1960, OR SC, 1960, Suppl. for July-September, p. 27.

180. UNTS, Vol. 260, p. 61.

181. S/5004, OR SC, 1961, Suppl. for October-December, p. 151. See the detailed analysis by Salmon: 'L'accord ONU-Congo (Léopoldville) du 27 novembre 1961', *Revue générale de droit international public*, 1964, pp. 60–109.

182 ST/SGB/ONUC/1. See the corresponding texts for UNFICYP *below*, pp. 427–47.

the Status Agreement and the Regulations were promulgated with effect from the date of arrival of the first elements of the United Nations Force in the Congo.[183] Arrangements with the States providing contingents were made by correspondence rather than by formal agreements.

In the absence of new resolutions, agreements and regulations, the Secretary-General and the Force relied greatly upon the precedents set by the basic documents of the UNEF and organized the Force in essentially the same manner. In his oral introduction requesting authority to establish the Force, the Secretary-General stated that if the authority was given, he would base his actions on his Summary Study of the experience derived from the establishment and operation of the UNEF.[184] And in his first report on the implementation of the Security Council Resolution of 14 July 1960 he characterized his prior oral introduction, in response to which the first resolution had been adopted, 'as a basic document on the interpretation of the mandate', and went on to restate and supplement the major principles expressed in the UNEF Regulations and in the Summary Study as they were to be applied to the Congo Force.[185] His report was unanimously 'commended' by the Security Council in its Resolution of 22 July 1960,[186] and was since used as a basic guide for the organization of the Force and the interpretation of its mandate.

In this report it is re-emphasized that the United Nations must reserve for itself the authority to decide on the composition of the Force, while avoiding elements from the permanent members of the Security Council [187] or from other States whose participation might give rise to complications, and taking into account, without being bound by, objections from the host State.[188] These principles were later formulated in the Status Agreement in the following terms:

183. A/4986, S/5004, OR SC, 1961, Suppl. for October-December, p. 151.—The agreement of 17 April 1961 between the United Nations and the President of the Republic of the Congo on the implementation of the Security Council Resolution of 21 February 1961 does not contain any provision specifically concerning the Force.

184. OR SC, 1960, 873rd meeting, par. 28; cf. pars. 175–6 and ibid., 885th meeting, par. 65. See the Summary Study in OR GA, 13th session, Annexes, A.i. 65, pp. 8 et seq., the relevant contents of which have been related above, pp. 47 et seq.

185. S/4389, OR SC, 1960, Suppl. for July-September, pp. 17 et seq.

186. S/4405, OR SC, 1960, Suppl. for July-September, p. 34.

187. As in the case of UNEF, these did, however, provide transportation and other services.

188. OR SC, 1960, 873rd meeting, pars 28, 89 and 147; cf. ibid., Suppl. for July-September, p. 18, cf. above, under 6 (a). The Secretary-General did not give effect to Congolese criticism of the employment of contingents from non-African States.

189. S/4986, par. 2, OR SC, 1961, Suppl. for October-December, p. 134. Cf. below, Chapter III,2(a), at notes 11 and 14, on attempts made to interfere with the exclusive responsibility of the United Nations in this respect.

The United Nations shall possess sole competence with respect to decisions concerning the composition of the military units sent to the Congo, it being understood at the same time that the United Nations shall in determining their composition, give every consideration to the opinion of he Government as one of the most important factors to be borne in mind in connexion with recruitment.[189]

In addition to equipped national contingents of field troops and supporting units,[190] the Force comprised a Supreme Commander with a general staff made up of officers seconded directly by member Governmets or transferred from UNEF and UNTSO [191] with the consent of the respective Governments, as well as other international and locally recruited personnel. It should be noted that the United Nations operations in the Congo (*Organisation des Nations Unies au Congo—ONUC*) —in contradistinction to UNEF—also included an important Civilian Operation, and that the head of the whole United Nations Operation was not the Commander of the Force but a political officer, the Special Representative of the Secretary-General. The Chief of the Civilian Operations was in rank and authority opposite number to the Supreme Commander, and also exercised the functions of Resident Representative of the Technical Assistance Board.[192] They were both subject to the authority of the Special Representative. The total strength of the Force ranged between 15,000 and 20,000 officers and men.[193] ONUC itself also included several hundred international and locally recruited personnel. The Force was equipped with a considerable number of motor vehicles and aircraft. These had been purchased or chartered by the United Nations or lent by various Member States for operation at United Nations expense. At Headquarters the Secretary-General had, as in the case of UNEF, an advisory committee of representatives of States providing contingents,[194] as well as military advisers seconded by Member States.[195]

The *costs* of the Force were covered by the United Nations in essentially the same manner as those of UNEF. In 1961 the expenses of

190. Field troops were provided by a number of African States and by certain States in Asia and Europe. Technical supporting units and services, including airlift of contingents and equipment, were also provided by other States, notably north American and western and eastern European.

191. *Above*, note 7.

192. S/4417/Add. 5, OR SC, 1960, Suppl. for July-September, p. 60.

193. The first units arrived within 48 hours of the Security Council decision to set up the Force. Within ten days the Force had risen to 8,000 officers and men. In September 1960 the Force totalled 19,341 and was composed of twenty-four national contingents ranging from 1 to 3,267 officers and men (*ibid.*, p. 202). Towards the end of 1961 the Force totalled about 16,000 officers and men.

194. *Ibid.*, 887th meeting, par. 36.

195. The above and other information on the organization of the Force may be found in the first report (*ibid.*, Suppl. for July-September, pp. 17 et seq.), and in the annual budgets for the United Nations Operations in the Congo.

ONUC averaged approximately $ 10 million per month, of which about 83 per cent. were for direct expenses and about 17 per cent were for reimbursement to the Governments providing contingents.[196] The budgets for 62–63 were of the same order.[197] The sums were assessed upon Member States after deduction for voluntary contributions and for waiver of reimbursement by States providing airlift services. The General Assembly had expressly decided that the expenses were 'expenses of the Organization' subject to legally binding assessment of Member States under Article 17 of the Charter,[198] but that they were nevertheless to be kept separate as being essentially different in nature from the expenses under the regular budget.[199] However, some Members refused to accept this decision and to pay the corresponding amounts assessed upon them in respect of UNEF and ONUC. Consequently, the General Assembly, by its Resolution 1731 (XVI), decided to submit the question to the International Court of Justice for an advisory opinion. In its opinion of 20 July 1962 on *Certain Expenses of the United Nations* the Court held, by nine votes to five, that the expenses did 'constitute "expenses of the Organization" within the meaning of Article 17, paragraph 2, of the Charter of the United Nations'.[199a]

It was pointed out in the first report of the Secretary-General on the implementation of the Security Council Resolution of 14 July 1960 that 'in accordance with the principles generally applied by the Organisation... the Force is necessarily under the *exclusive command* of the United Nations, vested in the Secretary-General under the control of the Security Council', a statement which has since been repeated in several communications to Congolese authorities [200] and to the Security Council.[201] The report reiterated, furthermore, that to all United Nations personnel used in the operations, 'the basic rules of the United Nations for international service should be considered as applicable, particularly as regards full loyalty to the aims of the Organisation and to abstention from actions in relation to their country of origin which might deprive the operation of its international character and create a situation of dual loyalty'. Accordingly, it has been pointed out that both the military and civilian personnel of the Force in the Congo were governed by the following two basic principles of international service:

196. *OR GA*, 15 session, Annexes, A.i. 49–50.
197. General Assembly Resolutions 1732 (XVI) and 1865 (XVII).
198. General Assembly Resolution 1583 (XV).
199. General Assembly Resolution 1619 (XV), cf. A/5066.
199a. *ICJ Reports*, 1962, pp. 179–80.
200. Second report, S/4417, *OR SC*, 1960, Suppl. for July–September, p. 45, and the documents cited *below*, Chapter III, 2 (a), at notes 11 and 14, in connexion with attempts by Governments to interfere with the exclusive command authority of the United Nations.
201. *Ibid.*, 885th meeting, par. 127, and 887th meeting, pars. 45–46.

1. The prohibition against seeking or accepting instructions of their governments with respect to their duties in the United Nations Force [United Nations Charter, Article 100].

2. The obligation to refrain from any activity incompatible with the proper discharge of their duties and particularly to avoid any act or pronouncement which may adversely reflect on their international status or on the independence and impartiality required by that status [United Nations Staff Regulation 1. 4].[202]

When the Secretary-General on one occasion complained to the President of one contributing Member State about the lack of protection offered to the United Nations personnel by an officer of its contingent, the President replied by referring to the fact that the officers had been restricted in their freedom of action by orders from the United Nations Command, and that if the latter were dissatisfied with the officer's action, he was under their command and they should tell him so.[203]

In the basic agreement with the United Nations, the Government of the Congo stated that it 'will ensure the freedom of movement of the Force in the interior of the country and will accord the requisite *privileges and immunities* to all personnel associated with the activities of the Force'.[204] Unfortunately, at times when relations between the United Nations and the Congolese Government were strained, several incidents took place where Congolese military units physically interfered with United Nations personnel or otherwise did not act in accordance with these undertakings. The violations gave rise to protests from, and counteraction by, the United Nations [205] and, in some cases, to expressions of regret by the Congolese authorities.[206] The privileges and immunities in the Congo were later set forth in detail in the Status Agreement of 27 November 1961 [207] on the same lines as provided for UNEF in the Status Agreement with Egypt. Like the latter, the Status Agreement with the Congo provided, on the one hand, that 'members of the Force shall be subject to the exclusive jurisdiction of their respective national States in respect of any criminal offences which may be committed by them in the Congo' (par. 9), and, on the other hand, that 'the Supreme Commander of the United Nations Force in the Congo shall take all appropriate measures to ensure the discipline and good order of members of the Force' and that the United Nations military police 'shall have the power of arrest over members of the Force' (par. 12). The Status Agreement al-

---

202. Schachter in *American Journal of International Law*, LV (1961) p. 11.

203. OR SC, 1960, Suppl. for July–September, pp. 99–102.

204. S/4389/Add. 5, *ibid.*, p. 28. Italics supplied.

205. See, for example, second report, S/4477/Add. 8, OR SC, 1960, Suppl. for July–September, p. 134; *ibid.*, 916th meeting, p. 2; and S/4753, OR SC, 1961, Suppl. for January–March, pp. 203–5.

206. OR SC, 1960, 888th meeting, p. 19.

207. OR SC, 1961, Suppl. for October-December, p. 151, see notably pars. 9 et seq.

so provided, like that of UNEF, for use of the United Nations flag (par. 26) and for distinctive United Nations identification marks on vehicles, aircraft and vessels of the Force (par. 32).

As the examples quoted above and the relevant provisions of the Status Agreement indicate, the *distribution of functions and powers* between the United Nations and the States providing contingents to the Force was the same as in the case of UNEF.[207a] The legal powers of the States providing contingents were confined to personnel matters, while all operational decisions were made by the United Nations, or by officers of national contingents acting under the instructions of the United Nations Command, which in turn was subject to the orders of the Secretary-General and, through him, of the Security Council and the General Assembly.[208]

While the organization of and the distribution of powers over the United Nations Force in the Congo were very similar to those of UNEF, the *functions and operations* of the Congo Force turned out rather differently. UNEF, during the second phase of its operations, had only one main task, that of patrolling the demarcation line and the international frontier. This it was able to do without any serious incidents involving military operations.[209]

The Congo Force had to perform a number of tasks throughout a vast territory in order to fulfil its mandate to assist in the maintenance of law and order and the protection of life and property, to prevent foreign intervention in the form of men, arms or military supplies, and to prevent civil war. Apart from a number of civilian activities, like maintenance of essential services, mediation and persuasion, the Force performed, *inter alia*, the following functions: patrolling areas threatened by disorders;[210] establishing and guarding United Nations protected areas where people in danger of arbitrary arrest or other persecution could take refuge;[211] guarding and defending the residences of Congolese political leaders and diplomatic representatives of foreign States[212]

207a. See, however, *below*, p. 398, note 270.

208. See *below*, pp. 93 et seq. on the implementation of this principle.

209. From August 1960 to July 1961 there were seven incidents involving firing on the UNEF troops, nine other incidents involving firing, 109 crossings of the demarcation line not involving firing, and 242 air violations of the line. In general, there was 'no resort to force by UNEF, the mere presence of armed personnel on the spot being adequate to prevent incidents. On one occasion, however, when an armed infiltrator fired at a patrol in order to resist apprehension, United Nations troops had to take appropriate action in self-defence' (Report of the Secretary-General, 30 August 1961, A/4857, pars. 1 and 15).

210. S/4557, pars. 67 et seq., *OR SC*, 1960, Suppl. for October-December, p. 22.

211. S/4590, *ibid.*, p. 94; S/4745, *OR SC*, 1961, Suppl. for January-March, p. 154; S/4750/Adds. 6–7, *ibid.*, pp. 162 et seq.; S/4757, *ibid.*, pp. 205 et seq.

212. *OR GA*, 15th session, Annexes, A.i. 85, pp. 35–36.

to protect them against arbitrary arrest or violence;[213] guarding government buildings;[214] guarding, isolating and neutralizing the meeting place of the Congolese Parliament and ensuring the free passage through the Congo of its members;[215] guarding, and in emergencies temporarily closing, ports and airfields to secure the supplies to and the movements of the United Nations Force and to prevent Congolese troop movements or external aid to the opposing sides in the civil war;[216] arrest and eviction of foreign military personnel or mercenaries;[217] disarming civilians[218] and military groups which have broken loose from their commanders;[219] rescuing civilians, wounded and dead out of areas affected by civil war.[219a] Last, but not least, the functions included occupying, patrolling and if necessary defending areas threatened by armed invasion, and establishing, guarding and defending road blocks [220] or neutral zones between opposing Congolese forces,[221] or removing road blocks or other obstacles and opposition to the United Nations movements and operations created by local military units;[222] guarding and defending United Nations personnel and positions.[223]

These and other activities could not avoid interfering with the plans of the various central and provincial authorities in the Congo—indeed, it

213. S/4557, pars. 66 et seq., OR SC, 1960, Suppl. for October-December, p. 22; OR GA, 15th session, Annexes, A.i. 85, pp. 41 et seq.; S/4571, par. 2, OR SC, 1960, Suppl. for October–December, p. 67; OR GA, 15th session, Annexes, A.i. 85, p. 27; S/4757, OR SC, 1961, Suppl. for January–March, p. 205.

214. S/4571, par. 2, OR SC, 1960, Suppl. for October-December, p. 67, cf. General Assembly Resolution 1600 (XV) par. 5.

215. S/4841, especially Annex III, pars. 6–8, OR SC, 1961, Suppl. for April-June, pp. 69 et seq.; S/4913, Annex II, OR SC, 1961, Suppl. for July–September, pp. 61 et seq.; S/4917, ibid., pp. 66 et seq.; cf. S/4865, S/4908, S/4911 and Add. 2, all in OR SC, 1961, Suppl. for July–September, pp. 14–5, 52–3, 54 et seq.

216. S/4531, par. 20, OR SC, 1960, Suppl. for July-September, p. 181; cf. ibid., pp. 16 et seq.

217. S/4557, pars. 73-74, OR SC, 1960, Suppl. for October-December, p. 24; OR GA, 15th session, Annexes, A.i. 85, pp. 103–6 and 108; S/4807, pars. 2 and 8, OR SC, 1961 Suppl. for April-June, pp. 43 et seq., S/4940, OR SC, 1961, Suppl. for July-September, pp. 99 et seq.

218. S/4557/Add. 6, OR SC, 1961, Suppl. for January-March, pp. 6 et seq.

219. Ibid., 1960, 901st meeting, p. 17; cf. Status Agreement, S/4986, par. 13, OR SC, 1961, Suppl. for October–December, p. 155.

219a. Annual Report of the Secretary-General, 1963—64, pp. 3–4.

220. See, for example, S/4750/Adds. 4 and 6, OR SC, 1961, Suppl. for January-March, pp. 162 et seq.

221. S/4557, pars. 74 and 79, OR SC, 1960, Suppl. for October-December, pp. 24-25; S/4750/Add. 7, OR SC, 1961, Suppl. for January-March, pp. 173 et seq.; A/4733, OR GA, 15th session, Annexes A.i. 85, pp. 107 et seq.

222. S/4940, and Add. 16, pars. 22–27, OR SC, 1961, Suppl. for July-September, pp. 99 et seq.; S/5053/Add. 14, pars. 46 et seq., OR SC, 1963, Suppl. for January-March, pp. 13 et seq.

223. OR GA, 15th session, Annexes, A.i. 85, p. 61.

was in many cases their purpose to restrict the freedom of action of these authorities in so far as they might upset order and security. However, the various Congolese authorities also had armed forces at their disposal, and they were not at all times willing to acquiesce in the UN interference. It was thus unavoidable that tension and armed clashes would occur during periods when the aims of the various central or provincial Congolese leaders and those of the United Nations diverged. And when the United Nations, pursuant to the Security Council's resolutions of 21 February and 24 November 1961, took active measures to arrest and expel foreign military personnel and mercenaries, this provoked attacks by Katangese forces which involved the United Nations in military operations on a larger scale in August and December 1961.[224] Extensive operations also took place during the final phase of the United Nations operation in Katanga in December 1962-January 1963.[225]

The numerous incidents of warfare which occurred between United Nations forces and Congolese forces (notably those of the Central Government and of the Katanga authorities) involved the use not only of small arms, but also of artillery, fighter planes, armoured cars and river boats, as well as bombing from the air.[226] There were considerable numbers of killed and wounded, and prisoners and equipment taken on both sides.[227] In some cases the United Nations troops, in other cases the other side, were forced to withdraw from ports, road blocks and other positions they had been holding.[228] In some cases the hostilities were ended by signed agreements for cessation of hostilities and withdrawal from positions held.[229]

The military encounters were, however, merely local operations. Most of them did not involve the entire armies of the United Nations and the

224. S/4940, Adds. 1–17, OR SC, 1961, Suppls. for July–September and October-December.
225. S/5053/Adds. 14 and 15, OR SC, 1963, Suppl. for January-March, pp. 13 et seq.
226. S/4758/Add. 2, OR SC, 1961, Suppl. for January-March, p. 218; OR GA, 15th session, Annexes, A.i. 85, p. 108; S/4940/Add. 2, par. 5; Add. 7; Add. 16, par. 12; Add. 17, pars. 2–4 and 12; S/5025, pp. 6 and 11; in OR SC, 1961, Suppl. for July–September, pp. 107 et seq., and Suppl. for October–December, pp. 48 et seq., 193, 196 and 199; S/5053/Add. 14, pars. 46 et seq., and Add. 15, OR SC, 1963, Suppl. for January–March, pp. 13 et seq., 61 and 66 et seq.
227. See, inter alia, S/4761, OR SC, 1961, Suppl. for January-March, p. 228; OR GA, 15th session, Annexes A.i. 85, pp. 36, 53, 61 and 108; S/4940; S/4940/Add. 7 and Add. 16, par. 27.
228. See notably on the fights in Banana and Matadi in March 1961, S/4761, OR SC, 1961, Suppl. for January–March, p. 228; in Elisabethville in August–December 1961, S/4940 and Adds. 1–17; and in Katanga December 1962–January 1963, S/5053/Add. 14, OR SC, 1963, Suppl. for January-March, pp. 13 et seq.
229. S/4761, OR SC, 1961, Suppl. for January-March, p. 228; S/4940/Add. 7 and Add. 11; cf. below, Chapter III, 3 (a).

Congolese authorities concerned. Public threats of countrywide military assault against the United Nations Force [230] and proclamations by the Katanga authorities of a state of 'war' with the United Nations [231] were never given full effect. Nor did the battles last long. Prisoners were usually returned to their units immediately or after a certain period of confinement.[232] Exceptions to this were foreign military personnel and mercenaries captured by the United Nations troops. These were detained, questioned and sent out of the country in implementation of Security Council and General Assembly decisions in that respect.[233]

Like UNEF, the United Nations Force in the Congo was not intended to carry out active military operations.[234] Its original instructions in respect of use of arms were, like those of UNEF, that

> ... men engaged in the operation may never take the initiative in the use of armed force, but are entitled to respond with force to an attack with arms, including attempts to use force to make them withdraw from positions which they occupy under orders from the Commander, acting under the authority of the Security Council and within the scope of its resolution.[235]

Thus the Force did not act when, at an early stage, the Central Government and certain States providing contingents put the Secretary-

---

230. S/4557, pars. 13 and 23, *OR SC*, 1960, Suppl. for October-December pp. 10 and 13.

231. S/4750, par. 11, *OR SC*, 1961, Suppl. for January-March, p. 162; S/5053/Add. 14, par. 45, *OR SC*, 1963, Suppl. for January–March, pp. 13 and 61.

232. In an agreement of 17 January 1963 between the United Nations and M. Tschombe, whereby the latter agreed to the entry of the United Nations Force into Kolvezi, the United Nations gave its assurance that the Katangese *gendarmerie* in that city would 'not be treated as prisoners of war or arrested' (*OR SC*, 1963, Suppl. for January–March, p. 84).

233. Security Council Resolution of 21 February 1961, A2, and General Assembly Resolution 1599 (XV) par 2. See quotation *below*, p. 138 and citations *above*, note 217.

234. In the instructions to Dr. Bunche for his mission to Katanga, in August 1960, the Secretary-General said that the aims of the Security Council should be 'speedily achieved, but without frictions ... which would compromise the impartial attitude and pacific status of a United Nations Force' (S/4417, par. 8, cf. also par. 10, *OR SC*, 1960, Suppl. for July–September, pp. 51–53).

235. First report, S/4389, *ibid.*, p. 20, cf. the Secretary-General's Summary Study of UNEF, *OR GA*, 13th session, Annexes, A.i. 65, p. 17; second report, S/4417, pars. 6 and 8–10, *OR SC*, 1960, Suppl. for July–September, pp. 48–52. Cf. *ibid.*, 885th meeting, par. 128. For a restrictive interpretation by the Special Representative of the Secretary-General in the Congo, see ibid., 888th meeting, p. 19. On the extension of the authority to use arms by General Assembly Resolution 1474 (ES-IV) of 20 September 1960, considered in the light of statements in the Assembly, see Schachter in *American Journal of International Law*, LV (1961) p. 20. On the further extensions, see below and Draper: 'The Legal Limitation upon the Employment of Weapons by the United Nations Force in the Congo', *International and Comparative Law Quarterly, XII* (1963) pp. 387–413.

General under intense pressure, employing notes, incidents, threats and appeals to the Security Council, to make the Force enter the province of Katanga despite the threats of the Katanga authorities to resist such entry with force.[236] Later, the Force rejected demands from the Central Government and from provincial governments, accompanied by ultimata, threats or other kinds of pressure, that it liberate Prime Minister Lumumba,[237] that it expel from Luluabourg invading forces of the Stanleyville Government,[238] or that it evict the troops which, upon the seizure of power by the Congolese Chief of Staff, had occupied airports and public buildings.[239]

However, the defensive policy was not pressed to the point where the Force could not act to re-establish its own positions and freedoms when these had been temporarily overthrown by larger contingents of Congolese troops. Thus, when an Austrian medical team had been arrested by Congolese troops, United Nations troops interfered and liberated them after a battle resulting in casualties to both sides.[240] Similarly, when Katanga gendarmes blocked the runway at the Elisabethville airport, they were disarmed and transported to their headquarters by United Nations troops.[241] When the United Nations garrison in Banana had beeen forced by shelling and superior number of Congolese troops to give up this naval base, reinforcements were sent up with instructions to reoccupy the base, but it was not specified whether they should do so by the use of force.[242]

When the threat of a full-scale civil war between the rival Governments in the various provinces became imminent after the murder of Prime Minister Lumumba, the Security Council, by a resolution of 21 February 1961, urged 'that the United Nations take immediately all appropriate measures to provent the occurrence of civil war in the Congo, including arrangements for cease-fires, the halting of all military operations, the prevention of clashes, and the use of force, if necessary, in the

236. Second report, S/4417, and Adds. 1 and 7 OR SC, 1960, Suppl. for July-September, pp. 54–17. See *ibid.*, 885th meeting, esp. par. 128. In the end the United Nations succeeded in taking up its positions in Katanga without resorting to force. This impelled the withdrawal of the last regular Belgian forces from the Congo.

237. S/4590, with text of United Nations protest against ultimative form, *ibid.*, Suppl. for October–December, p. 95.

238. S/4750/Add. 3, OR SC, 1961, Suppl. for January-March, p. 162.

239. S/4557, par. 17, OR SC, 1960, Suppl. for October-December, p. 17.

240. *Ibid.*, pp. 104–6.

241. S/4791, par. 25, OR SC, 1961, Suppl. for April-June, p. 22.

242. S/4758/Add. 2, OR SC, 1961, Suppl. for January-March, p. 210; and S/4761, *ibid.*, p. 228. The carrying out of the plans was prevented by the subsequent larger attack upon and forced withdrawal from Matadi, which was reoccupied only much later by unarmed Nigerian police.

last resort'.[243] This resolution—which for the first time in history authorized troops under United Nations command to use force if necessary to carry out the decisions of the Security Council—cleared the way for an active United Nations opposition to the civil war under way. However, it was in the execution of another task assigned to it by the same resolution, that of taking measures for the withdrawal of foreign personnel, that the Force became involved in military operations on a larger scale. The Force did not consider that it had the legal authority, on the basis of the resolution of 21 February 1961, to use force for the evacuation of foreign personnel. Instead, it found the legal authority in a request from the Central Government to assist in the execution of tis Ordinance of 24 August 1961 to this effect.[244] Later, the authority was specified in the Security Council's Resolution of 24 November 1961 where the Council:

> 4. *Authorizes* the Secretary-General to take vigorous action, including the use of the requisite measure of force, if necessary, for the immediate apprehension, detention pening legal action and/or deportation of all foreign military and para-military personnel and political advisers not under the United Nations Command, and mercenaries as laid down in paragraph A-2 of the Security Council resolution of 21 February 1961;
>
> 5. *Further requests* the Secretary-General to take all necessary measures to prevent the entry or return of such elements under whatever guise and also of arms, equipment or other material in support of such activities.[245]

The Status Agreement of 27 November 1961 provided that 'the United Nations shall not have recourse to the use of force except as a last resort and subject to the restrictions imposed by its mandate and by the resolutions of the Security Council and the General Assembly'.[246]

In the execution of its mandate under the Security Council Resolutions of 21 February and 24 November 1961 to evacuate foreign military personnel, political advisers and mercenaries, the United Nations Force took important preventive measures, including the placing of surveillance on Radio Katanga, on gendarmerie headquarters and on other key points and installations in the City of Elisabethville.[247] It was primarily attacks upon the positions thus taken up which caused the hostilities on a larger scale in Elisabethville in September and December and which

243. S/4741. At an earlier stage, the Secretary-General had transmitted to the Central Government and the Katanga authorities an interpretation of the Security Council Resolution of 9 August 1960 to the effect that the United Nations had no right to refuse either Government 'to ake any action which by their own means, in accordance with the Purpose and Principles of the Charter, they can carry through' in relation to the other Government (S/4417/Add. 6, OR SC, 1960, Suppl. for July–September, p. 64).

244. S/4940, pars. 1–2 and Annex, OR SC, 1961, Suppl. for July–September, p. 99.
245. S/5002, OR SC, 1961, Suppl. for October–December, p. 148.
246. S/5004, par. 43 (b), OR SC, 1961, Suppl. for October–December, p. 151.
247. S/4940, pars. 3 and 15, OR SC, 1961, Suppl. for July–September, p. 99.

later forced the United Nations to take preventive offensive action in several respects, such as bombardments from the air of railway lines, bridges, airports, artillery positions, ammunition dumps and military trucks, disarming Katangese gendarmerie and clearing defended road-blocks, inflicting heavy casualties upon the Kantagese forces.[248] This provoked strong protests to the United Nations from certain Member Governments, which spoke of 'war operations conducted by the United Nations in Kantanga'.[249]

Less violent, but more extensive military operations took place during the final phase of the United Nations action in Katanga in December 1962 and January 1963. After a six-day period of unanswered firing on United Nations positions and incidents involving seizure and detention of members of the United Nations Force by the Katangese gendarmerie, the United Nations on 28 December launched its final action against the forces of the provincial Katangese government. The United Nations Force first cleared the Katangese road blocks in Elisabethville and seized the key positions in that city. Subsequently, it advanced towards and occupied other cities in southern Katanga. This action cost 10 killed and 77 wounded on the United Nations side and nearly as many civilian casualities. One of the actions carried out during this phase—the advance on and occupation of Jadotville, which was carried out by the commanders in the field without consultation with headquarters at New York and Leopoldville—was termed by the Officer-in-Charge of the United Nations operation in the Congo as 'the first experience of a strictly United Nations armed force under United Nations command with combat conditions in the field'.[250] By 21 January 1963 the United Nations Force had under control all important centres hitherto held by the Katangese, the Katangese airforce had been eliminated and the Katangese gendarmerie as an organised fighting force had ceased to exist.[251] M. Tschombe ended the seccessionist activities and officials and security forces of the Central Government could gradually move into the Province, although these forces were, during the first period, placed under United Nations command (as a Congolese contingent of the United Nations Force).[252]

This ended the major United Nations military operations in the

---

248. S/4940, pars. 15—17, S/4940/Add. 2, and notably, Add. 16, pars. 22–27, and Add. 17, all in OR SC, 1961, Suppl. for July–September.

249. Telegrams to the United Nations from the Republic of the Congo (Brazzaville) an from Belgium, December 1961, S/5035, OR SC, 1961, Suppl. for October–December, p. 207, and S/5025, ibid., p. 190.

250. S/5053/Add. 14, par. 74, OR SC, 1963, Suppl. for January-March, p. 17.

251. S/5053/Add. 15, OR SC, 1963, Suppl. for January-March, pp. 67–68.

252. S/5240, par. 22, OR SC, 1963, Suppl. for January-March, p. 99; cf. p. 65; AnnualReport of the Secretary-General, 1962–63, pp. 11 and 12.

Congo. The Force remained in the country for another year-and-a-half, but it was gradually reduced in strength, not merely because of the restoration of national unity, but also because of the lack of funds. The last United Nations troops left the Congo in the summer of 1964.

In accordance with its mandate the United Nations Force in principle maintained neutrality in internal conflicts,[253] other than secession, confining its efforts to the prevention of offensive civil war operations, through persuasion, mediation, neutral zones or, if necessary, armed resistance.[254] During the period when more than one authority claimed to represent the constitutional Central Government these efforts were directed at either side. However, after the establishment in August 1961 of a new constitutional Central Government, recognized as such by the United Nations,[255] the Organization adopted the line that no military action would be directed against any offensive police operation undertaken by that Government.[256]

A neutral attitude was not called for when foreign activities were involved. Thus the United Nations Force itself took the initiative in detaining aircraft with crew bringing arms and military supplies into the

253. Security Council Resolution of 9 August 1960, par. 4 (S/4426, *OR SC*, 1960, Suppl. for July–September, p. 91), repeating earlier statements in the Secretary-General's Summary Study on UNEF and in his first report on the Force in the Congo (S/4389, *OR SC*, 1960, Suppl. for July–September, p. 16); S/4791, par. 25, *OR SC*, 1961, Suppl. for April–June, p. 22. Cf. the citations *below*, p. 137, note 46.

254. See, for example, S/4750, pars. 8–10, *OR SC*, 1961, Suppl. for January–March, p. 162.

255. In his letter of 13 August 1961 to the Prime Minister, the Secretary-General confirmed that the United Nations would deal with his Government as being the Central Government of the Republic of the Congo and agreed that 'whatever aid and support the United Nations is in a position to give to the Congo, within the limits of this mandate, should be rendered exclusively to your Government' (S/4923, *OR SC*, 1961, Suppl. for July–September, p. 74). See also *OR SC*, 1963, Suppl. for January–March, p. 98 , par. 21.

256. Confirmed in press statements by several United Nations officials in September 1961. In his report on the Protocol of 13 October 1961 of agreement between the Katanga authorities and ONUC subsequent to the cease-fire of 20 September 1961, the Officer-in-Charge of the United Nations Operation in the Congo stated that 'the freedom of action of the Central Government, representing the sovereign and constitutional authority of the Republic of the Congo, is of course unaffected'. In approving the Protocol, United Nations Headquarters set, *inter alia*, the following conditions: '(a) The conclusion of the agreement shall in no way affect the resolutions of the Security Council, including that of 21 February 1961, and of the General Assembly; (b) The agreement is of a strictly military nature and applies solely to the United Nations Force in Katanga and to the armed forces of Katanga'. The Protocol provided, on the other hand, in par. 10, that 'the representatives of ONUC shall not consider that the cease-fire has been violated in the event that the Katangese gendarmerie counters an attack from the outside'. (S/4940/Add. 11, pars. 9–10 and 12 and Annex II, *OR SC*, 1961, Suppl. for July-September, p. 99.)

Congo,[257] and in arresting and evicting foreign mercenaries and advisers. The United Nations also took a special interest when on New Year's Day 1961 Congolese troops from the Central Government invaded the Kivu Province from the Belgian trusteeship territory of Ruanda-Urundi, across the international frontier, although the United Nations Force confined itself to attempting to contact the invaders and the Belgian authorities with a view to obtaining a cease-fire, while not interfering with any defence action by the local Congolese troops.[258]

Nor was a neutral attitude taken in respect of seccessionist activities. This, like the attitude towards foreign advisers and mercenaries, was based upon specific resolutions of the Security Council,[259] and was of particular importance in respect of Katanga. In his summing-up report after the end of the last military operations in Katanga the Secretary-General stated:

37. . . . The Principle of non-interference in the internal political affairs of the Congo . . . has been observed and the United Nations has scrupulously avoided any support for or opposition to any Congolese official or candidate, whether in the national or provincial governments. The United Nations has avoided any intervention in the internal politics of the country beyond the opposition to secession in general required by the Security Council resolutions and the constitutional suggestions embodied in the Plan for National Reconciliation which, after all, was only a proposal which each party was free to accept or reject.

38. The United Nations operation in the Congo has also adhered to the principle of avoiding the use of force for political purposes, although it is true that the very presence and activity of the United Nations Force in the Congo has been an important factor in giving effective weight to United Nations opposition to secession, whether in Katanga, Kasai or elsewhere in the country. It is in the Congo, of course, for this and other purposes, at the specific request of the Government of the country. But the United Nations has never used the arms at its disposal to further the political aims of any group or individual in the country, or to interfere with its political processes. Even with regard to secession, civil war and the elimination of mercenaries, the employment of the Force has been in the most limited manner, with limited objectives, without the Force itself taking any military initiatives, and only then as a last resort.

257. S/4789, OR SC, 1961, Suppl. for April-June, p. 12, citing Security Council Resolution of 21 February 1961.

258. S/4606, Annex 4, OR SC, 1961, Suppl. for January–March, p. 1.

259. In its Resolution of 24 November 1961 (S/5002, OR SC, 1961, Suppl. for October–December, p. 148) the Security Council:

'8. Declares that all secessionist activities against the Republic of the Congo are contrary to the Loi fondamentale and Security Council decisions and specifically demands that such activities which are now taking place in Katanga shall cease forthwith;

9. Declares full and firm support for the Central Government of the Congo, and the determination to assist that Government in accordance with the decisions of the United Nations to maintain law and order and national integrity, to provide technical assistance and to implement those decisions.'

See also OR SC, 1963, Suppl. for January–March, p. 5, par. 14, and p. 100, par 25.

39. The only sound way to inject an international armed force into a situation of that kind is to ensure that it is for clearly defined and restricted purposes, is fully under control of the Organization and always maintains its primary posture of arms for defence.[260]

8. THE UNITED NATIONS SECURITY FORCE IN WEST NEW GUINEA (IRIAN BARAT) [261]

When in 1949 Indonesia achieved independence, the Netherlands did not transfer to the new State its sovereignty over West New Guinea (now Irian Barat), which was inhabited by Papuans rather than by Indonesians. However, Indonesia claimed this Territory, too, and the matter was repeatedly discussed in the General Assembly of the United Nations. At the end of December 1961 fighting started in the Territory between the Netherlands forces and Indonesian forces which had been landed by parachute and submarine.

On 15 August 1962 the two countries signed an Agreement and a number of attached documents.[262] These instruments provided for a cease-fire under United Nations observation and for the transfer to Indonesia of authority over the Territory after a transitional period during which it would be administered by a 'United Nations Temporary Executive Authority (UNTEA) established by and under the jurisdiction of the Secretary-General' (Article II). The latter was to appoint a United Nations Administrator, acceptable to both countries, who, 'as chief executive officer of the UNTEA, will have full authority under the direction of the Secretary-General to administer the territory for the period of the UNTEA administration in accordance with the terms of the present Agreement' (Articles IV-V).[263]

The Agreement was ratified by the two States on 20 September 1962. On the following day the General Assembly, by resolution 1752 (XVII), took note of it and authorized the Secretary-General 'to carry out the tasks entrusted to him in the Agreement'. Thereupon it entered into force.

On 1 October 1962 the Netherlands transferred the administration of the Territory to UNTEA, and on 1 May 1963 the latter retransferred it

260. S/5240, OR SC, 1963, Suppl. for January-March, p. 103.

261. The relevant documents are contained in OR GA, XVII, Annexes, A.i. 89 and Plenary meetings, I, pp. 49–58. See also OR GA, XVIII, Annexes, A.i. 20; Annual Report of the Secretary-General, 1962–63, pp. 35–40, and 1963–64, p. 26; and The United Nations in West New Guinea, UN Sales No. 63. I. 35. The question was not discussed in the Security Council.

262. OR GA, XVII, Annexes, A.i. 89.

263. See also Articles IX, on appointment of officials, and XI, on limitations upon the legislative power.

to Indonesia. During this period the United Nations flag was flown in the Territory, together with the Dutch flag until 31 December 1962 and thereafter together with the Indonesian flag. This may have been provided to mark the fact that the United Nations had merely been given the power of administration, not the sovereignty. However, the Agreement contained no other indication as to where the sovereignty would be vested. On the contrary, an aide-mémoire from the Secretary-General of 15 August 1962, which was attached to the Agreement and which specified the flag rules, stated that 'the *authority* [264] of the Government of the Netherlands over the territory will be terminated when the Special Representative of the Secretary-General takes charge' without making any mention of Indonesian authority before 1 May 1963.

At the time of the Agreement there were some 12,000 Netherlands Army troops and some 1,500 Indonesian troops in the Territory. The Agreement contained the following provision for new security forces:

> The Secretary-General will provide the UNTEA with such security forces as the United Nations Administrator deems necessary; such forces will primarily supplement existing Papuan (West Irianese) police in the task of maintaining law and order. The Papuan Volunteer Corps, which on the arrival of the United Nations Administrator will cease being part of the Netherlands armed forces, and the Indonesian armed forces in the territory will be under the authority of, and at the disposal of, the Secretary-General for the same purpose. The United Nations Administrator will, to the extent feasible, use the Papuan (West Irianese) police as a United Nations security force to maintain law and order and, at his discretion, use Indonesian armed forces. The Netherlands armed forces will be repatriated as rapidly as possible and while still in the territory will be under the authority of the UNTEA.[265]

The Memorandum of Understanding on Cessation of Hostilities of the same date provided, inter alia: 'A United Nations security force including an infantry battalion with ancillary arms and services will be placed by the Secretary-General at the disposal of the United Nations Temporary Executive Authority (UNTEA) in the territory primarily to supplement the existing Papuan police in the task of maintaining law and order'.[266]

The Secretary-General gave effect to these provisions by establishing a United Nations Security Force (UNSF), the major part of which was made up of a self-contained Pakistani unit (the 14th Punjab), consisting of six companies. The composition and functions of this Force were described in the Annual Report of the Secretary-General on the Work of the Organization 1962-63 as follows: [267]

264. Italics added.
265. Article VII. See also Article XIII.
266. Par. 7. See also par. 4.
267. OR GA, XVIII, Suppl. No. 1, pp. 36–37.

II. NATIONAL CONTINGENTS. UN CONTROL

In response to the Secretary-General's request, the Government of Pakistan provided a force of some 1,500 men to serve as the United Nations Security Force (UNSF). The Governments of Canada and the United States provided supporting aircraft and crews. Major-General Said Uddin Khan of Pakistan, appointed by the Secretary-General as Commander of UNSF, arrived in Hollandia on 4 September for preliminary discussions with the Netherlands authorities and for a survey of future requirements.

By 3 October an advance party of 340 men of UNSF had arrived in the territory. On 5 October the balance of the Pakistan contingent took up its positions. Also included in UNSF were some sixteen officers and men of the Royal Canadian Air Force with two Otter aircraft, and a detachment of approximately sixty United States Air Force personnel with an average of three DC-3's. These provided troop transport and communications. The Administrator also had under his authority the Papuan Volunteer Corps, the civil police and the Netherlands forces remaining until their repatriation, as well as Indonesian troops, totalling approximately 1,500.

In accordance with the terms of article VII [of the Agreement of 15 August 1962], the Papuan Volunteer Corps ceased to be part of the Netherlands armed forces upon the transfer of administration to UNTEA. The Corps, consisting of some 350 officers and men, was concentrated at Manckwari and was not assigned any duties in connexion with the maintenance of law and order. As Dutch officers and non-commissioned officers left the area, they were replaced by Indonesian officers. This process was completed on 21 January, when the command of the Corps was formally transferred to an Indonesian officer and the last Dutch officers left the territory.

During the period of UNTEA administration, the Papuan police were generally responsible for the maintenance of law and order in the territory. Before the transfer of administration to UNTEA, all the officers of the police corps were Dutch, there being no qualified Papuans. By the time UNTEA had assumed responsibility for the territory, almost all officers of Dutch nationality had left, being temporarily replaced by officers from the Philippines who, in turn, were later replaced by Indonesians. By the end of March 1963, the entire corps was officered by Indonesians. However, in accordance with the provisions of article IX of the Agreement, the chief of police continued to be an international recruit.

On 1 October, when authority was transferred to UNTEA, the Indonesian troops in the territory consisted of those who had been brought in by parachute during the Dutch-Indonesian conflict and those who had infiltrated the territory. Agreement was reached with the Indonesian authorities to replace a large number of these troops with fresh territorial troops from Indonesia. It was also agreed that the number of Indonesian troops in the territory would not exceed the strength of the Pakistan contingent of UNSF, except with the prior consent of the UNTEA administration.

The withdrawal of the Netherlands naval and land forces from the territory was effected in stages in accordance with a time-table agreed upon by the Temporary Administrator, the Commander of UNSF and the Commander-in-Chief of the Netherlands forces in the territory. By 15 November 1962, this process had been completed without incident.

The situation was generally calm throughout the period of UNTEA. On 15 December 1962, however, two incidents involving the police and a small group of Indonesian troops occurred in Sorong and Doom. One Papuan police constable was killed and four wounded. Order was immediately restored by units of UNSF while the civil administration continued to perform its normal functions. The area remained quiet for the rest of the temporary administration.

In general, the inhabitants of the territory were law-abiding and the task of maintaining peace and security in the territory presented no problems. The United Nations Administrator had no occasion to call on the Indonesian armed forces in connexion with the maintenance of law and order but only for the purpose of occasional joint patrols with elements of the Pakistan contingent.

The Force was, like the entire UNTEA, financed by the United Nations out of funds placed at its disposal by Indonesia and the Netherlands in equal shares. Like UNEF and the United Nations Force in the Congo, UNSF was under the command and control of the United Nations for operational purposes. It was less multi-national in its composition than the two other Forces. More significant differences were connected with the fact that the Force did not operate in 'foreign' territory, but in a territory under the temporary administration of the Organization itself. This fact and the nature of its tasks gave the Force more the nature of an 'internal' Force than any of its predecessors. Indeed, it was merely an arm of the United Nations Temporary Administration. Therefore it was not necessary to conclude any status (or host) agreement. Treaty provisions on privileges and immunities were not necessary in view of the fact that the United Nations itself had the legislative, executive and judicial powers in the Territory during the period of its administration. Nevertheless, Article XXVI of the Agreement provided for application of the Convention on the Privileges and Immunities of the United Nations 'to United Nations property, funds, assets and officials'. It is submitted that the Organization would have had the power to list the members of its Force as 'officials' for the purpose of the Convention, in accordance with its § 17,[268] if it had considered any treaty provisions necessary in this respect.

The functions of the Force were to maintain law and order in the Territory during the period of transition. However, this was not merely a regular function of internal police. It involved also the task of preventing incidents involving the large Dutch and Indonesian forces present in the Territory. This the Force succeeded in doing thanks to the co-operation of the two governments concerned and by trying to get to the place concerned before friction developed. Accordingly, the Force did not become involved in actual fighting.

9. THE UNITED NATIONS FORCE IN CYPRUS [269]

Cyprus was established as an independent State on the basis of the Lon-

268. Cf. *above*, under 6 (f). *Contra* apparently *Bowett: United Nations Forces* (London 1964), p. 260.

269. See, in addition to the Security Council documents cited below and subsequent Security Council documents, *Annual Report of the Secretary-General, 1963–64*, pp. 32–40, and *Introduction* thereto, pp. 7–8.

don Agreement of 19 February 1959—which laid down the basic constitutional structure of the new State and defined the rights of the Greek and Turkish groups of the population—and of the Treaty of Guarantee of 16 August 1960. By the latter the Governments of Greece, Turkey and the United Kingdom guaranteed 'the independence, territorial integrity and security of the Republic of Cyprus, and also the state of affairs established by the Basic Articles of its Constitution.' They reserved the right 'to take action with the sole aim of re-establishing the state of affairs created by the present Treaty . . . in so far as common or concerted action may not prove possible'.[270]

In 1963 hostilities occurred between the two groups of the population. These led to a cessation of the joint participation of the Greek and Turkish elements in the Government and to a crisis between Greece and Turkey, both of which, like the United Kingdom, were maintaining troops on the island.[271] The Turkish Government threatened to intervene to protect the Turkish minority, while the Cyprus Government, now composed of the Greek majority element only, claimed that the agreements referred to above had proved unworkable and proposed their revision.

An attempt was made to stop the internal disorders with the aid of the forces of the three guarantor Powers which were already on the spot. For this purpose, they were placed under United Kingdom command. Negotiations were then undertaken for the establishment of a broader international police force, still outside the United Nations, for the same purpose. These negotiations broke down, and on 15 February the matter was brought before the Security Council. After long negotiations the Council on 4 March adopted the following resolution:

> *The Security Council,*
> *Noting* that the present situation with regard to Cyprus is likely to threaten international peace and security and may further deteriorate unless additional measures are promptly taken to maintain peace and to seek out a durable solution,
> *Considering* the positions taken by the parties in relation to the Treaties signed at Nicosia on 16 August 1960,
> *Having in mind* the relevant provisions of the Charter of the United Nations and its Article 2, paragraph 4, which reads: 'All Members shall refrain in their international relations from the threat or use of force against the territorial integrity or political independence of any State, or in any other manner inconsistent with the Purpose of the United Nations',
> 1. *Calls upon* all Member States, in conformity with their obligations under the Charter of the United Nations, to refrain from any action or threat of action likely to worsen the situation in the sovereign Republic of Cyprus, or to endanger international peace;

270. Article IV, *UNTS*, Vol. 382, p. 3.
271. Pursuant to the four-power Treaty Concerning the Establishment of the Republic of Cyprus of 16 August 1960 (*UNTS*, Vol. 382, p. 8) and the Treaty of Alliance between Cyprus, Greece and Turkey of the same date, respectively.

2. *Asks* the Government of Cyprus, which has the responsibility for the maintenance and restoration of law and order, to take all additional measures necessary to stop violence and bloodshed in Cyprus;

3. *Calls upon* the communities in Cyprus and their leaders to act with the utmost restraint;

4. *Recommends* the creation, with the consent of the Government of Cyprus,[272] of a United Nations peace-keeping force in Cyprus. The composition and size of the force shall be established by the Secretary-General, in consultation with the Governments of Cyprus, Greece, Turkey and the United Kingdom. The commander of the force shall be appointed by the Secretary-General and report to him. The Secretary-General, who shall keep the Governments providing the force fully informed, shall report periodically to the Security Council on its operation;

5. *Recommends* that the function of the force should be, in the interest of preserving international peace and security, to use its best efforts to prevent a recurrence of fighting and, as necessary, to contribute to the maintenance and restoration of law and order and a return to normal conditions;

6. *Recommends* that the stationing of the force shall be for a period of three months, all costs pertaining to it being met, in a manner to be agreed upon by them, by the Governments providing the contingents and by the Government of Cyprus. The Secretary-General may also accept voluntary contributions for that purpose.[273]

All the Members of the Council voted in favour of the resolution as a whole, after the Soviet Union, Czechoslovakia and France had abstained on a preceding separate vote on paragraph 4, for reasons which will be explained in another context.[274]

After a further deterioration of the situation, the Council on 13 March adopted another resolution, reaffirming its first resolution and asking that it be implemented (meaning notably that the Force be established) as soon as possible.[275]

The establishment of the Force had been delayed that long because of difficulties in its financing and of certain matters which had to be clarified at the request of the States providing contingents. Accordingly it was not until 27 March that sufficient contingents had arrived in Cyprus to allow the Force to become operational, under the name of the United Nations Force in Cyprus (UNFICYP). By that time voluntary financial contributions to a total amount of $ 5.189.000 for the first three-months period had been pledged by fifteen States.[276] Moreover, some but not all the States providing contingents undertook to meet their own costs without reimbursement. (The costs of the Force, in contradistinction to those

272. This was given by letter the following day, circulated as S/5578.
273. S/5575. See also the discussion in S/PV/1094–1102.
274. *Below*, Chapter IV, 2 (g).
275. S/5603, cf. S/PV/1103.
276. These were, in addition to Cyprus and the three guarantor States: Australia, Belgium, Denmark, Federal Republic of Germany, Italy, Luxemburg, Netherlands, New Zealand, Norway, Switzerland and the United States (Press Release CYP/25, 31 March 1964). Later were added: Japan, Sweden, Austria, Liberia, Nigeria (S/5746/Add. 1, 19 June 1964).

of UNEF and ONUC, were not covered over the budget of the Organization.) The mandate of the Force was renewed by the Security Council for successive three-month periods, and, like UNEF, it was still functioning at the time of writing.

By the end of 1964 the Force totalled 6279 military personnel and 173 civilian police. Military contingents ranging from 800 to 1200 men were provided by Canada, Denmark, Finland, Ireland, Sweden and the United Kingdom. A medical unit was provided by Austria, and civilian police units by Australia, Austria, Denmark, New Zealand and Sweden.[278] The Secretary-General appointed as Commander, first General P. S. Gyani, and, upon his resignation at the end of June 1964, General K. S. Thimayya. Logistic support and air lift had been provided mainly by the United Kingdom and the United States, and by chartered flights. Efforts, on the lines of the New Guinea pattern,[279] to have also the Greek and Turkish Army contingents place themselves under the United Nations Command, failed.

A status agreement, modelled upon those of UNEF and ONUC, was concluded with Cyprus on 31 March.[280] Regulations for the Force, similarly modelled on those of the earlier peace-keeping Forces, were enacted by the Secretary-General on 25 April 1964, with effect from 10 May 1964.[280] The first agreement with a State providing contingents was concluded on 21 February 1966 with Sweden.[280]

The functions of the Force had been defined by the Security Council as 'in the interest of preserving international peace and security, to use its best efforts to prevent a recurrence of fighting and, as necessary, to contribute to the maintenance and restoration of law and order and a return to normal conditions'. This was supplemented in the Secretary-General's report of 29 April 1964, quoted *below*, pp. 83–85.

According to his first reports, in many cases the Force undoubtedly restrained both sides from having recourse to arms. Some defortifications also took place. However, blockades and other problems still persisted. And during the first period of operations serious clashes continued to take place, while the inventory of arms within Cyprus grew, through smuggling and importation by the Government. This led to criticism in a number of countries that the Force was not active enough, and that it must be given wider powers. In reply to this criticism, the Secretary-General on 10 April 1964 issued an aide-mémoire which partly summed up, and partly specified in greater detail than ever before, the guiding principles of a peace-keeping United Nations Force.[283]

278. Report by the Secretary-General of 12 December 1964, S/6102.
279. *Above*, under 8.
280. These three basic texts are reproduced in the Annex, *below*, pp. 427 et seq.
283. S/5653, 10 April 1964, reprinted in excerpts in *Bowett: United Nations Forces* (London 1964) pp. 555–6.

The major parts of this important document were subsequently summarized by the Secretary-General as follows: [284]

(a) The Force is under the exclusive control and command of the United Nations at all times. The Commander of the Force is appointed by and responsible exclusively to the Secretary-General. The contingents comprising the Force are integral parts of it and take their orders exclusively from the Commander of the Force.

(b) The Force undertakes no functions which are not consistent with the provisions of the Security Council resolution of 4 March 1964. The troops of the Force carry arms which, however, are to be employed only for self-defence, should this become necessary in the discharge of its function, in the interest of preserving international peace and security, of seeking to prevent a recurrence of fighting, and contributing to the maintenance and restoration of law and order and a return to normal conditions. The personnel of the Force must act with restraint and with complete impartiality towards the members of the Greek and Turkish Cypriot communities.

(c) As regards the principle of self-defence, it is explained that the expression 'self-defence' includes the defence of United Nations posts, premises and vehicles under armed attack, as well as the support of other personnel of UNFICYP under armed attack. When acting in self-defence, the principle of minimum force shall always be applied and armed force will be used only when all peaceful means of persuasion have failed. The decision as to when force may be used under these circumstances rests with the Commander on the spot. Examples in which troops may be authorized to use force include attempts by force to compel them to withdraw from a position which they occupy under orders from their commanders, attempts by force to disarm them, and attempts by force to prevent them from carrying out their responsibilities as ordered by their commanders.

(d) In connexion with the performance of its function and responsibilities, UNFICYP shall maintain close contact with the appropriate officials in the Government of Cyprus, which has the responsibility for the maintenance and restoration of law and order and which has been asked by the Security Council in its resolution of 4 March to take all additional measures necessary to stop violence and bloodshed in Cyprus.

An interesting elaboration of the partly novel tasks which were in fact assigned to the United Nations Force in Cyprus is contained in the Annex to another report of the Secretary-General, of 29 April 1964.[285] It reads as follows:

Objectives and interim aims of a comprehensive programme of action for UNFICYP

1. The task of the UN Force, as given in the Security Council resolution of 4 March 1964, is to use its best efforts towards the following objectives:
   (a) To prevent a recurrence of fighting.
   (b) To contribute to the maintenance and restoration of law and order.
   (c) To contribute to a return to normal conditions.

---

284. S/5950, 10 September 1964, par. 7.
285. S/5671, Annex II, 29 April 1964, see also the report on the implementation in S/5764, 15 June 1964, Part IV.

Efforts in any of these directions must, to have their maximum effect and durability, be made in a concerted manner, bearing in mind that (a) and (b) above are decisive steps leading to the over-all objective of the restoration of normal conditions in the daily life of the people.

2. The following is a suggested list of some of the objectives that could be defined as part of the programme of action designed to implement the mandates of UNFICYP:

(a) Achievement of freedom of movement on all roads in Cyprus, including the Kyrenia Road.

(b) Achievement of freedom of movement for all communities within the whole town of Nicosia and other cities under conditions of security.

(c) Progressive evacuation and removal of all fortified positions held by Greek and Turkish Cypriots, with priority given to Nicosia.

(d) Examination of the problem arising from the division that has taken place in the Cyprus police between the Turkish Cypriots and the Greek Cypriot members and the negotiation of necessary measures for their progressive reintegration.

(e) The progressive disarming of all civilians other than the regular police *gendarmerie* and the Cyprus army by the Cypriot Government and the Turkish community. UNFICYP, if requested, would assist in facilitating and verifying the disarming and the storage of arms under conditions of security.

(f) The control of extremists on both sides.

(g) The formulation of appropriate general amnesty arrangements.

(h) The arrangement of security measures and other necessary conditions to facilitate return to normal conditions and particularly of economic activity.

(i) The facilitation of the return of Turkish Cypriot civil servants and Government officials to their duties, including the public services, such as postal, telecommunications, public works, etc.

(j) The normal functioning of the judiciary.

The process of consultation and negotiation on these aims would continue side by side with the day-to-day efforts of the Force to carry out its mandate.

3. While efforts to make progress on the above points continue, certain interim aims should also be established and pressed in selected localities and on particular problems. The following are suggested:

(a) The removal of emplacements, fortifications and trenches in selected areas of Nicosia with a view to repeating this measure subsequently in other areas.

(b) A determined effort in selected areas of Nicosia to re-establish normality by returning to their homes, under United Nations security guarantee, refugees, as, for example, those from Hamed Mandres to Omorphita who would not carry arms, and attention to the development of a programme for the rehabilitation of their dwellings.

(c) A careful formulation of ways in which UNFICYP might be helpful in meeting the problem of the excesses by individual policemen in the course of searching and seizing civilians which at present causes much tension. Such a plan, which would largely depend on the use of UNFICYP police, would require a reliable system of reporting of abuses and a regular follow-through by UNFICYP in every case, and would also require a high degree of liaison and confidence with all Greek Cypriot and Turkish Cypriot members of the Cyprus police.

(d) The institution of procedures for inquiry into every serious instance of shooting, especially when casualties occur, so that a full record of such incidents, the reasons and responsibilities for them, can be determined and maintained.

(e) The elaboration of a plan for the reintegration, with UNFICYP assistance and guarantee, of the Turkish Cypriot policemen into the Cyprus police force, perhaps starting in one or two carefully selected Turkish Cypriot communities.

(f) The use of UNFICYP good offices with both sides to improve the existing unacceptable living conditions through resuming essential public utilities and services and finally to ensure normal living conditions for the Turkish Cypriot community in tense areas, such as Ktima and Polis.

(g) Initial efforts to facilitate the return of Turkish Cypriot officials and civil servants to their positions in Government service.

(h) An appraisal of the possibility of establishing in certain areas Cypriot Greek-Turkish-UNFICYP joint patrols as a means of restoring confidence and promoting a return to normality.

(i) Efforts, with UNFICYP if necessary providing security, to revive meetings of Greek and Turkish Cypriots, both official and non-official, and at all levels.

10. A PERMANENT UNITED NATIONS FORCE. PROPOSALS BY THE BIG POWERS. THE SCANDINAVIAN STAND-BY UNITS

Members of the United Nations have always been prepared to support the establishment of a United Nations Force in emergency situations when they felt that such a force was called for and knew what its tasks would be. But they have not so far been disposed to support the establishment of a permanent Force. Thus, the General Assembly did not, accept the Secretary-General's proposals for an individually recruited United Nations Guard in 1948 and for a United Nations Legion in 1952.[286] And both the Collective Measures Committee and, later, the Secretary-General have expressed the view that a standing United Nations Force would not be necessary or practical at the present stage.[287] Instead, they have made proposals for stand-by arrangements under which it would be possible, by drawing upon national contingents earmarked and prepared in advance, to organize an *ad hoc* force adapted to the circumstances of each particular case as it might arise.

The Collective Measures Committee, on the basis of the Uniting for Peace Resolution and having in mind a combat force to resist aggression, recommended in 1951-2 a Force on the Korean pattern organized and directed by one or more Member States.[288] The Secretary-General in 1958 submitted to the General Assembly a Summary Study of the experience derived from the establishment and operation of UNEF [289] as a

286. *Above,* Chapter I, 1.
287. Second Report of the Collective Measures Committee, OR *GA,* 7th session, Suppl. No. 17, p. 12; Secretary-General's Summary Study of UNEF, *ibid.,* XIII, Annexes, A.i. 65, pars. 152–4, cf. par. 123; Introduction to the *Annual Report of the Secretary-General,* 1959–60, pp. 3–4 (after the establishment of the Force in the Congo); U Thant's speech at Harvard University, 13 June 1963, text in *Toward World Peace, Addresses and Public Statements 1957–63* (New York 1964) at pp. 282–4.
288. *Above,* under 5.
289. OR *GA,* XIII, Annexes, A.i. 65, pp. 8–33.

'guidance for any future efforts looking towards the establishment or use of international United Nations instruments serving purposes of the kind met by UNEF'.[290] This study was not concerned with operations requiring combat activity.[291] It proposed flexible stand-by arrangements for a Force on the UNEF pattern, organized and directed by the United Nations. This scheme was further supplemented by the Secretary-General in the introductions to his later annual reports on the basis of the experience in respect of subsequent Forces.[292]

Neither of these proposals was passed upon by the General Assembly.[293] The military proposals of the Uniting for Peace Resolution and of the Collective Measures Committee have not been applied since Korea.[294] The conclusions contained in the Secretary-General's Summary Study on UNEF, on the other hand, were relied upon when another peace-keeping force was established in the Congo two years later [295] despite the fact that this force got involved in more active and military operations than UNEF.

It remains to be seen whether the conclusions of the Summary Study will also be extended, *mutatis mutandis*, to a genuine combat Force, if such a force should be established, or whether the United Nations in such case will revert to a Force under national command as proposed by the Collective Measures Committee, or whether the two systems can be married.[296] An indication of a proposal for such a marriage may be seen in the final statement on the British Commonwealth Prime Ministers' Conference issued in London on 17 March 1961. The relevant passage reads:

290. *Ibid.*, par. 3; cf. par. 154. The aims were further elaborated by the Secretary-General in his oral introduction of the Summary Study, see *ibid.*, Special Political Committee, 100th meeting, pp. 63–64, and see *Annual Report of the Secretary-General*, 1958–59, p. 10.

291. Secretary-General's Summary Study, *OR GA*, XIII, Annexes, A.i. 65, par. 178.

292. See *OR GA*, XV, Suppl. No. 1A, pp. 3–4, and subsequent Introductions.

293. *Above*, under 5, p. 45; *OR GA*, XIII, Annexes, A.i. 65, p. 34. In his oral introduction of the Summary Study on 5 November 1958 the Secretary-General indicated that there was no real need for the Assembly to take action at the time; *ibid.*, Special Political Committee, p. 64.

294. At that time some, but far from all, Members of the United Nations indicated that they might maintain within their national armed forces elements prepared for service as United Nations units in accordance with par. 8 of the Uniting for Peace resolution (*OR GA*, 6th session, Suppl. No. 13, p. 37, and 7th session, Suppl. No. 17, p. 21). However, these indications were not followed by any concrete action, and the Scandinavian initiatives in 1960–1 related below were for a peacekeeping Force rather than for a combat force.

295. *OR SC*, 1960, 873rd meeting, par. 28; cf. pars. 175—6. Earlier, on 13 October 1957, the Security Council had rejected a Pakistani proposal to deploy UNEF in Kashmir.

296. The constitutional question whether such a Force could be placed under United Nations command, is discussed *below*, in Chapter IV.

At the appropriate stage, a substantial and adequately armed military force should be established, to prevent aggression and enforce observance of the disarmament agreement; and an international authority should be created, in association with the United Nations, to control this force and to ensure that it is not used for any purpose inconsistent with the Charter.[297]

Later, both the Soviet Union and the United States included proposals for United Nations combat forces in the drafts of a disarmament treaty which they submitted to the United Nations Conference on Disarmament in Geneva in 1962. The Soviet proposal read:

1. To ensure that the United Nations is capable of effectively protecting States against threats to or breaches of the peace, all States parties to the Treaty shall, between the signing of the Treaty and its entry into force, conclude agreements with the Security Council by which they undertake to make available to the latter armed forces, assistance and facilities, including rights of passage, as provided for in Article 43 of the United Nations Charter.

2. The armed forces provided under the said agreements shall form part of the national armed forces of the corresponding States and shall be stationed within their territories. They shall be kept up to full strength, equipped and prepared for combat. When used under Article 42 of the United Nations Charter, these forces, commanded by the military authorities of the corresponding States, shall be placed at the disposal of the Security Council. [298]

The United States proposal read:

5. United Nations Peace Force
The Parties to the Treaty would undertake to develop arrangements during Stage I for the establishment in Stage II of a United Nations Peace Force. To this end, the Parties to the Treaty would agree on the following measures within the United Nations:

a. Examination of the experience of the United Nations leading to a further strengthening of United Nations forces for keeping the peace;

b. Examination of the feasibility of concluding promptly the agreements envisaged in Article 43 of the United Nations Charter;

c. Conclusion of an agreement for the establishment of a United Nations Peace Force in Stage II, including definitions of its purpose, mission, composition and strength, disposition, command and control, training, logistical support, financing, equipment and armaments.

6. United Nations Peace Observation Corps
The Parties to the Treaty would agree to support the establishment within the United Nations of a Peace Observation Corps, staffed with a standing cadre of observers who could be despatched promptly to investigate any situation which might constitute a threat to or a breach of the peace. Elements of the Peace Observation Corps could also be stationed as appropriate in selected areas throughout the world.[299]

297. Par. 3 (f) of the final statement, *The Times*, 18 March 1961. The principle of an international police force to replace the national armed forces was adopted one month earlier at the East-West Conference in Warsaw on 3–6 February 1961 (Report by Finn Moe, *Arbeiderbladet*, Oslo, 13 February 1961).

298. Conference of the Eighteen-Nation Committee on Disarmament, Doc. ENDC/2, 19 March 1962, Article 18.

299. ENDC/30, 18 April 1962, Stage I, H, 5–6.

Two years later, the Soviet Union submitted to the Members of the General Assembly a more detailed proposal for a combat force, for use in accordance with Article 42 of the Charter 'to prevent or stop aggressive acts, and protect the sovereignty and territorial integrity of a victimized State'. The Force was to be established and planned by the Security Council and the Military Staff Committee in accordance with the procedure laid down in Articles 43 et seq. The Force and its command would be composed of contingents from Western, neutral and socialist countries, *excluding* the permanent Members of the Security Council. The costs were to be reimbursed by the aggressor, but if necessary the Member States would take part in defraying them.[300]

In 1959 the Secretary-General of the United Nations suggested to those States which had contributed contingents to UNEF that they should take into consideration in their military planning the possibility that they might also in the future be called upon to provide contingents for a United Nations Force. In response, several countries, including Canada,[301] the Netherlands and the Nordic countries, established stand-by units for peace-keeping forces.[302] In particular, the Parliaments of Denmark, Finland, Norway and Sweden in 1964 decided to establish co-ordinated Scandinavian stand-by units totalling of some 5000 men which can be utilized either separately or as a joint force. It is not a standing force, but one composed of volunteers who have been prepared in advance and who may be called upon on short notice. In some of the countries the contingents form part of the (stand-by) national army, in others they do not. All costs of training, equipping and maintaining the force in the home countries are covered by the Governments concerned. Costs during periods of service are to be borne by the United Nations in the usual manner. The combined Scandinavian force comprises five infantry battaillons, one frigate, air-transport units, surgical and other sanitary units (which can also be called up separately for assistance in case of major catastrophies, such as earthquakes and floods), military police, staff officers, signal units and a port command. It is equipped with small arms, motor vehicles, bicycles, helicopters and transport planes. The Scandinavian contingents can be placed at the disposal of the United Nations by the King without prior approval by Parliament in

300. A/5721, 13 July 1964.

301. Cf. a lecture by Prime Minister Pearson in the Dag Hammarskjöld Memorial Series, at Carleton University, on 7 May 1964, and plans, dated 7 July 1964, for a Canadian Army Standby Batallion Group.

302. See also the Austrian Constitutional Act on the Dispatch of Austrian Units Abroad at the Request of International Organizations of 30 June 1965 (*Bundesgesetzblatt* 173/1965).

each case, while in Finland prior consultation with the foreign affairs committee of Parliament is required under the Statute.[303]

The problems of United Nations peace-keeping Forces have been studied by a number of non-governmental organizations, including the International Law Association,[304] the Norwegian Institute for International Affairs,[305] and two international conferences organized by the latter at Oslo in February 1964 [306] and December 1965.[307] In November 1964 there was also held a conference of governmental military and other experts at Ottawa.[308]

While the main emphasis of the non-governmental studies undertaken after the establishment of the Forces in the Middle East and the Congo were on peace-keeping Forces composed of national contingents, other types of Forces have not been completely ignored. Thus in 1963 there was formed in the United Kingdom a Council whose object was to gain support for an 'independent, integrated and trustworthy world police force, responsible to a strengthened United Nations, and based upon individual recruitment'.[309]

An interesting plan for a regionally organized peace-keeping force was the security force of the League of Arab States which was proposed for Kuwait in 1961.[310]

303. The units were established by: Decision by the Danish Parliament of 30 April 1964, approving a proposal of 13 March 1964 (No. XV) by the Ministry of Defence; decision by the Swedish Parliament of 6 May 1964, approving *Kungl. Maj:ts proposition nr. 81 år 1964, Bihang till Riksdagens protokoll 1964, 1 Saml. Nr. 81*, see also press communiqué published in *Nordisk Tidsskrift for international Ret og Jus gentium*, XXXIV (1964) p. 255; Law on a Finnish Security Force of 20 May 1964; Decision by the Norwegian Parliament of 8 June 1964, approving *Stortingsproposisjon nr. 61 (1963–64)*, cf. *Innst. S. nr. 248 for 1963–64*.

304. Notably by its United Nations Charter Committee, see *International Law Association, Report of the Forty-Eighth Conference, New York 1958*, pp. xiv and 507 et seq., especially pp. 519 and 549, and *Report of the Forty-Ninth Conference, Hamburg 1960*, pp. 98 et seq., especially pp. 126 et seq. Other studies undertaken are listed in footnote 1 to the Committee's Report to the Forty-Ninth Conference, *ibid.*, p. 131.

305. Report of study group in *Internasjonal politikk* (Oslo) 1963, Nr. 1–2.

306. Report in *Frydenberg: Peace-Keeping, Experiences and Evaluation – The Oslo Papers* (Oslo 1964).

307. Reference is also made to the interesting thoughts and conclusions advanced in *Attia: Les forces armées des Nations Unies en Corée et au Moyen-Orient* (Genève 1963) pp. 421–3.

308. Representatives from the following countries attended: Brazil, Colombia, Denmark, Finland, Ghana, India, Iran, Ireland, Italy, Liberia, Malaysia, Morocco, Netherlands, New Zealand, Nigeria, Norway, Pakistan, Senegal, Sierra Leone, Sweden, Tunisia, United Arab Republic.

309. *The Times*, 6 March 1963, p. 7.

310. See note verbale from the League of Arab States to the United Nations of 13 September 1961, *OR SC*, 1961, Suppl. for October–December, p. 162.

CHAPTER III

INTERNATIONAL REPRESENTATION OF AND
RESPONSIBILITY FOR THE FORCE

1. GENERAL

Who is internationally responsible for an international force? The State in whose territory it performs its functions or whom it assists? The States providing contingents? The Organization? Or its several Member States?

It has at once to be made clear that *Member States* as such have no legal responsibility vis-à-vis third parties for the acts of the Organization, whether on the international or on the civil law plane. The United Nations as an Organization has a juridical and an international personality of its own,[1] distinct from that of its individual Member States. It concludes treaties, convenes conferences, appoints representatives and performs other international acts in its own name, not on behalf of its several Member States. It cannot reasonably be maintained that all Member States would become parties to the treaties concluded by the Organization or would otherwise become externally liable for the acts of the Organization, be it in their capacity as Member States or in their capacity as members of the deliberative organ which might have decided upon the act.[2] This would require a clear delegation of powers, which the Charter does not contain,[3] quite apart from the fact that this would turn the United Nations into something like a federation, which was never

1. *Reparation for Injuries Suffered in the Service of the United Nations, ICJ. Reports*, 1949, p. 179; see also *below*, p. 156.

2. The latter possibility *may* have been in the minds of certain members of the Security Council during the discussion of the proposed Free Territory of Trieste reported *below*, pp. 148–149 (*OR SC*, 1947, No. 1, p. 7), although the words used in the discussion do not necessarily go beyond the scope of internal obligations.

3. Even the somewhat misleading provision in Article 24(1), that the Members of the United Nations agree that the Security Council 'acts on their behalf in carrying out its responsibility for the maintenance of international peace and security', cannot be given this wide interpretation. If this phrase has any legal significance at all, it can only be construed as a reference to the power of the Security Council (like that of any other principal organ), within its field of competence, to bind the *Organization* externally, or to the *internally* binding effect of its decision under Article 25 and Chapters VI–VIII.

intended. Similarly, the Members do not acquire any rights by the acts of the Organization unless these are addressed to them or constitute *pacta in favorem tertii*. This applies to the acts of any organ of the Organization when acting as such. It must apply also to the acts of an international Force if it is established and operated by the Organization and not by its Member States acting outside the deliberative organs of the Organization.[4]

As will be more fully explained below, *the State in whose territory the Force operates* and/or which it assists has no jurisdiction over and no other direct legal powers with respect to the force. The rights and duties of the host State are defined in international agreements with the United Nations and are in the nature of international rights and duties vis-à-vis this Organization as another subject of international law.

The only persons who could be seriously envisaged as bearing international rights and duties in respect of the Force are thus the Organization as such and *the 'participating' States*. If the Force is recruited individually by the United Nations, there are no 'participating' States, and there can be no question that the United Nations has the sole international representation and responsibility. Doubt arises only when the Force is composed of national contingents, whose members are concurrently members of the armed forces of 'participating' States.

The discussion which follows will be chiefly concerned with the five Forces established by the United Nations on the basis of national contingents and will aim primarily at establishing the distribution of international competences between the United Nations and the States providing these contingents. After summarizing the position with regard to operational control as discussed in detail in Chapter II, it will be appropriate to consider in turn the practice in the five Forces with respect to international agreements and to passive and active responsibility, before drawing general conclusions.

2. OPERATIONAL CONTROL

(a) *The peace-keeping Forces—Charter Articles 43 et seq.—Individually enlisted Forces*

It has been pointed out in Chapter II, 6 that the supreme power of decision in all operational and external matters relating to UNEF are vested in the United Nations, and that the legal powers retained by the

---

4. This must be what the writers cited *above*, p. 27, at note 6, meant when saying that the League of Nations could declare or be a party to a war or exercise a *jus belli*, and what *van der Molen*, p. 13, means when she says that the United Nations can wage war.

States providing contingents are confined to internal (personnel) matters of no direct concern to the parties to the dispute or to any other third parties. The Commander of the Force is appointed by the United Nations, takes his orders only from its organs [5] and acts exclusively in its name. He is responsible to the Organization and independent of the policies and control of any one nation. His, and through him the United Nations', operational command authority is not altered by the fact that each national contingent is under the direct command of its own national officers, since these take their orders in all operational matters relating to the Force, not from their national Government, but from the UNEF Commander.

It is even clearer from the basic documents and practice of UNEF mentioned in Chapter II,6 that the *host State* has no legal powers of direction over the Force which operates on its territory. It can present requests to the Commander or the Secretary-General, or it can make proposals in the deliberative organs of the Organization, but it can in no circumstances give any direct orders to the Force. The host State can, of course, insist upon compliance by the Force with the conditions laid down in the agreements concluded between the United Nations and the host State, but none of these conditions is of a nature to place the Force under the operational control of the host State.[6]

---

5. § 2 of the Austrian Constitutional Act of 30 June 1965 (*Bundesgesetzblatt* 173/1965) on the Dispatch of Austrian Units for Assistance Abroad at the Request of International Organizations provides that the question of to what extent the Austrian contingent commander 'an die Weisungen der Organe einer internationalen Organisation gebunden ist und inwieweit Organe einer solchen Organisation den Mitgliedern der Einheit ... unmittelbar Weisungen für ihre Verwendung erteilen dürfen, bestimmt sich nach dem zwischen der Republik Österreich und der internationalen Organisation über die Hilfeleistung abgeschlossenen Staatsvertrag'. The Act also contains the following relevant provisions:

'§ 3. Die Mitglieder der Einheit sind verpflichtet, den Weisungen des Vorgesetzten und hinsichtlich der Verwendung nach Maßgabe des § 2 Abs. 2 auch den Weisungen der internationalen Organisation im Ausland Folge zu leisten. Widersprechen einander Weisungen des Vorgesetzten und unmittelbar erteilte Weisungen der internationalen Organisation, so haben die betroffenen Mitglieder der Einheit die Weisungen des Vorgesetzten zu befolgen. Sie haben jedoch den Vorgesetzten unverzüglich von den widersprechenden Weisungen der internationalen Organisation in Kenntnis zu setzen. Der Vorgesetzte hat unverzüglich mit den Organen der internationalen Organisation, die die widersprechende Weisung erteilt haben, zum Zwecke der Beseitigung des Widerspruches Fühlung zu nehmen.

§ 4. Die nach österreichischen Rechtsvorschriften bestehende organisatorische Unterordnung von Mitgliedern der Einheit gegenüber ihren Vorgesetzten im Inland ruht auf die Dauer der Tätigkeit im Ausland.

...

§ 6. ... Während des Einsatzes hat der Vorgesetzte auf Verlangen der Bundesregierung jederzeit die gewünschten Berichte zu erstatten und die verlangten Auskünfte zu erteilen.'

6. On the question whether the host State has a unilateral right to demand the with-

2. OPERATIONAL CONTROL

It has been pointed out in Chapter II,7 that the *United Nations Force in the Congo* was organized in essentially the same manner as UNEF and that here too command authority in operational matters was vested exclusively in the Supreme Commander appointed by and acting under the orders of the United Nations.[7] Indeed, the basic relationship between the United Nations and the States providing contingents was the same in the Congo as in UNEF. The relationship to the host State had a somewhat different basis in so far as the United Nations Force was in the Congo to assist the Government in the maintenance of internal order, in addition to its task of preventing foreign intervention. (The close cooperation was well illustrated when on 24 August 1961 the Central Government enacted an *Ordonnance* providing for the expulsion of all non-Congolese officers and mercenaries serving in the Katangese forces, and requested United Nations assistance in the execution of this *Ordonnance*, a request which coincided with the United Nations own mandate and which was promptly complied with.)[8] However, the Secretary-General in his first report on the implementation of the Security Council resolution authorizing him to establish the Force made it clear that this would not affect the exclusive command authority of the United Nations. He stated that although the Force

> may be considered as serving as an arm of the Government for the maintenance of order and protection of life—tasks which naturally belong to the national authorities and which will pass to such authorities as soon as, in the view of the Government, they are sufficiently firmly established—the Force is necessarily under the exclusive command of the United Nations, vested in the Secretary-General under the control of the Security Council. This is in accordance with the principles generally applied by the Organisation. The Force is thus not under the orders of the Government nor can it, as I pointed out in my statement to the Council, be permitted to become a party to any internal conflict. A departure from this principle would seriously endanger the impartiality of the United Nations and of the operation.[9]

The Status Agreement between the United Nations and the Congo provided:

drawal of the Force, see the basic agreement with Egypt of November 1956 (OR GA, Annexes, A.i. 66, p. 9); Sohn in *American Journal of International Law*, LII (1958) pp. 239–40, citing the Egyptian statement in OR GA, 11th session, 597th plenary meeting, 27 November 1956, p. 348; Security Council Resolution of 14 July 1960; the basic agreement with the Congo, OR SC, 1960, Suppl. for July–September, p. 27; the subsequent resolutions of the Security Council amending the mandate; and Prime Minister Adoula's speech of 2 August 1961, S/4923, Annex, p. 6, OR SC, 1961, Suppl. for July–September, p. 74.

7. *Above*, pp. 65–66. Cf. Draper as quoted *below*, p. 362.

8. S/4940, par. 2, and Annex I, OR SC, 1961, Suppl. for July–September, p. 99, cf. *Gihl: Om freden och säkerheten* (Stockholm 1962) p. 366.

9. S/4389, OR SC, 1960, Suppl. for July–September, p. 18. This principle was reaffirmed by the representative of Ecuador, ibid., 886th meeting, par. 40.

The United Nations shall be as an international Force and as such its responsibilities shall be exercised for the purposes of maintaining public order, peace and security; in so doing it shall not apply domestic regulations and procedures, but shall act in accordance with its interpretation of the mission assigned to it by the Security Council.[10]

On some occasions the host Government and certain Governments providing contingents demanded that the United Nations Force in the Congo take a certain course of action and suggested or even demanded that certain contingents be employed for this purpose. In a few cases such demands were accompanied by threats to withdraw contingents from United Nations command and place them under the direct authority of the Congolese Government. All these demands were rejected by the Secretary-General, who in polite terms pointed out that it was for the competent organs of the United Nations to decide what actions the Force was to take and which contingents were to be employed for them.[11]

In his first report on the Congo Force, which was unanimously commended by the Security Council, the Secretary-General stated:

> The authority granted to the United Nations Force cannot be exercised within the Congo either in competition with representatives of the host Government or in co-operation with them in any joint operation. This naturally applies *a fortiori* to representatives and military units of other Governments than the host Government. Thus, *the United Nations operation must be separate and distinct from activities by any national authorities.*[12]

Although this statement, like the similar statements made earlier in respect of UNEF,[13] may at the time have been aimed primarily at the Congolese and Belgian Governments, the Secretary-General later quoted it to the Security Council in reference to news that a national contingent wanted 'to pull out from the Force until the United Nations "ceases its flagrant interference in internal Congolese affairs" '. And on this occasion the Secretary-General added:

---

10. S/5004, par. 43 (*a*), OR SC, 1961, Suppl. for October-December, p. 151.

11. Second report, S/4417, par. 7 and Adds. 1, 2 and 7 (OR SC, 1960, Suppl. for July–September, pp. 45 et seq.); *ibid.*, 888th meeting, pars. 32 and 109; 889th meeting, pars. 46 and 51; 896th meeting, p. 20; S/4531, par. 26 (OR SC, 1960, Suppl. for July–September, p. 183); S/4557, par. 17 (OR SC, 1960, Suppl. for October–December, p. 11). See also S/4809 and S/4811, (OR SC, 1961 Suppl. for April–June, pp. 48 and 50). See, on the other hand, the statement made in the Indian Parliament by Prime Minister Nehru who, according to press reports, when suggesting that the Indian contingent be deployed in Katanga, took care to emphasize that the contingent would act in accordance with the decisions of the United Naions (*Arbeiderbladet*, Oslo, 25 March 1961). See also *Documents on Swedish foreign policy 1961*, published by the Swedish Ministry for Foreign Affairs (Stockholm 1962) p. 58.

12. S/4389, par. 12, OR SC, 1960, Suppl. for July-September, p. 19 (italics supplied), restated orally, *ibid.*, 887th meeting, pars. 45–46. Cf. *below*, p. 435, par. 41.

13. See, for example, the Secretary-General's Summary Study, par. 165, OR GA, 13th session, Annexes, A.i. 65, p. 29.

2. OPERATIONAL CONTROL

> Were a national contingent to leave the United Nations Force, they would have to be regarded as foreign troops introduced into the Congo, and the Security Council would have to consider their continued presence in the Congo, as well as its consequences for the United Nations operation, in this light. [14]

Some Governments did at a certain time withdraw their contingents from the Force because of their dissatisfaction with the manner in which the Force was being deployed. But these contingents were withdrawn completely from the Congo. Had they been left in the country to act independently of the United Nations this would indeed have defeated one of the main purposes of the United Nations action, viz. to prevent intervention by foreign States.

It may be said both in respect of UNEF and the United Nations Force in the Congo that, legally, the States providing contingents can influence the operational (and external) decisions of the United Nations only through their regular participation in the deliberations and voting of the General Assembly and the Security Council in the same way as other Member States; or, in the case of some of them, as members elected by the General Assembly to the Advisory Committee. Any additional *factual* influence which they might be in a position to exercise through their contingents, notably by threatening to withdraw them, is weakened by the fact that they make no significant financial contributions in their capacity as 'participating' States,[15] and that the contingents are not large enough to make the United Nations dependent upon any single 'participating' State.[16]

The situation with regard to operational control was the same in respect of the United Nations Forces in *West New Guinea* and *Cyprus*.[16a] And it will probably be the same in respect of *a Force established by the Security Council under the procedure laid down in Articles 43 et seq.* of the United Nations Charter. As pointed out above, these articles appear to envisage supreme United Nations command authority over the Force [17] in operational matters, and the reports of the Military Staff Committee also point in this direction.[18]

---

14. *OR SC*, 1960, 896th meeting, p. 20.

15. *Above*, Chapter II, 6 (d). The major financial contributions to the Congo operation outside the regular assessments were made by other Member States in other forms, notably by those great powers which provided air transportation and waived their claims for reimbursement. Thus the US, the USSR, Canada and the UK alone waived reimbursement for air transport facilities which amounted to about $13,000,000 in the second half of 1960, *OR GA*, 15th session, Annexes, A.i. 49/50, p. 11. — In Cyprus the situation is different, see *above*, p. 81.

16. *Above*, Chapter II,6(b).

16a. *Below*, Annexes I and II, especially p. 435, par. 41 and *in fine*, and p. 438.

17. In this sense also *Kelsen: The Law of the United Nations*, pp. 765-8, and the Rapporteur of Committee III/3 of the San Francisco Conference, cited by him.

18. *Above*, Chapter II, 3, cf. notably Articles 44 and 47 (1) and (3) of the Charter.

Ross,[19] on the basis of an interpretation of the second sentence of Article 42 of the Charter, maintains that, despite any delegation of command to the United Nations from the contributing Governments by the terms of the special agreements, 'the command is and will remain national in the last instance, as surely as a breach of this obligation can only entail international effects for the state and does not affect the national duty of obedience. The individual soldier will be liable to punishment only for failing to obey his national superiors.'

It is certainly true that the members of national contingents may be subject only to their own national military code and jurisdiction, as indeed is the case under the articles elaborated by the Military Staff Committee, and also in the case of the United Nations peace-keeping Forces so far established. However, even though any disciplinary or criminal sanctions must be inflicted by the national authorities, this does not mean that such sanctions will not be inflicted for failure to obey a United Nations Commander. On the contrary, the contributing States must instruct their contingents to obey any orders from the United Nations Command, and must punish them if they fail to do so. At the very least the (national) commander of the national contingent must take direct orders from the United Nations Command and pass them on to the subordinate members of his contingent. But in the course of battle situations will clearly arise where it becomes necessary for the United Nations Command—whether this be one single command or separate commands for each region or for each service—to issue orders directly to smaller units detached from the main body of the national contingent or to separate services of the contingent. Even during the United Nations police operations in the Middle East and the Congo, it has been necessary to establish chains of command on these lines.[20] Indeed, in principle probably all members of the Force must be subject to United Nations orders, as was provided in the agreements concluded between the United States and the other States contributing forces to the United Nations action in Korea.[21] In these circumstances it would not be entirely fitting to say

19. *Constitution of the United Nations* (Copenhagen 1950) pp. 151—2. Draper takes a similar view in respect of Forces of the Congo type, *International and Comparative Law Quarterly*, XII (1963) at pp. 408–9, see *below*, Chapter V, note 110, and Chapter VIII,11(a) (iii), at note 212.

20. Cf. the deployment tables annexed to the second progress report to the Secretary-General from his Special Representative in the Congo, *OR SC*, 1960, Suppl. for October–December, p. 40, and on UNEF, *above*, p. 50, cf. p. 54, and *OR GA*, 12th session, Annexes, A.i. 65, p. 3.

21. *Above*, Chapter II, 4, at note 35. This is also clearly assumed in the Austrian constitutional Act cited *above*, note 5; However, this law provides that in case of conflict the orders of the contingent commander shall take precedence over those of the Organization. This contrasts with the Korean agreements, which provided that all

that command is 'national'. Indeed, it is only in respect of sanctions that the jurisdiction is clearly national. The 'substantive' (legislative and administrative) jurisdiction in operational matters—and this is the most important—is vested in the Organization. And this is not purely an international law jurisdiction—over States—as is usually the case when a State confers upon an international organization the power to make binding decisions. It is a jurisdiction exercised directly over the State organs concerned, which have for the time being and for the specific purpose become an organ of the United Nations [22] and the members of which have thus become subject to its internal law [22a] to the extent that the States concerned have not retained exclusive jurisdiction. This is going further than the usual case where a State undertakes to comply with the decisions of an international organization on the understanding that it will itself take all necessary measures to have the decision executed by its competent organs. To sum up, the States contributing contingents have ceded, not only the power to make decisions binding upon themselves as States, but the power to exercise direct legislative and administrative jurisdiction over the contingents in operational matters.

Whatever view one takes of the terminological question as to whether or not command can be said to be 'national', it can hardly be maintained that operational control, for the purpose of determining the international responsibility, is vested in the States providing contingents, if these States have placed their contingents under the direct command of a commander appointed by the Organization and exclusively subject to its orders, and especially if integrated. This must be so even if sanctions for disobedience of United Nations orders can be applied only under national law and by national authorities.

It should be added, moreover, that the system envisaged by the Military Staff Committee is not the only system which is permissible under the Charter. There is nothing in the Charter to prevent the 'air, sea or

---

orders of the Commander issued to the personnel of the contingent were to be carried out as given and that any disagreement might be presented subsequently. This special rule in the Austrian Constitutional Act may be viewed in the light of its stated purpose to provide a constitutional basis for the exercise abroad by Austrian officials of sovereign Acts on behalf of Austria, because, although they had not so far done so 'it might happen in future' that these officials would have to act 'not as organs of the United Nations or another international organization, but as representatives of the Austrian sovereign power, without prejudice to Austria's permanent neutrality' (Bundesgesetzblatt 173/1965, pp. 3–4).

22. This is clearly reflected in the Regulations; see especially UNEF Regulations 6, 11–12, and 29–33, and UNFICYP Regulations 6, 11–12 and 24–28.

22a. See *below*, Chapter IV, note 101, and the present writer's article on 'Jurisdiction over Organs and Officials of States, the Holy See and Intergovernmental Organizations' in *International and Comparative Law Quarterly*, XIV (1965) pp. 33–82 and 493–527, especially at p. 517.

land forces of Members of the United Nations' [23] from being subjected to a common, United Nations military code and discipline and even to prosecution before United Nations courts.[24] It was no doubt not the words of the Charter, but practical, political and national legal considerations, including in particular the presumed unwillingness of the States providing contingents to cede to the Organization the criminal jurisdiction over the members of their contingents, which caused the Military Staff Committee to propose that these matters should remain a national responsibility, as they are, for the same reasons, in the cases of the peace-keeping Forces. Indeed, it would be stretching the words of Article 42 and the intention of their drafters too far to attempt to deduce from them any restrictions upon the right of the Security Council (and the States providing contingents) to adopt such procedures of command and jurisdiction as may be found effective and legally and politically acceptable to the Member States concerned.

What has been stated above concerning the peace-keeping Forces applies *a fortiori* to any civilian or military *force enlisted individually by the Organization*.[25] The States providing individual officers for truce observation groups or genuine military Forces are, of course, even less in a position to exercise operational control than are States providing more or less self-contained contingents. And if the members of the Force are recruited directly by the United Nations as private individuals, as in the United Nations Guard, then they are not in any way national officials, but are entirely in the same position as civilian international officials.

(b) *Korea—Uniting for Peace Resolution—League of Nations Covenant*

In the case of *Korea*, on the other hand, the United Nations had no direct command authority. This, as already pointed out, was vested in the United States as the 'Unified Command'. Although the United States had been designated as such by the Security Council, and although it reported to the United Nations, it did not take operational orders from the United Nations. The Organization confined itself to making recommendations on major policy matters, and although the Unified Command in fact gave effect to these recommendations, it was not legally bound to do so.[26] This was true both of the conduct of the military operations, of

23. These are the terms of Article 42, upon which Ross bases his interpretation that 'the command must, according to the definition, be national'.

24. See *below*, pp. 365–72. This was envisaged, ultimately, by the abortive Treaty Constituting the European Defence Community, see *below*, p. 369, note 195.

25. *Above*, Chapter I.

26. *Above*, Chapter II, 4.

the treatment of prisoners of war and of the administration of occupied North-Korean territory.[27]

The Uniting for Peace Resolution does not go into the question of who is to control the Force. However, the Collective Measures Committee, as already pointed out above, pp. 43–44, proposed a system similar to that adopted in Korea, implying that operational control would be exclusively vested in a Member State or a group of Member States acting as 'executive military authority'. However, this proposal was not approved by the General Assembly. And even if it had been, it would not be binding upon any future session of the General Assembly. The question whether the Charter imposes any limitations upon the right of the Assembly and the Security Council to adopt whatever system of command they prefer is discussed below, in Chapter IV,4 (c).

It will be recalled that the position was similar in respect of military sanctions under the Covenant of *the League of Nations*.[28]

3. INTERNATIONAL AGREEMENTS [29]

(a) *The peace-keeping Forces*

The Regulations for the peace-keeping Forces provide that the Secretary-General of the United Nations 'shall be responsible for the negotiation and conclusion of agreements with Governments concerning the Force'.[30] Indeed, all agreements relating to the peace-keeping Forces have been concluded by the Secretary-General or under his autority by the Commander or the Commander's representative, in essentially the same manner as any other agreements concluded by the United Nations. The agreements with the States providing contingents[31] and those with the host State[32] were concluded by the Secretary-General. The more formal agreements expressly designated themselves as agreements between the United Nations and the State concerned and were registered

27. On the latter, see *Attia: Les forces armées des Nations Unies en Corée et au Moyen Orient* (Genève 1963) pp. 267 et seq.

28. *Above*, pp. 26–28, cf. *below*, pp. 125–6.

29. On the relationship to the Hague and Geneva Conventions on warfare see *below*, Chapters V, 2 (a) (pp. 182–197) and VIII (pp. 314–398).

30. UNEF Regulation 15, ONUC and UNFICYP Regulation 16. Cf. also UNEF Regulation 35 and ONUC and UNFICYP Regulation 30, which provide that 'members of the Force shall comply with such arrangements regarding customs and foreign exchange regulations as may be made between the Host State and the United Nations'.

31. *UNTS*, Vol. 271 (UNEF) and *below*, Annex 3 (UNFICYP).

32. *Ibid.*, Vol. 260, p. 61; *OR GA*, 11th session, Annexes, A.i. 66, p. 9 (UNEF); S/4389/Add. 5, *OR SC*, 1960, Suppl. for July–September, p. 27; S/4809, Annexes I–II, *OR SC*, 1961, Suppl. for April–June, p. 48; S/5004, *ibid.*, Suppl. for October–December, p. 151 (Congo); S/5634, *below*, Annex 1, p. 427 (Cyprus).

ex officio by the United Nations as provided for treaties to which the United Nations is a party.[33] Agreements of a technical nature providing for the entry of UNEF into the area to be evacuated by the Anglo-French and Israeli forces in the Middle East were concluded with the Commanders of these forces by the UNEF Commander on instructions from the Secretary-General.[34] Armistice agreements were also concluded by or on behalf of the UN both with the Central Congolese Government and with provincial authorities. Thus a 'provisional draft agreement on the cease-fire between the United Nations troops and those of the Kantaga authorities' of 20 September 1961 and an implementing 'protocol of agreement between the Katanga authorities and ONUC subsequent to the cease-fire' of 13 October 1961 were signed by 'President Tshombe, on behalf of the Katanga Government' and Mr. Mahmoud Khiari, on behalf of the United Nations, and entered into force upon subsequent approval by the United Nations Headquarters.[35] The legal situation was less clear when, earlier, on 5 March 1961, an agreement for the cessation of hostilities in the port of Matadi was concluded between 'Minister Delvaux, representing the Prime Minister and the Minister of the Interior of the Government of the Republic of the Congo, and the Sudanese captain, S. A. Hafiz, in charge of the United Nations troops at Matadi, in the presence of Major Clement Bouffard, representing the United Nations, and Kiembe, the Chief of Staff of the Congolese National Army'. The agreement provided for the withdrawal of 'the Sudanese troops' to Leopoldville and those who signed undertook to report to the Congolese Government and 'to the United Nations at Leopoldville' respectively, on the precise circumstances of the incidents. Whereas the two Congolese representatives signed the agreement 'for the Congolese Government', the United Nations Commander merely signed 'S. A. Hafiz, Sudanese captain'. In addition, Major Bouffard, who was a United Nations Liaison Officer and did not belong to the local garrison, signed as witness for the United Nations. One should probably not attach too great importance one way or the other to the form used by a local military commander under the pressure of battle conditions. However, a substantive reason for the forms of signature may be found in the fact that the United Nations Liaison Officer advised (but did not order) the local United Nations Commander not to agree to withdraw from Matadi, and that the Congolese representatives

---

33. Regulations for the registration and publication of treaties, Article 4.1(*a*), *UNTS*, Vol. 1, p. xxii.

34. Cf. *OR GA*, 11th session, Annexes, A.i. 66, pp. 29 and 43, and plenary meetings, pp. 1300–1.

35. S/4940/Adds. 7 and 11, *OR SC*, 1961, Suppl. for July-September, p. 99.

as a consequence forbade the former to act as interpreter.[36] Whatever the reason may have been, the text of the agreement refers twice to the United Nations and nowhere to the Sudanese Government (except for the title under the signature). There can thus be no doubt that the Sudanese captain was in fact concluding the agreement on behalf of the United Nations, under whose operational orders he stood, and not on behalf of the Sudanese Government, which would have had no right to give him instructions in the matter.

The fact that the agreements have been concluded by the Secretary-General or his representative in the name of the United Nations or its organ and never in the name of the States providing contingents, means that only the United Nations is a party to the agreements and bearer of the rights and duties arising from them. Consequently, only the United Nations can claim fulfilment of the treaty obligations from the other contracting party. Indeed, it is the United Nations, not the States providing contingents, which has presented the demands to the host State that it fulfil its treaty obligations and which has protested when these obligations have been violated, as they were on certain occasions in the Congo.[37]

It must probably be for the United Nations to present any claims to the host State even in respect of that provision of the Status Agreements between the Organization and the respective host States which provides that the immunity, inviolability and exemptions laid down for United Nations assets in Article II of the Convention on the Privileges and Immunities of the United Nations 'shall also apply to the property, funds and assets of Participating States used in Cyprus in connexion with the national contingents serving in the Force.'[38] Similarly, it must undoubtedly be for the United Nations to present any claims on the basis of those provisions of the Status Agreement which grant privileges and immunities to the members of national contingents. The 'participating' States have treaty relations only with the United Nations. It is true that the basic agreement between the United Nations and the 'participating' States refers to the Status Agreement, which is annexed to the basic agreement. This fact probably gives the 'participating' States a right vis-à-vis the United Nations to claim that the Organization maintains and

---

36. S/4761, with text of agreement in Annex II, *OR SC*, 1961, Suppl. for January–March, p. 228.

37. See, for example, second report, S/4417/Add. 8, Annex II, *OR SC*, 1960, Suppl. for July–September, pp. 78 et seq., cf. *ibid.*, 888th meeting, pars. 91–92; and *ibid.*, 916th meeting, par. 7. Cf. *below*, under 5, on the general legal protection of the members of the Force.

38. Agreement with Cyprus, par. 23, see also agreements with Egypt (*UNTS*, Vol. 260, p. 61) and the Congo, par. 23.

enforces such privileges and immunities as the Status Agreements accords to the 'participating' States and their personnel. However, the 'participating' States have no direct right vis-à-vis the host State, if this State and the United Nations did not intend by the Status Agreement to confer such direct right upon the 'participating' States (*pacta in favorem tertii*). It is hardly possible to deduce any such intent merely from the terms of the Status Agreement,[39] and if there was no such intent, one cannot admit that the United Nations could, by its subsequent agreements with the 'participating' States, unilaterally extend the scope of the host State's obligation by giving these States a direct right against it.

On the other hand, the host State cannot claim directly from the 'participating' States performance of the obligations undertaken by them in their agreements with the United Nations, for example to exercise jurisdiction with respect to any crime or offence which might be committed by members of their contingents. The agreements with the States 'participating' in the UNEF expressly [40] refer to paragraph 11 of the Status Agreement with Egypt, under which 'members of the Force shall be subject to the exclusive jurisdiction of their respective national States in respect of any criminal offences which may be committed by them in Egypt'. The agreements with 'participating' States add, moreover, that

> this immunity from the jurisdiction of Egypt is based on the understanding that the authorities of the participating States would exercise such jurisdiction as might be necessary with respect to crimes or offences committed in Egypt by any members of the Force provided from their own military services. It is assumed that the participating States will act accordingly.

However, the actual undertaking to exercise criminal jurisdiction, as contained in paragraph 7 of the agreements with the 'participating' States, hardly intended, by a *pactum in favorem tertii*, to establish a direct and irrevocable right for the host State to demand prosecution of members of national contingents. The host State must therefore address its demand to the United Nations, based on the Status Agreement, and leave it for the United Nations to present a demand to the 'participating' States, based on its agreements with them.

---

39. Cf. also the provision in the Status Agreements (Egypt and Cyprus, par. 10, Congo, par. 11, text p. 428) that the arrangements respecting criminal and civil jurisdiction are made having regard to the interests or special functions of the United Nations, and not for the personal benefit of the members of the Force. In practice, *pacta in favorem tertii* have been recognized only in exceptional circumstances; see *Rousseau: Principes généraux du droit international public* (Paris 1944) 1, pars. 295–301.

40. Par. 5, *UNTS*, Vol. 271, p. 38; cf. *above*, p. 56, and the corresponding provisions of the agreements relating to the Force in Cyprus, *below*, Annex 3, at p. 444.

(b) *Korea*

The international agreements entered into in connexion with the United Nations action in *Korea*,[40a] on the other hand, were concluded, not by the Secretary-General acting for the United Nations, but by the United States Government or the United Nations Command.

The four registered agreements with Member States providing armed forces or field hospitals were concluded by 'the Government of the United States of America (the executive agent of the United Nations Forces in Korea)'.[41] Of the agreements with the Republic of Korea, one—'regarding expenditure by forces under command of the Commanding General, Armed Forces of the Member States of the United Nations'—was concluded by 'the Government of the United States',[42] and another—'relating to economic co-ordination between the Unified Command of the United Nations and the Republic of Korea'—by 'the United States of America acting pursuant to the resolutions of the Security Council of the United Nations of July 7, 1950, and July 31, 1950 (hereinafter referred to as the Unified Command)'.[43] An agreement with the United Nations Korean Reconstruction Agency for the Relief and Rehabilitation of Korea (UNKRA), an organ of the United Nations, was concluded by the United States acting in its capacity as the Unified Command pursuant to resolutions of the United Nations.[44]

The first agreement which was concluded with the Republic of Korea, and which assigned to the Supreme Commander of the United Nations Forces the command authority over all military forces of the Republic of Korea, was embodied in an exchange of letters between President Rhee, as President of the Republic, and General MacArthur, as Commander of the United Nations Forces, on 15/18 July 1950, before the latter had formally established the United Nations Command.[45] The Agreement for the Repatriation of Sick and Injured Captured Personnel was concluded with the opposing side by 'the Senior Member of the

40a. On the Geneva Conventions for the protection of the victims of war, see *below*, pp. 182–9 and 318–20.

41. *UNTS*, Vol. 140, p. 314; Vol. 148, p. 78; and Vol. 177, pp. 234 and 242. Other agreements have not been registered, according to the *UNTS Cumulative Index*.

42. *UNTS*, Vol. 140, p. 62.

43. *Ibid.*, Vol. 179, p. 34. A third agreement with Korea relating to jurisdiction over offences by the United *States* forces in Korea was concluded on 12 July 1950 by 'the United States of America' (*ibid.*, Vol. 222, p. 229). It did not even mention the United Nations in the text or in the title or in the signature, and apparently was intended to cover only the United States contingent.

44. Summary in *US Department of State Bulletin*, XXV (1951), p. 232.

45. Text in *US Department of State Bulletin*, XXIII (1950), p. 206, and (in full) in S/1627 (mimeographed only).

United Nations Command Liaison Group'. And the Armistice Agreement was concluded by 'the Commander-in-Chief, United Nations Command'.[46] Although the North Korean and Chinese representatives insisted on treating the United Nations as a party to the conflict,[47] the Armistice Agreement, which was 'purely military in character', declared that it pertained 'solely to the belligerents in Korea', and provided on the other hand for commissions of 'neutral nations', which were 'defined as those nations whose combatant forces have not participated in the hostilities in Korea' (par. 37). In fact, all but one of the Members of the two 'neutral nations' commissions were Members of the United Nations. One of these (India) provided the armed forces necessary to assist the Neutral Nations Repatriation Commission in carrying out its functions.

Although the *execution* of the treaties concluded in respect of Korea was mostly in the hands of the United Nations Command and the United States Government, the United Nations did not refrain from invoking the provisions of the treaties concluded by the United Nations Command when the situation called for intervention of the Organization. Such a case occurred when the Republic of Korea, following the signing of the agreement on the exchange of prisoners on 8 June 1953, withdrew its representative on the armistice delegation of the United Nations Command and released some 25,000 anti-communist Korean prisoners of war held in United Nations prisoner-of-war compounds in the Republic. This caused the President of the General Assembly to send a message to the President of the Republic, in which it was stated, *inter alia*, that the release of the prisoners in question constituted a violation of the agreement on the exchange of prisoners of 8 June and of the undertaking contained in the agreement of 15 July 1950 between the President of the Republic of Korea and the Commander-in-Chief, United Nations Command, assigning to the latter the command authority over all military forces of the Republic during the period of hostilities.[48] This action may be viewed as having been undertaken by the United Nations acting on behalf of the United Nations Force and as a party to the treaty. However, it may also be viewed as having been undertaken in the exercise of the Organization's general responsibility with regard to the maintenance of international peace in conformity with the principles of justice and international law.[49] On another occasion, however, the United Nations presented a claim to the opposing side based on the Armistice Agreement in a manner which could normally be done only

46. *Above,* Chapter II,4, at note 48.
47. *Below,* p. 188, note 56.
48. *Annual Report of the Secretary-General,* 1952–53, p. 25.
49. United Nations Charter, Article 1 (1).

by parties to this agreement. By Resolution 906 (IX) the General Assembly

> 1. *Declares* that the detention and imprisonment of the eleven American airmen, members of the United Nations Command, referred to in document A/2830, and the detention of all other captured personnel of the United Nations Command desiring repatriation is a violation of the Korean Armistice Agreement;
> 2. *Condemns,* as contrary to the Korean Armistice Agreement, the trial and conviction of prisoners of war illegally detained after 25 September 1953;
> 3. *Requests* the Secretary-General, in the name of the United Nations, to seek the release, in accordance with the Korean Armistice Agreement, of these eleven United Nations Command personnel, and all other captured personnel of the United Nations Command still detained;
> 4. *Requests* the Secretary-General to make, by the means most appropriate in his judgement, continuing and unremitting efforts to this end.

The United States Government registered with the Secretariat of the United Nations all or most of the treaties it concluded in its own name with other United Nations Members and with the Republic of Korea. Under Article 102 of the United Nations Charter, every treaty entered into by a Member of the United Nations shall be registered. The agreements with Korea, a non-member State, could thus not have been registered if the United States had considered the United Nations rather than itself a party to them.[50] On the other hand, the agreement with UNKRA which was *not* registered,[51] should have been registered if the United States was a party, but could not have been registered if the United Nations was a party, since an agreement between the Organization and one of its organs is not an international agreement.

The agreements concluded by the United Nations Command (with non-member States) were none of them registered, as they should have been if the United States, alone or together with the other States contributing forces, was considered a party. Nor were they filed and recorded in accordance with Articles 10 (*a*) and 12 of the regulations for the registration and publication of treaties, which provide that the Secretariat shall 'file and record', and publish in the *Treaty Series,* treaties and international agreements which have been concluded by the United Nations and which are not subject to registration (because the other party is not a member State).[52] States frequently forget to register treaties, so a failure to register need not necessarily arise from legal doubts as to whether a Member State is a contracting party. However, the consistency of the failure to register the agreements concluded by the United Na-

---

50. The Secretariat accepts in the final analysis the views of the registering State as to registrability, see *Repertory of Practice of UN Organs,* Suppl. 1, II, p. 400, and the reservation made by the Secretariat in its notes in the *United Nations Treaty Series,* for example in Vol. 336, p. xiv.
51. According to the *UNTS Cumulative Index.*
52. *UNTS,* Vol. I, p. xxvi.

tions Command as opposed to those concluded by the United States Government may be taken as an indication that the United States Government was in doubt as to whether it was a party. On the other hand, the fact that they were not filed and recorded *ex officio* by the Secretariat demonstrates that the Secretariat, for its part, did not feel in a position to determine that the United Nations was a party.

The only other alternative would be to assume that the United Nations Command represented a distinct intergovernmental organization consisting of the Member States providing contingents and the Republic of Korea. However, no such organization existed.[53] The United Nations Command, in conducting military operations as well as in negotiating agreements, was subject only to the instructions of the United States Government, and the latter was not itself subject to the instructions of the Committee of Sixteen (and even less to those of any body which included Korean representation).

In paragraph 60 of the Armistice Agreement the military commanders of the two sides recommended 'to the Governments of the countries concerned on both sides' that a political conference 'of both sides' be held to settle 'the questions of the withdrawal of all foreign forces from Korea, the peaceful settlement of the Korean question, etc.' The question of the composition of the conference was thoroughly discussed by the General Assembly, where there was a large body of opinion in favour of expanding the conference to a round table conference with the participation of 'neutral nations' (India).[54] However, in the face of United States and Korean resistance, the Assembly finally decided, in Resolutions 711 A-B (VII) of 28 August 1953, to recommend that

> the side contributing armed forces under the Unified Command in Korea shall have as participants in the conference those among the Member States contributing armed forces pursuant to the call of the United Nations which desire to be represented, together with the Republic of Korea. The participating governments shall act independently at the conference with full freedom of action and shall be bound only by decisions or agreements to which they adhere.

It was also recommended that the Soviet Union participate 'provided the other side desires it'. The Resolution recommended, furthermore, that the United States Government, after consultation with the other participating countries, should arrange with the other side for the conference to be held. The People's Republic of China and the People's Democratic Republic of Korea, in cablegrams of 13 and 15 september 1953,[55] protested against the limitation of participation in the conference to bel-

---

53. *Below*, p. 122.
54. See *Annual Report of the Secretary-General*, 1953–54, p. 8–10, and Goodrich in *International Conciliation*, No. 494, pp. 184–6.
55. A/2469 and A/2476 incl. Corr. 1 (mimeographed only).

ligerent nations on both sides and proposed to add to the list the Soviet Union and certain neutral nations from South Asia.

The political conference convened in Geneva from 26 April to 15 June 1954. It was attended, on the United Nations side, by all States which had contributed armed forces except the Union of South Africa.[56] The conference did not reach agreement, but it was clear from the composition of the conference and the terms of the resolution of the General Assembly that the parties to any peace treaty would have been each of the nations providing forces (and participating in the conference) rather than the United Nations as an Organization.

Even in respect of the other treaties there does not appear to be sufficient basis for claiming that the United Nations was a party. The resolutions of the United Nations do not specifically confer upon the Unified Command or the United Nations Command the authority to conclude treaties on behalf of the Organization or otherwise to commit it legally. And it is hardly possible to read any such authority into the general clauses of the resolutions. The Security Council confined itself to authorizing the Unified Command [57] to use the United Nations flag. The Council would no doubt have found it even more necessary to be explicit had it intended to confer upon the Unified Command the much more far-reaching power to conclude treaties on the United Nations' behalf. Moreover, the parties to the treaties would no doubt have made themselves clearer had they meant that the United Nations was to be a party. The reference to the United States acting pursuant to the resolutions of the Security Council does not carry the matter any further than the resolutions themselves, as interpreted above. Only in one agreement did the United States refer to itself as agent, and even then not as agent of the United Nations, but of the United Nations Forces in Korea, and only in parenthesis. Finally, had the United Nations Secretariat felt that the United States concluded the agreements not on its own behalf, but on behalf of the United Nations, it would no doubt have raised the matter before the appropriate organ of the Organization when receiving the treaties for registration, even if, under its adopted policy, it would not in the final analysis refuse to register them in the manner requested by the United States.[58] Nor dit the United Nations in any other respect act unequivocally as a party to the treaties, by ex officio registration, filing and recording, or otherwise, except that on one occasion it presented a claim on the basis of the Armistice Agreement in a manner which only parties would normally be entitled to do.

56. Report to the United Nations on the Korean Political Conference at Geneva, OR GA, 9th session, Annexes, A.i. 17, p. 2; cf. General Assembly Resolution 811 (IX).

57. The United Nations Command, which was not established until 25 July 1950, was not mentioned in the Security Council resolutions.

58. Above, note 50.

It is accordingly submitted that the Armistice Agreement and the other military agreements with the opposing side were concluded by the United Nations Command on behalf of the United States Government and, probably, also of the other fifteen Governments providing contingents to the United Nations side,[59] and that the agreements with the Governments providing contingents, with UNKRA (an organ of the United Nations) and probably also those with the host State, were concluded by the United States Government (in one case through the United Nations Commander, before the formal establishment of the United Nations Command) on its own behalf.

It has already been pointed out that the Collective Measures Committee, in its first report on the implementation of *the Uniting for Peace Resolution*, proposed that the 'executive military authority' should negotiate agreements with the victim State and the contributing States.[60] The Committee did not specify in this context that this would be done on behalf of the United Nations. It may thus have envisaged the 'executive military authority' itself or its members, rather than the United Nations, as being party to the agreements.

4. CLAIMS AGAINST THE FORCE AND ITS MEMBERS

(a) The peace-keeping Forces

UNEF Regulation 15 and ONUC Regulation 16 provide that the Secretary-General 'shall make provisions for the settlement of claims arising with respect to the Force'. In practice, claims against UNEF and the United Nations Force in the Congo are settled by the United Nations, not by the State whose contingent or soldiers performed the act giving rise to the claim. The same is true of claims against members of the Force in respect of official acts [61] and other acts performed in the course of their service. Thus compensation to the dependants of civilians accidentally killed by members of UNEF and the Congo Force were paid by the United Nations and not by the Government providing the

---

59. On the position of the latter see *below*, pp. 123–4. — Also in respect of the conventions on warfare, the United Nations Command probably acted as an agent of all the States providing contingents, see *below*, Chapter V,2(a) especially the quotation at note 34. Otherwise each contingent was bound by the conventions to which its government was a party, see *below*, Chapter VIII,3.

60. OR GA, 6th session, Suppl. No. 13, pp. 25–26.

61. These are correctly claims against the United Nations, rather than against the member concerned. This appears to be recognized in par. 10 (*b*) of the Congo Status Agreement, while par. 38 (*b*), cf. par. 12, of the Status Agreements with Egypt and Cyprus do not give any indication one way or the other.

contingent concerned.[62] This has been done, even in cases where no official function or superior order required the member to fire and where he was therefore prosecuted in his home country for having shot the person in question.[63] Thus in 1965 the United Nations in an agreement with Belgium undertook to pay reparation for damage and injury inflicted upon a number of Belgian nationals by the United Nations Force in the Congo outside the course of hostilities.[63a] UNFICYP Regulation 16 provides that the Secretary-General, 'within the limits of available voluntary contributions... shall make provisions for the settlement of any claims arising with respect to the Force that are not settled by the Governments providing contingents or the Government of Cyprus'. The reservations must be viewed in light of the fact that the Force in Cyprus, unlike those in the Middle East and the Congo, is not financed over the budget of the United Nations, but partly by voluntary contributions, and partly by the 'participating' States themselves bearing the expenses relating to their contingent (above, pp. 81–82). Still, these reject legal responsibility for claims,[63b] and rightly so.[63c]

The United Nations, furthermore, lays down, unilaterally or together with the host State, the arbitral or other procedures under which claims advanced against the members of the Force personally should be settled.[64] Similarly, the host State may seek the good offices of the United Nations in order to obtain satisfaction of judgments by local courts or awards by a claims commission against members of the Force. In respect of awards by claims commissions established jointly by the Organization and the host State the United Nations even appears to have undertaken a responsibility for obtaining satisfaction.[65] Neither the Status Agreements with Egypt and the Congo, nor the UNEF and ONUC Regula-

---

62. See e.g. *below*, p. 195, on the death of 3 international Red Cross officials.

63. Cf. the Secretary-General's Summary Study, *OR GA*, 13th session, Annexes, A.i. 65, p. 26. At least in one case there was also a prior and additional collection among members of the contingent concerned for the benefit of the dependants. Total UNEF expenses for 'claims and adjustments' in 1959 were $31,100. In subsequent budgets $ 20,000 were allocated 'to cover costs of individual claims against the United Nations for personal injuries, damage to property and other losses arising from traffic accidents and other effects of the operation of the Force'. *Ibid.*, 15th session, Annexes, A.i. 27, pp. 3 and 8; cf. Summary Study, *ibid.*, 13th session, Annexes A.i. 65, par. 120.

63a. The agreement was signed on 25 February 1965. It entered into force (after ratification) on 17 May 1965 and was registered with the United Nations the same day.

63b. Agreement between UN and Sweden, *below*, pp. 445 (par. 12) and 446–7.

63c. See *below*, pp. 330 and 332.

64. Status Agreement with Egypt, *UNTS*, Vol. 260, p. 61, pars. 12 and 38 (*b*) (ii); UNEF Regulation 34 (*d*); Status Agreement with the Congo, par. 10 (*c*), *OR SC*, 1961, Suppl. for October–December, p. 151; Status Agreement with Cyprus, par. 38 (*b*).

65. Status Agreements with Egypt and Cyprus, pars. 12 *in fine* and 38(b) *in fine* with note 1. There is no similar provision in the Status Agreement with Congo.

tions, nor the agreements with the States providing contingents to UNEF mention any role to be played by the States providing contingents in respect of civil claims against members of their contingents. However, the agreements with the States providing contingents to the Force in *Cyprus,* provide that these States shall assist the United Nations in this respect, without themselves assuming responsibility.[65a]

It has already been pointed out that criminal jurisdiction over members of national contingents is vested exclusively in the State providing the contingent,[66] but that the host State must present any demand for such prosecution to the United Nations, not to the State concerned.[67] Indeed, when the host State has found it necessary to make official representations or protests in respect of actions by the Force, these have been made to the representatives of the United Nations, not to representatives of the States providing contingents.[68] However, the United Nations has accepted responsibility only in respect of actions under its authority. It has assumed no responsibility in respect of aircraft employed by States providing contingents for the purpose of transporting supplementary national supplies to their contingents in the Congo.[69]

(b) *Korea*

In Korea claims were settled, not by the United Nations, but by the Unified Command (or the United Nations Command acting under instructions from the Unified Command) or by the other participating States. None of these was acting under instructions from the United Nations and they paid any compensation out of their own funds. The agreements between the United States and the participating States provided that claims of any third Government or its nationals against the Government or nationals of the participating State or *vice versa* should be a matter for disposition between the Government of the participating State and the third Government or its nationals.[70] However, the agreements did not delimit the respective liability of the parties.

Early in September 1950 the Soviet Union presented to the United States Embassy in Moscow a note protesting against the shooting down of a Soviet military aircraft over the high seas and demanding reparation. The Embassy refused to receive the note on the ground that the

65a. *Below,* pp. 434, note; 440, par. 16; 445, par. 12; and 446–7.

66. Status Agreement with Egypt, par. 11, the Congo, par. 9 and Cyprus, par. 11; cf. *above,* pp. 56 and 66–67, and *below,* p. 428.

67. *Above,* under 3 (a) *in fine.*

68. See, for example, S/4531, par. 23, OR SC, 1960, Suppl. for July-September, p. 182, and S/4417/Add. 7, *ibid.,* p. 71.

69. S/4724, *ibid.,* 1961, Suppl. for January-March 1961, p. 127.

70. See, for example, Article 4 of the agreement with the Union of South Africa, *UNTS,* Vol. 177, p. 244.

action having been taken by United Nations forces, the protest should have been directed to the Security Council, to which the United States reported the incident in writing and orally. The Soviet Union also transmitted the text of its note to the Security Council, not for discussion, but only because the United States letter had been circulated earlier. The Soviet representative in the Security Council qualified the question as an intergovernmental one and the United States as the sole responsible party, adding that the United Nations had nothing to do with the matter.[71]

In early October 1950 the Soviet Union sent another note to the United States, alleging the strafing of a Soviet airfield. The Department of State asserted that the question of an attack was purely a United Nations matter and that the note was not officially before the United States. Later, the attack was admitted in a note from the United States to the United Nations, and apologies and reparations were offered, but only through the United Nations, since it was insisted that the attacking planes were under United Nations, not United States, control and that only through the United Nations could the United States be responsible.[72]

In a number of other cases the People's Republic of China, the People's Democratic Republic of Korea and the Soviet Union presented to the United Nations complaints of illegal warfare, including bombing of civilians and civilian property, bacterial warfare, mass murder of prisoners of war, invasion of neutral air space, bombing of neutral territory, shooting at neutral ships and aircraft, &C. However, the complaints always designated the United States, not the United Nations, as the party having committed the alleged violations of the generally accepted rules of international law on war and neutrality. The Soviet Union usually proposed resolutions to condemn the alleged acts of the United States. The terms of these draft resolutions demonstrated that the complaints were brought before the United Nations, not as the opposing side in the war responsible for the alleged violations, but rather as the world peace organization concerned with the settlement of international disputes.[73] The United Nations rejected the Soviet draft resolutions because the allegations had not been substantiated by proofs and not for the reason that they were directed at the United States. Also in some of these cases the United States admitted the possibility that its planes had inadvertently violated neutral territory and expressed its regret and its willing-

71. OR SC, 1950, No. 37, p. 5, and No. 38, pp. 2–4; Baxter in BYIL, 1952, p. 336.
72. Taubenfeld in *American Journal of International Law*, XLV (1951) p. 675–6.
73. Later the Soviet, North Korean and Chinese delegates appear to have taken the view that the United Nations was a party to the conflict, see *below*, p. 188, note 56.

ness to assume responsibility and pay compensation *through the United Nations* for any damage which an impartial investigation might show to have been caused by United States planes. The United States emphasized, moreover, that the action in Korea was being conducted in accordance with, and under the mandate of, the United Nations.[74]

The basic United States position in the cases referred to above appears to have been that it was the United Nations rather than the United States which was internationally responsible for the Force. However, this view was not pressed too clearly. Had it been, then the United States would not have admitted any responsibility at all, not even through the United Nations. It would at most have declared itself willing, as an internal matter within the Organization, to reimburse the United Nations for any compensation paid. Whatever may be the significance of this distinction, the United Nations does not appear to have accepted legal responsibility in the one form or the other. It is not known whether reparations were paid in any of the cases referred to or in any similar cases, but at least there is no indication that any such payment was made by or through the United Nations. The conclusion thus is that claims against the Force have been directed against the United States (or the other participating States) and that, although the United States has in some cases declined direct responsibility, the United Nations has not assumed it.

5. PROTECTION OF THE RIGHTS OF THE FORCE AND ITS MEMBERS

(a) *The Peace-keeping Forces*

Claims on behalf of the peace-keeping Forces have been presented and representations made by the United Nations, not by the States providing contingents. Similarly, it usually is the United Nations, not the Governments providing contingents, which intervenes on behalf of the members of the Force for the purpose of protecting their rights in that capacity. This is obvious in the case of the Commander and other international officials serving with the staffs, and also in respect of locally recruited personnel. But it also applies to members of national contingents. Indeed, the Regulations specifically provide that 'members of the Force are entitled to the legal protection of the United Nations and shall be regarded as agents of the United Nations for the purpose of such protection'.[74a]

---

74. See especially *Annual Report of the Secretary-General*, 1950–51, pp. 30 and 75–79, and *ibid.*, 1952–53, pp. 21–22; cf. OR GA, 7th session, 411th plenary meeting, pp. 531–60.

74a. UNEF Regulation 30, ONUC and UNFICYP Regulation 25.

The right of the United Nations to bring international claims in respect of injuries caused to its agents was defined by the International Court of Justice in its advisory opinion on *Reparation for Injuries Suffered in the Service of the United Nations.*[75] The Court, by 11 votes against 4, gave the opinion that in the event of an agent of the United Nations in the performance of his duties suffering injury in circumstances involving the responsibility of a State, the United Nations as an Organization has the capacity to bring an international claim against the responsible *de jure* or *de facto* Government with a view to obtaining the reparation due in respect of the damage caused to the victim or to persons entitled through him. It also held that the United Nations can base such a claim only upon a breach of obligations due to itself, not upon breach of obligations due to the State of which the agent is a national. Indeed, the Court assumed that both the Organization and the national State might have the right to bring such claims in respect of the agent, but on different bases. The Organization might exercise protection where there was 'a breach of an obligation designed to help an agent of the Organisation in the performance of his duties'. The national State could make claims in respect of 'breach of the general obligations of a State concerning the position of aliens'; this would not, 'as a general rule', be within the competence of the Organization. The distinction can also be expressed by saying that the Organization is competent to protect its agent as such (functional protection), while the national State is entitled to protect him as a private individual, i.e. on the basis of rules applicable to its nationals or to individuals generally (diplomatic protection).[76]

The division of functions and powers between the Organization and the national States must equally apply in respect of members of national contingents serving in a United Nations Force. In the case of UNEF this follows from the express provision in UNEF Regulation 30, which is annexed to the agreements between the United Nations and the States providing contingents. (It is also provided in ONUC Regulation 25 and UNFICYP Regulation 25.) However, it must also apply without express provision, if the members of the contingents during the period of their assignment to the Force are subject to the operational orders of the United Nations in essentially the same manner as other agents of the Organization.[77] Thus it applied in the Congo also during the two years which passed before the Regulations for the Force were enacted. This

75. *ICJ Reports*, 1949, pp. 181–8.
76. See Eagleton: 'International Organization and the Law of Responsibility', *Recueil des Cours*, 1950 I, pp. 452–84. See also *International and Comparative Law Quarterly*, XIV (1964) pp. 494–6.
77. UNEF Regulations 15–16 and 31–32, ONUC Regulations 16–17 and 26–27, UNFICYP Regulations 11 and 26–27.

was clearly confirmed by M. Tchombe, when he, in the telegram quoted *below*, Chapter VII, 3, replied to the Norwegian Prime Minister's intervention in favour of Scandinavian members of the United Nations Force, that these were not regarded as Scandinavians, but as United Nations military personnel, as already stated by the Swedish Minister for Foreign Affairs.

In cases of violence by Congolese forces against members of national contingents of the United Nations Force in the Congo, demands and protests were lodged by the United Nations with the Central Government and with provincial authorities.[78] The Governments of the States providing the contingents concerned also made protests or appeals in certain grave cases.[79] Similarly, the Central Government and provincial authorities presented regrets both to the United Nations [80] and to the national Government concerned.[81] Following the arrest on 3 March 1961 of three Swedish helicopter pilots in Boma, the Swedish Consulate in Leopoldville was instructed to protest to President Kasa-Vubu and to express 'the expectation of the Swedish Government that measures will be taken to prevent the recurrence of such acts of violence, which in the Swedish Government's view infringe the conditions for the presence and activities of the UN forces in the Congo in accordance with the relevant UN resolutions'.[82] No reply was received to this protest. After a much more serious incident in Port Franqui in April 1961, resulting in the killing of several United Nations personnel, the Swedish Government instructed its representative in the Congo to lodge with President Kasa-Vubu the following protest:

> The Swedish Government, which with deep concern has taken note of the reports of the incidents in Port Franqui on 27 and 28 April, protests sharply against the brutal acts of violence committed by units of ANC against three unarmed Swedes in the UN transportation service. Two of these are still reported missing and it is feared that they have been killed. The Swedish Government associates itself with the demands for prosecution of the offenders and the reservation of the right to damages already made by the Secretary-General of the UN.[83]

---

78. For example S/4417/Add. 8, Annex II, *OR SC*, 1960, Suppl. for July–September, p. 78; S/4753, *OR SC*, 1961, Suppl. for January–March, p. 203; S/4780, *ibid.*, Suppl. for April–June, p. 6; S/4940/Add. 16, Annex I, *ibid.*, Suppl. for July–September, p. 99.

79. See, for example, S/4780, *OR SC*, 1961, Suppl. for April–June, p. 6.

80. *OR SC*, 1960, *888th* meeting, pars. 91–92; S/4940/Add. 16, Annex II, *OR SC*, 1961, Suppl. for July–September, p. 105.

81. Press *communiqué* of 29 May 1961 from the Swedish Ministry for Foreign Affairs.

82. Text supplied by the Swedish Ministry for Foreign Affairs.

83. Press *communiqué* of 13 May 1961 from the Swedish Ministry for Foreign Affairs, as translated by the writer. An English translation may also be found in *Documents on Swedish Foreign Policy 1961*, published by the Royal Ministry for Foreign Affairs (Stockholm 1962) p. 57.

The reply from President Kasa-Vubu came to the Secretary-General of the United Nations, asking him to transmit a message to the delegations of Ghana, Sweden and the United Kingdom. In this the Congolese Government regretted 'the bloodsheds between units of the Congolese army and your contingent in the Congo' and the President presented his 'sincere regrets to your government and to the families concerned'.[84]

The acts committed by the Congolese armed forces in these and other cases where protests were made violated both the general obligations of a State concerning the position of aliens and special rules for the protection of the United Nations agents performing functions in the Congo pursuant to the invitation of the Congolese Government. The acts thus justified the concurrent exercise by the United Nations of functional protection of its agents, and by the national State of diplomatic protection of its nationals. It does not appear from the available texts that the United Nations protests have normally invoked grounds not connected with the United Nations mission of the personnel concerned (in many cases it was not considered necessary to invoke legal grounds at all). On the other hand, the second Swedish protest quoted above did not invoke grounds specifically related to the United Nations mission of the personnel.[85, 86] However, the first Swedish protest did so, and thus appears to conflict with the principle set forth above.[87] Even so, more important is the fact that also the Swedish protests correctly referred to the personnel as members of the United Nations Force rather than as representatives of a national force and the national Government.[88] Indeed, however the Swedish protest is viewed, it was never intended to preclude protection by the United Nations. The United Nations protests referred to the nationality of the personnel concerned, and sometimes

84. Press *communiqué* of 29 May 1961 from the Swedish Ministry for Foreign Affairs.

85. Nor did the Norwegian Prime Minister's request for release of two Norwegian officers, yet it was rejected on the grounds that they were not Norwegian, but United Nations personnel, see *below*, Chapter VII, 3.

86. *Bowett: United Nations Forces* (London 1964) p. 243 observes pertinently that this protest was 'in the nature of an association of the State with the formal United Nations protest and did not attempt to press a separate claim on the basis of the Congo's duties towards aliens'.

87. Unless *Bowett's* reasoning referred to in note 86 is applied here too (it is not clear whether he does).

88. According to an Associated Press report published in *Dagbladet*, Oslo, 19 August 1960, a Canadian protest to Prime Minister Lumumba against acts of violence committed by Congolese troops against Canadian soldiers at Leopoldville airport referred to the soldiers as 'representing the Canadian Government and the Canadian people'. This statement may not have been meant, and at any rate was not correct, in a *legal* (international law) sense. The text of the concurrent United Nations protest is reproduced in S/4417/Add. 8, Annex II, *OR SC*, 1960, Suppl. for July–September, p. 78.

to their contingent, but otherwise cited their official connexion with the United Nations Force rather than with the national Government.

In concluding its Status Agreements with the host States, the United Nations has in fact assumed protection of the members of national contingents also in matters which are not directly related to their functions for the United Nations. Thus, as already pointed out, it has secured for them wide immunity also in respect of non-official acts, and has assumed powers with regard to the settlement of civilian claims against them [89] which would normally have been a matter for the national State. However, all such rights and functions have been provided for in order to enable the Force to perform its special functions and to secure its independence in the interest of the United Nations.[90] The rights and functions are therefore based upon the status of the soldiers as members of the United Nations Force. Indeed, they could not nowadays have been assumed by a State in respect of its civilian nationals, but only in respect of its own officials, including members of its armed Forces. And the fact that they have been assumed by the United Nations and not by the States providing the contingents is evidence that the Force is treated externally as a United Nations Force and not as a combination of national forces.

It should be noted that the agreements concluded with the host State were couched in such wide and general terms that in most or all cases it was possible to base any claims or protests made on behalf of the Force or its members on the agreements, even if this was not always done. From this point of view, the cases which can be cited, apart from UNEF Regulation 30, might not appear to go beyond what has already been stated above (pp. 101–2). However, in fact the protest notes sent by the United Nations to the Central Government of the Congo rarely referred to the basic agreement or the other special undertakings of that Government.[91] Indeed, even if it is difficult to find any cases which are clearly outside the scope of treaties concluded by the United Nations, it is clear that, even without express provision, the Organization must be competent to present claims and exercise protection in respect of rights of

89. *Above*, at note 64.

90. See the express provision to this effect in the Status Agreements with Egypt, par. 10, and with the Congo, par. 11. The rights and functions secured by the United Nations on behalf of the members of the Force do not, therefore, constitute examples of the exception implied by the International Court of Justice when it stated that claims in respect of 'a breach of the general obligations of a State concerning the position of aliens... would be within the competence of the national State and not, *as a general rule*, within that of the Organization'; *ICJ Reports*, 1949 p. 182 (italics supplied).

91. An exception was the *note verbale* from the Secretary-General to the Central Government of 18 August 1960, S/4417/Add. 8, Annex II, *OR SC*, 1960, Suppl. for July–September, p. 78.

the Force, or for its members as such, irrespective of whether these derive from treaties or other specific undertakings, or from general rules of international law the purpose of which is to protect the Organization (and other subjects of international law) and its agents.

(b) *Korea*

It has been pointed out in Chapter II, 4, that direct action on behalf of the United Nations Force in Korea was taken by the Unified Command and, under its instructions, by the United Nations Command. Two exceptions were cited [92] where the United Nations itself protested to the Republic of Korea against its release of a number of prisoners of war, and presented a claim to the opposing side on the basis of the Armistice Agreement, respectively. The United Nations on certain occasions exchanged direct communications also with the Governments opposing the United Nations Force, in attempts to obtain a cease-fire. In this correspondence, however, the United Nations confined itself to making proposals and asking questions, and, as in its protest to the Republic of Korea, it may just as well have been acting in its capacity as the World-organization responsible for peace between all States, as in any capacity of legal representative of the Force.[93] Indeed, when concrete armistice negotiations started, these were conducted by the United Nations Command under the instructions of the Unified Command. The only case which appears clearly to imply protection by the United Nations is General Assembly Resolution 906 (IX).[94]

6. CONCLUSIONS

(a) *The host State*

There is no evidence with regard to any of the United Nations forces discussed above that the host State has any direct control over the Force or has in any respect represented it internationally, by concluding treaties, accepting responsibility or asserting rights on its behalf. This applies not only to UNEF, which had specific international functions fairly clearly distinguishable from those of the host State, but also to the Force in Korea, which went to assist the Government in a war to which the latter was already a party, and even to the Force in the Congo, which

---

92. *Above*, pp. 104–5.

93. See *above*, Chapter II,4, at notes 43 and 46–47, with reference to *International Organization*, V (1951) pp. 233 et seq.; *Annual Report of the Secretary-General*, 1950–51, pp. 47–52 and pp. 18–21; *International Conciliation*, No. 494, p. 182, and to relevant General Assembly Resolutions, especially Resolution 610 (VII).

94. Quoted *loc. cit.*, note 92.

went to assist the Government in the exercise of its internal tasks.[95] Indeed, the Secretary-General was thinking primarily of relations with the host State when he laid down the principle, in respect of UNEF and later even in respect of the Congo, that the United Nations action must be separate and distinct from activities by any national authorities and that it could not be part of any joint operation.[96]

The conclusion clearly is that the host State does not represent internationally any of the United Nations Forces so far established. Nor is there any reason to believe that any United Nations Force established pursuant to Articles 43 et seq. of the Charter or to the Uniting for Peace Resolution would be set up in a manner which would alter this situation. Only in the cases of the Saar and West New Guinea (Irian Barat) did the Organization, when establishing the international Force, place it at the disposal and under the authority of the local government.[97] However, these government were not sovereign governments, but were themselves appointed by and under the authority of the Organizations, which were in the last resort internationally responsible for their acts.

(b) *The peace-keeping Forces—Individually enlisted Forces—Charter Articles 43 et seq.—Saar*

The peace-keeping Forces are established by the United Nations under a Commander who is a United Nations official. The expenses are paid by the Organization or, to the extent that they are paid by the States providing contingents, reimbursed by the Organization unless reimbursement is waived by the States concerned. Operational command authority and control are in the hands of the Organization through the Commander appointed by it, and not in those of the States providing contingents. It is thus a true reflection of the facts when the Regulations for these Forces state expressly that the Force is a (subsidiary) organ of the United Nations.[98]

95. Cf. *above*, Chapter II,7 *in initio*, on the mandate of the Force, and Schachter in *Annual Review of United Nations Affairs*, 1960–61, p. 146, on the relationship to the host State.

96. See quotation *above*, under 2(a), at note 12, for the Congo, and par. 165 of the Summary Study, OR GA, 13th session, Annexes, A.i. 65, for UNEF.

97. The Council's Resolution of 11 December 1934, *Journal Officiel* (1934) p. 1762. See also the report approved on the following day by the Council's Committee on the Saar in execution of the resolution (*ibid.*, p. 1841). The report provides, *inter alia:* 'Sous réserve des exigences d'ordre militaire que pourra comporter la situation, et sans préjudice de toute action immédiate qui pourrait être nécessaire en cas d'urgence, le commandant en chef se conformera aux demandes qui pourront lui être faites par le Président de la Commission de gouvernement aux fins d'intervention de la force en vue de maintenir ou de rétablir l'ordre'.

98. UNEF Regulation 6, Status Agreement with Egypt *in initio* (*UNTS*, Vol. 260, p. 62); agreement with States participating in UNEF, par. 4, (*UNTS*, Vol. 271, p. 138); ONUC Regulations 5(b) and 6; UNFICYP Regulation 6.

6. CONCLUSIONS

It is logical that the Forces, as subsidiary organs of the Organization, established by it and under its exclusive operational control, form part of and represent its international personality, which is distinct from that of any State; and that their acts, including the official acts of the members of the Forces, create rights and obligations for the Organization, not for the several States providing contingents (nor for the host State). If it had been otherwise, the actions of the Forces would not have been 'separate and distinct from activities by any national authorities', as the Secretary-General rightly insisted in the case of UNEF as well as in respect of the United Nations operation in the Congo.[99] Indeed, it appears clearly from the facts set out under 3—5 above that the Forces are represented internationally by the United Nations. All agreements have been concluded by officials of the United Nations or by members of the Force acting on behalf of the United Nations or the Force as an organ of the United Nations. And most legal claims and official representations concerning the Force or its members as such have similarly been made to, or by, the United Nations (or the Force as an organ of the United Nations). Neither the host State nor the States providing contingents are known to have contested these competences of the United Nations in respect of the Forces.

The conclusion is therfore submitted that international responsibility for the United Nations peace-keeping Forces and for their members as such rests exclusively with the United Nations, in the same manner as for other organs of the Organization,[100] and that the United Nations alone is entitled to present international claims on behalf of these Forces and their members as such. This responsibility has been recognized by the United Nations.[101]

This conclusion applies *a fortiori* to Forces *recruited individually by the United Nations*, in respect of which there are no 'participating' States which could possibly pretend to represent the Force internationally.

99. See the full quotation *above*, under 2(a), at note 12.

100. Draper may take a different view, see *below*, Chapter V, note 110. Paul de Visscher in *Revue de droit international et de droit comparé* (Brussels) 1963, p. 169, takes the same view as the present writer, but tends towards the view that the States providing contingents may be responsible *too*. The latter view is not shared by the UN, see note 101.

101. *Ibid.*, p. 178, and the practice cited above. Dr. Schachter, Director of the General Legal Division of the United Nations, stated in a letter of 3 October 1963 to the present writer, referring to the Congo action: 'Our office has not taken the position in any specific case that responsibility would rest with the states providing the contingent which caused damage; in fact we have been quite prepared to acknowledge liability where the evidence shows that an illegal act has been caused by a member of an ONUC contingent'. In connexion with UNFICYP the United Nations had to make certain reservations with regard to the financing of the reparations, see *above*, pp. 109–10.

The position will presumably also be the same for a *Force established pursuant to Articles 43 et seq. of the Charter*,[102] although the Security Council probably is free to decide upon a different command system, which might entail a different international status of the Force.

As for *the League of Nations Force in the Saar*, the scarce relevant data contained in published documents give no indication that international responsibility would be vested in the several States providing contingents. Indeed, all available information [103] points to the League as the international person which was internationally responsible for the Force, through its responsibility for the Government of the Saar, at whose disposal and under whose authority the Council had placed the Force.

The question of whether the above conclusion, that the international responsibility for Forces under the Organization's command, applies also in relation to non-member States which have not 'recognized' the Organization as an international person, will be discussed separately below, in Chapter VII.

(c) *Korea—Uniting for Peace Resulution—League of Nations Covenant*

In *Korea*, the position was entirely different. The Force was established and operated by the United States Government, by which the Commander was appointed and dismissed, and to which he was responsible. He and the other members of the Force remained purely national officials and had neither the rights nor the duties of international officials.[104] The United States Government was also responsible for the external relations of the Force as a whole. The costs were paid by each participating Government in respect of its contingent.

102. Ross does not state whether his views on national command, set out *above*, under 2(a), at note 19, lead him to different conclusions with regard to responsibility. In any case such different conclusions could not apply to UNEF and the Congo Force, in view of the practice already referred to.

Kelsen: The Law of the United Nations, p. 767, although correctly pointing out that United Nations organs 'do not act on behalf of the members, but on behalf of the Organization', and that 'this becomes particularly clear when an enforcement action involving the use of armed force is taken by a majority decision of the Security Council adopted against the vote of members the armed forces of which are to be employed in this action', arrives at the conclusion that 'the Charter has created a type which is in the midst between an armed force of the United Nations distinct from the armed forces of the members' and execution of the enforcement action 'by the members through their own armed forces'. He does not discuss the question of responsibility.

103. See *above*, pp. 28–29 and 118, at note 97, with citations.

104. It may be related, as a *curiosum*, that a United States soldier convicted under United States military law appealed against the conviction on the ground that he had been tried by the United States forces. The appeal was rejected by a United States District Court (*American Journal of International Law*, LV (1961) p. 493). He would have suffered the same fate even under the UNEF-Congo set-up; cf. UNEF Regulation 34.

6. CONCLUSIONS

The United Nations thus had no legal powers over or in respect of the Force. It did not pay the costs. And except for General Assembly Resolution 906 (IX) [105] there is no clear evidence that the Organization acted externally as a bearer of rights and duties in respect of the Force. The main relationship of the United Nations to the Force was as follows. The international force was established by the United States on the recommendation of the United Nations. It reported to the Organization (through the United States Government) and was as a matter of fact operated in accordance with the major policy recommendations of the Organization. The United Nations on a few occasions communicated directly with the host State and the opposing side, but apart from the exception referred to above, without necessarily pretending to act as legal representative of the Force. The Force and the Command bore the name of the United Nations and used its flag. Otherwise the terminology employed reflected sometimes a genuine United Nations Force, sometimes a co-ordinated action of States. [106]

These relations, it is submitted, are not sufficient to establish the United Nations as bearer of the rights and duties in respect of the Force, either alone, or concurrently with the United States or other Governments. The terminology used, whatever its intention may have been, cannot give the Force a status which is not supported by the actual position. The significance of the appellations used to refer to the Force, and the other points of relation to the United Nations summarized above, is primarily political; for they fasten upon the United Nations the principal political and moral responsibility for the Force. It is not excluded that they may even have some legal significance. [107] But they cannot have the effect of making the Force an organ of the United Nations, for which the Organization would be legally responsible, [108] considering that

105. *Above*, p. 105.

106. *Above*, Chapter II,4.

107. Cf. *below*, pp. 125, 129–31, 161–2, 168, 269 et seq., especially pp. 296–7. In particular, the relations could have sufficed to bring the Force within the scope of Article 42; cf. the Soviet proposal for a Force to assist Egypt (*below*, p. 131).

108. In this sense also Kelsen: *Recent Trends in the Law of the United Nations* (London 1951) p. 940, cf. pp. 936–7, Baxter: 'Constitutional Forms and some Legal Problems of International Military Command', *BYIL*, XXIX (1952) pp. 335–7 and 316, and in *Proceedings of the American Society of International Law*, 1953, p. 97; and by *Attia: Les forces armées des Nations Unies en Corée et au Moyen Orient* (Genève 1963) e.g. pp. 267 and 419–20. *Contra* apparently *Weissberg: The International Status of the United Nations* (New York 1961) pp. 80 et seq. and 204–6, and, perhaps, Taubenfeld: 'International Armed Forces and Rules of War', *American Journal of International Law* XLV (1951) p. 675. The view in the text also appears to have been that of the Communist side initially and that of the United Nations side during the later phases of the war. Earlier the United Nations Command and the United States appear to have taken a contrary view, and so did the Communist side appear to do later, see *below*, Chapter V,2 (a) *in fine*, with citations.

it did not have operational control. For example, had the Force been an organ of the United Nations, the agreement with UNKRA discussed above,[109] would not have been an international agreement and, indeed, might more properly have been replaced by an internal (organic) decision of the United Nations.

Nor did the participating States establish any other intergovernmental organization, which as a separate subject of international law, distinct from the United Nations and the participating States, exercised control over and international rights and duties in respect of the Force. The United Nations Command, in conducting military operations as well as in negotiating the armistice agreements, was subject to the instructions of the United States, which in turn was not subject to instructions of any common organ of the participating States. The 'Committee of Sixteen'— which, moreover, did not include the Republic of Korea—was merely a forum for information and consultation and had no power to give instruction either to the Unified Command or directly to the United Nations Command.

In these circumstances the rights and duties in respect of the Force must be vested in the States which carried out the recommendations of the United Nations. How the international responsibility was divided between them is a complicated problem, which is essentially outside the scope of the present study. Indeed, the question falls within the sphere of law relating to coalition armies rather than that of the law of international organizations. Nevertheless, some tentative suggestions will now be put forward, as far as this seems possible on the basis of the very meagre information on intra-Force practice referred to above, and without having made a study of the practice of coalition armies.

First, however, it may be appropriate to make a few observations on the question of which States on the United Nations side were *parties to the war*.[110] The Republic of Korea obviously was at war with the Governments which had invaded its territory against its active military resistance. And so was the United States, which contributed a major part of the United Nations Force,[111] and which had operational control over the entire Force. The fact that Congress never declared war (although it did pass acts assuming a state of war) and that President Truman on one occasion even declared that the United States was not at war, but was only engaged in a 'police action' for the United Nations,[112] cannot, for

109. At notes 44 and 51.
110. 'War' is used in a broad, material, sense, see *below*, pp. 198–9.
111. About 90 per cent. of the non-Korean forces; Goodrich in *International Conciliation*, No. 494, p. 164. Cf. *below* Chapter IV,4(c), note 167.
112. Taubenfeld in *American Journal of International Law*, XLV (1951) p. 673, but see the contrary statement by President Eisenhower, cited *below*, Chapter V, 3(a), note 89.

6. CONCLUSIONS

the purpose of international law, overrule the factual nature of the hostilities,[113] even if they may be considered binding in municipal law. The holdings of some municipal courts in the United States that the Korean conflict could not be considered as a war 'within what may be termed the constitutional or legal sense' are, as their terms indicate, purely matters of municipal law; and one of these was, in any event, overruled.[114] Municipal practice was contradictory or inconclusive also in some of the other participating States.[115] As for their international position, one could hardly say that they were at war *ipso facto*, by virtue of their modest contingents integrated in United States units and placed under United States Command. However, they could no doubt become parties to the war by declaration or by other additional acts, made by these States themselves or by the opposing side.[116]

As for the question of international responsibility with regard to *treaties*, it has already been suggested [117] that the United States was a party to all international agreements concluded by it as the Unified Command or by the United Nations Command, and that the other fifteen participating Members of the United Nations and the Republic of Korea were probably also parties to the armistice agreement and the other agreements concluded by the United Nations Command with the opposing side. The latter point appears to follow from the terms of the armistice agreement and from general rules applicable to coalition armies. This may also have been the view of the President of the General Assembly when he, in his protest to the Republic of Korea mentioned above,[118] characterized the unauthorized release by Korean troops of the North Korean prisoners of war as a violation, not only of Korea's command agreement with the UN Command, but also of the agreement on exchange of prisoners between the Command and the opposing side, although he did not say expressly that the violation of the latter agree-

---

113. Cf. *below*, Chapter V,3.

114. See the cases reported by Brandon in *International and Comparative Law Quarterly* (1953) pp. 316–19; by Green in *Archiv des Völkerrechts*, VI (1956–57) pp. 420–1; and by Lauterpacht in *BYIL*, XXX (1953) pp. 221–2.

115. Thus the Australian Government and an Australian court considered Australia to be at war *de facto* but not *de jure*, while another court subsequently considered the country to be at peace. On this and UK practice, see Green in *International and Comparative Law Quarterly*, IV (1951) pp. 462–7, and in *Archiv des Völkerrechts*, VI (1956–57) pp. 422–4. See also Lauterpacht, *loc. cit.*, and the quotations *below*, Chapter V,3(a), at notes 90 and. 95.

116. Cf. General Assembly Resolution 711 (VII) which recommended that 'the side contributing armed forces under the Unified Command in Korea shall have as participants in the conference those among the Member States contributing armed forces pursuant to the call of the United Nations which desire to be represented, together with the Republic of Korea'.

117. *Above*, under 3 *in fine*.

118. At note 48.

ments had been committed by the Republic of Korea.[119] The States providing contingents were probably not co-parties with the United States to its agreements with the host State and UNKRA. They certainly were not parties to those of the agreements which did not even mention the United Nations, nor to the agreements with other participating States.

The United States, as having operational control, must clearly also be the party responsible for the *other acts* of the Force.

It is more difficult to determine the position of the other participating States in this respect. These were not, like the United States, entrusted by the United Nations with the conduct of the war, but were recommended to place their contingents under the command of the United States. Their contingents were integrated into the United States armed forces and the United States military commanders had direct command authority over all units of the contingents, without having to pass through the Government of the participating State, or necessarily through the contingent commander. Moreover, with the exception of the Republic of Korea, the participating States were not fighting to defend their national territory or for other specific national aims; they were helping the United States to carry out the recommendations of the United Nations.[120]

On the other hand, the role played by the participating States was in certain respects not so anonymous vis-à-vis the United States as was the role of the States providing contingents to UNEF and to the United Nations Force in the Congo vis-à-vis the United Nations. In the first place, the participating States in Korea paid their own costs and reimbursed the United States for the supplies and services provided by it.[121] (In UNEF and in the Congo the position was the reverse.) In the second place, the participating States assumed, by agreement with the United States, responsibility for claims by or against third parties,[122] although the agreements did not specify in what circumstances the claims were properly claims by or against the other participating Governments rather than by or against the United States. The relevant provisions in the agreements may have envisaged primarily civil claims, but there is nothing in the text to exclude international claims. Thirdly, all participating States were given the opportunity, if they so wished, to take part in the

---

119. The participating United Nations Members, in a Declaration of 27 July 1953, also appear to have considered themselves as parties to the Armistice Agreement, see *OR SC*, 1953, Suppl. for July–September, p. 11.

120. Cf. *Goodrich* in *International Conciliation*, No. 494, p. 165. Cf. *below*, pp. 130, 165 and 168.

121. For example, agreement between the United States and the Netherlands, Article 1 (*UNTS*, Vol. 177, p. 234).

122. *Ibid.*, Articles 4–5.

6. CONCLUSIONS

peace conference and to become parties to any resulting peace treaty.[123]

These three facts probably do not suffice to make the other participating States responsible jointly with the United States for the operation as a whole,[124] and probably not even for acts which cannot be attributed to any particular contingent. But the other participating States probably cannot be dissociated altogether from responsibility. It is suggested that they must be responsible, at least, for acts performed by their contingents on their own initiative, i.e. without or against orders from the United Nations Command or from other United States military authorities.[125] The participating States may also be responsible for other acts performed by their contingents, at least if they should constitute war crimes, since it is even less permissible to allow a *government* to evade its responsibility on the plea of superior orders than it is in the case of individuals.[126] Any responsibility for the participating States would not relieve the United States of its (joint) responsibility, at least not for acts performed pursuant to orders of United States commanders.

The suggestions made above may require some reconsideration in the light of the practice of coalition armies under a unified command, especially during the Second World War,[127] even though the United Nations Force in Korea differed in certain respects from the usual coalition armies and was not necessarily governed in all respects by the same rules.

The division of responsibility outlined for Korea may also hold for a Force constituted under *the Uniting for Peace Resolution,* if the recommendations of the Collective Measures Committee are given effect, despite the terminology employed by this Committee in suggesting that the Force would act 'on behalf' of the United Nations.

As for *Forces under the League of Nations,* the Covenant apparently envisaged an old-fashioned coalition war, conducted by the several participating Member States, which would all be parties to the war, without

---

123 General Assembly Resolution 711 (VII), quoted *above,* p. 106.

124. Such joint and equal responsibility might be the consequence of Kelsen's view that the Commander of the Unified Force was the common organ of the Members which had unified their action by a voluntary agreement *(Recent Trends in the Law of the United Nations,* p. 940).

125. The unauthorized release by Korean troops of some 25,000 North Korean prisoners of war would be an example. However, this was a treaty violation (cf. *above,* p. 104) rather than a violation of the general rules of international law.

126. Cf. Article 8 of the Charter of the International Military Tribunal of 8 August 1945 which provides that 'the fact that the Defendant acted pursuant to order of his Government or of a superior shall not free him from responsibility, but may be considered in mitigation of punishment if the Tribunal determines that justice so requires' *(UNTS,* Vol. 82, p. 288). A national contingent is, of course, in a much stronger factual position to resist superior orders than an individual member of a national force.

127. See on this Baxter in *BYIL,* XXIX (1952) pp. 325–32.

involving the legal responsibility of the League,[128] although it was considered by the Assembly and writers that the League itself might also become a party to the war if a declaration of war was made.[129]

(d) Scope of conclusions. Terminology

The conclusions arrived at above must in principle apply to all international rights and duties in respect of the Force and its members as such, both vis-à-vis the opposing side and neutrals, and to all external activities of the Force, including the conduct of hostilities, prizes, war booty, treatment of prisoners of war and civilians, administration of occupied territory, &c. Thus the United States must have over-all responsibility for the administration established by the United Nations Command in Korea north of the 38th parallel 'under the authority of the United Nations', since the United Nations did not have the effective control in regard to that part of the operation any more than to the rest of it.[130]

In accordance with these conclusions it appears that, while the term 'participating' States may be appropriate in cases such as Korea, Uniting for Peace and the League of Nations, where the individual States as separate international persons are wholly or partly engaged in the action, the term is not an adequate reflection of the legal position in cases of the UNEF-Congo (and, probably, Charter Article 43 et seq.) type, where the only international person involved in the operation is the Organization itself. In the latter cases it may be more adequate to speak of 'contributing' States, as has been done in several cases,[131] despite the fact that all Force Regulations use and define the term 'participating' States.[132] However, since 'contributing' States has been used also in a wider sense, as including States contributing supplies and services,[133] the present writer prefers to use a more specific term for example 'States providing contingents', as has been done in the budgets.[134]

---

128. *Schücking and Wehberg: Die Satzung des Völkerbundes* (2nd ed. Berlin, 1924), pp. 631–3, consider that the individual State which acts against the aggressor always acts as an organ of the League, that the costs of the military operations must be borne by the League if the aggressor is not capable of covering them, and that negotiations with the aggressor on the conditions for the restoration of normal relations must be conducted by the League. They do not indicate whether corresponding legal conclusions are to be drawn with regard to external responsibility.

129. *Above*, Chapter II,1, with citations.

130. See *Annual Report of the Secretary General*, 1950–51, p. 45, on the relief and other civilian activities of the United Nations organs in the area.

131. For example General Assembly Resolution 1151 (XII) and the Secretary-General's Summary Study, pars. 36 and 82.

132. UNEF Regulation 5(e), ONUC Regulation 5(f), UNFICYP Regulation 5(d).

133. *OR GA*, 11th session, Annexes, A.i. 66, p. 14.

134. *Ibid.*, 15th session, Suppl. No. 5 B, p. 4.

CHAPTER IV

COMPETENCE TO ESTABLISH AND OPERATE FORCES WITHOUT CONSTITUTIONAL PROVISIONS

The next question which arises is whether the Organization can establish an international military force [1] only on the basis, and within the limits, of the specific provisions in its constitution authorizing it to do so. The question is one of the capacity of the Organization as a whole. It is not intended to attempt to answer the questions of what organs of the Organization are competent under its constitution to create the Force [2] or under what procedures it should be established [3] or how it should be financed.[3a]

I. RELATION OF THE LEAGUE OF NATIONS FORCES TO ARTICLE 16 OF THE COVENANT

The one provision in the League of Nations Covenant which authorized the establishment of military forces was Article 16 (cf. Article 17) which applied only if a State resorted to war in disregard of its obligations under the Covenant.[4] This condition was not met in any of the cases

1. See, inter alia: Sohn: The Authority of the United Nations to Establish and Maintain a Permanent United Nations Force', *AJIL*, LII (1958) pp. 229–35; Schachter: 'Legal Aspects of the United Nations Action in the Congo', *AJIL*, LV (1961) pp. 1–28; and Halderman: 'Legal Basis for United Nations Armed Forces', *AJIL*, LVI (1962) pp. 971–996. See also the advisory opinion of the International Court of Justice on *Certain Expenses of the United Nations* of 20 July 1962 and the numerous discussions thereof, inter alia by T. S. Rama Rao in *Indian Year Book of International Affairs*, 1963, pp. 134–60 (with regard to p. 153, reference is made to the present writer's article in *Indian Journal of International Law*, IV (1964) pp. 1–74); by Amerasinghe *ibid.*, pp. 177–232; and by Erik Suy in *Rechtskundig Weekblad* (Antwerpen) XXVI (1962) pp. 922–955.
2. The principal provisions of the Charter which are relevant in this respect are indicated *below*, under 4(d). For a general discussion of the relative competence of the Security Council, the General Assembly and the Secretariat, see, inter alia, Sohn, *loc. cit.*, note 1; Report of the Committee on the Charter of the United Nations and discussion thereof, International Law Association, *Report of the Forty-ninth Conference, Hamburg 1960*, pp. 96–144; and *Kelsen: Recent Trends in the Law of the United Nations* (London 1951) pp. 953 et seq.
3. On the question whether an international force can be established by the Security Council in the absence of a permanent member, see the citations *below*, note 24.
3a. See *above*, p. 65, and *below*, p. 172.
4. *Above*, Chapter II,1.

where the League actually established, or prepared to establish, an international force. The task of the League of Nations forces in Vilna, Leticia and the Saar was not to repel an aggression which had taken place, but to maintain order in these disputed territories [5] and, conceivably, by their presence, to prevent any future aggression against these territories. The forces therefore could not be based upon Article 16 of the Covenant, and the resolutions establishing them rightly did not refer to this article or to any other article of the Covenant, neither as a legal basis for the establishment or operation of the force nor as a legal basis for requests to Member States for contingents, transit facilities or other assistance, or to the parties to the dispute for co-operation. Nevertheless, no member of the Council questioned the authority of the League to take these steps and all members voted for the establishment of the forces.[6]

2. RELATION OF THE UNITED NATIONS FORCES TO ARTICLES 42–43 OF THE CHARTER

The only provisions of the Charter which authorize the United Nations to establish international military forces are Article 42 and subsequent articles of the Charter. These only apply if there exists a 'threat to the peace, breach of the peace or act of aggression' (Article 39). In such cases the Security Council may, under Article 42, apply military force 'to maintain or restore international peace and security'.[7] Article 42 appears to leave the Security Council a somewhat wider margin than did the Covenant. Nevertheless, none of those forces which have so far been established by the United Nations has been, at least not at the time of their creation, based upon Article 42 or upon any other provision of the Charter dealing with military forces.

(a) *United Nations Field Service and observation groups*

The United Nations Field Service was established by the Secretary-General [8] under his own authority and without referring to Article 42. His action was preceded by a resolution of the General Assembly taking note of his intention to establish the Field Service. The resolution (297 [V]) did not refer to any provision of the Charter. The preamble merely stated that the Field Service would contribute to the more efficient

5. *Above*, Chapter II,2.

6. See the resolutions establishing the Saar force in *Société des Nations, Journal Officiel,* 1934, pp. 1730 and 1762, and the reports on and discussions of the forces in Vilna and Leticia cited *above*, Chapter II,2.

7. *Above*, Chapter II,3. On the implications of the term 'international' appearing only in the second context see *Kelsen: The Law of the United Nations* pp. 731–2.

8. *Above*, Chapter I,1.

operation of United Nations missions and that the Secretary-General had the authority to establish it. This may be read as a reference to the general power of the Secretary-General to appoint officials and establish such units of the Secretariat as are required to meet the needs of the several organs.[9]

The truce observation groups and the military observation missions [10] were established by the Security Council or the General Assembly, or by subsidiary organs under the authority of these organs, but again without referring to Articles 42 et seq. of the Charter.

It should be noted that the Field Service and the observation groups are not armed forces and are also with regard to their functions very remote form the articles referred to.[11] Thus they fall outside the scope of Article 42.

(b) *Korea*

The resolutions of the Security Council establishing the Force in *Korea* never referred to any provision of the Charter as a constitutional basis for the action. However, they referred to an 'armed attack'—which would point towards the provision on collective self-defence in Article 51 [13]—and determined the existence of 'a breach of the peace'.[14] Such determination is one of the three alternative conditions for the application of Article 39 and the following provisions of Chapter VII of the Charter. Indeed, Article 39 was cited by the representative of the United Kingdom in introducing the proposal which became the resolution of 7

9. This power was stated by the Secretary-General, as based upon Articles 97 and 98, in his original proposal of 1948 for a United Nations Guard, *OR GA*, 3rd session, 2nd part, Annexes, p. 9.

10. *Above*, Chapter I,2.

11. See the statement of the Special Committee on the United Nations Field Service quoted *above*, p. 22, and, for example, the Security Council's Resolution of 21 April 1948 authorizing the Kashmir Commission to establish observers.

13. *Kelsen: Recent Trends in the Law of the United Nations*, p. 927. He maintains (pp. 928–31 and 936–7) that this right of collective self-defence could not be invoked, for a number of reasons, and notably because the Security Council had already taken action. However, it cannot be admitted that the fact that the Security Council had already adopted a resolution which had failed to halt the aggressor, should constitute 'measures necessary to maintain international peace and security' and should thus suffice to deprive the victim and its helpers of their inherent right of collective self-defence. Even a strictly literal interpretation of Article 51 does not justify such a view. On the other hand, *Kelsen* (pp. 936 et seq.) also argues against the words of the President of the Security Council that 'this is a United Nations action', cf. *below*, note 161.

14. Both elements were contained in all three resolutions establishing and organizing the Force, viz. those of 25 and 27 June and 7 July 1950; cf. *above*, Chapter II,4 *in initio*.

July 1950.[15] In explaining paragraph 3 of the resolution, recommending that Member States make their contingents available to a unified command under the United States of America, he stated:

> Had the Charter come fully into force and had the agreement provided for in Article 43 of the Charter been concluded, we should, of course, have proceeded differently, and the action to be taken by the Security Council to repel the armed attack would no doubt have been founded on Article 42. As it is, however, the Council can naturally act only under Article 39, which enables the Security Council to recommend what measures should be taken to restore international peace and security. The necessary recommendations were duly made in the resolutions of 25 and 27 June, but in the nature of things they could only be recommendations to individual Members of the United Nations. It could not therefore be the United Nations or the Security Council which themselves appointed a United Nations commander. All the Security Council can do is to recommend that one of its members should designate the commander of the forces which individual members have now made available.[16]

The United Kingdom delegation thus appears to have assumed that Article 42 could only be applied on the basis of the agreements provided for in Article 43. A statement to this effect had also been made earlier by the Secretary-General in his report on a United Nations Guard.[17] However, any such interpretation conflicts with the broad wording of Article 42 and is not required by the *travaux préparatoires*.[18] Article 42 does not even provide that the Force must necessarily consist of national contingents,[19] but leaves the way open, e.g. also for individual enlist-

---

15. At subsequent meetings Chapter VII, but no specific article thereof, was cited by the representatives of Norway (*OR SC*, 1950, 488th meeting, p. 15), and India (*ibid.*, 494th meeting, p. 15). The Soviet representative pointed out that on 25 June 'no decision was taken as to what Article of the Charter should be applied and on what legal basis action should be taken' (*ibid.*, 494th meeting, p. 17). *Kelsen, op. cit.*, p. 932, considers that even Article 39 was not applicable, but his arguments do not appear very convincing.

16. *OR SC*, 1950, 476th meeting, pp. 3–4. The validity of the latter assertion, that the United Nations was precluded from itself appointing a commander, is discussed *below*, Chapter IV, 4 (c).

17. *OR GA*, 3rd session, 2nd part, Annexes, p. 10.

18. The reference in Article 106 to 'such special agreements referred to in Article 43 as in the opinion of the Security Council enable it so begin the exercise of its responsibillities under Article 42' does not necessarily imply that such agreements constitute the only basis upon which Article 42 can be implemented. *Kelsen: The Law of the United Nations*, p. 756, admits that the wording of Article 42 does not preclude the wide interpretation, but appears to draw unduly restrictive conclusions from the terminology of Articles 48 and 106, which, in the view of the present writer, were not intended to deal with this question. However this may be, Kelsen appears to be concerned with the question whether the Security Council can *compel* Member States to participate in a force otherwise than under Article 43. This is an entirely different question, which, as he points out, was answered in the negative at San Francisco, see *below*, note 21 and Chapter IV,4(a)–(c).

19. In this sense also *Goodrich and Hambro: Charter of the United Nations* (2nd edition, Boston 1949) p. 281; *Bentwich and Martin: A Commentary on the Charter of*

ment by the Organization.[20] Still less does Article 42 require that any national contingents must be provided under obligations undertaken persuant to Article 43, rather than voluntarily.[21] This broad interpretation was borne out by the proposal of the Soviet Union on 5 November 1956 that 'in accordance with Article 42... all States Members of the United Nations... should give military and other assistance to the Republic of Egypt'. The proposal was later explained as envisaging participation in the aid by the forces of all Member States prepared to take part.[22] As this proposal also seems to indicate, Article 42 does not even appear to exclude a force composed of national contingents under *national* command, such as the force actually employed in Korea.

Although the United Nations Force in Korea, like the United Nations Force proposed by the Soviet Union for the Middle East, could therefore have been based upon Article 42, it appears that the Security Council did not do so.[23] It thus considered itself legally entitled to establish the

the United Nations (London, 1950) p. 96; Sohn in *American Journal of International Law*, LII (1958) p. 230; and the Committee on Study of Legal Problems of the United Nations in *Proceedings of the American Society of International Law*, LI (1957) p. 207. While *Kelsen, loc. cit.*, appears to consider that even under Article 42 there can only be question of use of national contingents, Sohn, *loc. cit.*, considers that use of national contingents can be made only on the basis of Article 43. Neither view appears to be warranted.

20. Article 42 provides that the Security Council 'may take such action by air, sea, or land forces as may be necessary to maintain or restore international peace and security. Such action may include demonstrations, blockade, and other operations by air, sea, or land forces of Members of the United Nations.' Article 43 (1) provides: 'All Members of the United Nations, in order to contribute to the maintenance of international peace and security, undertake to make available to the Security Council, on its call and in accordance with a special agreement or agreements, armed forces, assistance, and facilities, including rights of passage, necessary for the purpose of maintaining international peace and security.'

In view of the general terms of Article 42 and the specific terms of Articles 43 and 45, one cannot attach decisive importance to a statement in the report of Committee III/3 at the San Francisco Conference, that the draft article which later became Article 42 'renders sacred the obligation of all states to participate in the operations'; *The United Nations Conference on International Organization, Selected Documents* (Washington 1946) Doc. 881, part II, p. 766. Indeed, as will be explained *below*, pp. 161–2, 4(a)–(b), the *duty* of Member States to contribute contingents is confined to the cases laid down in Articles 43–45.

21. In this sense also the Report of the Committee on the Charter of the United Nations, *International Law Association, Report of the Forty-Ninth Conference, Hamburg 1960*, pp. 137 and 143 n. Cf. also *Oppenheim, International Law*, II, § 52e. Contra: Sohn, *loc. cit.* The *travaux préparatoires* merely make it clear that Member States can be *required* to provide 'armed forces, assistance, and facilities' only pursuant to Article 43 (*Goodrich and Hambro, op. cit.*, pp. 279–80; *The United Nations Conference on International Organization Selected Documents* [Washington 1946] Doc. 881, part I D).

22. See *Repertory of the Practice of the Security Council*, Suppl. 1956–58, p. 172, with summary and citations of the relevant discussion.

23. Several writers, including Gross and Attia, consider that the action was not even

Force without basis in any of those provisions of the Charter which specifically authorized it to establish military forces. Yet nobody in the Council questioned the legality of the action. And the challenge which was made subsequently by the absent permanent member was based upon procedural grounds, viz. that one of the seven affirmative votes had been cast by someone who had no legal right to represent China, and that, moreover, no valid decision could be taken under Article 27.3 of the Charter in the absence of another permanent member.[24]

(c) *Uniting for Peace Resolution—China*

The Armed Force under part A of the Uniting for Peace Resolution [25] was to be established pursuant to recommendations of *the General Assembly* to Member States 'if the Security Council, because of lack of unanimity of the permanent members, fails to exercise its primary responsibility for the maintenance of international peace and security in any case where there appears to be a threat to the peace, breach of the peace, or act of aggression'. Any such force would thus be clearly outside the scope of the relevant articles of the Charter.[26] Nevertheless, 52 members of the General Assembly voted for the resolution, while 2 abstained. Five members voted against, considering that only the Security Council could establish military forces. The main emphasis in the discussion of this resolution was, naturally, upon the question of the distribution of powers between the Security Council and the General Assembly on the basis of Articles 11 (2) and 12 (2), on the one hand, and Article 24 of the Charter, on the other hand,[27] but Articles 43 et seq. were also brought into the picture.[28]

based upon Article 39, because of the absence of the Soviet Union from the Security Council.

24. USSR cablegram of 29 June 1950, *OR SC*, Suppl. for June–August, p. 29. Cf. the discussion thereof in the Security Council on 7 July 1950, *ibid.*, 476th meeting, pp. 2 and 7. On the question whether decisions can be made in the absence of a permanent member, see Leo Gross: 'Voting in the Security Council, Abstention from Voting and Absence from Meetings', *Yale Law Journal*, LX (1951) pp. 210–57, answering the question in the negative; and McDougal and Gardner: 'The Veto and the Charter. An Interpretation for Survival', *ibid.*, pp. 258–92, answering the question in the affirmative. According to *Kelsen: The Law of the United Nations* (London 1950) pp. 244–5, cf. pp. 940–1, pre-Korea practice was that absence of a member, even of a permanent member, does not prevent the Security Council from adopting a resolution.

25. General Assembly Resolution 377 (V), quoted and discussed *above*, Chapter II,5.

26. A different matter is that the military elements which Member States under part C of the Uniting for Peace Resolution are recommended to hold avaiable could *also* be placed at the disposal of the Security Council for action under Article 42.

27. See pp. 469–70 and *Kelsen: Recent Trends in the Law of the United Nations*, pp. 959 et seq.

28. *Repertory of Practice of UN Organs*, I, pp. 316 et seq.; cf. *OR GA* V, Plenary, 299th-302nd meetings, and First Committee, 354th-365th meetings.

The resolution, in its military aspect, was applied when the General Assembly, by its resolutions 498 (V) and 500 (V), found the People's Republic of China to have 'engaged in aggression' and endorsed the action already taken by the United Nations Force to resist this aggression.[29] The General Assembly had been convened in special emergency session on the basis of the Uniting for Peace Resolution when it established UNEF (and when it adopted further resolutions concerning the United Nations action in the Congo).[29a] However, this does not necessarily mean that UNEF (and still less the United Nations Force in the Congo) is to be considered a force under the Uniting for Peace Resolution.[30] Whatever view one takes of this, it will be recalled that the organization and command of UNEF (and the United Nations Force in the Congo) are basically different from those proposed by the Collective Measures Committee.[31]

(d) *UNEF*

As has been pointed out, UNEF was established by resolutions of the General Assembly, after the Security Council had demonstrated itself unable to act because of the veto. The resolutions do not cite Article 42 and subsequent articles or any other specific legal basis for the action. Indeed, there is no provision of the Charter authorizing the General Assembly to establish an international military force. Nevertheless, the decision was made unanimously, with 19 abstentions and no negative votes.[32] The Soviet delegation, however, disputed the power of the Assembly to establish the Force. In its explanation of vote the delegation stated that Chapter VII of the Charter empowers only the Security Council to set up an international armed force, and that the Charter envisages the use of such a force to repel aggression, not for controlling part of the territory of a Member State. When the Soviet delegation, nevertheless, abstained on the vote, this was because Egypt had agreed

---

29. *Above*, Chapter II,4, at note 41.

29a. *Above*, Chapter II,7, at note 71, and Chapter II,8, at notes 176–7.

30. Cf. Sohn in *American Journal of International Law*, LII (1958) pp. 233–4. In his second and final report on *UNEF*, approved in General Assembly Resolution 1001 (ES-I), the Secretary-General stated: 'Functioning, as it would, on the basis of a decision reached under the terms of the resolution 'Uniting for Peace', the Force, if established, would be limited in its operations to the extent that consent of the parties concerned is required under generally recognized international law.' The latter is, however, true of any decision not based on the specific provisions of the Charter, whether or not it is based on the Uniting for Peace resolution; *below*, Chapter IV, 4(a)–(b).

31. On these proposals, see *above*, Chapter II,5.

32. *Above*, Chapter II, 6, note 73.

to the introduction of an international force.[33] Contingents for the Force were also offered by eastern European countries.[34]

When questioned in the House of Commons as to the article of the Charter under which the Force had been created, the United Kingdom Joint Under-Secretary of State for Foreign Affairs correctly stated that it was not created under any specific article, but that it was set up as a result of resolutions passed by the General Assembly, and that no article of the Charter prevented its being set up.[35]

(e) Congo

The United Nations Force in the Congo was established by the Secretary-General, as authorized by the Security Council's Resolution of 13 July 1960. This resolution does not cite Articles 42 et seq. or any other provisions of the Charter, or indicate any other specific legal basis for the establishment of the Force. The resolution does not even employ any terms denoting 'threat to the peace, breach of the peace, or act of aggression', which are the conditions set out in Article 39 for the application of the articles of Chapter VII. Nevertheless, the resolution was adopted unanimously, with no negative votes and with China, France and the United Kingdom abstaining for reasons not connected with the establishment of the Force, which they supported.[36] No member of the Council at the time questioned its power to establish the Force.

The matter had been brought up by the Secretary-General in accordance with Article 99, which provides that 'the Secretary-General may bring to the attention of the Security Council any matter which in his opinion may threaten the maintenance of international peace and security'. In his letter to the Security Council the Secretary-General used exactly these words, not those of Article 39. In his oral statement in the Council, when he formulated the request which was taken over almost literally in the resolution adopted, the Secretary-General made no reference to a threat to the peace or to aggression. All he said on this point was that he

---

33. *OR GA*, ES-I, pp. 127–8. This was precisely the reason which, together with the consent of the States providing contingents, constituted a necessary and sufficient legal basis for the General Assembly to create the Force; see *below*, Chapter IV,4(c). See also the not very clear statement of the representative of Colombia (*OR GA*, ES-I, p. 87), who voted in favour of the resolution.

34. *Ibid.*, Annexes, A.i. 5, p. 24.

35. E. Lauterpacht in *International and Comparative Law Quarterly*, VI (1957) p. 322.

36. *Above*, Chapter II,7, at note 166.

must conclude from the communications received from the Government of the Congo that the presence of these [Belgian] troops is a source of internal, and potentially also of international tension. In these circumstances, the presence of the Belgian troops cannot be accepted as a satisfactory stopgap arrangement pending the re-establishment of order through the national security force.[37]

It appears that also the majority of the members of the Council conceived of the resolution as establishing a Force to assist in the maintenance of law and order and in the protection of life and property, thereby contributing to bringing about the withdrawal of the Belgian forces, rather than to resist external aggression, and it was in this sense that the mandate was executed. Indeed, at that stage it appears to have been the conception, not only of the Secretariat and of the majority of the members of the Security Council, but also of most of the States providing contingents, that what was being created was another non-combatant force of the UNEF type [38] to assist the Central Government in maintaining internal law and order,[39] although the Force, like UNEF, was to act independently and not as an organ of the Central Government. In these circumstances it was only natural that no reference was made in the resolution to any provision of Chapter VII or to international peace and security. Indeed, it is submitted that the majority of the members of the Security Council did not at the time conceive of the resolution as based upon Chapter VII,[40] and especially not upon Articles 42 et seq.

Subsequently, in view of the delay in the withdrawal of Belgian troops and in the introduction of the United Nations Force into the province of

37. OR SC, 1960, 873rd meeting, par. 26. In a *subsequent* report, dated 18 July 1960, the Secretary-General stated that it was implied in his first presentation that it was the breakdown of the instruments of the Government for the maintenance of order 'which had created a situation which through its consequences represented *a threat to peace and security* justifying United Nations intervention on the *basis of the explicit request of the Government of the Republic of the Congo'; ibid.,* Suppl. for July–September, p. 17 (italics supplied).

38. Indeed, prior to the adoption of the Resolution of 13 July 1960 the Secretary-General stated that he would base his actions on the UNEF experience. And he did so, see *above,* Chapter II,7.

39. This was reaffirmed, for example, by the representative of Ceylon when introducing the Resolution of 9 August 1960 (OR SC, 1960, 886th meeting, par. 31), and again by the Secretary-General on 7 December 1960 (*ibid.,* 913th meeting, pars. 34 and 60). Cf. *above,* Chapter II,7, *in initio,* on the discussion in the Council, with the minority views, and on the mandate of the Force.

40. Schachter: 'Legal Aspects of the United Nations Action in the Congo', *American Journal of International Law (1961)* pp. 2–9; cf. pp. 13 et seq., considers that the action was based upon Chapter VII (and more precisely upon Article 40). However, the main facts upon which he appears to base his well-argued conclusion appear to be events which occurred *after* 13 July 1960 or formulations which were made after that date.

Katanga, the fear of foreign intervention became more prominent,[41] and the Council in its resolution of 22 July 1960 made its first reference to international peace ('considering that the complete restoration of law and order in the Republic of the Congo would effectively contribute to the maintenance of international peace and security') and requested all States 'to refrain from any action which might undermine the territorial integrity and the political independence of the Republic of the Congo'. However, there was still no use of the terms employed in Article 39 and no reference to Chapter VII or any article therein. And the debate in the Security Council provided no further basis for the application of Chapter VII.[42]

On 4 August 1960 the Secretary-General stated in a message to the authorities of Katanga, who were then still refusing to admit United Nations troops to their territory:

> The Secretary-General wishes to draw attention to Article 25 of the United Nations Charter, as also to Article 49, which Articles confer on the Security Council an authority applicable directly to Governments, and *a fortiori* to subordinate territorial non-governmental authorities of Member nations. The same obligations must be regarded as applicable by analogy to nations which, like the Republic of the Congo, have been recommended for admission to the United Nations. Resistance by a Member Government to a Security Council decision has legal consequences laid down in the Charter. These sanctions necessarily apply also to the subordinate territorial organs of a nation to which the Charter rules apply.[43]

This was backed by the Security Council in its resolution of 9 August 1960 and by the General Assembly in its Resolution 1474 (ES-IV) of 21 September 1960. These bodies respectively 'called upon' and 'requested' 'all Member States, in accordance with Articles 25 and 49 of the Charter, to accept and carry out the decisions of the Security Council and to afford mutual assistance in carrying out measures decided upon by the Security Council'. The Central Government accepted this resolution and gave assurances that it would co-operate in its implementation in accordance with Article 49.[44] The Council and the Secretary-General

---

41. Cf. Schachter, *loc. cit.*, p. 14.

42. See, for example, the Ecuadorian statement in *OR SC*, 1960, 879th meeting, par. 73.

43. *Ibid.*, Suppl. for July-September, pp. 48–49, cf. pp. 52–53. See also the Secretary-General's statement on 8 August 1960, where, *inter alia,* he cited also Chapter VII and Articles 40 and 41 thereof, while reaffirming that the Security Council's Resolutions of 14 and 22 July were not explicitly adopted under Chapter VII, but on the basis of an initiative under Article 99 (*ibid.*, 884th meeting, pars. 22–26).

44. *OR SC*, 1960, Suppl. for July-September, p. 56 (see also pp. 99–102), cf. S/4807, Annex I, *OR SC*, 1961, Suppl. for April–June, p. 43. Similar statements were made by other Member States (see, for example, *ibid.*, p. 100). The Federal Republic of Germany, a non-member State, declared in a note of 13 April 1961 that it 'consistently has felt

still maintained the principles of resort to the use of arms in self-defence only and of non-intervention in the political struggles between the various authorities in the Congo.[45] Indeed, they considered that the United Nations had no right to violate these principles,[46] although they would not have been mandatory in the case of enforcement measures under Chapter VII.[47] Moreover, it has been considered in another context that the Security Council has the power to make binding decisions even outside the scope of Chapter VII.[48] Nevertheless, since the Security Council resolution refers to Article 49, which forms part of Chapter VII, it may be considered to have brought the operation of the Force within the province also of other articles of that Chapter, although no others were mentioned at the time.[49]

On 30 August 1960 the Secretary-General declared that the temporary administration, with exclusive authority, assumed by the United Nations over the earlier Belgian military bases in the Congo was 'regarded as a provisional measure in the sense of Article 40 of the Charter'.[50] As late as 9 December 1960 the Secretary-General stated before the Security Council that 'it is even doubtful if the Council ever has acted under Chapter VII. The very most that can be said is that the Council's actions may have been under Article 40 of the Charter'.[51] On 13 December he

bound by the resolutions concerning the Republic of the Congo (Leopoldville) adopted by the Security Council and the General Assembly and has acted accordingly' (S/4789, *ibid.*, p. 12).

45. See for example, *OR SC*, 1960, Suppl. for July-September, pp. 52–53.

46. As late as 7 December 1960 the Secretary-General stated that under the Charter the Organization had no right to interfere in domestic problems of a political nature or to intervene forcibly in internal constitutional and political conflicts (*ibid.*, 913th meeting, pars. 17, 29 and 31). Similar statements may be found in *ibid.*, 886th meeting, pars. 42–44 (Ecuador); 70–72 and 80 (Argentina); 887th meeting, par. 44 (the Secretary-General); 889th meeting, par 114 (China); and 915th meeting, par. 22 (the Congo). Cf. par. 4 of the Security Council Resolution of 9 August 1960, and *above*, Chapter II, 7 *in fine*.

47. Schachter, *loc. cit.*, pp. 5–6, points out that the prohibition in Article 2, 7 of intervention in domestic matters applies to provisional measures under Article 40, but not to enforcement measures under Articles 41 et seq. *Kelsen: The Law of the United Nations*, p. 757, states that the prohibition applies to ' "provisional measures" taken by the Security Council under Article 40 if not taken as enforcement measures, that is to say, under the sanction provided for in Article 39'.

48. See the Secretariat statement quoted *below*, Chapter IV,4(d).

49. The only reference in the discussion was to Articles 25 and 49; *OR SC*, 1960, 886th meeting, pars. 40 and 46.

50. *Ibid.*, Suppl. for July-September, p. 126, repeated in a letter of 14 December 1960 to the President of the Congo (*OR GA*, XV, Annexes, A.i. 85, p. 53).

51. *OR SC*, 1960, 915th meeting, par. 157 and 920th meeting, par. 75. See also his subsequent statement on 17 December 1960, *OR GA*, 15th session, plenary meetings, p. 1463, and his earlier statements on 21 August, *OR SC*, 1960, 887th meeting, pars 31 and 44.

stated that the resolutions might be considered as implicitly taken under Article 40, but that neither the Council nor the Assembly had ever endorsed this interpretation. He added that it was even more certain 'that the Council in no way directed that we go beyond the legal basis of Article 40 and into the coercive action covered by Articles 41 and 42'. It was, as a matter of fact, doubted whether Article 42, despite its broad terms, would have been applicable to a force for the performance of internal policing tasks.[52] Members of the Security Council also appeared to imply that Chapter VII was not applicable at that stage.[52a]

Only in its resolution of 21 February 1961, passed after the killing of Prime Minister Lumumba, did the Security Council use the terms of Article 39 and authorize the use of force for purposes other than self-defence. The relevant parts of the resolution read as follows:

> The Security Council,
> ...
> *Deeply concerned* at the grave repercussions of these crimes and the danger of widespread civil war and bloodshed in the Congo and the threat to international peace and security,
> ...
> 1. *Urges* that the United Nations take immediately all appropriate measures to prevent the occurrence of civil war in the Congo, including arrangements for cease-fires, the halting of all military operations, the prevention of clashes, and the use of force, if necessary, in the last resort.
> 2. *Urges* that measures be taken for the immediate withdrawal and evacuation from the Congo of all Belgian and other foreign military and para-military personnel and political advisers not under the United Nations Command, and mercenaries.[53]

In execution of paragraph 2 of the resolution and of a coinciding Ordinance of the Central Government of 24 August 1961, the Force in August—December 1961 got involved in larger and more active military operations against the Katanga forces.[54]

In its resolution of 24 November 1961 the Security Council, without repeating any parts of Article 39, but reaffirming its earlier resolutions, extended the authority to use force by authorizing the Secretary-General

---

52. Schachter, *loc. cit.*, pp. 7–8, who, moreover, considers the fact that no reference was made to Article 42 as 'persuasive evidence that the Council did not intend to apply it in this case'. He considers (pp. 4–6) that the action was based upon Article 40.

52a. Thus the representative of the United Arab Republic stated on 17 February 1961 that he might 'be compelled to come back to the Council to demand that measures be taken under Chapter VII' (*OR SC*, 1961 938th meeting, par. 26).

53. S/4741, *OR SC*, 1961, Suppl. for January–March, p. 147. On the interpretation of this resolution see, for example, S/4789, *ibid.*, Suppl. for April–June, p. 12, and S/4940, pars 1–2, *ibid.*, Suppl. for July–September, p. 99, cf. *above*, Chapter II,7 *in fine*.

54. *Above*, Chapter II,7 *in fine*.

to take vigorous action, including the use of a requisite measure of force, if necessary, for the immediate apprehension, detention pending legal action and/or deportation of all foreign military and para-military personnel and political advisers not under the United Nations Command, and mercenaries as laid down in paragraph A-2 of the Security Council resolution of 21 February 1961.

The instructions to the Force contained in the resolutions of 21 February and 24 November 1961 appear, by introducing the terms of Article 39, to have based further action upon Chapter VII. This appears to have been the contention of the United Nations. However, the International Court of Justice, in its advisory opinion of 20 July 1962 on *Certain Expenses of the United Nations,* stated categorically, as an *obiter dictum,* that neither UNEF nor ONUC were *'enforcement* actions within the compass of Chapter VII', and added:

> the operations of ONUC did not include a use of armed force against a State which the Security Council, under Article 39, determined to have committed an act of aggression or to have breached the peace. The armed forces which were utilized in the Congo were not authorized to take military action against any State.[55]

It is not quite clear whether the Court by these statements intended to preclude the application of all articles of Chapter VII. However this may be, it should be noted, in the first place, that Articles 39 et seq. nowhere talk of 'State', on the contrary, Article 40 merely talks of 'parties'. And the fact that Katanga is no 'sovereign independent nation', as expressly stated in the resolution of 24 November 1961,[56] does not deprive it of the capacity to constitute a 'threat to the peace' or even to comit a 'breach of the peace' under Article 39. Indeed, it has been pointed out that an enforcement action may constitutionally be applied not only against sovereign States,[57] and not only against an aggressor.[58] In the second place, when the Resolution of 21 February 1961 authorized the use of force, if necessary, to prevent civil war, it does not appear to

55. *ICJ Reports,* 1962, pp. 166 and 177.

56. S/5002, OR SC, 1961, Suppl. for October-December, p. 148. See also the following paragraphs of the preamble and operative paragraphs 1, 8 and 9 of the resolution.

57. *Kelsen: The Law of the United Nations,* p. 731, points out that an 'enforcement action may be directed against the state or against a group of the population not having the character of a state, or against both'. *Schachter, loc. cit.,* p. 8, gave a restrictive interpretation of Article 42 which, however, was not necessarily relevant to the new situation which arose subsequently, after 21 February 1961. Cf. *above,* note 7.

58. *Kelsen, op. cit.,* p. 727-30, points out that the Security Council is entitled 'to direct enforcement action against a Member which legally, that is, from the point of view of international law, is not wrong, since it has not violated any obligation expressly imposed upon it by the text of the Charter'. The Belgian Foreign Minister in his telegram of 9 December 1961 to the United Nations contended that the military measures taken by the United Nations in Katanga went 'beyond the requirements of self-defence' (S/5025, OR SC, 1961, Suppl. for October–December, p. 192), but see the Secretary-General's reply *ibid.,* p. 199.

have been the intention to exclude the application of force to prevent offensive operations even by the Central Government, i.e. by a sovereign State and Member of the United Nations, whose credentials had been recognized by General Assembly Resolution 1498 (V).[59]

If one considers that the action, as from the adoption of the 1961 resolutions and in the light of their mandatory terms, was based upon Chapter VII, the question arises of whether the basis was Article 42, or, as usually suggested,[60] merely Article 40. The resolutions offer little guidance in this respect, since they do not refer to any article. But in both resolutions the Council 'calls upon' all States, or all concerned, to take certain action, which is the terminology of Article 40. On the other hand, Article 40 is sufficient as a legal basis only if one considers that 'calls' under that Article may be mandatory, which is generally assumed,[60a] and only if one considers that these 'calls' may be enforced without recourse to Article 42, which does *not* appear to be the general view.[60b] It is submitted that when, through Article 39, one has entered the field of Chapter VII, not only Article 40, but also Article 42 becomes applicable in principle. It may be true that the drafters of the Charter had only actions against sovereign aggressor States in mind when they drafted Article 42.[60c] But if this was so, it might be true of Article 40 (and Article 39) too. And the intention of the drafters is not decisive if the terms are broader and if a broader interpretation is in accordance with the purposes of the Charter.[60d] The present writer believes that, if one considers that the action on 21 February 1961 became one under Chapter VII, it is more natural to consider it as being based upon Article 42 than upon Article 40. However, the view within the United Nations Secretariat appears to have been that the action was based upon Article 40 and not upon Article 42. The International Court of Justice, too, by refusing to consider it an *enforcement* action within the compass of Chapter VII, in fact rejected Articles 42 et seq.; it is not clear whether it also rejected Article 40.

Whatever may have been the legal basis introduced at this stage, it appears clear that the Security Council, when establishing the Force in

---

59. See also the statement quoted *above*, at note 43.

60. Thus Schachter in *Annual Review of United Nations Affairs*, 1960–61, pp. 146–7. See also the Danish written statement in *ICJ, Pleadings, Certain Expenses of the United Nations* (1962) p. 161, and *Franck and Carey: The Legal Aspects of the United Nations Action in the Congo*, Background Papers and Proceedings of the Second Hammarskjöld Forum (Dobbs Ferry, N.Y., 1963) pp. 66–67.

60a. In this sense *Bentwich and Martin*, *op cit.*, pp. 92–93; *Kelsen, op. cit.*, p. 740; and *Schachter, loc. cit.*, pp. 6–7.

60b. Thus, *Kelsen, op. cit.*, pp. 740–3 and *Goodrich and Hambro, loc. cit.*, p. 275, do not appear to think so.

60c. In this sense Schachter in *AJIL*, LV (1961) p. 8.

60d. Cf. *above*, p. 139, and *below*, pp. 350–2.

1960, considered itself entitled to do so without basing itself upon Article 42 or any other article of the Charter specifically authorizing it to establish a Force, and probably even without basing itself upon Chapter VII.

(f) *West New Guinea*

The United Nations Security Force in West New Guinea (Irian Barat) was established by the Secretary-General pursuant to Article VII of an Agreement of 15 August 1962 between Indonesia and the Netherlands. Under its terms the Agreement did not enter into force until the General Assembly had authorized the Secretary-General to carry out the several tasks entrusted to him in the Agreement. This the General Assembly did, in its resolution 1752(XVII), without making any special reference to Article VII or to the Security Force, and, still less, to Chapter VII of the Charter. The Security Council was not involved at all.

It is thus clear that Articles 42 et seq. of the Charter were not applied.

There was no challenge of the constitutionality of the Force. The resolution was adopted by 89 votes to none with 14 abstentions. The abstaining countries were France, and 13 French-speaking countries of Africa and America. Only two of them explained their abstention, stating partly that a *referendum* under neutral control should have been held before any transfer of the territory, and partly that this important decision should not have been made in such haste, without adequate study. None of the abstainers referred to the Force or its constitutionality.

(g) *Cyprus*

The United Nations Force in Cyprus (UNFICYP) was established by the Secretary-General pursuant to a *recommendation* (and authorization) given by the Security Council in its resolution of 4 March 1964. This resolution did not refer to Article 42 or to any other provision of the Charter. Nor had the Council on that or on any other occasion determined 'the existence of any threat to the peace, breach of the peace, or act of aggression', which is a condition for its power to take compulsory measures under Chapter VII of the Charter. In the preamble of the resolution the Council merely noted 'that the present situation with regard to Cyprus is likely to threaten international peace and security'. This was neither the terminology of Chapter VII ('threat to the peace'), nor that of Chapter VI ('is likely to *endanger the maintenance* of international peace and security'), although it comes close to the latter. The terms of the resolution were not as strong as those of Chapter VII, and, in the absence of any other evidence pointing to that Chapter, it would seem correct to conclude that the Council was not thinking in terms of Chapter VII, and that it did not base its decision upon Article 42. It may also be noted in this connection that, during the discussion at the meetings preceding the submission of the draft resolution, there was agreement that the Council could not revise the treaties on the basis of which Cyprus had been established as an independent State; this could only be done by the parties to them.[61] The terminology of the resolution—'recommends' rather than 'decides'—may also be significant in pointing to Chapter VI rather than to Chapter VII.

In connection with the vote on the resolution in the Security Council, the three delegates who abstained voiced certain reservations. The delegate of the Soviet Union stated that the procedures laid down in paragraph 4 of the resolution [61a] (vesting authority in the Secretary-General) would circumvent the Council. The delegate of France expressed

> reservations about the principle of United Nations intervention taking a military form, particularly if that were to lead to operations involving the use of force. Our reservations, moreover, are made even greater by the difficulties of implementation because of which, as is apparent from the text of the resolution, particularly heavy responsibilities are laid on the Secretary-General. The Security Council is thus divesting itself of responsibilities which belong to it but which would clearly be difficult to discharge. This can only confirm our reservations of principle. While, of course, not questioning in the slightest the Secretary-General's wisdom and prudence in these matters, the French delegation considers that this is really going very far in the direction of delegating powers to one man. We wish in any event to stress that this decision must not be regarded as a precedent.[61b]

The delegate of Czechoslovakia noted that 'the idea of an international force is not altogether in accord with the provisions of the Charter'. He also stated that 'we have serious doubts regarding the clause which transfers to the Secretary-General a responsibility that, under the strict letter of the Charter, belongs exclusively to the Security Council itself. That is why we abstained in the vote on operative paragraph 4'.[61b]

It is not clear from these statements what legal objections the two latter States may have had to the establishment of the Force, other than that the Council went too far in delegating its powers to the Secretary-General.

(h) *Conclusion*

It will be seen that *none of the Forces actually created by the League of Nations and the United Nations was established on the basis of those provisions in the constitutions of the two Organizations which specifically authorize them to establish military forces.* In particular, the League of Nations forces and the United Nations peace-keeping Forces in the Middle East, the Congo, West New Guinea and Cyprus demonstrate that

---

61. This was stated by the representatives of the United States, Norway, the Ivory Coast, France, Bolivia and Greece (S/PV/1096–1099).

61a. Quoted *above*, Chapter II,9.

61b. OR SC, 1102nd meeting, 4 March 1964, pp. 6–7.

the Council of the League, the General Assembly and the Security Council, respectively, consider themselves competent to establish a military force to perform non-combatant tasks without basis in those provisions of the Covenant or the Charter which authorize the establishment or utilization of military forces. The United Nations Force in Korea and the Uniting for Peace Resolution demonstrate that the Security Council and the General Assembly, respectively, consider themselves competent to establish a force for international enforcement without basis in the relevant specific provisions of the Charter. In the last two cases (Korea and Uniting for Peace) it was decided or proposed, respectively, that the Force, although acting in the name of or on behalf of the United Nations, should be under the command of one or more Member States, rather than of the United Nations. However, the Uniting for Peace Resolution does not lay down any *restriction* in this sense.[62]

Before proceeding to consider the question whether the United Nations really has the capacity to create forces in this manner and whether it can assume command over them, it is necessary to examine in general whether intergovernmental organizations also exercise powers in other respects in cases not specified in their constitution, or in circumstances other than those specified.

3. GENERAL INHERENT CAPACITY OF INTERGOVERNMENTAL ORGANIZATIONS

(a) *The doctrine of delegated powers*

It is still a widespread view that intergovernmental organizations possess only *delegated powers* and that consequently each Organization can exercise only the powers authorized by its particular constitution. This view is a basic premise of the major study of United Nations law, Kelsen's *The Law of the United Nations,* and was expressed, in a somewhat different form, by Judge Hackworth in his Dissenting Opinion in *Reparation for Injuries Suffered in the Service of the United Nations:*

> There can be no gainsaying the fact that the Organization is one of delegated and enumerated powers. It is to be presumed that such powers as the Member States desired to confer upon it are stated either in the Charter or in complementary agreements concluded by them. Powers not expressed cannot freely be implied. Implied powers flow from a grant of expressed powers, and are limited to those that are 'necessary' to the exercise of powers expressly granted. No necessity for the exercise of the power here in question has been shown to exist. There is no impelling reason, if any at all, why the Organization should become the sponsor of claims on behalf of its employees.[63]

62. See *above,* pp. 33–45 and 98–9, on the factual aspects of command in these cases, and *below,* pp. 162–9, on the constitutional power of the UN to assume command.

63. *ICJ Reports,* 1949, p. 198. The doctrine of delegated powers may also be the underlying premise of the current terminology when legal writers speak of powers 'conferred upon the organization by its constitution'.

However, a detailed study of the practice of intergovernmental organizations reveals that this view is in clear contradiction with the facts.

(b) *Exclusive jurisdiction over organs*

As has been more fully demonstrated in another study,[64] all intergovernmental organizations—no matter how small and technical they are or how limited their field of activity may be—exercise exclusive jurisdiction over their organs (*organic jurisdiction*, as opposed to territorial and personal jurisdiction, which is only exercised by certain intergovernmental organizations). They enact regulations which govern procedure, rights and duties of the staff vis-à-vis the Organization, and other relations within and between the several organs of the Organization. All intergovernmental organizations also make administrative decisions in these respects, and many of them establish tribunals to adjudicate upon disputes, notably between officials and the Organization.[65] This legislative, administrative and judicial jurisdiction is different from that exercised by non-governmental organizations over their organs; these organizations are, even in internal matters, subject to the legislative, administrative and judicial jurisdiction of the host State and can even internally act only within the limits of such jurisdiction.[66] As far as intergovernmental organizations are concerned, no State, host or otherwise, can interfere with their internal jurisdiction, which is entirely outside the legislative, administrative and judicial authority of any State. Indeed, municipal courts have declared themselves incompetent *ratione materiae* in disputes relating to the internal relations of the Organization,[67] with-

64. 'Jurisdiction over Organs and Officials of States, the Holy See and Intergovernmental Organizations', *International and Comparative Law Quarterly*, XIV (1965) pp. 31–82 and 493–527.

65. Such administrative tribunals or similar judicial bodies or procedures have been established by a number of organizations (UN, ILO, OEEC, Council of Europe, &c.) whose constitutions contain only a general provision authorizing the enactment of staff regulations, and by some organizations whose constitutions do not even contain that (League of Nations, International Court of Justice [without basing itself upon Article 101. 1 of the United Nations Charter or upon any General Assembly decision pursuant to that article]). The judicial nature, and the binding character *vis-à-vis* the administrative organs of the Organization, of the judgments of such administrative tribunals, was confirmed by the International Court of Justice in its Advisory Opinion on *Effects of Awards of Compensation Made by the UN Administrative Tribunal*, *ICJ Reports*, 1954, pp. 51–53, cf. p. 62. For a full discussion on this subject, see a study by the present writer on 'Settlement of Internal Disputes of Intergovernmental Organizations by Internal and External Courts' in *Zeitschrift für ausländisches öffentliches Recht und Völkerrecht*, XXIV (1964) pp. 1 et seq., at pp. 16–40. On the question of the capacity to exercise *criminal* jurisdiction, see *below*, Chapter VIII, 11 (a).

66. This is expressly stated in the United States Act quoted in *Nordisk Tidsskrift for international Ret og Jus gentium*, XXXIV (1964) at p. 94.

67. See *ibid.*, pp. 78–79, and *loc. cit. above*, note 64, at pp. 508–515. *Profili v. Inter-*

out basing themselves upon any particular provisions of the constitution of the Organization, or upon its immunity from suit *ratione personae*, in the same manner as they do in respect of disputes relating to the internal administration of foreign States.[68] Intergovernmental organizations thus exercise an exclusive legislative, administrative and judicial authority over their organs, similar to that of States over their organs (abroad). And this they do despite the fact that no provisions to this effect are included in any convention on privileges and immunities or in any headquarters agreement, and that no constitution contains any general provision in this respect. Most constitutions merely authorize some of the deliberative organs of the Organization to adopt their own rules of procedure, to establish subsidiary organs, and to adopt staff regulations. And some constitutions do not even provide for that.[69] None the less, the jurisdiction is being exercised and there can be no doubt that it is binding upon the organs of the Organization, including its officials in that capacity, and on Member States, in their capacity as members of such (deliberative) organs.

(c) *Capacity to conclude treaties*

Only in a few cases does the constitution contain a general authorization for the Organization to conclude treaties,[70] but many modern constitutions authorize it to conclude treaties of a certain type. Thus the United Nations Charter specifically authorizes the Organization to conclude agreements with Member States on the provision of military contingents (Article 43) and with specialized agencies bringing them into relationship with the United Nations (Article 63). Articles 77 et seq. and 105(3), too, could possibly be interpreted as authorizing the conclusion of

national Institute of Agriculture (Rome, 26 February 1931), *Rivista di diritto internazionale, XXIII* (1931) p. 386; *Chemidlin v. International Bureau of Weights and Measures* (Paris, 27 July 1945), excerpts in *Annual Digest, 1943–1945,* p. 231; *Diaz Diaz v. United Nations Economic Commission for Latin America* (Mexico, 28 April 1954). In the latter case, the Organization had a constitutional provision authorizing it to enact staff regulations (Article 101. 1 of the United Nations Charter), but this was not cited by the Court in support of its decision. The above decisions were *not* based upon the immunity from suit of the Organization, a distinct right which all organizations also enjoy irrespective of treaty provision, and which renders municipal courts incompetent *ratio personae*. See also the case reported in *Nordisk Tidsskrift, loc. cit.,* at p. 53.

68. See the cases reported in *Hackworth,* IV, pp. 732–4, and in *loc. cit. above,* note 64, at pp. 508–515.

69. Thus the OEEC adopted rules of procedure, the League of Nations staff regulations and a great number of organizations financial regulations, despite the absence of any relevant provisions in their constitution.

70. For example the constitution of the now dissolved International Refugee Organization, Article 2(2)(e).

trusteeship agreements and conventions on privileges and immunities with *Member* States, respectively.[71] However, these limited provisions have not stopped the United Nations from concluding a great number of other treaties, both with States and with other intergovernmental organizations. While no agreements on military contingents have been concluded by the Security Council in the manner provided in Article 43, a number of similar agreements have been concluded by the Secretary-General in respect of the peace-keeping Forces.[72] In addition to the relationship and other [73] agreements concluded with specialized agencies, the United Nations has concluded agreements with other intergovernmental organizations.[74] Agreements on privileges and immunities have been concluded also with non-member States.[75] However, the overwhelming number of agreements concluded by the United Nations relate to entirely different fields, notably to technical and other assistance rendered by the Organization or its autonomous organs to Member and non-member States.[76] Indeed, *only a small fraction of the treaties concluded by the United Nations fall within the categories authorized in the Charter.* The same applies to a number of other Organizations.[77] In addition, Organizations whose constitutions do not authorize the conclusion of any kind of treaties have, none the less, concluded treaties with States, e.g.

71. None of these articles specify that the United Nations may be a party to the agreements in question. For a closer examination of these provisions, see Parry in *BYIL*, XXVI (1949) pp. 122–31, and *below*, Chapter VIII,9(b).

72. *Above*, p. 47, cf. pp. 63 and 82, and *below*, Annex 3, p. 443.

73. For example agreements extending the competence of the United Nations Administrative Tribunal (see for example *Zeitschrift für ausländisches öffentliches Recht und Völkerrecht*, XXIV (1964) pp. 74–77, and, e.g. *UNTS*, Vol. 219, p. 388) and the agreement with WHO regarding a medical programme for Palestine refugees (*ibid.*, Vol. 103, p. 129).

74. See, for example, the many transfer and other agreements with the League of Nations and UNRRA listed in the *UNTS, Cumulative Index*, No. 1, pp. 476 and 478.

75. Interim arrangement with Switzerland on privileges and immunities, *UNTS*, Vol. 1, p. 163.

76. The United Nations Children's Fund (UNICEF, an autonomous organ of the United Nations set up by General Assembly Resolution 57 (I)) alone concluded more than 100 agreements and additional protocols in this category during its first ten years of operations only. For other examples of bilateral and multilateral treaties in this and other categories, see the *UNTS Cumulative Index* under the headings: United Nations, United Nations Appeal for Children, United Nations [International] Children's [Emergency] Fund, United Nations Relief and Works Agency for Palestine Refugees in the Near East (UNRWAPRNE), United Nations Emergency Force.

77. Thus ICAO, whose constitution provides merely for agreements with other Organizations (Articles 64–65), concluded—during the first ten years of its existence—about fifteen bilateral treaties with States on technical assistance, air navigation and privileges and immunities, as well as about fifty multilateral (standard) agreements to which several Organizations were parties on one side and individual States on the other. See *ibid.*, under the heading International Civil Aviation Organization. On *multilateral* conventions, see *below*, Chapter VIII,9(b).

headquarters agreements, and with other intergovernmental organizations, e.g. on co-operation. This has been done, not merely by large political organizations like the League of Nations, but also by the smallest and oldest technical Organizations.[78] It cannot be seriously argued that most of these treaties are merely contracts of municipal law, or that it is the several Member States rather than the Organizations as such which are parties to them.[79] Yet it has never been claimed in a concrete case that any of these treaties are invalid because the Organization did not have the power under any provision of its constitution to conclude them,[80] provided that no constitutional provision precluded it from so doing. Nevertheless, the invalidity of such treaties might have been pressed under the widely defended view that a treaty concluded in violation of constitutional restrictions is not binding.[81] Whereas this view has not been accepted in respect of States,[82] it has been maintained that it must in any case apply to treaties concluded by international organizations.[83]

78. Thus the Hague Conference on Private International Law has concluded a headquarters agreement with the Netherlands, despite the absence of any mention of treaty-making capacity or of privileges and immunities in its Statute of October 1951. Similarly, the International Bureau of Weights and Measures, whose constitution of 20 May 1875 is equally silent in this respect, has in 1949 concluded a co-operation agreement with UNESCO, as well as a 'convention' with France, dated 4 October 1875, concerning the placing of the *Pavillon de Breteuil* at the disposal of the Bureau. If the latter convention is recognized as a treaty in international law, as is the agreement between the United Nations and Switzerland concerning the Ariana site (*UNTS*, Vol. 1, p. 153), it may well be the oldest *existing* treaty concluded by an intergovernmental organization, any earlier treaties concluded by international river commissions being no longer in force. For other examples see under the various organizations in the alphabetical part of the *UNTS Cumulative Index*.

79. Cf. *above*, Chapter III,1, and *Nordisk Tidsskrift, loc. cit.,* at pp. 40–42.

80. Closest to such denial is probably *Kelsen: The law of the United Nations,* pp. 330–5 and 832–3. He states that 'the Charter does not contain a provision authorizing the United Nations to enter into other international agreements than those expressly mentioned in the Charter', and that 'among the many technical insufficiencies of the Charter one of the worst is the lack of a general authorisation of the Organisation to enter into international agreements'. (In the view of the present writer, no such general provision is necessary.) And he adds that 'the United Nations has legally only the power to enter into those international agreements which it is authorised by special provisions of the Charter to conclude'.

81. *Oppenheim: International Law*, 1, §§ 497 and 516; cf. *Castberg: Folkerett* (2nd edition, Oslo 1948) pp. 127–30.

82. See *Nordisk Tidsskrift, loc. cit.,* at pp. 32 et seq., and Articles 30 and 31 of the International Law Commission's 1963 draft articles on the Law of Treaties.

83. *Jessup: A Modern Law of Nations* (New York 1949) p. 130; and Parry, in *BYIL*, XXVI (1949) pp. 114–17. The present writer does not believe in this difference between States and intergovernmental organizations, see *Indian Journal of International Law*, IV (1964) pp. 28–35.

(d) *Jurisdiction over territory*

Although most intergovernmental organizations do not have a territory in the same sense as States, they have occasionally been granted full or limited powers of territorial jurisdiction, irrespective of whether or not their constitutions authorize them to exercise such powers.

Thus the *League of Nations*—which in the Covenant was only authorized to exercise limited territorial powers in respect of mandates, acting through mandatory States—exercised full powers of government in the Saar, through a Governing Commission appointed by it; [84] and limited powers in respect of Danzig, through a High Commissioner appointed by it.[85] This was provided in the Treaty of Versailles, which was only one of the five peace treaties in which the Covenant was incorporated and which was not ratified by all members of the League.

The *United Nations* has, on certain occasions, decided to assume limited governmental functions in disputed territories, despite the fact that the Charter only authorizes it to exercise territorial powers in respect of trust territories.[86]

Thus the annexes to the Treaty of Peace with Italy conferred upon the Security Council certain limited functions relating to the government of the proposed Free Territory of *Trieste*;[87] and the Council, after a juridical debate, adopted, on 10 January 1947 (by 10 votes to 0 and 1 abstention [Australia]), a resolution approving the relevant annexes to the Peace Treaty and accepting the responsibilities devolving upon it under the Treaty. Some members of the Council questioned its competence to assume these responsibilities in the absence of specific authorization in the Charter.[88] These objections were met, *inter alia*, by a reference to Article 24, which confers on the Security Council 'primary responsibility for the maintenance of international peace and security', without saying anything about the power to exercise territorial jurisdic-

84. Treaty of Versailles, Articles 45–50 with Annex; cf. Council Resolution of 13 February 1920, *Société des Nations, Journal Officiel*, 1920, p. 50.

85. Treaty of Versailles, Articles 100–8; cf. Council Resolution of 13 February 1920 defining the duties of the High Commissioner, *ibid.*, p. 53.

86. The limited territorial legislative power exercised by the United Nations in its headquarters district in New York, pursuant to § 8 of its headquarters agreement with the United States (*UNTS*, Vol. 11, p. 18) and by certain other Organizations, such as the International Atomic Energy Agency under its headquarters agreement with Austria, might be said to have been authorized under the constitutional provisions on privileges and immunities (Article 105 of the Charter), although active powers of jurisdiction are not normally granted as part of privileges and immunities. Cf *loc. cit. above*, note 64, pp. 518–521.

87. *UNTS*, Vol. 49, pp. 186 et seq.

88. *Kelsen: The Law of the United Nations*, pp. 833–4, denies the competence of the Security Council because no specific provision in the Charter authorizes it to exercise rights of sovereignty over a territory which is not a trust territory.

tion. However, the arguments of the opposition and the ensuing discussion referred only to the power of the Security Council, and thus, like Article 24 itself, appear to have been concerned primarily with the distribution of powers within the Organization,[89] rather than with the power of the Organization as a whole (acting through the General Asssembly), although this distinction was brought out by one delegate only.[90]

Later in the same year the General Assembly adopted a plan for the partition of Palestine whereby the United Nations assumed certain governmental functions in the country, notably in respect of the City of *Jerusalem,* which was to be established as a *corpus separatum* under a 'special international régime'. More specifically, the City was to be administered by the United Nations through a Governor, appointed by and responsible to the Trusteeship Council and assisted by an administrative staff classed as international officers within the meaning of Article 100 of the Charter. The Governor was to exercise on behalf of the United Nations all powers of administration, including the conduct of external affairs.[91] As was expressly stated in a subsequent report to the Trusteeship Council, this City was not to be a trust territory, and Chapters XII-XIII of the Charter were not generally applicable.[92] Nevertheless, the

89. Cf. *below,* under 4 (d).

90. The Polish delegate who very appropriately stated: 'We do not have any legal qualms about the Security Council accepting the responsibilities it is asked to accept. I know that it may be somewhat difficult to point to a specific phrase in the Charter which would justify the taking over of the functions we are asked to assume. However, I think it would be entirely within the general spirit of the Charter of the United Nations, if it were decided to form a Free Territory under a quasi-international administration. We believe it is only proper that the United Nations, as an Organization, should be given the responsibility of supervision over its administration. And since it is a matter which involves international peace and security, we believe that the Security Council is the logical organ to carry out these functions.' OR SC, 1947, pp. 4–19 and 44–61. See also Schachter in *BYIL,* XXV (1948) pp. 96–101.

91. General Assembly Resolution 181 (II), Annex, part III; cf. General Assembly Resolutions 194 (III) and 303 (IV), and Trusteeship Council Resolution 234 (VII).

92. *Kelsen: The Law of the United Nations* p. 687, with citations. On this basis the competence of the Trusteeship Council was denied by those opposed to the partition plan (*Kelsen, loc. cit.,* who also denies the competence pp. 133–4). This denial, which disregards the inherent power of the General Assembly to delegate its powers to other organs, appears to have been a matter of distribution of powers between the organs of the Organization rather than one of the competence of the Organization as a whole (acting through the General Assembly) to govern a territory. In addition, several speakers of the opposition challenged the legality of the entire partition plan because it violated the right of self-determination of the peoples, because it exceeded the terms of the mandate, and for other reasons, but apparently without alleging (at least in the plenary meetings) any incompetence of the Organization to assume territorial jurisdiction not specified in the Charter (*OR GA,* 2nd session, plenary meetings, pp. 1310–1427), although certain statements might be interpreted as hints in this sense (*ibid.,* pp. 1326–7, 1329, 1338–9, 1371).

partition plan was adopted by 33 votes to 13 (10 Moslem and 3 non-Moslem States) with 10 abstentions.[93]

While the League of Nations effectively carried out its governmental functions in the Saar, the United Nations was never able to exercise the functions assigned to it in respect of Trieste or assumed by it in respect of Jerusalem. However, this was not due to any legal incapacity of the Organization, but to the lack of co-operation of the States having control over the two territories. Indeed, if the United Nations and other modern Organizations have only to a limited extent exercised territorial jurisdiction, it is for the *external* reason that most territory is under the control of States, and that the United Nations, like any other authority, cannot assume jurisdiction over such territory unless these States cede their powers. An intergovernmental organization cannot without specific legal basis impose its jurisdiction upon States. But in those cases where the States concerned have ceded their powers, or where there is no territorial sovereign,[94] it has rightly not been considered necessary to look for a provision in the constitution of the organization concerned authorizing it to exercise territorial jurisdiction.[95]

An example of the latter was the succesful administration of *West New Guinea* (Irian Barat) by the United Nations from 1 October 1962 to 1 May 1963 through a Temporary Executive Authority comprising thirty-two nationalities, including Dutch and Indonesian personnel. As has already been explained in Chapter II,8, full authority to administer that Territory was conferred upon the Organization by a bilateral Agreement of 15 August 1962 between Indonesia and the Netherlands. The General Assembly confined itself to the adoption of a resolution in which it:

1. Takes note of the Agreement;
2. Acknowledges the role conferred upon the Secretary-General in the Agreement;

---

93. *Ibid.*, pp. 1325, 1327; cf. pp. 1370-1.

94. Cf. *below*, at note 110a, on *outer space*.

95. During the consideration of military enforcement measures at the San Francisco Conference, an amendment presented by the Norwegian delegation, to provide that the Security Council may 'take over on behalf of the Organization the administration of any territory of which the continued administration by the state in possession is found to constitute a threat to the peace', was withdrawn, after it had been indicated that such a reference to a particular procedure could be interpreted as restrictive and of such nature as to limit the field of application of measures at the disposition of the Council (Report of Rapporteur of Committee III/3 to Commission III on Chapter VIII, Section B (Doc. 881), part II B, *United Nations Conference on International Organization, San Francisco 1945, Selected Documents* (Washington 1946). This Conference thus appeared to take the view that a general provision authorizing the Council to make binding decisions and to apply military sanctions constituted sufficient authority for it to establish cession of jurisdiction, and that no specific mention of territorial jurisdiction was necessary to enable the Organization to assume such jurisdiction.

3. Authorizes the Secretary-General to carry out the tasks entrusted to him in the Agreement.[97]

As pointed out above, Chapter IV,2(g), no objection was made against this resolution on legal grounds. No Member voted against, and those 14 French-speaking Members who abstained, appear to have done so on other grounds.

(e) *Other acts*

As has been demonstrated in another study,[98] intergovernmental organizations also perform a number of *other international acts*, and establish organs entrusted with international functions, irrespective of whether such acts or organs have been authorized in their constitutions. Thus the United Nations and other intergovernmental organizations receive (and even send) 'diplomatic' representatives, convene intergovernmental conferences, present international claims on behalf of themselves and their officials, undertake to settle disputes with States by international arbitration, &c., even if their constitutions contain either no mention of such powers or only a limited one.[99] It is not possible within the scope of the present study to examine in detail these and other acts, which are performed only by subjects of international law, and which intergovernmental organizations perform without specific constitutional basis.

(f) *Conclusion: The inherent capacity*

The examples given probably sufficiently demonstrate that the capacity of intergovernmental organizations is not confined to such acts or rights as are specified in their constitutions. Indeed, it is submitted that this is a well-established principle of the customary law of intergovernmental organizations. If this were not so, then a large proportion of the treaties concluded, the courts established and the other acts performed by small and large intergovernmental organizations, including the United Nations, would be unconstitutional. And *no* organization would have been entitled, for example to send or receive 'diplomatic' representatives or to be a party to an international arbitration. Such unconstitutionality might entail internal invalidity. According to a widely supported school of thought, it might even, at least in some cases,

---

97. Resolution 1752 (XVII) of 21 September 1962.

98. 'Objective International Personality of Intergovernmental Organizations', *Nordisk Tidsskrift for international Ret og Jus gentium*, XXXIV (1964) at pp. 21–27.

99. The United Nations Charter contains no provision in any of these respects, except that Article 62 (4) authorizes the Economic and Social Council to convene conferences, a fact which, of course, has not prevented the General Assembly from doing likewise.

entail external invalidity.[100] Thus if one accepts the view referred to above, under (c) *in fine*, and if one were to deny the capacity of inter-governmental organizations to perform acts not specified in their con-stitutions, the vast majority of the treaties concluded for instance by the United Nations would have to be held null and void.

It will be seen that intergovernmental organizations, in this, as in many other respects (more than is generally realized),[101] are essentially in the same position as States. These too exercise exclusive organic juris-diction over their organs abroad (even over officials of foreign national-ity serving at diplomatic or consular missions abroad), exercise territorial jurisdiction, conclude treaties, send and receive diplomatic representa-tives, convene intergovernmental conferences, maintain armies and con-duct wars, irrespective of whether their constitutions authorize them to do so. There is no basic difference between States and intergovernmental organizations with regard to organic jurisdiction. With regard to terri-torial and personal jurisdiction and with regard to certain international acts, such as the creation of armies and the conduct of military opera-tions, there is, however, a considerable difference of fact. Intergovern-mental organizations exercise territorial and personal jurisdiction only in exceptional cases where States cede to them part of their jurisdiction over territory or individuals (which need not be done by constitutional provision or by another treaty to which the other Member States are parties). And when an Organization has no such jurisdiction, there are many international acts which it is not called upon, or is not in a prac-tical position, to perform to the same extent as the traditional subjects of international law, States. But this is difference of fact, not of inherent legal capacity.

100. See, however, *below*, under 5, on the external status of an international force established in violation of the constitution, and the more detailed discussion of the external effects of constitutional limitations in general in *Nordisk Tidsskrift, loc. cit.,* at pp. 32 et seq.

101. Thus, as will be more fully explained in a forthcoming study, it is submitted that intergovernmental organizations enjoy certain basic privileges and immunities, including notably immunity from suit in municipal courts, even where their constitu-tions or the applicable agreements do not so provide. Cf. *Godman* v. *Winterton and Others* (representing the Intergovernmental Committee on Refugees) *The Times,* 13 March 1940; see also the action against the Pan-American Union reported by Scott-Penfield in *American Journal of International Law,* XX (1926) p. 257 (in neither of these cases was a written opinion given, and it is thus not clear whether the courts (rightly) considered the organizations as juridical persons distinct from their several Member States). This immunity *ratione personae* is different from and embraces more than the exclusive jurisdiction *ratione materiae* discussed in (*b*) *above.*

Similarly, intergovernmental organizations have an internal law of their own, which is not, or not only, part of international law, as is generally assumed, but which is, in most respects, e.g. for purposes of conflict of laws, comparable to municipal law, cf. *Zeitschrift für ausländisches öffentliches Recht und Völkerrecht,* XXIV (1964) pp. 101 and 105–6, and *International and Comparative Law Quarterly,* XIV (1965) p. 517.

3. INHERENT POWERS OF ORGANIZATIONS

The International Court of Justice has taken cognizance of the fact that the capacities of the United Nations are not confined to those specified in its constitution. Thus, in the Advisory Opinion on *Reparation for Injuries Suffered in the Service of the United Nations*, the majority of the Court stated:

> Under international law, the Organization must be deemed to have those powers which, though not expressly provided in the Charter, are conferred upon it by *necessary* implication as being *essential* to the performance of its duties.[102]

The Court also stated that 'the capacity of the Organization to exercise a measure of functional protection of its agents arises by *necessary intendment* out of the Charter'.[103] Similarly, in its advisory opinion on *Effect of Awards of Compensation made by the United Nations Administrative Tribunal*, the Court pointed out that the Charter contains 'no express provision for the establishment of judicial bodies or organs and no indication to the contrary', but held that capacity to establish a tribunal to do justice as between the Organization and the staff members 'arises by *necessary intendment* out of the Charter'.[104]

Even these formulations might prove too restrictive if they were to be applied literally. However, this has not been done, neither by the Court, nor by the United Nations proper. Indeed, it is difficult to find in the practice of any of these bodies, or of other intergovernmental organizations, any indication that the conditions contained in the statements of the Court quoted above have ever been applied as a real limitation upon the powers of an intergovernmental organization. Thus, when the Genral Assembly decided to award United Nations distinctions to personnel which had fought in Korea, it by implication overruled the Polish objections that the United Nations was not a State, that the power was not laid down in the Charter, and that such distinctions were not *necessary* for the performance of the Organization's duties, as indicated by the Court.[105] This it did despite the fact that the last objection appeared to be well founded on the normal meaning of the terms 'necessary' or 'essential' used by the Court. Similarly, it may be recalled that Judge Hackworth, in the statement quoted above, under (a), took the view that 'there is no impelling reason, if any at all, why the Organization should become the sponsor of claims on behalf of its employees', the very thing which the majority considered to arise 'by necessary intendment' out of the Charter. Indeed, it is submitted that, if the constitutionally competent organs have decided, under the pro-

---

102. *ICJ Reports*, 1949, p. 182 (italics supplied). See Fitzmaurice in *BYIL*, XXIX (1952) pp. 5–6, for a comparison of three different views expressed in the Court on the question of implied powers.

103. *ICJ Reports*, 1949, p. 184 (italics supplied); cf. above, Chapter III,5(a).

104. *Ibid.*, 1954, pp. 56–57 (italics added).

105. *Above* Chapter II,4 at note 39.

cedure prescribed in the constitution, that the Organization shall perform a specific act in order to attain a purpose within the scope of its constitution, then a court cannot declare the act invalid because, in its view, the aim could have been attained without resorting to that act, or because it otherwise does not consider the act 'essential' or 'necessary' for the attainment of that aim. The Court may well have used these terms *ex abundante cautela,* or in application of the well-established judicial principle of not giving reasons which extend further than necessary to arrive at the conclusion called for in the case before the Court, without having necessarily intended them as restrictions upon the powers of an Organization, should it be faced with another case which would not be covered by that formula.

The factual and legal position appears to have been more adequately described in the United Kingdom Government statement, already reported, that UNEF was not created under any specific article of the Charter, but that *no article prevented its being set up,*[106] and by Mr. Hammarskjöld, two years before his tragic death, when he stated to Danish students:

> It may have struck some of you that the possibilities I have touched upon in connection with the present international debate, and the evolution I have just dealt with as well, have little explicit support in the United Nations Charter. This is true if you apply a restrictive literal interpretation to the Charter. But it is not true if the Charter is regarded as an international treaty, establishing certain common goals for international co-operation and creating organs which the member states may use in their cooperation towards these goals, but without aiming at limiting the development of its procedures. The statement of objectives in the Charter is binding, and so are the rules concerning the various organs and their competence, but it is not necessary to regard the procedures indicated in the Charter as limitative in purpose. They may be supplemented by others under the pressure of circumstances and in the light of experience.[107]

But for the reservations which may be deduced from the last sentence,[108] these two statements combined appear to contain the genuinely applicable limitations upon the constitutional power of intergovernmental organizations. Indeed, it appears that while intergovernmental organizations, unlike States, are restricted by specific provisions in their constitutions as to the aims for which they shall work, such Organizations are, like States, in principle free to perform any sovereign act, or any

106. *Above,* under 2(d), with citation.
107. Dag Hammarskjöld: 'Do we need the United Nations? An Affirmative Answer', text of an address by the Secretary-General before the Students' Association, Copenhagen, 2 May 1959, p. 15. Most of the text quoted above was repeated in the *Introduction to the Annual Report of the Secretary-General, 1958–59,* p. 2 (*OR GA,* 14th session, Suppl. No. 1A), adding the pertinent reservation 'if these additional procedures are not in conflict with what is prescribed'.
108. And from two sentences which followed it; see *OR GA,* 14th session, Suppl. No. 1A, p. 2.

act under international law, which they are in a factual position to perform to attain these aims, provided that their constitutions do not preclude such acts. While a minority of the members will always have the right to challenge the legality, from an internal point of view, of acts performed to attain aims other than those defined in the constitution, the minority cannot challenge acts performed in order to attain aims covered in the constituion merely on the basis that such acts were not 'essential' or 'necessary' to attain these aims. Thus, it is not necessary to look for specific provisions in the constitution, or to resort to strained interpretations of text and intentions, or to look for precedents or constructions to justify legally the performance by an intergovernmental organization of a sovereign or international act not specifically authorized in its constitution. As an intergovernmental organization it has an *inherent power* to perform such acts. This view appears to have been confirmed, in so far as the United Nations is concerned, by the International Court of Justice in its subsequent advisory opinion of 20 July 1962 on *Certain Expenses of the United Nations.*[109]

Indeed, it is submitted that international organizations are basically *general* subjects of international law, having an inherent capacity, within the constitutional limits indicated below, to perform all such acts as are performed by the traditional subjects of international law, States; but that most Organizations are not in a factual position to perform all such acts, because they have neither territory nor nationals, and because their purposes are limited in their constitutions.[110]

With these practical reservations, and within the limits outlined below in *(g)*, intergovernmental organizations must have the same legal capacity as States, for example to assume jurisdiction in stateless territory. If *outer space* were considered subject to unilateral occupation,[110a] then the United Nations could perform such occupation and enact legislation and exercise administrative and judicial powers binding upon verybody, if its assumption of sovereign rights were designed to prevent conflicts between States, to achieve international economic co-operation or to further any other purpose of the Organization.

109. See *below*, p. 404.

110. The writer thus does not share the widely held view that only certain (the 'larger' or the most 'important') intergovernmental organizations are international persons and only in certain respects. Whatever criteria one applies to determine the size or 'importance' of the Organizations, it is not possible to establish any differences of legal relevance in this respect, quite apart from the fact that they all perform international acts. – The inherent internal and international powers outlined in the text are discussed in detail in the study cited *above*, note 98. See also *below*, under 5(a), on the external position vis-à-vis non-member States.

110a. UN GA Resolution 1721 (XVI) A of 20 December 1961 merely provides that 'outer space and celestial bodies... are not subject to *national* appropriation' (Italics added).

In its Advisory Opinion on *Reparation for Injuries Suffered in the Service of the United Nations,* the International Court of Justice stated:

> The Court has come to the conclusion that the Organization is an international person. That is not the same thing as saying that it is a State, which it certainly is not, or that its legal personality and rights and duties are the same as those of a State... What it does mean is that it is a subject of international law and capable of possessing international rights and duties, and that it has capacity to maintain its rights by bringing international claims.

These passages appear in the first part of the Opinion, which lead to the *unanimous* conclusion that the United Nations has the capacity to bring an international claim.[111] It is not known whether, in saying that the legal personality is not necessarily the same as that of a State, the majority of the Court had in mind only the *factual* limitations referred to above, or legal restrictions in line with their statements quoted three pages above (which appear in the part of the opinion which was not unanimous), or both.

While the formula applied by the majority of the Court, in its point of departure, is theoretically more closely related to the doctrine of delegated powers, there is probably little or no difference as to the practical results between this formula and the doctrine of inherent capacity submitted above, provided that the criteria 'necessary implication' and 'essential to the performance of its duties' continue to be applied in the same liberal way as hitherto.

(g) *Limitations of the inherent capacity*

From an internal, constitutional point of view, the inherent powers of intergovernmental organizations thus appear to be subject to the following legal limitations only:

(i) The constitutions of most [112] intergovernmental organizations, as opposed to those of States, define and thereby limit the *purposes* of the Organization. In these cases the Organization is therefore not constitutionally entitled to perform acts designed to further other purposes.[113]

---

111. *ICJ Reports,* 1949, pp. 179 and 187; cf. pp. 205 and 217. See, however, p. 196, where Judge Hackworth stated that he concurred in the conclusion for different reasons.

112. For exceptions, see *Nordisk Tidsskrift,* XXXIV (1964) pp. 49–54.

113. This limitation was authoritatively stated (although in the context of internal distribution of powers rather than of capacity of the Organization as a whole) by the United Nations Secretariat in connexion with the decision of the Security Council to assume the functions assigned to it in respect of the proposed Free Territory of Trieste. Cf. *above,* under (d) and the text of the statement *below,* under 4(d). The statement refers to 'the fundamental principles and purposes found in Chapter I of the Charter'. In so far as the 'principles' contain any relevant restrictions directed at the Organization (which they probably do not, apart from those which would follow anyway from the sovereign rights of Member and non-member States), these would constitute

(ii) The Organization cannot perform *acts which are precluded by any other provision of its constitution*. Express provisions of this nature are rare. But most constitutions contain a number of provisions which expressly authorize the Organization to perform certain acts which would normally fall within the scope of its inherent powers. The question may then arise whether such provisions should be interpreted *a contrario*, as precluding the exercise of similar acts in cases or under conditions not provided for. In many or most cases such *a contrario* interpretation would lead to unreasonable or even impossible results, and has not been adopted in practice.[114] Only when the provision concerned lays down limitations or conditions for the performance of the act is there in most cases basis for an *a contrario* interpretation, although even then not necessarily to the exclusion of the inherent powers.[115] In many cases the provisions in question are concerned with the distribution of functions within the Organization and obviously cannot be interpreted *a contrario* with regard to the competence of the Organization as a whole.[116]

(iii) An act must be decided and/or performed by *the organ which is competent under the constitution, and in accordance with any procedures therein prescribed*. If the constitution has been badly drawn up, the competence of each principal organ may conceivably have been defined so narrowly that there is no organ which, under the internal distribution of powers, is competent to perform the act, although it falls within the inherent competence of the Organization as a whole. However, such a case is most unlikely to arise, since normally the plenary organ and the Secretariat between them must be deemed to have any residuary powers not assigned to any specialized organs. And the plenary organ can then either itself perform the act or authorize another organ

examples of (ii) *below*. Even the member of the Council who opposed the decision stated at one point that it was precisely this limitation he was referring to (*OR SC*, 1947, p. 57).

114. See the examples cited *above*, under (b)–(e). On the internal plane the fact that the Statute of the International Atomic Energy Agency expressly authorizes its Board of Governors to establish committees (Article VI. I) has, of course, not prevented the General Conference from doing likewise, despite the absence of any constitutional provision to that effect.

115. See *below*, under 4 (a)–(b).

116. In many cases provisions specifying otherwise inherent powers may be useful or even necessary precisely from the point of view of internal distribution of functions. But in other cases they are superfluous and merely create confusion, by tempting legal writers either to draw *a contrario* conclusions which would impose upon the Organization concerned restrictions which do not apply to other Organizations, which were not intended by the draftsmen and which have not been observed in practice (see, for example, *Kelsen: The Law of the United Nations*, p. 144, and *Julius Stone: Aggression and World Order* [London 1958] p. 193, note 37)—or else to resort to strained interpretations of provisions which were never meant to cover the point.

to do so, even if the act would be beyond the scope of the constitutional functions of that organ.[117]

(iv) In addition to these purely internal, constitutional limitations, it should be noted than an intergovernmental organization has no general inherent jurisdiction over its Members States, comparable to that of States over their nationals. It is true that the inherent organic jurisdiction extends also to the Member States in their capacity of members of the several deliberative organs of the Organization, whether or not the constitution of the Organization has authorized the organ concerned to adopt rules of procudure, financial regulations, &c., and whether or not it has authorized the chairman or, on appeal, the organ itself by a majority vote, to make rulings on disputed points. The Organization may also have a limited inherent jurisdiction over the Member States in their capacity as Members of the Organization as a whole, in such matters as their election to deliberative organs, their expulsion from the Organization, or the dissolution of the Organization.[118] But is doubtful whether this inherent jurisdiction over the Member States in organizational matters extends to financial matters in the sense that the Organization can oblige its Member States to contribute to the budget of the Organization if no such duty follows expressly or by implication from the constitution or another undertaking on the part of the Member States concerned; the existence and extent of such an obligation depends basically upon an interpretation of the constitution of the Organization concerned and the intention of its drafters rather than upon any inherent power of intergovernmental organizations generally. And in functional matters it is quite clear that the Organization cannot impose obligations upon Member States, or upon non-member States or other legal subjects not subject to its inherent organic jurisdiction, or assume powers belonging to them, without a specific legal basis. This, however, need not necessarily be sought in the constitution.[119] It may be embodied in another treaty, bilateral or multilateral, or in a unilateral act by the State concerned.[120] But in the case of Member States (and persons under their jurisdiction)

---

117. *Contra: Kelsen: The Law of the United Nations*, p. 685.

118. However, any such inherent membership jurisdiction is very limited and of little practical importance, since in most cases such powers may be deduced from the provisions of the constitution itself. In any case, such inherent membership jurisdiction is limited to certain purely organizational matters.

119. *Contra: Stone: Agression and World Order* (1958) p. 193. The constitutional difficulties referred to by him are, in the view of the present writer, nonexistent to the extent that he is not referring to (ii) or (iii) *above*, since intergovernmental organizations have the capacity, within the limits listed above, to assume any functions and powers ceded to them by the States which would thereby give up rights to, or come under the extended jurisdiction of, the Organization.

120. See the examples referred to *above*, under (d).

the legal basis will, as a matter of fact, in most cases be found in the constitution of the Organization. This important principle has been clearly borne out in the practice of intergovernmental organizations by the fact that in these cases the Organizations do not act without specific legal basis, whereas they do so when no obligations are imposed upon Member States. However, this fundamental distinction is not usually brought out in the debates or in legal writings; on the contrary, the talk is rather in terms of authority having been 'conferred' upon the Organization (or the organization having been 'authorized') by provisions in the constitution even in the case of inherent powers.[121] The principle is of particular importance in respect of confederations and so-called supra-national organizations,[122] which take over some of the regular functions of the member Governments and act on their behalf. In these respects a doctrine of 'delegated' powers is entirely appropriate, but not when the Organization exercises functions on behalf of itself as a new and distinct subject of international law, without binding its Member States.

The limitations listed under (i)-(iii), and in a sense even the limitation listed under (iv) in so far as Member States are concerned, are internal, constitutional matters, which do not, in principle, affect the external capacity of the Organization under international law [123] although, as has been indicated,[124] some writers consider that at least treaties concluded in violation of constitutional restrictions become externally invalid. In its advisory opinion of 20 July 1962 on *Certain Expenses of the United*

121. The correct viewpoint was adopted by General Romulo, the Philippine representative to the 2nd session of the General Assembly. Opposing the partition plan for Palestine, General Romulo confined himself to stating that the policy was not *'mandatory'* under any specific provision of the Charter (nor in accordance with its 'fundamental principles'), OR GA, II, plenary meetings, p. 1314 (italics added).

122. Cf. *Verdross: Völkerrecht* (5th edition, Vienna 1964) pp. 354-6, who, however, considers that the Member States have not delegated part of their sovereign powers to the supra-national organization.

123. This, inter alia, appears to have been overlooked by *Bowett: The Law of the United Nations* (London 1964) p. 309, when he states that exception must be taken to the present writer's above comments on constitutionality, inherent powers and binding obligations (as first published in *BYIL*, 1961, pp. 459-60) in the light of the Court's subsequent holding in the *Expenses* case that if the action is within the scope of the functions of the United Nations, but taken by the wrong organ, or in an irregular manner, any expense incurred vis-à-vis a third party was still an expense of the Organization within Article 17(2). See the full discussion *below*, Chapter IX, at notes 21-25.

The special question of the external effects of any unconstitutionality involved in the creation or operation of a United Nations military Force is discussed *below*, pp. 173-7. On the general question of external effects of unconstitutionality, see *Indian Journal of International Law*, IV (1964) pp. 27-35.

124. *Above*, under (c), at note 83, cf. (f), at note 100.

Nations, the International Court of Justice confirmed that *ultra vires* acts are not necessarily invalid externally.[125]

4. INHERENT CAPACITY OF THE UNITED NATIONS TO ESTABLISH AND COMMAND FORCES

It will be seen that there is complete concurrence between the practice of the League of Nations and of the United Nations in establishing international forces not based on constitutional provisions, and the practice of these and other intergovernmental organizations in exercising other powers not laid down in their constitutions, or being outside the field specified in their constitutions. Indeed, on the basis of the specific and general practice referred to under 1, 2 and 3 above, it is submitted that the United Nations has legal competence, within the limits indicated on pp. 156–8, to establish and operate military forces even in the absence of specific authority for it in the Charter. This is an inherent capacity of the Organization, and not something which was done in certain emergencies, when the Members present recognized the need for a force and therefore refrained from raising legal difficulties.[126] The capacity is well within the scope of the first purpose of the United Nations as stated in Article 1(1) of the Charter:

> To maintain international peace and security, and to that end: to take effective collective measures for the prevention and removal of threats to the peace, and for the suppression of acts of aggression or other breaches of the peace, and to bring about by peaceful means, and in conformity with the principles of justice and international law, adjustment or settlement of international disputes or situations which might lead to a breach of the peace.

This, like other inherent capacities of the Organization, could only be challenged if there were any provision in the Charter precluding the Organization from creating or operating a military force.[127] There is no provision which expressly does so, as there is in the constitutions of certain States.[128] However, the Charter provides, in Article 42 and subsequent articles (cf. Article 39), for the right of the Security Council to make use of an international force in certain circumstances.[129] The

125. *ICJ Reports,* 1962, p. 167, quoted and discussed *below,* Chapter IX, at notes 21–25.

126. It is thus not necessary to justify this in each case by strained interpretations of provisions of the Charter, or the 'essential' need for establishing 'a limited substitute Force able to perform at least some of the functions assigned by the Charter to the missing forces', as Sohn proposes in *American Journal of International Law,* LII (1958) p. 230; Sohn bases himself on the statement by the International Court of Justice in the *Reparation for Injuries* case quoted *above* p. 153.

127. Cf. the statement of the United Kingdom Government *above,* under 2(d).

128. See Article 9 of the Japanese constitution, quoted *below,* note 195.

129. See quotations *above,* Chapter II,3.

question then arises whether these provisions should be interpreted *a contrario*,[130] in the sense that no military [131] force can be established if the conditions laid down in these provisions are not fulfilled. Otherwise the provisions might seem meaningless and superfluous.

However, this interpretation has not been adopted in practice (any more than an *a contrario* interpretation has been adopted in most other cases where an international constitution specifies certain inherent powers),[132] despite the fact that Article 43 especially lays down certain conditions as to how the Force should be established. Indeed, it is submitted that the legal significance of Article 42 and the subsequent articles, and of any limitations contained in them, is a different one. In this connexion it is necessary to distinguish between three questions:

(*a*) The obligation of Member States to make available contingents, assistance and facilities to a United Nations Force.

(*b*) The obligation of Member States to permit a United Nations Force to operate on their territory.

(*c*) The competence of the United Nations to operate, command and exercise jurisdiction over a military Force.

(a) *Obligation of Member States to contribute contingents*
(b) *Obligation of Member States to admit the Force to their territory*

As has already been pointed out above, p. 158, it is a basic principle of the law of intergovernmental organizations that no obligations can be imposed upon Member States (otherwise than in their capacity as members of particular organs of the Organization), unless this is authorized by a specific provision in the constitution (or by another treaty, or by a unilateral act of the State concerned). It is this authorization which must be sought in Articles 42 and subsequent relevant articles of the Charter. And it is in this respect that the conditions and limitations contained in these articles (cf. Article 39) are relevant. In other respects the Organization can rely upon its inherent powers.[132a] Accordingly, no Member State has an obligation to contribute contingents or other direct [133] assistance to a United Nations Force except under the procedure laid down

130. This is Sohn's point of departure for the construction referred to in note 126.

131. The United Nations Field Service and the observation groups discussed *above*, pp. 21–24 and 128–129, are not military forces, and would not be preluded by any such *a contrario* interpretation.

132. *Above*, p. 157.

132a. Article 2(5), too, appears, by its terms, to reflect a distinction between actions which are and which are not based upon the specific provisions of the Charter, but see *below*, p. 206, note 131, and pp. 285–8.

133. The question of the obligation of all Member States to bear the *expenses* incurred by the Organization in connexion with the Force is a different matter. The authority for this must be sought, not in Articles 42 et seq., but in Article 17(2). The

in Articles 43-45.[134] Similarly, no party to a dispute [135] which has not committed aggression has a duty to admit a United Nations Force to operate in its territory except pursuant to a *decision* by the Security Council (not the General Assembly) under Articles 39 and 42.[136] [137]

(c) *Competence of the United Nations to assume command over a 'consent' Force*

In all other cases, i.e. when the conditions laid down in these articles are not fulfilled, or when action is taken by the General Assembly, a Force can only be created by individual enlistment or by utilizing national contingents *voluntarily* placed at the disposal of the Organization, pursuant to a recommendation or otherwise. Moreover, the Force can enter the territory of Member States only with their consent.[137] [138] This, in fact, is what has been done in all cases so far.[139]

International Court of Justice in its advisory opinion on Certain Expenses of the United Nations of 20 July 1962 held that Aricle 17(2) does impose such an obligation upon Member States (*ICJ Reports*, 1962, p. 179). See *above*, pp. 65, 158 and 172).

134. This, and no more, was expressly and authoritatively stated at the San Francisco Conference; see *Goodrich and Hambro: Charter of the United Nations* ad Article 42, and report of Committee III/3 (Doc. 881, II D). *Kelsen: The Law of the United Nations*, p. 756, appears to be in doubt on this point. Cf. also the Secretariat statement on Trieste quoted and discussed *below*, under (d).

135. The duty of third (Member) States to accord rights of passage is especially mentioned in Article 43 and thus appears, like other kinds of assistance, to depend upon the special agreements to be concluded under that article. In this sense *Colban: Stortinget og Utenrikspolitikken* (Oslo 1961) p. 73. This was not so under Article 16(3) of the League of Nations Covenant. Indeed, *Martin and Edwards: The Changing Charter* (London 1955) pp. 81–82, consider that the United Nations too has a right of passage even in the absence of special agreements. And so does *Bowett: United Nations Forces* (London 1964) p. 418 (cf. pp. 455–8), supporting himself upon the *travaux préparatoires* (*UNCIO*, XII, p. 510).

136. In view of the broad terms of Article 42 (quoted *above*, note 20, together with Article 43(1)), it is not necessary for the purposes of the present study to examine whether also other articles, such as Articles 24, 25, 40 or 53, confer a similar power upon the Security Council.

137. See, however, *below*, pp. 173–174 on the right of the United Nations under Article 2(4) of the Charter and general international law to fight an *aggressor* Member or non-member State. This right, as far as it goes, may be exercised even in the aggressor's own territory.

138. This distinction was brought out in the Soviet explanation of vote on the establishment of UNEF. As reported *above*, under 2(d), the Soviet Union justified its abstention by referring to the fact that Egypt had agreed to the introduction of an international force into its territory.

139. The territory of North Korea was entered, pursuant to General Assembly Resolution 376 (V), without the consent of its Government. However, the People's Democratic Republic of Korea, which was not a member of the United Nations, had committed aggression. On the position of a non-member State which has committed agression, see *below*, pp. 173–4.

But this, as practice demonstrates, does not mean that the Organization cannot make binding decisions with regard to the operation of such a Force. On the contrary, a Force established by the Organization by individual enlistment or secondment, such as the United Nations Field Service, UNTSO and the other truce observation groups, automatically becomes an organ of the Organization, and is subject to its exclusive organic jurisdiction in the same manner as other organs. The same applies to a Force composed of national contingents if and to the extent to which the states providing them have placed them under the authority of the Organization (or under a commander appointed by and taking his orders from it), and have thereby ceded their organic jurisdiction over them. In this manner also the UNEF and the other peace-keeping Forces have come under the exclusive organic jurisdiction of the Organization, subject to such powers as have been reserved for the States providing the contingents by their agreements with the Organization.[140] In respect of this organic jurisdiction there is no question of 'recommendations', but of 'decisions' which are directly binding upon the Force and its members, as described above.[141]

Only the Force in Korea (and the Forces envisaged by the Collective Measures Committee) was not subject to the organic jurisdiction of the United Nations, because the contributing States placed their contingents under a commander appointed by the United States, rather than under one appointed by the United Nations. This they did pursuant to a recommendation contained in the Security Council's Resolution of 7 July 1950, as proposed by the United Kingdom.

In his introductory statement (quoted above, p. 130), the United Kingdom representative took the position that the United Nations was precluded from itself appointing a commander, because the agreements provided for in Article 43 had not been concluded, and because the action could not therefore be based upon Article 42.

It has already been pointed out [142] that there appears to be no basis in the text of Article 42 or in the *travaux préparatoires* for assuming that the article can be applied only in the circumstances laid down in Articles 43 et seq.[143] In particular, there appears to be no basis for linking Art-

140. *Below*, p. 443.

141. pp. 91–98 and 144–5, cf. pp. 28–32, 48ff., 67, 79 and 82. It is therefore not appropriate, as has been done, to cite such cases as examples of the binding force of United Nations 'recommendations'. The latter question arises only outside the scope of the organic jurisdiction and the answer is that in principle the recommendations are not binding unless they have been given binding force by treaty or unilateral act, but that this can be done without basis in the constitution; cf. *above*, p. 158.

142. *Above*, under 2(b), with quotation of Articles 42 and 43(1) in note 20.

143. Most writers have taken a contrary view, see for example *Attia: Les forces armées des Nations Unies en Corée et au Moyen-Orient* (Genève 1963) pp. 271 and 420; and Quincy Wright: 'Legal Aspects of the Congo Situation' as cited by T. S. Rama

icle 43, and the hitherto unfulfilled conditions laid down therein, with the question of the obligation of Member or non-member States to admit a United Nations Force to operate in their territory. Still less is there any basis for linking Article 43 to the right of a United Nations Force to resist an aggressor (in the territory of the invaded State with its consent), as was the situation on 7 July 1950.[144] In both these respects, Article 42, the conditions of which were met in Korea, would have afforded ample legal basis.[145]

Even if one were to accept the view that Article 42 was not applicable, it would be difficult to find legal basis in the Charter for the second implication of the United Kingdom statement, namely that the United Nations could not itself appoint a commander (and thereby itself assume command over, and legal responsibility for, the Force). Not even the subsequent Uniting for Peace Resolution, which is clearly outside the scope of Article 42, imposes any restriction to that effect.[146] On the contrary, it recommends that each Member should maintain within its national armed forces elements which could promptly be made available.

> for service *as a United Nations unit or units,* upon recommendation by the Security Council or the General Assembly, without prejudice to the use of such elements in exercise of the right of individual or collective self-defence recognized in Article 51 of the Charter.[147]

This would appear at least to admit the possibility of an action different from the collective self-defence of States acting individually. Indeed, in the course of the discussion on the resolution, the opposition pointed out that under it the General Assembly would be empowered to assume command of armed forces and be responsible for their maintenance and allocation.[148] Nevertheless, the Collective Measures Committee in its first report proposed that

Rao in *Indian Year Book of International Affairs,* 1963, p. 146 (who erroneously implies that the present writer shares this view). However, *Stone,* at the Oslo Conference 1964, supported the present writer's view, see *Frydenberg: Peace-Keeping, Experience and Evaluation,* The Oslo Papers (Oslo 1964) p. 294.

144. Cf. *below,* under 5(a).

145. If the United Nations Force in the Congo is considered (after 21 February 1961) to operate under Article 42 (cf. *above,* under 2(e) *in fine*), then this constitutes a precedent against the United Kingdom interpretation.

146. See *above,* Chapter II,5.

147. General Assembly Resolution 377 (V). Italics supplied.

148. *Repertory of the United Nations Practice,* I, p. 317. The supporters of the resolution were less specific in this respect, cf. *ibid.,* p. 318, and *OR GA,* V, plenary, 299th-302nd meetings. One of them very correctly pointed out that the General Assembly could not make decisions which would automatically impose commitments or enforcement obligations upon the Member States (*ibid.,* p. 342). Another stated that the General Assembly was not empowered to order *or to take direct* enforcement action, but he derived this from Article 11(2) of the Charter (*OR GA,* V, First Committee, p. 127), which is a different matter; cf. *below,* pp. 171-2.

the Organization should authorise a State or group of States to *act on its behalf* as executive military authority, within the framework of its policies and objectives as expressed through such resolutions as it may adopt at any stage of the collective action.[149]

In searching for a legal basis for the United Kingdom view, the following further statement of the United Kingdom representative may be of relevance:

In conclusion, I should like to say a word regarding any possible constitution of further machinery by the Security Council. We believe that in spite of the suggestions which have been canvassed in the Press and elsewhere, there is no real need for such machinery, at any rate, at the present time. In any event, since we believe the Security Council is acting under Article 39 of the Charter, its function is not an operative one; all it should do is to make sure that the individual efforts of the Members concerned are properly coordinated.[150]

It appears from this statement that the legal reason invoked by the United Kingdom may have been based either upon the view that an intergovernmental organization must confine itself to such action as is specified in its constitution, or upon the view that Article 42 and subsequent relevant articles must be interpreted *a contrario* also in respect of assumption of command. As already pointed out, the first view is manifestly refuted by the general practice of the United Nations and other intergovernmental organizations.[151] The second view has been refuted by subsequent United Nations practice in respect of UNEF, Congo, West New Guinea and Cyprus, in so far as Forces not entrusted with a true military enforcement action against an aggressor are concerned.[152]

If one accepts the view submitted above, that Art. 42 and the follow-

---

149. First report, *OR GA*, VI, Suppl. No. 13, p. 25 (italics supplied); cf. also the third report, par. 10 i.f., *ibid.*, IX, Annexes, A.i. 19, p. 3.

150. *OR SC*, 1950, 18th meeting, p. 4.

151. *Above*, under 3.

152. *Kelsen*, in his post-Korea study: *Recent Trends in the Law of the United Nations*, p. 940, states that the commander of a force established by recommendation under Article 39 can 'probably' only be appointed by the Security Council, as a subsidiary organ of the United Nations, 'in case of an enforcement action taken by the Security Council under Article 42'. *Stone: Aggression and World Order* (1958) pp. 176 and 190 (cf. p. 178) considers the action in Korea and the Uniting for Peace Resolution constitutional only if based upon action by individual States rather than by the United Nations. This view appears to be based upon a proposition that the United Nations can take military enforcement measures only under Articles 42 et seq., although he cites also Article 11 as a basis of his proposition. The Secretary-General, after UNEF, and before the Congo, said that a fighting force could only be brought into being by the Security Council under Chapter VII (without, however, restricting his reference to Articles 42 et seq.); *Introduction to the Annual Report of the Secretary-General, 1957–58, OR GA,* 13th session, Suppl. No. 1 A, p. 2, Summary Study on the experience of UNEF, *ibid.*, Annexes, A.i. 65, pars. 177–80, cf. par. 167; *ibid.*, Special Political Committee, p. 63.

ing relevant articles should be interpreted *a contrario* only to the extent that they add to the inherent powers of the Organization—i.e. the view that it is necessary to rely upon these articles only when the United Nations imposes obligations upon Member States—then the question boils down to whether the United Nations resistance to aggression (by a Force enlisted individually or composed of voluntarily contributed contingents, and operating in the territory of States with their consent, or in that of the aggressor) constitutes imposition upon the aggressor of an obligation. Member States already have an obligation not to commit aggression under Article 2(4) of the Charter, and non-member States may have a similar obligation under the Briand-Kellogg Pact of 27 August 1928, under a bilateral non-aggression treaty, or under general international law.[153] And the enforcement by the United Nations of this already existing obligation can hardly require any specific legal basis.[154 155] It is not known whether the United Kingdom was pre-

153. *Below*, pp. 223–224. On the effects of the Briand-Kellogg Pact vis-à-vis non-contracting parties see Schwarzenberger in *International Law Association, Report of the Forty-Eighth Conference, New York 1958*, p. 581. He also points out (p. 580) that it is uncertain whether the Briand-Kellogg Pact, which outlaws war as an instrument of national policy, *a contrario* retains the legality of war as an instrument of international or supranational policy. Cf *Stone: Legal Controls of International Conflict* (New York 1954) p. 300.

154. Cf. the opposition of the representatives of El Salvador and India to the Canadian proposal that the consent of Israel, France and the United Kingdom should be obtained to the introduction of UNEF into Egyptian territory (*OR GA*, ES-I, pp. 69 and 70; cf. pp. 83 and 87, 3 November 1956). The Secretary-General, in his secound and final report on UNEF of 6 November 1956, confined himself to stating that the Force 'would be limited in its operations to he extent that consent of the parties concerned is required under generally recognised international law' (*ibid.*, Annexes, p. 20, see also pars. 9–10). This report was endorsed by General Assembly Resolution 1001 (ES-I) of 7 November 1956. It was not necessary to force the issue to a more clear decision because consent, and an undertaking to halt military aperations, were readily given by all parties, and because certain States providing contingents in any case insisted upon all parties agreeing. In a further part of the United Kingdom Government statement on UNEF (*above*, under 2(d)), the Government spokesman referred only to the need for the consent of the State in whose territory the Force would be stationed or operate, without mentioning a need for consent of the other parties (*International and Comperative Law Quarterly*, VI (1957) p. 322). And so did the Secretary-General in his Summary Study on the experience of UNEF, *OR GA*, 13th session, Annexes, A.i. 65, par. 15 (cf. par. 23 on the factual concurrence of the other parties to the dispute). Cf. also par. 10 of General Assembly Resolution 503 (VI), which, in implementation of the Uniting for Peace Resolution, 'recognizes that nothing in the present resolution shall be construed to permit any measures to be taken *in* any State without the free and express consent of *that* State' (italics supplied). Such consent can of course not be required of the aggressor, see *below*, p. 174.

It would, of course, involve the imposition of a new obligation if the Security Council should decide to apply military force against a State which has not violated any legal obligation (cf. *Kelsen: The Law of the United Nations*, pp. 727–30).

pared to argue that North Korea, not having ratified the Charter or the Pact, was legally entitled to go to war, and that the United Nations armed resistance thus constituted an attempt to impose a new obligation upon it. However this may be, the position of a non-member State is also in other respects a matter of general international law, rather than of the Charter.[156]

If the United Kingdom proposition (or a similar proposition based upon Article 42 only) that the United Nations was precluded from assuming command was not dictated by the terms of Article 39 or by the lack of any express power in the Charter for the United Nations to create a Force, it might conceivably have been based upon a strict interpretation of Article 47(3) which provided that 'the Military Staff Committee shall be responsible under the Security Council for the strategic direction of any armed forces placed at the disposal of the Security Council'. Since the Military Staff Committee was not functioning and was not in a position to perform its task, the United Kingdom may have felt that the forces in Korea could not be 'placed at the disposal of the Security Council', but had to be placed instead at the disposal of a Member State. If one adopts such a strict interpretation of Article 47(3), the effects will probably also extend, not only to a Force established under Article 43, but also to one established under Article 42. Indeed, it would probably extend to any force established by the Security Council under Chapter VII, but not to Forces established by the General Assembly.[157] Thus, it was natural that Article 47(3) did not prevent the General Assembly from assuming command over UNEF. However, it did not prevent the Security Council from assuming command over the United Nations Force in the Congo either. This cannot be reconciled with a strict interpretation of Article 47(3) if the United Nations Force in the Congo, as has been assumed,[158] is operated (since 21 February 1961) under Chapter VII (or even under Article 42) of the Charter. Moreover, there is no indication that the United Kingdom's proposition was based upon Article 47(3), or that anybody else has proposed any such strict interpretation of that article.[159]

---

155. The United Nations is not bound by any treaty not to use force against an aggressor. It can thus do so as a collective measure under the general provisions of the Charter (see Article 1 (1)) or in exercise of the right of collective self-defence under general international law (see *below*, pp. 173–4 and 404, note 2).

156. See *below*, under 5(a).

157. On the other hand, it might apply only to a Force composed of national contingents.

158. *Above*, under (e) *in fine*.

159. The United Nations Charter Committee of the International Law Association did not apply any such restrictive interpretation in relation to armed forces established under Article 42 and armed for defensive purposes; see the *Report of the Forty-ninth Conference* (1960) p. 137.

Should one accept the United Kingdom view—on the basis of a doctrine of delegated powers,[160] of an *a contrario* interpretation of Article 42 also in respect of command, or of assimilating resistance to an aggressor to the imposition of an obligation upon him—one might question whether the United Nations would have been entitled to call the action in Korea a United Nations action,[161] to authorize the Force to use its name and flag, to grant United Nations distinctions to members of the Force and exercise international protection on behalf of them,[162] to exercise political leadership of the action through resolutions (recommendations) of the Security Council and the General Assembly, and on the whole to assume moral and political responsibility for the action to the extent that it did.[163] Similarly, one might ask whether the United Nations would have been entitled to make national contingents act as 'United Nations unit or units' as provided in the Uniting for Peace Resolution, or even to let the 'executive military authority' act on behalf of the Organization in the manner proposed by the Collective Measures Committee.[164] Even if one accepts the earlier conclusion,[165] that the United Nations control over the Force in these cases was not sufficiently strong to render it internationally responsible for its acts, this does not necessarily mean that the relationship between the Organization and the Force can be ignored from a constitutional point of view.

After having offered all these alternative legal reasons which might have underlain the United Kingdom statement in connexion with the establishment of the command in Korea, it should be observed that it is extremely doubtful whether the legal considerations referred to by the United Kingdom's representative were the decisive reasons for conferring command authority upon the United States rather than upon the United Nations. It is more likely that this course was dictated by practical considerations.[166] Indeed, at the time it appeared to be the only

160. *Above*, under 3(a), cf. (f).

161. This was done by the President of the Security Council before calling upon the United Kingdom representative to introduce his draft resolution and to make the statement quoted *above*, p. 130; *OR SC*, 1950, 476th meeting, p. 2. *Kelsen, op cit.*, pp. 936 et seq., argues against this qualification, despite the fact that the Security Council action is one of the reasons why he is unwilling to recognize the action as collective self-defence (*above*, note 13).

162. General Assembly Resolution 906 (IX), quoted *above*, p. 105.

163. A great deal of this was done already on 7 july 1950; see *above*, note 161 and Chapter II,4 *in initio*.

164. *Stone: Aggression and World Order* (London 1958) pp. 178 and 186, who considers coordinated national action to be the only way in which the Uniting for Peace Resolution can be reconciled with the Charter, goes some way, but not very far, in permitting United Nations assistance to the action.

165. *Above*, Chapter III,6(c) *in initio*.

166. See the first report of the Collective Measures Committee, *OR GA*, 6th session, Suppl. No. 13, p. 45.

practical course, since the United States clearly was going to carry the main burden of the United Nations effort,[167] since it already had an organized command near the scene, and since there was no time to organize another. In these circumstances, and in view of the emergency situation which did not allow time for a discussion of legal niceties, it is only natural that no member of the Council found reason to question the legal grounds invoked by the United Kingdom in favour of a proposal which everybody agreed constituted the most, or only, practicable course.

In these circumstances, and in view of the fact that the United Kingdom representative did not clearly identify his legal basis and that the Collective Measures Committee did not invoke legal grounds at all, the action in Korea and the proposals of the Collective Measures Committee can hardly be cited as precedents in support of a proposition that the United Nations could not assume command over a Force established outside the scope of Article 42 and subsequent articles of the Charter. There are, on the other hand, four precedents against such a proposition: UNEF, Congo, New Guinea (Irian Barat) and Cyprus. However, neither of these constitutes a combat force to perform international enforcement measures against an aggressor. As for such a combat force, there is only the fact that the Uniting for Peace Resolution contains no restriction excluding United Nations command, although this Resolution has so far been clearly applied only in a case where the command was national.[168]

If, as submitted,[169] the application of Article 42 is not dependent upon the prior conclusion of agreements pursuant to Article 43, the second implication of the United Kingdom proposition, that the United Nations could not iself assume command, is of little practical importance in relation to the Security Council, in view of the wide terms of Article 42. It would in fact affect the power only of the General Assembly.

(d) Delimitation of powers of the Security Council and the General Assembly

The competence of the General Assembly is, however, also subject to express provisions of the Charter governing *the distribution of functions between the organs of the Organization*.[170] Although this problem, as

---

167. In fact, 50 per cent. of the total land forces, 86 per cent. of the total naval force and 93 per cent. of the total air force were supplied by the United States; Kunzmann, *Europa-Archiv*, XIII (1958) p. 10813. The greater part of the remainder was supplied by the Republic of Korea, a non-member State.

168. *Above*, p. 38, cf. pp. 45 and 133.

169. *Above*, under 2(b).

170. Moreover, the General Assembly, in contradistinction to the Security Council acting under Articles 41 et seq., is restricted by the domestic jurisdiction clause of Article 2(7) of the Charter.

pointed out in the introduction to the present Chapter, is essentially outside the scope of the present study, it should be pointed out for the sake of completeness that, even if it is determined that the Organization as a whole has the inherent power to establish and operate military forces with the consent of the Member States concerned, the organ making a decision to this effect can only do so within its field of competence as laid down in the Charter.[171]

Thus *the Security Council*, as a specialized organ with restricted membership, must keep within the scope of the functions assigned to it in the Charter. However, the relevant provisions of the Charter appear to be quite broad. Article 24 confers upon the Council 'primary responsibility for the maintenance of international peace and security'. And Article 39 imposes no restriction upon the power of the Security Council to make recommendations for the maintenance or restoration of international peace and security if there is a 'threat to the peace, breach of the peace, or act of aggression'. Moreover, both the San Francisco Conference and the Secretariat and Members of the Security Council have taken the view that the powers of the Security Council under Article 24 are not restricted to the specific powers listed in Chapter VII, or in other parts of the Charter. This means that the Council may act even if there is no 'threat to the peace', &c. as provided in Article 39 or 'dispute' as provided in Article 33. In the course of the discussion in the Security Council concerning the assumption by the Council of certain responsibilities in respect of the Free Territory of Trieste,[172] the Assistant Secretary-General for Political and Security Council Affairs, Mr. Sobolev, stated:

> Paragraph 1 of Article 24 provides: 'In order to ensure prompt and effective action by the United Nations, its Members confer on the Security Council primary responsibility for the maintenance of international peace and security, and agree that in carrying out its duties under this responsibility the Security Council acts on their behalf.' The words, 'primary responsibility for the maintenance of international peace and security', coupled with the phrase, 'acts on their behalf', constitute a grant of power sufficiently wide to enable the Security Council to approve the documents in question and to assume the responsibilities arising therefrom.
>
> Furthermore, the records of the San Francisco Conference demonstrate that the powers of the Council under Article 24 are not restricted to the specific grants of authority contained in Chapters VI, VII, VIII and XII. In particular, the Secretary-General wishes to invite attention to the discussion at the fourteenth meeting of Committee III/1 at San Francisco, wherein it was clearly recognized by all the representatives that the Security Council was not restricted to the specific powers set forth in Chapters VI, VII, VIII and XII. (I have in mind document 597, Committee III/1/30.) It will be noted that this discussion concerned a proposed amendment to limit the obligation of Members to accept decisions of the Council solely to those decisions made under the specific powers.

171. *Above*, under 3(g)(iii).
172. *Above*, under 3(d).

4. UN'S INHERENT POWER TO ESTABLISH FORCES

In the discussion, all the delegations which spoke, including both proponents and opponents of this amendment, recognized that the authority of the Council was not restricted to such specific powers. It was recognized in this discussion that the responsibility to maintain peace and security carried with it a power to discharge this responsibility. This power, it was noted, was not unlimited, but subject to the purposes and principles of the United Nations.

It is apparent that this discussion reflects a basic conception of the Charter, namely, that the Members of the United Nations have conferred upon the Security Council powers commensurate with its responsibility for the maintenance of peace and security. The only limitations are the fundamental principles and purposes found in Chapter I of the Charter.[173]

It will be noted that Mr. Sobolev's statement was not confined to recommendations to Member States and decisions binding upon the organs of the United Nations, as dealt with above, but was concerned also with decisions binding upon the Member States. However, in this respect Article 24 cannot justify circumvention of the limitations contained in specific articles of the Charter.[174] Thus, it would not be possible by a decision under Article 24 to compel Member States which have not concluded agreements under Article 43 to contribute contingents to the Forces envisaged in Article 42.[175]

The General Assembly, on the other hand, is the plenary and supreme organ which—in the United Nations as in other Organizations—exercises the general functions of the Organization, including any residuary functions not assigned to other organs. However, the General Assembly cannot exercise any functions reserved exclusively for the Security Council by any provision of the Charter. Thus the General Assembly cannot establish any Force in violation of Articles 11(2) and 12(1) (cf. Article 24), which limit the powers of the General Assembly in the field of peace and security, in recognition of the primary responsibility of the Security Council in this field. Article 12(1) debars the General Assembly from making recommendations with regard to any dispute or situation in respect of which the Security Council is exercising the functions assigned to it. Article 11(2) provides, *inter alia*, that any question on which 'action' is necessary shall be referred to the Security Council.[176] The General

---

173. OR SC, 1947, pp. 41–61. Cf. *above*, pp. 148–9. For a discussion of this and similar subsequent cases see Schachter: 'The Development of International Law through the Legal Opinions of the UN Secretariat', *BYIL* XXV (1948) pp. 96–101. See also *Goodrich and Hambro: Charter of the United Nations* (Article 24).

174. Cf. *above*, under (a)–(b). In this sense also Schachter, *loc. cit.*, pp. 99 and 101, opposing a contrary statement by Eagleton in *American Journal of International Law*, XL (1946), p. 526.

175. *Kelsen: The Law of the United Nations*, p. 756, appears to be in doubt on this point.

176. The term 'action' was interpreted in an *obiter dictum* of the International Court of Justice in its advisory opinion of 20 July 1962 on Certain Expenses of the United

171

Assembly has on three occasions (Uniting for Peace Resolution, UNEF and West New Guinea) acted on the assumption that these provisions do not preclude it from establishing, or authorizing the Secretary-General to establish, an international force without imposing such obligations as discussed under (a)-(b). That the General Assembly cannot impose 'commitments or enforcement obligations' upon Member States was clearly recognized by representatives who spoke in favour of the adoption of the Uniting for Peace Resolution.[177] And it was precisely the absence of any imposition of the force upon the host State which caused the Soviet Union not to vote against the establishment of UNEF by the General Assembly.[178]

(e) *Financing*

On the question of financing, which is also outside the scope of the present study, it has been pointed out above, pp. 55, 65 and 81, that the costs of UNEF and ONUC, in contradistinction to UNFICYP, were assessed upon the Members and that the ICJ has held that the General Assembly had the authority under Article 17(2) of the Charter to impose this obligation upon all Members. By its resolution 1854 (XVII) the General Assembly accepted this opinion. However, certain Members persisted in their refusal to contribute. This led to a grave financial and constitutional crisis, at the basis of which was the problem of the distribution of powers between the General Assembly and the Security Council.[179]

5. EXTERNAL STATUS OF FORCES ESTABLISHED IN VIOLATION OF CONSTITUTIONAL PROVISIONS [180]

The problem so far discussed has been whether the United Nations is competent *under its constitution* to establish and operate an international

Nations, see *below*, p. 285, note 253 and pp. 407–8. For earlier interpretation in practice of these and other relevant provisions, see *Repertory of Practice of UN Organs*, I, especially pp. 308 et seq., and Suppl. No. 1, pp. 140–3. See also *Goodrich and Hambro*, *op. cit.; Ross: Constitution of the United Nations* (Copenhagen 1950) pp. 153–4; *Kelsen: Recent Trends in the Law of the United Nations*, pp. 937 (on Article 24) and pp. 959 et seq.; *Martin and Edwards: The Changing Charter* (London 1955) pp. 27–28; and *Stone: Aggression and World Order* (London 1958) p. 178, who attaches importance to the term 'maintenance' (as distinct from 'enforcement') of international peace in Article 11. Cf. also the general citations *above*, note 2.

177. *OR GA*, V, Plenary, p. 342. Cf. also GA res. 503(VI), *above*, note 154.

178. *Above*, under 2(d); cf. *OR GA*, ES-I, p. 128.

179. See GA Resolutions 1854 (XVII) and 2006 (XIX) and the reports made pursuant thereto. On the legal aspects, see *above*, pp. 158 and 162, note 133.

180. See also *below*, Chapter VII.

force in cases other than those specified in the Charter. The conclusion arrived at is that in this as in other respects the United Nations as an Organization has an inherent power, but that it cannot impose obligations upon Member States to contribute contingents or services to the Force, or to receive it in their territories, without basis in specific provisions of the relevant articles of the Charter, and that the provisions on internal distribution of powers must be observed.

However, this constitutional problem is an internal one, which affects only the Member States and the Organization as such in their mutual relations. Only these may question the constitutionality of an action.

(a) *Vis-à-vis non-members*

Non-member States, insurgent governments and other external authorities, cannot derive any rights from the constitution of an Organization of which they are not members (or, if one prefers, from a treaty to which they are not parties).[181] They are therefore not in a position to invoke any unconstitutionality of a military action of the Organization even if it is directed against their forces or their territory.

All that external parties can do is to question the competence of the United Nations *under general international law to* conduct military operations against them. But they can hardly do this with success if they have committed aggression. The right to declare war was already recognized for the League of Nations,[182] despite the absence of any provision to that effect in the Covenant, and despite the fact that the international personality of the League was never clearly recognized. As for the United Nations, the International Court of Justice has recognized unanimously (except possibly for Judge Hackworth) that the United Nations possesses objective international personality, which is also valid with respect to non-member States.[183] It has been demonstrated that the United Nations performs such other acts under international law as it is in a factual position to perform, and it has been submitted, that it is indeed competent to perform any act under international law which it is in a factual position to perform.[184] It would be difficult to find a legal basis for making an exception for one particular capacity: to wage war.[185] Under general international law States have the right to exercise this in-

181. Except in the rare case of *pacta in favorem tertii*; cf. *above*, p. 102, note 39.
182. *Above*, p. 27 with citations.
183. Advisory Opinion on *Reparation for Injuries Suffered in the Service of the United Nations, ICJ Reports*, 1949, p. 185; cf. pp. 187, 196, 205 and 217. *Contra:* Bindschedler, *Archiv des Völkerrechts*, IX (1962) pp. 387–8. Discussion *below*, p. 308.
184. *Above*, under 3, especially (g) *in fine*.
185. See *below*, Chapter VII,5. At the Korean Political Conference 1954 the three Communist delegations maintained that the United Nations had been a belligerent, see *below*, p. 188, note 56.

herent capacity in individual or collective self-defence.[186] In the absence of any special rules or considerations, it must then be assumed that the United Nations can exercise its capacity in the same circumstances against the forces of the aggressor in the invaded territory and against his own territory.[187] Indeed, if the League of Nations and the United Nations did not have the capacity under general international law to conduct military operations and did not partake of the right of collective self-defence, it could be argued that the enforcement provisions of the two constitutions would not under general international law be valid against non-member States in so far as the provisions allow or require action by the Organization as such. In other words, even a military action decided and directed by the Security Council in accordance with Article 43 (and subsequent articles) could not be legitimately undertaken under general international law against a non-member State. This because, normally, a treaty creating an international organization, like any other treaty, could not create, vis-à-vis third parties, rights which the Organization does not possess under general international law, even if the constitution expressly provides for such rights as does the Charter in Article 2(6).[188] On the other hand, once the United Nations has this capacity and this right under general international law, as it is submitted that it has, no third party can invoke any limitations which might be

---

186. *Stone: Legal Controls of International Conflict* (London 1954) p. 245, denies the basis in general international law of the right of collective self-defence. He substitutes (p. 234) the liberty of each State to resort to war under customary international law. On the latter problem, see *below*, pp. 223–4.

The preamble of the Briand-Kellogg Pact provides that an aggressor should be denied the benefits furnished by the Pact. If this Pact were considered to exclude collective self-defence, then any treaty of defensive alliance would be legally inoperative against a Pact-breaking State. In his report on the the principle of self-defence in the United Nations Charter, Schwarzenberger points out that 'as a co-signatory of the Kellogg Pact, Norway would (in 1939–40) have had every right to discriminate in favour of the Allied Powers and against Germany as the initial aggressor in her lightning war against Poland'; *International Law Association, Report of the Forty-eighth Conference*, New York 1958, p. 569. See also *above*, p. 166, note 153, and *below*, pp. 260–1.

187. As indicated *above*, note 153, Schwarzenberger (*loc. cit.*, p. 580), raises the question whether the Kellogg Pact operates at all against war as an instrument of *international policy*.

188. See *Goodrich and Hambro, op. cit.* (2nd ed.) pp. 108–9, and *Kelsen, op. cit.*, pp. 109–10, on the relationship of this principle to Article 2 (6) of the Charter. In the view of the present writer, military enforcement measures against a non-member State pursuant to Article 2 (6) are, on the basis indicated in the text, in full accordance with general international law if the non-member State concerned has committed aggression. It is only in the unlikely case that Article 2 (6) would be used as a basis for enforcement measures against a non-aggressor non-member State that the Organization might be over-stepping its rights under general international law.—On the question of Article 2 (6), see *Nordisk Tidsskrift for international Ret*, XXXIV (1963) pp. 12–14.

derived from Articles 11(2) and 12(1) of the Charter, which curtail the competence of the General Assembly in favour of that of the Security Council, from an *a contrario* interpretation of Article 42 and subsequent articles, or from any other provision of the Charter, or from the fact that Member States have been compelled to provide contingents, assistance or right of passage despite the absence of the special agreements provided for in Article 43. This was the true legal position of the People's Democratic Republic of Korea and of Katanga.[189]

(b) *Vis-à-vis member States*

As for an aggressor Member State, opinions may differ as to whether, having itself violated the Charter by committing an act of aggression, it can still insist upon all its rights as a Member of the Organization.[190] If the answer is yes,[191] then it may, by virtue of its membership, be in a position to claim the 'privilege' of not being resisted, and of not having its own territory invaded, by a United Nations Force established in violation of the Charter. On the other hand, the other Member States retain their right under general international law to intervene in exercise of their right of collective self-defence. If one were to follow the reasoning which might have underlain the United Kingdom statement in the Security Council on 7 July 1950 and the subsequent proposal of the Collective Measures Committee, such action by Member States might in fact come very close indeed to action by the United Nations itself, and the 'privilege' of the aggressor Member State concerned would be reduced to a right to demand that the actual command of the Force be left to States.[192]

(c) *Responsibility for the Force and applicability of the laws of war*

Whatever view one takes of the constitutionality or otherwise of a Force established and operated by the United Nations, or of the right of Member and non-member States to invoke any unconstitutionality of the Force, or of the right of the United Nations under general international law to conduct military operations, it is submitted that if the United Nations establishes a Force and conducts military operations, and if genuine command and operational control are vested in the Organiza-

---

189. The actions against both of these were decided by the Security Council, and thus avoided the particular problems of Articles 11 and 12. Membership rights in respect of Katanga could be claimed only by the Government of the Republic of Congo.

190. This question would, of course, not arise if the Security Council should decide to direct an enforcement action against a State which has not violated its legal obligations under the Charter; cf. *Kelsen: op. cit.*, pp. 727–30.

191. Cf. *Stone: Aggression and World Order* (1958) pp. 186–7.

192. Cf. *above*, p. 168.

tion, the other parties involved in the hostilities must treat it as a United Nations Force rather than as a coalition of national armies.[193] Thus *international represensation of, and responsibility for, the Force* must vest in the Organization in the manner described above in Chapter III. Similarly, it is submitted that during its military operations, the Force is bound to observe humanitarian *laws of war* and is entitled to protection under them, to the extent discussed in the following chapters, whatever its constitutional position may be and whatever its status may be otherwise under international law.

From the point of view of international law it is generally the factual control which matters, irrespective of whether such control has been assumed in a constitutional or in an unconstitutional manner. Furthermore, war is a factual situation which must be taken into account irrespective of the legal right of the parties to resort to it.[194]

Indeed, if a national government were to create or utilize an armed force in violation of constitutional provisions prohibiting armed forces or belligerency,[195] or requiring the consent of other organs of the State concerned, the force would externally still be a national force of that State. The same applies if a State lacks the international 'capacity' to become a belligerent because it is not fully sovereign, or if it is neutralized,[196] or, of course, if it goes to war in violation of an obligation

193. *Contra: Attia:* Les forces armées des Nations Unies en Corée et au Moyen-Orient (Genève 1963) p. 420.

194. The external position of a military force is different from that of treaties, which, as indicated on pp. 450–1, many consider invalid if they have been concluded in violation of constitutional restrictions. In respect of treaties and other purely legal phenomena the question is merely: Does it exist or does it not? In respect of military forces there can be no question of the existence of the force—it does exist and it operates. Accordingly, the questions impose themselves: Who is responsible for the force, and what law applies to it? And they can hardly be solved by declaring the force invalid.

195. See, for example, Article 9 of the Japanese constitution of 3 November 1946, which renounces 'war as a sovereign right of the nation' and which goes on to provide that, in order to accomplish this aim, 'land, sea and air forces, as well as other war potential, will never be maintained. The right of belligerency of the state will not be recognized' (*Peaslee: Constitutions of Nations* (2nd edition, The Hague 1956) p. 512).

Even the provision contained in the last sentence probably does not deprive any Japanese army which might be established of the protection of the humanitarian laws of warfare, and it certainly does not relieve such forces of the duty to comply with such laws. Indeed, Japan on 21 April 1953 ratified the Geneva conventions of 1949.

On the internal plane, the Japanese Supreme Court has unanimously held that Article 9 does not preclude Japan, 'in the exercise of powers inherent in a state to maintain peace and security', from taking 'whatever measures may be necessary for self-defence'. On the scope and implications of this judgment, see Yokota. 'Renunciation of War in the New Japanese Constitution', *Japanese Annual of International Law* IV (1960), pp. 16 et seq., especially pp. 24–26.

196. *Oppenheim: op. cit.,* II §§ 74–76, and, somewhat differently, *Bowett: United Nations Forces* (London 1964) p. 498.

under international law. In none of these cases can the State concerned disclaim international responsibility for the force, nor can other States treat it as a private army, denying the State which created and commands it the right to exercise protection and other international rights in respect of the force. And, of course, neither the force or the Government controlling it, nor the forces opposing it or their Governments, could violate customary or conventional laws of war on the basis that the force was illegally constituted, or that the State did not have the international 'capacity' [197] or right to wage war, except that, in the latter case (lack of right), the State committing aggression can claim the benefit of the laws of war only to the extent which will be indicated in Chapter VI.

In the absence of any special considerations these principles must apply also to the United Nations, as a subject of international law, if it engages in military operations.

(d) Conclusion

In conclusion it may be stated that the constitutional problems involved in the establishment of an international force may form the subject of an internal dispute between Member States or between the Organization and some of its Members. But they do not, in principle, affect the external position of an established Force any more than the position in international law of the army of a State would be affected by the fact that it had been established in violation of its constitution. The issue may be obscured if the international force is employed against a *Member* State, but even in this case will in any event at least the international responsibility for the Force and the applicability of the laws of war remain unchanged.

197. *Oppenheim*, II, § 75 states that 'whenever a State lacking the legal qualification to make war nevertheless actually makes war, it is a belligerent, the contention is real war, and all the rules of International Law respecting warfare apply to it'. In fact, this means that the State has the *capacity*, although it may lack the right.

CHAPTER V

APPLICATION OF THE LAWS OF WAR. GENERAL [1]

I. INTRODUCTION

(a) *General*

It has been explained in the preceding chapters that the United Nations can establish military forces, composed of persons enlisted individually or of contingents provided by Member States, with or without
basis in Articles 42 et seq. of the Charter, and that the Organization
(like the League of Nations) has in fact established five military forces—
in Korea, the Middle East, the Congo, West New Guinea and Cyprus—
all composed of national contingents—without basing itself upon Articles
42 et seq. It has also been pointed out that Forces can be established in
this manner to combat aggression or to perform 'peace-keeping' functions, and that the Organization has done both.[2] Furthermore, it has
been demonstrated that the Organization can assume operational command over such Forces and thereby become internationally responsible
for the Force and entitled to exercise international protection of it and
its members, and that the United Nations in most cases (all except Korea)
actually did so.[3] In this connection it was also pointed out that if the
Organization assumes command, it bears the international responsibility
for the Force, even if the latter should have been established or employed in violation of the constitution of the Organization or of international law, and that any such illegality would also be irrelevant to the ques-

---

1. The following special studies on the question of the application of the laws of
war to United Nations Forces may be cited: Taubenfeld: 'International Armed Forces
and the Law of War', *American Journal of International Law (AJIL)*, XLV (1951)
pp. 671–9; Brandweiner: 'Sind die Vereinten Nationen den Kriegsgesetzen unterworfen?' in *Neue Justiz* (East Berlin) VIII (1954) pp. 225–7; Report of the Committee on
the Study of Legal Problems of the United Nations, *American Society of International
Law, Proceedings*, 1952, pp. 216–20; Baxter: 'The Role of Law in Modern War', *ibid.*,
1953, at pp. 95–98; Bivens: 'Restatement of the Laws of War as Applied to the Armed
Forces of Collective Security Arrangements', *AJIL*, XLVIII (1954) pp. 140–5; Draper:
'The Legal Limitations upon the Employment of Weapons by the United Nations
Force in the Congo', *International and Comparative Law Quarterly*, XII (1963)
pp. 387–413; *Bowett: United Nations Forces* (London 1964) pp. 484–516.
2. *Above*, Chapters II and IV.
3. *Above*, Chapter III.

tion of the application of the laws of war.[4] Finally, it has been pointed out that not only combat forces to fight aggression, but also peace-keeping forces may become involved in hostilities involving acts of warfare, and that both the combat Force in Korea and the peace-keeping Force in the Congo did so.[5]

It remains to consider whether and to what extent such military operations are governed by the customary and conventional laws of war which are valid as between States. This problem, which arose out of the provisions for collective security in Article 16 of the Covenant of the League of Nations and in Articles 42 et seq. of the Charter of the United Nations, was completely ignored at the Diplomatic Conference in Geneva in 1949 for the revision of the Geneva Conventions. Shortly thereafter it was highlighted by the United Nations actions in Korea and, later, in the Congo.

A number of institutions and writers have urged that this problem be studied.[6] Many have even suggested that a special code for United Nations Forces be elaborated.[7] Especially the latter suggestions seem to presuppose that United Nations Forces are not, *de lege lata*, or should not, *de lege ferenda*, be governed in all respects by the same laws of war as national armies.

The remaining chapters of the present study will be devoted to an examination of the problems of whether and in what circumstances and to what extent the general (customary) and conventional laws of war are applicable to United Nations Forces. The discussion will largely be one *de lege lata*. However, on the basis of the interpretation of existing law it may also be possible to evaluate whether there is any room for modifications *de lege ferenda*, and some comments will be made in this respect, too.

The problem arises primarily with regard to United Nations enforcement actions against an aggressor, and the following chapters will there-

4. *Above*, pp. 175–7.
5. *Above*, Chapter II,7.
6. Thus the American Society of International Law, see Bivens in *AJIL*, XLVIII (1954) pp. 140 et seq.; and McNair: *The Development of International Justice* (New York 1954) p. 29. Studies made so far are listed in note 1 *above*.
7. For recent proposals to this effect, see *Attia: Les forces armées des Nations Unies en Corée et au Moyen-Orient* (Genève 1963) p. 274; Yepes in 47 *Annuaire de l'Institut de droit international, Session d'Amsterdam 1957*, I, p. 504; van Asbeck, *ibid.*, 50, *Session de Bruxelles 1963*, I, p. 78 (citing Waldock, pp. 203–4), and Quadri, *ibid.*, p. 110, all as members of the relevant committees of the *Institut* (cf. *below*, Chapter VI,2(a)(ii)). Earlier similar suggestions were made by *Jessup: A Modern Law of Nations* (New York 1949) pp. 210–21; Scelle in *Yearbook of the International Law Commission*, 1949, pp. 51–53; Taubenfeld in *AJIL*, XLV (1951) p. 675; Baxter in *Proceedings of the American Society of International Law*, 1953, p. 97. See also Wright in *AJIL*, XLVII (1953) pp. 375–6.

fore be mainly concerned with such actions. However, some attention will also be paid to the possibility that peace-keeping Forces may become involved in hostilities which call for the application of the laws of war,[8] as they were in the Congo. Otherwise, the examination will take into account both Forces established on the basis of Articles 42 et seq. of the Charter and those which are not based on the applicable Articles of the Charter.[9] Similarly, both Forces under national command and responsibility and those under United Nations command and responsibility will be included in the examination.[10]

Before embarking upon the specific discussion, it is useful to review briefly the general (customary) and conventional laws of war and their sources (b), as well as the relevant practice of the United Nations Forces so far established (2).

(b) General (customary) and conventional laws of war

The laws of war have been developed between States over hundreds of years, first as customary law. Most of this has been codified during the last hundred years into a number of conventions and other international instruments. These have also introduced important new rules, some of which, in turn, have subsequently become customary law.

The most important conventions on the laws of war to-day [11] are the numerous *Hague Conventions* of 1907—notably the Fourth Convention, to which are annexed Regulations Concerning the Laws and Customs of War on Land (the *Hague Regulations*)—and the four *Geneva Conventions* of 1949, concerning the treatment and protection of wounded and sick in land (I) and sea (II) war, of prisoners of war (III) and of civilians (IV), respectively.[12] The Geneva Conventions were adopted under the auspices of the *Comité international de la Croix-Rouge*. They replace the Tenth and parts of the Fourth Hague Convention, as well as the two Geneva Conventions of 1929,[13] although these still remain in force for those very few States which have not acceded to the 1949 Conventions. The Geneva Conventions are by far the most comprehensive; indeed it has been said that 'they probably cover as much as two-thirds of the traditional law of war (as distinguished from the law of

8. See notably *below*, under 2(b) and 4, and Chapter VIII,5 and 13–14.

9. Cf. *above*, Chapter IV,4–5.

10. Cf. *above*, Chapter III.

11. A collection of the texts (in the original languages) of the important conventions and declarations on the laws of war, with lists of ratifications brought up to date as per 1 September 1961, has been published by the Norwegian Ministry for Foreign Affairs under the title: *Overenskomster verdrörende krigens rett som Norge står tilsluttet* (Oslo 1961).

12. *United Nations Treaty Series (UNTS)*, Vol. 75.

13. *League of Nations Treaty Series (LNTS)*, Vol. CXVIII, pp. 303 and 343, and *Overenskomster med fremmede stater* (Oslo) 1932, pp. 327 and 354.

neutrality)'.[14] Moreover, they are those which have obtained the greatest number of accessions. The 1949 Conventions have been ratified by nearly all States of the world,[15] including all the big powers. Indeed, their close-to-universality is unparallelled in international law.

The most recent convention in the field is the detailed *Convention for the Protection of Cultural Property in the Event of Armed Conflict*, adopted at the Hague on 14 May 1954 under the auspices of UNESCO, together with Regulations for the Execution of the Convention and a Protocol.[16]

The conventions as such are of course binding only upon the parties which have acceded to them. However, a great part of the law laid down in the conventions is recognized as binding upon all States, i.e. as part of the *general laws of war*. Thus the International Military Tribunal at Nürnberg stated in its judgment of 1 October 1946 against the major German war criminals that by 1939 the rules laid down in the Fourth Hague Convention 'were recognized by all civilized nations, and were regarded as being declaratory of the laws and customs of war'.[17] The same is probably true of many other of the older conventions on warfare or of parts of them.[18] It is similarly true of the *principles* of the Geneva Conventions, which were part also of the preceding Geneva and Hague Conventions. Indeed, the United States War Crimes Trib-

14. H. Lauterpacht in *BYIL*, XXIX (1952) p. 363.

15. By the end of 1964 103 States were formally bound by the Conventions, 88 following ratification or accession and 15 by a formal declaration of continuity in respect of ratification by the sovereign Power of their territory prior to independence. Other recently independent States are considered by the *Comité international de la Croix-Rouge* as bound for the same reason, even if they have not addressed a declaration of continuity to the Swiss Federal Council. Five States had not ratified and another five had not acceded, but most of these were bound by the 1929 Conventions. (*Implementation and Dissemination of the Geneva Conventions*, Report submitted by the International Committee of the Red Cross to the XXth International Conference of the Red Cross, Vienna October 1965, p. 1.)

16. *UNTS*, Vol. 249, p. 240.

17. *Miscellaneous*, No. 12 (1946), Cmd. 6964, p. 65. See also the similar, but less explicit, statements by the International Military Tribunal for the Far East in 1948 (*Law Reports of Trials of War Criminals* [London 1949] XV, p. 13), and by the United States War Crimes Court at Nürnberg in its judgments in the High Command (*ibid.*, XII, p. 87) and Krupp cases. Municipal courts have made similar statements, see for example *Annual Digest of Public International Law Cases*, 1947, Cases Nos. 121 and 125. In this sense also Brandweiner: 'Sind die Vereinten Nationen den Kriegsgesetzen unterworfen?' in *Neue Justiz* (East Berlin) VIII (1954) p. 225.

18. Brandweiner, *loc. cit.*, p. 225, points out that both the Nürnberg and the High Command judgments demonstrate that the courts did not consider the Fourth Hague Convention as the only convention which expresses customary international law. For a list (in the opinion of the present writer too comprehensive) of treaties in respect of which universal applicability is claimed, see *Guggenheim: Lehrbuch des Völkerrechts*, I (Basel 1948) p. 783. For exceptions, see Röed in *Nordisk Tidsskrift for international Ret og Jus gentium*, 1955, p. 31, citing notably the Sixth Hague Convention.

unal at Nürnberg, in its judgment against the German High Command, cited a number of provisions of the Geneva Conventions as an expression of recognized principles of civilized nations.[19] This was no doubt why the drafters of the Geneva Conventions considered it appropriate to add in the denunciation clause a reminder that any denunciation of the Conventions

> shall have effect only in respect of the denouncing Power. It shall in no way impair the obligations which the Parties to the conflict shall remain bound to fulfil by virtue of the principles of the law of nations, as they result from the usages established among civilized peoples, from the laws of humanity and the dictates of the public conscience.[20]

However, the Geneva Conventions also contain a great number of detailed and procedural provisions, many of which are new or have been recently revised, and which, despite the accession of nearly all States, have not as yet given rise to the establishment of customary law.[21]

2. PRACTICE

(a) *Korea*

The war in Korea broke out at a time when the four Geneva Conventions of 1949 had just been signed, but had not yet been ratified by any of the parties to the conflict.[22] The Geneva Conventions of 1929 had been ratified by most or all of the United Nations Members which pro-

19. Brandweiner, *loc. cit.*, p. 225.

20. First Convention, Article 63; Second Convention, Article 62; Third Convention, Article 142; Fourth Convention, Article 158. The second sentence in fact reproduces the so-called Martens' reservation clause (of the preamble to the Fourth Hague Convention), quoted *below*, p. 253, and explained in *Tidsskrift for rettsvitenskap*, 1945, pp. 113–6.

21. As an example may be cited Article 28, second and third paragraph, of the Prisoners of War Convention. *Guggenheim, loc. cit.*, and *Verdross: Völkerrecht*, 5th edition (Vienna 1964) p. 444, take a different view from that expressed in the text. Brandweiner, *loc. cit.*, p. 225, on the other hand, takes a view similar to that expressed in the text, partly for the same reason as the present writer and partly because not all States are parties. In the latter connexion it may be added that, since he wrote, also the People's Republic of China and both parts of the three divided States (Germany, Korea and Viet-Nam), which did not participate in the Geneva Conference, have acceded, except the Republic of Korea.—See also the United Kingdom statement quoted *below*, at note 30.

22. Only Switzerland and Yugoslavia had ratified before the war broke out. Even during the war, the Conventions were ratified only by three of the States providing contingents: The Philippines, France and South Africa. The main participants did not ratify until well after the armistice (the United States in 1955, the People's Republic of China in 1956, the Korean People's Democratic Republic in 1957. The Republic of Korea had still not ratified at the time of writing.).

vided contingents, but not by the Republic of Korea and the Korean People's Democratic Republic, which were established only after the Second World War.

On the day after the outbreak of the war, the International Committee of the Red Cross cabled North and South Korea proposing that they apply de facto the 'humanitarian principles protecting war victims' contained in the Conventions, referring specially to Article 3, common to all 1949 Conventions, which lays down certain minimum provisions to be applied 'in the case of an armed conflict not of an international character'.[23] The Republic of Korea responded by signing, on 4 July 1950, Article 3 of all four Conventions,[24] while the Korean People's Democratic Republic replied, on 15 July 1950, that it was 'strictly abiding by *principles* of Geneva Conventions in respect to Prisoners of War'.[25] It is thus clear, contrary to what is held by most writers on the subject,[26] that none of the parties undertook to apply the full provisions of any of the Conventions.

The International Committee of the Red Cross also cabled the United States and, in due course, the other States providing contingents to the United Nations Force, asking for information as to their intentions with regard to the application of the Geneva Conventions of 1929,[27] as well as with regard to the *de facto* application of the four Geneva Conventions of 1949.[28] The United States replied on 5 July 1950 that, without regard to the legal applicability of the Conventions to the conflict, it would be 'guided by humanitarian principles of Conventions particularly Article 3 of Geneva Convention 1949'.[29] The United Kingdom replied that, since Korea had not acceded to the Geneva Conventions,

23. *Le Comité international de la Croix-Rouge et le conflit de Corée, Recueil de documents*, I, 26 juin 1950–31 décembre 1951 (Genève 1952) pp. 3–7.

24. *Ibid.*, pp. 12–13, 15–16 and 30, where the text of the signed document is reproduced, introduced by the following note: 'Le 5 juillet 1950, le CICR était informé que le Président de la Corée du sud avait signifié son accord à l'application des Conventions de Genève et que, en témoignage, il avait signé le 4 juillet 1950 à 12 h. 30 le texte de l'article 3, commun aux quatre Conventions de Genève de 1949.'

25. *Ibid.*, p. 16, II, p. 9 (italics added).

26. Cf. Lauterpacht in *BYIL*, XXX (1953) p. 223; Mayda in *AJIL*, XLVII (1953) p. 424; Green in *Archiv des Völkerrechts*, VI (1956/57) p. 419; *Lie: Seven Years for Peace*, p. 340; *Greenspan, op cit.*, pp. 25–26; *Weissberg, op. cit.*, p. 105; *Attia, op. cit.* pp. 261–2; *Bowett, op. cit.*, p. 500. The United Nations Command accepted only the Prisoners of War Convention, see below. The People's Republic of China did not accept the Conventions until the main fighting was over.

27. To which they, but not the other side were parties (indeed, neither of the two Koreas had acceded even to the 1929 Conventions).

28. *Le Comité international de la Croix-Rouge et le conflit de Corée, Recueil de documents*, I, pp. 8–11. No such formal question was included in the cables sent to the People's Republic of China (*ibid.*, pp. 55, 58, 67 and 77) and no undertaking was received (cf. *ibid.*, pp. 60 and 63) from that country until 1952 (*below*, p. 186).

29. *Ibid.*, p. 13.

these were applicable only 'in so far as they are declaratory of accepted principles of international law'.[30] Some of the other United Nations members providing contingents replied in the same sense as the United States [31] or undertook to discharge their obligations under the 1929 conventions and to comply with the principles and spirit of the 1949 Conventions [32] or even to apply the latter Conventions, too, on a *de facto* basis.[33] Later some of these States and certain other United Nations Members providing contingents declared that they would

> observe any undertakings in regard to humane treatment of prisoners of war and sick and wounded entered into on behalf of United Nations forces by the United Nations Commander in Chief.[34]

These declarations, incidentally, are in line with the submission made above, Chapter III,3(b) and 6(c), that all States providing contingents to the United Nations Force became parties to the agreements concluded with the opposing side by the United Nations Command.

The United Nations Command does not appear to have entered into any such formal undertakings in respect of the Conventions. However, before his appointment as United Nations Commander, General Mac-Arthur stated that military and civilian persons of North Korea who were taken into custody would 'be treated in accordance with the humanitarian principles applied by and recognized by civilized nations involved in armed conflict', and that he would expect similar treatment from the other side.[35] In fact the United Nations Command went further, instructing the forces under its command to observe all the provisions of the Geneva Convention of 1949 Relative to the Treatment of Prisoners of War.[36] It also tried to designate a Protecting Power, but this was not accepted, and the whole war was fought without the assistance of Protecting Powers. On the other hand, the United Nations Command rejected the request of the International Committee of the Red Cross that it apply the detailed provisions of the other Geneva Conventions, too. In a telegram of 5 December 1951 to the International Committee of the Red Cross, the United Nations Commander stated:

> My present instructions are to abide by the humanitarian principles of the oneninefournine Geneva Conventions, particularly the common article three. In addition, I have directed the forces under my comd to abide by the detailed

30. *Ibid.*, p.14.
31. The Netherlands, *ibid.*, p. 18, and Luxemburg, *ibid.*, p. 30.
32. Canada, *ibid.*, p. 20, and Australia, *ibid.*, p. 22; cf. New Zealand, *ibid.*, p. 20.
33. Turkey and the Philippines, *ibid.*, pp. 23–4.
34. The United Kingdom, South Africa, Greece, Australia, New Zealand and Canada, *ibid.*, pp. 25–29.
35. Taubenfeld, *loc. cit.*, p. 678.
36. Cf. the Fifth Report of the United Nations Command, *OR SC*, 1950, Supplement for September–December, p. 75 (5 October 1950), and Taubenfeld, *loc. cit.*

provisions of the prisoner of war convention, since I have means at my disposal to assure compliance with this convention by all concerned; and have fully accredited the ICRC delegates accordingly. I do not have the authority to accept, nor the means to assure the accomplishment of responsibilities incumbent on sovereign nations as contained in the detailed provisions of the other Geneva Conventions, and hence I am unable to accredit the delegates to the UNC (United Nations Command) for the purposes outlined in those Conventions. All categories of non-combatants in custody of or under control of military forces under my command, however, will continue to be accorded treatment prescribed by the humanitarian *principles* of the Geneva Conventions.[37]

It thus appears clear that the United Nations Command did not, as generally assumed,[38] accept all four Conventions.

As for the United Nations itself, the Indian Delegation stated in the Security Council on 7 September 1950 that 'we should be justified in taking all possible steps to be sure that the military operations authorized by this Security Council are conducted in accordance with the laws of civilized warfare'.[39] Earlier, on 11 July 1950, the Secretary-General had cabled *both* Korean Governments and, referring to 'gravely disturbing reports of shooting of prisoners and other actions contrary to humanitarian principles', urged them to follow strictly the principles of the Geneva Conventions and to accept the offered services of the International Committee of the Red Cross. On 18 July 1950 the United Nations Commission on Korea unanimously adopted a resolution expressing gratification with the replies of the two Korean governments and hoping that they would take immediate steps to implement the Geneva Conventions 'to the fullest extent'.[40] Later, during the armistice negotiations, the General Assembly, by resolution 610 (VII), affirmed that:

> the release and repatriation of prisoners of war shall be effected in accordance with the Geneva Convention relative to the Treatment of Prisoners of War, dated 12 August 1949, the well-established principles and practice of international law and the relevant provisions of the draft armistice agreement.

37. *Le Comité international de la Croix-Rouge et le conflit de Corée*, I, p. 87 (italics added). See also Taubenfeld in *AJIL*, XLV (1951) p. 678. On the actual compliance with the principles of the Conventions, see note 38.

38. This assumption by many of the writers cited in note 26, *above*, is apparently based on earlier statements by the Unified Command and United States authorities, that all four Conventions were being observed, in addition to 'the applicable portions of the Hague Convention IV of 1907 as well as other pertinent principles of international law', see *Comité international de la Croix-Rouge et le conflit de Corée*, I, pp. 40 and 86, and letter of 5 July 1951 from the United States Mission to the United Nations (text in S/2232 and *Department of State Bulletin*, XXV [1951] p. 189). However, these statements of fact can hardly be regarded as acceptances in accordance with Article 2, common to the four Geneva Conventions, at least not in the light of the subsequent telegram quoted in the text.

39. *OR SC*, 1950, 497th meeting, p. 15, and Taubenfeld, *loc. cit.*, 677.

40. *Korea and the United Nations* (United Nations Publication 1950–I–8) p. 21; *OR GA*, VI, Supplement No. 13, pp. 29 and 47.

The Korean People's Democratic Republic did not even apply all the detailed provisions of the Prisoners of War Convention. Thus it did not, until after the Armistice, permit Red Cross representatives to inspect its prisoner of war camps,[41] as Articles 10 and 124 of the 1949 Convention Relative to the Treatment of Prisoners of War would have required it to do.[42]

At a late stage of the war, on 16 July 1952, after the serious fighting was over, the People's Republic of China informed the Swiss Government that it had decided to 'recognize' the four Geneva Conventions of 1949, subject to certain reservations.[43] The actual ratification did not follow until 28 December 1956.

It was not until the Armistice that both parties agreed to apply the specific provisions of one of the Geneva Conventions, by providing in paragraph 3 of the agreement on the exchange of prisoners of war that 'prisoners of war shall at all times be treated humanely in accordance with the specific provisions of the Geneva Convention, and with the general spirit of that Convention'.[44]

Each party repeatedly accused the other of violations or atrocities.[45] These accusations sometimes referred to the (general) laws of war,[46] sometimes to the Geneva Conventions,[47] and sometimes not to law at all.[48]

41. *Le Comité international de la Croix-Rouge et le conflit de Corée*, I and II, especially II p. 9, cf. Trygve *Lie: In the Cause of Peace* (New York) 1954 p. 340.

42. *UNTS*, Vol. 75, p. 145. The 1929 Convention (*LNTS*, Vol. CXVIII, p. 343) imposed this as a duty only in respect of the Protecting Power, cf. Article 86, not in respect of the International Committee of the Red Cross, cf. Article 88.

43. See also the comments by *Attia: Les forces armées des Nations Unies en Corée et au Moyen-Orient* (Genève 1963) p. 262.

44. Full text in *OR SC*, 1953, Supplement for July-September, p. 22, and in *United States News and World Reports*, 7 August 1953, p. 92.

45. See for example *Le Comité international de la Croix-Rouge et le conflit de Corée*, I, pp. 37 et seq. and 222, and II, pp. 79 et seq.; *Annual Report of the Secretary-General*, 1950–51, pp. 30 and 79, and 1952–53, pp. 21–22, cf. *above*, Chapter III,4(b).

46. The sixth report of the United Nations Command, *OR SC*, 1950, Supplement for October-December, p. 90, and Taubenfeld, *loc. cit.*, p. 679; *Annual Report of the Secretary-General*, 1950–51, pp. 30 (in these cases the accusations that the generally accepted rules of international law had been violated were made by the Soviet Union, see also *OR SC*, 1950, 497th meeting, 7 September 1950, p. 9, where the Soviet delegate cited provisions of the 1907 Hague Conventions as 'in full force to-day, and the armed forces of the United States are obliged to observe them' because it has made no declaration that it does not consider itself bound by them); *ibid.*, 1952–53, p. 22; *Department of State Bulletin*, XXXIII (1955) p. 77.

47. See for example *Le Comité international de la Croix-Rouge et le conflit de Corée*, I, p. 37, cf. p. 50, and p. 222; *Annual Report of the Secretary-General*, 1953–54, p. 14; *Department of State Bulletin*, XXXIII (1955) p. 77. See also *Annual Report of the Secretary-General*, 1952–53, pp. 14 *in initio* and 21 *in fine*.

48. See for example S/2092, *OR SC*, 1951, Supplement for April-June, p. 62.

It is clear from the facts discussed above that neither the Korean People's Democratic Republic, nor the United Nations Command, considered themselves bound under international law to apply the detailed provisions of the Geneva Conventions. The former had not ratified any of these conventions, and in these circumstances the latter was under no legal obligation to apply them, irrespective of whether it was considered legally as a representative of the United Nations, which had not ratified the Conventions, or of a coalition of States most of which had ratified the 1929 Conventions.

On the other hand, no State providing contingents maintained that the United Nations collective action was not governed by the general laws of war.[49] Indeed, both parties declared that they applied the 'principles' of the Geneva Conventions. This must be taken to include such parts of the Conventions as constitute what has been referred to under 1. above as general (or customary) laws of war. Although none of the parties clearly said so, they appear to have considered themselves bound under international law to apply these laws. This would go without saying if both parties fought as national armies, or as a coalition of national armies under a common commander who had not been appointed by, and was not under the orders of, an intergovernmental body, as clearly was the case in respect of the Communist forces in Korea. These also considered the United Nations Force as being a group of national armies, rather than as a United Nations army, during those phases of the war to which the practice reported above applies.[50] However, the United Nations Command and the United States Government did not take this view at the time. Thus the Acting Command Staff Judge Advocate stated in a letter of 6 September 1951 to the Delegation of the International Committee of the Red Cross to South Korea that

> it has been the consistent view of General Headquarters, United Nations Command, that the prisoners of war are United Nations' prisoners and that the United Nations is the Detaining Power.[51]

Earlier, the United States Government had refused to entertain Soviet claims for reparation for violations of the laws of neutrality, on the grounds that the action had been taken by United Nations forces and that the claim should therefore be addressed to the United Nations.[52]

---

49. Cf. also the facts referred to by *Bowett: United Nations Forces* (London 1964) p. 500.

50. *Above*, Chapter III,4(b). Cf. S/2092 *in fine*, OR SC, 1951, Supplement for April–June, p. 67.

51. *Le Comité international de la Croix-Rouge et le conflit de Corée*, I, p. 176. See *below*, note 54, on the different view taken in 1955.

52. *Above*, Chapter III,4(b).

The International Committee of the Red Cross, too, at one stage based its actions upon this assumption.[53]

It thus appears that, at the time (later the United States Government appears to have taken a different view),[54] the acceptance by the United States Government and the United Nations Command of the principles of the Geneva Conventions (i.e. of the general international laws of war)—to the extent that such acceptance reflected a feeling of an obligation under international law—must have been based upon the view that *the United Nations* as an Organization was bound by the general international law of war when carrying out an enforcement action (based *in casu* upon Article 39, but not upon Articles 42 et seq. of the Charter).[55] The declarations made by the Communists *at the time* (later they appear to have taken a different view) [56] could be given no such

53. As pointed out above, the International Committee of the Red Cross in the beginning requested each United Nations Member providing contingents to state its position with regard to the application of the Geneva Conventions. However, after these Member States began referring to any undertaking entered into by the United Nations Command (and the undertakings of the latter did not go so far as the early undertakings of some of the Member States)—the Committee addressed the Secretary-General of the United Nations on the subject, asking the Organization, on the one hand to recognize and accept Red Cross inspection and relief activities, and on the other hand to confirm that the Unified Command considered the four Geneva Conventions as applicable and to recommend to the Command that it recognize such applicability (*Le Comité international de la Croix-Rouge et le conflit de Corée*, I, pp. 82–85). However, the Secretary–General of the United Nations—who earlier, on 11 July 1950, had appealed to *both* Korean Governments to observe the principles of the Geneva Conventions—does not appear to have intervened at this points vis-à-vis the United Nations Command, at least not publicly, cf. *ibid.*, II, p. 16.

54. Thus, in an annex to its letter of 29 March 1955 to the Senate Foreign Relations Committee concerning ratification of the Geneva Conventions the Department of State stated inter alia: 'The fact that the centralized command was established before other U.N. units entered the field, and that few other contingents were of sufficient size to handle prisoners of war, resulted in centralized responsibility for prisoners in the hands of the United Nations Command. The United Nations Command—the military authority in the field—acted as the capturing force. The United States Government as the Unified Command—which exercised political authority over the United Nations Command—acted as the detaining power' (*Department of State Bulletin*, XXX (1955) No. 837, pp. 75 and 76).—Before that time the Communist representatives appeared to have modified their view in the opposite sense, see *below*, note 56.—Cf. also the interpretation given *below*, Chapter VIII,11(c), at note 229, of the United Nations Commander's statement quoted *above*, at note 37.

55. *Above*, Chapter IV,2(b).–Morris Greenspan: *The Modern Law of Land Warfare* (Berkeley and Los Angeles 1959) p. 25, states that 'by the time the armistice of July 27, 1953, had suspended hostilities in the Korean conflict, it was apparent that both sides had clearly recognized that a United Nations enforcement action, like other wars of an international nature, must be governed by the laws of war, and both sides had adduced such rules in matters relating to the conduct of the conflict'.

56. During the armistice negotiations and the subsequent Political Conference at Geneva in 1954, the Communist representatives treated or spoke of the United Nations

interpretation, since they were merely based upon the traditional concept of national armies. And this appears to have been the correct *legal*
view of the situation, as has been explained above.[57] Thus, while the
practice in Korea appears to demonstrate that one of the parties considered that the United Nations as an Organization was bound by the
general laws of war, and thus sets a precedent for this from a 'subjective'
point of view, from an *objective* point of view it sets a precedent only
with respect to the application of the laws of war to a United Nations
Force under national command and responsibility, i.e. for the binding
nature of these laws upon the participating States rather than upon the
United Nations as an Organization.

(b) *The peace-keeping Forces. Congo*

(i) The legal position is entirely different in the case of the League of
Nations police force in the Saar and the United Nations peace-keeping
Forces in the Middle East (UNEF), the Congo (ONUC), West New Guinea (UNSF) and Cyprus (UNFICYP). As has been explained, operational control over, and international responsibility for, these Forces
vests in the United Nations, not in the States providing contingents.[58]
Thus it is the United Nations which must ensure the application of the
laws of war and which is internationally responsible for violations thereof, despite the fact that disciplinary and criminal sanctions against individual members of the Forces are exercised by the States providing the
contingents, with respect to violations of the laws of war as with respect
to other offences. These Forces therefore squarely raise the question of
whether the United Nations as an Organization has the rights and
duties under the laws of war.

However, the Forces referred to above were all set up to perform

---

as a party to the conflict and as 'a belligerent', cf. *International Conciliation*, No. 494,
p. 182, and the report on the Korean Political Conference, *OR GA*, IX, Annexes,
A.i. 17, pp. 3–4. Even earlier, on 24 December 1951, the Commanders of the North
Korean and the Chinese forces addressed the United Nations Commander as 'Com-
mandant suprême de l'armée de l'ONU', see *Le Comité international de la Croix-
Rouge et le conflit de Corée*, I, p. 9.

57. Chapter III. In this sense also *Attia: op. cit.*, p. 27, and Baxter in *BYIL*, XXIX
(1952) pp. 336–7 and 316, and in *Proceedings of the American Society of International
Law*, 1953, p. 97. A contrary view appears to be taken by *Weissberg: The International
Status of the United Nations* (New York 1961) pp. 85 et seq. and 204–6, and perhaps
by Taubenfeld, in *AJIL* XIV (1951), p. 675. Cf. also *Bowett: United Nations Forces*
(London 1964) who states that 'all interested parties recognized the belligerent status
of the Organization'.

58. *Above*, Chapter III, esp. pp. 118–9; cf. the Secretary-General's Summary Study
of UNEF, pars. 168 and 171, *OR GA*, XIII, A.i. 65, p. 30. With regard to international
protection of the members of the Force, one may cite—in addition to the earlier practice
related *above*, Chapter III,5(a), pp. 112–6—the exchange of telegrams between President Tchombe and the Norwegian Prime Minister quoted *below*, Chapter VII,3.

peace-keeping functions and were not really intended to undertake genuine military operations. They were to fire only in self-defence.[59] Nevertheless, it could not be foreseen whether they could avoid military encounters in all circumstances which might arise. The Forces were therefore also given instructions covering this eventuality. The Regulations enacted by the Secretary-General for the Forces in the Middle East, Congo and Cyprus provide:

> The Force shall observe [and respect] the principles and spirit of the general international Conventions applicable to the conduct of military personnel.[60]

These provisions, like the declarations which had been made by the main parties in the Korean war, may be seen as a recognition of the applicability of the *general* (or customary) international laws of war, but not of those detailed provisions of the relevant conventions which do not as yet constitute customary international law. The Regulations are sometimes read as implying also the latter.[61] However, this does not follow from the words, nor did the United Nations intend or interpret them in this sense.

(ii) In 1956, after the establishment of UNEF, the International Committee of the Red Cross wrote to the United Nations proposing that the Force receive instructions that it comply with *the Geneva Conventions* if the circumstances should so require. The Committee pointed out, that, while the States providing contingents were all bound by the 1949 or the earlier Conventions, it appeared that the international police forces were directly dependent upon the United Nations, which was not, as an Organization, a party to the Conventions. After the establishment of the United Nations Force in the Congo, and again before the establishment of the Force in Cyprus, the Committee addressed new letters to the United Nations. In these it also offered its services.

The United Nations in reply gave assurances that the Forces had been or would be instructed to observe the principles and the spirit of the general international conventions concerning the behaviour of military personnel, citing UNEF Regulation 44 and the proposed similar Regulations for the other Forces. The Organization also accepted the offer of the Committee to provide the Forces with booklets summarizing the provisions of the Conventions.[62] However, the Organization did not undertake to comply with the detailed provisions of the Conventions, although it explicitly recognized that the importance of the Conventions, if the

59. *Above*, Chapter II,6–9.
60. UNEF Regulation 44, ONUC Regulation 43 and UNFICYP Regulation 40. Citations *above*, Chapter II, notes 78, 182 and 280, respectively. The two words in square brackets occur only in the Cyprus Regulation.
61. Thus Evensen in *Internasjonal politikk* (Oslo) 1963 p. 85.
62. *Comité International de la Croix-Rouge: Rapport d'ativité*, 1961, p. 49.

occasion arose, would be no less with regard to UNEF than with regard to national parties.[63] In particular the United Nations did not give effect to the proposal of the International Committee of the Red Cross that the Organization make a public and official declaration in which it would engage itself to apply (*respecter*) the Geneva Conventions in all circumstances.

In these circumstances the International Committee of the Red Cross on 10 November 1961 addressed a memorandum 'to Governments of States party to the Geneva Conventions and members of the United Nations Organization'. The most important parts of the memorandum, as translated by the International Committee, read as follows:

> Since 1956, the International Committee has drawn the attention of the Secretary-General of the United Nations to the necessity of assuring the application of the Geneva Conventions by the Emergency Forces which have been placed at their disposal. It made further representations when the United Nations Organization intervened in the Congo.
>
> In reply to these communications, the International Committee of the Red Cross received assurances that the United Nations Organization would respect the principles of the international humanitarian Conventions and that instructions to that effect had been given to the troops placed under its command. It was pleased to place these assurances on record.
>
> However, in view of the overwhelming importance of the interests involved, the International Committee judges it to be necessary that the matter should be very seriously considered, not only by the United Nations Organization, but also by each of the States bound by the Geneva Conventions.
>
> In fact, the United Nations Organization is not, as such, party to the Geneva Conventions. Consequently, each State is personally responsible for the application of these Conventions, when supplying a contingent to the United Nations.
>
> It would therefore be highly desirable that such contingents receive, before leaving their own countries, instructions to conform to the provisions of the Geneva Conventions in the event of their finding themselves having to use force. It seems to us no less desirable that the troops receive, in their own countries, appropriate instruction so that they may acquire a sufficient knowledge of these Conventions. This instruction could quite easily be included within the framework of study which the States, by virtue of Article 47/48/127/144 of the Geneva Conventions, have pledged themselves to incorporate in their programmes of military and, if possible, civilian instruction in such a manner that the principles are made known generally to their armed forces and to the civilian population.
>
> Finally, the International Committee wishes to remind States, which might supply contingents to an Emergency Force of the United Nations, that under the terms of Article I common to the four Geneva Conventions, the High Contracting Parties are bound not only to respect, but also 'to have respected' the provisions of these Conventions. It therefore expresses the hope that they will, each one, in

---

63. Some of these letters and those of the International Committee of the Red Cross have been summarized or quoted in *Comité international de la Croix-Rouge, Notes d'information;* see notably No. 2 of 29 September 1961, p. 2; No. 4 of 31 October 1961, p. 2; and No. 7 of 21 December 1961, p. 3; and document DD 2/1 (March 1963) of the Centenary Congress of the International Red Cross.

case of necessity, use their influence to ensure that the provisions of humanitarian law are applied by all contingents engaged as well as by the United Command.[64]

Thus the International Committee of the Red Cross—although it continued to consider, in accordance with its first letter to the United Nations in 1956, that the United Nations was internationally responsible for its Force's compliance with the humanitarian laws of war—appears to have taken the position that, since the United Nations had not acceded to the Geneva Conventions, each contracting party to these Conventions would remain responsible for their application by any contingents they might provide for the United Nations, and even that they had a moral obligation to do what they could to ensure such application by the other contingents, too.

The *Republic of Congo* (Léopoldville) was considered bound by the 1949 Geneva Conventions as a successor to Belgium, which had ratified them in 1952. This was confirmed by the Congolese Government in a letter of 24 February 1961 to the Swiss Federal Council.

The International Committee of the Red Cross made no proposal to the authorities in *Katanga* that they accept the Geneva Conventions. However, these authorities, like the other authorities involved, at an early stage, before the fighting between United Nations and Katangese forces, received an appeal from the *Committee* to respect the humanitarian principles generally recognized. In reply M. Tchombe affirmed his adherence to these principles.[65]

(iii) The League of Nations Force in the Saar and the United Nations Forces in the Middle East, West New Guinea and Cyprus have so far lived up to expectations and avoided becoming involved in *military operations* of a nature which would call for the application of the laws of war.[66] Some incidents of shooting at and/or by the Force had occurred, but casualties were few or none,[67] except that early in Cyprus the United Nations Force suffered several casualties and on several occasions had to return the fire and even to disarm the opposing group.[68]

However, the Force in the Congo became involved in fighting with another organized Force. This was referred to by some governments as

---

64. *Comité international de la Croix-Rouge, Notes d'information*, No. 6, 1 December 1961, pp. 3–4.

65. Exchange of telegrams with the *Comité international de la Croix-Rouge* in February 1961, cf. *Revue internationale de la Croix-Rouge*, March 1961, p. 140.

66. Cf. *below*, under 4(a).

67. On UNEF, see above, Chapter II,7, at note 209, and the Secretary-General's Summary Study on UNEF, par. 149, *OR GA*, XIII, A.i. 65, p. 27. On West New Guinea, see *Annual Report of the Secretary-General*, 1962–63, p. 37, quoted *above*, pp. 78–79.

68. Report by the Secretary-General to the Security Council on the United Nations Operation in Cyprus for the Period 26 April to 8 June 1964, S/5764, paras. 7–13.

'operations of war' conducted by the United Nations.[69] These incidents, as has been explained, involved the use of artillery, armoured cars, river boats and fighter and bomber planes, and led to the infliction of casualties, the capture of prisoners and equipment, forced withdrawals and cease-fire agreements.[70] These operations called for the application of the laws of war and gave rise to *accusations from both sides of violations* of these laws. Thus during two series of battles in Katanga in September and December 1961, each side accused the other inter alia of shooting at civilians, hospitals and cars marked with the Red Cross, as well as of abuse of the Red Cross emblem. Reciprocal accusations of maltreatment and killing of prisoners and civilians were also made.

In his report on developments in Elisabethville from 8 through 14 December 1961, the Officer-in-Charge of the United Nations Operation in the Congo stated:

> The Katanga forces consistently used the presence of civilians to shield their activities, while the United Nations forces, to their severe military disadvantage, tried their best to avoid endangering civilian lives and property. The Katangese placed their mortars near hospitals, schools, consulates and private houses. On the evening of December 10, Katangese armored cars used the international institute in the stadium area of northern Elisabethville as a base for an attack on United Nations positions. About 750 refugees had been gathered in the institute under the auspices of the Red Cross. One armored car was destroyed while it was attacking, but the United Nations forces could not engage the others because they returned to the shelter of the institute. The same area continued thereafter to be used for mortar and automatic weapon attacks on ONUC troops.
>
> The Katanga forces regularly abused the Red Cross symbol, *contrary to the law of war*. Many cases were reported. One of them was witnessed on December 8 by Mr. Ivan Smith, when a car bearing a Red Cross flag gave the signal for firing on the convoy in which he was riding back from the airfield. In another case, a Red Cross official saw a car bearing a large Red Cross which was filled with uniformed gendarmes carrying weapons. Though the number of legitimate Red Cross vehicles in Elisabethville was under 10, ONUC observers counted more than 50 cars bearing painted red crosses or red cross flags. On December 10 Mr. Olivet, the principal representative of the International Committee of the Red Cross in Elisabethville, asked Radio Katanga to broadcast hourly messages warning against misuse of the Red Cross.[71]

Charges were also made concerning maltreatment of prisoners. Thus the Officer-in-Charge, in his report on the last United Nations military action in Katanga in December 1962, reported an incident where the

---

69. S/5025, A II, 15 December 1961, and S/5035, IV, 19 December 1961 (*OR SC*, 1961, Supplement for October–December, pp. 191 et seq. and 210). The authorities in Katanga at one point, before the hostilities of August and December 1961, even proclaimed that they considered themselves in a 'state of war' with the United Nations, see S/4750, par. 11, *OR SC*, 1961, Supplement for January–March, p. 164.

70. Citations *above*, Chapter II,7, especially note 226.

71. *United Nations Review*, IX, No. 1 (January 1962) p. 52. Italics added.

Katangese troops fired at and brought down an ONUC helicopter, and added:

> At the time of the forced landing, one Indian officer in the aircraft, Lieuten-
> ant S. S. Kang, was gravely wounded by the bullets which brought it down. He
> died of his wounds, because the Katangese took hours to bring him to a hospital,
> which they did only after repeated demands had been made by the United Nations
> representative. The remaining five ONUC personnel on board—an Indian captain
> and two sergeants, one Norwegian lieutenant and one Swedish corporal—were
> savagely beaten by the Katangese and taken to gaol before being returned to
> ONUC custody. [71a]

Charges were also made against the United Nations troops. Thus the Belgian Government, in three cables to the Secretary-General of 8 and 9 december 1961, referred to 'the death of several Belgian civilians, kill-ed by United Nations forces in the course of the operations' and urged the Secretary-General 'to issue immediate instructions that United Na-tions troops should scrupulously respect the obligations of the Geneva Convention and take all necessary measures to safeguard the lives and property of the civilian population, as unfortunately does not appear to be the case at present'. The Belgian Government made the following spe-cific charges:

> (1) On several occasions, civilians could not be removed from areas of military
> operations, despite urgent request; in particular, the urgent representations of the
> delegate of the International Red Cross for the evacuation of persons trapped
> in the new hospital met with no reponse.
> (2) Hospitals have been hit, not by isolated shells, but by mortar fire appar-
> ently aimed at them, resulting in the wounding of hospital staff and in heavy
> damage and leading to protests by M. Olivet, delegate of the International Red
> Cross.
> (3) Civilians not taking part in any military operation have been wounded
> or even killed in their homes by mortar and machine-gun fire.

The United Nations refuted these charges, stating (1) that it never re-fused to evacuate civilians when it was physically possible and safe to do so, (2) that one of the 'hospitals' shelled was no hospital and had a mer-cenary observation post on its roof and that the other hospital had been hit by some shells aimed at the main base and headquarters of the Ka-tangese Gendarmerie 200 meters away, and (3) that much of the mortar firing directed on ONUC Headquarters by the Katangese gendarmes had gone wide in the surrounding residential area and that 'non-Congo-lese mercenaries and the Katangese gendarmes acting under their orders ... often use the civilian population as a shield during their attacks against ONUC troops'. [72]

71a. OR SC, 1963, Suppl. for January-March, pp. 9–10.

72. S/5025, 15 December 1961. See also S/5035, 19 December 1961, reproducing an exchange of telegrams between the Government of the Republic of the Congo (Brazza-

It will be noted from the quotations above that the United Nations referred to 'the law of war', whereas the Belgian Government referred to 'the obligations of the Geneva Convention'. As for the acts referred to in the reciprocal accusations, they would probably, had they been confirmed, constitute violations not merely of the specific conventional provisions, but also of the general (customary) laws of war.

Similar accusations against the United Nations troops were also made in the press and elsewhere by non-governmental sources, particularly by Belgians in Katanga and Belgium. These accusations, too, referred to the Geneva Conventions.[73]

During the fighting in Elisabethville in December 1961, M. Olivet, the principal representative in that city of the *Comité international de la Croix-Rouge,* and two other Red Cross personnel who rode with him in a marked Red Cross ambulance, were found killed.[74] An independent commission of enquiry was appointed by agreement between the United Nations and the *Comité.* It was composed of a Swedish judge, the Director of the medico-legal institute at Vienna and a Swiss Army officer. The Commission went to Elisabethville two months after the event. In view of conflicting evidence it was unable to establish all the facts, including the route the ambulance had been travelling to the spot where it was found and the military situation prevailing in the area at the time. However, the Comission was able to establish that the bullets which had killed the three victims were not of the type used by the Katangese forces at the time. Accordingly, the United Nations, without admitting any legal or financial obligation, paid to the *Comité international de la Croix-Rouge* a '*somme forfaitaire*' for the injury it had suffered. The *Comité* distributed the entire sum among the dependants of the victims.[75]

Complaints were also made that the members of the United Nations Forces concerned were not brought to trial, and proposals were made to the *Comité international de la Croix-Rouge* for the establishment of a

---

ville) and the Secretary-General of the United Nations. These documents may be found in *OR SC,* 1961, Supplement for October–December, pp. 190 and 207.—Reference may also be made to *OR SC,* 1963, Suppl. for January–March, p. 19.

73. See, notably, a booklet entitled '46 hommes en colère, les 46 médicins d'Elisabethville déconcent les violations par l'ONU au Katanga de sa propre Chartre, de la Déclaration universelle des droits de l'homme, des Conventions de Genève' published in Brussels on 12 April 1964. An English translation entitled '46 Angry Men' was published in Brussels on 28 August 1962.—Accusations were also distributed by INDAF (*Informations et Documentations Africaines*) Brussels 6.

74. See, inter alia, *Comité international de la Croix-Rouge, Rapport d'activité,* 1961, pp. 12–14.

75. Letter of 23 October 1962 from the *Comité international* to M. A. Vroonen, husband of one of the victims, published, together with the latters' reply, in *Essor du Katanga,* 13 November 1962.

'Commission d'enquête internationale impartiale' and a 'Tribunal suprême permanent'.[76]

(iv) As already indicated, the *Comité international de la Croix-Rouge* maintained representatives in the Congo (and later on Cyprus) who intervened on a number of occasions in order to secure observance of the humanitarian principles laid down in the Geneva Conventions.[77] In particular they sought to protect wounded and to evacuate these and civilians from the battle zones.[78] The *Comité* also offered its services and intervened directly with the parties where appropriate. Thus it cabled the President of the Congo, reminding him that by acceding to the Geneva Conventions his Government had undertaken to observe its provisions and that it should therefore prevent such atrocities as had been committed in various parts of the country.[79] Direct appeals, referring to the Geneva Conventions merely as generally accepted norms of humane treatment, were also made to the Katangese authorities.[80] The representatives of the *Comité* were authorized to and did regularly visit the prisoners detained by the United Nations and the Katangese authorities, and also negotiated their release.[81] Reports on visits to prisoners taken during the hostilities between United Nations and Katangese forces were communicated both to the United Nations and to the Katangese authorities. In addition, the reports were sent to the State which had provided the contingent to which the prisoner belonged. In the case of prisoners held by the United Nations troops, the *Comité* referred to the Organization as the 'Detaining Power'.—The *Comité* also took measures, in co-operation with the United Nations and the Congolese authorities to make the members of the United Nations and Congolese forces acquainted with the contents of the Geneva Conventions.[82]

(v) The *conclusion* may be drawn from the practice related above that the United Nations has accepted the applicability of the general (customary) laws of war to its own forces and to those of its adversaries in military operations in which their peace-keeping forces might become involved, and that it felt that external responsibility, in this respect, international as well as civil, vested in the Organization, not in the States

76. Letter of 10 February 1962 from the 46 civilian doctors of Elisabethville to the *Comité international de la Croix-Rouge*. The *Comité* did not consider itself competent to do this and therefore never did it. But the *UN* took some action, see *below*, p. 398.

77. See notably *Comité international de la Croix-Rouge: Rapport d'activité, 1961*, pp. 9–15 and 48–49.

78. See, inter alia, *Comité international de la Croix-Rouge, Notes d'information*, No. 4, 31 October 1961, p. 2; and *ibid.*, No. 7, 21 December 1961, pp. 1 and 9.

79. *Comité international de la Croix-Rouge, Notes d'information*, No. 6, 1 December 1961, p. 2.

80. *Ibid.*, No. 7, 21 December 1961, p. 2.

81. See notably *Comité international de la Croix-Rouge, Rapport d'activité 1961*, pp. 10–11.

82. *Ibid.*, No. 6, 1 December 1961, pp. 3–4; No. 7, 21 December 1961, p. 3.

providing contingents.[83] However, the Organization did not consider itself bound by the detailed provisions of the Geneva Conventions, despite the fact that these had been ratified by most [84] of the States providing contingents and by some of the parties to the conflict.[85] Other parties tended rather to cite the Geneva *Conventions,* and in one case even in terms which would indicate that they considered the United Nations Force bound to observe their provisions.

3. THE PRINCIPLE OF APPLICABILITY OF THE LAWS OF WAR TO UNITED NATIONS ENFORCEMENT ACTIONS

(a) *General. Analogy to war between States*

So far, no special rules governing the conduct of military operations in the course of a United Nations enforcement action have been established. The conventions on warfare ignore the problem.[86] Strangely enough, this is true even of the 1949 Geneva Conventions.[87] And no special conventions have been concluded concerning the conduct of United Nations actions. Nor has the United Nations enacted any special or detailed regulations for its Forces. It has simply instructed them to apply the general (customary) laws of war in the humanitarian field and—in Korea, but not in the Congo—also one of the four Geneva Conventions. The opposing side, too, has demonstrated that it expected the United Nations Forces to abide by the laws of war in the humanitarian field, just as it has considered these laws applicable to itself.[88] The practice which has occurred so far in Korea and the Congo probably does not suffice to constitute customary international law. However, it does consistently point to the application of the regular laws of war in the humanitarian field, as developed between States, to both parties during a United Nations enforcement (resistance of aggression) or peace keeping action when organized hostilities develop.

When the United Nations intervenes to resist aggression, there will

83. See also the practice reported *above,* Chapter III,4(a) and 5(a).

84. An important exception was Canada, which, however, was bound by the 1929 Conventions.

85. France, Israel and Egypt had ratified the 1949 Conventions before the Suez war. The United Kingdom did not ratify the 1949 Convention until afterwards, but made a declaration of application at the beginning of the operations in accordance with Article 2 common to the four Conventions. The Republic of the Congo (Léopoldville) was considered bound by the 1949 Conventions as a successor to Belgium, see *above,* under (ii).

86. See, however, the resolution adopted by the Hague Conference on the protection of cultural property, quoted and discussed *below,* Chapter VII,10(b).

87. See *below,* p. 346.

88. *Above,* under 2(a) and (b).

normally be a regular war in progress between the aggressor and the victim of the aggression, both of whom will continue to fight after the United Nations intervenes. The United Nations action in Korea was itself in certain cases also referred to as 'war' by the participating governments, although more frequently it was not.[89] In their interpretation of national statutes, municipal courts and arbitration tribunals appear to have considered the action in Korea as 'war' as frequently as the converse.[90] However, for international purposes the general tendency appears to be not to refer to a United Nations enforcement action as 'war',[91] even if the action, like that in Korea, is carried out under national command.[92] But even if it is inappropriate to consider a United

89. President Truman on 29 June 1950 told his press conference that the United States was not at war, but was executing a United Nations police action. However, on 19 March 1953 President Eisenhower told his press conference that a war, not a police action, was being fought in Korea. (Greenspan: *The Modern Law of Land Warfare*, Berkely and Los Angeles 1959, p. 25, citing inter alia the *New York Times* for 30 June 1950 and 20 Mach 1953.) Prime Minister Eden stated that 'we are not engaged in a war'. Other United Kingdom Government spokesmen consistently avoided speaking of the action as 'war'. (See the statements cited by Green in *International Law Quarterly*, IV [1951] p. 463, by H. Lauterpacht in *BYIL*, XXX [1953] p. 222, note, and by *Weissberg: The International Status of the United Nations* [New York 1961] pp. 103–4.) See, on the other hand, the Australian Government statement quoted in the text *below*, at note 95.

90. See the cases reported and the general discussion by Green: 'The Nature of the "war" in Korea' in *International Law Quarterly*, IV (1951) pp. 462–7 and in *Archiv des Völkerrechts*, VI (1956–57) pp. 419–24; by Brandon: 'Is the Korean conflict "war"?' in *International Law Quarterly*, II (1953) pp. 316–19; by H. Lauterpacht in *BYIL*, XXX (1953) pp. 221–2; by Bishop in *AJIL*, XLVI (1952) p. 165, note, and in *AJIL* XLVIII (1954) pp. 155–8; by *Greenspan, loc. cit.;* and by *Weissberg, op. cit.,* p. 104.

It should be noted that decisions by municipal courts of Members of the United Nations denying a state of war do not necessarily imply a holding that the action in general did not constitute war. They might merely imply that the particular Member State concerned was not a party to any such war. This is particularly true in respect of those States which provided only limited contingents, see notably the Australian Communist Party Dissolution case quoted by Green in *International Law Quarterly*, IV (1951) p. 467. See *above*, Chapter III,6(c), pp. 122–3, on the general question of which of the States providing contingents were parties to the war.

91. In this sense Hsu Mo in *The Grotius Society, Transactions for the Year 1949*, p. 10 and van Asbeck in 47 *Annuaire de l'Institut de droit international*, Session de Bruxelles 1963, I, p. 78. *Contra:* Bindschedler in 50 *Annuaire de l'Institut de droit international*, Session de Bruxelles 1963, II, p. 315.

92. In this sense H. Lauterpacht in *BYIL*, XXX (1953) p. 221 and in *Oppenheim, International Law*, II, § 65, and Baxter in *BYIL*, XXIX (1952) p. 359. Cf. Johnson in *Nordisk Tidsskrift for international Ret*, XXVI (1956) p. 31, and *Kunz: Kriegsrecht und Neutralitätsrecht* (Wien 1935) p. 17, who considers the common action under Article 16 of the Covenant to be 'international execution' from the point of view of legal theory. See also the statements by a legal committee of the League quoted *below*, at note 114, and by the Committee on Legal Problems of the United Nations of the American Society of International Law, in the *Proceedings* of that Society for 1952, p. 217.

Nations enforcement action as 'war' in a *formal* or traditional sense,[93] it must still be considered as war in a *material* sense,[94] since in fact it exhibits the characteristics of a war. This, at least, must have been the view of the Australian Government when it stated to an Australian court, for the purpose of a dispute of municipal law relating to the action in Korea:

> The Government has sent land, sea and air forces to Korea to assist in taking military measures in order to restore international peace and security in Korea as provided in Chapter 7 of the Charter of the United Nations. The Australian forces are engaged in active hostilities and have suffered intensive casualties. That Australia is at war de facto is clear. Whether or not Australia is at war de jure depends on the interpretation of the Charter as applied in the circumstances.[95]

Even an action conducted under the command of the United Nations itself may be considered as war in a material sense if it in fact exhibits the characteristics of a war.[96] Indeed, the Secretary-General of the United Nations has stated, in June 1963, that the application of military sanctions put bluntly is war.[97]

However, it is not the terminology which determines the field of applicability of the laws of war.[98] Whether the term 'war' is defined broadly or narrowly, it is a fact that the *laws* of war also apply to armed conflicts between States where no declaration of war has been made or where the state of war is not recognized by both parties.[99] They also

93. *Oppenheim: International Law*, II, § 54, defines war as 'a contention between two or more States through their armed forces, for the purpose of overpowering each other and imposing such conditions of peace as the victor pleases'.

94. In this sense also *Guggenheim: Lehrbuch des Völkerrechts, II (Basel 1951)* p. 780 and *Bowett: United Nations Forces* (London 1964) p. 500. On this distinction in general, see *Siotis: Le droit de la guerre et les conflits armés d'un caractère non-international* (Paris 1958) pp. 20–21, with citations; *Guggenheim, op. cit.*, II, pp. 779 et seq.; *Hyde: International Law* (Boston 1947) III, p. 1692; *Kotzsch: The Concept of War in Contemporaty History and International Law* (Geneva 1956) p. 56, cf. pp. 288–93. Cf. also *Oppenheim, op. cit.*, II, § 96, and Wright in *AJIL,* XLVII (1953) p. 365.

95. For complete quotation and context, see Green in *International Law Quarterly*, IV (1951) p. 465. He states (p. 468, cf. p. 466) that 'from the point of view of international law a war is being fought in Korea whether the parties to it describe it as a de facto or a de jure war'.

96. *Greenspan: The Modern Law of Land Warfare* (Berkeley and Los Angeles 1959) p. 24, terms United Nations actions under Article 42 of the Charter 'war' without even specifying whether in a formal or a material sense. Cf. also *Guggenheim, loc. cit.*, speaking of enforcement measures in general.

97. Speech at Harvard University 13 June 1963, *Toward World Peace, Addresses and Public Statements* 1959–63 (New York 1964) at p. 274.

98. Cf. H. Lauterpacht, *loc. cit.*, p. 221.

99. As for treaty law, Prime Minister Eden declared in the House of Commons, after the British-French intervention in the Israeli-Egyptian war of 1956, that 'there was also no declaration of war in the Korean conflict, but the Geneva Convention does

apply to armed conflicts between States and other independent bodies which are treated as subjects of international law, whether generally or in this particular respect only.[100] Thus, when an insurrection turns into an armed conflict exhibiting the characteristics of a real war and involving two armies under the direction of organized civilian authorities, the insurgents are treated as belligerents and the laws of war are applied by and to both parties.[101] Even governments which have not obtained control over any territory, but have been established in exile, with the consent and recognition of the government of the host country, to fight for the overthrow of the 'legal' government or for the establishment of a new State or the re-establishment of a State which has been extinguished, have been considered as belligerents, with belligerent rights and duties under the laws of war,[102] although certain writers deny the validity of this.[103] The Geneva Conventions of 1949 provide that they ap-

apply to any state of armed conflict' (*Parliamentary Debates, Fifth Series*, Vol. 558, col. 1643, cf. cols. 1645, 1647 and 1649, House of Commons' Official Report, Session 1955–56). Article 2 common to the four Geneva Conventions of 1949 provides that the Conventions 'shall apply to all cases of declared war or of any other armed conflict which may arise between two or more of the High Contracting Parties, even if the state of war is not recognised by one of them.' The 1954 Hague Conference decided to add the words 'or more' after 'one' in the corresponding article (18) of the Convention for the Protection of Cultural Property in the Event of Armed Conflict, see the *Records* of the Conference (The Hague 1961) p. 385.

It has already been pointed out *above*, Chapter IV, 5(c), that the laws of war apply even if the State lacks the 'capacity' and the right under its constitution or under international law to go to war.

100. On the similar question in respect of the Geneva Conventions, see *below*, Chapter VIII,10(a). On the *capacity* to wage war, see *Guggenheim, op cit.*, II, pp. 786–8, and *above*, pp. 176–7, with note 197, and *below*, p. 348, note 117.

101. On the question whether recognition is required, see *below*, Chapter VII,1.

102. See *below*, Chapter VII, 1. The inter-allied agreements and declarations of 12 June and 24 September 1941, of 1 and 13 January and 17 December 1942 and of 5 January 1943 concerning inter alia the war aims, war crimes and the invalidity of property transfers in occupied territories, were also signed by the Czechoslovak Government in exile and, except for the declaration of 1 January 1942, by the French National Committee. And Germany treated captured members of the Free French Forces as prisoners of war, despite a contrary provision in the armistice agreement of 1940, see *Les Conventions de Genève du 12 Août 1949, Commentaire*, III (Genève 1958) pp. 69–70.

On the recognition of the Czechoslovak Government in exile, see *Guggenheim: Lehrbuch des Völkerrechts*, I (Basel 1948) p. 201, note 100, and *Hyde: International Law*, I, (2nd edition, Boston 1947) p. 30, cf. pp. 154–5. On the general problem of the status of governments in exile, see *Mattern: Die Exilregierung* (Tübingen 1953) pp. 29 et seq., and Brandweiner: 'Zur Lehre von den Exilregierungen' in *Österreichische Zeitschrift für öffentliches Recht*, III (1950) pp. 497–519. As pointed out by these and other writers, the French National Committee and the Free French Forces, which obtained control over French overseas territories, may be considered as regular insurgents against the Vichy Government. However, they also fought the Axis powers.

103. Brandweiner, *loc. cit.* preceding note, pp. 510–2 (with citations) denies that

ply to 'members of regular armed forces who profess allegiance to a Government *or an authority* not recognized by the Detaining Power'.[104] Indeed, it is submitted that the laws of war in the narrow sense—including the military and humanitarian rules, but not necessarily those relating to economic warfare and neutrality [105]—apply to all types of armed conflict of an international character, i.e. to any armed conflict between subjects of international law [106] which has the factual characteristics of war, even if it does not constitute 'war' in a formal, or traditional, sense.[107] This must be true, not only of such types of international armed conflicts as have occurred in the past and where the occasion for the application of the laws of war has already arisen, but also of other types of international armed conflict, if and to the extent that they present similar factual characteristics, whether or not one wishes to refer to these as 'war'. The need to prevent unnecessary suffering and destruction, which is the purpose of the laws of war, is as strong in one case as in the other. The fact that collective action of the United Nations against an aggressor had not 'been contemplated at the time the laws of war were in process of formation' [108] cannot be decisive, as long as there is no practice or other special basis in support of a different law for such actions.

Thus, as long as no special law has been laid down, the general laws of war [109] must be applicable, directly or by analogy, to a United Na-

such new governments in exile can become subjects of international law even through recognition, and cites Kunz, Anzilotti and *Hyde* (now *op. cit.*, pp. 154–5, but see p. 30, note) in support of this view. He also denies (p. 518) that the laws of war apply to the forces of such a government if it operates on its own. According to him these laws apply only if the forces are incorporated in the forces of another belligerent power [and then presumably under the protection and responsibility of that power]. Brandweiner takes a constitutive view of recognition in other respects, see for example *loc. cit.*, p. 511.

104. Article 13(3) common to the two wounded and sick conventions and Article 4(3) of the prisoners of war convention (italics added). Brandweiner, *loc. cit.*, considers that these provisions deviate from general international law. See *below*, Chapter VII, 1, note 4.

105. Cf. *Guggenheim, op. cit.*, II, pp. 780–1.

106. The general question whether recognition is a condition for belligerent rights is discussed *below*, Chapter VII.

107. Kunz, basing himself on the term 'force' in Article 2(4) of the Charter, states that the laws of war apply 'in any situation of large-scale international fighting, whether or not it is called war, whether or not the fighting groups are states in the sense of international law' (*AJIL*, L [1956] p. 317).

108. *Fenwick: International Law*, p. 551, who suggests that, for this reason, the laws of war should not apply to such action 'properly speaking'.

109. On the corrsponding question in respect of the *conventions* on warfare, see *below*, Chapter VIII, especially under 10(a), at note 117.

tions enforcement action,[110] to the extent that no special considerations arising out of the differences between such actions and 'war' require deviations from these laws.[111] The International Court of Justice, in holding that the United Nations 'is an international person', made the reservation that 'its legal personality and rights and duties are not necessarily the same as those of a State'.[112] It is submitted however that, to

---

110. In this sense also *Oppenheim, op cit.,* II, § 65; *Guggenheim, op cit.,* II, p. 780; Kunz in *AJIL,* L (1956) p. 320; and the majority of the members of a committee of the *Institut de droit international, Annuaire,* XLVII (1957) I, pp. 332–3. These writers speak of United Nations actions in general terms, without mentioning any special types. See also Paul de Visscher in *Revue de droit international et de droit comparé,* 1963, p. 170, cf. pp. 177–8, having in mind particularly the action in the Congo. Verdross in *Recueil des Cours,* 1953, II, p. 67; *Greenspan, op. cit.,* pp. 24–26, and Brandweiner: 'Sind die Vereinten Nationen den Kriegsgesetzen unterworfen?' in *Neue Justiz* (East Berlin) 1954, p. 225, support the applicability of the laws of war to actions pursuant to Article 42, and would then presumably *a fortiori* take the same view in respect of other actions against an aggressor. In the same sense, but less clearly, Taubenfeld: 'International Armed Forces and the Rules of War', in *AJIL,* XLV (1951) pp. 673–9 et seq., referring to actions under Article 43, actions of the Korea type and, possibly, actions under the Uniting for Peace Resolution. The Greek Delegate to the Hague Conference of 1954 spoke in the same sense, although less clearly, but apparently having in mind only actions under national command, see *Records of the Intergovernmental Conference on the Protection of Cultural Property in the Event of Armed Conflict* (The Hague 1961) pp. 183 and 267, cf. p. 385. *Greenspan, op. cit.,* cites U.S. Law 8 a, which provides specifically that the laws of war are applicable to the exercise of armed force by the United Nations. Similarly it is stated in the United Kingdom *Manual of Military Law, Part III (The Law of the War on Land,* London 1958) par. 7: 'Although there may be room for argument as to whether hostilities waged for the collective enforcement of international law—in particular under the Charter of the United Nations—constitute war, both the Hague Rules and the customary rules of warfare are applicable to hostilities of that character.'

Draper: 'The Legal Limitations upon the Employment of Weapons by the United Nations Force in the Congo', *International and Comparative Law Quarterly,* XII (1963) at pp. 408–9, submits that, in the existing state of the law of war, an international Force which is part of a subsidiary organ of the United Nations may not, so far as the use of weapons is concerned, be subject to the customary law of war. It is not quite clear whether he is speaking only of peace-keeping actions of the Congo type, but his main arguments are equally relevant to enforcement actions against an aggressor under United Nations command. His main argument appears to be based upon the view that the Organization and its commander cannot be responsible for all acts committed by the members of the Force if they do not have disciplinary and criminal jurisdiction over them, a view which would appear to imply a denial of the international responsibility of the United Nations for a Force under its command as set forth *above,* pp. 118–120. As has already been demonstrated *above,* pp. 96–97, cf. pp. 118–120, in the view of the present writer such jurisdiction is *not* a condition for the capacity of the Organization to be internationally responsible for a Force.

111. Hsu Mo states that 'the existing rules of warfare, with, perhaps, certain changes necessitated by new conditions, would still apply' (*The Grotius Society, Transactions for the Year 1949,* p. 10).

112. Full quotation *above,* Chapter IV,3(f) *in fine.*

the extent that this reservation does not envisage merely factual differences, it applies only where the factual differences between the Organization and States require different legal rules.[113] And in the present case, as will be demonstrated in detail below, Chapter VI,3-5, there is little or no basis for such differences, not even *de lege ferenda*.

The applicability of the laws of war was recognized in respect of military sanctions under the Covenant of the League of Nations by a special legal committee of the League, which stated:

> Certain members of the Committee drew its attention to the question whether, in the case of resistance to aggression or the execution of international police measures, the laws of war *(jus belli)* would continue to be applicable. In such circumstances, it might, indeed, be doubtful whether the case was one of war properly so called. In the Committee's opinion, whatever name may be given to such operations, the rules of the laws of war would remain applicable.[114]

While Forces of the League never became involved in actual hostilities, the United Nations Forces in Korea and the Congo have been, and their practice, as described under 2 above, confirms the principle of the applicability to United Nations actions of the general laws of war in their military and humanitarian aspects. In the same vein, the Collective Measures Committee, established by the Uniting for Peace Resolution of the General Assembly,[115] stated in its first report (1951):

> In any future operations, the executive military authority designated by the United Nations should follow the humanitarian principles applied and recognized by civilized nations involved in armed conflict.[116]

(b) *Forces under national command*

There is a particularly strong legal basis for the application of the laws of war in those cases where the enforcement action is carried out by forces of one or more Member States acting under national command, rather than under binding directives of the United Nations. Thus it was admitted that the laws of war apply to military sanctions under Article

---

113. Cf. *ibid.* and *Indian Journal of International Law*, IV (1964) p. 49.

114. Report of 8 March 1930 by a committee of eleven lawyers set up to propose amendments to the Covenant to harmonize it with the Kellogg-Pact, *League of Nations: Committee for the Amendment of the Covenant of the League of Nations in Order to Bring It into Harmony with the Pact of Paris*, doc. C.160.M.69.1930.V, p. 118. Cf. also an earlier report by the Secretary-General of 17 May 1927, *Reports and Resolutions on the Subject of Article 16 of the Covenant* (Geneva 1927) pp. 84 and 87.

115. *Above*, Chapter II,5.

116. *OR GA*, VI, Suppl. No. 13, par. 246. The applicability of the laws of war to United Nations enforcement actions was also recognized, by implication, in Resolution II proposed by the second Francois committee of the *Institut de droit international*, quoted *below*, p. 269.

16 of the League of Nations Covenant.[117] Similarly, none of the States participating in the United Nations action in Korea maintained during that action that it was not governed by the general laws of war, on the contrary, they acted on the assumption that it was.[118]

Indeed, as has been demonstrated, even if the Member States have undertaken their action pursuant to a recommendation or even a decision of (the League of Nations or) the United Nations, and even if, in *fact*, they comply with any further recommendations made by the Organization in the course of the action, as they did in Korea, they are themselves internationally responsible for the conduct of the operations and become themselves parties to any international agreements concluded in respect of the Force.[119] The States must then observe their own obligations under general and conventional international law, including the general laws of war and such conventions on warfare as have been accepted by them and the other party to the conflict. The fact that the action is not 'war' in a formal sense cannot relieve the Member States executing the enforcement action, or any other party to the conflict, of their duty as States to observe the laws of war to the extent that no valid special considerations require exceptions from these laws.[120]

(c) *Forces under United Nations command*

When the action is carried out by a Force under United Nations command and responsibility, the States providing contingents, as has been demonstrated, are not internationally responsible for the conduct of the operations and are not parties to the conflict or to any international agreements concluded in respect of the Force. They are only responsible vis-à-vis the United Nations for ensuring that their contingents obey United Nations' orders and for prosecuting the members thereof for any offences in accordance with the internal agreements concluded by these States with the Organization. It is the United Nations which, although

---

117. See the statement by the special legal committee quoted *above* at note 114. See also *Schücking und Wehberg: Die Satzung des Völkerbundes*, 2nd edition (Berlin 1924) p. 632, who state: 'Zwischen den Mitgliedern des Völkerbundes und dem rechtsbrüchigen Staate kommt im Kriegsfalle das geltende Land- und Seekriegsrecht zur Anwendung'. Similarly, *Kunz: Kriegsrecht und Neutralitätsrecht* (Wien 1935) p. 17, states that 'die gemeinsame Aktion des Art. XVI V.B.P. ist rechtstheoretische internationale Exekution, steht aber unter *Kriegsrecht*'.

118. *Above*, under 2(a). *Attia: Les forces armées des Nations Unies en Corée et au Moyen-Orient* (Genève 1963) p. 260 also takes the view that they did apply.

119. *Above*, Chapter III, especially 6(c).

120. *Below*, Chapter VI. On the position in respect of the *various types* of national command, see the detailed discussion of the legal situation with regard to the Geneva Conventions below, Chapter VIII,2–4.

it does not itself have disciplinary and criminal jurisdiction over the members of the Force,[121] is externally responsible and which alone is a party to the conflict and to any external agreement.[122] And the United Nations is not bound by the accession of the States providing contingents to the Geneva Conventions or to any other relevant agreements.[123]

In these cases the question of the application of the laws of war depends, not merely upon an analogy from traditional war to enforcement action, but also upon the question of an analogy from States to the United Nations as a intergovernmental organization.[124]

This analogy would appear obvious in cases where the capacity of the United Nations to take military action is itself based upon an analogy from the right of the traditional subjects of international law, i.e. States, to wage war in collective self-defence.[125] In such cases it appears clear that, as long as no special law has been established for the United Nations by treaty or custom, and to the extent that no valid special considerations require exceptions for enforcement actions by that Organization, it can exercise its right under general international law only in the manner prescribed by the laws of war as developed between States.[126] This viewpoint would apply notably to United Nations actions against aggressor *non*-member States.[127] It would probably also be the most adequate view in respect of any enforcement action against *Member* States, if the action is not taken under the specific provision in Article 42 of the Charter.[128]

On the other hand, the Charter also provides an independent legal basis for the capacity of the Organization to conduct military operations. It may be argued that, insofar as the Organization acts on this basis, it is not bound by any direct analogy from general international law. This would particularly be so in respect of an action taken on the

---

121. *Above*, pp. 56 and 96–98 and *below*, pp. 322 and 365–372.

122. *Above*, Chapter III, especially 3(a) and 6(b).

123. Cf. *below*, Chapter VIII,5 et seq.

124. Cf. *above*, Chapter IV,3, and *The Indian Journal of International Law*, IV (1964) pp. 1 et seq., especially p. 49. Draper in *International and Comparative Law Quarterly*, XII (1963) pp. 408–9 and 411–2, has difficulty with this analogy, for reasons which have been discussed *above*, Chapter III,2(a) and *below*, Chapter VIII,11(a)(iii). He doubts whether, 'in the existing state of the law of war, an international Force which is part of a subsidiary organ of the United Nations can be a belligerent to which the customary law of war applies'.

125. *Above*, Chapter IV,5(a).

126. On the capacity of the United Nations to *implement* the laws of war, see *below*, Chapter VIII,11.

127. *Above*, Chapter IV,5(a), cf. *Nordisk Tidsskrift for international Ret og Jus gentium*, XXXIV (1964) pp. 12–15 and *below*, Chapter VII.

128. Cf. *above*, Chapter IV,4(c) (and, on the other hand, (d)).

basis of Article 42 of the Charter [129] against a Member State, or even against a non-member State, if one considers the Charter binding upon these, too, to the extent provided in Article 2(6).[130] The view might even be advanced in respect of actions not based upon Article 42, if the general provisions of the Charter, and in particular Article 1(1), are considered to provide a sufficient constitutional basis for such military action.[131]

However, even if in these cases there is no formal basis for an analogy from traditional war, there is no more substantive difference between an enforcement action and traditional war in these cases than there is in those cases where the legal basis of the action is sought in general international law; both are likely to take the form of regular hostilities. In these circumstances the application by analogy of the laws of war, to the extent that no special considerations apply, would seem well justified. Accordingly it is submitted that, at least as long as the United Nations has enacted no different instructions for its Force, the laws of war apply by analogy to this Force if it becomes involved in an armed conflict. The question is merely whether the Organization, when it acts on the basis of its own constitution rather than upon that of general international law, is entitled unilaterally to lay down a law which differs from that applicable to traditional war between States,[132] i.e. whether the Organization has the power in this respect to make decisions binding upon its Member States, or even upon non-members. Such power would require specific basis. As will be demonstrated below, in Chapter VI, 3(f)(i), there is no specific provision to this effect in the Charter or elsewhere in respect of the laws of war in the narrow sense, i.e. in respect of the military and humanitarian laws of war. Furthermore, it is doubtful whether any of the provisions concerning enforcement action could be considered to confer this power by implication. Only in the economic field and in respect of neutrality does the Charter provide for

---

129. This is the case discussed by Brandweiner in *Neue Justiz* (East Berlin), 1954, pp. 225–7, and by *Attia: Les forces des Nations Unies en Corée et au Moyen-Orient* (Genève 1963) pp. 254–5. However, both of these conclude, rightly, that the United Nations is bound by the laws of war.

130. This question has been briefly discussed by the present writer in *Nordisk Tidsskrift for international Ret og Jus gentium, loc. cit.*

131. Cf. Halderman: 'Legal Basis for United Nations Armed Forces' in *AJIL,* LVI (1962) pp. 971 et seq. The distinction between actions based upon the Charter and other actions would appear to be reflected in Article 2(5) of the Charter, which provides: 'All Members shall give the United Nations every assistance *in any action it takes in accordance with the present Charter,* and shall refrain from giving assistance to any state against which the United Nations is taking preventive or enforcement action' (italics added, cf. *above,* Chapter IV,4(a)–(b)). However, the commentaries written at the time offer no indication that the Conference had this distinction in mind, see *below,* Chapter VI,3(i), at notes 259a et seq.

132. Cf. *Jessup: A Modern Law of Nations* (New York 1949) p. 214.

a power to make decisions binding upon States. But this power is not confined to those cases where the *United Nations* takes *military* action, and, still less, to those cases where it does so by a Force under its own command.[133]

It has been maintained that the United Nations does not have the capacity to *implement* the laws of war, and that therefore its Forces cannot be subject to those laws. This objection has been particularly linked to the question of the applicability to United Nations Forces of the *conventions* on warfare. It will therefore be discussed in that context, below, in Chapter VIII,11(a).

(d) *Analogy to internal police actions*

Certain writers emphasize that a United Nations enforcement action is not war, but a police action, and that under municipal law there is no question of equal rights for the police and the criminal; if the criminal kills the policeman who tries to arrest him he is guilty of murder of a no less serious, or even more serious, nature than if he kills a private person who has taken no action against him. From this they draw the conclusion that an enforcement action cannot necessarily be governed by the regular laws of war, and in particular that the United Nations cannot be bound by all parts of those laws. Most of the writers concerned do not specify whether they have in mind United Nations actions under national or United Nations command, or both. Nor do they usually specify whether they are thinking of actions based upon the constitution (Articles 42 et seq. of the Charter), in respect of which their view has a stronger legal basis, or also of actions based upon the right of collective self-defence under general international law; however they are presumably thinking of the former.[134]

Thus the Committee on the Study of Legal Problems of the United Nations of the American Society of International Law, in a study entitled 'Should the Laws of War Apply to United Nations Enforcement Actions?' concluded as follows:

> The Committee agrees that the use of force by the United Nations to restrain aggression is of a different nature from war-making by a state. The purposes for which the laws of war were instituted are not entirely the same as the purposes of regulating the use of force by the United Nations. This we may say without deciding whether United Nations enforcement action is war, police enforcement of criminal law, or *sui generis*. In the present circumstances, then, the proper answer would seem to be, for the time being, that the United Nations should not feel bound by all the laws of war, but should select such of the laws of war as may seem to fit its purposes (*e.g.*, prisoners of war, belligerent occupation), adding

133. *Below*, pp. 282, 284, 285. Chapter VI,3(i). *Contra: Kotzsch: The Concept of War in Contemporary History and International Law* (Geneva 1956) p. 296.

134. Because writers generally appear to assume that United Nations actions must be based upon the specific provisions of the Charter (*contra*: above, Chapter IV).

such others as may be needed, and rejecting those which seem incompatible with its purposes. We think it beyond doubt that the United Nations, representing practically all the nations of the earth, has the right to make such decisions.[135]

In recent years a number of proposals have been made that the laws of war applicable to collective enforcement actions be studied and that a special revised code of the laws of war for such actions be elaborated.[136] Some of these proposals were inspired by similar ideas.[137]

Logically and theoretically it certainly is true that a United Nations enforcement action performs functions in the international community corresponding to those of the police in a national community. Naturally, it would be ideal if it were in fact possible to place a United Nations enforcement action against one or more aggressor States on a footing similar to that of a national police action against individual criminals. Indeed, this must be the final goal of a fully organized world community, where enforcement is decided automatically by an organ whose authority is generally recognized and is carried out by a Force which is sufficiently overwhelming to establish law and order without becoming involved in any large-scale and protracted armed conflict.[138] However, at the present, primitive stage of the development of international organization, an enforcement action is much more likely to involve large-scale use of arms over a longer period, in the same manner as a traditional war between States.[139] And even an internal police action may be

---

135. *Proceedings of the American Society of International Law,* 1952, p. 200, cf. pp. 217–8 and Bivens in *AJIL,* XLVIII (1954) p. 141. See the criticism of these views by Brandweiner in *Neue Justiz* (East Berlin) 1954, pp. 226–7; Lauterpacht in *BYIL,* XXX (1953), pp. 220–1 and pp. 241–3; Baxter, *ibid.,* XXIX (1952) pp. 358–9, and in *Proceedings of the American Society of International Law,* 1953, pp. 95–98; Kunz in *AJIL,* L (1956), p. 320; *Kotzsch: The Concept of War in Contemporary History and International Law* (Geneva 1956) pp. 288 et seq.; *Greenspan, op. cit.,* p. 25; and the views expressed in *Annuaire de l'Institut de droit international,* XLVII (1957) I, pp. 332–3. See also *below* p. 275, note 212.

136. Citations *above,* notes 6–7.

137. See for example Attia, Bivens, Quadri, Wright and Yepes, *loc. cit.*

138. Taubenfeld, *loc. cit.,* p. 674, states: '... if the United Nations developed constitutionally and approached progressively nearer to the form of a world government, it would, of course, grow even more difficult to show the binding force on it of pre-existing rules, which were created by actions of its subordinates.'

139. Jessup states: 'If a nation goes berserk, force is let loose, and if the international community seeks to restore order, it must use greater force. We may cease to call it war, but there will be fighting, and people will be killed. The analogy is not to the single citizen who assaults and kills, but rather to major rioting or civil war which requires the troops to be called out.' (*A modern Law of Nations,* New York 1949, p. 189.) Brandweiner, who takes the same view of United Nations action as that submitted in the text, states on civil war: 'Für den Bürgerkrieg überlässt es das Völkerrecht im allgemeinen der innerstaatlichen Rechtsordnung, Art und Mass der anzuwendenden Gewalt normativ zu bestimmen' (*Neue Justiz,* East Berlin, 1954, p. 225). *Kotzsch, op. cit.,* p. 289, states: 'Apart from certain legalistic theorism, however, it has become abundantly

governed by the laws of war, if it develops into a civil war displaying the same factual characteristics as an international war.[140] International law is a primitive law which, to a greater extent than municipal law, must base itself upon factual situations. Since the factual nature of the hostilities carried out on both sides during an enforcement action is hardly distinguishable from that of hostilities in traditional war, the situation calls for the application of the laws of war, rather than of that of internal police actions. Furthermore, since the hostilities are conducted by, and in most cases, between,[141] independent subjects of international law, it must be the laws of international war, rather than those of civil war, which are applicable in the absence of any special considerations or rules.

However, even if this principle is adopted, it is necessary to consider whether these laws must be modified in certain respects when applied to United Nations actions because of their nature as police actions or for other reasons. Such a detailed study is even called for to verify the submission just made, that United Nations Forces are really governed by the laws of war applicable to States. This requires a separate examination of each type of sanction and each field of the laws of war. An attempt at this, confined to actions against an aggressor, will be made in the following chapter. However, before entering into this detailed study, it is appropriate to add some remarks on the general problem of whether the laws of war apply also to United Nations peace-keeping Forces and to intervention by the United Nations in internal conflicts.

4. PEACE-KEEPING FORCES. INTERNAL CONFLICTS

(a) *Peace-keeping Forces when not engaged in organized hostilities*

Even if the analogy to internal police actions does not at the present stage of development apply to United Nations enforcement actions against an aggressor, it does apply, in most cases, to United Nations police actions in the narrow sense, or to peace-keeping actions as they are now called. Neither in the Middle East, nor in West New Guinea (Irian Barat), nor on Cyprus, have the United Nations police forces, up to the time of writing, become involved in military operations against another organized force. The few cases of firing at and/or by the United Nations Force and of apprehension and disarming of individuals or groups

evident under the League as well as under the United Nations that its military enforcement actions, if they were resisted by the Charter-breaking State, necessarily consisted of armed contests prolonged in duration and precarious in progress and outcome. These circumstances are the very characteristics and concomitants of war.'

140. *Below*, Chapter VII,1.
141. See, however, *below*, under 4(c)–(d).

which have occurred [142] bear no resemblance to war, not even in the material sense, and are governed by different legal rules, more comparable to those governing internal police actions. These rules, for example on the right to fire, to seize arms and supplies and to take and retain prisoners, will depend upon the mandate of the Force and upon any agreements concluded with the host State and with the other parties involved in the conflict. They will thus vary from case to case. Similarly, the rights and duties of the Force in the territory of the host State will depend upon its mandate and the agreement with that State, not upon the laws of belligerent occupation.[143] In most cases, the powers and the action of the United Nations Force will be less rigorous than those of a fighting army, and its actions will thus stay well within the limits of the laws of war, for example in respect of employment of arms, seizure and destruction of supplies and public and private property and seizure and retention of hostile persons. However this may be in any particular action, it goes without saying that the United Nations Force will be guided in these respects at least by the same humanitarian principles as underlie both actions of national police forces and the laws of war, and that it will take any action within its power to ensure that its opponents do likewise.

(b) *Peace-keeping Forces when engaged in organized hostilities*

However, it may happen that a peace-keeping United Nations Force becomes involved in genuine hostilities with another organized force, even if this was not expected when the Force was set up and when national contingents for it were provided. This was what happened in certain phases of the United Nations action in the Congo. In such cases the hostilities may bear more resemblance to war in the material sense than to internal police actions, and it is accordingly submitted that the limits of the general (customary) laws of war become applicable to both parties, for the reasons outlined under 3 above,[144] even if the Force is under United Nations command and responsibility, as all peace-keeping Forces have been. This is probably what is envisaged by the standing clause in the Regulations for United Nations peace-keeping Forces, that 'the Force shall observe (and respect) the principle and spirit of the general

---

142. *Above*, under 2(b)(iii) *in initio*.

143. The Secretary-General stated in par. 12 of his second and final report on UNEF that that Force was 'more than an observers' corps, but in no way a military force temporarily controlling the territory in which it is stationed' (*OR GA*, First Emergency Special Session, Annexes, A.i. 5, p. 21).

144. As pointed out by Kunz in *AJIL*, L (1956) p. 321, it makes no difference in relation to the laws of war whether the war is 'small' or 'big', limited or total. As for Katanga, it is recalled that aircraft and artillery were used, cf. *above*, Chapter II,7 at note 226.

international Conventions applicable to the conduct of military person-nel'.[145] Indeed, as was pointed out under 2(b) above, both parties to the conflicts in Katanga appear to have assumed that the general humanitar-ian laws of war were applicable, even if they did not always exercise to the full their positive belligerent rights under these laws. Thus they did not usually retain prisoners for long. The United Nations merely held them for exchange as prisoners (under cease-fire agreements concluded between the United Nations and the Katangese authorities or under spe-cial exchanges arranged by the representatives of the *Comité internatio-nal de la Croix-Rouge* [146]) or for evacuation as foreign military or para-military personnel within the terms of the Security Council's resolutions of 21 February and 24 November 1961. At an early stage the United Nations did not even consider itself *entitled* to take prisoners. However, this was abandoned when on 7 April 1961 white mercenaries attacked and killed members of the United Nations Force. The Force then had the choice between a military attack or simply taking the mercenaries pris-oners. They did the latter. The thirty prisoners were treated according to the Geneva Convention and the International Red Cross was invited to visit them.[147]

In view of the failure to make full use of the positive rights under the laws of war, and of the fact referred to at the end of subsection (a), it is not of great practical importance to determine at what point a conflict develops into hostilities subject to the general laws of war. This problem becomes acute only if both parties have accepted the *conventions* on warfare, in particular the Geneva Conventions with their detailed pro-visions which go beyond what has as yet become customary law. In such case the answer must be found by an application of the same principles as would be applied to determine whether the conventions become appli-cable to limited hostilities between States. In the case of the Geneva Conventions, this is notably a question of the interpretation of the term 'armed conflict' in Article 2 common to these Conventions. Under these Conventions it is the nature of the conflict, rather than the legal status of the parties, which is the determining criterion, as long as the conflict is of an international character.[148]

145. *Above*, under 2(b)(i).
146. *Comité international de la Croix-Rouge: Rapport d'activité 1961*, pp. 10–11.
147. Information supplied by Lieutenant-Colonel Björn Egge, Royal Norwegian Army, formerly with ONUC.
148. Cf. *below*, Chapter VIII,10(a).

(c) *Internal conflicts and the general laws of war* [149]

It is, however, necessary to consider the question whether the situation would be different if a United Nations Force became involved in hostilities, not with the forces of a State or another subject of international law, but with those of another organized group (insurgents). This question may arise even in respect of enforcement actions; indeed, it was debated whether the only such action so far undertaken, Korea, was an example of United Nations intervention in an internal or an international war.[150] However, the question is of greater practical importance in respect of peace-keeping Forces. These have always been established with the consent of the States concerned and have, to a greater or lesser extent, been entrusted with functions of internal peace-keeping.[151] Thus, in the Congo the most serious clashes were, not with the forces of the Central Government, but with those of the secessionist Province of Katanga, whose independence had been recognized, neither by the United Nations, nor by the Central Government, nor by any other government. It was argued at the time that the hostilities between the United Nations Force and the forces of Katanga for this reason did *not* constitute an international conflict.

(i) If the 'United Nations Force' were placed at the disposal and *under the orders of the government of the host State* and were employed by the latter for internal purposes as part of its own forces, the conflict must be considered as part of the internal conflict between the central government and dissident groups within that State. It would then be governed by the law governing internal conflicts. However, as will be explained below, in Chapter VII,1, the practice of courts and governments clearly tends towards applying the general laws of war even to internal conflicts, if the insurgents have established a political organization and the hostilities have assumed the characteristics of a real war. Contrary to the view advocated by most writers, this is not restricted to those cases where the insurgents have been recognized as belligerents.

However, it has never happened that a United Nations Force has been placed under the authority of the host State. Indeed, it might be asked whether it could properly be termed a United Nations Force if it were. In two cases, Saar and New Guinea, the international force was

---

149. On the general aspects of this problem, see *Siotis: Le droit de la guerre et les conflits armés d'un caractère non-international* (Paris 1958) and *Castberg: Studier i folkerett* (Oslo 1952) pp. 83–124.

150. See *below,* under (d) *in fine.*

151. The internal nature of many disputes in which the United Nations intervenes was stressed by a number of speakers during the non-governmental Conference on United Nations Peace-Keeping Forces in Oslo 20–21 February 1964. It was urged that this aspect be further studied. See also Schachter in *AJIL,* LV (1961) p. 8, speaking of the action in the Congo.

placed at the disposal of the territorial authorities, but in these cases the territorial authority was itself an organ of the United Nations and any military action would have been internal for this reason, see under (iii) below. In Korea the Force was placed under the command of a Member State other than the host State and the conflict was therefore clearly international, cf. under (iv) below.

(ii) In the other cases, including the Middle East, Congo and Cyprus, the Force was maintained *under the* direct and exclusive *control of* the Secretary-General of *the United Nations*, as guided by any relevant decisions of the General Assembly and/or the Security Council. In these cases the Secretary-General emphasized very strongly that 'the United Nations operation must be separate and distinct from activities by any national authorities' [152] and that 'the Force is under the exclusive control and command of the United Nations at all times'.[153] In these circumstances the Force is operating as an organ of the UN, an independent subject of international law. It would then be hard to consider it as a party to an internal conflict, even if the other party to the conflict is not a sovereign State. Thus, any armed conflict which might occur between the United Nations Force and organized groups of the Greek or the Turkish element of the population on Cyprus could not be regarded as internal, even though any conflict between such groups or between one such group and the Cyprus Government would be internal. Similarly, while in the Congo any conflict between the Central Government and the authorities in Katanga would have been internal, the armed clashes which occurred between the latter and the United Nations Force were not. This is clearly true if the United Nations action pursues independent aims, as it did during the hostilities in Elisabethville in 1961.[154] However, it is submitted that it must apply even if the United Nations Force assists and co-operates with the host government (or any other government) in the execution of its internal aims,[155] as long as the United Nations Force acts as an independent Force which takes its orders from the Organization and not from the host government. Thus

152. *Above*, Chapter III,2(a), see also the other similar statements cited *loc. cit.*, notes 11–13.

153. See this and the other very clear statements contained in paragraphs 3–9 of the Secretary–General's Aide-Memoire Concerning Some Questions Relating to the Function and Operation of the United Nations Peace-Keeping Force in Cyprus, quoted *above*, Chapter II,9—Another indication that the United Nations Force must be regarded as a *foreign* Force, is the fact that 'the Force, as a subsidiary organ of the United Nations, enjoys the status, privileges and immunities of the Organization...' (UNEF, ONUC and UNFICYP Regulation 10).

154. *Above*, Chapter II,7.

155. The United Nations will of course not do so unless the internal troubles have international implications, which notably will be the case if the dissident groups receive support from abroad.

the United Nations actions in Katanga could not be considered as internal, despite the fact that one of them arose out of action taken to assist the Central Government in the execution of its Ordinance of 24 August 1961 providing for the expulsion of all non-Congolese officers and mercenaries serving in the Katangese forces.[155a]

This view is based upon the assumption that the same would apply if a *State* intervened in an internal conflict of another State with an army acting as an independent unit under the former State's command.[156] This is certainly true if the foreign State intervenes on the side of the insurgents. But it is submitted that the conflict must be considered international also if the foreign State intervenes on the side of the government; this quite apart from the difficulty of distinguishing between these two cases if both sides claim to be the legal government. The reluctance in practice to recognize the applicability of the Geneva Conventions in such cases may be primarily due to the natural reluctance of the intervening State and the party it assists to admit the intervention to that extent, a reluctance which of course does not apply to the United Nations. Indeed, it is submitted that the current view that a conflict is internal if *one* side is not a subject of international law [157] does not apply in respect of foreign or international intervention.

Accordingly it is submitted that in none of the cases discussed above could the conflict be considered internal. It must be assimilated to an international conflict (unless one would wish to create a third category, which would neither be internal, nor international, but this would hardly be called for). And it must be governed by the laws of war by virtue of the analogy discussed under 3(a) above, rather than by virtue of the principle and practice discussed below, in Chapter VII,1.

(iii) Only if the Force operates *in a territory under United Nations sovereignty or administration* could the conflict be considered as internal. This would have been the case had hostilities occurred in Leticia in 1933–34, in the Saar in 1935, or in Western New Guinea while this Territory was being administered by the United Nations. However, even in these cases the conflict would only be internal if the other side were an internal group, for example a part of the population in the Saar or West New Guinea, or, possibly, any foreign forces stationed in the territory that might have taken action on their own, contrary to the orders of the United Nations and their own governments. If the United Nations Force on the other hand should become involved in hostilities with external forces, for example of a neighbouring State—or with for-

155a. *Above*, p. 72, cf. *Gihl: Om freden och säkerheten* (Stockholm 1962) pp. 366–7. See also the Cyprus Status Agreement, *below*, p. 435 *in initio* and *in fine*.
156. Cf. below, under (iv) with note 160.
157. See for example *Siotis: Le droit de la guerre et les conflits armés d'un caractère non-international* (Paris 1958) p. 21.

eign troops which were stationed in the territory and which, acting on the orders of their home governments, were defying the United Nations under whose authority they had originally been placed,[158]—the conflict would clearly be international and governed by the general laws of war. Even in the former cases, where the conflict would have to be considered internal, the general laws of war would apply on the conditions described below in Chapter VII,1.[159]

158. Cf. *above*, Chapter III,2(a), at note 14.

159. *Bowett: United Nations Forces* (London 1964) pp. 486 et seq. has a different approach to the problem of the application of the laws of war to United Nations peace-keeping Forces. He attaches decisive importance to the *mandate* of the Force and makes the basic distinction as to whether the Force has a mandate capable of authorizing armed hostilities under *international* law, or of authorizing armed action under *municipal* law. He proposes 'to consider each individual use of force by the United Nations within the context of the proper purposes *for which it was lawfully constituted* and the means it must use to accomplish these purposes' (italics added). He does not specify the criteria which would determine whether the mandate falls within one or the other category. However, he mentions as examples of the first category armed observer groups, UNEF, ONUC and a United Nations Force entrusted with the defence and security of a zone or area under United Nations control. As examples of the second category he lists the Force in West New Guinea and a Force entrusted with plebiscite functions. The latter example may indicate a substantive difference. However, if this only envisages the Saar and other territories under United Nations administration, Bowett's examples indicate that he arrives at the same results as the present writer. If this is so, the latter is not convinced that Bowett's basic criterion is really helpful, for the following reasons:

1. As pointed out in the text, under (c)(ii), a conflict with dissident internal groups, which would be internal if they were opposed by forces of the central Government, would, in the view of the present writer, be external if they were opposed by a United Nations Force under the command of the Organization or of Member States other than the host State. (In another context [*below*, note 164] Bowett appears to take the same view in respect of the action in the Congo.) In Bowett's second category would therefore fall only the cases discussed in the text under (a), where no question of the laws of war arises, under (c)(i), where the Force would not be a genuine United Nations Force, and under (c)(iii), where the territory is under United Nations administration (but not in all respects, cf. under 2 below).

2. The actions of the same Force may be governed by different legal systems, depending upon the identity of the opponent and the nature of the particular conflict. An example of the former is given by Bowett himself when he makes an exception for the case where the Force in West New Guinea might be called upon to defend that Territory against an external attack; another example is given in the text, under (c)(iii). An example of the latter *might* be a Force which on some occasions becomes involved in genuine fighting which, as suggested under (c)(ii), is governed by the laws of war, and on other occasions performs pure police functions which, as suggested under (a), are governed by other legal norms.

3. Except for the case discussed in the text under (a), it is not the *mandate*, but the nature of the conflict in which the Force *in fact* becomes involved, which determines the applicable law. Whether the conflict is inside or outside the mandate of the Force as defined by the competent organs of the United Nations and/or agreed with the host State or any other State concerned is not decisive, cf. *above*, pp. 175-7.

(iv) If the United Nations Force is placed *under the command of one or more States, other than the host State,* as it was in Korea, the conflict is international, cf. the submissions already made under (ii) that an internal conflict becomes international insofar as foreign States [160] (or organizations) intervene and that the current view that a conflict is internal if *one* side is not a subject of international law does not apply in cases of foreign or international intervention. This is largely confirmed by the corresponding practice in respect of the Geneva Conventions in Korea, cf. below, under (d).

(d) *Internal conflicts and the conventions on warfare*

As will be explained in Chapter VIII,5 et seq., those provisions of the conventions on warfare which do not reflect customary international law do not apply to any United Nations Force under the Organization's command and international responsibility, unless the Organization has acceded to these conventions, which it has not. However, if the Organization accedes, formally or informally, the conventions would apply to all armed conflicts of an international nature. The delimitation between conflicts of an international nature and those of an internal nature must be the same here, in relation to the conventions on warfare, as submitted above, under (c), in relation to the general laws of war. Thus the conventions would apply to the conflicts discussed under (c)(ii) above.

The modern conventions—and these are the important ones, because they go beyond what constitutes customary law [161]—are also directly applicable to internal conflicts, but only on a reduced scale. Thus the

160. On the civil war in Spain 1936–39, see *Oppenheim: International Law,* II, § 76, who states that as a result of the illegal intervention of foreign States it had lost the character of a civil war in the accepted meaning of the term, citing a statement to this effect by the Secretary of State on 25 June 1937, *House of Commons Debates,* 325, col. 1608 (Oppenheim does not indicate whether the Italian and German forces fighting with the insurgents, were under the latters' command or under that of their own States.) Oppenheim adds that recognition of belligerency was correctly refused for that reason. However, one must agree with *Chen: The International Law of Recognition* (London 1951) p. 361, that the participation by foreign States 'would be all the more reason for the application of the laws of war'. Similarly it is submitted that the laws of (international) war were applicable in Yemen in 1963, and that they would have been applicable had United States forces become involved in an armed conflict in the Lebanon in 1958 despite the fact that these forces were in that country at the request of its Government.

When the *Comité international de la Croix-Rouge* in July 1965 appealed to the parties to the conflict in Viet-Nam to observe the Geneva Conventions, it stated expressly that all the provisions (*l'ensemble*) of these Conventions (not merely Article 3), were applicable, and it addressed this appeal not merely to the Governments of North Viet-Nam and the United States, but also to the Government of South Viet-Nam and to the Viet-Cong insurgents in that country (*Comité international de la Croix-Rouge,* Communiqué de presse No. 808, 26 July 1965).

161. *Above,* under 1(b).

four Geneva Conventions of 1949 provide in their common Article 3 that 'in the case of armed conflict not of an international character occurring in the territory of one of the High Contracting Parties, each Party to the conflict shall be bound to apply, as a minimum' certain specified basic humanitarian principles.[162] The 1954 Hague Convention for the Protection of Cultural Property in the Event of Armed Conflict contains a similar provision in its Article 19. To this extent these Conventions would apply even to such conflicts of the United Nations Force as are *not* governed by the general laws of war, cf. above, under (c)(i) and (iii), if the State concerned or the United Nations, respectively, is a party to the conventions.

It has been suggested that only this reduced regime would be applicable even in other cases, such as the United Nations action in the Congo. However, it is submitted that the reduced regime could apply only to the relations between internal authorities, not to those between the latter and the United Nations, for the reasons set forth under (c)(ii) above. In the case of the Conventions, there is an additional reason for this, namely that Article 3 and Article 19 only apply if the conflict occurs 'in the territory' of one of the contracting parties. It is then clearly assumed that it is that contracting party which is involved in the conflict with a dissident group, and not an external power. This quite apart from the fact that the territorial sovereign, theoretically, might not be a party to the Conventions, and then Article 3 would, according to its own terms, not be applicable.[163] For these reasons, too, and considering that the Geneva Conventions are clearly intended to make sure that no armed conflict falls between two stools, there can be little doubt that conflicts with a United Nations Force must be governed by the regular provisions

162. The questions of the field of application and the scope of this provision have been studied by two committees of experts appointed by the *Comité international de la Croix-Rouge*, in 1955 and 1962, respectively. Their reports are reproduced in *Commission d'experts chargée d'examiner la question de l'application des principes humanitaires en cas de troubles intérieurs* (Genève 1955) and *Commission d'experts Chargée d'examiner la question de l'aide au victimes des conflits internes* (Genève October 1962, CICR document D 780), see also the preceding *Mémorandum du CICR sur la Croix-Rouge et l'aide aux victimes des conflits internes*, document D 759. The second committee's report is also reproduced in the *Comité's* report to the *XXth International Conference of the Red Cross, Vienna October 1965*, entitled *Protection of Victims of Non-International Conflicts* (Document Conf. D 6/1).

163. Reference is also made in this connection to Article 13(3) of the two wounded and sick conventions and Article 4(3) of the prisoners of war convention, which provide that the Conventions apply to 'members of regular armed forces who profess allegiance to a government *or an authority* not recognized by the Detaining Power' (italics added). As pointed out in the commentary by the *Comité international de la Croix-Rouge*, the term 'regular' is merely a reference to the general conditions listed in the preceding paragraphs of the Article (*Les Conventions de Genève du 12 août 1949, Commentaire*, III, pp. 70–71).

of the Geneva Conventions [164] in the same cases as they are governed by the general laws of war, cf. above, under (c)(ii), if the Organization is a party to the Conventions.[165] Only in those cases where the conflict —in accordance with what has been submitted above, under (c)(i) and (iii)—is governed by the law of internal conflicts, would the reduced regime of Article 3 and Article 19, respectively, be applicable, if the host State *or* the United Nations, respectively, is a party to the Conventions. As for practice, it is recalled that the United Nations in the Congo recognized only the applicability of the 'principles and spirit' of the conventions. It has already been submitted that this in fact referred to the general laws of war [166] rather than to Article 3 of the Geneva Conventions, to which the Congo (but not the United Nations) was a party.

Similarly it must be the regular provisions, rather than the reduced regime, which applies if the United Nations Force is under the command of one or more Member States (other than the host State) which have acceded to the conventions. In this respect reference may be made to practice in Korea. When the war in Korea broke out, it was debated whether the original war between North and South Korea was civil or international war. Accordingly, the *Comité international de la Croix-Rouge*, in its appeals of 26 June 1950 (i.e. before the intervention of United Nations Forces) to these two parties that they should apply the Geneva Conventions, referred 'specially' (*'notamment'*) to their common Article 3.[167] South Korea did in fact confine its acceptance of 4 July 1950 to that Article, while North Korea on 15 July stated that it was strictly abiding by the principles of the Conventions in respect to Prisoners of War. In its subsequent appeals (after the intervention of the United Nations Forces) to the States providing contingents to the United Nations Force and to the Command of that Force, the *Comité international* correctly did not refer to Article 3, but to the Conventions as a whole. However, the *Comité* quoted for information its earlier appeals to 'the two Korean governments'. It may have been this latter fact which induced the United States, in its first reply of 5 July 1950, to state that it would 'be guided by humanitarian principles of Conventions particu-

164. *Contra:* Draper in *International and Comparative Law Quarterly*, XII (1963) p. 410, cf. pp. 408–9, speaking of the action in the Congo, cf. also note 124 *above*. He also considers it doubtful whether *Article 3* applies, although on grounds different from those of the present writer. His conclusion is thus that the action in the Congo falls between two stools. Also *Bowett: United Nations Forces* (London 1964) p. 509 finds difficulty in accepting the view that Article 3 was applicable in the Congo, apparently for the same basic reason as the present writer.

165. On its capacity to accede and to exercise the rights and comply with the obligations of the Conventions, see *below*, Chapter VIII, especially under 9–11.

166. *Above*, under 2(b)(i).

167. *Above*, under 2(a) *in initio*, and *Le Comité international de la Croix-Rouge et le conflit de Corée*, I, pp. 4 and 6.

larly Article 3 of Geneva Convention 1949'. Later the United States correctly made no reference to this Article, nor did the other States providing contingents or the United Nations Command.[168]

(e) *Practical problems if two different regimes apply to one conflict*

It may be asked, finally, whether practical difficulties would not arise if the United Nations Force were to act together with troops of the host State in one common action. Two different regimes might then be applicable to the same action if the United Nations' part of it is regarded as international and subject to the laws of war, while the host State's part is regarded as internal and subject to the laws on civil war.

However, as has already been indicated, the practice of governments and courts tends towards applying the general laws of war even to internal conflicts which fulfil certain criteria. In these cases, no practical difficulties are likely to arise in so far as the general laws of war are concerned. The situation would be similar in respect of those (older) conventions on warfare, like the Fourth Hague Convention of 1907, which largely reflect customary international law.

The situation would be different in respect of the Geneva Conventions and the 1954 Hague Conventions, which contain a number of detailed provisions that do not as yet constitute customary law. Although these conventions are directly applicable to internal conflicts, they provide, as already explained, for a different, reduced regime for such conflicts. Accordingly, if the submissions made above are accepted, conflicts between the host State and dissident groups would be governed by the reduced regime, while the United Nations action would be governed by the regular provisions if that Organization were a party to the Conventions. In the case of the 1907 Hague Conventions and other early conventions on warfare it was considered to be an intolerable situation to have two even less different regimes apply to the same international conflict, and they therefore all contained the *clausula si omnes,* which provided that they would apply only if *all* parties to the conflict were parties to the Conventions. However, the Geneva Conventions and the 1954 Hague Convention do not take such a serious view of the concurrent application of different regimes to different parties to the same conflict. The Geneva Conventions provide on the contrary that 'although one of the Powers in conflict may not be a party to the present Convention, the Powers who are parties thereto shall remain bound by it in their mutual relations'.[169] It is submitted that the practical difficulties would not be essentially different in the case of a United Nations action combined with an internal State action.

168. See *above,* under 2(a) with citations.
169. Article 2, common to the four Geneva Conventions.

However this may be, the problem is probably largely theoretical. Joint military actions of the United Nations Force and the host State in an internal conflict have not occurred so far (unless the war in Korea properly could be considered internal) and are probably not very likely in future either.[170] Moreover, if they were to occur, it might well be that one force would be placed under the command of the other in such a manner that it would assume that other force's status for the purposes of the military action.

---

170. As correctly pointed out by *Bowett: United Nations Forces* (London 1964) pp. 256–7, there is, for a number of reasons, no justification for regarding West New Guinea (*above*, Chapter II,8) 'as a precedent for the United Nations supplying any State with internal security forces simply because its own security forces were inadequate for their tasks'.

EXTENT OF APPLICABILITY OF THE LAWS OF WAR TO ACTIONS AGAINST AN AGGRESSOR. DISCRIMINATION IN FAVOUR OF THE UNITED NATIONS?

1. INTRODUCTION

A United Nations Force will normally become involved in genuine military operations only against an aggressor, i.e. a State or other community which has attacked another State or the United Nations itself. It is true that no such limitation is laid down in the Charter for actions under the specific provisions of Articles 42 et seq. From this Kelsen [1] draws the conclusion that the Security Council is entitled 'to direct enforcement action against a Member which legally, that is, from the point of view of international law, is not wrong, since it has not violated any obligation expressly imposed upon it by the text of the Charter.' However, whatever may be the law under the Charter, it is hardly conceivable that the Security Council would decide to undertake a genuine military action against an independent State which is not an aggressor.[2] And action not based on Articles 42 et seq., as well as any action against non-member States, may have to be based upon general international law and then obviously can only be undertaken when permitted by that law, namely in individual or collective self-defence,[3] i.e. in defence of a State victim of aggression or of the United Nations itself.

If the action thus is directed against an aggressor, it is submitted that the United Nations, as well as any individual States which come to the aid of the victim State, must be entitled to claim the benefit of any preferential status vis-à-vis the aggressor which the victim State is entitled to claim with regard to the conduct of the war. It is therefore necessary to attempt to establish whether and to what extent the existing laws of

---

1. The Law of the United Nations, pp. 727–30. See also Verzijl in 50 *Annuaire de l'Institut de droit international, Session de Bruxelles 1963*, I, p. 48.

2. As for the nature of the military operations of the peace-keeping Force in the Congo against Katanga, see Draper: 'The Legal Limitations upon the Employment of Weapons by the United Nations Force in the Congo', *The International and Comparative Law Quarterly. XII* (1963) pp. 387–413. See also Torsten *Gihl: Om freden och säkerheten* (Stockholm 1962) pp. 364 et seq.

3. Cf. *above*, Chapter IV,5(a).

war applicable between States discriminate between the aggressor and the victim. This question shall be examined below, under 2, to the extent that it is possible to do so within the scope of the present study. Thereupon it will be attempted to establish, under 3 and 4, whether further deviations from the regular laws of war apply, or can be introduced by the United Nations, on the ground that the action is a United Nations enforcement action rather than (defensive) war, or that it is conducted by the United Nations under its own command and responsibility rather than by Member States acting pursuant to its recommendation, or that it is based on constitutional provisions rather than upon the right of collective self-defence under general international law.

It is these questions which give room for genuine doubt and which probably are at the root of the divergence of views referred to above, in Chapter V,3(d), and of the demands for a study of the problem and for the elaboration of a revised code for United Nations military actions.[4] The divergence appears to have arisen out of relatively abstract discussions. It can be resolved only on the basis of a separate examination of each sanction and each field of the laws of war. This will be attempted below.

2. DEVIATIONS FROM THE TRADITIONAL LAWS OF WAR IN FAVOUR OF THE STATE VICTIM OF AGGRESSION

(a) *The prohibition of aggressive war. Discrimination against the aggressor. General*

(i) Under the traditional laws of war there was no discrimination between aggressor and defender. The predominant opinion until the Second World War was stated in the sixth edition of Oppenheim's International Law (1940) as follows (§ 61):

> Whatever may be the cause of a war that has broken out, and whether or no the cause be a so-called just cause, the same rules of International Law are valid as to what must not be done, may be done, and must be done by the belligerents themselves in making war against each other, and as between the belligerents and neutral States. This is so, even if the declaration of war is *ipso facto* a violation of International Law, as when a belligerent declares war upon a neutral State for refusing passage to its troops, or when a State goes to war in patent violation of its obligations under the Covenant of the League or of the General Treaty for the Renunciation of War. To say that, because such a declaration of war is *ipso facto* a violation of International Law, it is 'inoperative in law and without any judicial significance', is erroneous. The rules of International Law apply to war *from whatever cause it originates*.[5]

4. *Above*, pp. 179 and 208.
5. This passage was quoted by the United States Military Tribunal in the Hostages Case, but in the context of war crimes, see *below*, under (d).

However, the customary laws of war, the Hague Conventions and some of the other conventions on warfare were established at a time when it was legal to commence a war. Since then, the Covenant of the League of Nations has *excluded the right to go to war* in certain circumstances,[6] a number of non-aggression pacts and similar bilateral treaties have been concluded, the Briand-Kellogg Pact of 27 August 1928, to which practically all States of the world adhered, has excluded war 'as an instrument of national policy' against such other parties to the Pact as have not themselves violated it,[7] and the Charter of the United Nations has provided in Article 2(4) that 'all Members shall refrain in their international relations from the threat or use of force against the territorial integrity or political independence of any State, or in any other manner inconsistent with the Purposes of the United Nations'.

The Charter of the International Military Tribunal at Nürnberg of 8 August 1945 declared as an international crime the 'planning, preparation, initiation or waging of a war of aggression, or a war in violation of international treaties, agreements or assurances',[8] and the Tribunal, in its judgment of 1 October 1946, declared that the Charter was 'the expression of international law existing at the time of its creation'.[9] The General Assembly of the United Nations, in its unanimous resolution 95(I), *affirmed* 'the principles of international law recognized by the Charter of the Nürnberg Tribunal and the judgment of the Tribunal'. Thus the Nürnberg Tribunal and the General Assembly considered aggressive war to be a crime, not only as between the parties to the treaties referred to above, but under *general* international law. The principle that aggression is the gravest of all crimes against peace was specifically and solemnly reaffirmed by the General Assembly in resolution 380 (V).

The International Law Commission has included similar statements in its Draft Formulation of the Nürnberg Principles and its Draft Code of Offences against the Peace and Security of Mankind.[10] The latter provides in Article 2:

> The following acts are offences against the peace and security of mankind:
> (1) Any act of aggression, including the employment by the authorities of a State of armed force against another State for any purpose other than national or

6. See Articles 12(1), 13(4) and 15(6)–(7). In 1927 the Secretary-General of the League refused to draw discriminatory conclusions therefrom in relation to *non*-member States, see *Reports and Resolutions on the Subject of Article 16 of the Covenant* (Geneva 1927) p. 87, cf. pp. 84 and 86.

7. See Article I and the fourth paragraph of the preamble.

8. Article 6(a), *UNTS*, Vol. 82, p. 288.

9. *AJIL*, XLI (1947) pp. 216–20; *Miscellaneous*, No. 12 (1946), Cmd. 6964, pp. 38–39, cf. p. 36.

10. *Yearbook of the International Law Commission*, 1950, II, p. 376, and 1951, II, p. 135.

collective self-defence or in pursuance of a decision or recommendation by a competent organ of the United Nations.

The Commission's draft Declaration on the Rights and Duties of States provides:

> Every State has the duty to refrain from resorting to war as an instrument of national policy, and to refrain from the threat or use of force against the territorial integrity or political independence of another State, or in any other manner inconsistent with international law and order.[11]

The result of this development is, as pointed out by Brandweiner, that war, i.e. application of military force by States, will always constitute either a delict (aggression) or a sanction (in the exercise of the right of individual or collective self-defence).[12]

(ii) In these circumstances, as has been demonstrated in greater detail in a war-time study by the present writer,[13] *it can no longer be maintained that the laws of war apply in all respects equally to the aggressor and the defenders.* Basically, the aggressor could not derive from his illegal act any rights under the customary laws of war or under conventions adopted before the treaties outlawing war.[14] On the other hand, as was also pointed out in the above-mentioned study, the interests of humanity and of the defenders themselves make it impossible to draw all the logical consequences from this in itself just principle. In particular, all humanitarian rules protecting individuals, whether military personnel or civilians, must remain in force equally for both parties.

---

11. Article 9, *ibid.*, 1949, p. 288; text also annexed to General Assembly resolution 375 (IV) which took 'note' of the draft Declaration.

12. Brandweiner in *Neue Justiz* (East Berlin) 1954, p. 226. On United Nations sanctions against non-aggressors, see *above*, under 1 *in initio*.

13. 'Okkupantens "rettigheter"', *Tidsskrift for rettsvitenskap* (Oslo) 1945, pp. 114–38, written during the German occupation of Norway, and concerned especially with the law of military occupation in cases where the illegal aggression had *not* been authoritatively determined; see also the corresponding, but somewhat more radical practice reported *ibid.*, 1946, pp. 267–75. More general and somewhat more radical studies in the same sense are the articles by Quincy Wright in *AJIL*, XXXIX (1945) pp. 365–76 and XLVII (1953) pp. 365–76, and by H. Lauterpacht in *Law and Politics in the World Community* (Berkeley and Los Angeles 1953) pp. 89–113. Above all reference is made to Lauterpacht's excellent subsequent study: 'The Limits of the Operation of the Law of War' in *BYIL*, XXX (1953) pp. 206–43, where he partly went back on his earlier views in the light of court practice after the Second World War (i.e. on the basis of cases where the aggression had not been determined by the Security Council). His then more conservative views are based partly upon the jurisprudence in respect of war crimes, which is irrelevant in other fields (*see below*, under (d) *in fine*), and partly upon a more heavy reliance upon court practice and a less heavy reliance upon State practice than in the present study.

14. See Lauterpacht in *BYIL*, XXX (1953) pp. 208–9, on the application in this context of the principle that new law supersedes earlier law inconsistent therewith. On other possible theoretical bases for discrimination, see *below*, under (e)(ii).

A view in this sense was expressed in the seventh edition of Oppenheim's International Law (1952, § 61) where it is stated, inter alia:

> An illegal war ... can no longer confer upon the guilty belligerent all the rights which traditional International Law, characterised as it was by the unlimited right of States to wage war for the purpose both of enforcing and challenging legal rights, conferred upon the belligerent. *Ex injuria jus non oritur* is an inescapable principle of law. At the same time, in view of the humanitarian character of a substantial part of the rules of war it is imperative that *during the war* these rules should be mutually observed regardless of the legality of the war ... However, ... these considerations apply only for the duration of the war. After the end of the hostilities there is full room for the application of the principle that no rights and benefits can accrue to the aggressor from his unlawful act.

Ten years later the principle of discrimination was accepted also by the *Institut de droit international.* This association took up the question, first in 1955-58 as part of the studies of a committee on 'Reconsideration of the Principles of the Law of War' and later, from 1962 onwards, through a special committee on 'Equality of Application of the Rules of the Law of War to Parties to an Armed Conflict'. Professor *François,* the Rapporteur of both committees, wrote several reports, which proposed a number of resolutions on the subject. While the majority of the first committee opposed discrimination even in the case of a United Nations action,[15] only two or three members of the second committee did so, the rest supported discrimination to varying degrees.[16] On the basis of Professor François' report for the second committee the *Institut,* at its session in Brussels in September 1963, adopted the following resolution:

> *The Institute of International Law,*
> *Considering,* on the one hand, that obligations whose purpose is to restrain the horrors of war and which are imposed on belligerents for humanitarian reasons by Conventions in force, by the general principles of law and by the rules of customary law, are always in force for the parties *in all categories of armed conflicts and apply equally to actions undertaken by the United Nations;*
> *Being of the opinion,* on the other hand, subject to the above reservation, that there cannot be complete equality in the application of the rules of the law of war when the competent organ of the United Nations has determined that one of the belligerents has resorted to armed force in violation of the rules of the law of nations consecrated by the Charter of the United Nations;
> *Invites* the fourth Commission to continue its study of the question to what extent and under what conditions this inequality must be accepted.[17]

---

15. See the report in 47 *Annuaire de l'Institut de droit international, Session d'Amsterdam 1957,* I, p. 531, cf. pp. 323 et seq.; especially pp. 326-35, 498-505 and 531.

16. *Ibid., 50 Session de Bruxelles 1963,* I, pp. 115 et seq.

17. *Ibid.,* II, p. 376, discussion pp. 306-56. This resolution supersedes a contrary earlier *draft* resolution cited by *Bowett: United Nations Forces* (London 1964) p. 499 from *loc.cit. above,* note 15, p. 531. Italics added.

Support for the principle of discrimination now comes from both Western and Communist [18] jurists, as well as from the United Nations.[19] However, the principle is still strongly opposed by a number of writers, including prominent lawyers from neutral countries,[20] and by the *Comité international de la Croix-Rouge*, primarily on the basis of the difficulty of defining and determining aggression and the resulting risk that the principle may benefit the victor, rather than the victim.

(iii) It is frequently maintained, as in the above quotation from Oppenheim's International Law,[21] that the basis criterion is one of time: While no discrimination can take place *durante bello*, discrimination can take place after the war. However, this is not the relevant legal criterion. As will appear from the discussion below, it is necessary to distinguish according to the nature of the norms concerned and the sanctions to be applied, rather than according to the time of their application. Each type of sanction and each main field of the laws of war must be evaluated separately, and the results thus arrived at must in principle be applied both during and after the war. Or, expressed in the Latin terms usually employed in discussions of this problem, the *jus ad bellum* must be taken into account in determining the *jus in bello* as well as the *jus post bellum*. A different matter is that some of the sanctions in respect of which the discrimination applies, are in fact usually applied only after the war, and then it is possible to apply them only if the aggressor is defeated. This is true notably of reparation, but not necessarily of restitution. It is also true that politically weak neutral States are not in a position to discriminate during the war, at least not as long as no determination of aggression has been made by the Security Council. However, this is not true of politically strong States, as practice during the Second World War demonstrates.[22]

(iv) A main subject of contention among those who support discrimination is the question of to what types of conflicts it should apply. Some

18. See Zourek's interventions, *ibid.*, II, pp. 317–9 and 350. However, Brandweiner earlier expressed a contrary view in *Neue Justiz* (East Berlin) 1954, p. 225.

19. Liang, Director of the Codification Division, as reported in *Yearbook of the International Law Commission*, 1949, p. 53.

20. For exposés of their views, see notably Bindschedler in 50 *Annuaire de l'Institut de droit international, Session de Bruxelles 1963*, II, pp. 314–6 and 347–8; Castrén, *ibid.*, pp. 311–3; and Ruegger, *ibid.*, pp. 328–9; but see Guggenheim, *ibid.*, p. 330. See also Kunz, *ibid.*, I, pp. 86–95; Rosenne, *ibid.*, II, pp. 316–7; Paul de Visscher in *Revue de droit international et de droit comparé* (Bruxelles) 1963, p. 170; Huber in *Revue internationale de la Croix-Rouge*, XXXVII (1955) at p. 433, cf. p. 420; and *Attia: Les forces armées des Nations Unies en Corée et au Moyen-Orient* (Genève 1963) pp. 258–9. For a fuller presentation of the view opposing discrimination, see Kunz: 'The Laws of War' in *AJIL*, L (1956) at pp. 317–20.

21. See also Lauterpacht in *BYIL*, XXX (1953) p. 214, cf. p. 232, but see pp. 236–7. Cf. also Attia, *op. cit.*, p. 257.

22. See *below*, under (i).

maintain that it must apply to all cases of aggression, while the majority seem to require *determination of aggression and designation of the aggressor* by the Security Council of the United Nations in accordance with Article 39 of the Charter. Extensive practice exists only with respect to the situation where no determination of aggression has been made by a political world organization. The following discussion shall be based mainly upon practice in connexion with the Second World War, where this was largely [23] the case, and which took place *after* the conclusion of the general conventions outlawing war and where, fortunately, the aggressors were finally overpowered and thus prevented from resisting the execution of the law.

The question of discrimination shall be discussed, first in relation to the various forms of sanctions against the aggressor [(b)-(e)], then in relation to four main, broad substantive fields of the laws of war [(f)-(i)] and, finally, in relation to the conventions on warfare [(j)].

(b) *Reparation and restitution*

There can be no doubt that the aggressor State, in accordance with a general principle of international law, is bound to provide restitution or reparation for all damage caused in the course of the war illegally startted by it, irrespective of whether the acts by which it caused the damage were within or without the limits of the traditional laws of war.

(i) Thus the aggressor must pay *reparation* for all contributions imposed upon an occupied territory and for *ususfructus* of property therein even if such contributions or *ususfructus* did not exceed the limits laid down in Articles 46-56 of the Regulations Concerning the Laws and Customs of Warfare on Land, annexed to the Fourth Hague Convention. Even before the general outlawry of war by (the Covenant of the League of Nations and) the Briand-Kellogg Pact, this principle was stated in Article 231 of the Treaty of Versailles as follows:

> The Allied and Associated Governments affirm and Germany accepts the responsibility of Germany and her allies for causing all the loss and damage to which the Allied and Associated Governments and their nationals have been subjected as a consequence of the war imposed upon them by the aggression of Germany and her allies.

However, in the following Article the Allied Governments confined their claim mainly to damage inflicted upon their civilian population.[24] Only in respect of Belgium was full compensation insisted upon, including reimbursement of costs incurred by the Government for waging the war against the aggressor. This was done on the explicit basis of Germany's violation of the Treaty of 1839 which guaranteed Belgium's neutral-

---

23. See *below*, at note 186.

24. Annexes I, III and IV to Article 244 partly go further. Cf. also para. 1 of the Annex to Article 297.

ity. The violation of this treaty had, incidentally, been voluntarily admitted in the German *Reichstag* on 4 August 1914 by Reichschancellor von Bethmann-Hollweg [25] who, however, (invalidly) pleaded self-defence (*Notwehr,* not *Notstand*) and indicated that Germany would try and repair the injustice (*Unrecht*) after the war.[26]

After the conclusion of the Covenant of the League of Nations and the Briand-Kellogg Pact, the principle adopted in respect of Belgium was extended to all defenders, without regard to whether they were direct victims of aggression or whether they had voluntarily come to the assistance of the victims. The leading commentary to the Covenant, written by two outstanding German jurists, had already established the aggressor's duty to pay reparation for all expenses and losses incurred by the Members of the League of Nations as a result of his violation of the Covenant, including costs and losses involved in military and economic sanctions.[27] This principle was applied after the Second World War. Although no Peace Treaty has yet been concluded with Germany and although only a small part of the reparations have been paid, the percentages laid down in part I, Article I B, of the inter-allied reparation agreement of 21 December 1945/14 January 1946 for each Allied Power's share of the total German reparations, were based on a computation of their total losses and expenses in connexion with the war,[28] without regard to whether the damage had been caused by acts which did or did not exceed the limits of the traditional laws of war.

Later the Federal Republic of Germany has attempted to confine its voluntary reparation payments to cases where the traditional laws of war had been violated, including in particular the persecution of the Jews.[29] In the agreements concluded with the formerly occupied countries of Western Europe concerning reparation to individual victims the Federal Republic did not accept an express reference to those victims who had been arrested, tortured and killed because of resistance to the occupant. Thus the agreement with Norway of 7 August 1959 provides in Article I for reparation for the benefit of Norwegian nationals who had fallen victim of 'national-socialist measures of persecution because

25. 'Das widerspricht den Geboten des Völkerrechts.'

26. *Verhandlungen des Reichstages,* 13te Legislaturperiode, Zweite Session, 1914, Band 306 (Berlin 1916), 1. Sitzung, 4. August 1914, pp. 6–7. He went somewhat back on it four months later, see *ibid.,* 4te Sitzung, 2. Dezember 1914, p. 18.

27. *Schücking und Wehberg: Die Satzung des Völkerbundes,* 2nd edition (Berlin 1924) p. 633, as quoted *below,* note 205.

28. See for example *Preliminary Report on Germany's Crimes Against Norway* (Oslo 1945) pp. 34–36.

29. See the Agreement with Israel and the appended Protocol with the Conference on Jewish Material Claims against Germany of 10 September 1952 (*UNTS,* Vol. 162, pp. 206 and 270; *Bundesgesetzblatt* II, 1953, p. 94) on the reparation to the Jews.

of their race, faith or conviction'. However, an additional provision leaves the distribution of the sums to the discretion of the Norwegian Government,[30] and this cleared the way for payments to members of the resistance movement,[31] who accordingly received payments on the same footing as victims of racial or political persecution. Nevertheless, the absence of a formal German admission of liability without regard to the provisions of the Hague Convention was strongly criticized during the ratification debate in the Norwegian Parliament, where speakers of different political parties emphasized the absence of any legal or moral right on the part of the German authorities to invoke that Convention as a limitation of their obligations.[32]

The peace treaties concluded after the Second World War with Italy and the smaller Axis Powers provided for fixed sums as reparation to the countries they invaded, without indicating how these sums had been computed.[33] It is, however, obvious that the bases are the fact of invasion and the amount of damage caused, rather than the question of the incompatibility of the acts causing damage with the traditional laws of war. The Treaty of Peace with Japan recognizes 'that Japan should pay reparations to the Allied Powers for the damage and suffering caused by it during the war', but 'that the resources of Japan are not presently sufficient . . . to make complete reparation for all such damage and suffering . . .' [34] It is clear from this and the subsequent provisions that the duty to pay reparation is not limited to damage caused in violation of the traditional laws of war.

The principle of the complete liability of the aggressor has now been recognized in the Report to the *Institut de droit international* of the second François Committee referred to under (a) above. The Rapporteur proposed the following draft resolution (X):

---

30. *Overenskomster med fremmede stater* (Oslo) 1960, p. 482. Article I reads:
'1) Die Bundesrepublik Deutschland zahlt an das Königreich Norwegen sechzig Millionen Deutsche Mark zugunsten der aus Gründen der Rasse, des Glaubens oder der Weltanschauung von nationalsozialistischen Verfolgungsmassnahmen betroffenen norwegischen Staatsangehörigen, die durch diese Verfolgungsmassnahmen Freiheitsschäden oder Gesundheitsschädigungen erlitten haben, sowie zugunsten der Hinterbliebenen der infolge dieser Verfolgungsmassnahmen Umgekommenen.
2) Die Verteilung des Betrages bleibt dem Ermessen der Königlich Norwegischen Regierung überlassen.'
31. During the negotiations the German Government agreed to drop a clause which would have precluded members of the resistance movement from the reparation, *Stortingsproposisjon nr. 29* (1959–60) pp. 4–5, *Stortingsinnstilling nr. 99* (1959–60) p. 307.
32. Partly because of the illegal aggression and partly because of the German disregard for the laws of war. *Stortingstidende*, 1959–60, pp. 1565 et seq.
33. For example, the treaties with Italy, Article 74 (*UNTS*, Vol. 49, p. 154), and with Bulgaria, Article 21 (*UNTS*, Vol. 41, p. 64).
34. Article 14, *UNTS*, Vol. 136, p. 62.

La responsabilité de l'agresseur pour les conséquences de son agression en matière de réparation financière, reste entière, même s'il s'est conformé aux droits des belligérants quant à la façon dont il a fait la guerre.

(ii) As for *restitution,* it was the policy of the Allies after the Second World War [35] to return to the original owner property which Germany had acquired from or in Allied countries, irrespective of whether the Germans had seized them as prizes or booty or requisitioned or otherwise acquired them in accordance with the traditional laws of war. This policy was embodied in the decisions of the Allied Control Council for Germany with regard to identifiable objects found in Germany which the owners had not ceded voluntarily to the German authorities, irrespective of whether the latter had re-transferred them to German nationals. The principle was also embodied in bilateral agreements concluded between the Allied Powers concerning the restitution of ships and other property recaptured from, or left behind in the occupied countries by, the German invaders.[36] Although exceptions were made to this principle in relations between Allied governments and nationals (notably in cases where an Allied government had taken the property as war booty and subsequently transferred it to Allied nationals),[37] there is no indication that such exceptions were made in respect of property which was still held by German authorities or German nationals and where therefore the principle *ex injuria jus non oritur* applied with particular force. The question of restitution will be discussed in more detail below, under (g) (ii).

(iii) On the other hand, it is submitted that even the illegal aggressor must be entitled to *reparation and restitution from the defenders* (the victim of aggression and his allies) for injury and loss inflicted upon the personnel and nationals of the aggressor by acts which violate those traditional laws of war which are binding even upon the defenders,[38] including the provisions of the Geneva Conventions. If these are to be

35. As for the First World War, see Article 238 of the Treaty of Versailles and Article 184 of the Treaty of St. Germain.

36. See for example the agreements concluded between Norway and the United Kingdom, on 24 September 1945 concerning the Disposal of Property Falling into the Hands of the Allied Forces in Norway, Articles I–II, and on 11 October 1945 concerning the Use and Disposal of United Nations Vessels Captured or Found by their Forces in the Course of Operations for the Liberation of Europe, part II (*Overenskomster med fremmede stater inngått i årene 1940–45,* Oslo 1950, pp. 313 and 362), and the similar agreement concluded between the United States and the United Kingdom on 7 May/15 June 1945 (*UNTS,* Vol. 89, p. 327, *United Kingdom Treaty Series,* No. 28 [1946]. On these 'Liberated Ships Agreements', see *below,* pp. 258–9.

37. See *below,* pp. 249–50.

38. See *below,* under (f)–(j). In this sense also Wright, *AJIL,* XLVII (1953) pp. 372–3.

legally binding upon the defenders, then at least this sanction must apply to them if they violate this obligation. The individual victims of their violations must be entitled to reparation and restitution. And at the present stage of development of international law their government, even if in principle 'outlawed', must probably be allowed to present their claims.[40] As far as grave breaches of the Geneva Conventions are concerned, this submission is reinforced by provisions therein to the effect that no contracting party shall be allowed to absolve himself of liability in respect of grave breaches of their provisions.[41] In the view of the *Comité international de la Croix-Rouge* these provisions are intended to:

> empêcher que, dans une convention d'armistice ou dans un traité de paix, le vaincu ne soit contraint de renoncer à toute réparation due à raison d'infractions commises par des personnes se trouvant au service du vainqueur.[42]

As for practice, it may be noted that in the peace treaties concluding the Second World War, the Axis Powers waived all claims of their governments or nationals against the Allied Powers arising out of the war.[43]

(c) *Criminal and civil liability of the leaders responsible for the aggression*

Those political and military leaders of the aggressor State who are responsible for the decision to go to war, must personally carry criminal and civil liability for damage and cost inflicted upon other States and their nationals as a consequence of the war unleashed by them, including damage caused by acts which are not outlawed under the traditional laws of war.

As for *criminal* responsibility, this principle was laid down in Article 6 of the Charter of the International Military Tribunal in Nürnberg of 8 August 1945.[44] This provided that 'leaders, organisers, instigators and accomplices participating in the formulation or execution of a common plan or conspiracy to commit any of the foregoing crimes [including aggressive or illegal war] [45] are responsible for all acts performed by any persons in execution of such plan'. It has already been pointed out that the principles of international law recognized by the Charter and

40. Cf. *below*, under (f)(ii) *in initio*.
41. See for example Article 131 of the Geneva Convention on the Treatment of Prisoners of War.
42. *Comité international de la Croix-Rouge, Commentaire à la Convention de Genève relative au traitement des prisonniers de guerre* (Genève 1958) p. 664.
43. See for example Article 76 of the Italian Peace Treaty (*UNTS*, Vol. 49, p. 158).
44. *UNTS*, Vol. 82, p. 288. This does not mean that such acts constitute 'war crimes', cf. *below*, under (d)(i), on the judgment of the Tribunal.
45. Article 6(a), quoted *above*, p. 223.

the judgment of the Nürnberg Tribunal were unanimously affirmed by resolution 95(I) of the General Assembly of the United Nations.[46]

The question of *civil* liability is rather theoretical. It has not been brought before international courts. National courts will of course be bound by municipal law. When the applicable municipal law contains no clear rule, national courts may apply the principle of international law submitted above. However, this does not necessarily mean that this principle, in the absence of appropriate provisions in treaties, constitutes a limitation upon the freedom in this respect of national legislators.

(d) *Criminal and civil liability of personnel executing the aggression*

On the other hand, only violations of the traditional laws of war constitute *war crimes* for which individuals may be prosecuted under international law. The personnel of the aggressor cannot be prosecuted merely for having borne arms against the peaceful victim of aggression, or for acts not exceeding the limits of the traditional laws of war, at least not if they have acted pursuant to superior orders.

(i) This was no doubt the intention when Article 6(b) of the Charter of the *International Military Tribunal* defined war crimes as 'violations of the laws and customs of war'. The Tribunal, in its judgment over the German major war criminals, stated that such crimes were covered by specific provisions of the Regulations annexed to The Hague Convention concerning the Laws and Customs of War on Land and of the Geneva Convention on the Treatment of Prisoners of War. It refused to find, for example, Admiral Dönitz guilty of war crimes in respect of such inhuman acts as could be justified under the traditional laws of war,[47] although the Tribunal avoided pressing the point too far.[48] A similar attitude was taken by the United States Military Tribunal at Nürnberg

46. The International Law Commission did not include the principle discussed here in the text of its 'Formulation of the Nürnberg Principles' and its 'Draft Code of Offences Against the Peace and Security of Mankind', elaborated pursuant to the same resolution (*Yearbook of the International Law Commission*, 1950, II, pp. 374 et seq., and 1951, II, pp. 133 et seq.; cf. General Assembly resolutions 177 (II), 488 (V) and 1186 (XII)).

47. *AJIL*, XLI (1947) pp. 248 and 304; *Miscellaneous*, No. 12 (1946), Cmd. 6964, p. 109.

48. Thus the judgment also contains the following *obiter dictum*: 'A further submission was made that Germany was no longer bound by the rules of land warfare in many of the territories occupied during the war, because Germany had completely subjugated those countries and incorporated them into the German Reich, a fact which gave Germany authority to deal with the occupied countries as though they were part of Germany. In the view of the Tribunal it is unnecessary in this case to decide whether this doctrine of subjugation, dependent as it is upon military conquest, has any application where the subjugation is the result of the crime of aggressive war.' (*AJIL*, XLI [1947] p. 249).

in the *Hostages Trial* against von List, Rendulic and others.[49] Thus General Rendulic, although found guilty on several counts, was found not guilty for having systematically burnt and devastated every house and every cottage in Norwegian Lappland and for having deported the entire population in order to prevent them from assisting the advancing Soviet (and Norwegian) troops. The Court referred to Article 23g of the Hague Regulations which prohibits destruction which is not 'imperatively demanded by the necessities of war' and stated that, although there was in fact no such necessity, the conditions as they appeared to the defendant at the time were sufficient to justify a conclusion that urgent military necessity existed.[50]

This principle, too, must be considered to be one of those principles of international law recognized by the Charter of the Nürnberg Tribunal and the judgment of the Tribunal which were affirmed by the General Assembly of the United Nations in its resolution 95(I).

The International Law Commission, in its Formulation of the Nürnberg Principles and its Draft Code of Offences against the Peace and Security of Mankind, similarly defined war crimes as violations of the laws or customs of war. It was even in doubt as to whether 'every violation of the laws or customs of war should be regarded as a crime under the code or whether only acts of a certain gravity should be characterised as such crimes'.[51]

It is thus clear that war crimes do not include such (less grave) acts as do not constitute violations of the traditional laws of war. Indeed, it would be unreasonable to apply criminal (or even civil) sanctions for such acts of the military personnel of the aggressor who had no part in deciding to wage the aggressive war. Even in respect of those political and military leaders who were responsible for this decision, and who are thus responsible also for such acts as are not forbidden under the traditional laws of war, such acts must be dealt with as part of the charge of

---

49. See the quotations by Lauterpacht in *BYIL*, XXX (1953), pp. 215 and 218, from the judgments of the United States Military Tribunal at Nürnberg in the Hostages and High Command Cases (*contra:* The Ministries Case, cited *ibid.*, p. 219). However, these judgments do not *state* that the principle of discrimination does not apply to war crimes. In the Hostages Case the non-application of that principle is stated in general terms, quoting inter alia the passage from the 6th edition of *Oppenheim's International Law* which was quoted *above*, under (a) (*Law Reports of Trials of War Criminals, selected and prepared by the United Nations War Crimes Commission*, London 1949, VIII, p. 59), it was the context rather than the terms of the reasoning which was confined to war crimes.

50. *Trials of War Criminals before the Nürnberg Military Tribunals*, IX, (Washington 1950) pp. 1295–7, cf. pp. 1113–36.

51. *Yearbook of the International Law Commission*, 1950, II, p. 377, and 1951, II, pp. 59 and 136.

aggressive war and should not be stigmatized as 'war crimes'. This may have been the view of the International Military Tribunal at Nürnberg, when finding Admiral Raeder guilty on count two of planning aggressive war without finding him guilty on count three for war crimes in respect of acts of unrestricted submarine warfare which could be justified under the traditional laws of war.[52]

(ii) The principle that even the nationals of the aggressor cannot be punished for acts which do not violate the traditional laws of war must probably apply also in *criminal proceedings before national courts*.[53]

Reference has already been made to the judgments of the United States Military Tribunal at Nürnberg. This adjudicated on the basis of the Allied Control Council for Germany's Law No. 10 of 20 December 1945, which authorized the prosecution of war criminals before the courts of each zone of occupation in Germany, and which defined war crimes as 'atrocities or offences against persons or property constituting violations of the laws or customs of war'.[54] Like its model, the Charter of the International Military Tribunal, this must be interpreted as referring to the traditional laws of war.

The same principle was applied when national courts of the formerly occupied countries prosecuted German war criminals under their own criminal law. Thus § 1 of the Norwegian Provisional Ordinance of 4 May 1945, provided that 'acts which according to their nature are covered by Norwegian criminal law shall be punished under Norwegian law if they were committed, in violation of the laws and customs of war, by enemy aliens or other aliens who have been in enemy service or have belonged under him...' This law, too, was applied by the Norwegian courts only against violations of the traditional laws of war.[55]

---

52. *AJIL*, XLI (1947) p. 308; *Miscellaneous* No. 12 (1946), Cmd. 6964, p. 112. The judgment in respect of Raeder merely refers to the judgment in respect of Dönitz (*ibid.*, pp. 108–9), who was not found guilty on the count of planning aggressive war. It is thus not clear how comprehensive the reference is, or whether the Tribunal thought of the point at all.

53. See the more detailed discussion in *Tidsskrift for rettsvitenskap*, 1945, p. 124–5, and the practice reported *ibid.*, 1946, pp. 269–71.

54. Text reprinted in *International Conciliation*, No. 450 (April 1949) p. 359, from the *Official Gazette of the Control Council for Germany*, No. 3, 31 January 1946, p. 501.

55. In its first war crime judgment after the Second World War (against Karl-Hans Herman *Klinge*) the Norwegian Supreme Court stated: '... one cannot hold the individual German responsible for having come to this country—no matter how illegal the German aggression was. He can only be prosecuted for the misdeeds he committed during his stay here.' (*Norsk Retstidende*, 1945, pp. 210–1.) See also the decision reported in *Norsk Retstidende*, 1948, p. 1089, where the Norwegian Supreme Court rejected an appeal by the Prosecution against an acquittal of SS-Hauptmann Hans Latza for having passed death sentences on Norwegian nationals (lower court judgment in *Archiv des Völkerrechts*, I [1948–49] p. 120).

This appears to have been the practice, in respect of German nationals, also of the courts of a number of other Western European countries which had been occupied by Germany during the Second World War,[56] although in some cases the courts took the contrary view that, since Germany was the aggressor, German officials could not escape charges of theft, murder etc. by invoking 'rights' which would have followed from the traditional laws of war.[57] After the Second World War a Belgian court even held that an Austrian national could be punished for violation of legislation which had been enacted by the Belgian Government in exile and which forbade assistance to the enemy. The basis of this decision was that the attack upon and occupation of Belgium constituted violations of international law.[58] This is no doubt going too far.

(iii) The State which has been the victim of illegal aggression is of course free to prosecute *its own nationals* for assistance to the enemy even if the assistance was rendered pursuant to laws or orders, e.g. requisitions, of the aggressor which did not violate the traditional laws of war.[59] A different matter is that the victim of aggression may not wish to extend its criminal legislation so far,[60] and that its courts will not normally do so unless the criminal code so provides.[61]

On the other hand, the personnel and nationals of the defenders can-

56. See for example the Christiansen and Zuhlke cases, *Annual Digest of Public International Law Cases*, 1948, Cases Nos. 121–2.

57. See, for example, the cases reported by Lauterpacht in *BYIL*, XXX (1953) p. 219.

58. Judgment of 16 December 1919, reported by *Fraenkl: Military Occupation and the Rule of Law* (New York 1944) pp. 57–58.

59. In this sense also Quincy Wright in *AJIL*, XXXIX (1945) p. 271.

60. As for Norwegian law, see § 2 (2) cf. § 5, of the Provisional Ordinance on Treason of 15 December 1944, which hardly goes that far, cf. also the commentary thereto by *Solem: Landssvikanordningen* (Oslo 1945) p. 56, and Röed in *Tidsskrift for rettsvitenskap*, 1946, pp. 67 and 72. See also Mellbye, *ibid.*, 1945, p. 59.

61. See, however, a number of Dutch cases reported by Morgenstern, *BYIL*, XXVIII pp. 293–4, from *Annual Digest of International Law Cases*, 1946, Cases Nos. 144–5 and *Na-oorlogse Rechtspraak*, V (1949) No. 1381, where Dutch nationals were prosecuted for assistance rendered to the German occupant. Their pleas that under the Hague Regulations the Germans were entitled to demand from them the assistance concerned were rejected by the courts, not on the grounds that their acts were beyond the limits of the Hague Regulations (Morgenstern considers that in fact they did exceed these limits), but on the grounds that this question was irrelevant; only general principles of national penal law, such as those relating to *force majeure*, were relevant. A Norwegian judgment of 21 January 1946, reported in *Tidsskrift for rettsvitenskap*, 1946, p. 270, and *Norsk Retstidende*, 1946, p. 1040, also rejected a similar plea as irrelevant. The Supreme Court on appeal imposed an even more severe punishment, but, in contradistinction to the lower court, acted on the assumption that the defendant had in part assisted the Germans *voluntarily*. Although the judgment does not refer to the illegality of the German occupation of Norway, it nevertheless fails to take into account the Hague Regulations, which otherwise probably would have been considered part of Norwegian law in any case where they do not conflict with any statute.

235

not escape punishment for war crimes because of the fact that they have been committed against the personnel or nationals of an illegal aggressor. To the extent that the traditional laws of war, notably in the humanitarian field, are recognized as binding even upon the defenders,[62] it is necessary to maintain also the relevant criminal sanctions. A different question is whether *the aggressor State* has the right to perform the prosecution of the war criminals of the defender, or whether this should be left to the courts of the defender or to neutral courts. In practice nobody can prevent the aggressor from prosecuting the war criminals during the war, or even after the war if he wins it. The question therefore boils down to whether the defenders must recognize the validity of the aggressor's judgments if and to the extent that such a duty might exist at all. However, even these questions are largely theoretical, because the Geneva Conventions, which cover the major part of the humanitarian laws of war, provide for trial of war criminals by the Contracting Parties without discrimination.[65] As will be explained below, under (j), these Conventions are not subject to discrimination between aggressor and victim. To the extent that States have an *obligation* under international law to prosecute their own personnel and nationals for war crimes, this obligation must devolve upon the victim of aggression and its allies in respect of violations of those parts of the laws of war which are binding even upon these States. Indeed, the Geneva Conventions provide that all contracting parties shall take measures necessary for the suppression of all acts contrary to the Conventions and shall prosecute those who have committed certain specified grave breaches.[65]

(iv) The fact that only violations of the traditional laws of war are punished as war crimes is frequently cited by the opponents of the principle of discrimination, and even by others, as evidence that both parties are equally bound by these laws during the war despite the illegal character of the war undertaken by one of them.[66] However, this does not necessarily follow. Even municipal law does not impose criminal sanctions in respect of all illegal acts. Similarly, in international law the criminal responsibility of the individuals acting for the aggressor does not embrace *all* acts which the aggressor is not entitled to perform. Even if the persons performing the acts cannot be prosecuted as war criminals,

62. See *below*, under (f) et seq.

65. See for example Article 129 of the Convention on the Protection of Prisoners of War.

66. See for example Lauterpacht, *BYIL* XXX (1953) pp. 217 and 220; Bowett: *United Nations Forces* (London 1964) pp. 495–6; and the judgment by the Singapore Court of Appeal cited by him: N.V. de Bataafsche Petroleum Maatschappij and Others v. The War Damage Commission, *International Law Reports*, XXIII (1956) at p. 845. This judgment applied a dictum of the United States Military (criminal) Tribunal at Nürnberg in the Krupp case to a civil dispute concerning title to property. However, this application by the Singapore court was itself merely a dictum.

or as murderers or thieves under municipal law, it does not follow that their acts were lawful. In particular, it does not follow that the State on whose behalf they acted must be spared of other kinds of legal sanctions, such as invalidity of the act and duty to provide reparation or restitution. Thus, the fact that the criminal responsibility (*during and after* the war) of the individuals concerned is confined to violations of the traditional laws of war, does not necessarily mean that the aggressor has a legal 'right',[67] even during the war, to perform all acts which do not constitute violations of these laws. Some examples of this have been given above, under (b) and (c). Others shall be given below, under (g)-(i). On the contrary, as has been pointed out above, under (b), he must pay reparation for *all* acts which cause damage, and he must restitute all seized property. Even the title of those to whom he might have transferred the property may be invalidated, as shall be demonstrated under (g) and (h).

This distinction was rarely, if ever, brought out in the judgments of the International and the United States Military Tribunals at Nürnberg. However, one aspect not specified above was brought out by the Netherlands Special Court of Cassation in a judgment given in 1948. The Court held that, although the illegality of the German war of aggression would have entitled Holland to answer Germany's crime by reprisals, even to the extent of suspending the normal operation of the laws of war on land, at sea and in the air, the lower court had gone too far when it considered as war crimes all war-like acts, including those which were in accordance with the laws and customs of war, performed against Holland or against Dutch subjects by Germany's military forces or other State organs, on the sole ground of the illegality of her war of aggression. Article 27(a) of the Special Criminal Law Decree was intended to apply to acts which, apart from the fact that the Second World War was a war of aggression on the part of Germany, ran counter to the laws and customs of war, or to the laws of humanity.[68] Even if it cannot be admitted that the Netherlands would have been entitled to violate the traditional laws of war in the humanitarian field,[69] it does not go without saying that it could not legally do so in the economic field.[70]

(v) Indeed, one must probably go further and relieve the individuals who happen to have acted on behalf of the aggressor State even of *civil liability* for those of their acts which do not violate the traditional laws of war. It would not be reasonable to require them to pay *reparation* for

67. Cf. *below*, under (e)(iv).
68. The Zuhlke case, as summarized in *Annual Digest of Public International Law Cases*, 1948, Case No. 122.
69. *Below*, under (f).
70. Cf. *below*, under (g)–(h).

the damage caused by such acts performed pursuant to superior orders. On the other hand, one could theoretically require them to pay reparation if they have performed them upon their own initiative (or have carried out the superior orders more extensively than necessary) and they must have been aware of the aggressive nature of the war. The writer is not aware of any practice in respect of individual reparation. Even if it is assumed that the individuals concerned have no duty to pay reparation, it does not follow that the acts are lawful. It is not illogical that the duty to pay reparation vests in the person on whose behalf an act was performed rather than in his agent.

On the other hand, there is nothing to prevent the defending States from requiring those of their own nationals who have collaborated with the aggressor to pay reparation to their own government (or its allies). This was done on a large scale by the Norwegian Government after the Second World War, without basis in any specific pre-war legislation.

Whatever the situation may be in respect of reparation, there can be little doubt that the members of the armed forces (as well as civilian personnel, nationals and inhabitants) of the aggressor must *restitute* any property or other rights which have been acquired from the victim or his allies or their nationals or inhabitants otherwise than by a genuinely voluntary sale, even if the acquisition did not violate the traditional laws of war.[71]

(e) *Other sanctions. Reprisals. Theoretical basis of discrimination. 'Rights' for the aggressor?*

For the sake of completeness, a few words shall be said also about two other types of sanctions: Reprisals and invalidity.

(i) According to *Schwarzenberger*, the legality of *reprisals* depends, in the law of peace, on three conditions being fulfilled:

> (1) A prior illegal act must be the reason for the act of reprisal against the wrongdoer.
> (2) The application of reprisals must be preceded by an unsuccessful attempt to obtain redress for the alleged international tort.
> (3) The reprisals taken must not be patently excessive, that is to say, out of all proportion to the original wrong committed or run counter to the minimum requirements of the standard of civilization.

In addition, there is an absolute prohibition of certain acts, even by way of reprisals, under the conventions on warfare [72] and possibly under the general laws of war.[73]

71. See *above*, under (b), and *below*, under (g)(ii) and (h).

72. Geneva Conventions on Prisoners of War, Article 13, and on Civilians, Article 33; Hague Convention 1954 for the Protection of Cultural Property, Article 4(4).

73. *International Law Association, Report of the Fiftieth Conference, Brussels 1962*, pp. 220–1. See also *Castberg: Studier i Folkerett* (Oslo 1952) pp. 78–81, who in addi-

Within these limits the *defender* can of course apply reprisals against the aggressor in respect of such of his acts as violate the traditional laws of war (*jus in bello*). The question whether the *aggressor*, too, can resort to reprisals against acts by the defender which violate those, primarily humanitarian, laws of warfare which even they must observe,[74] is more doubtful. It should be remembered that the right of reprisals, i.e. the right to violate international law in order to force another violator of international law to stop doing so, is a dangerous principle.[75] It may be argued that, while the aggressor can claim reparation and restitution for the benefit of individual victims, and while he can possibly even apply criminal sanctions to the individual offenders as a deterrent against further violations, it would not be reasonable to allow him to inflict further sufferings upon the victim of his aggression by applying reprisals against the defender States and their forces in general. On the other hand, the latter may be the only practicable and effective deterrent. And it is not possible to prevent the aggressor from applying such reprisals. The question is whether others must recognize their validity, whether the aggressor is liable to pay reparation for them and whether his officials can be punished as war criminals for having resorted to reprisals. On the latter, the Netherlands Special Court of Cassation held in 1949 that a German war criminal could not invoke the usual belligerent right of reprisals in a war unleashed by the German aggression.[76]

(ii) A different question is whether the victim and his allies are entitled to apply *reprisals against the aggressor because of his illegal aggression*, i.e. even if he does *not* violate the traditional laws of war.[77]

tion criticizes the practice of reprisals against individuals for acts of their State or their compatriots, see now Article 34 of the Geneva Convention on the Protection of Civilians, which prohibits the taking of hostages.

74. *Below*, under (f)–(j).

75. *Castberg, op. cit.*, pp. 80–81.

76. The Rauter case, as reported by Lauterpacht, *BYIL*, XXX (1953) p. 219. But see another, somewhat confused and contradictory, Dutch judgment in *Annual Digest of Public International Law Cases*, XV (1948) Case No. 121 (the Christiansen case).

77. The Netherlands Special Court of Cassation has declared in a war crimes case that the Netherlands was entitled to answer the German aggression with reprisals, even with regard to the normal operation of the laws of war, and that Germany had no right to take counter reprisals (the Zuhlke case, *Annual Digest of Public International Law Cases*, 1948, Case No. 122, also cited *above* under (d)(iv); cf. also the Rauter case, *ibid.*, Case No. 131 and Albrecht in *AJIL*, XLVII [1953] p. 593). The United States Military Tribunal at Nürnberg stated in the *Ministries Case* that 'he who initiates aggressive war loses the right to claim self-defence against those who seek to enforce the Treaty' (*ibid.*, p. 219). On the other hand, the Netherlands Special Court for War Criminals at Arnhem held that the occupant waging an illegal war was entitled, in principle, to punish members of the resistance movement, except when such resistance was due to the unlawful acts of the occupant (Lauterpacht in *BYIL*, XXX (1953) p. 217). This was correct for the purposes of prosecution for war crimes, cf. *above*, under (d)(iv).

This they are only entitled to do within the limits outlined under (b)-(d) above and (f)-(i) below. Indeed, the question of reprisals against the aggressor's violation of the *jus ad bellum* is the same as the question of discrimination under discussion in the present chapter, and the difference is merely one of theoretical basis.

Some writers take the law of reprisals as the *theoretical basis of the discrimination*.[78] It would seem more natural to use as such basis the related right of *Notwehr* (individual and collective self-defence), i.e. the right to perform otherwise illegal acts in defence against an illegal attack.[79] Or one may, as suggested above under (a), base the discrimination upon the principle of *ex injuria jus non oritur*. (Schwarzenberger, *loc. cit.*, also suggests 'outlawry' of the aggressor as the theoretical basis; this may coincide with the principle of *ex injuria jus non oritur*, cf. below.) From this it follows, basically, that an illegal aggressor cannot claim any of those rights which the traditional laws of war confer upon belligerents. However, this principle can be given effect only to the extent that it does not conflict with humanitarian or other interests which must be protected in all circumstances or with other overriding principles of law.

Any of these three bases justify a *limited* discrimination in favour of the victim of aggression *and those coming to his assistance*.[80] The present writer, for his part, prefers the third basis.

It should be noted, however, that all of these three bases justify otherwise illegal acts only vis-à-vis the aggressor.[81] The right of the defenders to disregard certain neutral rights [82] must be based upon the illegality of assisting a criminal, now expressed in Article 2(5) of the United Nations Charter,[83] or upon *Notstand*, or upon the duty of 'neutral' Members of the United Nations under the Charter to assist the victim.

(iii) A final important type of sanction which ought to be mentioned is *invalidity of the acts of the aggressor*. The question of to what extent his acts are invalid shall be discussed in detail below, under (g)-(i). As

78. See notably Schwarzenberger in *Völkerrecht und rechtliches Weltbild, Festschrift für Alfred Verdross* (Wien 1960) p. 245, and in *International Law Association, Report of the Fiftieth Conference, Brussels 1962*, pp. 204–5, cf. pp. 211 and 220. Holloway, *ibid.*, p. 166, prefers to speak of sanctions.

79. Cf. *Tidsskrift for rettsvitenskap* (Oslo) 1945, p. 119. On the distinction between these two concepts, see *Castberg: Studier i Folkerett* (Oslo 1952), p. 75.

80. The latter extension can be justified even under Schwarzenberger's theory of reprisals, by the right of all contracting parties to the Kellogg Pact and the United Nations Charter to apply reprisals against the State violating these treaties, see *Völkerrecht und rechtliches Weltbild*, p. 246.

81. Cf. *Castberg, op. cit.*, pp. 75 and 79.

82. Cf. *below*, under 3(h)(ii).

83. *Below*, under 3(i).

for the occupant's and his personnel's acquisitions of property or other economic rights, it has already been indicated above, under (b), that he must restitute all property still in his possession (or within his territory). However, the question of the validity of his acquisitions arises also in relation to third parties who have acquired the property or right from him, by voluntary transfer or by seizure as prize or booty.

(iv) With regard to the question of which of the sanctions discussed under (b)-(e) above constitutes the crucial criterion for the existence and extent of a 'right', it would seem appropriate to deny the existence of a 'right' in all cases where *any* sanction is *permitted*. It is not necessary for the purposes of the present study to go further into this theoretical question, except to state that the terminology used in the following will be based upon the broadest of the sanctions discussed above. Thus, the aggressor will be considered to have no 'right' in those cases where he is liable to pay reparation or where his act is considered invalid. This in fact probably covers also all cases where any of the other sanctions apply.

It might be added that the present writer's view, as explained more fully in his wartime study on 'The "Rights" of the Occupant',[84] coincides with that so well expressed by Sir Humphrey Waldock in the following statement at the 1963 Brussels Conference of the *Institut de droit international*:

> L'Institut doit éviter tout texte de Résolution qui puisse suggérer, pendant une guerre d'agression, qu'il existe un *droit* à utiliser des armes conventionelles. Ce droit n'existe pas et ne peut pas exister. Il en est de même pour les mesures économiques, d'une importance particulière pour les Etats tiers: il n'y a pas de *droit* de recourir à ces mesures. Employer dans ce contexte le mot *droit* serait reprendre le langage du passé.[85]

After having thus established, on the basis of, an in most respects, relatively clear and consistent practice, that the fields of application of the various sanctions do not necessarily coincide, and that the applicability of one sanction suffices to deny the existence of a right, it is possible to turn successively to the main fields of the substantive laws of war and neutrality.

(f) *Humanitarian rules of warfare*

(i) There is a large measure of agreement—although partly on the basis of such conclusions from the law of war crimes as have been discarded above, under (d)(iv)—that the obligations arising out of the humanitarian rules of warfare, which are intended to protect individuals,

---

84. *Tidsskrift for rettsvitenskap* (Oslo) 1945, pp. 113 et seq.; see also *below*, under (f)(ii).

85. 50 *Annuaire de l'Institut de droit international, Session de Bruxelles 1963*, II, p. 325. See, however, *below*, under (f)(ii), on the Geneva Conventions.

military and civilian,[86] and cultural property, are binding both upon the aggressor *and the defender State*. This includes the rules for the protection of the members of the fighting forces, sick and wounded military personnel, prisoners of war, civilians, and cultural property.[87] To relieve the defender, vis-à-vis the aggressor, of his humanitarian duties under the traditional laws of war, would result, directly, in increased suffering for the military personnel and the civilian population of the aggressor, and, by way of (legal or illegal) reprisal, in suffering for the personnel and population of the defender. Indeed, there would be little or no hope of having the humanitarian laws respected by the aggressor if they were not also observed by the defender. Accordingly, it is submitted that, even under the modern laws of war, the defender is obliged to comply with those traditional laws of war which have a humanitarian purpose, and that he is liable to pay reparation for damage inflicted upon personnel and nationals of the aggressor in violation of these laws. This would also accord with the principle that the rights of reprisals and self-defence, as well as the principle of *ex injuria jus non oritur*, usually cited as the theoretical basis of the discrimination, strictly apply only against the aggressor *State*.[88] However, there are also other principles, such as the duty not to assist in the commission of a crime[89] and *Notstand,* which may interfere even with the rights of *individuals* under traditional law in the *economic* and related fields (this may be more practical in respect of individuals in enemy and neutral territory than in occupied territory).[90] In the strictly humanitarian field, however, even the defenders are obliged to observe the traditional laws of war.

(ii) More doubtful is the question whether this obligation of the defender corresponds to a right vested in *the aggressor State,* or whether it, as appears to be Quincy Wright's view,[91] constitutes merely a direct right under international law for the individuals concerned. At the present preliminary stage of development of direct individual rights under international law and of remedies available to individuals, it is probably necessary to retain the right of the aggressor State to protect its nationals in this as in other respects.

86. This is accepted, although on the different basis described under (ii) *below,* also by Quincy Wright (*AJIL,* XLVII [1946] pp. 373 and 375, cf. pp. 370–1), who otherwise goes further than most writers in drawing legal consequences from the illegality of aggressive war.

87. On the use of nuclear weapons, see *below,* under 3(f)(iv).

88. As for the two former (reprisals and self-defence), see *Castberg: Studier i folkerett* (Oslo 1952) pp. 75 and 79.

89. Now confirmed in Article 2(5), cf. Article 2(6), of the United Nations Charter.

90. Cf. *below,* under (g)–(i). Article 33 of the Geneva Convention for the Protection of Civilians prohibits 'reprisals against protected persons *and their property*'.

91. *Loc. cit. above,* note 86.

However, this does not mean that the aggressor has a legal *'right'* to impose such personal or economic sufferings or burdens upon enemy or neutral nationals as do not exceed the limits set by the traditional laws of war. Thus he has no legal 'right' under general [92] international law to retain prisoners of war who have not committed war crimes. Nor does he have a 'right' to prosecute spies or other civilians who assist the victim State. Even if it is not possible to prevent the aggressor from performing such acts during the war, he must bear the full international (and civil) responsibility for them, as described under (b) above. Similarly, other States are entitled to consider his judgments [93] and other acts as illegal and invalid, although his agents bear no criminal responsibility for the acts as independent crimes.[94] The aggressor's legal 'rights' are confined to that of claiming the protection of the humanitarian laws of war for his own military personnel and civilian nationals. This is why the traditional laws of war in the humanitarian field may be termed the 'minimum rules' [95] or the 'minimum standards',[96] because they represent the minimum which *both* parties must apply and are entitled to claim of each other, while, on the other hand, they exhaust the legal obligations of the defender only, not those of the aggressor.

The principle of non-discrimination in the humanitarian field and its limitation to the *obligations* and the corresponding passive rights, rather than the active rights, arising out of the humanitarian laws of war, have now been reflected in draft Resolution V unanimously supported by the Committee on Equality of Application of the Rules of the Law of War to Parties to an Armed Conflict of the *Institut de droit international*.[97] It reads:

> Les obligations, ayant pour but de restreindre les horreurs de la guerre et imposées aux belligérants pour des motifs humanitaires par les conventions en vigueur, par les principes généraux du droit ou par les règles du droit coutumier, sont toujours de rigueur pour les parties dans toutes les catégories de conflits armés, y compris l'action coercitive de la part de l'O.N.U. Il en est de même pour les règles concernant la participation de non-combattants aux opérations de la guerre.[98]

92. As for the Geneva Convention Relating to the Treatment of Prisoners of War, see *below*, p. 244.

93. This does not refer to the judgments referred to *above*, under (d)(iii).

94. *Above*, under (d); see, however, under (c).

95. Used by the present writer in *Tidsskrift for rettsvitenskap* (Oslo) 1945, pp. 119–21, where the practical aspects of the legal problems discussed in the text were considered in greater detail.

96. Used by *Kotzsch: The Concept of War in Contemporary History and International Law* (Geneva 1956) p. 294, and by Quadri, 50 *Annuaire de l'Institut de droit international, Session de Bruxelles*, I, p. 33. This term is probably better in English and French than the term used earlier by the present writer in Norwegian.

97. *Above*, under (a)(ii).

98. *Annuaire, loc. cit.*, p. 14. The last sentence was added, without explanation, upon

Even those who admit discrimination in respect of prohibited weapons [99] or other humanitarian aspects could not extend the discrimination to the *Geneva Conventions* and the 1954 Hague Convention for the Protection of Cultural Property. These conventions, in contradistinction to the Hague Conventions of 1907, were concluded *after* the conventions which outlawed aggressive war, and thus at a time when the contracting parties could have been expected to make specific provisions for discrimination against the aggressor if they had intended such discrimination to take place within the scope of the Conventions. These conventions must therefore in all circumstances be applied equally by defender and aggressor.[100] It may even be necessary to go so far as to hold that the aggressor has a legal 'right' to confine prisoners of war, because Article 21 of the Prisoners of War Convention expressly provides that 'the detaining Power may subject prisoners of war to internment.'[101] The result might then be that the aggressor would not be liable to pay reparation for the mere detention of the prisoners (but of course for any other hardships inflicted upon them). This would be very unreasonable. However, it might be seen as a lesser evil to the aggressor not taking prisoners at all, i.e. to killing all enemy military personnel. The Hague Convention, at the insistence of the smaller powers, attempted as far as possible to avoid language which would seem to confer similar active rights upon the occupant.[102]

(g) *Military occupation. Invalidity of economic and other acts*

While most of the principles laid down above are either confirmed in practice or the subject of fairly general agreement, there is considerably more room for doubt and for divergent views when one turns to the law of military occupation [103] and of economic warfare. In the present

a proposal by Wengler. Presumably this sentence too, concerns only the *obligation* to treat as prisoners of war etc. the persons who fulfil the conditions for belligerency, and not the *right* under the traditional laws of war to execute those who do not fulfil these conditions. See also draft Resolution VI, *ibid.*, p. 15.

99. *Below*, under 3(f)(iv).

100. In this sense also Schwarzenberger.

101. Cf. *below*, under (g), pp. 252–253 and 256, on the interpretation of certain other, similar provisions of the Geneva conventions.

102. *Tidsskrift for rettsvitenskap* (Oslo) 1945, pp. 114–6. See for example, Articles 48–49.

103. On this subject, see, in addition to the present writer's wartime study cited *above*, at note 13, the more recent studies by Morgenstern: 'Validity of the acts of the belligerent occupant', *BYIL*, XXVIII (1951) pp. 291–322, and Feliciano: 'The Belligerent Occupant and the Returning Sovereign—Aspects of the Philippine law of belligerent occupation', *Philippine Law Journal*, XXVIII (1953) pp. 645–703. Morgenstern's study is, in contradistinction to the present writer's wartime study, based upon the assumption that the occupation is legal.

sub-section will be examined the problems relating to *illegal occupation,* i.e. occupation by the aggressor of the territory of his victim or of the latter's allies. The situation in respect to lawful occupation, i.e. occupation by the latter of the territory of the aggressor, will be briefly examined below, under 3(g)(ii).

(i) It is clear, for the same reasons and to the same extent as indicated under (f), that both parties must observe the humanitarian rules of the law of occupation which are intended to protect individuals and cultural property. But this does not necessarily mean that one has to recognize the validity of the legislation enacted by the illegal occupant within the limits of Article 43 of the Hague Regulations. Nor does it necessarily mean that one must recognize such property and other economic rights for the illegal occupant as are inferred from Articles 48-55 of the Hague Regulations concerning requisitions, taxes, contributions, and seizure and use of the property of the legal government.

The United States Military Tribunal at Nürnberg made a rather sweeping statement that 'International Law makes no distinction between a lawful and an unlawful occupant in dealing with the respective duties of occupant and population in occupied territory'.[104] However, this and similar statements in other judgments against war criminals were made in the context of *criminal* responsibility and of the rules relating to the conduct of hostilities, i.e. in the context of the *humanitarian* laws of war and occupation. As has already been pointed out, the principle of discrimination does not apply in any of these respects.[105]

It has been argued that any legal theory which denies to the aggressor the *rights* under the traditional laws of war would act as an inducement for him to disregard limitations upon, and conditions for, these 'rights' laid down in the relevant articles.[106] Although this argument may have some force, it should not be forgotten that the illegal occupant himself does not usually consider or admit that his occupation is illegal. Moreover, as pointed out under (d), the individual (criminal and civil) sanctions are, even against the personnel of an aggressor, confined to such acts as violate the traditional laws of war.[107]

Another argument against considering invalid the legislation enacted by the aggressor and his acquisitions and transfers of title to property is

---

104. The Hostages Trial (against List, Rendulic and others), *Law Reports of Trials of War Criminals,* VIII (London 1949) p. 59.

105. *Above,* under (d) and (f)(i).

106. Lauterpacht in *BYIL,* XXX (1953) p. 231, who however adds that 'a belligerent will not necessarily permit his conduct to be determined by consideration of the standard which foreign courts and authorities—largely on the hypothesis that he will be defeated—may apply to his acts'.

107. Except for the duty to render restitution, see *above,* under (b)(ii) and (d)(v) *in fine.*

that the resulting uncertainty would create disorder and inconvenience for authorities, courts and persons in the occupied territory and elsewhere.[108] Although this argument, too, has some force, it should be remembered that any legal order must strive at making it difficult for the law-breaker to enjoy the benefits of his crime, and that the inconveniences which might be caused in the occupied territory will inconvenience him, too.

These and other practical arguments for the traditional view [109] cannot be disregarded. On the other hand, an important practical argument against the traditional view (in addition to the legal argument of *ex injuria jus non oritur*) should be added. After the war it is probably equally difficult for the aggressor and his victims to *prove* whether the defender's private and public property which is found in the hands of the aggressor and his nationals in his own territory and in liberated territories, was 'legally' or 'illegally' seized. Litigation of this question would be an enormous waste of effort, to which the aggressor or those who acquired the property from him have no moral right to put the victim governments and their nationals.

(ii) There can be no doubt that governments,[110] belligerent as well as neutral, are free to give effect to the principle *ex injuria jus non oritur*, by holding invalid, even in respect of foreign nationals, *acquisitions and transfers by the illegal occupant of public or private property or other economic rights* of the invaded countries and their allies, even if these do not violate the traditional laws of war. Indeed, this is what the Allies partly did after the Second World War.[111] In the St. James Declaration of 5 January 1943 the Allied Powers

> reserve all their rights to declare invalid any transfers of, or dealings with, property, rights and interests of any description whatsoever which are, or have been, situated in the territories which have come under occupation or control,

108. Cf. Lauterpacht, *loc. cit.*, pp. 231–2.

109. See the excellent exposition by Lauterpacht, *BYIL*, XXX (1953) pp. 231–2, cf. p. 225, although he overshoots the mark in some of his statements, for example when he maintains generally that the logical rule of the invalidity of the acts of the aggressor cannot be acted upon during the war by the courts of a neutral State. This is true of politically weak States, at least as long as there is no determination of aggression (and sanctions) by the Security Council. However, politically strong States and their courts took a different position even during the Second World War, when there was no such determination, cf. *below*, under (i), and Lauterpacht, *loc. cit.*, p. 238.

110. *The inhabitants of the occupied territory* are in a different position if they wish individually to pursue their claims vis-à-vis the occupant, see *Tidsskrift for rettsvitenskap* (Oslo) 1945, p. 126.

111. As for the First World War, reference may be made to par. 1 of the Annex to Article 297 of the Treaty of Versailles. This confirmed all measures taken by either side in respect of enemy property except such 'as have been taken by the German authorities in invaded or occupied territory'. It may be noted that this exception was not confined to Belgium, cf. *above*, under (b)(i).

direct or indirect, of the Governments with which they are at war, or which belong, or have belonged, to persons (including juridical persons) resident in such territories. This warning applies whether such transfers or dealings have taken the form of open looting or plunder, or of transactions apparently legal in form even when they purport to be voluntarily effected.[112]

Many writers assume that this Declaration and other similar declarations [113] comprise only such transfers as would have been illegal under the traditional laws of warfare.[114] However, the Declaration makes no reference to this law. The term 'transactions apparently legal in form' was presumably added in order to make it clear that forced *sales* (against compensation) were also included. It cannot be read as precluding from restitution other forms of forced acquisition, be they in the form of requisitions under international law, expropriations under municipal law or otherwise. Indeed, some of the governments which signed the Declaration had already at that time promulgated legislation which invalidated German property transactions without regard to whether or not they were in accordance with the traditional laws of war.[115] The only transfers which the text of this and other declarations indicate that it was intended to exclude, were genuinely *voluntary* transfers.

Indeed, this was in many cases the only exception actually made when the Allies gave effect to the Declaration. One may refer in this connection to the fact that the decisions of the Allied Control Council for Germany and the bilateral inter-allied agreements on liberated ships and property cited above, under (b)(ii), made no exception for property

112. *Miscellaneous* No. 1 (1943), Cmd. 6418; *Overenskomster med fremmede stater inngått i årene 1940–45* (Oslo 1950) p. 84.

113. See for example Resolution VI incorporated in the Final Act of the Bretton Woods Conference of 22 July 1944. After citing the fact that the United Nations had 'reserved their right to declare invalid any transfers of property belonging to persons within occupied territory', this resolution called upon neutral countries 'to prevent any disposition or transfer within territories subject to their jurisdiction of any (1) assets belonging to the Government or any individuals or institutions within those United Nations occupied by the enemy; and (2) looted gold, currency, art objects, securities, other assets looted by the enemy'. Here again there is no trace of the distinction drawn in Articles 48 et seq. of the Hague Regulations (but of Article 47), unless this is deduced from the following paragraph of the preamble: 'Whereas, enemy countries and their nationals have taken the property of occupied countries and their nationals by open looting and plunder, by forcing transfers under duress, as well as by subtle and complex devices, often operated through the agency of their puppet governments, to give the cloak of legality to their robbery and to secure ownership and control of enterprises in the postwar period.' However, the only thing which this paragraph appears to exclude is voluntary transfers.

114. Lauterpacht, *BYIL*, XXX (1953) pp. 225–6 and 230; Woolsey in *AJIL*, XXXVII (1943) p. 286; Schwarzenberger in *International Law Association, Report of the Fiftieth Conference, Brussels 1962*, p. 210. See, however, Downey in *AJIL*, XLIV (1950) p. 502.

115. See *below*, at note 124, on the Norwegian Provisional Ordinance of 18 December 1942.

which had been requisitioned or otherwise acquired in accordance with the traditional laws of war. The Inter-Allied Reparation Agreement of 21 December 1945/14 January 1946 provided in part III—in execution of the St. James Declaration, the specific Inter-Allied Declaration on Looted Gold of 22 February 1944 and Resolution VI of the Bretton Woods Conference of 22 July 1944 [116]—that all contracting parties who had lost monetary gold 'through looting or by wrongful removal to Germany' should be entitled to share in the restitution of the monetary gold found in Germany. This passage was clarified by the Tripartite Commission (composed of the three Western Occupying Powers) in a letter to the contracting and other interested parties of 13 March 1947. Here the term 'monetary gold'—and, by implication, the term 'wrongful' ('illégitime')—was defined as follows:

> Tout or qui, au moment de sa spoliation ou de son transfert illégitime, figurait comme faisant partie de la réserve monétaire du pays demandeur, soit dans les comptes *du gouvernement demandeur lui-même,* soit dans ceux de la banque centrale du pays demandeur ou d'une autre autorité monétaire sur son territoire ou à l'étranger. [117]

This definition, quoted and approved by Saucer-Hall in his arbitral award on the *Gold of the National Bank of Albania,*[118] makes it clear that inter alia the Inter-Allied Reparation Agreement also comprises what the occupant would have been 'entitled' to seize under Article 53 of the Hague Regulations.—Similarly, the delegates of the formerly occupied countries, in a resolution annexed to the Inter-Allied Reparation Agreement

> agree to accept as the basis of a restitution policy the following principles:
> (a) The question of the restitution of property removed by the Germans from the Allied countries must be examined in all cases in the light of the United Nations Declaration of 5th January, 1943.
> (b) In general, restitutions should be confined to identifiable goods which (i) existed at the time of the occupation of the country concerned, and were removed with or without payment; (ii) were produced during the occupation and obtained by an act of force.
> (e) With respect to the restitution of looted goods which were produced during the occupation and which are still in the hands of German concerns or residents of Germany, the burden of proof of the original ownership of the goods

116. Quoted *above,* note 113.

117. Italics added.

118. Of 20 April 1953, *United Nations, Reports of International Arbitral Awards,* XII, pp. 42–43. He states that the definition 'est en tous points compatible avec la partie III de l'Acte de Paris' [the inter-allied Agreement on Reparation from Germany, on the Establishment of an Inter-Allied Reparation Agency and on the Restitution of Monetary Gold of 21 December 1945/14 January 1946] and that it 'n'est en opposition, ni avec les antécédents de l'Acte de Paris, ni avec ses effets, ni avec le résultat voulu par les Parties signataires et accepté par celles qui y ont adhéré ultérieurement'.

shall rest on the claimants and the burden of proof that the goods were acquired *by a regular contract* shall rest on the holders.'

Here again it seems clear from the italicized parts that voluntary transfers are excluded ('regular contract'), but that forced transfers are included, even if paid for, and that no exception is made for acquisitions purusant to Articles 52-55 et seq. of the Hague Regulations.

Indeed, generally these decisions and agreements were carried out in State practice without making any exception for property acquired in accordance with the traditional laws of war and without regard to whether the property had been 'validly' re-transferred to private persons. This is particularly true in those cases which were governed by statutes enacted by the Occupation Powers or agreements entered into by the Allied powers. However, outside the scope of these there were exceptions in individual cases. Thus those Allies whose territory had not been occupied by the Germans were not always willing to restitute property of military significance which they had captured on the battlefield. In such and certain other cases they might distinguish between 'looted' and 'legally requisitioned' or conquered property, considering, in the latter cases, that the requisitioning or seizure had validly transferred title to Germany, thereby extinguishing the original owner's title.[119]

The restitution clauses in the peace treaties with the other European Axis powers also appear to include all property which had not been transferred voluntarily to the occupant. Thus Article 75 of the Treaty of Peace with Italy provides:

> 1. Italy accepts the principles of the United Nations Declaration of January 5, 1943, and shall return, in the shortest possible time, property removed from the territory of any of the United Nations.
> 2. The obligation to make restitution applies to all identifiable property at present in Italy which was removed by force or duress by any of the Axis Powers from the territory of any of the United Nations, irrespective of any subsequent transactions by which the present holder of any such property has secured possession.[120]

The subsequent Treaty of Peace with Japan of 8 September 1951 is quite clear when it provides for the return of all property and rights of Allied Powers or nationals 'unless the owner has freely disposed thereof without duress or fraud'.[121] The peace treaties with Italy and the small

119. Cf. Lauterpacht, *BYIL*, XXX (1953) p. 230, with citations; Downey in *AJIL*, XLIV (1950) p. 503; cf. Smith in *BYIL*, XXXIII (1946) pp. 235–6.

120. *UNTS*, Vol. 49, p. 157. See also the similar clause for example in Article 22(1)–(2) of the Treaty of Peace with Bulgaria, *UNTS*, Vol. 41, p. 64. Italy and the minor Axis Powers which withdrew from the Axis before the end of the war were, however, not in all respects treated as aggressors, cf. the preambles to their respective peace treaties.

121. Article 15, *UNTS*, Vol. 136, p. 66.

European Axis Powers even contain provisions for restitution *to* these countries and their nationals of identifiable property which the Germans had removed from their territory by force or duress after these powers had withdrawn from the German war of aggression and consequently were forcibly occupied by the Germans.[122]

However, the validity of transfers of property and rights is governed by municipal law. And even as late as the Second World War States had no *duty* under international law to invalidate such acquisitions or transfers by the aggressor in those cases where they had not undertaken to do so, in the treaties referred to above or in other treaties.[123] Indeed, neither the legislative, nor the judicial authorities in the occupied territories and in the territories of the occupant and his allies would during the war consider such acquisitions and transfers invalid. However, this does not prevent the legislative and judicial authorities of the legal government of the occupied territory, of its allies and of neutral States from so doing, not only after, but also *during the war*, to the extent that they consider this expedient or appropriate, even if they have not concluded any treaty to this effect. Thus the Provisional Ordinance enacted by the Norwegian Government in exile on 18 December 1942 concerning the invalidity of transactions etc. in connection with the occupation of Norway by the Germans declared in § 4 invalid any sale of public property or other assets undertaken by the occupant, without making any exception for those acquisitions which are considered legal and definitive under the traditional laws of war, cf. Article 53, first paragraph, and Article 55 of the Hague Regulations.[124]

In the absence, or outside the scope, of special invalidating legislation, courts of Western European countries have been inconsistent, but largely reticent, in holding invalid acquisitions made in accordance with the traditional laws of war.[125] This accords with the text of the St. James Declaration, where the Allied Powers did not declare the transactions invalid *ipso facto*, but merely 'reserve all their rights' to declare them

---

122. See for example the treaties with Hungary, Article 30(2) (*UNTS*, Vol. 41, p. 200) and with Italy, Article 77(2) (*UNTS*, Vol. 49, p. 160).

123. As for the situation after the establishment of the United Nations, see *below*, under 3(i).

124. On these provisions, see Franz *Scholz: Privateigentum im besetzten und unbesetzten Feindesland* (Berlin 1919) pp. 104–8, with citations. It is hardly conceivable that the Norwegian Government would subsequently have signed the St. James Declaration if this had excluded some of these acts. See *Tidsskrift for rettsvitenskap*, 1945, pp. 130–1, for further details of the Ordinance and its interpretation. It and the subsequent Ordinance of 21 September 1945 also declared invalid confiscations and transactions in respect of confiscated property, without making any exception in respect of property confiscated as punishment, cf. *Scholz, op. cit.*, pp. 155–6, and Lauterpacht in *BYIL*, XXX (1953) p. 225. But see the French Decree of 1945, interpreted *ibid.*, p. 230, note.

invalid, presumably by legislative action. This formulation *may* be viewed as a partial waiver of a right existing under general international law, and the court practice may be viewed as an implementation of this waiver. However, the court practice may alternatively have been based upon the assumption that the still obtaining principle of international law, when applied in *interpretation and supplementation* of municipal law, is that acquisitions by the aggressor are not invalid *ipso facto* when they do not violate the traditional laws of occupation or war,[126] but that this principle is in no way imposed by international law as a limitation upon the freedom of action of States. Indeed, even the practice of holding invalid transactions which violate the *traditional* laws of war is a fairly recent one which was not as a matter of law, or not completely, applied after the First World War.[127] As late as 1936 it was maintained that, under Norwegian law, seizure of moveable property as war booty or otherwise in violation of the traditional laws of war could be invalidated by the courts of the dispossessed State or its allies, but not by neutral courts or the courts of the seizer or his allies.[128] Even during the Second World War it was not unequivocally established in practice that the invalidity of illegal acts operates *ipso facto* and that States were *bound* to apply this sanction even to such acts, although writers after the war have expressed themselves in this sense on the basis of practice in connection with the Second World War.[129] If automatic invalidity

125. Thus the majority of the cases cited by Lauterpacht in *BYIL*, XXX (1953) pp. 229–30 and some of the cases cited by Morgenstern, *ibid.*, XXVIII (1951) pp. 296, 298 and 316, although the latter include also judgments rendered in occupied territory during the occupation. See also *Annual Digest of Public International Law Cases*, 1948, Case No. 200, where the French invalidating ordinance of 21 April 1945 was interpreted *a contrario.*—See, on the other hand, some of the cases cited *above*, under (d)(ii) and (iii), note 61, where even criminal sanctions were considered applicable to acts which did not violate the traditional laws of war. A Luxemburg court held that Germany had no *ususfructus* in respect of Luxemburg State forests, see *Archiv des Völkerrechts*, II (1949) p. 494. See also the Swedish divorce case cited *below*, note 146.

126. Morgenstern *loc. cit.*, pp. 291 *et seq.* and 320, demonstrates that the provisions of the Hague Regulations relating to belligerent occupation have become part of the municipal law of most States. She does not deal with *illegal* occupation.

127. Thus Saucer-Hall points out, in his arbitral award on the Gold of the National Bank of Albania of 20 April 1953, that 'ce nouveau principe n'a d'abord reçu qu'une application incomplète, notamment dans le Traité de Versailles de 1919 et dans les autres traités de paix qui mirent fin à la Première guerre mondiale' (*United Nations, Reports of International Arbitral Awards*, XII, p. 40).

128. Gjelsvik: *Norsk Tingsrett*, 3rd edition (Oslo 1936) pp. 411–3.

129. Lauterpacht, *BYIL*, XXX (1953) p. 225 takes the view that 'any court free to administer the law impartially is entitled and bound to treat such purported title as invalid.' This appears to be the view also of Morgenstern, see her discussion of different views and of practice *loc. cit.*, pp. 300–320. She concludes that there is some authority for the view that the invalidity operates *ipso facto*. Earlier, *Hyde: International Law*, 2nd edition (Boston 1947), III, p. 1886 took the contrary view that there is no obliga-

of acts violating the traditional laws of war is assumed to have been the rule of international law during the Second World War, then the St. James Declaration and similar instruments, which merely reserved the right to *declare* the acts invalid, would make no sense unless they covered also acts which did not violate the traditional laws of war. On the other hand, if the said rule of automatic invalidity did not apply, then the cases where courts treated as valid those acts of the aggressor which did not exceed the limits of the traditional laws of war, are not really relevant to the question of discrimination against the aggressor.[130] Indeed, in several cases where courts of third ('neutral') countries have considered invalid forced transfers of property in occupied countries, this was based upon the view that the acts of the occupant have no extraterritorial effect, at least not if the property at the time of judgment is situated outside the occupied territory, without attaching decisive importance to the fact that the transfers had been forced in violation of the traditional laws of war.[131]

It may, finally, be asked whether the legal position has changed as a result of the new Geneva Convention of 1949 Relative to the Protection of Civilian Persons in Time of War. This Convention was concluded after the treaties outlawing aggressive war, and thus cannot be superseded by the latter. In a special section on 'occupied territories' the Convention contains specific provisions on the occupant's requisitioning of 'foodstuffs, articles or medical supplies' and of civilian hospitals (Articles 55 and 57). It may be asked whether these confer positive *rights* upon the occupant, with the effect that requisitions by the illegal occupant must be upheld as valid transfers of title. However, the terms in which these provisions speak of the occupant's requisitions are similar to, and no more positive than those of Article 52 of the Hague Regulations. As has been explained in detail elsewhere,[132] these Regulations did not intend to recognize any *rights* for the occupant.[133] In view of the strong divergencies of views on this point at the Hague Conference

---

tion under international law. As for neutral practice, see also the Swedish Law on Restitution of Certain Property Originating in Occupied Territory of 29 June 1945 and the similar Swiss law, both of which apparently implied a deviation from existing municipal law (cf. Saucer-Hall in *Reports of International Arbitral Awards*, XII, p. 41). As for the situation after the establishment of the United Nations, see *below*, under 3(g).

130. Cf. also Morgenstern, *loc. cit.*, pp. 300–1 and 310.

131. See the Swiss judgment of 30 October 1917, reported by Morgenstern, *loc. cit.*, pp. 315–7; the Austrian Supreme Court judgment of 20 July 1955, reported in *Revue critique de droit international privé*, XLV (1956) p. 482; and some of the judgments cited in the preceding Austrian Supreme Court judgment of 10 May 1950 reported in *Entscheidungen des Österreichischen obersten Gerichtshofes in Zivil- and Justizverwaltungssachen*, XXIII (1950, 1. Halbjahr, Wien 1951) at pp. 325–6.

132. *Tidsskrift for rettsvitenskap* (Oslo), 1945, pp. 113–8.

133. *Contra*: Morgenstern in *BYIL*, XXX (1953) pp. 295 and 320, citing a judgment

between the big and the smaller powers, all that the Conference could do was to define what everybody agreed that the occupant was *not* entitled to do, without admitting any *a contrario* interpretation to the effect that the occupant was entitled to do what the Regulations did not so forbid, but leaving this question to other sources of law ('les principes du droit des gens, tels qu'ils résultent des usages établis entre nations civilisées, des lois de l'humanité et des exigences de la conscience publique'),[134] including those which were older than the Convention. It is hardly conceivable that the Geneva Conference of 1949, forty years later, after the outlawry of war and the experience of the two aggressive World Wars, would have intended, by those of its provisions which are similar or no more positive than those of the Hague Regulations, to go further in the sense of recognizing genuine 'rights' for the occupant than the Hague Conference had done—in disregard of the basic principle both of 'international law' and of 'public conscience' that *ex injuria jus non oritur*—except perhaps insofar as the requisitions (and not merely their limitation) had a *humanitarian* purpose.

Although practice is inconsistent with regard to the validity of title acquired or transferred by the illegal occupant, it may be stated in *conclusion* that States are, no doubt, entitled to invalidate even titles which he has acquired or transferred without violating the traditional laws of war. During and after the Second World War the Allied *governments* did so in most cases where they dealt with this matter by treaty and in many cases where they dealt with it by legislation. However, courts in most, but not all, cases have refrained from holding the acquisitions and transfers invalid in the absence of any applicable legislation or treaty to that effect. This practice of the courts may have been based upon a view that only transactions which violate the traditional laws of war are invalid *ipso jure*, i.e. in the absence of invalidating legislation. However, it *may* also be seen as a reflection of the still existing uncertainty, in particular in view of the terms of the St. James Declaration, as to whether violation of *any* laws of war led to invalidity *ipso jure*, or, alternatively, as an application of the waiver of any such automatic invalidity which (waiver) their governments would have undertaken by the terms of the St. James Declaration.

(iii) The legal position is basically similar with regard to the question of the validity of the *legislation enacted by the illegal occupant*. Under the traditional laws of occupation it is assumed that those legislative acts of the occupant which do not violate the traditional laws of occupation (in particular the limitations laid down in Articles 43 et seq. of the Hague

by a court in *occupied* Belgium and a German writer (cf. the present writer's criticism of this and other German writers' views in *Tidsskrift for rettsvitenskap*, 1945, *loc. cit.*).

134. The so-called 'Martens' reservation clause' in the preamble of the Fourth Hague Convention, adopted as a compromise to solve this very issue.

Regulations and Articles 47 et seq. of the Geneva Convention of 1949 on the Protection of Civilian Persons) and which are not in the nature of special occupation legislation retain their validity even after the end of the occupation.[135] However, during the Second World War this view was rejected by the Norwegian Ministry of Justice, which stated that it would be contrary to the general sense of justice to attribute to 'foreign conquerors' the authority to legislate with effect after the end of occupation.[136] Indeed, in accordance with what has been said above about the invalidation of the economic acts of the occupant, it is submitted that the legal government must be entitled to invalidate *any* legislation enacted by the illegal occupant, and to do so with effect already during the occupation. Such invalidation can hardly be contested under constitutional provisions protecting acquired rights.[137] Nor can it be contested by foreign courts (on the basis of *ordre public* or otherwise) in those cases where they under their own conflict of laws are to apply the law of the occupied territory. Thus, a French ordinance of 9 August 1944 provides: 'Les lois ... que l'autorité de fait qui s'est imposée à la France a promulgées ... ne peuvent tirer de sa volonté aucune force obligatoire'.[138] However, usually the legal government will not wish to invalidate legislation which was enacted purely for the purposes of the normal administration of the occupied territory, for example to control prices.[139] Similarly, courts—and other States—are not likely to consider such legislation invalid unless it has been declared invalid by legislative

135. *Castberg: Postliminium* (Uppsala 1944) pp. 19–24.

136. See the full quotation in *Tidsskrift for rettsvitenskap* (Oslo) 1945, p. 129, note.

137. *Contra:* Morgenstern, *BYIL,* XXVIII (1951) p. 299 and the many writers quoted by her. See also *Castberg, loc. cit.,* pp. 5 and 24. However, these are writers who apply the traditional laws of war and disregard the illegality of the occupation.— Quincy Wright, on the other hand, extends the invalidation to *criminal* law, when he states that if the occupation is a consequence of illegal aggression, the existing criminal law continues during the occupation even if modified by explicit acts of the occupant necessitated by considerations of order and safety (*AJIL,* XXXIX [1945] p. 271). He makes no reservation for application to the detriment of the accused.—§ 2 of the Norwegian Provisional Decree of 8 May 1945 on insurance against war damage and subsequent legislation on that subject offer examples of retroactive revision (to the detriment of private individuals) of acts performed pursuant to the occupation legislation, cf. *Tidsskrift for rettsvitenskap* (Oslo) 1946, p. 271.

138. *Sirey,* 1944, *Lois,* p. 1585, as quoted by Morgenstern, *BYIL,* XXVIII (1951) p. 298, note. She doubts the relevance of the ordinance because of the considerable degree of independence possessed by 'the *de facto* French Government established during the occupation'. In the view of the present writer the ordinance is directly relevant insofar as it relates to legislation enacted by authorities in occupied France (Vichy was occupied before the promulgation of the ordinance). Another French invalidating ordinance, of 21 April 1945, was interpreted *a contrario* by the courts, see *Annual Digest of Public International Law Cases,* 1948, Case No. 200.

139. Cf. the other examples given by *Castberg, loc. cit.,* p. 23.

act of the legal government.[140] However, even without basis in statute, courts on some occasions have held the occupant's legislation to be invalid although it did not exceed the limits of the Hague Regulations.[141]

It is submitted, moreover, that the *legal government* is entitled to enact during the occupation its own legislation with effect for the occupied territory and to apply it to acts and transactions committed or performed during the occupation by its own and foreign nationals in the occupied territory. The Norwegian Government in exile even enacted *criminal* legislation for the prosecution of Norwegian traitors and German war criminals,[142] and applied this after the Liberation to acts which had been committed during the occupation and partly even before the enactment of the legislation. The validity of this legislation was contested, partly on the basis that the legislative power was vested in the occupant rather than in the legal government and partly on the basis that the legislation violated the provision in § 97 of the Norwegian Constitution which prohibits the retroactive effect of statutes. The Supreme Court rejected these objections,[143] however, mostly on bases other than the illegality of the aggression and the occupation.[144]

(iv) The legal position may be basically similar with regard to the question of the validity of the *other acts* of the illegal occupant. Thus the Norwegian statute on the Revision of Administrative Decisions During the Occupation was primarily aimed at the invalidation of admi-

---

140. See for example Aboitiz v. Price (1951) 99 F. Supp. (D. Utah) 602, as reported by Lauterpact in *BYIL*, XXX (1953) pp. 218–9, and some of the judgments cited by Morgenstern, *BYIL*, XXVIII (1951) p. 297, although some of them were pronounced by courts in German-occupied territory and are thus not relevant to the question under discussion.

141. See for example the Belgian World War I case and the two Dutch World War II cases reported by Morgenstern, *BYIL*, XXVIII (1951) p. 294 from *Annual Digest of Public International Law Cases*, 1919–22, Case No. 329, and 1946, Case No. 143, and *Na-oorlogsche Rechtspraak*, IV (1948) No. 1309 g. It is recalled that, although the First World War preceded the Briand-Kellogg Pact, the German attack upon Belgium was in clear and admitted violation of the Treaty of 1839 which guaranteed Belgium's neutrality. See also the U.S. cases cited *below*, pp. 261–2.

142. Cf. Quincy Wright's view, as cited in note 137 *above*.

143. See notably the *Klinge* case, *Norsk Retstidende*, 1945, pp. 199 *et seq.*, cf. also the *Haaland* case, *ibid.*, pp. 13 et seq.

144. Cf. *above*, under (d), on the inapplicability of this criterion to the prosecution of war criminals, although the present context is somewhat different. The speaker for the majority in the Klinge case stated that it would be unreasonable if § 97 of the Norwegian Constitution, 'which has been established for the protection of the society, could be invoked also by foreign criminals (voldsmenn), nationals of a State which have attacked that same society in order to subjugate it, and who, as part of the attempt to subjugate it, have applied the most ruthless and brutal methods' (*Norsk Retstidende*, p. 202). See also Chief Justice Berg's motivation (*ibid.*, p. 213). *Contra:* the speaker for the minority, *ibid.*, p. 208.

nistrative acts and judgments which had been designed to further the interests of the occupant or which had been influenced by the extraordinary conditions during the occupation. Some of its provisions were confined to acts which were illegal under the traditional laws of occupation,[145] others were not.[146] No exception from the latter provisions was made in favour of German or other foreign nationals.

It is not possible in the present study to discuss practice in relation to all types of acts. Nevertheless, some brief submissions shall be made with regard to the questions of the competence of the occupant and the legal government, respectively, to appoint officials for the occupied territory and to represent it internationally.

The legal government must, in principle, be entitled to disregard the illegal occupant's *appointment of officials* for the occupied territory and to consider the acts of these invalid even in relation to foreign nationals, even if the appointment does not violate the traditional laws of war. Conversely, the legal government must, in principle, be entitled to consider its own officials as still being in office, even if they have been removed by the occupant in accordance with Article 54 of the Geneva Convention on the Protection of Civilian Persons of 1949. It may be asked whether this right has not now been superseded by Article 54 of the Geneva Convention of 1949 on the Protection of Civilian Persons, which states that it 'does not affect the *right* of the Occupying Power to remove public officials from their post'.[147] However, this is merely a reference to a 'right' existing under general international law, and it was hardly intended by Article 54 to give it a wider scope than it has under that law. Accordingly it is submitted that it pertains only to the lawful occupant.

However, in respect of officials, too, the legal government will hardly

---

145. Notably the provisions providing for automatic invalidity, see for example § 1 and, largely, § 14.

146. For example §§ 2, 4, 5, 7 and 9, cf. § 25. Most of these provisions did not provide for automatic invalidity, but for new administrative or judicial decision, either to invalidate or to confirm the earlier decision. In these cases the authorities might of course, if they wished, choose to exercise their power of invalidation only when the act was illegal under the traditional laws of war. See, on the other hand, a judgment of the Swedish Supreme Court of 18 August 1947 reported in *Nytt juridisk arkiv*, 1947, p. 346. This judgment disregarded a Norwegian post-war executive decision (the validity of which had subsequently been upheld by a Norwegian court) invalidating a divorce pronounced by the 'Norwegian' Ministry of Justice in occupied Norway during the German occupation.

147. Italics added. Cf. *above*, under (ii) *in fine*, and *below*, under (j)(ii). On the other hand, the Article confirms that the officials have a right to resign, as earlier submitted and discussed in detail by the present writer in *Tidsskrift for rettsvitenskap* (Oslo) 1946, pp. 276–308, although the provision in the first sentence of the second paragraph of Article 54 opens the door to requisition in respect of certain services, cf. *ibid.*, pp. 299–302.

wish to make unreasonable use of its right to the detriment of the inhabitants of the occupied territory. And as long is it has not enacted legislation to this effect, its courts—and other States—will probably consider the officials appointed by the occupant in accordance with Article 43 of the Hague Regulations as lawful and their acts as valid if they do not exceed the limits of the traditional laws of occupation. As for practice, the Norwegian Supreme Court has, in the absence of legislation invalidating with retroactive effect the appointment of officials by the occupation regime, and without entering into the question of the legality or illegality of the appointment, in one case considered that a Norwegian Nazi official who had been dismissed after the Liberation was entitled to refund of payments made in respect of him to the State Pension Fund, and in another case that such an official was not entitled to back-payment of salary for the period up to the Liberation.[148]

Finally, the illegal occupant obviously has no 'right' to *represent the occupied territory internationally*. In 1942, during the German occupation of Norway great numbers of reindeer were stolen or wandered across the border between Norway and Finland. Norwegian police and Lapps entered Finnish territory and brought a number of reindeer back to Norway. The German occupation authorities concluded an agreement with the Finnish authorities under which the Norwegian State would pay reparation for the reindeer taken from the Finnish Lapps, while no provision was made for reparation to the Norwegian Lapps for the reindeer they had lost. The agreement was concluded in Norway in German. It was signed by Finnish representatives, by local Norwegian Nazi officials at the request of the German *Reichskommissar für die besetzten norwegischen Gebiete,* and by a local representative of the latter. The agreement stated that it would become binding 'für den norwegischen und den finnischen Staat'. After the Liberation the Norwegian Government refused to recognize the agreement and negotiated a new agreement with Finland. It is submitted that the Norwegian Government would have had a right to claim a new settlement (and refund) even if the agreement concluded by the Germans had been fully carried out before the Liberation.

(v) To the extent that it is possible to draw a *general conclusion* from practice in connection with the Second World War in the various respects relating to military occupation, it appears to be that if international law contains a rule of interpretation of the applicable municipal law in this field to the effect that the acts of the occupant are presumed to be invalid *ipso jure,* this is confined to those acts which violate the *traditional* laws of occupation. It is not desirable to extend any rule of *automatic* invalidity to all acts of the occupant, because even the legal

148. *Norsk Retstidende,* 1950, p. 84, and 1951, p. 903.

government will never wish to invalidate all such acts. However, the legal government has an apparently unlimited *right* to invalidate any acts of the illegal occupant which it wishes to invalidate. Neither its own nationals, nor foreign nationals or their governments, can contest the legality of such invalidation.

(h) *Economic warfare. Prizes*

The principles outlined above in respect of forced transfers and other economic measures undertaken by the *aggressor* in occupied territories must probably apply also to similar measures in his own territory, on the battlefield and elsewhere. There is hardly any more reason to recognize the validity of prizes and booty which he has captured in battle or of his other measures of economic warfare, including blockade, sequestration of private enemy property etc.[149] The aggressor cannot be considered entitled to apply such measures even within the limits of the traditional laws of war; on the contrary, he must be liable to pay reparation and render restitution even in such cases. Nor can any State be obliged to recognize the validity of transfers effected by such measures or protest if others fail to do so.

It has, on the other hand, been suggested that the *defender* is entitled to undertake such measures against the aggressor (and neutrals) even *beyond* those permitted under the traditional laws of war.[150] However, the latter may lead to reprisals, and even if these are considered illegal, this does not help the victims of these reprisals.

It is not possible within the scope of the present study to discuss practice in all these respects.[151] It must suffice to mention a few examples of State practice in respect of *prizes*.

In the Liberated Ships Agreements, concluded at the end of the Second World War,[152] the Allied powers agreed that all ships captured or found by the Allied forces should be returned to those Allied governments under whom they originally belonged (not to the capturing Allied Power), without making any exception for ships acquired by the Ger-

---

149. See the further examples listed by *Kotzsch: The Concept of War in Contemporary History and International Law* (Geneva 1956) p. 295.

150. Verzijl in 50 *Annuaire de l'Institut de droit international, Session de Bruxelles 1963*, I, p. 102, cf. pp. 17–18. See also the Norwegian Supreme Court judgment in *Norsk Retstidende*, 1957, p. 942, cf. p. 949, criticized by Carsten Smith in *Tidsskrift for rettsvitenskap* (Oslo) 1962, pp. 200–1. *Contra:* Wright in *AJIL*, XLVII (1953) p. 371. The Secretary-General of the League of Nations in 1927, before the conclusion of the Briand-Kellogg Pact, stated that vis-à-vis neutrals, Article 16 of the Covenant 'appears to contemplate all or any measures consistent with the laws of war' (complete quotation *below*, note 162).

151. The relationship to neutral States shall be briefly discussed under (i) *below*.

152. Cited *above*, note 36.

mans without violating the traditional laws of war. It was added, however, that 'some form of prize proceedings will be required to divest the enemy of their title', while it was made clear that such prize proceedings would be merely a legal formality. This addition was natural in view of the rule of prize law that it is the decision of the prize court and not the legality of the seizure which determines the transfer of title. Thus, under the traditional laws of war, prize judgments were considered to transfer title with binding effect for nationals of allied, enemy and neutral States even if the seizure violated the traditional laws of naval warfare, while no valid transfer was considered to be effected without such judgment even if the vessel had been seized in conformity with the traditional laws of war.[153]

The peace treaties with the other Axis Powers, however, were in this respect based upon the traditional laws of war. Thus the Treaty of Peace with Italy of 1947 merely provided for revision of those Italian prize decisions or orders 'as may not be in conformity with international law',[154] which clearly referred to the traditional laws of war. The Peace Treaty with Romania contained the same clause.[155] However, the Allied Powers refrained also in other respects from treating Italy and the smaller Axis partners as aggressors on the same footing as Germany, cf. the preambles of the peace treaties which referred both to their initial aggression and to their subsequent active participation in the war against Germany. Japan was, four years later, in fact given the same mild treatment.[156] Still, it is an anomaly, as compared to the restitution provisions discussed above, under (b)(ii) and (g)(ii), if these provisions on prize decisions really imply that these countries were allowed to retain ships and cargo captured at sea from States which had been victims of aggression. On the other hand, the Axis Powers in the peace treaties accepted as valid *all* Allied prize decisions.[157]

The Report to the *Institut de droit international* in 1963, referred to above, under (a), avoids the controversial subjects of military occupation [158] and neutrality. It contains, however, the following draft resolutions, which largely conform with what has been submitted above:

---

153. Gjelsvik: *Norsk tingsrett* (Oslo 1936) § 43 IV 1–2(a).

154. Annex VII A, *UNTS*, Vol. 49, p. 235.

155. Annex VI A, *UNTS*, Vol. 42, p. 90.

156. Article 17(a) of the Treaty of Peace with Japan of 8 September 1951 provides for revision 'in conformity with international law' (*UNTS*, Vol. 136, p. 68).

157. See for example Article 76 (1)(c) of the Italian Peace Treaty (*UNTS*, Vol. 49, p. 159).

158. The Report cites in this connection Röling's statement that 'perhaps in no other part of war-law is there more uncertainty and more difference of opinion than in the field of occupation law' (*Receuil des Cours*, 1960 II, p. 400).

Résolution VIII

L'agresseur doit être privé du recours à des mesures économiques qui ont pour but de diminuer la force de résistance de son adversaire.

Résolution IX

L'agresseur doit être privé du droit de confiscation de navires marchands en mer, de pose de mines sous-marines, de bombardement naval de villes et de ports, du droit d'interception de la contrebande de guerre. Un jugement de prise prononcé par un tribunal de l'agresseur devrait être frappé de nullité.

It is expressly stated in the Report that the list given in Resolution IX is not intended to be exhaustive.[159]

(i) *Neutrals*

After the outlawry of aggressive war, neutral States must be entitled to discriminate against the aggressor without regard to the traditional laws of neutrality.[160] They may assist the victim of aggression with civilian and military supplies, arms [161] and financial means, while prohibiting such assistance to the aggressor.[162] (They may even assist him with armed forces and other measures of warfare, in the exercise of the right under general international law of collective self-defence.) [163] Furthermore they must, like the belligerent States, be entitled to consider the acts of the aggressor unlawful and invalid even if these do not violate the traditional laws of war and occupation. By acting in this manner, the neutral States would not make it lawful for the aggressor to

---

159. 50 *Annuaire de l'Institut de droit international, Session de Bruxelles 1963*, I, pp. 17 and 31.

160. In this sense also Zourek, basing himself upon logics, juridical conscience and Article 2(5) of the United Nations Charter (50 *Annuaire de l'Institut de droit international, Session de Bruxelles 1963*, II, pp. 318–9) and Schwarzenberger, stating that the parties to the broken treaties are entitled by way of reprisals to disregard any of their duties as neutral powers and to discriminate as they see fit against the aggressor (*Völkerrecht und Rechtliches Weltbild, Festschrift für Alfred Verdross*, Vienna 1960, p. 246).

161. In this sense also Zourek, *ibid.*, p. 350.

162. Quincy Wright, with the approval of François, states that this may be done 'in spite of commercial treaties including the most favoured nation clause' (50 *Annuaire de l'Institut de droit international, Session de Bruxelles 1963*, p. 123). Earlier, prior to the Briand-Kellogg Pact, the Secretary-General of the League of Nations took the position that vis-à-vis the aggressor this followed *a fortiori* from the right to conclude treaties for collective military self-defence; however, it was 'prudent to conclude that, in applying the economic sanctions of Article 16 [of the Covenant] without resort to war, the Members of the League must fully respect the rights of *third* States.' If they declared war, however, 'Article 16 appears to contemplate all or any measures consistent with the laws of war' (this clearly referred to the *traditional* laws of war). Other Member States, however, had no such rights, cf. Article 20 of the Covenant. (*Reports and Resolutions on the Subject of Article 16 of the Covenant*, Geneva 1927, pp. 84–87.)

163. In this sense already a League of Nations Report of 28 August 1921, *ibid.*, p. 17.

attack them, too,[164] or resort to illegal acts as reprisals; any such action by the aggressor must be treated as illegal aggression or illegal reprisals, respectively. A different matter is that the aggressor, having committed one crime, will hardly refrain from committing another, and that politically weak States therefore may find it safer not to make use of their right to discriminate.

The present writer earlier took the view that the neutral States would be entitled to discriminate only if the illegality of the aggression had been authoritatively recognized.[165] He now has modified this view, inter alia in the light of practice in connection with the Second World War.[166] Without attempting to list and evaluate this practice, it may be recalled that the St. James Declaration—which the preceding and subsequent practice of its authors indicates covered all forced transactions, even such as did not exceed the limits of the traditional laws of war [167] —was particularly addressed to 'persons in neutral countries'.

The governments of several neutral countries enacted special legislation on the subject after the conclusion of the war. The Swedish Act of 29 June 1945 on Restitution of Certain Property Originating in Occupied Countries provided in § 2 for restitution of property which the occupant had requisitioned or seized 'in violation of the rules of international law'. This no doubt refers to the *traditional* laws of war. The Swiss Ordinance of 10 December 1945 is in similar terms.[168] On the other hand, as pointed out by Lauterpacht, practice in politically stronger neutral countries partly points the other way. While the United States was still neutral in the Second World War, it enacted legislation (Lend-Lease) which provided for a clear discrimination against Germany in violation of the traditional laws of neutrality. This was justified by the Attorney-General precisely by reference to the Briand-Kellogg Pact and similar treaties.[169] Even without specific legislation certain courts in the

---

164. In this sense also Lauterpacht in *BYIL*, XXX (1953) p. 237 (but cf. pp. 232 and 238), speaking of the position of neutrals generally, without going into specific aspects. The same position was taken by the Secretary-General of the League of Nations, in respect of economic sanctions under Article 16 of the Covenant, speaking of relations between the Members of the League and basing himself upon an *a fortiori* conclusion from the right to conclude treaties of alliance involving collective *military* action against an aggressor contracting party, see note 162 *above*.

165. *Tidsskrift for rettsvitenskap*, 1945, pp. 132–3 and 135–7.

166. See also the arguments adduced by Schwarzenberger, *loc. cit. above*, note 160; and Lauterpacht in *BYIL*, XXX (1953) pp. 237–8; and in *Oppenheim: International Law*, II, § 292 h.

167. *Above*, under (g)(ii).

168. Quoted by Lauterpacht in *BYIL*, XXX (1953) p. 226, note.

169. In a statement reported by Jenks in *The Grotius Society Transactions for the Year 1951*, p. 27.

United States declined in strong terms to give effect to decrees of the German occupant on the ground that the occupation had not been 'recognized'; instead they recognized as valid the contrary acts of the legal government in exile.[170] This legislation and these judgments must be considered as entirely legal,[171] and the war which Germany declared upon the United States on 11 December 1941 must be considered as illegal aggression notwithstanding this practice.[172]

The legal governments of the occupied countries are not known to have made any exception for foreign nationals in the legislation which they enacted during and after the occupation and which invalidated the acts of the occupant even where these might have been legal under the traditional laws of occupation. On the contrary, some of these laws related specially to foreign nationals.[173] Indeed, it is submitted that no neutral State can protest if the belligerent States extend to its nationals the effect of their measures of discrimination, as long as such measures are kept within the limits discussed above.

However, neutral States have no *duty* under customary international law to discriminate against the aggressor [174] and to treat as unlawful those of his acts which do not violate the traditional laws of war. Such duty may, however, follow from a regional or global treaty. Thus Article 16 of the Covenant of the League of Nations provided for automatic economic sanctions against the aggressor by all Member States.[175] The Charter of the United Nations also contains relevant provisions and

170. *Annual Digest of Public International Law Cases*, 1941–42, Cases Nos. 171 and 172.

171. In this sense also Zourek, *loc. cit.*, II, pp. 319 and 350. So also Schwarzenberger, with respect to Norway's position before it became a belligerent, in *International Law Association, Report of the Forty-Eighth Conference, New York 1958*, p. 569.

172. The judgment of the International Military Tribunal at Nürnberg fails to talk directly of 'aggressive' war against the United States by Germany (*AJIL*, XLI 1947 p. 213–4). This probably must be due to other reasons, for example that the United States was already at war with Japan and that the United States was not *invaded* by Germany. None of these reasons can be admitted to be legally relevant and, indeed, the judgment states generally that the Briand-Kellogg Pact 'was violated by Germany in all the cases of aggressive war charged in the Indictment' (*ibid.*, p. 216).

173. Thus for example § 6, cf. § 9(2), of the Norwegian provisional law of 19 July 1946 on insurance of real estate against war damage.

174. In this sense the United States Attorney-General, see a preceding note. *Contra* apparently Valladao in 50 *Annuaire de l'Institut de droit international, Session de Bruxelles 1963*, I, p. 340.

175. On the legal aspects of these, in relation to the aggressor, other Member States and non-member States, see a report of the Secretary-General of 17 May 1927, in *Reports and Resolutions on the Subject of Article 16 of the Covenant* (Geneva 1927) pp. 83–88. On practice during the Italian aggressive war against Ethiopia, see Taubenfeld in *AJIL*, XLVII (1953) pp. 382–3.

authorizes the Security Council to make decisions in this sense. These shall be discussed below, under 3.

(j) *The Hague and Geneva Conventions*

(i) The principle of discrimination, to the extent admitted above, applies not merely to the general (customary) laws of war, but also to the *Hague Conventions* of 1907, whether or not their provisions constitute customary international law, because these Conventions must be considered to have been superseded, *to that extent,* by the subsequent conventions outlawing war. The fact that, later, two of the Geneva Conventions of 1949 state that they shall be 'complementary' to the relevant parts of the Hague Regulations [176] cannot be interpreted as nullifying the modifications of these Regulations which result from the treaties outlawing war. Moreover, as has been more fully explained in another context,[177] international conventions like the Hague Conventions cannot in the same manner as national statutes be interpreted *a contrario,* as permitting everything that they do not prohibit. National legislation is adopted by a majority vote and can thus in a binding manner lay down the *limit* between right and wrong. International conventions, however, require unanimity or a large measure of agreement. And at the Hague Conference it was quite clear that agreement could be reached only as to what the belligerents could *not* do. The Hague Regulations therefore had to be confined to stating that, and had to leave other questions to other sources of law, including sources which were older than the Regulations as well as more recent sources.[178] The Hague Regulations thus present no barrier to drawing the legal consequences from the subsequent treaties outlawing war.

(ii) The *Geneva Conventions* of 1949, however, as explained above,[179] are in a different position. They were concluded after the conventions outlawing war, and the contracting parties could then have been expected to make provisions for discrimination if they had intended to allow this vis-à-vis the aggressor. In fact, neither the first drafters, nor the Diplomatic Conference, had any such intentions. Indeed, the first Article of the Conventions provides that they shall be respected 'in all circumstances', which has been interpreted by the drafters as implying inter alia that they apply even in a war of aggression.[180] The provisions of these Conventions must therefore be applied equally by both parties,

---

176. Prisoners of War Convention, Article 135; Civilians Convention, Article 154.
177. *Tidsskrift for rettsvitenskap* (Oslo) 1945, pp. 113–8.
178. Cf. *above,* (g)(ii) *in fine,* with citation of a contrary view in note 133.
179. p. 244.
180. *Comité international de la Croix-Rouge, Les Conventions de Genève du 12 août 1949, Commentaire,* III, p. 24.

even when they fall outside the purely humanitarian field.[181] Moreover, *if* any provision of these Conventions clearly confers a positive right upon the belligerents, then this must probably be recognized as a 'right' even after the war, and may thus in so far nullify the duty of the aggressor under general international law to pay reparation for all damage he has caused.[182] Finally, the new Geneva Conventions expressly provide that the rights they confer upon the protected persons may not be waived, neither by these persons nor by agreements between the belligerent States.[183] Thus even the aggressor State cannot in the armistice agreement confer upon the victim State a right, for example, to retain for reconstruction work those of his soldiers who have not been convicted of war crimes, in view of the provision in Article 118 that 'prisoners of war shall be released and repatriated without delay after the cessation of active hostilities'.

(k) *General*

It will be seen from the discussion above that in certain respects the traditional laws of war have been modified to take into account the fact that aggression has become illegal. Governments have to some extent effected discrimination in practice, in particular during and after the Second World War, and a growing number of jurists now accept this as a principle of the modern laws of war, on one or more of the theoretical bases listed above, under 2(e)(ii). However, this discrimination is limited to certain sanctions and certain fields of the laws of war. Many of these are such as tend to arise in connection with the liquidation of the war rather than with its actual conduct, and the discrimination can then be implemented only if the aggressor is defeated. Still, these facts must not be allowed to prevent the adoption and application of the principle of discrimination in those respects where this is possible. It must be the aim of any legal order to hamper the criminal and to assist the victim as far as this can be done without violating other aims of overriding importance.

(i) It follows from the discussion above that the principle of discrimination is basically applicable also *durante bello*. The still rather current view that discrimination is applicable only after the war, may have arisen from the fact that the humanitarian laws, which are binding upon both parties, are to be applied during the war, while the question of

181. Castberg in 50 *Annuaire de l'Institut de droit international, Session de Bruxelles 1963*, II, pp. 336–7, arrives at the same conclusion on a different basis.

182. Thus possibly Article 21 of the Prisoners of War Convention (*above*, under (f)(ii), p. 244), but hardly Articles 54 et seq., cf. *above*, pp. 252–3 and 256.

183. Articles 6–7 common to the three first Conventions and Articles 7–8 of the Convention on Civilians.

reparation, where discrimination is admitted, usually arises only after the war. Indeed, not only payment of reparation, but also restitution of seized property, invalidation of forced transfers and other acts of the aggressor, as well as prosecution of leaders responsible for the decision to attack, mostly take place, for practical reasons, only after the war. However, should they arise during the war, the rules to be applied must be the same. Indeed, the duty to pay reparation, the criminal responsibility, and the right to invalidate forced transfers and other acts of the aggressor arise as soon as the acts have been committed. And restitution and invalidation have even in practice been effected during the war, for example upon the liberation of occupied territory. They can also be effected already during the war in third countries, to the extent that the property or the other objects of the rights concerned are located there. Similarly, prosecution of political leaders could take place during the war if these fall into the hands of the defenders, although in practice they are more likely to be detained for prosecution after the war, like Rudolf Hess, if they are not executed by the people, as Mussolini was.—On the other hand, there are important aspects of the laws of war which usually are implemented only *after* the war and where *no* discrimination is applicable. This is to a great extent true of prosecution for war crimes and of individual duty to pay reparation. This, too, proves that the crucial criterion is not one of time, but one of the substantive field of law and type of sanction.

It is submitted that the discrimination discussed above must apply, at least in most respects,[184] also in favour of those who come to the aid of the victim, whether these be States acting independently or pursuant to a United Nations resolution, or a United Nations Force however composed and commanded.

(ii) The present writer tends to the view that the discrimination outlined above must apply in all cases of flagrant aggression, even if *the fact of illegal aggression has not been authoritatively determined*.[185] The practice reported above from the Second World War, where the League of Nations had taken no action to determine the aggression (except that committed by Japan against China, by Italy against Ethiopia

---

184. Practice and writers seem to confirm that this applies even in respect of reparation from the aggressor State, see *below*, pp. 270–1.

185. In this sense also Zourek, as cited in the text *below* (from 50 *Annuaire de l'Institut de droit international, Session de Bruxelles 1963*, II, p. 356) and *ibid.*, p. 319, as well as the President of the *Institut de droit international* (Rolin). The latter stated during the 1963 discussion of the second François report on discrimination: 'Plusieurs orateurs ont évoqué la difficulté de définir l'agresseur. Mais l'agression est souvent flagrante, comme en 1935, en 1938 ou en 1939. Il ne faudrait pas que tout le droit soit frappé d'une hypothèque en raison d'une difficulté éventuelle.' (50 *Annuaire de l'Institut de droit international, Session de Bruxelles 1963*, II, p. 333.)

and by the Soviet Union against Finland),[186] tends to support this view. It is true that the principle of discrimination against the aggressor could not have been given effect if the Axis Powers had won the war, just as a theft in municipal law cannot be nullified and prosecuted if the police do not succeed in seizing the stolen goods and the culprit. However, as has been so well pointed out by Lauterpacht,[187] it must be assumed in a legal study that the forces of law and order will prevail over the forces of crime. Fortunately this has in fact been so in most modern wars.

It is true that this doctrine of discrimination may lead to confusion if the aggressor, too, claims to be a victim of aggression and draws the legal consequences therefrom (although it does not appear to have been reasoning along these lines which produced the Axis violations of the laws of war in the Second World War), even if neutral parties can have no reasonable doubt as to who is the aggressor. For this reason it might be a more prudent alternative view to confine the application of the principle of discrimination to those cases where the fact of aggression has been authoritatively determined. This may be the main reason underlying the widely held view that the principle of discrimination applies only in cases where the Security Council has determined the existence of aggression.[188] Thus, the (second François) Committee on the Equality of Application of the Rules of the Laws of War to Parties to an Armed Conflict of the *Institut de droit international* proposed the following Resolution I:

> L'inégalité de traitement des parties *durante bello* est justifiée si le Conseil de Sécurité de l'O.N.U. a désigné l'une des parties comme agresseur et pourvu que cette inégalité de traitement ne dépasse pas les limites indiquées par les Résolutions suivantes.

The Report adds, however, that this does not intend to answer the question of whether discrimination is justified also if the aggressor has not been designated by the Security Council. This question is left open. It is for that reason that the draft resolution says 'est justifié' rather than 'ne saurait être justifiée qu'en cas où'.[189] Moreover, it should be noted that the draft resolution speaks only of discrimination *durante bello*. Since the draft resolutions clearly (and *a fortiori*) admit discrimination *post bellum*, the specification of *durante bello* might be interpreted to

---

186. See the Assembly's resolutions of 24 February 1933, of 11 October 1935 and of 14 December 1939, respectively. The two latter resolutions also requested the Member States to assist the victims of aggression.

187. *BYIL*, XXX (1953) pp. 235–6.

188. Thus Scheuner in *International Law Association, Report of the Fiftieth Conference, Brussels 1962*, p. 160, and Yepes, when opposing the majority stand of the first François Committee *against* discrimination, *loc. cit. above*, note 15.

189. 50 *Annuaire de l'Institut de droit international, Session de Bruxelles 1963*, I, p. 117. See also Resolutions II and III, quoted *below*, pp. 268–9.

mean that the limitations which are prescribed for the discrimination shall not apply *post bellum*. This, however, would be very dangerous, because it might be used as a justification for imposing the determination and the law of the victor.

However, if the need to prevent uncertainty and abuse or similar reasons are decisive, then any other forms of objective determination must be taken into account, too. Thus the same effect must be given to any *voluntary* admission by the aggressor,[190] to a judgment by a *neutral* international tribunal,[191] to a decision by a regional intergovernmental organization [192] if both aggressor and victim are Members of it, and to a decision by the General Assembly of the United Nations.[193] Even if Article 39 (cf. Article 11(2)) of the Charter, despite the broad wording of Article 10, is interpreted *a contrario* as precluding the General Assembly from exercising in other respects its otherwise inherent right as the plenary organ of the world organization, the Assembly certainly must be recognized as a spokesman for the world community with sufficient authority to provide the objective determination which many consider necessary in order to prevent uncertainty and abuse arising from the in itself just application of the principle of discrimination against the aggressor. It must be remembered that the outlawry of aggression and the right of individual and collective self-defence were not created, but merely confirmed, by the Charter. Accordingly, the legal consequences

190. Cf Prime Minister Bethmann-Hollweg's implicit admission in the German *Reichstag* on 4 August 1914 of the German violation of the Treaty of 1839 which guaranteed Belgium's neutrality (citations *above*, note 26). Cf. also the admission after the Second World War by the Government of the Federal Republic of Germany, for example by Prime Minister Erhard in his radio speech on 31 August 1964. Forced admissions, like those contained in the Treaty of Versailles, cannot be given this legal effect; otherwise it would be possible also for the aggressor to force his victim to 'admit' aggression.

191. The Nürnberg Tribunal was established by the Allied Powers with only allied participation. Although its judgment in fact was just and sound, this principle would have enabled the Axis Powers to establish their own tribunal had they won the war. What is required is a tribunal established by a neutral organization or neutral States and composed of neutral nationals. Proposals for an international tribunal for war crimes, as outlined, for example in *Oppenheim: International Law*, II, § 257b, have been considered by the United Nations as part of the question of the establishment of an international criminal jurisdiction. The study was however interrupted by General Assembly resolution 898 (IX), which linked it to a definition of aggression, the subsequent efforts at which did not succeed. See also General Assembly resolutions 260 B(III), 489 (V), and 687 (VII), and the reports of the two special committees which elaborated a draft statute for an international criminal jurisdiction (the second is contained in *OR GA*, IX, Suppl. No. 12).

192. Cf. Articles 3 and 5 of the Inter-American Treaty of Reciprocal Assistance of 2 September 1947 (*UNTS*, Vol. 21, p. 95) and Article 6 of the Pact of the League of Arab States of 22 March 1945.

193. *Contra:* Lauterpacht in *BYIL*, XXX (1953) p. 207.

which this prohibition and this right entail for States engaged in a conflict, viz. the principle of discrimination, must not necessarily be contingent upon compliance with a procedure prescribed in the Charter for United Nations action.—The above mentioned (second) committee of the *Institut de droit international* also admitted the relevance of Assembly recommendations, although only pursuant to the Uniting for Peace Resolution. Its draft resolution III reads:

> Une recommandation de l'Assemblée Générale, en vertu de la Uniting for Peace Resolution, doit être assimilée, en ce qui concerne l'inégalité des parties, à une décision du Conseil.[194]

However, the report indicates that this question was controversial in the Committee. And the resolution which the *Institut* adopted at its session in Brussels in 1963 and which is quoted in full above, under 2(a), provides that 'there cannot be complete equality in the application of the rules of the law of war when *the competent organ of the United Nations has determined* that one of the belligerents has resorted to armed force in violation of the rules of the law of nations consecrated by the Charter of the United Nations'.[195] The words in italics were added by a last-minute amendment by *Jessup*, which caused *Zourek* to vote against the resolution, stating that the amendment could result in no discrimination being applied if the Security Council took no decision.[196]

The majority view, that discrimination can be applied only if the Security Council has determined aggression, might be defended in this strict form if one, in contradistinction to the present writer, were to deny that the right of discrimination flows from the general outlawry of war and were to assume that it follows only from the relevant provisions of the United Nations Charter, such as Articles 2(5)-(6), 25 and 41 et seq.[197] In *that* case it might be argued that the discrimination can be given effect only pursuant to the procedure prescribed in Article 39 of the Charter, i.e. determination by the Security Council that an act of aggression has taken place.[198] However, as will be explained below, the

---

194. 50 *Annuaire*, I, p. 119. *Contra:* Kunz and Quadri, *ibid.*, pp. 89 and 96. Once this principle is accepted, there is no legal basis for confining it to recommendations made pursuant to the Uniting for Peace Resolution. The General Assembly cannot by its own resolutions establish new powers for itself vis-à-vis States which do not accept these resolutions and powers, nor can it limit its existing powers with binding effect for the future, unless an external legal commitment has been entered into or new customary law is created.

195. *Annuaire de l'Institut de droit international, Session de Bruxelles 1963*, I, p. 376; italics added.

196. *Ibid.*, I, p. 356.

197. Cf. *below*, pp. 280–9.

198. See however, *below*, p. 285, note 253, on the interpretation of the term 'any action' in the first (active) part of Article 2(5).

relevant provisions of the Charter provide only a limited basis for discrimination and are mostly concerned with steps to be taken by 'neutral' States.[199]

3. FURTHER DEVIATIONS IN FAVOUR OF THE UNITED NATIONS

(a) *Introduction*

Whichever of the views discussed under 2(k)(ii) one takes, it would probably be agreed that, if the discrimination outlined under 2 shall apply at all, it must apply in favour of a United Nations Force, if this, as assumed above, is employed against an aggressor.

The question of whether the principle would apply to a United Nations Force even if there is no aggressor was raised by a member of the second François committee (Verzijl), who referred to the fact that 'les forces de l'O.N.U. sont en fait intervenues également par des actes de belligérance sans qu'il y eut un agresseur, notamment pour faire cesser des hostilités, ou pour imposer par la force à un Etat indépendant certaines solutions politiques qui concernaient sa compétence interne'.[200] The Rapporteur replied that the discrimination must apply in all cases where military action has been taken pursuant to a decision of the Security Council. Accordingly he formulated the relevant resolution (II) as follows:

> Sous réserve des stipulations des Résolutions qui suivent, l'inégalité de traitement est également justifiée quand il s'agit d'une action militaire des forces de l'O.N.U., opérant en vertu d'une décision du Conseil de Sécurité.[202]

However, as indicated above, Resolution III attributed the same effect to a recommendation by the General Assembly pursuant to the Uniting for Peace Resolution.—The present chapter is, as already stated, concerned exclusively with the situation where the United Nations Force resists an *aggressor*.

In his comments to draft Resolution II the Rapporteur stated:

> En faisant précéder cette Résolution d'un renvoi aux Résolutions suivantes, le rapporteur espère donner satisfaction aux membres qui désirent ne pas ouvrir la porte à une trop grande liberté d'action des forces de l'O.N.U.[202]

It now remains to consider precisely this question. It may be formulated as follows: Can or must yet further modifications be made in favour of the United Nations, as the supreme World Organization carrying out

199. See *below*, pp. 280–9.
200. 50 *Annuaire de l'Institut de droit international, Session de Bruxelles 1963*, I, p. 48.
202. *Ibid.*, p. 118.

an enforcement action against an aggressor (comparable to a police action against criminals) rather than a regular war of defence against the aggressor (comparable to self-defence under municipal law)? This question will be discussed in the following subsections, dealing successively with each of the sanctions and each of the main fields of the laws of war discussed under 2. In each case a summary will be given of the law which applies to a war of aggression between States, followed by indications of what further modifications are possible if a United Nations Force is involved.

In the latter respect little support can be drawn from practice. There has only been one relevant case, Korea, and practice there was mainly confined to the humanitarian field, where it was recognized that the customary laws of war apply to a United Nations Force without discrimination.[203] Otherwise the following discussion must be rather in the nature of abstract and preliminary speculation, based on considerations of what is reasonable and expedient, while seeking guidance in some cases in provisions of the United Nations Charter which, although hardly intended to deal with the subject of the laws of war, may be of some relevance.

(b) Reparation and restitution

(i) It has been demonstrated under 2(b) above that the *aggressor* is liable to pay reparation for all damage caused by his acts of war and for all costs incurred by the victim in resisting the aggression, even if the acts of the aggressor did not exceed the limits of the traditional laws of war. Similarly it has been demonstrated that the aggressor has a duty to restitute property which he has seized or requisitioned, even if the seizure or requisition did not violate the traditional laws of war.

Practice in connection with the First World War might indicate that this is a right only for the direct victim of aggression, not for those who come to his assistance, in so far as Article 232 of the Treaty of Versailles provided for full reparation only to Belgium and not to Great Britain which came to its assistance. However, practice in connection with the Second World War makes no distinction between the direct victims of aggression and those States which, like France and the United Kingdom, came to their assistance. If this is not regarded merely as an exercise of the power of the victor, this suggests that the right to full reparation (and, of course, restitution) pertains to the assisting States too. If both they and the aggressor are parties to any of the treaties outlawing aggressive war, their claim to reparation could probably be based upon that treaty. However, if the outlawry of aggressive war and the related right of collective self-defense is now accepted as a principle of general

203. *Above,* Chapter V,2(a).

international law,[204] it may well follow that any State making use of that right is entitled to claim, not only restitution or reparation for damage suffered, but also reparation for all costs incurred. The United Nations must then have the same right, based upon breach of the Charter and/or general international law, if this Organization takes action against the aggressor. This view was taken already in the leading commentary upon the Covenant of the League of Nations by two prominent German writers, in respect of the costs incurred by the Members of the League taking part in sanctions against the aggressor.[205] The principle was also expressed, forty years later, by the Soviet Union in the following terms:

> The Soviet Government considers that the question of the reimbursement of expenditure required for the execution of emergency measures adopted by the Security Council to deter or repel aggression through the use of United Nations armed forces should be decided in conformity with the generally recognized principle of international law that aggressor States bear political and material responsibility for the aggression they commit and for the material damage caused by that aggression.[206]

If the view is accepted that the United Nations is entitled to reimbursement from the aggressor for all costs the Organization has incurred in order to defeat him, there is a full discrimination in favour of the United Nations already under the general laws of war, and no further benefit could be conferred upon it in this respect.

(ii) It has been submitted under 2(b)(iii) above that the illegality of the aggression cannot relieve the *defender* of his obligation to pay reparation and to provide restitution in respect of any of his acts which violate those of the traditional laws of war which remain binding upon him, i.e. in particular the humanitarian laws and the Geneva Conventions. This must *a fortiori* apply to those who come to his assistance. It is submitted that there is not sufficient reason to make an exception in this respect for the United Nations, on the basis of an analogy to national police forces or otherwise. If it is considered essential that a Unit-

---

204. As submitted *above*, Chapter IV,5(a) and Chapter VI,(a)(i).

205. *Schücking and Wehberg: Die Satzung des Völkerbundes*, 2nd edition (Berlin 1924) p. 633: Der Rechtsbrecher ist, wie in der Note Clemenceaus vom 22. Mai 1919 an die deutsche Delegation ausdrücklich festgesetzt ist und wie es auch der Natur der Sache entspricht, verpflichtet, alle Kosten zu übernehmen und jeden Schaden zu ersetzen, der den Mitgliedern des Bundes durch einen Verstoss gegen den Vertrag erwächst. Ist der Rechtsbrecher aus irgend einem Grunde dazu nicht imstande so muss angenommen werden, dass die Kosten der vom Bunde ausgegangenen Unternehmungen, also namentlich von militärischen Massnahmen, dem Bunde zur Last fallen, während die den einzelnen Mitgliedern bei der Durchführung der Absperrung entstehenden Kosten und Schäden solchenfalls von ihnen selbst zu tragen sind. Doch hat der Völkerbund auch hier die Möglichkeit, besonders schwer geschädigten Staaten den Verlust ganz oder teilweise zu ersetzen.

206. Letter dated 10 July 1964 to the United Nations, A/5721.

ed Nations Force, as well as any other defender, observe the humanitarian rules of warfare, then the relevant sanctions should be maintained and applied, in order to secure compliance with these obligations and in order to provide reparation to those individual victims who are not personally responsible for the aggression. Indeed, the United Nations has not contested its obligation to pay reparation for any violation of the general laws of war which might have been committed by its troops in Katanga, although this is not a relevant precedent, because it was not a case of aggression by one sovereign State against another. On the other hand, it may be argued that, in the case of the United Nations, this should be a direct obligation to the individual victims, rather than a right for the aggressor State.[207]

(c) Criminal and civil liability of the leaders responsible for the aggression

It has been pointed out under 2(c) above that the *criminal responsibility* of political and military leaders of the aggressor State who are responsible for its decision to attack, extends to all acts performed by any persons in execution of the aggression. This is the maximum, and it is neither possible, nor would there be any reason, to go any further because the victim of aggression receives assistance from the United Nations.

Similarly, it was submitted that the same leaders should personally bear *civil liability* for the damage inflicted upon States and their nationals as a result of the aggressive war, including damage caused by acts which do not exceed the limits of the traditional laws of war. There is no known practice to confirm this and to indicate whether it also applies in respect of damage suffered by the States coming to the victim's assistance. However, there is no apparent reason why it should not extend to such States and to the United Nations.

(d) Punishment for war crimes

It was pointed out under 2(d) above that the personnel of the *agressor* who have no part in the decision to attack cannot be prosecuted as war criminals for acts which do not violate the traditional laws of war, at least not as far as they have acted pursuant to superior orders. This principle must, it is submitted, be maintained even in an action against a United Nations Force.

On the other hand, it was submitted that even the personnel of the *defenders* cannot escape punishment for war crimes because of the fact that they have been committed against an illegal aggressor, and that any

---

207. Cf. *above*, p. 242, and *below*, p. 276. As pointed out there, Wright takes this view even in respect of violations committed by personnel of a defender *State*.

obligation to prosecute war criminals must devolve also upon the defenders in respect of acts which are forbidden even to them, including primarily violations of the humanitarian traditional laws of war. This, too, must apply to a United Nations Force, as long as one accepts the view, submitted below, under (f), that such a Force remains bound by these laws. On the other hand, it may be argued that to the extent that the aggressor has the right himself to prosecute war criminals of the defending forces, this could not extend against the members of a United Nations Force as a world police force; the policing of these must be left to the World Organization. However, at present it is not possible for the United Nations to do this in respect of a Force composed of national contingents, because the States providing these contingents have not transferred to the Organization any powers of criminal jurisdiction. Experience in the Congo demonstrated that this is a weak aspect of the present system. If the UN became a party to the Geneva Conventions, the question of depriving the aggressor of the right to prosecute members of a UN Force would become academic also for the reason set forth above, p. 236. The various questions of criminal jurisdiction will be discussed more fully below, pp. 365–76 and 397.

(e) *Reprisals*

It has been pointed out under 2(e) above that, if the normal conditions for reprisals are fulfilled, the *defenders* can resort to reprisals against the aggressor in respect of those of his acts which violate the traditional laws of war, except that the Geneva and 1954 Hague Conventions prohibit reprisals against the persons they protect and their property, as well as against cultural property. It would hardly be consistent with humanitarian principles if one were to relax the normal conditions for reprisals in favour of a United Nations Force. And outside the humanitarian field the problem is of little practical importance, because of the discrimination which already applies in favour of the defenders and a United Nations Force, as set forth in other subsections of the present Chapter. This discrimination is considered by many as reprisals against the aggression. In this respect it may thus be said that a United Nations Force is entitled to apply reprisals to the extent which follows from the substantive parts of the present section [(g)-(j)].

On the other hand, if it should be felt that even the *aggressor* has a right to resort to reprisals in respect of any violations by the defenders of such, primarily humanitarian, rules of the traditional laws of war as are binding even upon them, it could be argued that such reprisals could not be taken against a United Nations Force. Even if war crimes were committed by the members of such a Force, it could be argued that the aggressor must confine himself to appeal to the Organization to stop such crimes and to prosecute the offenders.

(f) *Humanitarian rules of warfare. Nuclear weapons*

(i) It has been pointed out under 2(f) that it is widely accepted that the obligations arising under those laws of war whose purpose it is to protect individuals from suffering, and cultural property from destruction, *must be observed by both parties*. There can be no doubt that this fundamental principle must be maintained even if a United Nations Force is involved;[208] indeed, the Charter reaffirms in its preamble faith in fundamental human rights and 'in the dignity and worth of the human person'.[209] This is also confirmed by practice during the Korean war.[210] Resolution V proposed to the 1963 Brussels Conference of the *Institut de droit international*, quoted above, under 2(f), expressly states that the humanitarian obligations apply also to a United Nations enforcement action. And so does the resolution adopted, see above, p. 225.

The Charter does not contain any provision which would authorize deviation from the humanitarian laws of war. It is true that the relevant articles (Articles 42 et seq.) confer upon the Security Council and the Military Staff Committee broad powers to 'take such action by air, sea or land forces as may be necessary' and to make 'plans for the application of armed force', and that none of the articles refer to the laws of war, or even to 'war'; nor do they contain any other relevant restrictions. Nevertheless, they talk of the United Nations Force, its composition and its employment in terms similar to those employed in respect of national armies, and it is submitted that the drafters of the Charter should have expressed themselves more specifically, had they intended the United Nations Force to differ from national armies to an extent where it could conduct military operations in a manner which would be inconsistent even with those humanitarian and related rules of the laws of war which are applicable to all types of genuine military action [211] and which are considered so important that they cannot be abandoned even vis-à-vis an illegal aggressor. To impose upon Member States, not to mention non-member States, an obligation to accept this would require a clearer legal basis. Such a basis may be found in Articles 2(5) and 41 of the Charter, which will be discussed in detail below, under

---

208. In this sense also Giraud in 50 *Annuaire de l'Institut de droit international, Session de Bruxelles 1963*, II, p. 337, and Baxter in *Proceedings of the American Society of International Law, 1953*, p. 96. The latter states that 'it cannot seriously be asserted that especially severe measures must be taken against nationals of a state which has resorted to the unlawful use of force', these will already have been enslaved by a totalitarian regime.

209. See also the provisions on human rights in Articles 1(3) and 55(c).

210. *Above*, Chapter V,2(a).

211. 'Armed conflict', 'war in the material sense', *above*, pp. 199–201, cf. *below*, pp. 348–50.

(g)-(i).[212] However, these are hardly relevant to the humanitarian aspects, although they may be relevant to private economic interests.[213]

(ii) It was also pointed out under 2(f) above that, even if the aggressor enjoys the passive rights which follow from the traditional laws of war in the humanitarian field for the protection of his personnel and nationals, he does not genuinely possess those *active rights* which the traditional laws of war leave open for the belligerents to exercise vis-à-vis enemy (or neutral) personnel or nationals, except for such rights as have been clearly laid down in conventions concluded after the treaties outlawing war. With the latter exception, the defenders may claim *reparation* also for damage caused by such acts and they may consider the aggressor's judgments and other acts invalid. This must apply also if the aggressor is opposed by a United Nations Force. On the other hand, it has already been pointed out that, even if a United Nations Force is involved, it would not be reasonable to apply *criminal* sanctions to such acts committed by personnel of the aggressor who have had no personal part in the decision to commit aggression.[214] And reprisals in respect of such acts are allowed only to the extent that they can be applied

---

212. It may be these provisions which *Kotzsch* has in mind when he states that 'although an examination of the principal provisions of the Charter directly dealing with enforcement action shows that the Security Council is not necessarily bound to act in accordance with international law, this does not mean that the general principles of international law are reduced to a "platonic" significance'. (*The Concept of War in Contemporary History and International Law*, Geneva 1956, p. 274). It is more difficult to interpret such a limitation into *Attia's* relevant statement at p. 255 of his study on 'Les forces armées des Nations Unies en Corée et au Moyen-Orient' (Genève 1963). After citing Articles 24, 25, 39, 42 and 48, he states that vis-à-vis Member States, the Security Council occupies 'une position juridique supérieure', by virtue of which it does not consider itself bound by the laws of war, whether conventional or customary, while United Nations forces vis-à-vis non-member States from a legal point of view should observe the customary laws of war, subject to Article 2(6); all of this being subject to limitations established unilaterally by the Security Council. Reference may also be made to the following statement by the Committee on legal problems of the United Nations of the American Society of International Law:

'Since no other rules have been stated it was natural that the United Nations should accept existing rules insofar as they seem relevant and proper; this was especially true as regards humanitarian principles. It is not true, however, that the United Nations considers itself to be a combatant in the sense of the old laws of war, and bound to apply all of them. It is maintained by some that acceptance of the Charter by Member States meant acceptance by them of the superior legal position of the United Nations as regards the use of force and that, consequently, the United Nations may apply such rules as it wishes. It might, for example, forbid use of atomic bombs by a state while reserving the right to use them itself. Presumably, its rules would be of high humanitarian character and it would respect them carefully'. (*Proceedings*, 1952, p. 217.) This statement also goes too far, in the view of the present writer.

213. See *below*, p. 284.

214. *Above*, under 2(d) *in initio* and 3(d).

against the illegal aggressor as such, i.e. to the extent set forth in the substantive parts of the present section.[215] In these respects, too, a United Nations Force must be governed by the same law as any other defender.

However, special considerations may arise in two other respects:

(iii) In the first place, there would in the case of the United Nations be some more reason to accept Quincy Wright's view that the obligation of the defender to observe the humanitarian law creates *a right only for the individuals concerned, not for the aggressor State*.[216] This because one would have more confidence in the United Nations' willingness to satisfy claims presented by individuals without active support of their government than one would have in the willingness of a State victim of aggression to do so.

(iv) Secondly, the question of a special position for a United Nations Force has been raised in respect of *nuclear weapons*.[217] One of the reasons for this may be the fact that, while those humanitarian laws of war which are directly concerned with individuals (the protection of sick, wounded, prisoners and civilians) have been worked out in great detail and are fairly clear, this is not true of the law relating to the modern means of mass destruction, including aerial bombardment, nuclear weapons and guided missiles. That the legal situation of these weapons is not clear is recognized also by those who support their illegality *de lege lata*.[218]

The General Assembly of the United Nations on 24 November 1961 adopted a resolution declaring the use of nuclear weapons to be 'a direct violation of the Charter of the United Nations' and declaring that 'any *State* using nuclear and thermonuclear weapons is to be considered as violating the Charter of the United Nations, as acting contrary to the laws of humanity and as committing a crime against mankind and civilization'.[219]

This resolution was adopted by 55 votes against 20 and with 26 abstentions.[220] In his Report on Self-Defence under the Charter of the

215. (f)–(i), cf. (e).
216. *Above*, p. 242, cf. pp. 272 and 273 and *below*, p. 281.
217. Cf. *Jessup: A Modern Law of Nations* (New York 1949) pp. 215–6; the report of the Committee on Study of Legal Problems of the United Nations, *Proceedings of the American Society of International Law*, 1952, pp. 217–8; and *Clark and Sohn: World Peace through World Law*, second edition (Cambridge, Mass., 1960) pp. 294–5 and 319. *Contra:* Quadri in 50 *Annuaire de l'Institut de droit international, Session de Bruxelles 1963*, I, p. 97.
218. See for example Eide and Opsahl in *Atomvåpen* (Oslo 1962) at p. 86.
219. Resolution 1653(XVI). Italics added. In this sense also Eide and Opsahl, *loc. cit.*, pp. 82–86.
220. The separate vote on each of the phrases quoted was 56–19–26 and 52–20–23,

United Nations and the Use of Prohibited Weapons, discussed at the International Law Association's Conference in Brussels 1962, *Schwarzenberger*, while contesting part of the legal basis of this declaration as incompatible with the practice of both parties during the Second World War (indiscriminate aerial bombardments),[221] submitted as a general proposition (i.e. not expressly confined to the question of weapons of mass destruction) that 'in strict law, it appears impossible to deny the right to a belligerent whose opponent has broken obligations *juris ad bellum* to retaliate by way of reprisals, including such as may involve breaches *juris in bello*' and that 'discrimination is permissible in strict (customary) law against the armed forces or civilian population of an aggressor State on the ground of reprisal'.[222] This view had also been adopted by the British Branch of the Association in a resolution of 7 December 1961 in the special context of weapons of mass destruction.[223] However, the competent committee of the Brussels Conference rejected, by 29 votes against 21 and with 14 abstentions, a draft resolution which would have declared 'the use of biological, chemical and nuclear weapons of mass destruction' (to be) contrary to international law, but permissible if

> (a) one of the parties to an international conflict has committed a breach of the rules of warfare (*jus in bello*) or (b) has broken treaty obligations not to resort to force or to war (*jus ad bellum*) provided always that such use of prohibited weapons, being permissible only as a form of reprisals, is not disproportionate to the occasion.[224]

respectively, and the vote on that part of the resolution as a whole was 56–19–26 (*OR GA*, XVI, Plenary Meetings, II, p. 807).

221. *International Law Association, Report of the Fiftieth Conference, Brussels 1962*, pp. 218–21 and 229–33.

222. *Ibid.*, pp. 211 and 221. He warned, however, that in view of 'the chain reaction of negative reciprocity which such retaliatory measures are likely to set in motion, it can rarely, if at all, be advisable to take such reprisals'. He also added that 'in the case of conventions which, as, for instance, the Geneva Red Cross Conventions of 1949, are intended to be applied in all circumstances or which expressly prohibit reprisals against protected persons, retaliation against such individuals is prohibited'.

223. *Ibid.*, p. 234.

224. *Ibid.*, pp. 184 and 190. The resolution had been proposed by Messrs. Nagendra Singh and Krishna Rao of India. Cf. the discussion *ibid.*, pp. 157–91, and the text of the resolution finally adopted, *ibid.*, p. xi.—As for the *Institut de droit international*, the Rapporteur of its Committee on Equality of Application of the Rules of the Law of War to Parties to an Armed Conflict confined himself to proposing, in draft Resolution VII, that 'l'agresseur doit être privé de l'emploi de l'arme nucléaire', considering this to be the least that could be done as long as no agreement had been reached on the total prohibition of such weapons. Other members of the Committee proposed prohibition for *all* participants, with the self-evident reservation 'except that the defender or the United Nations may use such arms in retaliation against their use by the aggressor'. (50 *Annuaire de l'Institut de droit international, Session de Bruxelles 1963*, I, p. 16.)

At a subsequent vote, the first part alone (prohibiting the weapons without qualification) was rejected by 34 votes against 24 and with 9 abstentions.[225]

It might be argued that the *United Nations*, acting as the supreme world organization for the maintenance of peace, is, in this respect too, in a position which is somewhat different from that of a victim State or another *State* coming to its assistance. One would probably have more confidence in the United Nations not resorting to nuclear weapons without having assured itself that there is no other way of halting the aggressor. Moreover, possession by the United Nations of nuclear weapons might in some, but not in all, cases be sufficient to deter aggression, which would be the purpose of any rule of international law in this respect. The idea has therefore been aired that the United Nations alone might be allowed to use nuclear weapons against an aggressor.[226] This would represent a compromise between the opposing views referred to above. However, the discussions at the Geneva Disarmament Conference demonstrate that, unless this is coupled with other steps in the field of disarmament, it would not satisfy those who believe that nuclear weapons are necessary as a deterrent against aggression even in cases where the Security Council is unable to act. Nor may it suffice to satisfy those who consider that nuclear weapons can only be legally justified in defence against an attack with atomic weapons or similar weapons of mass destruction.[227] Indeed, the latter view is the basis of one of the important proposals which have been made for vesting in the United Nations the exclusive right to possess, produce and use nuclear weapons.[228] Another problem, not dealt with here, is whether the United Nations would in fact be prepared to use nuclear weapons, even if it had the right to do so.

225. *Ibid.*, p. 191.

226. Cf. Jessup and the American Society of International Law committee cited in note 217 *above*, both speaking *de lege ferenda*. The committee is quoted in full *above*, note 212. *Jessup* considers that international forces should be forbidden to use poison gas or bacteriological warfare, while he raises the question of whether such forces should be allowed to use nuclear weapons as a last resort even if these weapons, too, are outlawed for States. It may be recalled in this connexion that the preamble of the Charter provides that 'armed force shall not be used, save in the common interest'.

227. See, for example, Eide and Opsahl in *Atomvåpen* (Oslo 1962) at p. 85.

228. *Clark and Sohn: World Peace through World Law* (2nd edition, Cambridge, Mass., 1960) pp. 294–5 and 319. The reason why these writers propose that a 'United Nations Peace Force shall have the potential capacity to use nuclear weapons is that it seems impossible to devise any system of inspection which can afford an *absolute* guarantee that no nuclear weapons whatever will be concealed during the disarmament period or that no such weapons whatever will be clandestinely produced thereafter'. Accordingly, the weapons shall never be used 'save by the order of the General Assembly itself and then only if such weapons have actually been used against the United Nations or such use is imminently threatened'.

However this may be, the prohibition of nuclear weapons, and any limitation of such prohibition, cannot be implemented without an agreement between the powers concerned. Such agreement was therefore expressly called for in the resolutions adopted by the General Assembly and the International Law Association.[229] The problem is therefore, from a practical point of view, one *de lege ferenda* rather than *de lege lata*, and depends upon a political decision. *De lege lata* it may suffice to state that the United Nations is not a party to the St. Petersburg and Brussels Declarations, the Hague Conventions of 1907 and the Geneva Protocol of 1925,[229a] to which the General Assembly's resolution and others refer as a basis for the prohibition of nuclear weapons, although this fact is irrelevant if one, with the majority, considers these Conventions to be declaratory of general international law.[230] The United Nations is of course directly bound by its own Charter, to which the resolution refers in its operative part. It should be noted, however, that the prohibition in the operative part is directed at use by any 'State' and at use for 'war' purposes,[231] although these terms may not have been chosen deliberately for the purpose of excluding from the prohibition enforcement actions by the United Nations.

(g) *Military occupation* [232]

(i) As has been pointed out under 2(g) above, the *aggressor* has no 'right' to impose upon the territory occupied by him any sufferings or burdens, even such as do not exceed the limits of the traditional laws of occupation, except insofar as such rights exceptionally might have been specifically laid down in the Geneva Conventions or in other modern conventions. This is true if the aggressor is opposed by States, and of course also if he is opposed by a United Nations Force. Accordingly it was submitted above, on the basis of practice during and after the Second World War, that governments, belligerent as well as neutral, are free to treat as invalid the acts of the aggressor occupant relating to economic, legal and other matters, even if these acts do not violate the traditional laws of occupation. This, too, must apply if a United Nations

---

229. *Loc. cit.*, p. xi.

229a. And it could accede only to some of them, see *below*, p. 361.

230. Schwarzenberger, *loc. cit.*, note 221, at p. 230, doubts this, pointing to the small number of States which are parties to the Conventions.

231. Paragraphs 1(d) and 2, respectively. However, paragraph 1(a) speaks of the use of nuclear weapons in general.

232. On the occupation of parts of North Korea by the United Nations Force in Korea and their administration by the Unified Command and, after the armistice, by South Korea, pursuant to successive resolutions (recommendations) adopted by the United Nations Commission for the Unification and Rehabilitation of Korea and its Interim Committee, see *Attia: Les forces des Nations Unies en Corée et au Moyen-Orient* (Genève 1963) pp. 268–271.

Force intervenes. Thus any government, as well as the United Nations, may consider void the laws enacted by the occupant and his executive acts, such as the appointment and dismissal of officials, as well as judgments rendered by courts under his authority. No foreign State can protest if the legal government during or after the occupation enacts legislation which invalidates such acts of the aggressor or the illegal occupant with effect even for foreign nationals. The same is true if another State enacts such invalidating legislation, with effect also for foreign nationals or property within its jurisdiction. Nor can the inhabitants of the occupied territory contest the validity of such invalidating legislation on the basis of constitutional provisions protecting acquired rights. This despite the fact that the provisions of the Hague Regulations relating to belligerent occupation have become part of the municipal law of most States.

More doubtful is the question of what applies if the governments concerned have not enacted invalidating legislation. In most, but not all, cases national courts have then refrained from considering invalid acts of the occupant which did not violate the traditional laws of war. The courts may thus have considered that, even if the traditional laws of occupation do not constitute limitations upon the freedom of action of the legislator in the case of illegal aggression, they still form part of the law of the land insofar as no legislation has been enacted, i.e. for the purposes of interpretation and filling of *lacunae*. Indeed, no government would wish to invalidate *all* acts of the illegal occupant. And it is difficult to draw a line *de lege lata*. The drawing of the line may, at least in many fields, be better left to the legislative and executive authorities. This may have been the real reason why most courts did not, in connection with the Second World War, apply *on their own initiative* the modification to the traditional laws of war which would seem logically to follow from the outlawry of aggressive war and the principle *ex injuria jus non oritur*.

Nevertheless, there is no doubt room for further utilization of the right to discriminate. Although this in principle can be done unilaterally, being a matter for the municipal law of each State to decide, it could be much more effectively achieved if the United Nations were to adopt appropriate recommendations or decisions, for example on the basis of Article 41 of the Charter.[233] However, there appears to be no reason to confine such recommendations or decisions—or, indeed, any further utilization of the right to discriminate—to those cases where the aggressor is opposed by a United Nations Force. Those reasons which speak in favour of the invalidity of the acts of the aggressor as a belligerent and as an occupant are directly linked to the illegality of the aggression and the principle *ex injuria jus non oritur*, rather than to the nature of the

233. Cf. *below*, under (i).

action resisting the aggression. Accordingly, while there is room in this field for a more radical discrimination, it would be hard to justify a limitation of such discrimination to cases where a United Nations Force has intervened against the aggressor.

Even if the United Nations has made no relevant recommendations or decisions, the Member States, as shall be demonstrated below, under (i), have an automatic *obligation* under Article 2(5) of the United Nations Charter to passive discrimination against the aggressor in any case where the Organization is taking 'preventive or enforcement action' against him. This must imply a duty to refrain from recognizing as valid those acts of the occupant which the legal government has declared invalid, even if they do not violate the traditional laws of war.

(ii) It has been submitted in an earlier study [234] that if the *defenders* occupy the territory of the aggressor, they must observe the traditional laws of occupation (the minimum standards), at least insofar as these protect private interests. This must be maintained at least within the humanitarian field.[235] However, if the occupant is the United Nations, this might be held to be a duty directly vis-à-vis the inhabitants, rather than a right of the aggressor State.[236]

Outside the humanitarian field, there might be room for giving a United Nations Force a privileged position.[237] It might be possible to accord to a United Nations Force the right to take certain legal and economic measures in an occupied territory which an occupant is not permitted to take under the traditional laws of war. Certain arguments in favour of such privileges might be drawn from the fact that a United Nations Force is acting as a police force on behalf of the world community. Thus, the United Nations might more easily than a victim State or its allies be considered entitled to alter the political structure of the occupied territory of the aggressor,[238] notably in order to render it more democratic in recognition of the fact that it is very difficult for a democracy to commit aggression. However, in many other cases it would seem that more arguments for extended rights could be drawn from the fact that the Force is used to stop illegal aggression. In other words,

234. *Tidsskrift for rettvitenskap* (Oslo) 1945, pp. 118–9. In the same sense largely Castberg in 50 *Annuaire de l'Institut de droit international, Session de Bruxelles 1963*, II, pp. 336–7.
235. Castberg, *loc. cit.*, goes further, see *below*, note 238.
236. Cf. *above*, under (f)(iii).
237. Thus van Asbeck takes the view that 'une force militaire de l'O.N.U., occupant un territoire ou pays, devra, en tant qu'organe de la Société des Etats, pouvoir disposer de pouvoirs plus larges qu'une armée d'un Etat ou de quelques Etats individuels', 50 *Annuaire de l'Institut de droit international, Session de Bruxelles 1963*, I, p. 79. Cf. also Quadri, ibid., p. 110, who proposes the elaboration of special regulations for the occupation of the aggressors' territory in the course of a collective action.
238. Castberg, *ibid.*, II, pp. 336–7 rejects this right for the victim State and the UN.

while it might be possible to defend certain privileges for a United Nations Force as occupant of the territory of the aggressor, there would be strong reasons to extend many of them also to a national force which resists aggression. The strongest—and perhaps decisive—argument against such discrimination is the risk of the aggressor retaliating by applying similar measures. And this probably applies with equal force in the case of a United Nations action, if the aggressor is powerful.

If and to the extent that the defenders for this or other reasons cannot, as a matter of general law, be considered as entitled to exceed in this respect the limits of the traditional laws of war, the question arises of whether this right cannot, nevertheless, be created, and even turned into duty, by specific decisions of the Security Council. Articles 41 and 42 of the Charter authorize that Council to decide what military and non-military measures shall be taken to stop the aggression.[239] Thus, Article 41 authorizes the Council to decide upon measures 'not involving the use of armed force', including complete interruption of economic relations and communications with the aggressor. The Article does not state that such measures may not go beyond what a (belligerent or) neutral would have been entitled to do under the laws of war. Even if Article 41 is directly concerned with the case where no military enforcement measures have been undertaken, it can hardly be claimed that the Security Council could no longer take these measures if it goes to the extent of military sanctions under Article 42. However, it is doubtful whether Article 41 is relevant to the territory of the aggressor after its occupation by the defending forces through the 'use of armed force'. Nor do the terms of Article 42, which deal with the use of armed force, appear to authorize acts in an occupied territory which would be forbidden to a defender State under the modern laws of war, whatever these may be.

On the other hand, *Jessup* submits, *de lege ferenda,* that because 'international forces are operating for the entire world community, attempts to defray the expense of the military operations through forced loans and similar devices should be prohibited', and that the old 'relic of the ancient right of booty which is found in the stipulation that the occupant may take property of the enemy government, should similarly be waived in favour of such subsequent international steps as may be taken'.[240] Similarly *Baxter* suggests that 'the occupation of enemy territory by United Nations forces will give rise to a fiduciary obligation to rehabilitate the area concerned so that it may resume its rightful place in the international community'.[241] A similar idea may be underlying draft Resolution IV of the second François Committee, which reads:

239. Cf. Wright in *AJIL,* XLVII (1953) pp. 371–2 and 375.
240. *A Modern Law of Nations* (New York 1949) p. 217.
241. *Proceedings of the American Society of International Law,* 1953, p. 97.

Les buts spécifiques que la Charte a prévus pour les actions de coercition, de
l'arrêt de l'envahisseur, du rétablissement de la paix et de la sécurité internatio-
nales, déterminent les limites des mesures militaires permises contre un agresseur.[242]

It is certainly true that a United Nations Force will be expected to act
in a particularly humane manner [243] and that it should and will not
make use of its rights under the laws of war and occupation in those
respects where this may not be necessary to achieve its purpose, viz. to
stop the aggression and prevent further aggression. This should be clearly
expressed in any internal standing or *ad hoc* instructions issued by the
Organization to its Force. However, it is difficult to agree that the Organization should be prevented from using its rights under the laws of
war and occupation set forth above as a matter of (external) international law. This would tie its hands unduly and may, indeed, not have
been Jessup's intention.

(h) *Economic warfare*

The situation in respect of economic warfare is essentially similar to
that of the non-humanitarian aspects of the laws of occupation.

(i) As was pointed out above, pp. 258–60, the *aggressor* has no 'right'
to appropriate booty, to sequestrate enemy property, to declare a blockade, to interfere with 'enemy' or 'neutral' shipping, to seize and condemn
prizes etc. He must pay reparation and render restitution for all such
acts. And no other State has a duty to recognize their validity. This will
of course apply, *a fortiori*, if a United Nations Force intervenes.[244] In
the case of a United Nations military or non-military action there may
even be a *duty* for Member and non-member States to refuse to accept
such measures on the part of the aggressor, as shall be demonstrated below, under (i).

(ii) On the other hand, there would be room for permitting the *defenders* to apply even such measures of economic warfare as exceed the
limits of the traditional laws of war and neutrality, except that this, as
pointed out above, under 2(h), would create an undesirable risk of reprisals on the part of the aggressor. This risk will hardly be less if such

242. *50 Annuaire de l'Institut de droit international, Session de Bruxelles 1963*, I,
p. 119.

243. In this sense, speaking generally (i.e. not specially in the context of occupation)
also *Fenwick: International Law*, p. 551; *Clark and Sohn: World Peace through World
Law* (2nd edition, Cambridge, Mass. 1960) p. 319; and Eustathiades *50 Annuaire de
l'Institut de droit international, Session de Bruxelles 1963*, I, p. 34.

244. Jessup takes the same position, but expressly only as a *de lege ferenda* proposition for a *United Nations* action. He states: 'It should be agreed that the state against
which international enforcement action is taken shall have no right of interference with
ships or aircraft of other states. Any act of force by the war vessels or aircraft of that
state on or over the high seas should be considered an act of piracy'. (*A Modern Law
of Nations*, New York 1949, p. 220.)

measures were applied by a United Nations Force. Nevertheless, as was submitted above, under (g)(ii), the Security Council no doubt has the authority under Article 41 of the Charter to recommend or decide upon measures of economic warfare which exceed the limits of the traditional laws of war and neutrality.[245] Indeed, as will be explained under (i) below, Article 2(5) probably confers upon Member States an *automatic duty* to apply such measures.[246] These may even be directed against individuals, insofar as their actions may assist the enemy. This is particularly true of individuals in enemy or neutral territory.[247]—However, these Articles are not confined to cases where the United Nations has taken military action. The Security Council may impose these obligations in any case where it has determined that aggression has taken place even if it does not take any other, military or non-military, action.[248]

(i) *Neutrals. Article 2(5) of the Charter* [249]

It has been pointed out above, under 2(i), that 'neutral' States are free to discriminate against the aggressor in economic, legal, military and other respects, and that a 'neutral' State cannot complain if other States discriminate in a manner which also affects its interests and those of its nationals.

While this legal right to discriminate will be the same if the United Nations intervenes, its factual utilization may be much more extensive, because it may then become easier even for politically weak States to make use of their right to discriminate against the aggressor. However, to this end a determination by the United Nations that aggression has taken place (and related recommendations and decisions) is enough, even if it is not followed by action of a United Nations Force.

On the other hand, it was pointed out above, under 2(i), that 'neutral' States have no *obligation* to discriminate, unless this follows from treaty. On this point even the legal position is radically altered if the United Nations intervenes, because an obligation to discriminate against the aggressor follows from the Charter of the United Nations, for Member States and even for non-member States if one considers the Charter

---

245. In this sense also Wright, *AJIL*, XLVII (1953) pp. 371–2 and 375. He construes also Article 2(5) and even Article 42 (*contra: above*, under (f)(i)) in the same sense.

246. Wright, *ibid.*, p. 375, appears to take a contrary view, but see p. 371.

247. Cf. *above*, p. 242. Bowett: *United Nation Forces* (London 1964) p. 491, referring to Articles 2(5) and 25, states that 'these obligations of the Charter cannot be said to inure to the individual'. However, he does so in the context of *occupation*, where, as has been pointed out *above*, p. 282, these Articles, and particularly Article 41, are less relevant.

248. *Below*, under (i) *in initio*.

249. See Taubenfeld: 'International Actions and Neutrality' in *AJIL*, XLVII (1953) pp. 377–396.

binding upon these in accordance with Article 2(6).[250] The basic provisions are Articles 2(5) and 41.[251] The latter provision confers upon
the Security Council the power to make decisions calling upon Members
to apply non-military sanctions, including interruption of economic relations and of communications.[252] Article 2(5) provides:

> All Members shall give the United Nations every assistance in any action it
> takes in accordance with the present Charter, and shall refrain from giving
> assistance to any state against which the United Nations is taking preventive or
> enforcement action.

According to the words, these obligations to discriminate do not apply
in all cases of aggression. They apply only where the United Nations
has decided to take enforcement action, or, as for the first (active) part
of Article 2(5), 'any action'. Whatever the difference between these
terms may be,[253] none of the provisions involves a substantive limitation,[254] since the action does not have to be military action but may be
confined to non-military measures of compulsion and, indeed, to the
very measures of discrimination. Thus, the second part of Article 2(5),
too, applies even if the Security Council has merely decided upon certain measures of discrimination, without taking any active steps. Indeed,
the second part applies in all cases of *aggression*, because it follows already from the outlawry of war that nobody is entitled to assist the
aggressor.[254a]

If such military or non-military action has been decided upon, the
question arises whether a duty to discriminate arises *automatically* out of
Article 2(5), even if no specific decision to this effect has been made by
the Security Council. This legal question arises if the Organization has

250. On the latter question, see *Nordisk Tidsskrift for international Ret og Jus
gentium*, XXXIV (1964) pp. 12–14.

251. Other relevant provisions are Articles 2(6), 25, 42–53 (especially Articles 48(2)
and 49) and 103.

252. Cf. *above*, under (g)(ii).

253. *Bowett: United Nations Forces* (London 1964) pp. 224–5 takes the view that
the United Nations action in the Congo fell under the first, but not under the second,
part of Article 2(5). On the other hand, the International Court of Justice, in its advisory opinion on Certain Expenses of the United Nations, interpreted 'action' *in
Article 11(2)* to mean 'coercive or enforcement action' and 'such action as is solely
within the province of the Security Council', i.e. action under Chapter VII, namely
'Action with respect to threats to the peace, breaches of the peace, and acts of aggression' (*ICJ Reports*, 1962, pp. 164–5). Verdross, as quoted by *Attia: 'Les forces armées
des Nations Unies en Corée et au Moyen-Orient (Genève 1963)* p. 274, takes a wider
view of both parts of Article 2(5). *Attia, op. cit.*, p. 276, takes the same view as the
Court.

254. Cf. *Oppenheim: International Law*, II, §§ 292h and 292i, whose somewhat
different discussion of this problem appears to lead to the same practical results.

254a. In this sense apparently also Verdross in *Recueil des Cours*, 1953 II, pp. 69
when he states that it applies also to self-defence pursuant to Article 51.

not adopted relevant decisions, or if it has done so only in the form of recommendations. It is recalled in this connexion that in the only case where the United Nations has taken enforcement action against an aggressor, namely against North Korea and the People's Republic of China during the Korean war, the Security Council and the General Assembly in their relevant resolutions *called upon* all Members, or all States and authorities, to render assistance to the victim of aggression and to the United Nations action and to refrain from giving assistance to the aggressors. Some relevant provisions also used the term 'recommends'.[255]

There can be no doubt that the duty laid down in the *second* part of Article 2(5) to *refrain from giving assistance* to the aggressor, which follows from the outlawry of war, is automatic,[256] as it was under Article 16(1) of the Covenant of the League of Nations, which was far more specific in setting forth what the Member States were to do. However, it should be recalled that in practice the Members of the League only applied economic sanctions once, against Italy, and then only specific sanctions which had been decided by the Council. The great majority of the Member States took part in these sanctions. During the war in Korea, the General Assembly similarly adopted a resolution [500(V)] that every State should apply an embargo on arms and certain specified strategic materials. Despite the fact that this was merely a recommendation, forty out of the then 61 Member States reported full compliance with the provisions of the resolution.[257]

The obligation to refrain from giving assistance to the aggressor must clearly imply a duty to prevent even such types of assistance as neutral States would have been entitled to permit to be rendered to both belligerents under the traditional laws of neutrality, such as the exportation of arms or the departure of persons wanting to join the armed forces of the belligerents.[258] But the Article goes further than that. It probably must be interpreted as also prohibiting acts which neutral States under the traditional laws of war are *obliged* to perform or permit, if such acts would involve assistance to the belligerent. This interpretation is strengthened by the fact that at the San Francisco Conference 'it was understood in subcommittee that the statute of permanent neutrality is incompatible with the principles declared in paragraphs 5 and 6 of Chapter

255. Security Council resolutions of 25 and 27 June and General Assembly resolutions 498(V) of 1 February 1951 and 500(V) of 18 May 1951.

256. In this sense also *Attia: Les forces armées en Corée et au Moyen-Orient* (Genève 1963) p. 272, quoting Verdross at p. 274.

257. Taubenfeld, *loc. cit.*, pp. 393–4.

258. In this sense also Wright in *AJIL*, XLVII (1953) p. 371, who states (citing Articles 2(6) and 41) that this obligation may be enforced by the States taking part in the enforcement action 'if specifically authorized by the proper authority of the United Nations'.

II'.[259] Thus 'neutral' States are, at least if they are Members of the United Nations, deprived, not only of some of their rights as neutrals, but even of their right to stay neutral in all respects.

Also the *first* part of Article 2(5), if read as it stands, would seem to impose upon States an automatic duty to give the United Nations *active assistance* in any action it takes.[259a] The words 'in accordance with the present Charter' would seem to refer to the immediately preceding words 'any action it takes', and the meaning would then be that the duty to render active assistance is confined to actions undertaken on the basis of the specific provisions of the Charter.[260] However, the United States Delegation to the San Francisco Conference clearly interpreted these words as referring to 'every assistance' when it reported the provision as requiring Members 'to give to the Organization any assistance which their obligations under the Charter require of them'.[261] Goodrich and Hambro, after quoting this, state that the provision 'imposes no obligations not provided for in other parts of the Charter', in particular in Chapter VII.[262] This is the logical conclusion of the United States interpretation. But it means that the first part of Article 2(5) is legally meaningless and superfluous. On the other hand, if the provision is interpreted otherwise, the words '*every* assistance' might carry too far and render Article 43 and partly even Article 41 meaningless. Article 43 provides that all Members 'undertake to make available to the Security Council, on its call and *in accordance with a special agreement* or agreements, armed forces, assistance, and facilities, including rights of passage . . .' This explicit call for special agreements may render it difficult to maintain that there is an automatic duty under Article 2(5) to give those

259. *United Nations Conference on International Organization*, Doc. 739, I/1/A/ 19(a), VI, at p. 722.

259a. In this sense apparently Verdross in *Recueil des Cours*, 1953 II, p. 69.

260. Cf. *above*, Chapter V,3(c), note 131. This is the interpretation of *Attia: Les forces armées des Nations Unies en Corée et au Moyen-Orient* (Genève 1963) p. 271. He even believes that the action must have been taken on the basis of Article 43, a proposition which must be rejected both for the reason set forth *above*, Chapter IV, 2(b) and 4(c) *in initio* and because Article 2(5), as pointed out above, is not even confined to military action.

261. *Report to the President on the Results of the San Francisco Conference*, Department of State Publication 2349, p. 42.

262. Charter of the United Nations, at Article 2(5). Cf. also the draft Declaration of Rights and Duties of States (taken note of by and annexed to General Assembly resolution 375(IV)), Article 10 of which imposes upon *every* State the 'duty to refrain from giving assistance to any State which is acting in violation of article 9, or against which the United Nations is taking preventive or enforcement action', but which does not establish any duty to assist the United Nations actively. See the account of the discussions concerning Article 10 given by Taubenfeld, *loc. cit.*, pp. 388–390. He states that *Member* States have a clear duty under Article 2(5) of the Charter not to aid the aggressor and 'usually' a duty to aid in the United Nations action.

types of assistance which are enumerated in Article 43.[263] This despite the fact that under Article 16(3) of the Covenant of the League of Nations there was a clear automatic duty to 'afford passage' to the international force [264] (but not to participate actively in military sanctions). As for practice, it should be noted that during the Korean war about half the Member States rendered or offered assistance to the military effort, either in the form of troops or in the form of other services (this apart from the forty-three governments who offered assistance in the form of relief supplies).[265] The relevant resolutions of the Security Council and the General Assembly had *called upon* all Members, or all States and authorities, to (refrain from giving assistance to the aggressors and to) render every assistance to the United Nations action.[266] The basic resolution had *recommended* that Members furnish assistance to the Republic of Korea.[267]

If the first (active) part of Article 2(5) is interpreted as not imposing an automatic duty, it becomes important to draw a distinction between what constitutes, respectively, abstention from assistance to the aggressor and assistance to the United Nations action. As already pointed out, this must not be tested in relation to the traditional laws of neutrality. The test must rather be that between passivity and activity. Thus it is submitted that even those Member States which do not take part in the United Nations action are automatically prevented, under the *second* (passive) part of Article 2(5), from admitting warships of the aggressor to their ports, even within the limits permitted by the traditional laws of neutrality. They probably even have an automatic duty to refrain from such indirect assistance to the aggressor as it would be to recognize any

---

263. Cf. *Stone: Legal Controls of International Conflict* (New York 1954) p. 198.

264. *Martin and Edwards: The Changing Charter* (London 1955) pp. 81–82, consider that 'even today, no Member could lawfully deny rights of passage through its territory to a foreign army marching against an aggressor branded as such by the Council'. *Contra: Colban: Stortinget og utenrikspolitikken* (Oslo 1961) p. 73. *Bowett: United Nations Forces* (London 1964) pp. 417–8 and 455–8, points out that United Nations *practice* is to require agreement, although this was not the intention of the drafters.

265. *Report of the Collective Measures Committee*, OR GA VI, Suppl. No. 13, p. 46, see also Taubenfeld, *loc. cit.*, p. 392 .

266. Security Council resolution of 25 June 1950 and General Assembly resolution 498(V) of 1 February 1951.

267. Security Council resolution of 27 June 1950.—*Bowett, op cit.*, pp. 224–30, discusses the partial lack of assistance to the United Nations action in the Congo. This action was not an enforcement action against an aggressor decided on the basis of the specific provisions of the Charter (*above*, Chapter IV, 2(e)). Bowett considers that even the Congo action falls under the first, active part of Article 2(5). Whether or not one accepts this view, most of the non-co-operation discussed by him may have been in contradiction with the specific resolutions adopted by the Security Council, cf. notably that of 21 February 1961 quoted *above*, Chapter IV, 2(e).

'rights' arising out of his illegal aggression and to give effect to these. Thus, if the aggressor has occupied the territory of the victim State, a 'neutral' State cannot reject claims presented by the legal government of that territory on the basis that the authority over the occupied territory now is (or was) exercised by the occupant in accordance with Article 43 of the Hague Regulations. Similarly, the 'neutral' State must recognize as valid the legislation which the legal government enacts for the occupied territory, even if this conflicts with legislation which the occupant has enacted within the limits of the traditional laws of war, and even if the legislation of the legal government directly aims at invalidating acts which the occupant has performed within these limits.[268] But 'neutral' States cannot be expected to be 'plus royaliste que le roi' and to treat as invalid even such acts of the occupant the validity of which is not contested by the legal government.

There are even good grounds for holding that the duty to refrain from assisting the aggressor must include a duty not to hamper the United Nations action even if the latter violates the 'neutrality' (in the traditional sense) of the Member State concerned. Thus, it has been submitted that 'where the international police force is operating, it will undoubtedly be illegal, for example, for even a non-Member to insist on such a right and duty as that requiring it to fire upon international aircraft flying over its territory, as the Swiss considered it their duty in two world wars'.[269] This despite the fact that neutral States are *obliged* to do this under the traditional laws of neutrality.

Even within the scope of the automatic obligation under Article 2(5) there is, of course, room for appropriate United Nations recommendations or decisions to indicate to Members which specific measures they should take in execution of their obligation. Outside the scope of the automatic obligation under Article 2(5), the Security Council *must* make specific *decisions* if it wishes to impose upon Member States an obligation to discriminate against the aggressor. This it can do under Article 41, which is wide enough to cover all measures which do not involve use of armed force by the Members concerned. However, if this Article should not be considered sufficient, it may be recalled that the competent committee of the San Francisco Conference, as well as the United Nations Secretariat, are on record in favour of the view that the obligation of the Members to accept the decisions of the Security Council is not limited to the specified powers. The Security Council could thus act

268. See *Tidsskrift for rettsvitenskap* (Oslo) 1945, pp. 135–7.
269. Taubenfeld in *AJIL*, XLVII (1953) p. 396. The validity of this particular submission depends upon whether air transit is considered to fall under the 'rights of passage' referred to in Article 43, and, if it does, whether the agreements referred to in Article 43 are understood merely as execution of a pre-existing obligation.

directly on the basis of Articles 24 and 25. The only limitations appear to be that it must be acting to maintain peace and security in accordance with the purposes and principles of the United Nations.[270]

(j) *The Hague and Geneva Conventions*

The question of in what circumstances the conventions on warfare are binding upon a United Nations Force will be discussed in Chapter VII below. The question of whether discrimination is permitted in the application of the conventions in those cases where they are binding upon the United Nations Force, is governed by the principles set forth above, under 2(j). Thus discrimination in the application of the Hague Conventions of 1907 is permitted to the extent set forth in the substantive discussion in the preceding subsections. The Geneva Conventions, on the other hand, are binding according to their terms, with no discrimination permitted. If it is felt that even in respect of certain of their provisions special rules must apply to a United Nations Force, the Organization must make the necessary reservations upon its accession to the Conventions.

(k) *Conclusions*

If the discrimination in favour of a victim of aggression outlined under 2 above is accepted as part of the existing laws of war and is extended to those coming to the victim's assistance, little room is left for further discrimination in favour of a United Nations Force resisting aggression. In most respects such further discrimination would run counter to the fundamental principles of humanity and justice which must be respected in all circumstances, and/or might provoke reprisals which would violate these principles and be against the interests of the defenders themselves. In other words, it would run up against the very same considerations that dictate the limitations upon the general right of discrimination set forth under 2 above. In only a few respects would there be room for further discrimination in respect of the United Nations:

In the first place, the United Nations, as the political world organization, must be entitled to exercise its political functions under the Charter, for example in occupied territory,[271] without being bound by the restrictions which the laws of war impose upon States in this respect, as long as this does not violate overriding humanitarian considerations. This right of the United Nations is of course not confined to those cases where the Organization intervenes by a military Force of its own; thus it will apply even in a territory occupied by a national army, but it may

270. *Above*, Chapter IV,4(d) (statement by Mr. Sobolev).
271. See *above*, under (g)(ii).

be more readily exercised in a territory occupied by a United Nations Force.

Furthermore, the Charter contains certain provisions, including notably Articles 2(5) and 41, which oblige the Member States, or authorize the United Nations to oblige its Member States (or even non-members) to take economic and other measures, without stating or implying that these measures must be kept within the limits of what States are permitted to do under the laws of war and neutrality. These provisions are of particular importance in respect of the law of neutrality, but they are of importance also in respect of direct economic and other non-military measures by the active defenders against the aggressor and his allies. However, again the authorization or obligation to take such measures is not confined to those cases where the Organization itself takes military action against the aggressor. It applies in all cases where the Organization has determined that aggression has taken place and has decided upon measures against the aggressor, whether the military resistance is rendered by the Organization or by the victim State and those other States which come to its aid.[272] Indeed, the right to discriminate in these respects existed to a large extent, as a permissive rather than an obligatory rule, even before the Charter, as part of the modification of the traditional laws of war which resulted from the treaties outlawing aggressive war.

The Charter does not contain comparable provisions relating to military measures. It is true that Article 42, which authorizes such measures, does not refer to 'war' or to the laws of war. Nevertheless, it would probably take a more explicit provision, reflecting a real intention of the contracting parties, to establish, with binding effect for Member States or even for non-members, that the United Nations could deviate from those parts of the laws of war which apply to all types of armed conflict,[273] including notably the law governing the conduct of hostilities and the treatment of prisoners, sick and wounded.

An exception would be the right to use nuclear or similar weapons in defence even against aggression with conventional arms, if an agree-

272. Contra: Attia: Les forces armées des Nations Unies en Corée et au Moyen-Orient (Geneva 1963) p. 255 and Kotzsch: The Concept of War in Contemporary History and International Law (Geneva 1956) pp. 274 and 293–6, who appear to confine the discrimination to United Nations military actions. Kotzsch even appears to confine it to actions of a Force under United Nations control. See also the report of the Committee on Legal Problems of the United Nations of the American Society of International Law (Proceedings, 1952, p. 217) and Baxter, ibid., 1953, p. 97.—Even Article 2(5) probably is not confined to United Nations military 'preventive or enforcement action', cf. above, at notes 253 and 254a.

273. Cf. above, Chapter V,3—4. As for conflicts of an internal nature, see below, pp. 299–304.

ment were arrived at in this field, and if this were to outlaw the use of such weapons by States, but not by the international police force. Even *de lege lata* some arguments for such a distinction might be drawn from the facts that the United Nations resolution outlawing nuclear weapons refers only to *States*, and that the United Nations is not a party to those instruments upon which the outlawry declared in this resolution is based. However, these facts are decisive only if a prohibition of nuclear weapons is based upon these instruments alone.[274]

On the other hand, the United Nations should, and no doubt will, whenever possible, conduct its military operations in a *more* humane manner than the laws of war require. However, this must be ensured by internal regulations and instructions. It could not be imposed upon the Organization as a limitation of its rights under international law without endangering the success of its actions.[275] At least there appears to be no basis for such limitation *de lege lata*.

With these possible reservations, the relevance of which to international law *de lege lata* is doubtful, the United Nations must be bound by the substantive aspects of the traditional laws of war in the humanitarian field, i.e. those which protect individuals and cultural property, in the same manner as a defending State. However, in respect of violations of these laws by a United Nations Force operating under United Nations command and responsibility, there is a stronger theoretical case than in respect of violations committed by the forces of a defending State, for holding that the said right is not vested in the aggressor *State*, but in the individuals concerned.[276] This would imply that the aggressor is not entitled to apply reprisals against any violations of these laws by the United Nations, even if the aggressor were entitled to do so vis-à-vis a defending national force.[277] This result would not be unreasonable even if the United Nations Force is not under the command and responsibility of the Organization. Nor would the aggressor State have the right to prosecute United Nations personnel for such violations, this should be left to the United Nations itself.[278] This, too, would not be unreasonable, if the latter were possible, as it theoretically is when the United Nations has command and control. However, as long as the States providing contingents to the United Nations Force have not conferred upon the Organization any criminal powers over the members of the Force, there would probably be no more reason to deprive the aggressor of this right than there would be to deprive him of the right to prosecute members of a defending national force. In the third place, the aggressor

274. *Above,* under 3(f)(iv).
275. *Above,* under 3(g) *in fine.*
276. *Above,* pp. 242, 272, 273, 276 and 281.
277. *Above,* under 3(e).
278. *Above,* under 3(d).

would be deprived of his right to claim reparation and restitution from the United Nations, this would have to be settled directly between the United Nations and the individuals who had suffered loss or injury [279] possibly with the assistance of a Protecting Power. The duty of the United Nations with respect to public cultural property would then have to be enforced by the Protecting Power and the other authorities referred to in the 1954 Hague Convention for the Protection of Cultural Property in the Event of Armed Conflict and in the attached Regulations. Whatever weight one attaches to these practical disadvantages which would ensue from a denial of any right for the aggressor *State*, it may be stated that in none of the respects discussed above does a special rule for a United Nations Force impose itself.

Of much greater importance is the possibility of a *further utilization* by the United Nations of the *general* right of discrimination which exists for all defenders, notably in the economic field, and which has been discussed under 2 above. In this respect the provisions of the United Nations Charter and the decisions and recommendations of the competent organs of that Organization may be of great assistance, notably with reference to the law relating to neutrality, economic warfare and military occupation. In all these respects it is possible, through the provisions and machinery of the United Nations, to increase the practical significance of the partly theoretical submissions made under 2. However, this is not confined to those cases where the Organization intervenes against the aggressor by means of a United Nations Force. The fuller utilization of the right to discriminate and the use of the provisions of the Charter are in most respects equally justified and possible in other cases where the Organization has determined that aggression has taken place. The reasons for and against discrimination are essentially the same in both cases.

Broadly speaking it may thus be concluded that, with a few possible exceptions, mostly *de lege ferenda*, a United Nations Force does not have any more far-reaching rights vis-à-vis the aggressor than a State victim of aggression has under the existing modern laws of war. This is particularly true in the military and humanitarian field. However, it is also true in other fields and even vis-à-vis third States if the comparison is to those cases where the United Nations has determined that aggression has taken place and has taken *non*-military action, as the Organization is entitled to do in any case of aggression. Where the laws of war must still persist in their traditional, non-discriminatory form, this is dictated by impelling considerations of a humanitarian nature and of public order, and these apply with essentially the same force if the defence is carried out by a United Nations Force rather than, or in addition to,

---

279. *Above,* under 2(f), 3(b) and 3(f)(iii).

a national force. Indeed, if the United Nations Force is operating *together* with a national Force, there would be confusion if different laws applied to different parts of the defending force.[280]

Only if one refuses to allow discrimination to the extent possible in favour of a State victim of aggression, does the question of further discrimination in favour of a United Nations Force become a real one.[281] But even then it will probably turn out that the reasons which motivate the refusal to admit discrimination in favour of a victim State apply equally against discrimination in favour of a United Nations Force. This is true, for example, if the reason is the fear that, once admitted in certain respects, the principles of discrimination might endanger the reciprocal application of even the humanitarian laws of warfare. Indeed, most of those who still oppose discrimination as between States, oppose it also in respect of a United Nations Force.[282]

Indeed, the crucial criteria for the application of the principle of discrimination is not whether the aggressor is resisted by a national force or a United Nations Force, but whether aggression has taken place and/or whether this has been authoritatively determined. To the extent that the considerations which speak against discrimination in favour of a national defending force are felt to be too strong to admit discrimination, it is in most respects logical to take the same view in respect of a United Nations Force.

4. FURTHER DEVIATIONS IN FAVOUR OF ANY SPECIAL TYPE OF UNITED NATIONS FORCE?

Having established under 3 that the fact that the aggressor is resisted by a United Nations Force, rather than by national forces, does not in itself alter the rights and duties under the laws of war, it now remains to consider whether the situation might be different in respect of any special type of United Nations Force. In this context, two types merit consideration, viz. Forces established pursuant to the specific provisions for a United Nations Force in Articles 43 et seq. of the Charter, and Forces under United Nations command and responsibility. The United Nations Force in Korea belonged to neither of these types, and the limited prac-

---

280. The latter has been pointed out by Eustathiades, who opposes discrimination in all cases (50 *Annuaire de l'Institut de droit international, Session de Bruxelles 1963,* I, pp. 34–35). See, however, *above,* p. 219.

281. Thus to *Kotzsch, loc. cit.,* note 272.

282. Thus for example Bindschedler and Eustathiades in 50 *Annuaire de l'Institut de droit international, Session de Bruxelles 1963,* I, pp. 25 and 47–48. See, however, *Kotzsch* and *Attia, loc. cit. above,* note 272.

tice of that war cannot therefore be relied upon in the following discussion.

(a) *Forces established pursuant to the relevant specific provisions of the Charter*

It has been demonstrated above, Chapter IV,2, that none of the Forces so far established by the League of Nations and the United Nations have been established on the basis of those Articles of the Covenant or the Charter which provide for the establishment and operation of a United Nations Force. However, future developments might bring about a change. If so, the question would arise whether any more far-reaching discrimination would be justified or applicable if a Force were established and utilized on the basis of these provisions.

If action of a United Nations Force is based upon general international law and its inherent right of individual and collective self-defence,[283] it follows logically that the action must be subject to the laws of war laid down in general international law. If on the other hand the action is based upon the specific provisions of the Charter, the situation might be different, at least in relation to Member States.[284] Indeed, it may well be actions by a Force established pursuant to the specific provisions of the Charter in Articles 42 and 43 [285] which have been in the mind of those writers who argue that a United Nations Force is analogous to a police force and therefore cannot be bound by all the laws of war.[286]

However, as has been pointed out in Chapter V,3(a), the general laws of war *stricto sensu*, i.e. the rules relating to the military and humanitarian aspects, govern any kind of international conflict which displays the factual characteristics of a war. Accordingly it is submitted that even the fact that the Force is established and operates pursuant to the specific provisions of the Charter could not justify exceptions to the modern laws governing these aspects of a war against an aggressor, unless and to the extent that such exceptions follow from the said or other provisions of the Charter. In this respect it has been pointed out above, under 3(g)(ii) et seq., that Article 41 (cf. Article 49) authorizes the Security Council to decide upon discriminatory measures in the political, economic and related fields, beyond those permitted under the traditional laws of (war and) neutrality, but that Article 42 does not appear to

---

283. *Above*, Chapter IV,5(a).

284. On non-members, see *Indian Journal of International Law*, IV (1964) pp. 235–7.

285. The current view is that Article 42 covers only forces established pursuant to Article 43, cf. *above*, Chapter IV,2(b). As pointed out there, this view is not justified.

286. *Above*, Chapter V,3(d) *in initio*. This is clearly the position of *Kotzsch: The Concept of War in Contemporary History and International Law* (Geneva 1956) p. 274.

authorize measures exceeding the limits of the traditional laws in the military and humanitarian field.[287] Even in the absence of any decision by the Security Council, Article 2(5) imposes upon Member States an obligation to refrain from giving assistance to the aggressor even in cases where they would have been bound to do so under the traditional laws of neutrality.—However, Article 2(5) is not confined to cases where the Organization takes military action, and Article 41 is specifically concerned with cases where the Organization has *not* decided to use armed force. These provisions are thus relevant to any type of preventive or enforcement action taken by the Organization, and could not be relied upon as a basis for authorizing a different regime for actions based upon the specific provisions for actions by a United Nations Force.

(b) *Forces under United Nations command and responsibility*

It has been pointed out above, under 3(k), that there might be certain reasons for restricting the sanctions applicable against a United Nations Force if the Force is under the Organization's command and responsibility, because one would have more confidence in the will of the Organization, than in that of a defending *State*, to observe its obligations under the laws of war and to prosecute infractions and compensate victims. However, at the present stage of development, the Organization's means of doing so may be more limited than those of States. In the first place it may have more difficulty in raising funds to pay damages. And if the United Nations Force is composed of national contingents, the Organization may be unable to prosecute offenders because the States concerned have not ceded to it any criminal and disciplinary powers. It may therefore be inadvisable to admit further discrimination, even in the field of enforcement, except that *reprisals* against a United Nations Force may be prohibited even if they are not prohibited against a national defending force; however, even this latter distinction does not impose itself *de lege lata*.

In respect of the substantive rights and duties under the laws of war it cannot make any difference whether the United Nations Force is operated under national command and responsibility, as in Korea, or under that of the United Nations, as in the Congo.[288] Those reasons

287. It is not always clear whether the writers referred to *above*, in note 272, disagree with the latter. Thus *Kotzsch, loc. cit.*, merely states in general that 'an examination of the principal provisions of the Charter directly dealing with enforcement action shows that the Security Council is not necessarily bound to act in accordance with international law'.

288. *Contra: Kotzsch, op. cit.*, p. 296, who takes the view that 'a belligerent State can claim the benefits flowing from that discrimination only in the event that it is engaged in enforcement action authorized *and directed* by the United Nations' (italics added).

which set limits to the discrimination apply in the latter case too. And the Charter provides no basis for a distinction between the two types of United Nations Force in respect of the laws of war. It is true that Articles 43 *et seq.* appear to envisage a Force under the direction of the United Nations.[289] However, these articles contain no provisions relevant to the laws of war. And even if the preceding articles, as was demonstrated above, under (a), contain certain relevant provisions, the application of these provisions is not confined to the cases envisaged in Articles 43 et seq. As has been demonstrated in Chapter IV,2(b), not even Article 42 is so limited. The latter Article envisages any type of Force, whether composed of persons recruited individually, of national contingents contributed pursuant to Articles 43 et seq. or of national contingents contributed voluntarily. It also comprises forces under national command as well as forces under United Nations command.[290]

5. CONCLUSION [291]

In the absence of any relevant practice—other than that of the Korean war, which is largely confined to the humanitarian field—it is not possible to point to any customary law bearing on the laws of war applicable to a United Nations Force resisting aggression. However, a theoretical examination, field by field and sanction by sanction, in the light of the relevant provisions of the United Nations Charter, leads to a confirmation of the submission, already made on a more abstract basis in Chapter V,3, that a United Nations Force is (with few or no exceptions) bound by the laws of war as developed in and applicable to wars between States (as modified, in respect of such wars, by the treaties outlawing war and by the United Nations Charter).

This is in particular true *de lege lata*. But even *de lege ferenda* there is only very limited scope for a distinction between United Nations Forces and defending national forces,[292] if the principle of discrimination against an aggressor is applied to wars between States to the extent indicated under 2 above. And if one, for fear of reprisals or for other reasons, does not wish to admit discrimination in wars between States, the same reasons would probably prevent discrimination in United Na-

289. *Above*, Chapter II,3 *in fine*.
290. *Above*, Chapter IV, 2(b), cf. 4(c).
291. See also the more detailed conclusions *above*, under 3(k).
292. Baxter, *Proceedings of the American Society of International Law*, 1953, p. 97, appears to imply the contrary. However, he also quotes Lauterpacht, *BYIL*, XXX (1953) p. 221, who correctly states that a future code of rules governing the collective use of force cannot differ appreciably from those governing the principal aspects of the relations of belligerents in an ordinary war.

tions actions as well, if these involve hostilities which are comparable to wars. Indeed, in many respects it might be difficult to apply two different sets of rules to the national and the international defending forces taking part in the same conflict.

CHAPTER VII

POSITION VIS-A-VIS NON-MEMBERS. IS RECOGNITION OF THE UNITED NATIONS REQUIRED?

While States can exercise belligerent rights and are subject to belligerent duties even if the opposing side has not recognized them as States or as belligerents, this is not generally considered to be so in the case of insurgents and new governments in exile. The question then arises whether such recognition must be required in the case of the United Nations. It is a fact that, despite the near universality of the Organization, the most serious military encounters in which United Nations Forces have been involved have been with States or communities which were not Members of the United Nations. In these circumstances it is important to determine whether the application of the laws of war to a United Nations Force—and, more especially, the Organization's right to invoke, and duty to observe, these laws in respect of such Force—is dependent upon 'recognition' of the international personality or belligerent rights of the United Nations by the opposing side. Similarly, it is necessary to establish whether the conclusions arrived at above, in Chapters III-IV—that the United Nations as an Organization has the capacity to establish, and is the bearer of international rights and duties in respect of, a Force under its command—apply even in relation to States and other communities which have not 'recognized' the Organization. In short, the question arises whether the conclusions arrived at in Chapters III-VI, and in particular in Chapters III and V, apply also in relation to non-member States. This will be discussed in the present chapter.

Before entering into this question, it will be useful to review briefly the relation to the laws of war, in the absence of recognition, of other communities which are not States and in respect of which practice and doctrine exist, notably insurgents.

I. RECOGNITION OF INSURGENTS AND NEW GOVERNMENTS IN EXILE

Many writers maintain that even if insurgents and new governments in exile satisfy the objective requirements for the exercise of full belligerent rights,[1] they are not entitled to do so until they have been recog-

1. Cf. *above*, p. 200.

nized as governments or as belligerents, and that they can claim rights under the laws war only in relation to those States which have granted such recognition.[2] This fact is also acknowledged in Article 3 common to the four Geneva Conventions, which provides for automatic application only of the most basic humanitarian principles to armed conflicts not of an international character, although the reasons for this limitation are connected with other considerations.[3] However, practice gives a different picture.

As for *governments in exile*, it is recalled that the three military Geneva Conventions of 1949 apply to 'members of regular armed forces who profess allegiance to a government or an authority not recognized by the Detaining Power'.[4] However the *Comité international de la Croix-Rouge*, in its commentary to this provision, considers that recognition by *third* States is necessary. It also, rightly, considers that, if the authority concerned does not consider itself as representing a contracting party, it must declare its acceptance of the Conventions in accor-

---

2. In this sense, for *governments in exile, Mattern: Die Exilregierung* (Tübingen 1953) p. 73, cf. pp. 62 and 72; and *Guggenheim: Lehrbuch des Völkerrechts*, I (Basel 1948) p. 200; and, for *insurgents: Verdross: Völkerrecht*, 4th edition (Vienna 1959) pp. 145–7; *Guggenheim, op. cit.*, p. 198; *Hyde: International Law*, I, pp. 198–202, and III, p. 1692; Bindschedler in *Archiv des Völkerrechts*, IX (1962) p. 388. Cf. also *Castrén: The Present Law of War and Neutrality* (Helsinki 1954) p. 90, and, less rigidly, *Siotis: Le droit de la guerre et les conflits armés d'un caractère non-international* (Paris 1958) pp. 22 and 228–9. The contrary view has been well and convincingly presented, in respect of insurgents, by Alf *Ross: Laerebog i Folkeret* (3rd edition, Copenhagen 1951, English translation of the second edition entitled *A Textbook of International Law*, London 1947, German translation of the second edition entitled *Lehrbuch des Völkerrechts*, Stuttgart 1951) § 18 V, and by *Chen: The International Law of Recognition* (London 1951) pp. 333 et seq., especially pp. 350 and 362–3. *Oppenheim: International Law*, I, § 76, and *Lauterpacht: Recognition in International Law* (Cambridge 1947) pp. 175 et seq., consider recognition of belligerency, like recognition of States, as necessary, but consider that the States concerned have a *duty* to grant such recognition as soon as the insurrection satisfies the objective requirements, and that States are not entitled to grant such recognition before this stage has been reached. For more complete citations of writers holding the differents views, see *Oppenheim, loc. cit.*

3. See the commentary of the *Comité international de la Croix-Rouge: Les Conventions de Genève du 12 août 1949, Commentaire*, III, pp. 34 et seq., where it is regretted that the advantages of this legal innovation are offset by the fact that, as a compromise, it is no longer the provisions of the Conventions as a whole which will be applicable (p. 43).

4. Article 13(3) common to the two wounded and sick conventions and Article 4(3) of the prisoners of war convention. Brandweiner: 'Zur Lehre von den Exilregierungen' in *Österreichische Zeitschrift für öffentliches Recht*, III (1950) pp. 497–519, while recognizing that the Conventions are applicable between new governments in exile and (other) *contracting parties*, appears to consider that new governments in exile otherwise cannot exercise belligerent rights *even if they have been recognized*.

dance with their common Article 2.[5] Writers cite in connection with new governments in exile the judgment of the Permanent Court of International Justice in the case concerning *Certain German Interests in Polish Upper Silesia.* It is true that in this case the majority of the judges refused to consider Poland as a party to the Armistice Convention of 11 November 1918 and the Protocol of Spa of 1 December 1918 because it had not been recognized as a belligerent by Germany and because it was 'only on the basis of such recognition that an armistice could have been concluded between those two Powers'. The Court stated that the fact that the Principal Allied Powers had recognized the Polish armed forces, which were under the supreme political authority of the Polish National Committee with headquarters in Paris, as an autonomous allied and co-belligerent army, could not 'be relied on as against Germany, which had no share in the transaction'.[6] It would, it is submitted, be to press the point too far to conclude that the laws of war did not apply to the hostilities between the Polish and the German forces. But one might draw the conclusion from the judgment that vis-à-vis Germany the relevant rights and duties arising out of these laws did not vest in the Polish National Committee, but in the Allied power under whose command the Polish forces had been placed[7] or from whose territory they, or the Polish National Committee, were operating. However, even this does not necessarily follow from the judgment. This was concerned, not with military matters or the laws of war *stricto sensu,* but with the question of whether Poland was entitled to invoke economic rights arising out of the armistice and peace treaties. Moreover, the Court only pronounced itself upon the question of whether Poland was a party to certain treaties. This is different from the question of whether the government in exile is the subject of such rights and duties as are automatic under general international law. The conclusion of a treaty, like the establishment of diplomatic relations, is a positive and voluntary act, even in respect of recognized States. One cannot lightly assume such acts

---

5. The *Comité's* commentary states: '... il n'est pas dit expressément que ce Gouvernement ou cette Autorité doivent du moins être reconnus par des Etats tiers. Cette condition est cependant conforme à l'esprit de la présente disposition, fondée sur le cas particulier des troupes gaullistes.—Il faut de surcroit que cette Autorité, non reconnue par l'adversaire, se considere elle-même comme représentant l'une des Hautes Parties contractantes ou qu'elle déclare accepter les obligations prévues par la Convention et soit désireuse de les appliquer.' (*Les Conventions de Genève du 12 août 1949, Commentaire,* III, Genève 1958, p. 71.) *Guggenheim, loc. cit.,* II, p. 787, requires recognition by the host State.

6. *Permanent Court of International Justice, Ser. A,* No. 7, pp. 27–28, cf. Lord Finlay's contrary observations on p. 84.

7. Cf. *above,* Chapter III,6(c), on the somewhat different effect of placing the contingents of other United Nations Members under United States command.

to have been performed tacitly with a non-recognized State.[8] These may

8. It may be recalled in this connexion that the conclusion of a bilateral treaty normally amounts to an act of recognition, although this does not apply to an armistice (for example those concluded between Israel and the Arab States in 1949, *UNTS*, Vol. 42). It may also be recalled that it is *not* generally admitted that adherence to a multilateral convention (which is *not* considered to imply recognition of all the other parties thereto) suffices to establish treaty relations between contracting parties which have not recognized each other (*Lauterpacht: Recognition in International Law*, Cambridge 1947, pp. 371–4; *contra:* Jean *Charpentier: La reconnaissance internationale et l'évolution du droit des gens*, Paris 1956, pp. 59–63, and, apparently, Hudson in *AJIL*, XXIII (1929) pp. 126–32), despite the fact that the adherence is *express*, in contradistinction to the situation discussed in the text. In the view of the present writer, treaty relations must be presumed to be established, and the only question which arises is whether a State can make a reservation to prevent this. Such reservation would probably have to be explicit, a mere declaration that it does not recognize the acceding party pursues another aim and cannot normally be interpreted as a reservation against the application of the treaty in relations between the non-recognizing and non-recognized States. This appears to be the basic conception of the case relating to recognition of *governments* reported by Hudson, *loc. cit.*, pp. 130–1. See also *below*, Chapter VIII, p. 349.

In the case of the *constitutions of intergovernmental organizations* there can be no doubt that these must create the rights and duties laid down in their provisions also as between Member States which have not recognized each other (cf. *Castberg: Folkerett*, 2nd edition, Oslo 1948, p. 60); reservations on this point cannot be accepted. However, this does not necessarily imply a recognition for other purposes by each Member State, as suggested by Bindschedler in *Archiv des Völkerrechts*, IX (1962) p. 382, *Verdross: Völkerrecht*, 4th edition (Vienna 1959) p. 186, and many other writers. The examples cited by Bindschedler (Lithuania 1921, the Byelorussian and Ukrainian Soviet Socialist Republics 1945, Israel 1949, cf. also the statements on Israel and Indonesia cited in the Secretary-General's memorandum of 8 March 1950 on the legal aspects of the problem of representation in the United Nations, *OR SC*, 1950, Supplement for January-March, p. 20, note) suffice to demonstrate that such recognition is not implied *ipso facto*, although practice before the Second World War *partly* tended the other way (the League of Nations first refused to admit Colombia because it made the reservation that it did not recognize the independence of a Member State [Panama]; the Commercial Tribunal of Luxemburg in *USSR v. Luxemburg and Saar Company* held that the admission of the Soviet Union to the League of Nations constituted a general recognition of its *Government* even on the part of those Member States which abstained from voting [or voted against], *Annual Digest of Public International Law Cases*, 1935–37, p. 114; *but* later Colombia was admitted to the League despite its reservation that this did not imply a [general] recognition of Panama; the United States ratified the 1924 Universal Postal Convention without thereby recognizing the *Government* of the Soviet Union, and certain States asserted their right to continue in their refusal to recognize the *Government* of that country after its admission to the League of Nations). In this as in other respects, a distinction must be made between the Organization as a distinct subject of international law and its several Member States. The admission to membership of an Organization whose constitution permits only States to become Members, involves a general recognition of the admitted State by the Organization as such, but not necessarily by the several Member States. (On the divergent views and practice in this respect, see notably *Rousseau: Droit international public*, Paris 1953, pp. 296–7, cf. p. 313; *Lauterpacht: Recognition in International Law*, Cambridge

have been some of the reasons underlying the otherwise apparently somewhat rigid ruling of the Court, although it did not say so.

While no practice has been found which is directly relevant to the question of the application of the customary laws of war to the forces of new governments in exile, studies of such practice in respect of *insurgents* are available. Reference is made in particular to the thorough examination by *Chen*, who demonstrates that practice clearly tends towards belligerent rights (under the general laws of war and neutrality) irrespective of recognition, when the insurgents have established a political organization and when the hostilities have assumed the characteristics of a real war.[9] Most of the cases reported concern the exercise of (active) belligerent rights vis-à-vis neutral States.[10] However, some neutral courts and governments have stated in broad terms that 'the existence of this civil war gave to both parties all the rights of war *against each other*'.[11] It was also specifically emphasized in many other cases that the laws of war must apply equally to both parties.[12] It

---

1948, pp. 400–403; *Oppenheim: International Law*, I, § 75d; and the writers cited by these authors. See also *ibid.* and *Jessup: A Modern Law of Nations*, New York 1949, pp. 44 et seq., for *de lege ferenda* proposals to give recognition by the Organization effect also for the Member States. A Norwegian proposal in this sense was rejected by the San Francisco Conference on 3 May 1945, cf. *Rousseau, loc. cit.* By its resolution 396(V) the General Assembly of the United Nations declared that the attitude adopted by the General Assembly or its Interim Committee concerning the question of which *government* is entitled to represent a Member State in the United Nations 'shall not of itself affect the direct relations of individual Member Sates with the State concerned', cf. also *OR GA*, V, Plenary Meetings, pp. 675–7, and Annexes, Vol. II, pp. 13–16.)— A different matter is that under the declarative view, to which both Bindschedler and Verdross (and the present writer) adhere, States are general subjects of international law even in relation to States which have not recognized them.

9. *The International Law of Recognition* (London 1951) pp. 337 et seq. Already in his (earlier) *Textbook of International Law*, § 18 V, Alf Ross had pointed out that Kunz' briefer 'survey of the practice of the states since the American war of independence shows that in many and important cases the legitimate government has treated the insurgents as belligerents' (see *Kunz: Die Anerkennung von Staaten und Regierungen im Völkerrecht*, pp. 174–7).

10. *Ross, loc. cit.*, appears to be more prepared to make concessions to the constitutive view in respect of active belligerent rights for the insurgents against neutrals than in the relations between the contending parties.

11. The Santissima Trinidad (1822), United States Supreme Court, and Lord Russell's letter to Lord Lyons of 19th July 1861, both quoted by *Chen, op cit.*, pp. 339 and 343; italics added by the present writer. See also the practice reported by Kunz as summarized in the quotation *above*, note 9, from Ross.

12. See the cases cited by *Chen, op. cit.*, pp. 338–9, 340, 345–6, 357 and 358. An exception is *Prats v. United States*. It is true that in this case the United States-Mexican Mixed Claims Commission held that the United States was entitled to belligerent immunity in the American Civil War, despite the fact that neither the United States nor Mexico had recognized the Confederates as belligerent. (See, however,

would seem reasonable to conclude from this practice that recognition of belligerency by the legal government or by other States is not a condition for the application, on an equal basis, of the laws of war to a civil war which has objectively reached the warlike character referred to above,[13] and that this applies in the relations between the contending parties as well as in relation to third parties.[14]

2. RECOGNITION OF THE UNITED NATIONS? SCOPE OF THE PROBLEM

Despite the contrary practice referred to under 1, the majority of writers still assume that insurgents and new governments in exile—the only communities, other than States and intergovernmental organizations, which are known to have engaged in war or warlike activities—cannot claim full rights under the laws of war in the absence of recognition. In these circumstances it is not possible to ignore the question of whether such recognition must be required also in respect of the United Nations. As already pointed out in the introduction to this Chapter, this problem arises, not only in connexion with the question of the applicability of the laws of war, but also as a question of whether the conclusion arrived

Jessup: A Modern Law of Nations, New York 1947, p. 189.) The first Commissioner stated, inter alia:
    'The subsequent history of the contest shows how truly it must be characterized as war *and be governed by its laws* although carried on within the State...
    . . .
    ...had Great Britain never recognized the Confederates as belligerents at all, the consequences of the state of war as a fact to Great Britain, as to all other neutral powers, would have been the same: such as the liability of their vessels on the high seas to search and seizure as prize by the armed cruisers of the United States, and to capture for attempts to violate the blockade. These rights the United States exercised against Mexico and all other nations, and did it in virtue of the fact of war, and not because of the recognition of the belligerency of the insurgents by those powers or any of them...'(*Moore: International Arbitrations,* III, Washington 1898, pp. 2887-9; italics added by the present writer.)
    This passage is frequently quoted in support of the declaratory view of recognition of insurgents as belligerents. However, it appears from other parts of the judgment that the Commissioner assumed that the United States could claim belligerent rights (at sea, and belligerent immunities in its own territory) against neutrals even if the *insurgents* did not possess such rights. Such discriminatory view conflicts with most other cases and would hardly be accepted to-day with regard to *internal* conflicts which, like the American Civil War, have reached the warlike stage referred to above. And even if it were, this would not necessarily be conclusive for the question *of the equal application* of the laws of war to relations *between the two parties to the civil war.*
    13. For particulars on this point, see *Chen, op. cit.,* pp. 364-8.
    14. Cf. *Chen, op. cit.,* pp. 350 and 362-3, and *Ross, loc. cit.*

at in Chapter III above, that the Organization is the international person which represents the Force internationally and is responsible for its acts,[15] is applicable in relation to non-member States.

No problem of recognition arises if the United Nations action is conducted under national command and responsibility, on the League Covenant or the Korean pattern, since it is then the international personality of the participating States rather than that of the Organization which is directly involved. Nor does the problem become acute in respect of United Nations actions conducted against Member States. It appears to be a general assumption that Member States, as parties to the Charter, have accepted the international personality of the Organization,[16] despite the fact that the Charter, deliberately,[17] contains no provision on this subject, and despite the fact that membership of an Organization in itself does not presuppose that that Organization has international personality.[18] However, for the purposes of the present context, it is sufficient to note that Articles 42 et seq. of the Charter presuppose that the Organization has the capacity to conduct military operations.[20] The problem with which the present chapter is concerned therefore becomes acute only in respect of actions undertaken by the United Nations, under its own direction and control, against States or other communities which are not Members of the Organization.

It has already been pointed out that the three military Geneva Conventions of 1949 provide that they shall apply to 'members of regular armed forces who profess allegiance to a government or an authority not recognized by the Detaining Power'.[21] The term 'authority' must include the United Nations. However, as long as that Organization has neither acceded to the Geneva Conventions, nor made a declaration pursuant to the last sentence of Article 2 common to the four Conven-

---

15. *Above,* Chapter III,6(b).

16. In this sense, for example, Bindschedler in *Archiv des Völkerrechts,* IX (1962) pp. 383 and 387.

17. *United Nations Conference on International Organization, San Francisco 1945,* Doc. 524, IV/2/26, Doc. 554, IV/2/28, Doc. 933, IV/2/42, par. 8, Vol. 13, pp. 622–3, 710 and 763; see also *Report to the President on the Results of the San Francisco Conference* (Washington 1925), Department of State Publication 2349, pp. 157–8; and *Kelsen: The Law of the United Nations* p. 330.

18. Cf. *Indian Journal of International Law,* IV (1964) p. 264, note 341. Since, as will be demonstrated *below,* under 4, the international personality of the United Nations is not established by the Charter, it is submitted that even vis-à-vis Member States the validity of this personality, and notably its extent, do not follow from their membership, but from the objective existence of the United Nations as an intergovernmental organization.

20. Cf. *above,* Chapters II,3 and III,6(b) *in fine.*

21. *Above,* under 1, at note 4.

tions,[22] the answer to the problem depends entirely upon general international law.

To require recognition, in a constitutive sense, of the United Nations as an international person or as a belligerent, would mean that the Organization would have no international responsibility for its Force vis-à-vis non-recognizing non-member States, and no right to present claims to such States on behalf of the Force. The conclusion arrived at earlier,[23] that the Organization has the international responsibility for Forces of the UNEF-Congo or Article 43 et seq. type, would thus become inoperative in relation to such States. This would mean that neither party to the conflict would have a legal right to insist upon the other party applying the laws of war. In order to make sure that the laws of war would nevertheless remain applicable, and that they would in fact be applied, even as between the United Nations Force and those of the non-recognizing non-member State, one would then have to treat the States providing contingents as parties to the conflict, each in respect of its contingent. However, this would conflict with the considerations evolved in Chapter III. In particular it would conflict with and prejudice the position of the Force as a genuine United Nations Force, independent of the several Member States. In respect of a Force individually enlisted by the United Nations there would not even be any States providing contingents to whom the responsibility could conceivably be transferred.[24] Such forces, and even those composed of national contingents if one maintains their independent United Nations character, would thus assume the same precarious position as insurgents who have not reached the stage of recognized belligerency, and in respect of whom there is no generally recognized rule as to what extent the laws of war apply. It would thus create grave difficulties if one were to require recognition of the United Nations as a condition for its rights and duties under the laws of war.

3. PRACTICE IN KOREA AND KATANGA

It has already been pointed out that the general laws of war have been considered or accepted as applicable by both parties in those armed con-

---

22. See *below*, Chapter VIII,8–14.

23. *Above*, Chapter III,6(b).

24. The position would thus be rather different from that of new governments in exile. In respect of these one would have less hesitation in placing responsibility on the State under whose command the new government's forces have been integrated or from whose territory they or the new government operate.

flicts in which the United Nations has so far become involved.[25] This despite the fact that both of the major military conflicts were with non-members, and that none of these had recognized the United Nations as a subject of international law or as a belligerent. However, the action in *Korea*, as has been mentioned, did not involve the United Nations as an international person, but particular Member States. It is therefore not relevant to the question under discussion in the present chapter.

The action in the *Congo*, on the other hand, was undertaken by the United Nations as an international person in its own right. And the United Nations was, on the whole, treated as the international person responsible for the action and the Force by the authorities in *Katanga*.[26] This was clearly evidenced for example in an exchange of telegrams between M. Tshombe and the Norwegian Prime Minister after the second round of fighting in Katanga in December 1961. In a telegram of 23 December 1961 the Norwegian Prime Minister requested the release of "LES DEUX OFFICIERS NORVEGIENS DE LONUC SOUSLIEUTENANT STEINAR FREDRIKSEN ET SERGENT OLAV SKARET QUI AINSIQUE LES 10 RESSORTISSANTS SUEDOIS FURENT FAITS PRISONNIERS PAR LA GENDARMERIE KATANGAISE A ELISABETHVILLE LE 2 DECEMBRE 1961." M. Tshombe replied, in a telegram of 25 December 1961, inter alia:

> LES PRISONNIERS QUE NOUS DETENONS N'ETANT PAS CONSIDERES COMME SUEDOIS
> OU NORVEGIENS MAIS COMME UN PERSONNEL MILITAIRE DE L'ONU SELON DES
> PROPRES DECLARATIONS DU MINSTRE SUEDOIS DES AFFAIRES ETRANGERES LE GOU-
> VERNEMENT DU KATANGA SERAIT HEUREUX CEPENDANT QUE LES GOUVERNEMENTS
> QUI ONT DES REPRESENTANTS AU KATANGA DANS L'ONU INTERVIENNENT AUPRES DE
> CETTE ORGANISATION POUR QU'ELLE RESPECTE LA CHARTE A LAQUELLE ELLE
> PRETEND SE REFERER STOP IL EST EVIDENT QU'A L'HEURE ACTUELLE A LA SUITE DES
> ACTES COMMIS PAR CERTAINS CONTINGENTS DE L'ONU ET AUX EMPRISONNEMENTS
> ARBIRITRAIRES DONT SE RENDENT COUPABLES LES NATIONS UNIES LE GOUVERNE-
> MENT KATANGAIS CERTAIN DE SON HONNETETE MALGRE CE QUE L'ONU DIT NE PEUT
> ACTUELLEMENT LIBERER LES PRISONNIERS.

This clearly demonstrates that M. Tshombe considered the United Nations Force in the Congo as one single Force, for which the United Nations and not the governments providing contingents was internationally responsible. On the other hand, despite their many negotiations and other relations with the United Nations, the authorities in Katanga are not known to have performed, before the practice referred to, any specific act which under general international practice is considered as an implied recognition.[27] Indeed, Katanga's relations with the United Na-

---

25. *Above*, Chapter V,2
26. Cf. the practice referred to *above*, pp. 100 and 114.
27. The first agreements which were concluded between the United Nations and Katanga were the cease-fire agreements of 20 September and 13 October 1961, cf. *above*, Chapter III,3(a). However, cease-fire agreements are not considered as implying recognition.

tions had not at that time developed much beyond those of Israel and Jordan with the United Nations at the time of the killing of Count Bernadotte and Ole Helge Bakke, respectively.[28] However, Katanga was not an independent non-member State, but an insurgent province of a Member State.[29] It thus does not constitute a direct precedent for the application of the laws of war to hostilities between the United Nations and non-member States.

4. OBJECTIVE INTERNATIONAL PERSONALITY OF THE UNITED NATIONS

However, the International Court of Justice has given a clear answer to the question of the international personality of the United Nations vis-à-vis non-member States in another context. In its advisory opinion on *Reparation for Injuries Suffered in the Service of the United Nations* the Court held unanimously that the Organization had the capacity to bring an international claim even against a non-member State. In this connexion it stated in its *reasoning* that 'the Organization is an international person' and that

> ... fifty states, representing the vast majority of the members of the international community, had the power, in conformity with international law, to bring into being an entity possessing objective international personality, and not merely personality recognized by them alone, together with capacity to bring international claims.[30]

This statement of the Court has, however, been criticized by writers. Some criticize the *reason* given by the Court, on the (strong) grounds that the number of Members is irrelevant from a legal point of view.[31] Others express disagreement with the Court's conclusion on the grounds that, in their (and the general) view, it is the convention establishing the Organization which creates, and determines the scope of, its international personality, and that this convention, like other treaties, is

28. In its advisory opinion on *Reparation for Injuries Suffered in the Service of the United Nations,* the International Court of Justice might not have found it necessary to deal specifically with the question of the *objective* international personality of the United Nations (*see below,* under 4) if it had considered that Israel and Jordan had recognized it as an international person.

29. Cf. the message quoted *above,* Chapter IV,2(e), at note 43, which the Secretary-General addressed to Katanga at an early stage, and in which he stated that the legal consequences of resistance by a Member Government to a Security Council decision 'necessarily apply also to the subordinate territorial organs of a nation to which the Charter rules apply'.

30. *ICJ Reports,* 1949, pp. 185 and 187, cf. pp. 218–9. Even the two statements quoted seem to be unanimous, except possibly for Judge Hackworth, see *ibid.,* p. 196.

31. *Schwarzenberger: International Law,* I, 3rd edition (London 1957) pp. 128–30; *Zemanek: Das Vertragsrecht der internationalen Organisationen* (Vienna 1957) p. 27. The latter, nevertheless, supports the Court's *conclusion,* on other grounds.

binding only upon the contracting parties.[32] However, as has been demonstrated elsewhere, a closer examination of practice reveals that intergovernmental organizations, like States, perform 'sovereign' and international acts—and that they act, and are treated, as bearers of corresponding (and other) international rights and duties—even when the convention establishing the Organization contains no provision which authorizes this (expressly or by implication) and even if there is no such convention at all. The provisions of any convention or other document which embodies the constitution of the Organization are significant only in a negative sense, i.e. if they *preclude* the performance of certain capacities.[33] Moreover, even such limiting provisions are hardly applicable vis-à-vis non-member States in cases where corresponding restrictions in the constitutions of States are not effective vis-à-vis other States.[34] In particular, it has already been submitted that constitutional restrictions of a procedural or substantive nature upon the right of the United Nations to establish, command or employ armed forces cannot be invoked by (or against) a non-member State.[35]

Consequently it is submitted that the international personality of the United Nations, like that of States, arises *ipso facto* out of its existence as an intergovernmental organization, no matter how the Organization was established. In these circumstances the rule of international law that a treaty is binding only upon the contracting parties is not relevant, and this reason for denying the objective international personality of the

32. Bindschedler: 'Die Anerkennung im Völkerrecht' in *Archiv des Völkerrechts*, IX (1961–62) pp. 387–8; cf. *Schwarzenberger, op. cit.*, pp. 137–8,

33. *Above*, Chapter IV,3, and the present writer's article on 'Objective International Personality of Intergovernmental Organizations, Do Their Capacities Really Depend upon the Conventions Establishing Them?', in *Nordisk Tidsskrift for international Ret og Jus gentium*, XXXIII (1963), at pp. 21–31.

34. *Ibid.*, pp. 32–40, and, more fully, in *Indian Journal of International Law*, IV (1964) pp. 27–35. Chapter II of the International Law Commission's 1963 draft articles on the Law of Treaties, on 'Invalidity of Treaties', does not provide for invalidity because of substantive restrictions in national constitutions (Article 30, cf. Articles 31–37). As for procedural restrictions, they provide that, when the consent of a State to be bound by a treaty has been expressed by a Head of State, a Head of Gavernment or a Foreign Minister or by a representative who presents full powers from one of these, 'the fact that a provision of the internal law of the State regarding competence to enter into treaties has not been complied with shall not invalidate the consent expressed by its representative, unless the violation of its internal law was manifest' (Article 31, *Yearbook of the International Law Commission*, 1963, II, p. 190, cf. Article 4, *ibid.*, 1962, II, p. 164). This draft article is based upon the principle that international law determines who is competent to bind a State and that 'the declaration of a State's consent to a treaty is binding upon that State, if made by an agent ostensibly possessing authority under international law to make the particular declaration on behalf of his State' (A/CN.4/156, Commentary to Article 5, para. 13, *Yearbook of the International Law Commission*, 1963 II, p. 44).

35. *Above*, Chapter IV,5(a).

Organization therefore cannot be admitted. Nor are the other reasons which have been advanced against the objective international personality convincing,[36] and no relevant practice has been cited which can support the denial of such personality.[37]

Indeed, the United Nations is, legally, in basically the same position as States in respect of external relations of international law, and the reasons which support the objective international personality of States support that of the United Nations, too. Accordingly, there does not appear to be any reason to deny the objective international personality of the Organization if one, with the majority of writers (including the present), recognizes the objective international personality of States, as both practice and logic appear to warrant.[38] This must certainly be so if one, in conformity with practice, admits the objective international personality or belligerency also of other sovereign communities, such as the Holy See[39] and insurgents. But even if one does not admit this, it would seem that the United Nations is more comparable to States than to insurgents and new governments in exile, in respect of which special considerations might more easily apply. It is therefore submitted that the conclusion of the International Court of Justice, that the United Nations has the capacity to present international claims even to non-member States, and its statement that the Organization has objective international personality, are justified on the basis of the general law of intergovernmental organizations, even if one, on good grounds, is not prepared to admit the relevance of the *reason* indicated by the Court.

5. OBJECTIVE BELLIGERENT RIGHTS OF THE UNITED NATIONS

After having, through this brief excursion into the advisory opinion of the Court and the general law of intergovernmental organizations, established that the international personality of the United Nations is objective, it now remains to consider whether this objective personality comprises rights and duties under the laws of war.

It has already been submitted, on the basis of the general practice of intergovernmental organizations, that their international personality comprises the capacity to perform any 'sovereign' and international acts which they are in a practical position to perform (and which are not

36. *Nordisk Tidsskrift for international Ret og Jus gentium*, XXXIII (1963) pp. 62–75 and 88–98.

37. *Ibid.*, pp. 76–79.

38. See, for example, Alf *Ross, op. cit.*, § 18; *Verdross: Völkerrecht* (5th edition, Vienna 1959) pp. 246–8; and Bindschedler, *loc. cit.* note 32, p. 386.

39. See the practice reported in *Nordisk Tidsskrift for international Ret og Jus gentium*, XXXIV (1963) p. 104, note 250.

precluded by any provision of their constitutions, if and to the extent that constitutional restrictions are effective at all vis-à-vis non-members).[40] It has also been submitted that the United Nations has an inherent capacity to establish and employ military forces under its own command and international responsibility,[41] and that it has the right under general international law to use these forces against an aggressor non-member State.[42] It must be a concomitant of this capacity and this right that the Organization enjoys rights and duties under the laws of war, whether these be identical to those of States conducting a defensive war, as submitted above, or different, as submitted by certain others.[43] And there is no basis for holding that this concomitant should apply vis-à-vis non-members to any lesser extent than vis-à-vis Members. Accordingly, if one admits that the international personality of the United Nations is objective, i.e. that the Organization has the capacity to exercise rights and duties under international law even vis-à-vis non-members, then there is no reason why this should not extend also to rights and duties arising under the laws of war in all cases where the Organization becomes involved in military operations, whether or not these cases have been provided for in the Charter. Recognition of belligerency, therefore, cannot be required as a condition for the exercise by the Organization of belligerent rights. The Organization is entitled, in relation to non-members as well as to Member States, to exercise the rights arising under the laws of war as described in the preceding chapters, and its opponents are entitled to exercise vis-à-vis the Organization the corresponding rights under these laws. The problem of recognition of belligerent rights thus does not arise at all.

This is the final conclusion as far as the present writer is concerned. However, as has been pointed out,[44] other writers derive the international personality of an intergovernmental organization from the provisions of its particular constitution and from the intention of the contracting parties thereto, and accordingly hold that the international personality of an intergovernmental organization is a limited one, and includes only such powers as follow (explicitly or by implication) from the constitution. In *this* respect they might have found some support in certain *dicta* of the International Court of Justice in its advisory opinion on *Reparation for Injuries*, especially in the statement that the Court's conclusion that the United Nations is an international person is not the

40. *Above*, Chapter IV,3; *Nordisk Tidsskrift for international Ret og Jus gentium*, XXXIII (1963) pp. 15–45; *above*, under 4, at note 34. *Contra*, inter alia: *Schwarzenberger: International Law*, I, 3rd edition (London 1957) p. 138.
41. *Above*, Chapter IV,4, cf. Chapter III.
42. *Above*, pp. 173–4, cf. p. 166.
43. See *above*, Chapter V,3(d).
44. *Above*, under 4, cf. *The Indian Journal of International Law*, IV (1964) pp. 1–6.

same thing as saying 'that its legal personality and rights and duties are the same as those of a State',[45] except that such restrictive application of this statement would appear to conflict with the Court's statement in its later advisory opinion on *Certain Expenses of the United Nations*.[46] At any rate, the question does not arise in respect of military operations, because the capacity to conduct such operations is expressly laid down in Article 42 of the Charter, and in broad terms. And even on that basis, the capacity, and the concomitant rights and duties under the laws of war, must be valid vis-à-vis non-members, if one accepts the Court's conclusion relating to the objective international personality of the United Nations.

Only if one disagrees with this conclusion of the Court, as many of the writers referred to do, precisely because they make the international personality depend upon the constitution, is it necessary to rely upon Article 2(6) of the Charter, if one considers that this provision imposes obligations upon non-member States,[47] and that these obligations include the duty to accept the exercise by the United Nations as an Organization of rights and duties under the laws of war. If one does not admit this either, then the question arises how far the adherents of the constitutive view would press their view. If they are not prepared to press it to the point of considering a United Nations action against a non-member as falling outside the scope of the laws of war, then they run into the problems described above, under 2, *in fine*, of trying to find substitutes which could assume the rights and duties under these laws, despite the fact that the Forces are under the United Nations operational control. Whatever solutions are chosen in these respects, they but serve to demonstrate the impractical and illogical results to which the constitutive theory leads, in the case of intergovernmental organizations no less than in the case of States. If, as a way out, the adherents of the constitutive view chose to consider the action of the aggressor non-member to imply recognition of the belligerency of the United Nations, they would in many cases be resorting to an obvious fiction.

It has already been pointed out [48] that the *capacity* of the United Nations to conduct military operations vis-à-vis non-members is not affected by any procedural or substantive unconstitutionality of the Force or the action, or by any violation of international law which such action might constitute, any more than a State is deprived of its capacity

45. *ICJ Reports*, 1949, p. 179. See, however, the interpretation given *above*, Chapter IV,3(f) *in fine*, and in *Nordisk Tidsskrift for international Ret og Jus gentium* XXXIII (1963) p. 17, note 16.

46. *ICJ Reports*, 1962, p. 168, quoted *below*, Chapter VIII,9(a). See also *Nordisk Tidsskrift for international Ret og Jus gentium*, XXXIII (1963) pp. 80–81.

47. See *ibid.*, pp. 9–11.

48. *Above*, Chapter IV,5(a).

to wage war by any such unconstitutionality or violation. Accordingly, the laws of war apply, and the United Nations retains its right and duty to invoke and apply these on behalf of a Force under its operational control, even if the Force has been constituted in violation of the Charter or if it is employed in violation of the Charter, of general international law or of any special obligation which the Organization might have assumed.[49]

The conclusion thus is that the laws of war apply to the United Nations when taking enforcement action against non-members, even if these have not recognized the Organization as a subject of international law or as a belligerent, and even if the action had been taken in violation of the Charter or of general or particular international law. Only if one, in contradistinction to the International Court of Justice, were to deny the international personality of the Organization in relation to non-member States, and if one does not consider Article 2(6) of the Charter binding upon these, would the question of a special recognition of belligerency by the non-member States arise.

---

49. Indeed, this applies even to military operations against a Member State, for the somewhat different reasons stated *above*, Chapter IV,5(c).

CHAPTER VIII

THE CONVENTIONS ON WARFARE

I. GENERAL

The problem of the application of the conventions on warfare to United Nations actions is of little practical importance in respect of the Hague Conventions and the other older conventions, because many of these conventions, and in particular, the Regulations Concerning the Laws and Customs of Land Warfare annexed to the Fourth Hague Convention, merely express what is now recognized as general (customary) international law and what is therefore binding *ipso facto* upon all States, as well as upon the United Nations, in the manner which has been set forth in Chapters V and VI above. This is, however, not true of all provisions of the modern and detailed conventions, notably the Geneva Conventions of 1949 and the Hague Convention of 1954 for the Protection of Cultural Property in the Event of Armed Conflict.[2] The following discussion will therefore primarily be concerned with these conventions.

In the application of the conventions on warfare, as in the application of the general laws of war, a basic distinction must be made between a United Nations Force under national control and responsibility and a Force under the control and responsibility of the Organization. In respect of the former, which shall be dealt with under 2-4 below, the legal situation is, in principle, that the troops of each participating State must, subject to the general participation clause in the Hague Conventions,[3] comply with those conventions to which that State is a party, vis-à-vis the troops of any opposing State which is also a party to those conventions. In respect of a Force under United Nations control and responsibility which shall be dealt with under 5-14, only the conventions to which the Organization is a party are directly applicable.[4] In one case as in the other, certain problems arise. These shall be discussed in the following, with regard to each particular type of situation.

2. *Above*, Chapter V,1(b).
3. See *below*, at note 50.
4. It is not clear whether *Bowett: United Nations Forces* (London 1964) pp. 503 et seq. applies the distinction between United Nations command and national command to the question of the applicability of the conventions. In the context of forces

2. ACTIONS UNDER THE COMMAND OF THE PARTICIPATING STATES

The first type of situation is the traditional coalition system, where the troops of the several participating States have not been placed under the control of the Organization or of any particular State, but merely under an individual common commander who acts on behalf of each State severally, or under no common command at all. This was the system which apparently was envisaged under Article 16 of the Covenant of the League of Nations.[5] In such cases there can be no doubt that, legally, each State providing troops is a party to the conflict and that its troops consequently must apply the conventions to which that State is a party, except that the general participation clause in the Hague Conventions and in the other older conventions in such a case may easily operate to render these conventions technically non-applicable.[3]

This situation may give rise to great practical and even to legal difficulties, because certain matters for practical reasons cannot be adequately dealt with on the basis of national responsibility if the Force is composed of a great number of contingents, and particularly if some of these are small and cannot operate as self-contained units.

Thus it may be neither practical, nor in harmony with the spirit and purposes of a United Nations action, to vest rights to, and responsibility for, prizes and war booty in the national State whose soldiers happen to physically seize the prize or the booty, or in the national State of the commander of the capturing unit. Similarly it may be neither in the interests of the United Nations action, nor in those of the inhabitants of an occupied territory, if this, or the various parts of it, were to be administered by and under the responsibility of those States whose forces happened to have entered it first, or who happen to be there at an any given moment. Moreover, it may be impossible to determine or agree as to which State is in fact and law responsible for the prize, the booty or the occupied territory, because the units have become mixed during the

composed of national contingents, 'whether or not under direction of a United Nations Command *stricto sensu*' he states, inter alia: 'A United Nations Force in which only some of the States contributing national contingents have acceded to the Geneva Convenions of 1949 would very probably be at cross-purposes in its treatment of various classes of protected persons. Of more consequence to the Force itself is the possibility that an opponent engaged in armed conflict with an integrated United Nations Force composed of national units, some adhering to, others not bound by, the Geneva Conventions, might lawfully be entitled to treat the entire Force as not within the reciprocal protection of those laws. The obvious and distressing result could be that combatants whose State, by formal accession, had achieved for them the benefits of the conventional laws of war in all other circumstances, may find themselves unprotected when engaged in United Nations service.'

5. *Above*, Chapter II,1.

battle, or because of uncertainty as to whether the crucial criterion is the nationality of the soldiers or of the smallest unit, or that of the commander, and if so, at what level. Such uncertainty or dispute may jeopardize the proper application of the conventions.[7]

This aspect is particularly prominent in respect of *prisoners of war*. Article 122 of the Geneva Convention Relative to the Treatment of Prisoners of War provides that each of the parties to the conflict shall give, within the shortest possible period and through its official Prisoners of War Information Bureau, detailed information on each prisoner of war who has fallen into its power. And article 12 of the same Convention provides inter alia:

> Prisoners of war may only be transferred by the Detaining Power to a Power which is a party to the Convention and after the Detaining Power has satisfied itself of the willingness and ability of such transferee Power to apply the Convention.[8] When prisoners of war are transferred under such circumstances, responsibility for the application of the Convention rests on the Power accepting them while they are in its custody.

These provisions have been commented upon as follows:

> Prisoners of war have that status from the moment when they fall into the hands of the enemy and it is from that moment that there must be one State functioning as the Detaining Power and responsible for the various obligations imposed upon it by the Convention. That Detaining Power will, in the first instance, be that State whose armed forces or other agencies first captured the prisoners of war concerned. Thereafter any transfer of such prisoners out of the control of the capturing State, *i.e.*, the Detaining Power, must comply with the provisions of the Convention, Arts. 12 and 122, dealing with transfer, and any such transfer can be made only by individual States who are parties to the Convention.[9]

Under the duress of battle, it may be practically impossible to comply with the requirements of these two provisions at each transfer from the capturing unit through other front-line units of different nationalities to the authorities responsible for prisoners of war in the rear, considering that these transfers have to be effected quickly upon the decision of the officers on the spot, in order to comply with those provisions of the Convention which require early evacuation from the battle zone, proper catering and medical care and a number of administrative mea-

---

7. See also the criticism of the great number of Commissioners-General for Cultural Property in *Records of the Intergovernmental Conference on the Protection of Cultural Property in the Event of Armed Conflict* (The Hague 1961) p. 196, paras. 800 and 804.

8. This requires prior investigation, for example through the future Protecting Power, according to the *Commentaire à la Convention de Genève relative au traitement des prisonniers de guerre*, published by the *Comité international de la Croix-Rouge* (Geneva 1958) p. 146.

9. United Kingdom War Office: *The Law of War on Land Being Part III of the Manual of Military Law* (London 1958) edited by H. Lauterpacht, par. 134.

sures which cannot be performed in the battle zone.[10] On the other hand, under Article 5 of the Prisoners of War Convention, that Convention 'shall apply from the time the military personnel fall into the hands of the enemy'. In these circumstances many transfers would not be valid under the Convention, and the State of whatever may be considered as the capturing unit in accordance with Article 5, would therefore, from a legal point of view, remain the Detaining Power for the purposes of the Convention while the prisoners are under the factual control of units of another State and possibly even work for a third State in whose territory they are kept. Or it may be impossible to identify the State which is responsible under the Convention because the identity of the original captors is not known (it could not make the list required by Article 122) or because several units co-operated in the capture, or because of doubt as to whether the nationality of the soldiers or of their commanders is decisive, and in the latter case what level of commander is to be considered decisive. Or it may be impossible to identify the State which is responsible under the Convention because the prisoners are for example interned and work in the territory of one State, but are guarded by troops of another State under the general command of an officer of a third State. Such complications and doubts may prejudice the position of the prisoners, and they certainly will render the tasks of the Protecting Power and the International Red Cross very difficult. There does not appear to be any solution based upon the principle of national responsibility which at the same time conforms with the Convention, is possible to carry out, and protects the interests of those persons which the Conventions are designed to protect.

The *Comité international de la Croix Rouge* takes the view that if it is not possible to establish which of the parties in a coalition is responsible, then 'all the States concerned' (i.e. all those States whose forces participate in the coalition) must be held severally and jointly responsible.[11] (The reservations which a number of States have made to Article 12 to the effect that no Power which transfers prisoners to another Power is thereby liberated from its obligations as Detaining Power would have a similar effect.) [12] However, in practice this will hardly prevent the States concerned from referring to each other, and this solution would therefore not be likely to protect the interests of the prisoners.

10. See notably Articles 15 and 18–19 of the Prisoners of War Convention.

11. *Commentaire à la Convention de Genève relative au traitement des prisonniers de guerre*, published by the *Comité international de la Croix Rouge* (Geneva 1958) p. 145.

12. On the question of the validity of these reservations, vis-à-vis the other contracting parties, see Pilloud: 'Les réserves aux Conventions de Genève 1949' in *Revue internationale de la Croix-Rouge*, August 1957, pp. 404–37.

Moreover, this solution affords no answer to those many cases where the provisions of the Convention are based upon the assumption that there is *one* Detaining Power, as for example Articles 82 et seq. of the Prisoners of War Convention, which refer to the law and the authorities etc. of the Detaining Power.[13]

In all these cases the uncertainty as to which State is responsible and the dispersal of responsibility among several States may seriously jeopardize the proper application of the conventions and render precarious the position of the persons and interests which the conventions are designed to protect.

3. ACTIONS UNDER THE COMMAND OF ONE STATE

If the participating States place their troops under the command of *one* State—as was done in Korea and as apparently was envisaged under the Uniting for Peace Resolution [14]—the question arises whether the same principle as described under 2 applies, or whether the entire Force is bound by the conventions to which the commanding State is a party, and by these only. The answer must, it is submitted, be that each contingent is bound by the conventions concluded by its national government,[15] unless it has become part of the forces of the commanding State in such a manner that it has lost its original nationality for the purposes of the conflict and that its national State has no direct external responsibility for it. However, such absorption would hardly be politically acceptable to the United Nations or to the Member States concerned.

As for Korea, it has been pointed out that the contingents of the Member States, other than the United States, were of modest size (altogether they constituted only about 10 per cent of the non-Korean forces) and that their integration into the United States forces had been taken very far in most cases.[16] It was submitted that the United States, as having operational control, must be considered responsible for the acts of the entire Force. But it was also submitted that the role of the govern-

---

13. See *below*, under 11, especially pp. 377–9.

14. *Above*, Chapter II, 4–5.

15. Taubenfeld: 'International Armed Forces and the Rules of War' takes the view that it is not self-evident that the Geneva Conventions signed by most nations could be shown to be technically binding on the unified forces of the United Nations (*American Journal of International Law*, XLV (1951) p. 674). He may, however, have based this upon the view, rejected *above*, pp. 121–2, that international responsibility for the action in Korea was vested in the United Nations as an Organization, rather than in the participating States, cf. *above*, p. 121, note 108, and pp. 188–9.

16. *Above*, pp. 35–6.

ments providing contingents had not been reduced to such an extent that they could escape concurrent responsibility for the acts of their contingents. Thus, from a legal point of view, the Force could not in its entirety be considered as a United States Force, but each contingent must be considered as having preserved its character as a national force. The States providing contingents must be considered as parties to the conflict for the limited purposes of their participation in the action, even if they are not considered *ipso facto* as full-scale parties to a war.[18] In these circumstances each contingent must be bound by the conventions concluded by its government. Indeed, this appears to have been the view of the parties concerned. As already pointed out above, in Chapter V,2(a), each State providing a contingent to the United Nations Force was approached individually on the subject by the International Committee of the Red Cross. They also gave individual replies, partly similar and partly different, even after the adoption on 7 July 1950 of the Security Council's resolution on the Unified Command and the establishment of the United Nations Command on 25 July 1950. Several States replied by undertaking to observe any undertakings 'entered into on behalf of United Nations forces by the United Nations Commander-in-Chief'. However, this can hardly be read as more than a delegation to the latter of the power to commit also the governments concerned. And the Commander himself referred in this context to 'responsibilities incumbent on sovereign nations'.[20]

A more doubtful question is whether the United States was obliged to see to it that the contingents, *in addition*, applied the conventions to which the United States was a party. The answer is probably no. If the United States must be considered to be responsible also for the acts of national contingents, it is because it had operational command, not because the contingents legally formed part of its own national force. The situation was different from that of the United Nations Forces in the Middle East, the Congo and Cyprus, where the national contingents legally were no more national, but formed part of the United Nations Force, and where the States providing contingents clearly were not parties to any conflict in which the Force might become involved.

As for the factual situation, it has been pointed out above, Chapter V,2(a), that the Geneva Conventions were not legally applicable in Korea. Contrary to what writers on the subject maintain, none of the parties involved did in point of fact accept or undertake to apply the Conventions before or during the serious fighting, except that the United Nations Command undertook to apply *one* of the Conventions.

18. *Above*, pp. 106 and 122–5.
20. *Above*, pp. 184–5. Italics added.

The Collective Measures Committee based its proposals, which were made during the Korean War, upon the pattern followed there. It must therefore be presumed that under their system, too, each national contingent would be bound only by the conventions to which its State was a party.

As shall be explained below, under 7, it may give rise to certain practical problems if different parts of a United Nations Force are bound by different conventions, or can invoke different reservations to the same conventions.

The situation could be partly remedied, in respect of the Geneva Conventions and the 1954 Hague Convention, by a declaration by the authorities of the State in command, acting on behalf of all participating States, that the Force as a whole would apply all the relevant Conventions for the purposes of that particular action. This would then constitute joint informal acceptance in accordance with Article 2 common to the four Geneva Conventions. Indeed, as recalled above, several of the States participating in the action in Korea in their replies to the International Committee of the Red Cross undertook to observe any such undertaking by the United Nations Command. However, this was not fully followed up by the Commander, because he did not 'have the authority to accept, nor the means to assure the accomplishment of, responsibilities *incumbent on sovereign nations* as contained in the detailed provisions of the other Geneva Conventions' [20] other than the Prisoners of War Convention, and presumably also because the other side had not accepted these other Conventions. In respect of the Hague Conventions and the other older conventions, such a common declaration would hardly have any binding effect upon the other side, since these conventions do not contain any clause on informal accession for the purposes of a particular conflict, but only the normal clause on formal and general accession.[21]

4. ACTIONS UNDER THE COMMAND OF A GROUP OF STATES

For obvious political reasons it may in many, or most, cases not be appropriate or feasible to entrust control over the Force and responsibility for the action to one particular State. It was probably considerations of this nature which led the Collective Measures Committee to recommend, in 1951, that control might alternatively be vested in a *group* of States, which similarly would act on behalf of the United Nations as executive military authority.[22] From a legal point of view this would involve three possible set-ups:

21. Cf. *below*, under 12.
22. *Above*, Chapter II,5.

(a) The natural solution would be to set up the 'executive military authority' as an organ of the United Nations. It would then by its acts commit the Organization, not only morally and politically, but also legally. However, it appears that the Collective Measures Committee based itself on the Korean pattern, which, as submitted above, means that the 'executive military authority' would not be an organ of the United Nations in the legal sense.[23] If this assumption is maintained, there remain the following two possibilities:

(b) Each State in the 'group' may be severally and jointly responsible for the acts of the Force. In this case the principle indicated under 2 above would apply, and the same, legally insuperable, difficulties as were described there would arise. In some ways the situation would be still more confused, because one would not know which of the States in the group were to be considered, for example, as the Detaining Power in respect of prisoners taken or held by contingents of those participating States which did not belong to the group.

(c) These difficulties could be solved if the 'group' would constitute a new, separate, intergovernmental organization which would assume responsibility in lieu of the several Members of the 'group'. However, if one is prepared to resort to the international personality of a new Organization, it would seem preferable, and create no more legal problems, to utilize that of the already existing Organization, the United Nations, i.e. to apply the solution indicated under (a), which, in turn, is merely one possible form of the solution which shall be discussed in detail in the following sections.

5. ACTIONS BY NATIONAL CONTINGENTS UNDER THE ORGANIZATION'S COMMAND

The remaining parts of the present Chapter shall be devoted to the problems which arise when an enforcement or peace-keeping action is carried out under the control of the United Nations itself in such a manner that the Organization as such—rather than one, some or all of the States providing contingents—has the international responsibility for the Force.[24] This was the situation in the Congo (as well as in the Middle East, West New Guinea and Cyprus), and it would presumably also be the position of a Force established pursuant to Articles 43 et seq. of the Charter. (Some authorities involved in the action in Korea, as well as certain writers, maintained that this was the position in Korea, too.) [25]

Even in such cases the States providing contingents have certain func-

23. See *above*, pp. 108 and 125, cf. pp. 121–2.
24. *Above*, pp. 99–102 and 118–9.
25. Citations *above*, Chapter III,6(c), note 108.

tions. Thus the Regulations for the Forces in the Middle East, the Congo and Cyprus provide that 'members of the Force shall remain subject to the military rules and regulations of their respective national States without derogating from their responsibilities as members of the Force as defined in these Regulations and any rules made pursuant thereto' and that 'members of the Force shall be subject to the criminal jurisdiction of their respective national States in accordance with the laws and regulations of those States'[26] and also that 'responsibility for disciplinary action in national contingents provided for the Force rests with the commanders of the national contingents', subject to certain rights and the general responsibility of the United Nations Commander.[27] Similarly, the 'General Principles Governing the Organization of the Armed Forces Made Available to the Security Council by Member Nations of the United Nations', elaborated by the Military Staff Committee and provisionally adopted by the Security Council in 1947, provide that the national contingents 'will be subject at all times to the discipline and regulations in force in their national armed forces.'[28]

However, the obligations and responsibility which devolve upon the States providing contingents from these and similar provisions are obligations vis-à-vis the United Nations, not vis-à-vis third parties,[29] if the United Nations has full operational control over the Force and the power to issue (superseding) substantive regulations and orders relating to the operations of the Force. This is normally true even if these obligations of the States providing contingents have been expressly referred to in agreements concluded by the United Nations with third parties.[30] Indeed, as has already been submitted, it is the United Nations, acting in its own name only, which represents the Force in treaty relations with

26. UNEF Regulation 34(c) and (a), ONUC Regulation 29(c) and (a), and UNFICYP Regulation 29(c) and (a). On the question of criminal jurisdiction, see *below*, under 11(a).

27. UNEF, ONUC and UNFICYP Regulation 13. Otherwise the ONUC and UNFICYP Regulations give stronger powers to the Commander than the UNEF Regulations, inasmuch as ONUC and UNFICYP Regulation 13 adds that the Commander 'may make investigations, conduct inquiries and require information, reports and consultations for the purpose of discharging this responsibility'.

28. Article 39, quoted in full *above*, Chapter II,3.

29. The United States even took this position in Korea, where the United Nations did *not* have operational control, see *above*, Chapter, III,4(b).

30. *Above*, Chapter II,3(a).

31. In Korea the United Nations Command was in these respects acting *on behalf of the participating States*, see *above*, Chapter, III,3(b). And these were alle invited to the concluding political (peace) conference, where they should 'act independently at the conference with full freedom of action and shall be bound only by decisions or agreements to which they adhere' (General Assembly resolution 711 A-B [VII], *above*, p. 106).

third parties, including the opposing side,[31] as in all other external and operational respects, and which alone is a party to the conflict.[32]

The United Nations is not bound by treaties concluded by its Member States, nor is it entitled to rights under such treaties. Therefore, as long as the Organization has not acceded to the conventions on warfare, it has no obligations and no rights *under these* vis-à-vis the opposing side.[33] Even if all its Member States have acceded to the conventions, the United Nations is not legally bound and entitled by their provisions, except in so far as they coincide with general (customary) international law.[34] This is also the position taken by the United Nations itself, as evidenced by the fact that the Regulations it has enacted for its peace-keeping Forces merely require these to observe 'the *principles and spirit* of the general international Conventions applicable to the conduct of military personnel.'[35] This may also have been the assumption upon which the 1954 Hague Conference acted when it adopted its resolution expressing the hope that the United Nations would ensure application of the Convention by the armed forces taking part in a military action in implementation of the Charter, although the resolution, according to its text, might also be read as designed to meet a different situation.[36]

The States providing contingents will in most or all cases be parties to the conventions, and in particular to the Geneva Conventions, which have been ratified or acceded to by nearly all States.[37] However, their treaty rights and obligations are not directly relevant to their contingents in a Force under United Nations control and responsibility.[38] The Geneva Conventions and the 1954 Hague Convention for the Protection of Cultural Property in the Event of Armed Conflict 'apply to all cases of declared war or of any other armed conflict which may

32. *Above*, Chapter III, especially 6(b). It would, of course, be a different matter if a contingent were to operate on its own, ignoring the United Nations orders and carrying out instead orders issued by its national government in pursuance of national aims, cf. the Secretary-General's statement quoted *above*, Chapter III,2(a), at note 14.

33. In this sense also *Attia: Les forces armées des Nations Unies en Corée et au Moyen-Orient* (Geneva 1963) p. 254. He states: 'Les forces des Nations Unies agissent dans ce cas au nom d'une entité juridique indépendante, qui ne peut pas être considérée comme liée par le droit conventionnel tant que l'Organisation des Nations Unies, comme entité juridique, n'a pas adhéré aux conventions sur le droit de la guerre'.

34. Cf. *above*, Chapter V,1(b). *Bowett* may take a different view, see *above* note 4.

35. *Above*, Chapter V,2(b)(i). Italics added.

36. Cf. the account of the discussions which led up to the resolution *below*, under 10(b)(i).

37. *Above*, Chapter V,1(b), note 15.

38. Taubenfeld, in *American Journal of International Law*, XLV (1951) p. 674, cf. pp. 678–9, takes this view also in respect of the United Nations Force in Korea. *Contra: above*, under 3.

arise *between two or more of the High Contracting Parties*.[39] Accordingly, the decisive criterion for the application of the conventions on warfare to a soldier is not his nationality, but to whose force he belongs.[40] Indeed, the three military Geneva Conventions specify that they apply to 'members of the armed forces of a Party to the conflict', without referring to their nationality.[41] Since the national States of the members of national contingents or of individual members of the staff of a United Nations Force are not parties to the conflict, these States have no direct rights and duties under the conventions in respect of their contingents or individual personnel participating in the conflict between the United Nations and the other side. This means that, as long as the United Nations has not acceded to the conventions, these do not apply to an action involving a genuine United Nations Force, and in particular that the members of such Force legally have no protection under the conventions.

It may be asked, however, whether in these circumstances the States providing contingents have a subsidiary responsibility. Indeed, in its circular letter of 10 November 1961 to the contracting parties to the Geneva Conventions, the International Committee of the Red Cross stated, *inter alia:*

> In fact, the United Nations Organization is not, as such, party to the Geneva Conventions. Consequently, each State is personally responsible for the application of these Conventions, when supplying a contingent to the United Nations.[42]

Is there any legal basis for this statement? Article 1 common to the four Geneva Conventions provides: 'The High Contracting Parties undertake to *respect and to ensure respect for (faire respecter)* the present Convention *in all circumstances*'. It may be asked whether the broad wording of the italicized parts can be read as imposing upon the con-

39. Article 2 common to the four Geneva Conventions, Article 18 of the Hague Convention of 1954. Italics added.

40. The possibility of service in a foreign army is admitted by implication in Article 23, last paragraph, of the *Règlement concernant les lois et coutumes de la guerre sur terre* annexed to the Fourth Hague Convention. Under Article 17 of the Prisoners of War Convention, the detaining Power is not even entitled to require prisoners to state their nationality, which they of course would have had to know, had it been relevant for the prisoners' status under the Convention.

41. Article 13 of the two Conventions on Wounded and Sick and Article 4 of the Prisoners of War Convention. Article 4 of the Convention on the Protection of Civilians, which is not relevant to the question of the protection of the members of a United Nations Force, provides that the Convention protects persons who 'find themselves in the hands of a *Party to the conflict* or Occupying Power, of which they are not nationals' (italics added), but that 'nationals of a State which is not bound by the Convention are not protected by it'. Cf. also Article 13, and Article 2 as discussed *below,* under 5 *in fine.*

42. Full text *above,* Chapter V,2(b)(ii). This view has also been expressed by the *Commission médico juridique* in *Annales de droit international médical,* No. 11, 1964.

tracting parties an obligation to ensure that even *non*-contracting parties apply the Conventions, and as conferring upon the contracting parties a subsidiary responsibility vis-à-vis the other parties to the conflict if they do not. The International Committee of the Red Cross' own commentary to the Article does not appear to go quite that far.[43] And in its circular letter of 10 November 1961 mentioned above the Committee confined itself to reminding those who might supply contingents to a United Nations Force of their obligation under Article 1 to 'have respected' (*'faire respecter'*) the provisions of the Conventions and to expressing the *'hope'* that they will 'use their influence to ensure that the *provisions of humanitarian law* are applied by all contingents engaged, as well as by the United Command'. This despite the fact that in this particular case it might be said that the States concerned are in a position to impose accession as a condition for providing contingents. It may be, however, that the last quoted, non-mandatory passage from the circular letter was referring only to the *other* contingents.

On the other hand, it might be argued that, having ratified the Conventions, the States providing contingents are not entitled voluntarily [43a] to place their contingents at the disposal and under the control of another subject of international law, whether this be a State or the United Nations, if this other subject is not itself a party to the Conventions. If States nevertheless do so, it might be argued that they incur responsibility directly vis-à-vis the other party to the conflict for the damage he may suffer as a result thereof. If this view were accepted, the States providing contingents to a genuine United Nations Force might, on this indirect basis, be held responsible for violations of the conventions committed by their soldiers in the service of the United Nations, and the practical result might in so far be the same as if these States had been directly responsible for compliance with the conventions by their contingents. However, unless such responsibility is based upon Article 1 of the Geneva Conventions, to which the International Committee of the Red Cross did not refer *in that context*, this indirect responsibility vis-à-vis the other party to the conflict would be logically and technic-

---

43. Interpreting the words 'faire respecter', the commentary states: 'Si une autre Puissance manque à ses obligations, chaque Partie contractante (neutre, alliée ou ennemie) doit chercher à la ramener au respect de la Convention. Le système de protection prévu exige en effet, pour être efficace, que les Etats Parties à la Convention ne se bornent pas à l'appliquer, mais encore fassent tout ce qui est en leur pouvoir pour en assurer le respect universel' *(Les conventions de Genève du 12 août 1949, Commentaire, III, La Convention de Genève relative au traitement des prisonniers de guerre*, Genève 1958, p. 24). See also the resolution adopted by the XVIIIth International Red Cross Conference at Toronto 1952 (Resolution No. XVI, text in *Handbook of the International Red Cross*, Geneva 1953, p. 390).

43a. If they have an obligation to do so under the Charter, this obligation takes precedence under Article 103 of the Charter.

ally confined to violations of such provisions of the Conventions as do not constitute part of general international law, since the general laws of war are binding also upon the United Nations.

Even if Article 1 or general principles of international law are considered to form a sufficient legal basis for the duty of the States providing contingents to see to it that their contingents apply the Geneva Conventions and the other conventions to which they are parties, this does not constitute a satisfactory legal protection of the troops of the adversary and of civilians in the battle area and in occupied territory. In the first place, concerning the prevention of violations, it should be noted that the governments of the States concerned have jurisdictional powers only in respect of certain parts of the Force and that they lack operational control over and international responsibility for even these parts. More important from a practical point of view, in respect of the opportunity of obtaining reparation and preventing repetitions, are the difficulties of identifying the offenders and their nationality. Indeed, one would have the same difficulties as were described above, under 2, in respect of a Force under national command. It should also be noted that any indirect responsibility of States providing contingents would not cover members of the United Nations Secretariat who have been attached to the Force or make decisions relating to it. Nor would it cover military or civilian personnel who have been recruited individually to serve in the Force, for example on the staff of the Commander, or the Commander himself. Acts committed by any of these are in the position described below, under 6. It may also happen that not all States providing contingents are parties to the conventions.

Moreover, it should not be forgotten that the protection of the troops of the opposing side is only one aspect of the problem, which was given great prominence during the hostilities in Katanga by the allegations which were made against the United Nations Force for having violated the laws of war.[44] In these circumstances the question of the protection of the members of the United Nations Force itself receded somewhat into the background in public discussions, despite the fact that the *Comité international de la Croix-Rouge* had to intervene for their protection on a number of occasions. However, the problem of the protection of the United Nations personnel is of major importance. And it cannot be settled on the basis of the indirect responsibility outlined above for States providing contingents, since this does not appear to give these States any *rights* vis-à-vis the opposing side. The latter has a legal obli-

44. *Above*, Chapter V,2(b)(iii).

gation to apply those provisions of the conventions which do not reflect general international law only if both parties to the conflict are bound by them. And the other party is the United Nations, not the States providing contingents. Indeed, as already pointed out, the latter States probably cannot even invoke (vis-à-vis the opposing side) the rights arising under the *general* laws of war, they are merely entitled to exercise diplomatic protection of their nationals as such, not functional protection of the members of a genuine United Nations Force in that capacity.[45]

As for civilians, the Convention Relative to the Protection of Civilian Persons in Time of War, like the other Geneva Conventions, provides in Article 2 that it applies to any 'armed conflict which may arise between two or more of the High Contracting Parties'. This means that the Convention does not apply if the United Nations is the only party to the conflict on its side, but has not acceded to the Conventions. Civilians may, nevertheless, benefit from the indirect responsibility described above for the States providing contingents. However, this covers only acts of the United Nations Force. Civilians are thus not protected even in this manner against the acts of the opposing side.

The conclusion is thus that the United Nations as an Organization has neither rights nor duties under those provisions of the conventions which do not reflect general international law, that the States providing contingents may be indirectly responsible for violations of these provisions committed by their contingents, but that these States hardly can invoke rights under the conventions in respect of members of a Force which is not theirs, but an organ of the United Nations. Moreover, even if they could, this would prejudice the independent position of the Force as a genuine United Nations Force.[46] Thus, while there may be a certain legal basis for the protection of the troops of the aggressor and of the civilian population against acts of the United Nations Force, there is no adequate legal basis for the protection under the *conventions* of the troops of the United Nations, or of the civilian population against acts of the aggressor. The obligation of both parties to observe the *general* laws of war [47] of course remains. And so does the will of the United Nations to apply these laws, or even the Geneva Conventions, and the fact that it will as far as possible conduct its military operations in a *more* humane manner then required by these laws.[48]

45. *Above*, Chapter III,5(a).
46. Cf. *below*, under 8 *in fine*.
47. *Above*, Chapter V,3(c) *in fine*.
48. *Above*, pp. 282–3 and 292.

6. ACTIONS BY A FORCE RECRUITED INDIVIDUALLY BY THE ORGANIZATION

If the Force has been recruited by the Organization by individual enlistment, as the United Nations Guard and the United Nations Field Service,[49] there are no States providing contingents which could have even an indirect responsibility for the acts of the Force. In such cases the legal situation is clear beyond doubt. If the United Nations as an Organization has not acceded to the conventions of warfare, the Force and its members have no legal obligation to apply those provisions which do not reflect general international law. Nor has the opposing side. In such cases, therefore, not only the members of the United Nations Force, but also those of the opposing forces, as well as the civilian population, are deprived of legal protection under the conventions, but are of course protected by the general laws of war.

7. COMPARATIVE EVALUATION OF THE VARIOUS COMMAND SYSTEMS

The unsatisfactory legal situation described under 5 and 6 could be avoided in one of two ways: The United Nations as an Organization could accede to the conventions, or it could refrain from itself assuming command over the Force and leave this instead to the participating States. This latter alternative shall be considered in the present section, and the first alternative in the following sections.

In Korea the United Nations was able to leave command to the United States, which had both armed forces and an organized command near the scene of aggression and which was prepared to supply the bulk of the military forces. But the situation in Korea was rather exceptional. There may not always be one State which is able and willing to assume responsibility for the United Nations action. And even if there is, there may be strong political objections, both from the point of view of the United Nations and from that of the other participating States, to leaving command and control over a United Nations action in the hands of one particular State, at least if that State is not willing to provide the vast preponderance of the forces involved.

These difficulties would be somewhat eased if control were left to a *group* of States. However, as has been demonstrated under 4, this would create new legal problems which would render this method legally less attractive than to leave supreme control and responsibility in the hands of one State or the United Nations as an Organization.

49. *Above,* Chapter I,1.

Another alternative is that discussed under 2, viz. a regular coalition Force, where each State providing forces is a party to the conflict and responsible directly vis-à-vis the other side. However, as was pointed out, it would not be possible for such a Force to comply with *all* provisions of the conventions. Moreover, it may not be the most effective way of conducting a United Nations action, even if the participating States agree upon the appointment of an overall commander. It is indicative that this system has never been applied in a League of Nations or United Nations action. It is true that this solution was envisaged by the drafters of the League of Nations Covenant, but the actions which have in fact been undertaken by the League and the United Nations, and the plans which have been adopted after the Second World War, imply a stronger central control and responsibility.

Under all the three alternatives discussed above under 2-4, each contingent is bound by the conventions on warfare to which its government has acceded. This may of course give rise to certain practical problems.—The Hague Conventions and the other older conventions contain the general participation clause (*clausula si omnes*), which provides that they shall apply only if *all* belligerents are parties to them.[50] This will in many cases mean that the conventions technically do not apply at all if the United Nations action is carried out under national command (i.e. by resort to any of the systems discussed under 2-4). However, this may not be serious, insofar as many of these conventions are merely declaratory of general international law.—The Geneva Conventions and the 1954 Hague Convention do not contain the general participation clause. These conventions may thus become applicable in respect of certain contingents of the United Nations Force, even if it is not applicable in respect of others. Such partial application would, of course, give rise to certain practical problems. However, as far as the Geneva Conventions are concerned, these have been ratified or acceded to by most Members of the United Nations. Nevertheless, it may always happen, as it did in Korea, that the host State or the victim of aggression is a new or divided State which has not yet had a proper chance to accede to the conventions. And even if all the participating States are parties to the Geneva Conventions, and to the same version of them (1949), practical difficulties may arise out of the fact that some States have made reservations to certain provisions of the 1949 Geneva Conventions.[51]

In addition to the legal and practical difficulties referred to above, there is another important consideration which militates against any sys-

50. See for example Article 2 of the Fourth Hague Convention of 1907.

51. On these, see Pilloud in *Revue internationale de la Croix-Rouge*, August 1957, pp. 409–37. Some of the reservations which have been made would indeed be relevant to a United Nations action under national command.

tem of national command as discussed above. In many cases, such as the police operations in the Middle East and the Congo, it is of great importance for the success of the operation that it is purely international in character, i.e. that control and responsibility vest exclusively in the United Nations and that the national policies and interests of the States providing contingents are not brought into play.[52] This is an interest, not only of the United Nations and the host State and the other parties to the conflict which gave rise to the creation of the Force, but also of the States providing contingents themselves, since these may not want to become involved in the struggle as States.[53]—Also in the case of genuine enforcement actions against an aggressor it may be important, whenever possible, to organize the action in a manner which clearly distinguishes it from a traditional coalition war or a war by certain particular States, and which corresponds to its true nature as the beginning of a genuine international police power under the control of the world community as a whole. Here, too, not only the general interests of the United Nations and the world community are involved, but also those of the States providing contingents, which may want to avoid becoming full-scale parties to a war in the traditional sense.

These may have been some of the reasons which induced the drafters of the Charter and the members of the Military Staff Committee to abandon the concept of an enforcement action by several national forces on the coalition pattern which had underlain the provisions in Article 16 of the Covenant of the League of Nations, in favour of a force under the direction of the United Nations. The contrary proposals which the Collective Measures Committee made in 1951 may be viewed, not as indications of any new trend in the opposite direction, but rather as a measure prompted by the special situation during the Korean War against the background of the earlier failure to execute the provisions of Articles 43 et seq. of the Charter. Indeed, the more recent police actions have demonstrated that a Force can be operated under United Nations command, even if many problems still have to be solved.

8. NEED FOR UNITED NATIONS ACCESSION TO THE CONVENTIONS

It follows from the preceding discussion that national command over a United Nations Force is not a satisfactory system, and in particular that it does not allow a satisfactory application of all provisions of the Ge-

52. Cf. *above*, Chapter III,2(a).
53. See the statements in this sense in the Secretary-General's Summary Study of the Experience Derived from the Establishment and Operation of UNEF, paras. 168 and 171, *OR GA*, XIII, A.i. 65, p. 30.

neva Conventions. From the latter point of view, the least inconvenience attaches to the system of command by one State, but this will usually not be politically possible.

Command by the Organization is the preferable system and, except for Korea, the only system which has been adopted in practice. However, it is then an indispensable condition for the application of the conventions on warfare that the United Nations as an Organization accedes to these conventions, and more specifically to the Geneva Conventions.[54] This is true, not only of a Force established by individual enlistment, but also of a Force composed of national contingents exclusively, or of national contingents supplemented by United Nations officials and other personnel recruited individually, as is the usual case.

In either case of United Nations command, accession by the Organization is the only way of imposing upon the opposing side a legal obligation to apply the conventions, and is thus the only way of providing a legal basis for the protection under these of the members of the United Nations Force and of the civilian population against acts of the opposing side. If the adversary is already a party to the conventions, his obligations automatically become effective once the United Nations accedes. If the adversary is not a party to the Geneva Conventions, he must make a declaration of acceptance pursuant to Article 2 of the Geneva Conventions before the accession of the United Nations can produce legal effects with regard to the conflict concerned. In the absence of such accession by both parties, the United Nations has no legal right to present claims to the other side on the basis of the provisions of the conventions. Nor, as already pointed out, have the States providing contingents any legal basis for so doing.

Accession by the United Nations is also necessary in order to secure full *legal* protection under the *conventions* of the military personnel of the opposing side and of the civilian population against acts of members of the United Nations Force.[55] The indirect responsibility of the States providing contingents, as described above, is only a partial solution, and it does not at all protect against acts committed by those members of the Force who are officials of the United Nations or who have been recruited individually by that Organization. It is necessary that the United Nations—as the international person who is a party to the conflict, who has the operational control over and the international responsibility for the Force and who represents it externally—takes on a direct commitment in relation to the other side to apply the conventions. It will then be the responsibility of the United Nations—through the agreements it concludes with the States which provide the contingents and which train

54. Cf. *above*, under 1, and *below*, under 13 *in initio*.
55. Cf. Article 4 of the Convention on Civilians, quoted *above*, under 5, note 41.

them, enact military regulations for them and exercise criminal and disciplinary powers over them—to require these States, whether or not they themselves are parties to all of the conventions, to undertake an obligation vis-à-vis the Organization [56] to do everything in *their* power to ensure that the members of their contingents conform to the conventions. This the States can do in particular by informing the members of their contingents of their rights and obligations under the conventions, by instructing the officers to watch over compliance with their provisions, and by punishing any offenders.[57] It is also up to the United Nations whether, particularly in the light of the experiences in the Congo, it wishes to establish some central procedure and machinery under which the Organization may assist the States providing contingents in the detection and prosecution of offenders and thus may play its limited part in ensuring that these are effectively prosecuted.

If matters are left on the basis of the (indirect) responsibility of the States providing contingents—upon which the International Committee of the Red Cross has found it necessary to rely in the absence of United Nations accession—even the principles of exclusive United Nations operational control and of the non-commitment and non-intervention of the States providing contingents may be prejudiced, because these States may claim that, if they as States are to carry the external responsibility for the application of the conventions, then they must also as States have corresponding operational powers.[58a]

For these reasons the remaining parts of the present chapter will be devoted to the question of United Nations accession to the conventions on warfare. In view of the fact that there appears to be a general tendency among international lawyers to assume, or even take for granted, that the United Nations cannot accede to these conventions,[58] the first and major parts will be devoted to the questions of *whether* the United Nations legally can accede to the conventions and implement their provisions. The subsequent parts will then deal, more briefly, with the questions of *how* the Organization can accede and whether it is *proper*

56. During the Korean War the United States Government offered to pay reparation *through the United Nations* for violations of neutral territory, see *above*, Chapter III,4(b). This may be viewed as a recognition of an obligation vis-à-vis the United Nations to see to it that the United States contingent observes the laws of neutrality.

57. Article 129 of the Geneva Conventions, quoted and discussed *below*, pp. 372–4, provides for the handing over of offenders for trial to another Contracting Party.

58a. This has been emphasized also by Paul de Visscher in *Revue de droit international et de droit comparé*, 1963, p. 168.

58. Thus for example Baxter, inter alia in 'Forces for Compliance with the Law of War', *Proceedings of the American Society of International Law*, 1964; Bowett: *United Nations Forces* (London 1964) pp. 507 and 509, cf. pp. 511–16; see also Draper in *International and Comparative Law Quarterly*, XII (1963) pp. 408–10.

for it to do so considering the fact that the conventions were elaborated with a view to traditional wars between States.

9. FORMAL CAPACITY OF THE UNITED NATIONS TO ACCEDE TO CONVENTIONS BETWEEN STATES

(a) *Capacity to conclude treaties*

The United Nations Charter contains neither a general provision authorizing the Organization to conclude treaties, nor a special provision authorizing it to accede to multilateral conventions between States like the Hague and the Geneva Conventions. It merely provides, in Articles 43 and 63,[59] for the conclusion of certain other types of treaties.

However, it has been pointed out in the first part of this study that the United Nations has concluded a very great number of treaties with States and other intergovernmental organizations, and that only a small fraction of these fall within the categories which have been specifically authorized in the Charter.[60] In many cases it would also be stretching the fiction too far to maintain that the capacity was *implied* in the Charter by 'necessary intendment',[61] especially when the treaties were concluded in connexion with functions which are not specified in the Charter and which its drafters never thought of, as for example the agreement of 28 March 1951 with the United States establishing the United Nations Postal Service (*UNTS*, Vol. 149, p. 414). Indeed, no case is known where the UN has refrained from concluding a treaty because it or the other party considered that it lacked the legal capacity to do so, or where any court or other authority has denied the validity of any treaty because it had been concluded without basis in any provision of the Charter. On this basis, and on the basis of similar practice in respect of other international acts and of other Organizations,[62] it was submitted that, despite the more restrictive views maintained in

---

59. See also Articles 77 et seq., as discussed by Parry in *BYIL*, XXVI (1949) pp. 122 et seq., and Article 105(3), as discussed *below*, under (b).

60. *Above*, Chapters III,3(a) and IV,3(c).

61. Reparation for Injuries Suffered in the Service of the United Nations, *ICJ Reports*, 1949, p. 184, cf. *ibid.*, 1954, pp. 56–57.

62. Thus the League of Nations, despite the absence of any provision on treaties in its constitution, concluded a number of agreements with Switzerland—notably on privileges and immunities (18 September 1926, *Journal officiel*, 1926, p. 1422, and *Hudson: International Legislation*, I, p. 224), the Ariana site, and the League's radio-station (21 May 1930, *ibid.*, V, p. 494)—and with other Member States, for example with Greece on the protection of Bulgarian minorities (29 September 1924, *Journal officiel*, 1924, p. 1352). Even if not all of these were concluded in the *form* of treaties, they all had the *effect* of treaties.

legal theory,[63] the United Nations has a general inherent capacity to perform international acts, and in particular to conclude treaties—without any positive, express or implied, authority in the constitution being necessary—and that this capacity is limited by the Charter only in a negative sense, by the following three requirements: (i) that the treaty must be designed to promote one of the purposes of the Organization as laid down in the Charter, (ii) that there is no other provision of the Charter which precludes the Organization from concluding treaties, or the treaty concerned, and (iii) that the treaty is concluded by the organ which has general competence under the Charter and in accordance with any procedure laid down in the Charter for the conclusion of treaties.[64]

This general submission, with the first limitation, has now been confirmed, in respect of the United Nations, by the *International Court of Justice* in the following statement in its advisory opinion of 20 July 1962 on *Certain Expenses of the United Nations*: '...when the Organization takes action which warrants the assertion that it was appropriate for the fulfilment of one of the stated purposes of the United Nations, the presumption is that such action is not *ultra vires* the Organization'.[65] It is submitted that the 'presumption' must refer to the limitations laid down in the constitution—i.e. to the two other limitations listed above as (ii) and (iii), to the extent that they have external validity [66]—and to any limitations deriving from general international law and thus applicable also to treaties.[67] Requirement (i) obviously is ful-

---

63. See, for example, the writers cited in *Nordisk Tidsskrift for international Ret og Jus gentium*, XXXIV (1964) pp. 15–18. The strictest view is taken by *Kelsen: The Law of the United Nations* (London 1950) who states: 'The Charter of the United Nations neither contains a general provision authorizing the Organisation to enter into international agreements nor a provision determining the organ competent to conclude on behalf of the United Nations such agreements. Consequently the United Nations has legally only the power to enter into those international agreements which it is authorised by special provisions of the Charter to conclude; and these agreements are to be concluded, on behalf of the Organisation, through the organs determined by these special provisions' (p. 330). See also Pescatore in *Recueil des Cours*, 1961 II, p. 61, who is partly forced into a restrictive view by his failure to distinguish clearly between the question of whether the Organization can bind *itself* by treaty and whether it can bind its *Member States*, cf. on this question, *Nordisk Tidsskrift, loc. cit.*, pp. 37–44.

64. *Above*, Chapter IV,3(c)–(g).

65. *ICJ Reports*, 1962, p. 168.

66. On this question, see *above* Chapter VII,4, at note 34, and, more specifically *Indian Journal of International Law*, IV (1964) pp. 27–35.

67. The most important such limitation is that the act must not impose new obligations upon Member States or third parties (listed as limitation (iv) *above*, Chapter IV, 3(g)). This is not relevant to treaties because these are not unilateral, but bilateral or multilateral acts which establish obligations only for those who have voluntarily become parties to them. Other, less practical examples of limitations derived from general international law are treaties designed to promote an illegal purpose.

filled by a treaty designed to secure the humane conduct of actions to maintain peace. With regard to requirement (ii) there is no provision in the Charter which precludes the capacity of the United Nations to conclude treaties or, specifically, to accede to the conventions on warfare. Nor are there any procedural provisions in the Charter relevant to the third requirement, and this can therefore be met simply by a resolution of the General Assembly authorizing the Secretary-General to accede to the conventions.

Immediately before the advisory opinion referred to, the *International Law Commission*, by nine to eight votes with two abstentions,[68] adopted, as part of its 1962 draft articles on the Law of Treaties, the following provision (Article 3[3]): 'In the case of international organizations, capacity to conclude treaties depends on the constitution of the organization concerned.' It has been pointed out in an earlier study that this is true only in the negative sense indicated above, and only to the extent that constitutional limitations have external effect. If the proposal of the International Law Commission was intended to imply more than that, as the Commission's commentary seemed to indicate, it had no support in practice. The commentary (4) stated that the capacity to conclude treaties 'does not depend exclusively on the terms of the constituent instrument of the organization but also on the decisions and rules of its competent organs'.[69] However, as was submitted in the earlier study, this is a fiction. Intergovernmental organizations rarely, if ever, enact 'rules' before they conclude their first treaty, and nobody appears to be prepared to deny the validity of those hundreds of treaties which have been concluded in the absence of such 'rules'. Moreover, it is hard to see how an Organization can authorize itself by 'rules' or 'decisions' to do something which it does not already possess the capacity to do.[70] However this may be, the draft article does not necessarily indicate that the International Law Commission would deny the general capacity of the *United Nations* to conclude treaties,[71] or its capacity to accede to

---

68. *Yearbook of the International Law Commission*, 1962, I, p. 243.

69. *Yearbook of the International Law Commission*, p. 164. The commentary also referred to some of the facts referred to *above*, Chapter IV,3(c), and quoted the passage on implied powers from the advisory opinion on *Reparation for Injuries*. The advisory opinion on *Certain Expenses of the United Nations* was rendered only after the adoption of the Report.

70. See the full discussion in *Nordisk Tidsskrift for international Ret og Jus Gentium*, XXXIV (1963) pp. 82–86. A different matter is that an organ of the Organization by its own rules and decisions can *limit* the powers of subordinate organs, or even its own (e.g. by rules on a 2/3 majority); what the external effect of such limitations is, is another matter.

71. The summary records *(Yearbook of the International Law Commission*, 1962, I, pp. 57 et seq.) offer little guidance, because paragraph 3 was elaborated and proposed by a drafting committee of which there are no official records. However, in the plenary

the conventions on warfare, because the United Nations Regulations on Registration of Treaties, to which 'rules' may refer,[72] are general in scope, and because commentary (4) to the Article quotes also the well-known statement on implied powers from the advisory opinion on *Reparation for Injuries,* without, however, relying upon it to the extent that the *travaux préparatoires* did.[73]

The governmental comments to Article 3 revealed a reluctance to include in the draft articles on the law of treaties a provision which in fact attempted to settle the difficult and controversial question of international personality. Only two comments, viz. those of Austria and the United States, went into the substance of paragraph 3 on international organizations, and they both indicated that the draft paragraph was too restrictive.[74] In the end, the Commission in 1965 decided to omit paragraph 3 as a consequence of its earlier decision to confine the articles to treaties between States.[75] Instead, it adopted the following provision as Article 2:

> The fact that the present articles do not relate
> (a) to treaties concluded between States and other subjects of international law or between such other subjects of international law; or
> (b) to international agreements not in written form shall not affect the legal force of such treaties or agreements or the application to them of any of the rules set forth in the present articles to which they would be subject independently of these articles.[75a]

meetings some speakers indicated that the paragraph was too restrictive or that it gave too great effect to the will of the parties to the constitution. Moreover, several Members of the Commission very appropriately emphasized, in connexion with *States,* that the draft articles were concerned with general international law rather than with restrictions arising from constitutions and treaties, and that lack of *capacity* is different from lack of *right* to conclude certain treaties, since the latter does not entail invalidity, cf. *Nordisk Tidsskrift, loc. cit.,* pp. 55–57.

72. *Yearbook of the International Law Commission,* 1962, II, p. 32. However, as explained in *Nordisk Tidsskrift,* 1964, p. 83, note 198, the Regulations appear merely to assume a *pre-existing* capacity of the United Nations and the specialized agencies to conclude treaties, whatever its scope might be.

73. *Yearbook of the International Law Commission,* 1962, II, pp. 32 and 36–37, citing *ICJ Reports,* 1949, p. 179.

74. A/CN.4/175, 23 February 1965, pp. 17–18 and 159–60. The Austrian comments were along the same lines as the text above, emphasizing that the constitutions may contain negative limitations upon the inherent power to conclude treaties, but that constitutional provisions are not required to establish this capacity. The United States comments stated that the term 'constitution' was too restrictive and should be replaced by 'authority'.

75. A/CN.4/SR 776–780, May 1965, cf. A/CN.4/177, 19 March 1965, pp. 39–40.

75a. *Report of the International Law Commission on the Work of its Seventeenth Session,* OR GA, XX, Suppl. No. 9, p. 6; cf. doc. A/CN.4/SR 810–811.

(b) *Capacity to accede subsequently to multilateral, law-making conventions between States*

Most of the treaties concluded formally by Organizations are bilateral, but some agreements have been concluded with a greater number of States or other intergovernmental organizations. Thus, the Agreements of 22 February 1957 and 21 October 1963 Relating to Technical Assistance for the Benefit of the Advanced School of Public Administration for Central America (ESAPAC), were concluded between the United Nations and five, respectively six, Central-American States.[76] Similarly the Agreements of 29 January 1963 for the Establishment in Cairo of a Middle Eastern Regional Radioisotope Centre for the Arab Countries was concluded between the International Atomic Energy Agency, the United Arab Republic and, initially, three other Arab States, and was subsequently acceded to by other Arab States;[77] all these parties, including the Agency, are Members of the intergovernmental organization set up by the Agreement. The Revised Basic, and, later, Standard Agreements for the Provision of Technical Assistance are concluded jointly by the United Nations and five to seven specialized agencies with each State.[78]

It is submitted that, from a legal point of view and in particular from the point of view of legal capacity, it makes no difference whether the number of parties is six or sixty or one hundred,[78a] or whether the Organization becomes a party at the time of the original conclusion or later.

76. *UNTS*, Vol. 274, p. 93, and Vol. 480, p. 197, respectively. Reference may also be made to the agreement on the Scandinavian training hospital in Korea, concluded on 13 March 1956 between the United Nations Korean Reconstruction Agency (UNKRA), the Republic of Korea and the three Scandinavian countries (*UNTS*, Vol. 427, p. 256); the Indus Basin Development Fund Agreements of 19 September 1960 and 6 April 1964 between seven States (Australia, Canada, Federal Republic of Germany, New Zealand, Pakistan, United Kingdom and the United States) and the International Bank for Reconstruction and Development (*UNTS*, Vol. 444, p. 260); and the Agreement of 16 November 1962 between the Bank, the United Nations Special Fund and five Central-American States providing for a study of telecommunications needs in these five countries, and to the conventions (cited by Lachs: 'Le développement et les fonctions des traités multilatéraux' in *Recueil des Cours*, 1957 II, p. 264) concerning the loan to Austria which were approved by the Council of the League of Nations.

77. IAEA document INFCIRC/38 + Add. 1/Rev. 1. Similar multilateral agreements may be found in INFCIRC/49, 55, 56 and 9/Rev. 1.

78. See for example, the numerous agreements listed in *UNTS*, *Cumulative Index*, under 'United Nations, multipartite'. The European Economic Community has concluded agreements with a larger number of States, such as the *Convention d'association entre la Communauté Economique Européenne et les Etats Africains et Malgache Associés à cette Communauté* of 20 July 1963, which was concluded between the Community and its six Member States on the one hand and 18 African States on the other. However, this has been concluded pursuant to Article 238 of the constitution of the Community, which authorizes it to conclude association agreements with 'un [sic] Etat tiers, une union d'Etats ou une organisation'. Other agreements have been concluded pursuant to Articles 111–4 and 228.

78a. Even the European Economic Community, whose constitution *might* be inter-

Indeed, it has been pointed out that the various drafts presented to the International Law Commission and the draft articles it adopted in 1962 on the law of treaties do not differentiate between capacity to conclude bilateral and multilateral treaties, and that the Final Protocol annexed to the International High Frequency Broadcasting Agreement of 1949 provides that 'should the Secretary-General of the United Nations accept this Agreement on behalf of the United Nations' telecommunications services, [*the United Nations*] *shall be regarded as a Party to the Agreement* for the purposes of this Agreement.'[78b]

If the UN has not yet concluded more conventions with a larger number of States, or acceded to conventions subsequent to their original conclusion, it is because the practical need has not yet arisen, or because the terms of the conventions concerned did not permit it to accede, and not because the Organization itself lacked the legal capacity to do so. Indeed, once one admits the capacity of the United Nations to conclude treaties with States, one cannot deny that capacity merely for the reason that the number of States exceeds a certain figure or that the Organization was not among the original parties.[79]

Nor is it possible to deny the legal capacity of the United Nations to accede to any particular category of multilateral treaties,[80] at least not if the treaties are relevant to the functions and purposes of the Organization, and it is mostly [80a] in such cases that the question will arise in practice. It is true that the United Nations has so far formally concluded only '*traités-contrats*', and that it has not formally acceded to conventions which lay down general legal rules or '*traités-lois*'. However, this distinction, too, is submitted to be legally irrelevant for the question of treaty-making capacity. A number of writers have pointed out that the distinction between *traités-contrats* and *traités-lois* is merely of descriptive or methodological value and has no legal significance.[81] As

preted to limit the number of parties to *one*, has not hesitated to conclude an agreement with *eighteen* States, see note 78.

78b. *Chiu: The Capacity of International Organizations to Conclude Treaties* (The Hague 1966) pp. 70–72.

79. This, apparently, is also the view of *McNair: The Law of Treaties* (Oxford 1961) when he states, in the course of the discussion of what States may (be invited to) accede to treaties: 'There is no reason why accession should not be made available to international organizations possessing the treaty-making power in relation to the subject matter of the treaty in question' (p. 151, note).

80. For a mild example of such denial, see *below*, under 10(b)(i) (French statement).

80a. See *Nordisk Tidsskrift*, 1964, p. 85, for examples of acts which go beyond the stated purposes of the Organization.

81. *Rousseau: Principes généraux du droit international public*, I (Paris 1944) p. 136, citing Anzilotti, Basdevant, Heilbron, Hostie, E. Kaufmann, Lauterpacht, Rapisardi-Mirabelli, Scelle, etc. Cf. also Lachs in *Annuaire français de droit international*, 1956, p. 340. *Castberg: Folkerett* (2nd edition, Oslo 1948) takes a contrary view in certain

will be demonstrated below, the practical need to accede may arise in respect of these conventions, too. And even if it does not, an accession by the United Nations may be useless, but not void.

As a matter of fact, practice is quickly moving towards accession by intergovernmental organizations to general international conventions between States. Already at present the United Nations and other intergovernmental organizations are in fact parties to general international conventions between States, even *traités-lois*, although they usually have become parties—not by signature and ratification, or formal accession, in the same manner as the contracting States—but by different methods. This is true of at least some of those many conventions which have been elaborated and approved by the Organization and submitted to Member (and non-member) States for accession.

Thus, the United Nations, the specialized agencies and other Organizations are parties to their general conventions on privileges and immunities.[83] These conventions clearly establish direct rights *and obligations*[84] for the Organization vis-à-vis the contracting Member States. The Organizations also act as parties in so far as, for example, reservations to the Convention on the Privileges and Immunities of the Specialized Agencies are submitted, not only to the other contracting States, but also to the Organizations, and are not accepted if these object. The position of the Organizations as parties to the conventions has even been clearly expressed, notably in § 35 of the Convention on the Privileges and Immunities of the United Nations, which provides: 'This convention shall continue in force as between the United Nations and every Member which has deposited an instrument of accession . . .'[85] In its first report, the sub-committee which later prepared the text of the Convention stated:

> The general Convention on immunities and privileges of the United Nations is, in a sense, a Convention between the United Nations as an Organization, on the one part, and each of its members individually on the other part. The adoption of a Convention by the General Assembly would therefore at one and the same time fix the text of the Convention and also imply the acceptance of that text by the United Nations as a body.[86]

respects, but none of the respects he refers to has any bearing upon the question of treaty-making capacity.

83. In this sense also *ICJ Reports*, 1949, p. 179, and several writers. Parry took a somewhat different view in *BYIL*, 1949, pp. 129 and 142–3.

84. Examples of obligations may be found for example in §§ 23 and 29 of the Convention on the Privileges and Immunities of the United Nations, adopted by the General Assembly's resolution of 13 February 1946 (*UNTS*, Vol. 1, p. 15).

85. *UNTS*, Vol. 1, p. 30. See also the preamble and §§ 30, 32 and 36 of the same Convention, and Article 13(3) of the constitution of the International Refugee Organization of 15 December 1946 (*UNTS*, Vol. 18, p. 3).

86. *OR GA*, I, First Part, Sixth Committee, p. 45. A contrary view was (erroneously) taken by the Executive Directors of the International Monetary Fund in respect of

The capacity of the United Nations to be a party to this convention might conceivably be deduced from Article 105(3) of the Charter, which provides: 'The General Assembly may make recommendations with a view to determining the details of the application of paragraphs 1 and 2 of this Article or may propose conventions to the Members of the United Nations for this purpose.' However, it has been pointed out that 'a convention to which each of its Members but not the United Nations itself is a party is exactly what Article 105(3) would appear to envisage'.[87] However this may be, it should be noted that, although such provisions occur in the constitutions of the United Nations and many of the specialized agencies, they do not occur in the constitutions of all specialized agencies.[88] Thus at least the latter constitute examples of intergovernmental organizations being parties to law-making multilateral conventions between States although no provision of their constitution authorizes them to conclude such conventions.

The position may be partly similar in the case of other multilateral conventions adopted by the Organization for accession by Member States. Even if it is not a party in a formal sense, the Organization may itself be subject to the substantive rights and duties laid down in the convention in so far as they are applicable to the Organization, or at least to such provisions as specifically refer to the Organization. Thus it is submitted, for example, that the United Nations—by virtue of the General Assembly's approval of the Convention on the Prevention and

the Convention on the Privileges and Immunities of the Specialized Agencies (*UNTS*, Vol. 33, p. 261). In a letter of 3 September 1948 to the Board of Governors of the Fund, they stated that 'formal approval by the Board of Governors is not necessary since the Fund will not be a party to the Convention'. Nevertheless, the letter stated that 'the Executive Directors intend to approve the Convention together with an Annex . . .' (Text of the letter in *International Monetary Fund, Summary Proceedings, Third Annual Meeting, 1948*, p. 99.) A different matter is that the accession by the Fund (and the International Bank) was not of great importance, because its constitution contains detailed provisions on privileges and immunities (*UNTS*, Vol. 2, pp. 72–76) which were maintained above those of the Convention, by the Annex adopted by the Fund (and the Bank, *UNTS*, Vol. 33, p. 298) in lieu of that recommended by the United Nations (General Assembly resolution 179 (III)).

87. Parry: 'Treaty-Making Power of the United Nations' in *BYIL*, 1949, p. 129. He criticizes the advisory opinion of the International Court of Justice on Reparation for Injuries for deducing the capacity of the United Nations to conclude agreements from Article 105(3). However, it does not follow from the text of the opinion that the Court necessarily envisaged Article 105(3) when it stated that the Charter provides 'for the conclusion of agreements between the Organization and its Members' (*ICJ Reports*, 1949, p. 179). It might have thought of Article 43.

88. For example, not in the constitutions of the International Bank, the International Monetary Fund, the Universal Postal Union, the International Telecommunication Union and the International Finance Corporation, who are all parties to the Convention on the Privileges and Immunities of the Specialized Agencies.

Punishment of the Crime of Genocide on 9 December 1948 [89]—has undertaken a contractual obligation vis-à-vis each acceding State *at least* to perform those specific (depository and related) functions which have been assigned to the Organization under Articles XI-XIX of the Convention.

Similarly, it has been pointed out that the International Labour Conventions establish obligations between the International Labour Organization and the contracting States as well as between these States *inter se,*[90] although this does not necessarily illustrate the inherent power, since it may find some support in the constitution itself (Article 26(4) cf. (1)). It is also interesting to note that the International Court of Justice, in its judgment of 21 December 1962 on the preliminary objections in the *South West Africa Cases,* considered both the League of Nations and its several Member States to be parties to the Mandates,[91] although again this does not necessarily flow from the inherent power, because it might find some basis in Article 22(8) of the Covenant of the League. In this case not even the Member States had acceded formally to the agreement.

As a final example the International Telecommunication Convention of 21 December 1959 may be cited. Although open for accession only by governments of countries ('pays', Article 18), this Convention provides, in Article 28, that, in accordance with Article XVI of the *bilateral* agreement between the United Nations and the International Telecommunication Union of 1947 'les services d'exploitation des télécommunications des Nations Unies jouissent des droits et sont soumis aux obligations prévus par cette Convention et les Règlements administratifs y annexés'.

The latter Convention even provides an example of a *formal* and *subsequent* accession by the United Nations when it represents a territory under trusteeship. Article 20 provides: 'Les Nations Unies peuvent adhérer à la présente Convention au nom d'un territoire ou groupe de territoires confiés à leur administration et faisant l'objet d'un accord de tutelle conformément à l'article 75 de la Charte des Nations Unies'. A similar, but not so clear, provision is contained in Article 35(5)(b) of the constitution of the International Labour Organization, in respect of

89. General Assembly resolution 260 (III), text of the Convention also in *UNTS,* Vol. 78, p. 277.

90. Gascon y Marin: 'Les transformations du droit administratif international' in *Recueil des Cours,* 1930 IV, p. 33. This notwithstanding the fact that the signature of the conventions by its President and Secretary-General in accordance with Article 19(4) of the ILO-constitution does not make the Organization a formal party, see Ingrid Detter: *Law Making by International Organizations* (Stockholm 1965) pp. 160-1.

91. *ICJ Reports,* 1962, pp. 332 and 341, cf. pp. 343-4.

accession to the International Labour Conventions. However, these are special cases where the Organization acts as a territorial sovereign,[92] and the capacity to conclude treaties on behalf of the territory might be said to be implied in Article 81 of the Charter. Moreover, the United Nations has never itself assumed the tasks of an administering authority in accordance with the last part of that Article,[93] and for this reason it has not become necessary for the Organization to accede formally to the International Telecommunication Convention or the International Labour Conventions.

An *informal subsequent* accession has taken place in respect of the Universal Postal Convention. Under its terms, this Convention is open for accession only to 'Pays-membres' of the Universal Postal Union. However, the Secretary-General of the United Nations has declared that the Organization undertakes to apply the Convention to its postal service, and the XIIIth Congress of the Union has taken note of this.[94] —A provision allowing the UN to become a party to an international Broadcasting Agreement by subsequent acceptance was quoted *above*, p. 338.

It is submitted that in those cases where no formal accession was made, this was due, not to any lack of legal capacity on the part of the United Nations, but to the fact that the practical need for a formal accession was not felt to be strong enough, or that the conventions concerned had been made open for accession only to States [95] because the drafters of these had not, at the time of their conclusion, realized the practical need for United Nations accession or had not found the need to be strong enough. It is true that, as shall be more fully explained below, under 10(b), certain delegates to the 1954 Hague Conference on the Protection of Cul-

92. Indeed, under Article 1(3)(d) of the International Telecommunication Convention it is the trust territory which becomes an Associate Member of the International Telecommunication Union, cf. *Indian Journal of International Law*, IV (1964) p. 17.

93. The abortive schemes for United Nations administration of the Free Territory of Trieste and the City of Jerusalem were not covered by the said Articles because they were not designed to be trust territories under Chapters XII–XIII of the Charter. The same was true of the UN administration of New Guinea in 1962–63. See *above*, p. 150.

94. *Les actes de l'Union Postale Universelle, revisés à Ottawa 1957 et annotés par le soin du Bureau international*, 1er fascicule (Bern 1959) pp. 52–53. In actual fact, the Secretary-General only communicated his *readiness* to make such a declaration, and the Postal Congress took note of this with satisfaction. The Universal Postal Union considers this sufficient to establish the obligations and has therefore not required any formal declaration (information supplied by the Secretariat).

95. It was obviously this fact which forced the Special Rapporteur of the International Law Commission, in his report on the operation of ships under United Nations flag, to propose a general agreement between the Members of the United Nations to extend to the United Nations all international agreements relating to navigation to which they are a party (Report of the International Law Commission Covering the Work of Its Eighth Session, *Yearbook of the ILC*, 1956, II, p. 279).

tural Property in the Event of Armed Conflict claimed, first that the United Nations could not adhere to a Convention, and later that there were technical difficulties in the way of the United Nations signing a Convention of that nature, and that this may have been one of the reasons why the Conference decided to settle for a resolution. However, as shall similarly be explained below, there were also practical reasons why it was not necessary for the United Nations to accede formally to the Convention, indeed, the United Nations representative expressly said so. On the other hand, in the case of trust territories, where the need to be a party to the International Telecommunication Convention was obvious, no legal hesitations appear to have prevented the contracting parties from permitting the United Nations to accede on behalf of territories administered by it. This is evidenced by Article 20 of that Convention, which has been quoted above, although this, as already mentioned, is rather a special case. Indeed, it is only in special cases, where the Organization exercises State-like functions, that the practical need is likely to arise for the Organization to accede and for the contracting parties to open up the convention for accession by it. In particular, the need may arise in respect of Organizations with supra-national powers, i.e. when States have not merely undertaken to abide by certain decisions of the Organization, but have ceded to it part of their own jurisdiction over their territory, their nationals or their organs, as is the case of United Nations Forces composed of national contingents under the Organization's operational command [96] and of the European Comunities. Indeed, the European Economic Community has already formally signed its first regular multilateral convention between States [97] in the same manner as the contracting States, including its six Member States, in this case the constitution contained provisions which authorized the conclusion of agreements with third States.[98] A need may arise also in cases where the Organization has established its own State-like services, or has assumed other special State-like functions, such as the United Nations' operation of ships or aircraft under its own flag and registra-

96. Cf. *above*, Chapter III,2(a) *in fine*.

97. The Protocol of 16 July 1962 to the General Agreement on Tariffs and Trade Embodying Results of the 1960–61 Conference, see pp. 7–10 and 362 of the GATT-publication bearing the same title and *UNTS*, Vol. 440, pp. 2–13, cf. Vol. 441, pp. 64 and 295.

98. Articles 111–4. Cf. Pescatore: 'Relations extérieures des Communautés européennes' in *Recueil des Cours*, 1961 II, p. 154. He also gives, pp. 155–8, an exposé of the practical reasons why the Communities may not make too much use of this treaty-making power. However, it is submitted that these reasons do not apply against conclusion or accession by the Community jointly with its several Member States, as the example in the text demonstrates. At any rate, these reasons are related to the fact that the Community in many respects represents and binds its Member States, and they are thus not relevant to the United Nations.

tion,[99] of its own postal and telecommunications services or of a military force recruited by individual enlistment.[100] In the cases referred to it may be highly appropriate, or even necessary, that the United Nations takes on the same obligations, and acquires the same rights, as States under international conventions governing the subject matter.[101]

In conclusion it is submitted that the United Nations has a general inherent capacity to conclude treaties, and that there is no basis for making an exception in respect of law-making multilateral conventions between States. This is confirmed in practice by the fact that the United Nations and other intergovernmental organizations have in fact become parties to such conventions, fully or in part. The question whether the United Nations has acceded formally and subsequently to these conventions in the same manner as the other parties is submitted to be irrelevant to the question of the inherent capacity of the Organization to do so. The crucial test is whether the Organization *is* a party, rather than *how* it became one; indeed, once it is admitted that the Organization can be a party it would be hard to deny its capacity to become a party in the same formal manner as States if the terms of the particular convention concerned permits it to. Thus there can be no doubt that the United Nations has the inherent capacity to become a party to the conventions on warfare if their terms permit it to accede.

10. ARE THE CONVENTIONS OPEN FOR ACCESSION BY THE UNITED NATIONS?

After having demonstrated the inherent capacity of the United Nations to accede to the conventions on warfare, it is now necessary to deal with

99. The United Nations operated ships under its own flag on some occasions in Korea, the Middle East and West New Guinea, see *United Nations Conference on the Law of the Sea, Official Records,* IV, p. 138, and *United Nations Review,* IX (1962) No. 12, p. 26. See also Article 7 of the Convention on the High Seas of 29 April 1958, *ibid.,* II, p. 136, and the draft new Article XXV bis to the Brussels Convention on Liability of Operators of Nuclear Ships of 25 May 1962, elaborated 1964 by the Standing Committee of the Diplomatic Conference on Maritime Law (International Atomic Energy Agency document CN-6/SC/13, 1965 pp. 70–71, cf. pp. 15–20).

The possibility of intergovernmental organizations registering their own *aircraft* was foreseen in Article 18 of the Tokyo Convention on Offences and Certain Other Acts Occurring on Board Aircraft of 14 September 1963. As for *space vehicles,* reference is made to par. 5 of General Assembly resolution 1962 (XVIII), to Article 6 of the agreement concerning the Kiruna launching base in Swedish Lapland between the European Space Research Organization and Sweden of 29 July 1964 (quoted in *Indian Journal of International Law,* IV (1964) p. 248), and to the reports of the United Nations Committee on the Peaceful Uses of Outer Space and its legal sub-committee from 1964 onwards. See also *below,* pp. 363–4 and 370, note 199.

100. See *above,* Chapter I, Chapter III,2(a) *in fine* and 6(b) *in fine.*

101. Cf. *above,* note 95.

the different question of whether the conventions on warfare themselves are open for accession by the United Nations, or whether their terms are such as to preclude the Organization from making use of its inherent capacity to accede. This is, in the first place, a question of the interpretation of the *accession clauses*—do they comprise States only or the United Nations as well?

It may be noted, preliminarily, that the *Holy See* is an *original* party both to the Geneva Conventions and to the 1954 Hague Convention on the Protection of Cultural Property. As for the latter Convention it appears to be a party in its capacity of territorial sovereign of the Vatican City; indeed, the Holy See was the first contracting party to request inclusion in the International Register of Cultural Property under Special Protection, and pursuant to its request the entire area of the Vatican City State was entered in the Register on 10 February 1960.[102] However, it does not appear to have acted in the same capacity in respect of the Geneva Conventions. This is clearly the case of the 1864 Geneva Convention, to which it acceded in 1868, at a time when it had no territorial sovereignty. It was because it was a party to that Convention that it was invited to the 1949 Geneva Conference, where its delegation defended notably the religious interests.[103] Thus, indications are that even when it signed the new Geneva Conventions in 1949 and ratified them in 1951, it did not necessarily do so in its capacity of territorial sovereign, or at least not exclusively in that capacity. The Holy See has even acceded to a number of multilateral conventions between States of which it was not an original signatory and which were open for accession by States only. In most cases it appears to have done so in its capacity as sovereign of the Vatican City,[104] even if it is now, at its own request, listed as the 'Holy See'. However, in some cases it may well have acceded in the capacity of the Holy See, for example in respect of cultural conventions.[104a]

Except for the 1954 Hague Convention for the Protection of Cultural Property, which will be discussed separately under (b), the question of United Nations Forces or a United Nations enforcement action was not considered during the elaboration and adoption of the conventions on warfare. This is obvious in the case of the pre-war conventions. But even at the Diplomatic Conference at Geneva in 1949, four years after the

102. *Records of the Intergovernmental Conference on the Protection of Cultural Property in the Event of Armed Conflict* (The Hague 1961), Foreword.

103. See for example *Actes de la Conférence diplomatique de Genève de 1949*, II A, p. 615.

104. This was made quite clear in one case in ECOSOC resolution 507 (XVI), which resolved 'to admit the Vatican City State as a Party' to the Convention on Road Traffic of 19 September 1949.

104a. Thus the Holy See on 26 November 1962 acceded to the European Cultural Convention of 19 December 1954 (*UNTS*, Vol. 218, p. 139).

adoption of the Charter of the United Nations which provided for a Force under United Nations command,[105] the problem was not considered. This may seem strange, but it is nevertheless a fact which has been confirmed both by the organizers of the conference and by the United Nations. The United Nations was represented by an observer at the Conference, but his report to the United Nations does not refer to the matter. Nor is there any reference in the records of the discussions or the other *travaux préparatoires*.[106] One of the drafters [107] has suggested that the reason was that at that time prospects for a United Nations military action seemed completely unrealistic, despite the clear words of the Charter, in the light of the failure of the League of Nations to implement military sanctions under the Covenant. Indeed, the Conventions were adopted at the, from this point of view, most unfortunate moment, after the failure of the Military Staff Committee and before Korea.

(a) *The Hague and Geneva Conventions*

The accession clause common to the Hague Conventions of 1907 reads:

> Les Puissances non signataires sont admises à adhérer à la présente Convention.
> La Puissance qui désire adhérer notifie par écrit son intention au Gouvernement des Pays-Bas en lui transmettant l'acte d'adhésion qui sera déposé dans les archives dudit Gouvernement.
> Ce Gouvernement transmettra immédiatement à toutes les autres Puissances copie certifiée conforme de la notification ainsi que de l'acte d'adhésion, en indiquant la date à laquelle il a reçu la notification.[108]

The accession clauses common to the Geneva Conventions of 1949 read:

> From the date of its coming into force, it shall be open to any Power in whose name the present Convention has not been signed, to accede to this Convention.
>
> Accessions shall be notified in writing to the Swiss Federal Council, and shall take effect six months after the date on which they are received.
>
> The Swiss Federal Council shall communicate the accessions to all the Powers in whose name the Convention has been signed, or whose accession has been notified.[109]

It is also possible to become a party to the Geneva Conventions in an informal manner, under the third paragraph of Article 2, common to the four Geneva Conventions, which reads:

105. *Above*, pp. 29–32.

106. In the *Actes de la Conférence diplomatique de Genève de 1949* there are references to the United Nations only in connection with the registration of the Conventions.

107. M. Pilloud, Directeur-adjoint des Affaires générales, Comité international de la Croix-Rouge.

108. See for example Article 6 of the Fourth Hague Convention.

109. See for example Articles 139–40 of the Prisoners of War Convention.

Although one of the Powers in conflict may not be a party to the present Convention, the Powers who are parties thereto shall remain bound by it in their mutual relations. They shall, furthermore, be bound by the Convention in relation to the said Power, if the latter accepts and applies the provisions thereof.

In respect of all these provisions the question arises whether the terms 'Puissance' and 'Power' mean 'State' in the technical sense or whether they mean something more.

There was no discussion at the Diplomatic Conference in Geneva in 1949 or at the preparatory conference of these terms as used in the accession clauses and throughout the Conventions.[110] Indeed, there is no indication in the *travaux préparatoires* of the Geneva Conventions why these terms were chosen in preference to 'State' or the equivalent terms which are used in most modern conventions.[111] At the time of the adoption of the Hague Conventions the term 'Puissance' was not as unusual as it is to-day, although even then that term was not applied in the majority of *non*-military conventions.[112] As for the Geneva Conventions, there have been peculiar changes in the terms used. The 1864 Conventions used 'Gouvernements' (Article 9), the 1906 Convention used 'Puissances' (Article 32, adding, however, that the accession would take effect only if, within one year, no Contracting Power objected to the accession), the 1929 Conventions used 'pays' (Articles 35 and 93, respectively) and the 1949 Conventions use 'Puissance'. The switch to the term 'Puissance' in 1949 contrasts sharply with the general trend in the opposite direction in respect of other conventions (it may have been this trend which caused the switch in 1929 from 'Puissances' to 'pays', which is closer to, but still not as narrow as 'State'). Indeed, after the Second World War the term 'Puissance' has practically or completely disappeared in non-military conventions.[113]

110. Information supplied by MM. Pictet and Pilloud, Directeur et Directeur-adjoint des Affaires générales, Comité international de la Croix-Rouge.

111. The term 'Puissance' was taken over from the accession clauses of the draft conventions which were adopted by the XVII International Conference of the Red Cross at Stockholm in August 1948 and which served as the basis of discussion for the Diplomatic Conference in 1949, see for example Article 126 of the Stockholm draft of the Prisoners of War Convention, *Actes de la Conférence diplomatique de Genève de 1949*, I, p. 99. Indeed, the Geneva Diplomatic Conference adopted the accession clause proposed by the Stockholm Conference without discussion, subject only to two irrelevant modifications made by the Drafting Committee (*Actes de la Conférence diplomatique de Genève de 1949*, II B, pp. 25, 30, 68, 108, 178, 370).

112. Out of the non-military multilateral conventions listed in *Recueil des Traités de la Norvège* for the period 1864–1898 only two conventions refer to 'Puissances', while three refer to 'Etats' and one to 'pays'. During the period 1905–28 the corresponding proportion was twelve 'Etats' to two 'Puissances'.

113. Thus not one of the conventions listed in the United Nations' Handbook on Final Clauses (ST/LEG/6, 5 August 1957, pp. 4–19) contains that term among the great variety of (more restrictive territorial) terms used ('State', 'country', 'government' and 'Member of the United Nations').

Viewed in the light of the purposes of the Geneva Conventions and of their other provisions, there is every reason to assume that the drafters had substantive reasons for avoiding the term 'State'. As a matter of fact, they were very anxious to make sure that the Conventions should apply to every conflict of an international character, no matter the formal status of the conflict or of the parties thereto. (They even wanted the Conventions to apply to armed conflicts of an internal nature, but, since views differed in this regard, they included as a compromise a provision [Article 3 common to the four Conventions] prescribing, as a minimum, the application of the basic principles of the Conventions.) [114] To this end the drafters carefully avoided all technical terms which might be given a restrictive interpretation. Thus, the Geneva Conventions deliberately do not speak of 'war', but of 'armed conflict'.[115] And as the chief Finnish delegate to the Geneva Conference, Castrén, points out, 'the new Geneva Conventions are carefully framed and do not mention "States" [116] but instead either the "Contracting Parties" or the "Parties to the conflict" ' [117] (in addition to "Detaining Power", "Occupying Power", "Power upon which the prisoners depend" or merely "Power"). The three military Geneva Conventions even provide expressly that they apply to 'members of regular armed forces who profess allegiance to a Government *or an authority* not recognised by the Detaining Power'.[118] It would have rendered the efforts to broaden

114. *Siotis: Le droit de la guerre et les conflits armés d'un caractère non-international* (Paris 1958) pp. 193–219, especially p. 204. However, it is submitted that the conventions apply fully if the insurgents have been recognized as belligerents or fulfil the objective criteria therefor, cf. *above*, Chapter VII,1.

115. Draper considers that the United Nations Force may not be subject to those older conventions which apply only in 'war' (*International and Comparative Law Quarterly*, XII [1963] p. 408). In the view of the present writer, 'war' must mean war in the material sense, cf. *above*, pp. 199–201, with note 99.

116. On one exception, see *below*, under (a) *in fine*.

117. *Castrén: The Present Law of War and Neutrality* (Helsinki 1954) p. 90. He adds that the intention was that 'those parts of the Conventions which concern the observance of rules of humane conduct should also be applied during internal conflicts'. However, his statement quoted in the text is made to illustrate his (correct) assertion that 'the rights of belligerents should not ... be limited to (certain kinds of) States and unions of States'. As for 'unions of States' he considers that the position of the League of Nations was uncertain, but that the United Nations 'may be regarded as being qualified to become a belligerent'. In addition to *sovereign States*, he mentions as parties which can wage war: 'other communities whose right to make war has not been restricted by treaties or other international arrangements and who have not become so dependent on another country that they have lost their own right to wage war', non-sovereign countries and permanently neutralized States. Finally he points out that *insurgents* have the rights of a belligerent if they have been recognized as belligerents or, according to some authors, if they fulfil the objective criteria (cf. *above*, Chapter VII,1).

118. *Above*, Chapter V,3(a), note 104. Cf. also *above*, Chapter VII,1, at notes 5 and 8.

the scope of the Convention vain in so far as international conflicts are concerned, if the clauses on formal and informal accession had precluded parties other than States, or parties whom not everybody was prepared to recognize as States. It was therefore *necessary* to use a broader term than 'State'. Whether or not the term 'Power' was chosen deliberately for this purpose, it cannot, in the light of the purposes of the Convention as reflected in its other provisions and its general terminology, be interpreted restrictively, as if it had read 'States', or as synonymous with that technical term.

This conclusion, drawn from the *travaux préparatoires* and the other articles of the Conventions, is confirmed by practice after their conclusion. Thus, if the term 'Gouvernement' (which followed the term 'Puissances') in the accession clause of the 1864 Geneva Convention had been interpreted as synonymous with the government of a *State,* then the Holy See could not in 1868 have acceded to the Convention which sprung out of the wars during which it lost its statehood. Similarly, although the question of the United Nations as a party has not yet been posed to the contracting parties to the 1949 Conventions,[119] these have on a number of occasions been faced with formal accessions of other (territorial) communities which many contracting parties did not recognize as States. And, indeed, there is a marked difference between the attitude which these contracting parties have taken in this respect towards the Geneva Conventions and that which they have taken towards other international conventions. In respect of other conventions they frequently, not merely refuse to recognize the communities as States, but they also refuse to recognize their accession to the conventions as valid. However, in respect of the Geneva Conventions a number of these same States have contented themselves with a declaration of non-recognition (as States), while avoiding statements which would imply a denial of the applicability of the Conventions to conflicts involving such communities. (On the other hand, to the knowledge of the International Committee of the Red Cross, no government has ever invoked its accession to the Geneva Conventions to establish its legal existence as a State.) These States thus appear to act on the view that parties other than States may become parties to these Conventions.

Indeed, it is obvious that Conventions such as the Geneva Conventions must be applicable (subject to ratification, accession or acceptance) to any armed international [119a] conflict, whoever may be parties to it, as long as they are subject to the general laws of war.[120] They even cover conflicts involving parties which have no international status, inas-

---

119. See, however, the comments transmitted to the *Comité international de la Croix-Rouge,* referred to *below,* under 14.

119a. On internal conflicts, see *above,* Chapter V,4(d).

120. As the United Nations is, see *above,* Chapter V.

much as Article 3 common to the four Geneva Conventions provides for the application of the basic principles of the Conventions to 'armed conflicts not of an international character'. It would certainly be contrary to the purpose of the Conventions and of those who inspired them if they were considered to be inapplicable to armed conflicts of an international character because one of the parties, although a subject of international law, was not a State. Such conflicts could not be allowed to fall between two stools because they are neither internal nor between States. A restrictive interpretation in this respect could only be maintained if the contracting parties had clearly precluded such a subject of international law from acceding, either by clear words in the Conventions, or by unclear terms in the Conventions whose interpretation in a restrictive sense was clear from the *travaux préparatoires* (or from the substantive provisions of the conventions, cf. below, under 11).

However, neither is the case in respect of the Hague and the Geneva Conventions. It is true that the term 'Puissance' is normally used in treaties as synonymous with 'States', simply because the contracting parties only thought in terms of States. However, the term does not in itself preclude other subjects of international law who may be parties to an armed conflict of an international and warlike character. Indeed, it is submitted that the United Nations, too, is a 'Power'.[121]

The fact that the drafters never thought of including the United Nations in this context is not decisive, as long as they did not think of it at all, and thus did not indicate any intention to preclude it. No convention can be interpreted as including only what the drafters actually thought of. Nor can the failure to discuss United Nations actions be interpreted as an intention to preclude them, if the reason for the failure was that the drafters did not consider this as a realistic possibility, as one of them has suggested.[122] A convention must, within the limits of its terms, be interpreted to include what is necessary to achieve its purpose. This must apply both with regard to new aspects which arise in the course of the development of the international community and to aspects which existed at the time of conclusion of the convention, but which the drafters did not consider. As for the former, it has been rightly pointed out that the interpretation of an old constitution cannot be the same to-day as

121. The Soviet Union in 1920 declared itself willing to grant a League of Nations Commission of Investigation 'the same liberty for studying the situation as is enjoyed by the representatives of *other Powers* within the boundaries of a Sovereign State' (*Martin Hill: Immunities and Privileges of International Officials*, Washington 1947, p. 73, italics added). Cf. also the statement quoted *above*, Chapter V, 2(a) *in fine*, according to which it had been the consistent view of the United Nations Command in Korea that the United Nations was the 'Detaining Power' in respect of Prisoners of War.

122. *Above*, at note 107.

it was when the constitution was adopted, but that all interpretation must be undertaken in the light of the general legal development, changes in social conditions and new concepts of the functions of the State organs.[123] This must be true of international conventions, too. And it must apply even to a convention which is only sixteen years old (or less), when the international community and concepts of its organization have changed so rapidly as they have since the establishment of the United Nations. Therefore, even if the drafters in 1949 had only States in mind as 'Powers', it must be admitted that there is to-day also a new 'Power', the United Nations, which, after 1949, has established armed forces and which under its Charter shall direct military action against an aggressor.

While some Judges of the International Court of Justice have been willing to adopt quite far-reaching teleological interpretations, the majority of the Court has usually been reluctant to adopt interpretations which went too far in that direction and which did not conform with the text of the treaty in question.[124] Thus, in its second advisory opinion on the *Interpretation of Peace Treaties with Bulgaria, Hungary and Romania* of 11 July 1950 the Court refused to consider the Secretary-General of the United Nations as entitled to appoint a 'third member' to an arbitration Commission under the Peace Treaties, when one of the parties had failed to appoint its representative. The Court stated:

> The principle of interpretation expressed in the maxim: *Ut res magis valeat quam pereat,* often referred to as the rule of effectiveness, cannot justify the Court in attributing to the provisions for the settlement of disputes in the Peace Treaties a meaning which, as stated above, would be contrary to their letter and spirit.[125]

However, as pointed out above, it would neither be contrary to the letter, nor to the spirit of the Geneva Conventions to consider the United Nations as entitled to accede.

McNair[126] is also rather critical of the rule of effectiveness. After citing the above case, and another, very obvious, case states:

> We doubt whether this so-called rule means more than to say that the contracting parties obviously must have had some purpose in making a treaty, and that it is the duty of a tribunal to ascertain that purpose and do its best to give effect to it, unless there is something in the language used by the parties which precludes the tribunal from doing so. Thus in its Advisory Opinion on *Reparation for Injuries* the International Court remarked that it was impossible to see how

---

123. Castberg: 'Grunnlovsfortolkning og internasjonalt samarbeid', *Dagbladet*, Oslo, 28 September 1960, citing, in particular, the constitutions of the United States and Norway.

124. Fitzmaurice in *BYIL*, XXVIII (1951) pp. 7–8.

125. *ICJ Reports*, 1950, p. 229.

126. *The Law of Treaties* (Oxford 1961) pp. 383–5.

the United Nations could recover reparation for the death of, or injury to, one of its agents 'unless it possessed capacity to bring an international claim' against the State responsible and held that the United Nations must be deemed to have the power to do this; although that power was not expressly conferred by the Charter, there was nothing in the Charter which excluded the exercise of such a power.

If one, with McNair and most other writers, were to assume that the capacities of intergovernmental organizations depend upon an interpretation of their constitutions,[127] one might add: nor is there anything in the Charter to say that the United Nations could, or should, have the capacity to 'recover reparation for the death of, or injury to, *one of its agents*'. And it is extremely doubtful whether the drafters of the Charter intended to confer this power. They probably never thought of it. *At most*, it might be argued that they would have conferred the power, had they thought of it. But even that is doubtful. It is quite conceivable that thinking in 1945, although only four years before the advisory opinion of the Court, might not have been far enough advanced to give an affirmative answer if the delegates to the San Francisco Conference had thought of the question. Yet the International Court of Justice considered the power to follow from the Charter by 'necessary intendment'.

Although it is thus not an indispensible condition that the drafters would have made a provision if they had thought of the problem, it is submitted that in the case of the Geneva Conventions the delegates would, in one way or another, have made it clear that the United Nations could accede, if they had thought of United Nations actions as a real possibility,[128] and if they had been aware of the fact that these might in future be organized under United Nations command and responsibility in such a manner that the members of the United Nations Force would be without protection unless the United Nations were a party, and if they had considered that the existing text was not clear enough.

It is accordingly submitted that both the 1907 Hague and the 1949 Geneva Conventions are open for accession by the United Nations.[129] It is submitted, furthermore, that if the Organization accedes formally under the accession clause, it becomes a contracting party not only in a substantive, but also in a formal sense, i.e. it acquires the same rights and duties as contracting States, not only under the substantive provi-

127. The present writer does not share this view, see *above* Chapter IV,3(f), and 'International Personality of Intergovernmental Organizations' *Indian Journal of International Law*, IV (1964) pp. 1–74.

128. As shall be explained *below*, under (b), the 1954 Hague Conference did think of the United Nations, but chose a different solution, which was sufficient to meet the needs of *that* Convention.

129. *Contra* Baxter, *loc. cit., above*, note 58, and apparently *Bowett: United Nations Forces* (London 1964) pp. 507 and 509.

sions of the conventions, but also under the final clauses, all of which speak of 'Power' or 'Party'.

However, in the latter context a curious anomaly may be found in the signature clause. While, as already pointed out, all the substantive and final clauses of the Geneva Conventions carefully avoid the term 'State', that term suddenly crops up as the very last word of all four Geneva Conventions.[130] After the final clauses, the Conventions are concluded by the usual signature clause which reads:

> IN WITNESS WHEREOF the undersigned, having deposited their respective full powers, have signed the present Convention.
>
> DONE at Geneva this twelfth day of August 1949, in the English and French languages. The original shall be deposited in the archives of the Swiss Confederation. The Swiss Federal Council shall transmit certified copies thereof to each of the signatory and acceding States.

Even if the term 'State' is interpreted literally, it could only restrict the right to claim certified copies. It could not of itself operate to restrict the right of accession under the separate accession clause, which, like the other final clauses, speaks of 'Power'. A different question is whether the fact that the term 'State' is used in a clause which obviously should have the same scope as the accession clause, can be taken as an indication that the drafters intended the term 'Power' to mean 'State'. However, it is submitted that the term 'State' in the signature clause was a mere slip of the pen, which can be accorded no significance beyond its own field. It is well known to those who have participated in diplomatic conferences that the signature clause is added in great haste at the very last moment by some exhausted member of the Secretariat or of a Drafting or Final Clauses Committee, that it is copied from some other convention which happens to be at hand, that the delegates regard it as a matter of pure routine, and that they in any event are far too exhausted to check it even if they would have considered checking necessary. Even *after* the Conference participants do not appear to have noticed that the term 'State' slipped in at the very end.[131] In these circumstances it would be highly inappropriate to attribute any deeper meaning to this term. If interpreted literally, it means that the Swiss Government has no *duty* to transmit certified copies to the United Nations if it accedes. But it does not mean that the Swiss Government could not do so, indeed, it should, and, no

---

130. Another exception, of even less significance, may be found in the model identity card contained in Annex IV to the Prisoners of War Convention. This contains a space to be filled in by the 'name of the *country* and military authority issuing this card' (italics added). Under Article 4A(4) of the Convention cards 'similar to' this model shall be issued to 'persons who accompany the armed forces without actually being members thereof' by 'the armed forces which they accompany'. It is obvious that the United Nations would be free to fill in the name of that Organization.

131. See for example the quotation *above,* at note 117, from the Finnish chief delegate.

doubt, would. Still less does it mean that *other* provisions, which do not use the term 'State', should be interpreted restrictively. On the contrary, if there has to be conformity, there would be stronger reasons for giving an *extensive* interpretation to the slip of the pen in the signature clause.

(b) *The Hague Convention for the Protection of Cultural Property in the Event of Armed Conflict of 14 May 1954*

The accession clause of this Convention (Article 32) reads:

> From the date of its entry into force, the present Convention shall be open for accession by all States mentioned in Article 30 which have not signed it, as well as any other State invited to accede by the Executive Board of the United Nations Educational, Scientific and Cultural Organization. Accession shall be effected by the deposit of an instrument of accession with the Director-General of the United Nations Educational, Scientific and Cultural Organization.

It will be noted that this invitation is addressed to *States*. On the other hand, Article 18(3) reproduces the substance of the third paragraph of Article 2 of the Geneva Conventions, quoted above, under (a) *in initio*, retaining the term '*Power*'.

(i) This Convention was concluded after Korea, and this may have been the reason why the Conference which adopted it did take into consideration the possibility that the United Nations might undertake a collective action.[132] The Greek delegation proposed to add to Article 18 the following new paragraph 2: 'The Convention shall also be binding on High Contracting Parties taking part in collective action in compliance with a decision taken by the competent organs of the United Nations',[133] explaining that, although it might be admitted that in the case of collective action the laws of war would be respected, it was important enough to state so, there or elsewhere, for the purposes of the Convention. Dr. Saba, the Legal Adviser of UNESCO, the sponsoring Organization, stated that he thought that the Convention would apply, even without being expressly mentioned, in the event of United Nations collective action. It would be necessary for the Security Council and the General Assembly to take a resolution deciding to apply the Convention. The Conference could vote a resolution expressing the hope that the United Nations adopt the principles of the Convention. Nevertheless, the Secretariat had, after consultation with the United Nations Secretariat envisaged the drafting of a text, which could be inserted among the final provisions or elsewhere, reading:

---

132. *Records of the Intergovernmental Conference on the Protection of Cultural Property in the Event of Armed Conflict* (The Hague 1961) pp. 78, 183–4, 267, 292, 385, 414.

133. *Ibid.*, p. 385.

Where an international authority—by the terms of the article (Final Provisions)—would state its acceptance of all or some of the provisions of the present Convention, which it would be capable of applying, the High Contracting Parties shall be bound, in relation to the said international authority, by the provisions of the Convention accepted in the terms of the aforementioned statement.

This proposal was accepted by the Greek delegate, who withdrew his own. However, the new proposal was ruled out of order because it had not been introduced in writing.[134]

Instead, the French delegation, claiming, first, that in practice the United Nations could not adhere to a convention, and, later, that there were technical difficulties in the way of the Organization signing a convention of that nature,[135] proposed a *resolution* recommending that the United Nations ensure application of the *principles* of the Convention by the armed forces taking part in a military action in implementation of the Charter.[136] This was supported by the Greek delegate, who explained that his draft provision had raised legal problems which had appeared complicated. Although he felt that, by the general principles of the laws of war, the provisions, or at least the general principles, of the Convention would have to be taken into account in a collective action by the United Nations, he thought that a resolution on that point would contribute positively to clarifying the situation.

The representative of the United Nations, M. Giraud, said that the problem was well put in the French resolution. Practical and political adjustments would be made so that the resolution might bring about the application of the Convention by the United Nations in the event of collective action. In fact, all action would be undertaken with national contingents. If all States were Parties to the Convention, no difficulties would arise, but if some contingents were provided by States that were not Parties to the Convention, the French resolution would be useful.[137] After deciding to refer to the 'provisions' of the Convention rather than to its 'principles', the Conference adopted the French proposal in the following form:

---

134. *Ibid.*, pp. 183–4, cf. p. 213.

135. The invalidity of this assertion has been discussed *above*, under 9(b), cf. *below*, under 11.

136. *Records of the Intergovernmental Conference on the Protection of Cultural Property in the Event of Armed Conflict* (The Hague 1961) p. 414, cf. pp. 267 and 292.

137. *Ibid.*, p. 267, cf. *above*, 2–4.

The Conference expresses the hope that the competent organs of the United Nations should decide, in the event of military action being taken in implementation of the Charter, to ensure application of the provisions of the Convention by the armed forces taking part in such action.[138]

The General Conference of UNESCO at its eighth session in Montevideo in November-December 1954 adopted a resolution (IV.1.4-133) accepting the responsibilities devolving upon UNESCO under the Convention, recommending all States which had been invited to the Conference to accede to the Convention, and endorsing the above resolution of the Conference. The Secretariat of UNESCO thereupon transmitted both resolutions to the United Nations with a letter of 16 February 1955, requesting that they be brought to the attention of the competent organs of the United Nations. Accordingly, the United Nations Secretariat informed the General Assembly, the Security Council and the Economic and Social Council. No further action was taken by these organs.[139] However, the Convention was one of those envisaged when the Regulations for UNEF, ONUC and UNFICYP, which the Secretary-General enacted subsequently instructed these three Forces to 'observe the *principles and spirit* of the general international Conventions applicable to the conduct of military personnel'.[140]

The reason why Dr. Saba proposed a separate clause on accession by international organizations under a special procedure, rather than that they be included in the regular accession clause, appears to have been that he felt that the Organization might not be in a position to apply all the provisions of the Convention. Thus it could not iself take the measures required by Article 8 for the special protection of its property in the host States. Although the immediate reason why the proposal was not pursued, was that it was ruled out of order, it appears that there were also some substantive hesitations. Thus the French representative appears, at least at the first discussion of his draft resolution, to have felt, wrongly,[141] that the United Nations lacked the capacity to adhere to a Convention. It may also have been felt that there were practical difficulties in the way.[142]

Of greater importance was probably the fact that the Conference took place in 1954, after Korea and the Uniting for Peace Resolution, with their systems of national command, and before the establishment of the genuine United Nations Forces in the Middle East and elsewhere under

---

138. *Op. cit.*, p. 78.
139. UNESCO/CA/RBC 1/4, of 15 June 1962, UN/A/3119 and S/3557 of 13 March 1956 and E/2838 of 16 April 1956.
140. *Above*, p. 190, and *below*, p. 445, par 11.
141. *Above*, under 9.
142. Cf. *below*, under 11.

United Nations command and international responsibility. This is probably why the United Nations representative stated that any United Nations Force would be composed of national contingents and that no difficulties would arise if all the States providing contingents were parties to the Convention. Indeed, this is partly true even of a genuine United Nations Force, because the United Nations has no territory properly speaking, and because its cultural property, at least that outside New York, would therefore be protected under the Convention as cultural property in the territory of the host State. To the extent that this is so,[143] the Organization has nothing to gain by becoming a contracting party, as it would have by becoming a party to the Geneva Conventions. It would only have been a one-sided party to the 1954 Hague Conventions, and it is therefore sufficient if it in fact applies the Convention unilaterally (and makes a unilateral decision or declaration to that effect).

Nevertheless, the discussion at the 1954 Hague Conference demonstrated again the reluctance of participants in diplomatic conferences, including the United Nations representatives thereto, to discuss an eventuality which has not in fact occurred, even if it has been provided for in the Charter, not because they want to exclude it from the Conventions, but because they either do not think of it, or else consider it academic. The 1949 Geneva Conference, one year before Korea, did not consider United Nations actions at all. The 1954 Hague Conference, one year after Korea and two years before UNEF, considered United Nations actions, but only those of the Korea type, i.e. actions under

---

143. This is certainly true of its property in Geneva, because the Ariana site is Swiss territory; it enjoys only inviolability (see § 2 of the 'interim' agreement on privileges and immunities between the United Nations and Switzerland of 11 June 1946, *UNTS*, Vol. 1, p. 164). The headquarters district in New York is in a different position, cf. *International and Comparative Law Quarterly*, XIV (1965), pp. 518–20. It is under 'the control and authority [but not sovereignty] of the United Nations'. However, United States law is applicable unless otherwise provided by the United Nations. The headquarters agreement does not specify whether the reference to United States law also comprises treaties concluded by the United States (which are part of the law of the land).—Article 13(1) of the Regulations for the Execution of the 1954 Hague Convention (attached to the latter) provides that 'any High Contracting Party' may apply for the entry into the 'International Register of Cultural Property under Special Protection' of cultural property 'situated within its territory' (see also Article 16(1)). In respect of United Nations property in Geneva this must therefore be done by the host State (in agreement with the Organization). The same is true of United Nations property in New York if the headquarters district is considered United States territory. If not, it must be entered by the United Nations; however, this the Organization could not do if it is not a party to the Convention. The problem of cultural property of intergovernmental organizations was not discussed during the preparation of the 1954 Hague Convention. Up to the time of writing no host State had registered the cultural property of an intergovernmental organization.

national command,[144] not those of the type envisaged in the Charter.

(ii) The resolution adopted by the Conference leaves it entirely to the United Nations to decide what action it should take to ensure application of the Convention. The resolution does not in itself preclude the Organization from formally accepting or acceding to the Convention. But it is submitted that *the accession clause* in Article 32 does so, by referring to '*States*'.

It has been maintained that this term cannot always be interpreted strictly, to the exclusion of intergovernmental organizations. This view has been advanced in respect of the similar provisions in Article 34 of the Statutes of the Permanent Court of International Justice and the International Court of Justice, the latter of which reads: 'Only states may be parties to cases before the Court'. This despite the fact that the word 'only' makes this provision more explicitly limitative than the Hague Convention.[145] Thus, when a proposal was made to a Committee of Jurists, appointed by the League of Nations in 1929, that Article 34 be amended to provide that the League might be a party before the Court, President Anzilotti expressed the view that the text of Article 34 did not 'prejudge the question whether an association of States could, in certain circumstances, appear before the Court' and that 'if the League possessed a collective personality in international law, Article 34 would not exclude it from appearing before the Court.' [146] Similarly, the Belgian Government, in its oral statement before the Court in *Reparation for Injuries Suffered in the Service of the United Nations*, raised the question of whether Article 34(1) of the Statute of the Court precludes only individuals and non-governmental organizations and not entities composed of States.[147] And Eagleton, although he points out that the San Francisco Conference considered and rejected a proposal to admit inter-

144. Cf. in addition to the statement of the United Nations representative reported above, at note 137, that of the French representative, who spoke of 'combined' military action by the United Nations; this rather points to action by several States on the League and the Korea pattern *(Records, op. cit.,* p. 267). See also the Greek statement and proposal, *ibid.,* pp. 267 and 385.

145. This question has been discussed by the present writer in an article on 'Settlement of Internal Disputes of Intergovernmental Organizations by Internal and External Courts' in *Zeitschrift für ausländisches öffentliches Recht und Völkerrecht,* XXIV (1964) at pp. 96–99.

146. Minutes of the 1929 Committee of Jurists, League of Nations document C.166.M.66,1929.V, pp. 59–60, as reported by *Hudson: The Permanent Court of International Justice 1920–1942* (New York 1943) p. 187, cf. p. 186, and *El-Erian: First report to the International Law Commission on relations between States and intergovernmental organizations, Yearbook of the International Law Commission,* 1963, II, p. 182.

147. *ICJ Pleadings, Reparation for Injuries Suffered in the Service of the United Nations,* p. 99.

governmental organizations,[148] submits that 'it would not be unreasonable or illogical for the Court to hold, if opportunity presented, that the word 'states' was used in the sense of 'international legal persons' and that, consequently, international organizations having legal personality could be allowed to appear before the Court.[149] Similar views have been taken by several other writers, including Lauterpacht and Weissberg, although the latter points out that the question was raised, not only at San Francisco, but also during the elaboration of Article 34 of the Statute of the Permanent Court of International Justice, upon which Article 34(1) of the Statute of the International Court of Justice was modelled.[150] On the other hand, he points out that the term 'State' has been used in different ways for different purposes. Also within the Court itself have divergent opinions on the question been expressed.[151]

There may no doubt be cases where it would be unduly rigid to confine a provision in a statute or treaty to States if its drafters used that term merely because it did not occur to them that there are other subjects of international law (or, as *Eagleton* puts it: 'because most delegates regarded states as the only legal persons') or because no intergovernmental organizations existed in the field at the time when the convention was concluded. Application by analogy to intergovernmental organizations may be justified in cases where this conforms with the purposes of the convention and the *presumed* intention of the parties, and in particular where it was clear that the purpose of using the term 'State' was merely to preclude private parties (individuals and non-governmental organizations), as it was the case of Article 34(1) of the Statute

148. On this, see *Jessup: A Modern Law of Nations* (New York 1949) pp. 25–26, who points out that the reasons for the rejection were more political than juridical and that 'the result has no significance in law or logic relating to the legal personality of international organizations'.

149. Eagleton: 'International Organization and the Law of Responsibility', *Recueil des Cours*, 1950 I, p. 418.

150. *Weissberg: The International Status of the United Nations* (New York, 1961) pp. 189–200, citing the *League of Nations Advisory Committee of Jurists, Procès-Verbaux of the Proceedings of the Committee, 16 June–24 July 1920*, p. 579. In the same sense Lauterpacht in *Annuaire de l'Institut de droit international*, XLV (1954) I, p. 535, and the writers cited by Hambro in *Recueil des Cours*, 1950 I, p. 160. Some writers (cited and opposed by the present writer, *loc. cit., above*, note 145) submit the broad interpretation of Article 34 in favour of the International Labour Organisation in order to allow for implementation of Articles 29(2), 26(4), 31 and 37 of its constitution.—On the other hand, the Secretary-General of the United Nations has taken the view that Article 34(1) precludes the United Nations (A/AC.78/L.10 of 13 April 1955, cf. A/2909, Annex II, p. 38, 10 June 1955). And so has the United States *(ICJ Pleadings, Reparation for Injuries*, p. 21). Other writers content themselves with proposing a revision of Article 34(1), see those cited by *Weissberg, op. cit.*, note 136.

151. *ICJ Reports*, 1952, p. 133, as contrasted with *ibid.*, 1956, pp. 106 and 168, cf. *Weissberg, loc. cit.*

of the Court. However, it is difficult to do so when the *travaux prépara-toires* demonstrate that the drafters were aware of the problem, but rejected or failed to press or adopt proposals tending to open up the convention for accession by the Organization. And this was the factual position, not only in respect of Article 34(1) of the Statute of the Court, but also in respect of the Hague Convention on the Protection of Cultural Property. In these circumstances it is submitted that Article 32 of that Convention must be interpreted literally, as permitting only 'States' to accede, upon the invitation of the Executive Board of UNESCO.[152]

(iii) More doubtful is the question of whether the United Nations could become a party by making *a declaration in accordance with Article 18(3)* referred to above, under (b) *in initio*. When this Article speaks of *'Powers'* it is probably only because it was taken from Article 2 of the Geneva Conventions, so that the difference in wording probably does not represent any deliberate distinction on the part of the drafters. Nevertheless, it does not appear reasonable to interpret this provision any more restrictively here than in the Geneva Conventions, as long as the drafters of the Hague Convention did not manifest any positive desire to prevent the admission of the United Nations (but merely refrained from adopting an explicit provision on such accession because of [erroneously] presumed legal and/or technical difficulties on the side of the UN and because of a [largely justified] belief that there was no practical need for such accession). On the contrary, in a resolution the drafters of the Convention asked the Organization to ensure its application, without restricting the methods by which it should do so. It is accordingly submitted that the United Nations may accede informally to the Hague Convention of 1954 by a declaration under Article 18(3). Otherwise it would not be possible to obtain legal protection under the Convention for cultural property in territory which might come under United Nations authority.[153]

152. A strict interpretation of the term 'State' may also have been the assumption upon which the Special Rapporteur of the International Law Commission based his proposal that the Members of the United Nations extend to the United Nations all international agreements relating to navigation to which they are a party, cf. *above*, note 95. Similarly the term 'le gouvernement d'un pays' in Article 18 of the International Telecommunication Convention of 1959 and 'tout Pays souverain' in Article 3 of the Universal Postal Convention do not comprise the United Nations, cf. *above*, under 9(b).

153. Cf. *above*, Chapters II,8 and IV,3(d), on West New Guinea and other internationalized territories. See also Article 13(2) of the Regulations for the Execution of the 1954 Hague Convention, which provides that, in the event of occupation, the Occupying Power shall be competent to make such application.

(c) *Other conventions. Conclusions*

The conclusion thus is that the United Nations is entitled to accede to the 1907 Hague and the 1949 Geneva Conventions. The same must apply in respect of other conventions on warfare whose accession clauses use similar terms, viz. the Hague Declaration of 29 July 1899 renouncing the use of bullets which expand or flatten easily in the human body, which is open for accession by 'les Puissances non signataires'. On the other hand it is submitted that the United Nations is not entitled to accede formally to the 1954 Hague Convention on the Protection of Cultural Property. The same may even be true of the earlier conventions which are open for accession by 'States' only, since it may be inappropriate to apply an *accession* clause by analogy, even if the object of the analogy manifestly came into being only after the convention had been concluded. This would then apply to the Paris Declaration of 16 April 1856 on maritime warfare, to the St. Petersburg Declaration of 29 November and 11 December 1868 on the use of certain projectiles, and to the Geneva Protocol of 17 June 1925 prohibiting the use of asphyxiating, poisonous or other gases and of bacteriological methods of warfare.[154] But the United Nations may probably accede to the 1954 Hague Convention in the informal way laid down in its Article 18(3).

Even in those cases where the United Nations is not entitled to accede under the terms of the convention, there is nothing to prevent the Organization from making a declaration of acceptance which the depository State or Organization [155] can submit to the contracting parties. The convention will then become binding in relation to any power which accepts the declaration.

11. SUBSTANTIVE CAPACITY OF THE UNITED NATIONS TO IMPLEMENT THE LAWS OF WAR AND THE CONVENTIONS ON WARFARE. CRIMINAL JURISDICTION

Before giving a final answer to the question of whether the United Nations can accede to the Geneva Conventions and the other conventions on warfare, it is necessary to ascertain whether the substantive provisions of these conventions lend themselves to application by the Organization.

It has already been pointed out that the drafters of the conventions had only States in mind and did not take United Nations actions into

---

154. This protocol has been largely relied upon in connexion with the outlawry of nuclear weapons, see *above*, Chapter VI,3(f)(iv).
155. UNESCO is the depository of the 1954 Hague Convention.

consideration. They therefore drafted the provisions on the assumption that these would be applied by States (although the drafters of the Geneva Conventions carefully avoided to use that restrictive term).[156] This may of course lead to difficulties in certain respects, because the United Nations is not a State and does not have the same physical and legal means at its disposal as States have.

It is not possible within the scope of the present study to discuss all aspects of these problems, and especially not the practical aspects. The latter clearly call for a separate study. It is necessary to concentrate mainly upon the legal aspects, and to deal with these in a general way, singling out for concrete study only those provisions which appear to present the greatest difficulties.

(a) *Capacities relevant to the laws of war in general*

(i) Difficulties do not, in principle, arise in respect of those conventions, or parts of conventions, which deal with purely military operational matters. The basic conditions for ability to implement such provisions are possession of armed forces and command over these. And the present discussion is precisely concerned with cases where the United Nations has armed forces, and where these are under the operational command of the Organization; if they are under national command accession to the conventions is required of the participating States, rather than of the United Nations.[157] That the relevant operational control over the peace-keeping Forces is vested in the Organization is clearly reflected in the following statement by Draper on the United Nations Force in the Congo:

> The really effective operational decisions affecting the Force, particularly those relating to the use of particular weapons, their employment against specified objectives and the occasions for their use, are made at the frequent meetings between the Secretary-General and his Advisory Committee.[157a]

Nevertheless, problems arise in connection with the internal enforcement of the laws of war and the conventions on warfare; these will be discussed below, under (ii).

Several conventions, and in particular the Geneva Conventions, refer to *agreements* to be concluded between the parties to the conflict. It has already been pointed out that the United Nations has the capacity to conclude international agreements.[158] This capacity extends also to agreements incidental to military operations. Indeed, as already point-

---

156. *Above*, pp. 346 and 348.
157. *Above*, under 2–4.
157a. *International and Comparative Law Quarterly*, XII, (1963) p. 395.
158. *Above*, under 9, cf. Chapter IV,3(c).

ed out, the United Nations has in fact concluded such agreements, not only with the host State and the States providing contingents, but also with the opposing side, for example armistice agreements.[159] There is no doubt that the Organization has the capacity to conclude also the many other types of agreements envisaged in the Geneva Conventions.[160]

It has also been pointed out above that the United Nations has an inherent capacity to exercise *territorial jurisdiction,* and that it and its predecessor, the League of Nations, have in fact exercised full territorial jurisdiction in certain cases (West New Guinea and the Saar).[161] The inherent capacity of the United Nations in this respect appears to have been assumed already at the San Francisco Conference, in connexion with the withdrawal of the Norwegian proposal to state explicitly in the Charter that the Security Council may 'take over on behalf of the Organization the administration of any territory of which the continued administration by the state in possession is found to constitute a threat to the peace'.[162] Thus there is no legal obstacle to the United Nations assuming the legislative, administrative, judicial and other functions which devolve upon an occupying power under Articles 42 et seq. of the Regulations on Land Warfare annexed to the Fourth Hague Convention of 1907 and under the Geneva Convention of 1949 Relative to the Protection of Civilian Persons in Time of War.

Even if it has no territory in the proper sense, the United Nations can still exercise similar powers outside the territorial jurisdiction of any State [163] in respect of *ships, aircraft and space vehicles* which have been registered with the Organization (and fly its flag), rather than with a State. So far there has been little need for the Organization to exercise territorial jurisdiction over these, because in most cases ships and aircraft have been lent by Member States and have remained on their register, even if they fly the United Nations flag. However, it has happened that ships have been acquired by the United Nations as its property and have been registered with that Organization in lieu of national

159. *Above,* Chapter III,3(a).

160. See, for example, the agreements referred to in Article 6 of the first three Geneva Conventions and in Article 7 of the fourth Geneva Convention and in the many articles cited in these provisions, including e.g. Articles 65, 66, 73, 111, 118 and 119 of the Prisoners of War Convention. Most of these provisions refer to agreements concluded between 'the High Contracting Parties' or 'the Parties to the conflict'.

161. *Above,* Chapter IV,3(d).

162. *Ibid. in fine,* note 95.

163. On the position of ships in the territorial sea, see Articles 14–23 of the Convention on the Territorial Sea and the Contiguous Zone of 29 April 1958. On criminal jurisdiction over aircraft while in the air above national and international land or sea territory, see Articles 1 and 3–4 of the Convention on Offences and Certain Other Acts Committed on Board Aircraft of 14 September 1963.

registration.[164] In such cases the Organization has the legal capacity to exercise the territorial legislative, administrative and judicial powers in respect of the vessel while it is outside the territory of any State, or, if the Organization prefers (because it has no law, or no land territory in which its courts may sit, or for other practical reasons), to delegate these powers to a State of its choice.[165] This is, in principle, true also of criminal jurisdiction, although, as will be discussed in greater detail below, under (ii)-(iii), the competence to exercise such jurisdiction over *military personnel* is governed by the terms of the agreements concluded by the United Nations with the States providing contingents, rather than by territorial criteria.—Accordingly it is submitted that the Organization has the legal capacity to exercise even 'territorial' jurisdiction, both in respect of the ships, aircraft and space vehicles of its own Force, to the extent that these are not subject to the jurisdiction of the State providing them or of the State in whose territory they operate, and in respect of any *prizes* taken by its Force.

However, the jurisdiction over the members of the Force and officials of the Organization, including the crew of its ships and aircraft, is to a great extent based, not upon territorial, but upon *organic* criteria. It has already been pointed out that the Organization has an inherent capacity to exercise organic jurisdiction over the members of its Force and its other organs, including fuctional protection.[166] It will be demonstrated below, under (ii), that this organic jurisdiction implies a competence to assume even criminal jurisdiction over officials and other members of the Force,[167] even outside territory under United Nations jurisdiction, to the extent that the host State is not entitled to exercise such jurisdiction (on a territorial basis) and to the extent that the States providing contingents have not retained an exclusive right to do so (on a personal or organic basis).

These are but three examples of the earlier submission that the United Nations has an inherent legal capacity to perform any type of sovereign or international act which it is in a practical position to perform.[168] The Organization also has the legal capacity to perform other acts incidental

---

164. See the practice listed *above*, note 99.

165. See the present writer's article on 'Jurisdiction over Organs and Officials of States, the Holy See and Intergovernmental Organizations' in *International and Comparative Law Quarterly*, XIV (1965) at p. 49, and, for criminal jurisdiction, *below*, note 199.

166. *Above*, pp. 144–145 and 163, cf. pp. 91–98 and 112–6, and, more fully, in *International and Comparative Law Quarterly*, XIV (1965) pp. 33 et seq. and 493 et seq.

167. Cf. the case of the Casablanca deserters, as reported *ibid.*, pp. 35–36.

168. *Above*, Chapter IV,3 (f)—(g) and, more fully, in *Indian Journal of International Law*, IV (1964) pp. 1 et seq.

to warfare. Thus there is no legal obstacle to it establishing its own prize law and prize courts,[169] except that it needs the permission of any State in whose territory such courts would sit. In this respect there is no practice.

(ii) Problems arose in the Congo out of the fact that national contingents are not as effectively under United Nations control as are the component parts of a national army, and in particular out of the fact that responsibility for criminal and (largely) disciplinary matters vests in the national authorities.[170] The Military Adviser to the Secretary-General of the United Nations, Maj. Gen. Rikhye, referred to this at the Oslo Conference in 1964, in the following terms:

> The fact that the UN Force Commander does not have disciplinary powers over the national contingents under his command is a potential liability that should be, and probably could be partially avoided if a set of regulations could be formulated and accepted by all countries earmarking units.
>
> Equally there is need on the part of some countries to authorise special disciplinary powers in the field. At present their men are tried for offences committed on UN service under national codes in their national courts. Since these courts cannot meet in the field this is often a cumbrous and ineffective process.
>
> UN troops enjoy immunities in regard to local laws under UN status agreements with the governments of the area of operations. Such immunities place a heavy responsibility upon the UN organisation and its Secretary-General. It would therefore be extremely undesirable if breaches and flagrant violations of local laws, rules and regulations occur without check and the culprits go without suitable disciplinary action. It is said with great regret that there have been a few cases, including major crimes, in which the governments concerned were not disposed to make the necessary investigations and to take suitable disciplinary action against the culprits. The impact of this attitude on the reputation, discipline and morale of a UN force, and the great concern that it causes to the government of the country where UN troops are deployed, as well as on other governments, needs no emphasis. The whole question of discipline in the field in a UN military command needs the urgent attention of Member States who intend to continue generously supporting the UN efforts in this field.[171]

The best way of avoiding these difficulties would of course be *if the United Nations itself could assume criminal and disciplinary jurisdiction over the members of the Force.*[172] In the case of an individually re-

---

169. This problem and that dealt with two paragraphs above have been raised by *Bowett: United Nations Forces* (London 1964) p. 515.

170. *Above*, Chapter II,7(e).

171. *Frydenberg: Peace-Keeping, Experience and Evaluation—The Oslo Papers* (Oslo 1964) p. 191. The summary of the subsequent discussion at the conference, as summarized *ibid.*, p. 310, appears to have been concerned rather with the question of external responsibility (which the United Nations *has* assumed, cf. *above*, Chapter III,4(a)), pp. 108–10. Nevertheless, the measures suggested by Gen. Rikhye have since been taken or proposed in Scandinavia. See also *below*, p. 376.

172. *Clark and Sohn: World Peace through World Law*, 2nd edition (Cambridge, Mass. 1960) p. 311, proposes this, although only within the areas leased by the United Nations for the use of the Peace Force. They do not seem to be specifically concerned

cruited Force the Organization would probably *have* to do so. However, the Forces which have so far been established have been composed of national contingents, and the States providing these have not been willing to cede to the Organization their powers in this respect, for the reasons set forth above Chapter III,2(a) *in fine*. Many international lawyers appear to assume that the Organization would not even have the legal *capacity* to accept and exercise such jurisdiction.[173] This assumption is probably based upon the common view, discussed above, Chapter III,3, that an intergovernmental organization can only exercise such powers as its particular constitution authorizes it to exercise, expressly or by implication. As has been demonstrated, this view is contradicted by practice,[174] nor is it theoretically well founded.[175] It was submitted that the correct view is that, subject to certain limitations, the Organization can exercise any sovereign (and international) act which it is in a factual position to perform. The capacity to exercise criminal jurisdiction can be no exception. A different matter is that the United Nations rarely has been in a factual positon to exercise this capacity, because it would require a cession to the Organization of powers which States usually do not cede to others. However, in those few cases where intergovernmental organizations have been in a factual position to exercise criminal jurisdiction, they have not hesitated to do so. In view of the negative attitude of international lawyers on this point, it is necessary to go into some detail in order to explain why, in the view of the present writer, there can be no doubt that the UN has this capacity.

It has already been pointed out that the United Nations, like other intergovernmental organizations, exercises exclusive jurisdiction over its organs and officials in that capacity. This comprises both legislative, administrative and judicial powers.[176] This jurisdiction extends also to the members of national contingents placed under the authority of the Organization, to the extent that the States providing them have not retained such powers.

---

with war-time offences. *Bowett: United Nations Forces* (London 1964) pp. 353 and 488, straightly considers that it would be preferable if the Command of a permanent United Nations Force could have disciplinary authority. United Nations criminal jurisdiction is also proposed by La Ligue Belge pour la Défense des Droits de l'Homme and by Paul de Visscher in *Revue de droit international et de droit comparé* (Brussels) 1963 pp. 176 and 180.

173. The writers cited in the preceding note can hardly be worried about this (cf. however, *Bowett, op. cit.*, p. 515, and the fact that *Clark and Sohn* tend to make it a territorial power).

174. *Above*, Chapter IV,3(b)—(e) and Chapter VIII,9 and *Indian Journal of International Law*, IV (1964) pp. 1 et seq.

175. *Ibid.*, especially pp. 59 et seq.

176. *Above*, Chapter IV,3(b) and, more fully, in *International and Comparative Law Quarterly*, XIV (1965) at pp. 52 et seq. and 496 et seq.

Thus there can be no doubt about the legal capacity of the United Nations to enact the necessary *legislation* (regulations) and to issue the necessary administrative instructions of a substantive nature. This power it exercises in part already to-day in respect of its peace-keeping Forces. The Organization assumed and partly exercised the power by paragraph 7 of General Assembly resolution 1001 (ES-I), by the Regulations which the Secretary-General enacted for the several Forces [177] and by the numerous supplemental instructions and command orders which were issued pursuant to these.[178] This was confirmed by references to that part of the resolution and to the Regulations in those formal agreements which were subsequently concluded with States providing contingents and to which the Regulations were annexed.[179] It is true that these same Regulations provide that 'members of the Force shall remain subject to the military rules and regulations of their respective national States'. However, the Regulations go immediately on to make the reservation 'without derogating from their responsibilities as members of the Force as defined in these Regulations and any rules made pursuant thereto'.[180] This means that United Nations regulations supersede national regulations outside those fields which have been reserved for national competence in accordance with the other provisions of the Regulations. Even the United Nations Command in Korea found it necessary to enact certain regulations valid for the Force as a whole; despite the fact that in this case the international responsibility, including responsibility for the application of the laws of war, was vested in the participating States;[181] it is recalled, however, that the United Nations Command for its part appears to have assumed that it vested in the United Nations.[182] In particular, the United Nations Command on 14 October 1952 issued 'Operation Instructions Reference Enemy Prisoners of War' to supplement the Geneva Convention and to provide for uniform administration, security and treatment of prisoners of war captured by the Forces of the United Nations Command,[183] including those guarded by South Korean forces.[184]

On the other hand, the United Nations has not yet assumed *criminal jurisdiction* in respect of violations of the laws of war or of its own sub-

---

177. See notably the Regulation quoted *above*, Chapter V,2(b)(i).
178. See UNEF Regulations 2–4, cf. Regulations 6, 11–12 and 31, and ONUC and UNFICYP Regulations 2–4, 6, 11–12 and 26.
179. See, for example, *UNTS*, Vol. 271, pp. 136–7.
180. UNEF Regulation 34(c), ONUC and UNFICYP Regulation 29(c).
181. *Above*, Chapter III,6(c).
182. *Above*, Chapter V,2(a) *in fine*.
183. *United Nations Command Pamphlet No. 1*.
184. *Vachter: The Story of the Korean Military Armistice Negotiations* (New York 1953) p. 197.

stantive regulations. Although the Organization has a limited power of arrest over members of its peace-keeping Forces,[185] it has neither enacted criminal law, nor has it established courts by which offenders could be tried. On the contrary, the Regulations for the United Nations peace-keeping Forces reserve criminal jurisdiction and (largely) disciplinary powers to the national authorities,[186] despite the fact that the international responsibility also in this respect vests in the United Nations.[187]

Intergovernmental organizations generally exercise *disciplinary* powers over their officials.[188] The disciplinary measures may include not only demotion, suspension (with or without salary) or dismissal, but also financial sanctions, such as reduction of salary for a specified period,[189] reduction or revocation of pension,[190] or a direct fine.[191]

However, no intergovernmental organization is known to have exercised genuine *criminal* jurisdiction over its *officials*. Indeed, even if an Organization did enact criminal law, it could not enforce it in the territory of the host State or any other State without its consent. On the other hand, certain intergovernmental organizations have exercised criminal jurisdiction in territory or over persons placed under their full or partial jurisdiction by their constitution or by other agreement,[192] although, in those cases where the Organizations did not have the full

185. Host agreements with Egypt, par. 14 (*UNTS*, Vol. 260, p. 68), with the Congo, par. 12 (*OR SC*, 1961, Suppl. for October–December, p. 155), and with Cyprus, par. 14; UNEF Regulation 14, ONUC and UNFICYP Regulation 15.

186. UNEF Regulation 13–14 and 34, ONUC and UNFICYP Regulations 13–15 and 29. Text *below*, p. 439.

187. *Above*, p. 102 and *below*, Annex 1, p. 428, see also paras. 6 *in fine* and 9 *in fine* of the host agreement with Egypt, para. 1 of the host agreement with the Congo, and paras. 5 and 9 of the host agreement with Cyprus.

188. As for the United Nations, see *Repertory of Practice of United Nations Organs*, V, pp. 254 et seq.

189. *Règlement de l'Institut international pour l'unification du droit privé*, adopted by the General Assembly on 18 January 1952, Article 64 (not exceeding two months), *UNIDROIT, Assemblée générale, 1ère session (1951–52), Procès-verbaux et documents*, p. 55 and Annexe IV.

190. *Statut des fonctionnaires de la Communauté économique européenne et de la Communauté européenne de l'énergie atomique*, Article 86 (*Journal officiel des Communautés européennes*, V [1962] p. 1406).

191. Staff Regulations of the Scandinavian Training Hospital in Korea, adopted by the (Scandinavian) Committee on 7 June 1957, Chapter XIII(1)(b)(iii) ('fine not exceeding ½ month's salary').

192. Thus in the case of *condominia* or *coimperia* governed by an intergovernmental organization set up for that purpose (see, however, the case concerning the Inter-Allied Rhineland High Commission reported in *Annual Digest of Public International Law Cases*, 1925–26, Case No. 36) and of certain internationalized territories, for example the Saar as governed by the League of Nations under Articles 45–50 of the Treaty of Versailles from 1920 to 1935.

territorial jurisdiction, the sanctions so far consisted in fines rather than in confinement.[193]

Similarly, it is submitted that the United Nations has the capacity to establish criminal law and to enforce it vis-à-vis any persons who may be placed under its jurisdiction also in this (criminal) respect by the State concerned, provided that the State in whose territory the criminal law is enforced agrees. Thus, as has already been submitted,[194] the Organization would be fully competent to establish a criminal code and to set up courts to try members of its Forces accused of violations of the laws of war if the States providing contingents should cede their criminal jurisdiction to the Organization or place their contingents under the authority of the Organization without reservation as to criminal jurisdiction,[195] and if the Organization does not enforce its criminal law in the territory of any State which does not agree.

However, the competence of the United Nations goes further than that. It is submitted that its competence is not contingent upon the consent of the States under whose jurisdiction the individuals normally belong [195a] (but only upon the consent of the State in whose territory the jurisdiction is enforced if it is enforced in territory under the jurisdiction of any State), if the offence has such points of attachment to the Organization as under general principles of international criminal law entitle it to exercise jurisdiction. It is not necessary for the purposes of the present study to determine what these principles are [196] and whether or

193. Thus in the cases of international river commissions, including the European Commission of the Danube (cf. *Cour permanente de Justice internationale*, Sér. B, No. 14) and the Central Commission of the Rhine, and the European Coal and Steel Community (Articles 65(5) and 66(5)–(6), cf. Articles 33 and 36 and 92, of the constitution provide for 'amendes', 'astreintes' and 'sanctions pécuniaires', see on these measures *Krawielicki: Das Monopolverbot im Schuman-Plan* (Tübingen 1952) pp. 36 et seq. and 86 et seq.).

194. *Above*, Chapter III,2(a) *in fine*.

195. This was envisaged, ultimately, by the abortive Treaty Constituting the European Defence Community of 27 May 1952, under which a common criminal code and a common judicial system was to be established at a future date, see Article 79 of the Treaty and Articles 18 et seq. of the *Protocole juridictionnel*. Meanwhile the national courts would function 'par délégation de la Communauté'.

195a. Except to the extent that these States have specifically reserved exclusive jurisdiction, as they have in respect of members of their national contingents.

196. Cf. *Skeie: Den norske strafferett*, 2nd edition (Oslo 1946) I, pp. 82 et seq., and *Andenaes: Alminnelig strafferett* (Oslo 1956) pp. 499 et seq. Wright defines them in a negative sense, in *AJIL*, XXXIX (1945) p. 270, as follows:

'While it is often held that a state must show a positive authority from international law or treaties for any exercise of criminal jurisdiction over aliens beyond its own domain or its ships at sea, it was held by the Permanent Court of International Justice in the case of the Lotus that:

Restrictions upon the independence of states cannot be presumed ... all that can be required of a state is that it should not overstep the limits which inter-not they apply to intergovernmental organizations, which have no territory of their own, in the same manner as to States, by simple analogy, and in particular where the relevant *limits* under *public* international law are to be drawn. It will suffice to state certain cases, relevant to United Nations enforcement actions, where the United Nations no doubt can assume criminal jurisdiction without asking the permission of national authorities in whose territory the jurisdiction is not actually exercised.

In the first place the United Nations can assume jurisdiction, and indeed has assumed jurisdiction, on the basis of *territorial* attachment, in respect of offences committed in a territory which has been brought under its jurisdiction. Such jurisdiction it may obtain by virtue of a cession from the State to which the territory belongs, as it did in West New Guinea (Irian Barat) in 1962.[197] Or it can obtain jurisdiction by occupation, including military occupation in the course of an armed conflict.[198] The same is true of offences committed outside the jurisdiction of any State on board ships flying the United Nations flag, on aircraft registered with the United Nations and on space ships launched by it.[199] On the other hand, the Organization is debarred from exercising crim-

national law places upon its jurisdiction; within these limits, its title to exercise jurisdiction rests in its sovereignty ... The territoriality of criminal law, therefore, is not an absolute principle of international law and by no means coincides with territorial sovereignty.

There appears to be a general rule of international law forbidding states to exercise criminal jurisdiction over acts committed by aliens in foreign territory but there is an exception if the act was directed against the security of the state and was not protected by the law of the state where committed'.—§ 12 of the Norwegian Criminal Code of 22 May 1902 goes much further, but see § 14.

197. The United Nations constituted its first court of justice in West New Guinea on 10 November 1962 *(United Nations Review,* IX [1962] No. 12, p. 26, cf. *above,* Chapters II,8 and IV,3(d)).

198. Cf. Articles 64 et seq. of the Geneva Convention on the Protection of Civilian Persons.

199. Cf. *above,* under (i) and note 99. A different matter is that the Organization in many such cases might find it more convenient to delegate the jurisdiction to one Member State. Thus Article 18 of the Tokyo Convention of 14 September 1963 on Offences and Certain Other Acts Occurring on Board Aircraft provides that 'if Contracting States establish joint air transport operating organizations or international operating agencies, which operate aircraft not registered in any one State those States shall, according to the circumstances of the case, designate the State among them which, *for the purposes of this Convention* [i.e. for purposes of criminal jurisdiction], shall be considered as the State of registration' (italics added). Cf. Article 77 of the Convention on International Civil Aviation of 7 December 1944 (the ICAO constitution). As for ships, see Article 7 of the Convention on the High Seas of 29 April 1958, *United Nations Conference on the Law of the Sea,* Official Records, IV, pp. 138–40, and *Yearbook of the International Law Commission,* 1956, II, pp. 102–3 and 279.

inal jurisdiction on the basis of *territorial* attachment over crimes committed within its headquarters district, by § 10 of its headquarters agreement, under which the United States has expressly reserved for itself the power to impose penalties other than expulsion or exclusion from the headquarters district.

In the second place, the United Nations could probably exercise criminal jurisdiction over its *officials* with regard to their official acts. Actually, the Organization is the only authority which can do this, because States are debarred from doing so without the consent of the Organization. Those Member States which have acceded to the Convention on the Privileges and Immunities of the United Nations have expressly recognized the immunity of United Nations officials in respect of official acts (§ 18a of the Convention). Other Members have the same obligation under Article 105(3) of the Charter.[200] And even in the absence of any such express provision, it is submitted that international officials enjoy immunity in respect of official acts to the same extent as State officials do.—The Organization would exercise any such criminal jurisdiction on the basis of *organic* attachment. This competence therefore exists irrespective of *where* the act was committed. It exists even in respect of acts committed within the headquarters district, since §§ 7-10 of the headquarters agreement and the reservations contained therein only concern powers exercised on the basis of territorial attachment.

In the third place it is submitted that the United Nations, on the basis of the customary laws of war, has the same right as other belligerent Powers to prosecute members of the opposing forces who have committed war crimes,[201] and prisoners of war who have committed postcapture offences.[202] The United Nations Command in Korea enacted a number of articles, rules and regulations on these subjects,[203] although

---

200. On the partly parallel problem in respect of civil disputes arising out of official acts of international officials, and out of any acts of members of United Nations Forces, see an article by the present writer, entitled 'Settlement of Internal Disputes of Intergovernmental Organizations by Internal and External Courts', in *Zeitschrift für ausländisches öffentliches Recht und Völkerrecht*, XXIV (1964) at pp. 22–31.

201. The unfounded objection that this would require *national* regulations has been adequately answered by Quincy Wright: 'War Criminals' in *AJIL*, XXXIX (1945) at pp. 276–7, although in the context of the Allied 'United Nations' during the Second World War.

202. Both of these rights have been recognized in the Geneva Conventions, see notably Article 99, cf. Article 85, of the Prisoners of War Convention and Article 70 of the Convention on Civilians.

203. Concerning the trial of war criminals, see 'Rules of Procedure for Military Commissions of the United Nations Command' of 22 October 1950. Concerning prisoners of war, see 'Supplemental Rules of Criminal Procedure for Military Commissions of the United Nations Command' conducting trials of prisoners of war charged with postcapture offences of 6 October 1951; Rules of 'Procedure Governing Nonjudicial Punishment of Prisoners of War' applicable to all prisoners of war or other

these would be relevant in the present context only if one were to accept the view, which appears to have been that of the United Nations Command at the time, that the United Nations had the international responsibility for the Force in Korea.[204]

It should be added, however, that the United Nations could not actually exercise its criminal jurisdiction in the territory of any State without its consent. Therefore the examples given above will remain theoretical unless the United Nations Forces have occupied the aggressor's territory or unless the Organization obtains the consent of the State where its Force is stationed or operates, or of another friendly State, to establish courts in its territory, and to confine accused or convicted persons there (or, alternatively, delegates the power to execute the judgments to the State).

(iii) However, even if such consent is obtained, the question of the United Nations assuming *criminal jurisdiction over the members of its Forces* will remain theoretical as long as these are composed, not of personnel recruited individually, but of national contingents, and as long as the States providing these contingents—for the political, legal and other reasons referred to above—wish to retain the criminal powers for themselves. Some States may even be required to do so by their constitutions, although the new provisions which many States have adopted in recent years in order to allow delegation of powers to intergovernmental organizations will overcome such constitutional difficulties.[205]

In these circumstances the question arises whether the Conventions require the Organization itself to exercise criminal jurisdiction, or whether they permit it to rely upon the States providing contingents to do so. On this subject the Geneva Conventions contain a provision which obviously was not written with the United Nations in mind. It reads:

> The High Contracting Parties undertake to enact any legislation necessary to provide effective penal sanctions for persons committing, or ordering to be committed, any of the grave breaches of the present Convention defined in the following Article.
>
> Each High Contracting Party shall be under the obligation to search for persons alleged to have committed, or to have ordered to be committed, such grave breaches, and shall bring such persons, regardless of their nationality, before its own courts. It may also, if it prefers, and in accordance with the provisions

persons detained or interned by the United Nations Command of 19 October 1951; 'Articles Governing United Nations Prisoners of War' of 23 October 1951, which list and define the offences for the commission of which a prisoner of war 'shall be punished as a military commission may direct' (the penalties were not specified, except for a specification of those cases where the death sentence might be imposed); and 'Regulations governing the penal confinement of prisoners of war' of 23 September 1952. (*United Nations Command Pamphlet No. 1.*)

204. Cf. *above*, pp. 110–2 and 187—8.

205. Thus for example § 93 of the Norwegian constitution, as adopted in 1962.

of its own legislation, hand such persons over for trial to another High Contracting Party concerned, provided such High Contracting Party has made out a *prima facie* case.

Each High Contracting Party shall take measures necessary for the suppression of all acts contrary to the provisions of the present Convention other than the grave breaches defined in the following Article.[206]

It follows from the second paragraph that the United Nations need not itself prosecute war criminals if it instead hands them over to another contracting party which has made out a *prima facie* case. The last words seem to indicate that the drafters had in mind States victims of the breaches. However, the words are not confined to such States. They are not even confined to parties to the conflict. It has been pointed out above, pp. 351–352, that conventions must not be interpreted to cover only such cases as the drafters had in mind, if neither the words, nor the purpose and spirit, of the conventions require such restrictive interpretation. In the present case the purpose of the specific provisions concerned —just and effective prosecution of the offender—will be achieved if he is handed over to a State which is able and willing to prosecute him. If the provisions were to preclude handing over to the States providing contingents, the result would be that, as long as these are unwilling or unable to cede jurisdictional powers to the United Nations, the Geneva Conventions could not be made applicable to United Nations Forces under the Organization's command, and that neither the members of the Forces, nor their opponents, would be legally protected by the Conventions insofar as their provisions go beyond customary law. This result would contrast sharply with the purpose and the wide scope of the Conventions.[207] Such an interpretation could therefore not be admitted unless the words of the provisions really were restrictive, which they are not. Accordingly it is submitted that the provisions quoted above do not require the United Nations to try persons who have committed war crimes before its own courts, but that they permit the Organization to *leave it for the States providing contingents to try any member of their contingent*, provided that these States are parties to the Geneva Conventions.[208] However, the United Nations must see to it that they real-

206. First Convention, Article 49; Second Convention, Article 50; Third Convention, Article 129; Fourth Convention, Article 146.

207. *Above*, pp. 348–50.

208. The drafters of the Geneva Conventions did not wish to exclude the handing over of the accused to an *international* criminal court whose competence has been recognised by the contracting parties (*Comité international de la Croix-Rouge: Commentaire à la Convention de Genève relative au traitement des prisonniers de guerre*, Genève 1958, p. 658 [Article 129(2)]). An international court would legally be very different from an internal court of the United Nations, as discussed in the text, see an article by the present writer on 'Settlement of Internal Disputes of Intergovernmental Organizations by Internal and External Courts' in *Zeitschrift für ausländisches*

ly do so and becomes internationally responsible if it does not. It is submitted, furthermore, that the United Nations does not have to require these States to make out a *prima facie* case if the Organization itself has sufficient evidence for this purpose and turns this over to the State concerned.—The third paragraph of the provisions must be interpreted in the light of this, i.e. also in respect of minor offences the United Nations must have a choice as to whether prosecution shall be performed by the Organization or by the States providing contingents.[209] It would seem to follow logically that even the criminal legislation referred to in the first paragraph could be enacted by the States providing contingents in lieu of the Organization, provided that they are parties to the Conventions. However, the wording of the first paragraph may also lend itself to a strict interpretation, requiring the Organization itself to enact the legislation. In that case the United Nations will have to do so — but it can, if it prefers, do so by adopting by reference the criminal law of each contracting party which has provided a contingent for the members of that contingent.[210] In these circumstances it would hardly be necessary for the Organization to make any reservation in this respect upon accession to the Conventions.[211]

Draper takes a different view. He considers that the United Nations, because it lacks disciplinary and criminal powers over the commander and the members of the Force, is not in a position to implement Article 3 of the Fourth Hague Convention of 1907, which provides that the belligerent party shall be 'responsable de tous actes commis par les personnes faisant partie de sa force armée' or Article 1(1) of the attached Regulations Concerning the Laws and Customs of Land Warfare, which provide that 'corps de volontaires' shall have 'à leur tête une personne responsable pour ses subordonnés'. He admits that this objection logically applies also in respect of the *customary* laws of war, and he appears to

---

öffentliches Recht und Völkerrecht, XXVI (1964) at pp. 61 et seq.—This may have been realized by the 46 civilian doctors in Elizabethville when they demanded the establishment of an *international* tribunal, see *above*, Chapter V,2(b)(iii).

209. According to the *Comité international de la Croix-Rouge's Commentaire à la Convention de Genève relative au traitement des prisonniers de guerre* (Genève 1958) pp. 658–9, the third paragraph, too, requires criminal prosecution and not merely administrative measures.

210. Article 16 of the Prisoners of War Convention provides that 'all prisoners of war shall be treated alike by the Detaining Power, without any adverse distinction based on race, nationality, religious belief or political opinions, or any other distinction founded on similar criteria'. A similar provision is contained in Article 27 of the Civilians Convention. This appears to preclude discrimination based upon the varying conditions of the prisoners or civilians, rather than such discrimination as derives from the varying conditions of the Detaining or Occupying Power.

211. See *below*, p. 382.

draw the conclusion that neither the conventions on warfare, nor the customary laws of war may be applicable to a United Nations Force. He is speaking only of 'an international Force which is part of a subsidiary organ of the United Nations' and only of laws relating to 'the use of weapons'.[212] However, if his conclusion were adopted, it would probably logically have to apply to any Force under United Nations command and responsibility and to any other parts of the laws of war.

In the view of the present writer the provisions referred to by Draper do not raise the question of *what* laws are applicable, but of who is externally responsible for the observance of whatever laws are applicable. It has already been explained why, in the view of the present writer, the crucial criterion of international responsibility is who has operational command, rather than who has criminal and disciplinary jurisdiction over the members of the Force.[213] If it were a condition for the international responsibility of the Organization that it can itself exercise direct criminal and disciplinary jurisdiction over the members of the Force, the answer could not be that the laws of war (or some special laws, if the conclusions in Chapters V-VI above are not accepted) do not apply, but that the international responsibility for the Force would have to vest in the States providing contingents. The problems discussed in sections 5-14 of the present chapter would then not arise at all. The international responsibility for the Force would vest in the States providing contingents also for the purpose of the *general* laws of war, and the problems discussed above in Chapter V,3(c) would not arise either.

The present writer must, however, retain his earlier conclusions (which conform with practice) that, if the United Nations has operational control over the Force, and this it had in the Congo,[213a] it must also bear the international responsibility for it, and that it is bound to observe the general laws of war, and even the conventions on warfare if it is a party to these. It is the international responsibility of the Organization to ensure that the Force complies with these laws. But it does not *have* to fulfil this responsibility by itself directly inflicting the necessary sanctions upon any offenders. It can leave this for the States providing the contingents to do in conformity with their national law,[213b] provided that this conforms with the applicable conventions and other rules of international law, and provided that the Organization sees to it that this law is enforced. However, within its own field of competence the

212. 'The Legal Limitations upon the Employment of Weapons by the United Nations Force in the Congo', *International and Comparative Law Quarterly*, XII (1963) pp. 408–9.

213. *Above*, Chapter III,2(a) *in fine*, cf. 6(b).

213a. See Draper as quoted *above*, at note 157a.

213b. Cf. the discussion of Ross' contrary view *above*, Chapter III,2(a).

Organization must of course itself take any measures to ensure compliance. In particular it must conform its own operational instructions to the applicable laws of war. For the rest, it must make arrangements with the States providing contingents to ensure that these take the necessary measures within those fields of competence where they have retained authority or where they have a factual control. If the States are themselves parties to the conventions on warfare, they even have a pre-existing duty to do their part to ensure the observance of the provisions of these conventions.[214] In particular, the States concerned must teach the members of their contingents the laws of war and instruct them to observe these. Since 1966 the United Nations has included specific provisions in this sense in its agreements with the States providing contingents. Moreover, the States providing contingents must undertake to prosecute offenders. Provisions to this effect were included already in the agreements between the United Nations and the States providing contingents to UNEF.[215] Firmer provisions were included in the agreements with the States providing contingents to Cyprus, see below, pp. 444–5, esp. pars. 7 and 11. The latter paragraph also refers specifically to enforcement of the Geneva (and 1954 Hague) Conventions.

Even if the criminal jurisdiction rests with the 'participating' States, this does not preclude the United Nations from establishing certain services and procedures of its own to assist them in their tasks and to verify —to the satisfaction of the Organization and of the authorities representing the persons who have suffered, or would be liable to suffer, injury or damage—that the necessary measures have been taken. The Organization has, in the Regulations for its more recent Forces, provided that the Commander of the Force 'may make investigations, conduct inquiries and require information, reports and consultations for the purpose of discharging' his 'general responsibility for the good order and discipline of the Force'.[216] Thus, the United Nations may establish its own investigation service and turn the evidence it obtains over to the State responsible for the prosecution.

(b) *Conventional provisions referring to the party's law, courts and conditions*

As already indicated, the problems which have been discussed above are not special to the conventions on warfare. They arise also under the general laws of war, which, in any event, are binding upon the United Nations.[217] The problems referred to therefore arise even if the Organization does *not* accede to the conventions.

214. *Above,* under 5, cf. Articles 129 and 131 of the Prisoners of War Convention.
215. *UNTS,* Vol. 271, pp. 227–8 (para. 7).
216. ONUC and UNFICYP Regulations 13, cf. 14–15, text *below,* p. 439.
217. *Above,* Chapters V–VI. *Contra:* Draper, as reported *above,* at note 212.

Nevertheless, certain problems special to the conventions may arise in respect of those provisions, primarily in the Geneva Conventions, which have not as yet developed into customary law or which have been given a more precise formulation than required under the general laws of war. However, strangely enough, despite the fact that the Geneva Conventions were formulated to fit States, they do not appear to contain any provision which the United Nations could not implement.

The most difficult provisions in addition to the common article on penal sanctions quoted and discussed under (a)(iii), are Articles 82 et seq. of the Prisoners of War Convention. These, like Articles 64 et seq. of the Convention on Civilian Persons, refer on a number of occasions to the (criminal) laws and courts of the Detaining or the Occupying Power.[218] The United Nations does not have any law and courts of its own in these fields. However, as has been pointed out above, the Organization is legally competent to establish its own law, including criminal law, and its own courts.[219]

If the United Nations has the control over the Force and alone is party to the conflict and internationally responsible for the Force, it will probably find that even under the general laws of war the most convenient method of fulfilling its responsibility in respect of prisoners of war, trial of war criminals, occupation of enemy territory, condemnation of prizes, taking of booty etc., is for the Organization to enact its own, uniform regulations and to establish its own courts. Indeed, even the United Nations Command in Korea did this in certain respects,[220] despite the fact that this was an action under *national* command.

On the other hand, there is hardly any of these provisions which pre-

218. See for example Articles 82, 85, 99, 100 and 129 of the Prisoners of War Convention and Articles 64, 68, 71 and 73 of the Convention on Civilians. Some of these provisions are merely permissive. Article 5 *in fine* of the Prisoners of War Convention refers to a non-criminal (civil or military) tribunal of the Detaining Power.

219. In the United Kingdom War Office's *Manual of Military Law*, Part III: The Law of War on Land (London 1958) par. 134, it is stated, inter alia: 'For the purposes of the Convention the Detaining Power must be one State and not a group of States, and cannot be any organisation other than a State. This means in practice that any system of 'international control' of prisoners of war would be inconsistent with the Convention'. In a footnote it is added that an international organization 'would not be entitled to apply a common legal code framed for the purpose of imposing penal and disciplinary sanctions against prisoners of war captured by the armed forces operating on behalf of such an organisation or association. Such a code would be contrary to the requirements of Art. 82'. This is of course true if the United Nations has not itself acceded to the Convention. In Korea, where such a common legal code was enacted (*above*, at note 203), the United Nations Command had accepted the Convention, although in that case, in the view of the present writer (cf. *above*, Chapters III,3(b) and V,3(b)), it did so merely on behalf of the participating States. Baxter *(BYIL,* XXIX [1952] p. 354) considers the Unified Command as distinct from the United States.

220. *Above,* at note 203.

vents the Organization from utilizing the law and the courts of the States providing contingents, under appropriate arrangements, in those respects where it does not find it convenient to establish its own.[221] If the provisions require the party to the conflict to apply *uniform* provisions, the Organization would probably be justified in selecting one of the States providing contingents, provided that it makes its selection in good faith.

The most difficult problems arise out of those provisions which require the Detaining or the Occupying Power to apply the *same* law, courts or conditions as are applicable to members of its own forces or to its own civilian nationals doing similar work,[222] or laws, courts or conditions which are not more severe than those applied to members of its own forces or to its own national workers.[223]

An example of the latter is Article 51 of the Prisoners of War Convention, which provides:

> Prisoners of war must be granted suitable working conditions, especially as regards accommodation, food, clothing and equipment; such conditions shall not be inferior to those enjoyed by nationals of the Detaining Power employed in similar work; account shall also be taken of climatic conditions.

Since the United Nations does not have any nationals, it has no conditions applicable to them. However, it may satisfy the requirements by relying upon the conditions it has established for civilian workers employed by it. This may present certain difficulties if the Organization has civilian workers in different regions of the world, but this is a problem which may arise also in respect of war between national States having territories in several regions. In one case as in the other the Detaining or Occupying Power must be allowed to apply standards adapted to the laws and other conditions of the region where the work is performed. The provisions in Article 16 of the Prisoners of War Convention and in Article 27 of the Convention on Civilians, that the Detaining and Occupying Power shall treat all prisoners and all protected persons alike, can hardly preclude this.

As an example of a provision which refers to the laws, courts and conditions applicable to the members of the Party's own forces the following provision may be quoted:

> Prisoners of war may not be sentenced by the military authorities and courts of the Detaining Power to any penalties except those provided for in respect of

221. The most doubtful provision in this respect is probably that quoted and discussed *above*, under (a)(iii).

222. See Articles 32, 51, 82, 84, 87, 102, 105 and 108 of the Prisoners of War Convention, cf. also Article 73 of the Convention on Civilians.

223. See Articles 20, 25, 46, 51–53, 60, 82, 84, 87, 88, 95, 103 and 106 of the Prisoners of War Convention.

members of the armed forces of the said Power who have committed the same acts.[224]

It has already been pointed out that the Organization has the legal capacity to establish law, and courts (and conditions) if the States providing contingents agree to submit the members thereof to such laws, courts and conditions. However, it has also been pointed out that these States have been unwilling to cede their powers in this respect, because it would meet with internal practical and political difficulties and might require amendment of their laws. At any rate, this could hardly be improvised and would therefore not be possible in respect of contingents placed at the disposal of the United Nations in an emergency, if adequate preparations have not been made in advance.[225] The Organization will therefore at present in most respects have to apply as a (minimum) standard the national laws, courts and conditions of one of the States involved in the action. It is submitted that if the Organization makes its selection of a State for these purposes in good faith, no violation of the conventions is thereby committed. Thus, in respect of labour, the Organization might apply the laws and conditions of the 'participating' State in which the work is performed.[226] In respect of criminal matters, it might apply the law and courts of one of the States providing contingents; at least if the standards of that State are not below the average standards of the other States providing contingents [227] this could not constitute a violation of the Conventions.

(c) *Conclusions. Significance of the Korean experience*

There thus does not appear to be any provision in the conventions on warfare which the United Nations does not have the legal capacity to implement.[228]

224. Article 87 of the Prisoners of War Convention. See also Article 82.

225. Cf. *above*, p. 369, note 195.

226. Cf. Article 23 of the Prisoners of War Convention, which provides that 'prisoners of war shall have shelters against air bombardment and other hazards of war, to the same extent as the local civilian population', and that 'any other protective measure taken in favour of the population shall also apply to them'. These conditions may be inferior to those prevailing in the home country of the prisoners, but this is inherent in the system of the Convention also in respect of war between States, cf. also Article 16 which provides that all prisoners shall be treated alike by the Detaining Power without any adverse distinctions based on nationality or similar criteria.

227. The non-discrimination provision in Article 16 of the Prisoners of War Convention would probably prevent the application of the standards of the prisoners' home countries as a yardstick of 'good faith' in this respect.

228. Strictly the United Nations may not be in a position to benefit fully from the Hague Convention of 21 December 1904 on Hospital Ships, even if it accedes, because that Convention refers to Articles 1–3 of the Hague Conventions of 29 July 1899 for the Adaptation to Maritime Warfare of the Principles of the Geneva Convention of 1864, and because Article 1 of that Convention speaks of 'Etats' (while Articles 2 and 3

In most respects it can implement the conventions without any cession or renunciation of powers normally vested in the States which provide contingents without themselves being parties to the conflict. The action in the Congo has demonstrated that it would be a great advantage if these States would cede part of their criminal jurisdiction to the Organization even if the United Nations does *not* accede to the Conventions. However, no provision of the conventions *requires* that they do so, as long as they themselves effectively exercise such jurisdiction at the request of the Organization. The *host* State may have to concede certain rights to the Organization, but none which it would appear legally or politically impossible for it to concede.

In several respects the Organization will have to enact law and to establish administrative and judicial machinery which it does not possess to-day, or to designate law and courts of the States providing contingents. The problems which arise *for the Organization* in this connexion are of a practical rather than of a legal nature.

It is not possible within the scope of the present study to discuss these and other practical problems which might arise. It must suffice to note that, basically, the practical, like the legal, problems arise in connexion with the application of the general laws of war to a United Nations action under the Organization's own control and international responsibility, even if the United Nations does not accede to the conventions, although in certain respects the problems may become more acute as a result of the fact that many provisions of the Geneva Conventions lay down more precise and detailed obligations than follow from the general laws of war.

It may have been partly the latter consideration which induced the United Nations Command in *Korea* to reject the request of the International Committee of the Red Cross that the United Nations Command undertake to apply the Geneva Conventions. One-year-and-a-half after the outbreak of the war the United Nations Commander stated:

> I have directed the forces under my command to abide by the detailed provisions of the prisoner of war convention, since I have means at my disposal to assure compliance with this convention by all concerned ... I do not have the

speak of 'Puissances'). However, the situation will be different if the reference to the 1899 Convention is considered to have been replaced by a reference to the new Geneva Convention of 1949 on the Amelioration of the Condition of Wounded, Sick and Shipwrecked Members of Armed Forces at Sea, as between those contracting parties which are also contracting parties to the latter Convention, since in that Convention the term 'Puissances' has been substituted for 'Etats' (Article 22). On the interpretation of these terms, see *above*, under 10. Or one may consider that the 1899 Convention has now become customary law and that the applicability of its provisions no longer is confined to the field which their precise terms cover.

authority to accept, nor the means to assure the accomplishment of, responsibilities *incumbent on sovereign nations* as contained in the detailed provisions of the other Geneva Conventions.[229]

However, the words in italics appear to indicate that the reply may have been partly based upon the fact that, legally, the United Nations action in Korea was a joint action by the forces of several sovereign States [230] as indeed it was. Only in respect of prisoners of war had the United Nations Command, nevertheless, been able to assume control and had enacted the uniform regulations referred to above, at note 203, and could therefore, as it had stated earlier, consider itself as the 'Detaining Power'.[230a] Another reason may have been that the Korean People's Democratic Republic had only committed itself in respect of the Prisoners of War Convention, although even there it had only accepted the principles and refused to apply all the detailed provisions.[231] Indeed, some of the States participating on the United Nations side had emphasized earlier that the Conventions could not apply since Korea was not a party to them, although they would 'observe any undertakings in regard to humane treatment of prisoners of war and sick and wounded entered into on behalf of United Nations forces by the United Nations Commander in Chief'.[232]

The refusal of the United Nations Command in Korea to apply the other three Conventions therefore cannot be taken as evidence of their inapplicability to a United Nations Force, and certainly not to a Force under the control and international responsibility of the Organization as envisaged in Articles 43 et seq. of the Charter.[233] On the contrary, the fact that the United Nations Command, even without the inducement which full reciprocity would have constituted, accepted the Prisoners of War Convention with itself as the 'Detaining Power', indicates that the Geneva Conventions can be implemented by the United Nations. Indeed, it may be seen as an indication that this is the only practical course for a United Nations Force to take in respect of the Prisoners of War Convention, no matter whether the international responsibility otherwise vests in the Organization or in the participating States.

---

229. Italics added. Quoted in full *above*, Chapter V,2(a), at note 37.

230. It was rather during the initial phases of the action that the United States and the United Nations Command appear to have assumed the contrary, cf. *above*, p. 187.

230a. *Above*, pp. 187–8, with note 54.

231. *Above*, Chapter V,2(a).

232. UK statements to the International Committee of the Red Cross, quoted in *Le Comité international de la Croix-Rouge et le conflit de Corée*, I, pp. 14 and 25, cf. *above*, Chapter V,2(a).

233. Cf. *above*, Chapter II,3 *in fine*, and Bowett: *United Nations Forces* (London 1964) p. 488.

In conclusion, it seems that those difficulties which arise if the United Nations is to act as a Detaining Power, Occupying Power, etc., are not more serious than those which arise if a United Nations action is carried out under national responsibility in such a manner that the several participating States, or a group of them, act as Detaining and Occupying Powers. As pointed out above, under 2, it may in the latter case be virtually impossible to comply with the provisions of Article 12, cf. Article 122, of the Prisoners of War Convention. And the *practical* problems involved in the United Nations acting as Detaining and Occupying Power are probably considerably less than those involved in a number of States doing so.

If for practical or other reasons the Organization should not be in a position to implement any particular provision of the Conventions according to its letter, for example, if it should be found that a transfer of certain functions to the States providing contingents would constitute a violation of certain provisions, the Organization would have to make an appropriate reservation in connexion with its accession to the Conventions, as other contracting parties have done in other respects.[234] It is hard to envisage that the Organization should find it necessary in this context to make any reservations which would prejudice the aims, principles and effectiveness of the Conventions and which would therefore not be acceptable to the other contracting parties. It would merely be a question of employing somewhat different legal or practical techniques to achieve the protection provided for in the Conventions.—On the other hand, those difficulties which arise out of the application of the Conventions to a United Nations action under national command cannot be solved by such reservations, because United Nations accession will then be irrelevant, while parallel reservations by all Member States likely to provide contingents would be impracticable, and would, moreover, come too late after they have already ratified.

12. MODES OF ACCESSION

It has been pointed out above that the United Nations, like other parties, can accede to the conventions in two different ways.

First, it can accede formally in accordance with the accession clauses, if these refer to 'Puissance', as do the Hague and Geneva Conventions,[235] but hardly if they refer to 'State', as does the 1954 Hague Convention on the Protection of Cultural Property.[236]

234. Cf. Pilloud in *Revue internationale de la Croix-Rouge*, August 1957, pp. 409–37.

235. See quotations *above*, under 10(a) *in initio*.

236. *Above*, under 10(b)(ii).

In the second place, the United Nations can accept the conventions informally, by a declaration in accordance with the last sentence of Article 2 common to the four Geneva Conventions [237] and (probably) the similar provision in Article 18(3) of the 1954 Hague Convention, both of which refer to 'Puissance'. The latter provision reads:

> If one of the Powers in conflict is not a Party to the present Convention, the Powers which are parties thereto shall nevertheless remain bound by it in their mutual relations. They shall furthermore be bound by the Convention, in relation to the said Power, if the latter *has declared that it accepts the provisions thereof and so long as it applies them.*

It will be noted that the italicized part differs somewhat from the corresponding part of Article 2 of the Geneva Conventions, which merely requires that the non-contracting Power 'accepts and applies the provisions thereof'. However, it is submitted that this is only a matter of precision.[238] Indeed, the records of the 1949 diplomatic conference demonstrate that even under the Geneva Conventions the contracting parties are bound to apply the conventions in relation to the non-contracting Power only if the latter makes a declaration of acceptance [239] and only so long as it applies the conventions.[240]

The declaration referred to in Article 2 of the Geneva Conventions and in Article 18(3) of the 1954 Hague Convention and the resulting obligations were no doubt envisaged as referring to a particular conflict; a *general* obligation could of course more appropriately be undertaken by formal accession. However, the wording does not preclude a declaration from being made in advance and from covering more conflicts. Accordingly it is submitted that even a general acceptance, comprising any present or future conflict, could be effected in this informal manner.

237. Quoted *above*, under 10(a) *in initio*. This mode of accession was applied inter alia by the United Kingdom in the Suez war in 1956, cf. *La Convention de Genève relative au traitement des prisonniers de guerre*, Genève 1958, p. 33, note.

238. Article 18(3) follows word by word a draft submitted by UNESCO, with only two changes, both of which are irrelevant in the present context ('who' was replaced by 'which' and 'principles' by 'provisions') and the discussion at the Diplomatic Conference dealt only with these changes (*Records of the Intergovernmental Conference on the Protection of Cultural Property in the Event of Armed Conflict*, The Hague 1961, pp. 347 and 385). That otherwise no substantive change was intended is confirmed by the fact that the written comments which accompanied UNESCO's draft referred to the proposed text of (what became) Article 18(3) by the same terms as Article 2 of the Geneva Conventions ('if the latter accepts and applies' its principles, *ibid.*, p. 312).

239. *Actes de la Conférence diplomatique de Genève de 1949* (Bern 1950–51) II B, p. 103. A contrary view is expressed in the Commentary published by the *Comité international de la Croix-Rouge* (*La Convention de Genève relative au traitement des prisonniers de guerre*, Genève 1958, p. 32, cf. pp. 28 and 31).

240. *Ibid.*, pp. 103–4. The report of the Special Committee stated that the declaration would cease to be applicable as soon as it would have been 'démentie d'une façon claire par la conduite du belligérant non contractant'.

This is important in respect of the United Nations. In the first place, as has been pointed out under 10(b)(iii), the informal procedure by declaration of acceptance and application probably is the only procedure under which this Organization can become a party to the 1954 Hague Convention. And even in respect of the Geneva Conventions, where formal accession is open to the United Nations, the informal acceptance procedure may be useful, partly in order to distinguish United Nations actions from war in the traditional sense [241] and partly because many still find it a strange thought that an intergovernmental organization should accede formally to a convention between States, but might more easily accept accession if it took a different form. A declaration pursuant to Article 2 would then be the obvious answer. Indeed, it was probably such a declaration which was envisaged by the Council of Delegates of the International Red Cross in paragraph (a) of the resolution which it adopted at the Centenary Congress [242] and the preamble of which refers to the necessity for protection of the United Nations Forces by the Geneva Conventions.

The informal acceptance clauses refer only to the case where 'one of the Powers in conflict' is not a party to the conventions. Thus, the Article is not applicable if *none* of the parties has acceded formally to the conventions, as was the situation in Korea and Katanga. In such cases it is not possible to make the conventions binding through an informal accession (declaration) by both parties on the basis of Article 2. The *Comité international de la Croix-Rouge* in such cases instead attempts to obtain an independent *ad hoc* agreement between the two parties that they will apply the Conventions. This was what was attempted in Korea.[243] In deciding whether the United Nations should accede to the Geneva Conventions by formal accession or by informal acceptance, it should be taken into account that, if the other party to the conflict is not a party to the Conventions, only formal accession would make Article 2 applicable.

With this exception, there is hardly any legal differences between formal and informal accession from the point of view of capacity and eligibility to accede. In particular, there is no basis for assuming that the United Nations could accede informally if one does not admit that it could do so formally. Once it is admitted that the United Nations is a 'Power' under the informal acceptance clauses, it can hardly be denied that it is also a 'Power' under the formal accession clauses.[244] And,

241. *Below*, under 13(b).
242. Quoted in full *below*, under 14. The same was true of the proposal of the Legal Adviser of UNESCO at the 1954 Hague Conference (*Records, op. cit.*, p. 184).
243. *Above*, Chapter V,2(a).
244. It should be noted that *internal* conflicts are governed by Article 3 rather

from the point of view of capacity, if the United Nations, as demonstrated above, has an inherent capacity to become a party to multilateral, law-making conventions between States, it makes no difference by what method it becomes a party.

Nor is there any difference with regard to the substantive legal effects of accession. All the substantive articles of the conventions become applicable to all acceding parties, irrespective of whether their accession is formal or informal (as long as the informal acceptance is in force and in respect of the conflict to which it applies). However, there is a difference in respect of the final clauses. Not all of these are applicable to informal acceptance. In particular, informal acceptance would not give the United Nations the formal rights of a contracting party under these provisions to receive certified copies of the convention and to be notified of any ratification, accession or denunciation by other parties.

On the other hand, the fact that the Organization by formal accession under the accession clauses would also acquire the formal rights of a contracting party in respect of other final clauses [245] would present no obstacle to such accession, since the Organization has an inherent capacity to become a contracting party also in the formal sense.

13. CONCLUSIONS. SHOULD THE UNITED NATIONS ACCEDE?
REASONS WHICH HAVE HELD UP ACCESSION

It has already been pointed out under 1. that the Hague Regulations on land warfare and other older conventions on warfare which are still applicable and relevant to United Nations actions largely reproduce what has now become general international law, and that there may therefore be no urgent practical need for the United Nations to accede to these conventions. Also in respect of the 1954 Hague Convention it has been pointed out that full accession is not necessary. If the cultural property of the United Nations is protected by the accession of the State in whose territory it is located, it will suffice if the Organization applies the Convention unilaterally, although it would be desirable if it would formally declare its intention of doing so.[246] A full accession, formal or informal, is primarily required in respect of the *Geneva Conventions,*

---

than by Article 2. As for the accession clause, see *above,* under 10(a), on the liberal way in which it has been applied vis-à-vis territorial units not recognized as States, and on the insignificance of the word 'State' in the signature clause.

245. For example under Articles 137, 140, 142 and, probably, 143 of the Prisoners of War Convention.

246. Cf. the resolution adopted by the Hague Conference, quoted *above,* under 10(b)(i).

which contain a large number of provisions that cannot as yet be considered as part of general international law.

There is no need for accession by the United Nations if the Force is under national command and responsibility, except in so far as the Organization may have assumed direct control over and responsibility for certain aspects, for example prisoners of war. Otherwise the need for accession arises only if the United Nations establishes Forces under its own command—as envisaged in Article 43 et seq. of the Charter and as done in practice in the Middle East, in the Congo, in Cyprus and elsewhere. If in such cases the Organization does not accede, any armed conflicts in which such Forces might become involved are not governed by the Geneva Conventions. This means, as explained under 5-8, that the civilian population and the members of the opposing forces do not enjoy full legal protection under the Conventions, and that the members of the United Nations Force itself enjoy no legal protection at all under the Conventions, insofar as their provisions do not constitute general international law. The situation would be even worse if the United Nations were to recruit a Force by individual enlistment, since then the civilian population and the members of the opposing force, like the members of the United Nations Force, would be deprived of *any* protection under the Conventions. United Nations accession may also be necessary in order to relieve the States providing contingents from any indirect responsibility for the acts of the Force and in order to prevent them from invoking such responsibility as a legal basis for intervention in the direction of the Force's operations.[247]

The main reasons why so far no steps have been taken with a view to formal accession to, or informal acceptance of, the Geneva Conventions appear to be connected with the following legal and political considerations and facts:

(a) The existing *disagreement as to whether the United Nations is bound to apply the same laws of war as States* waging a war in the traditional sense. It has been demonstrated above, in Chapter V, that if the United Nations becomes involved in organized hostilities, this constitutes war in a material sense and is governed by the laws of war. It also constitutes an 'armed conflict' of an international character, and thus falls within the scope of the Geneva Conventions. Furthermore, it has been demonstrated in Chapter VI that even in a war between States there is room for discrimination between those fighting on the side of the aggressor and those fighting on the side of the victim of aggression, in the economic and legal fields and in the field of neutrality. However, it was also demonstrated that such discrimination cannot extend to the *humanitarian* laws which are designed to protect individual victims of

247. *Above*, pp. 330 and 332.

the hostilities, and in no circumstances to the Geneva Conventions which have been concluded *after* war was outlawed and yet make no distinction between aggressor and victim. Finally, it was demonstrated that the reasons why no discrimination can be allowed in the humanitarian field and why the discrimination even within other fields must be contained within certain limits, apply in most or all respects, with equal force to United Nations actions which take the form of genuine fighting between two organized military forces rather than of policing by an overwhelming force against which organized resistance is not possible.[248]

(b) The most important political obstacle is the general feeling that a *United Nations action,* even if governed by the same laws as war in the traditional sense, *must be clearly distinguished from war,* and the apprehension that accession by the United Nations to the conventions on warfare might blur this distinction. However, the Secretary-General of the United Nations himself has stated that application of military sanctions as provided for in the Charter is war.[249] Whatever terminology is used, it is submitted that this apprehension must not be allowed to prevent the individual victims of military operations, and particularly the members of the United Nations Force from enjoying full legal protection under the conventions. Indeed as was pointed out under 10(a), the drafters of the Geneva Conventions made every effort to emphasize in the text of the Conventions that their provisions apply to any armed conflict, whatever its denomination and legal nature. To this end, they ignored legal and political distinctions which are no less important than that between United Nations actions and wars between States. Thus, as pointed out under (a), they made no distinction between war of aggression and war of defence. Indeed, the vast majority of States have acceded to the Conventions with a view to defensive war, since they do not envisage embarking on any aggression. It would seem hard to justify that the United Nations, which in fact is in the same position of preparing to take military action against an aggressor by coming to the assistance of these States, should fall outside the Conventions merely because such action technically is not 'war'. On the contrary, it is submitted that there is *less* reason to distinguish in this respect between a United Nations action and individual or collective self-defence than there is to distin-

248. Evensen: 'Folkerettslige problemer forbundet med opprettelsen av internasjonale sikkerhetsstyrker for FN', *Internasjonal politikk* (Oslo) 1963, p. 85, emphasizes that even if the United Nations does not accede to the conventions, the requirements of the Hague and Geneva Conventions in respect of the treatment of sick and wounded, prisoners of war, civilians etc. must constitute absolute *minimum requirements* for the conduct of the actions of a United Nations security force if these assume the nature of armed actions.

249. *Above,* Chapter V,3(a), at note 97.

guish between the latter and aggressive war.[250] This is borne out in respect of the general laws of war by the fact that those members of the competent committee of the *Institut de droit international* who oppose discrimination in respect of States do so in respect of the United Nations, too. Indeed, a detailed analysis of the various fields of the laws of war demonstrates that in few or none of these is there sufficient reason to admit *any* further discrimination against the aggressor if he is resisted by a United Nations Force than if he is resisted by a national force.[251]

The United Nations Charter provides expressly for United Nations military action against aggressors. And as long as it is clear that the military aspects of such action, including its impact upon civilians and military personnel on both sides, are not likely, at the present stage, to differ substantially from those of war between States, it would not appear justified to deny these individuals legal protection under the Conventions on the basis that the United Nations action is politically or legally different from an action of individual or collective self-defence.

The political apprehensions based upon the distinction between a United Nations action and war in the traditional sense have been emphasized particularly in connexion with the *Hague* Conventions, and particularly in respect of any accession which might take place in connexion with peace-keeping Forces.[252] It has already been pointed out that there is little practical need for United Nations accession to the Hague Conventions, and that peace-keeping Forces are less likely to become involved in hostilities which call for the application of the laws of war than combat Forces are. Furthermore, as shall be explained below, there is no reason why any general accession should be linked specially to peace-keeping Forces or any other particular type of forces. It is only when no general accession has been made in advance that the UN is forced into the position that it may have to accede in respect of a specific peace-keeping Force. Indeed, as shall be explained below, under (f), the United Nations in fact was not too far from (informal) accession for the specific purposes of its peace-keeping Forces in the Middle East, the Congo and Cyprus, respectively.

It should be noted, moreover, that if the United Nations refrains from acceding to the Geneva Conventions, this would render the Conventions inapplicable to actions under United Nations command, but it would not prevent their application to United Nations actions under national command. These are, as was demonstrated above, under 2-4, governed by the conventions on warfare even if the United Nations does

250. Cf. *above*, Chapter V,3(d) and Chapter VI.
251. *Above*, Chapter VI,3–5.
252. Evensen, *loc. cit.*

not accede. The distinction would thus not be between United Nations actions and traditional war, but between traditional war and United Nations actions under national command, on the one hand, and United Nations actions under the command of the Organization on the other.

If it nevertheless is insisted that (the latter type of) United Nations actions must be kept separate even in respect of the Geneva Conventions, it is submitted that the distinction may be sought in the *manner* of accession, by having the United Nations accede informally,[252a] rather than in preventing the Organization from acceding at all.

(c) The legal objection most commonly invoked against United Nations accession is the assertion *that the United Nations is not eligible to accede* to the Conventions. Some even assert that the United Nations itself does not have the capacity to accede to that kind of conventions. As has been demonstrated above, this view is not justified. The United Nations has the legal capacity to accede to conventions of any type, provided that their text does not preclude accession by subjects of international law other than States. And this the Geneva Conventions do not do. Neither their text, nor their purpose and spirit preclude the United Nations from acceding and from thereby following the example of the Holy See which signed and ratified the 1864 Geneva Convention at a time when it was not a State and had no territory.[253] In particular, it cannot be presumed that the drafters of the 1949 Geneva Conventions chose to use the now unusual term 'Puissance' in Article 2 and the accession clause with the intention that it should be interpreted as strictly as the usual term, 'State'—which is used in all other modern conventions— or as the term 'pays' which had been used in the 1929 Geneva Conventions. This all the more so considering the purposes and the broad scope of the Conventions, as reflected in their other provisions, which require the application of the Convention to any 'armed conflict' of an international character.

(d) A fourth argument invoked against United Nations accession is *that the United Nations is unable to implement the provisions of the Conventions*, and in particular that it cannot enact criminal law and exercise criminal jurisdiction because the Charter does not authorize it to do so. As has been explained, the notion that an intergovernmental organization can only perform such acts as its constitution authorizes it to do is manifestly contradicted by practice; it also lacks theoretical basis in international law and has now been refuted by the International

---

252a. See *above*, under 12.

253. *Above*, under 9–10. Evensen, *loc. cit.*, p. 84, also appears to consider that the United Nations can accede; however, he seems to deal only with the question considered under 9(a) *above* (the capacity of the United Nations to conclude treaties), rather than with the controversial aspects dealt with under 10 and 11.

Court of Justice.[254] The United Nations has an inherent power to exercise any sovereign act which it is in a factual position to perform, including criminal jurisdiction over persons placed under the Organization's jurisdiction. A different matter is that political and internal legal considerations have forced the States providing contingents to reserve to themselves the power to exercise criminal jurisdiction over the members of their contingents. However, the Geneva Conventions hardly require the United Nations to do this itself, as long as it sees to it that it is done. And this the Organization must do even under the general laws of war, i.e. even if it does not accede to the Conventions.[255] Similarly, most of the other problems posed by the fact that the Geneva Conventions were drafted with States only in mind, arise in respect of the general laws of war too, and can be solved. And so can those, less numerous, problems which are special to the conventions.

(e) A fifth reason for the failure of the United Nations to accede to the Geneva Conventions is the fact that no Force has yet been established under United Nations control in accordance with Articles 43 et seq. of the Charter and that the planning which was well started by the Military Staff Committee in 1946-47 was broken off before it had reached the question of the application of laws of war. However, recent proposals made by the big Powers indicate a desire to take steps to establish a United Nations Force to combat aggression.[256]

(f) A final reason is the fact that the Forces which have effectively been established under United Nations command in the Middle East, the Congo, New Guinea and Cyprus were peace-keeping Forces which were not supposed to engage in military operations of a warlike nature. Indeed, in his Summary Study of the Experience Derived from the Establishment and Operation of the UNEF, upon which the Congo Force was based, the Secretary-General stated that 'the use which could be made of the units provided could never include combat activities'.[257] If the United Nations had acceded in respect of any one of these Forces, it might have cast doubt on this (peace-keeping) nature of the Forces and might have caused uneasiness, not only in the host country and in the countries in the area, but also in the countries providing contingents, since an accession which was meant as precaution might have been interpreted an expectation of, or even an intention to engage in, genuine military operations. The result was that when fighting nevertheless broke out in the Congo,[258] neither the United Nations Force itself, nor the opposing

254. *Above*, pp. 143–60, *below*, pp. 402–4 (cf. also *above*, pp. 333–6) and more fully in *Nordisk Tidsskrift*, 1964, pp. 18–27, 80–81 and 88–96,

255. *Above*, under 11(a).

256. *Above*, Chapter II,10.

257. Par. 178, *OR GA*, XIII, Annexes, A.i. 65. p. 31.

258. On the gradual development of the basis for the military operations of the

side, nor the civilian population, enjoyed adequate legal protection under the Conventions.[259] And if the United Nations had acceded at *that* late point, its accession might have had additional undesirable effects, by contributing to inducing the parties to treat the hostilities as a full-scale war even in those respects where they had not so far done so; they might, for example, have been induced to retain prisoners longer than they actually did, even if the Conventions merely say that prisoners of war *may* be interned. Accession at that late stage might also (wrongly) have been interpreted as a recognition of a state of 'war', or of statehood for Katanga.

Nevertheless, both before and after Congo the United Nations had no hesitation in making special provisions for each of its peace-keeping Forces to the effect that 'the Force shall observe the principles and spirit of the general international Conventions applicable to the conduct of military personnel'.[260] These provisions were communicated informally to the *Comité international de la Croix-Rouge*, but this did not transmit them to the other side. Had the provisions been officially transmitted, they would have constituted declarations under Article 2 of the Geneva Conventions and Article 18(3) of the 1954 Hague Convention if they had referred specifically to these Conventions and if they had referred to the 'provisions' thereof rather than to the 'principles and spirit'. In its subsequent agreements with States providing contingents the UN has moved further in both these respects, see below, pp. 397–8 and 445, pars. 10–11. There is thus little which remains to make the Organization a party to the Conventions in respect of its peace-keeping Forces.

The inconveniences referred to under (f) could be avoided if the United Nations were to accede to the Conventions before a peace-keeping action is decided upon, and especially if it does so, not with special regard to peace-keeping actions at all, but with regard to *any* situation where the Organization might become involved in military operations which would constitute an 'armed conflict' and where the military and civilian personnel involved would therefore require the protection which the Conventions offer. Such general (abstract) accession, which is not con-

United Nations, starting from the concept of self-defence as employed in respect of UNEF, see Draper: 'The Legal Limitation upon the Employment of Weapons by the United Nations Force in the Congo', *International and Comparative Law Quarterly*, XII (1963) pp. 387–413.

259. The Congo was a party to the Conventions, see *above*, Chapter V,2(b)(ii). Katanga, a province of the Congo, was not a party as such, but would no doubt have been asked to make a declaration under Article 2 if the United Nations, for its part, had been a contracting party. Cf. *above*, Chapter V,4 and under 12.

260. *Above*, Chapter V,2(b)(i). No Regulations are known to have been enacted for the Force in New Guinea.

fined to any particular conflict or type of Forces, can most appropriately be effected by formal accession pursuant to the accession clauses. However, as was pointed out above, under 12, it can also be effected informally, by declaration pursuant to Article 2.

The real difficulty is, however, that when the United Nations is not actually involved in an action of the said nature, the pressure upon its organs to take steps to accede is not strong enough. And when a peacekeeping action is under way, accession is complicated by the considerations referred to under (f). Indeed, the United Nations has so far found itself in the position of the tribe which never got the roofs of its huts repaired because when it was raining, they could not do so, and when the sun was shining, it was not necessary. Whether rain or sun, the time would appear to have come for the United Nations to take the necessary steps to become a party to the Geneva Conventions in an abstract (formal or informal) manner, neither linked specifically to an action against an aggressor pursuant to Articles 43 et seq. of the Charter, which have not so far been implemented, nor linked specifically to peace-keeping actions or any particular peace-keeping action, but with a view to covering both. Such abstract accession would apply automatically, as a protection of the individual victims of the hostilities, in any case where a Force under United Nations control might become involved in an armed conflict, whatever its origin, purpose and denomination.

14. INVITATIONS TO THE UNITED NATIONS TO ACCEDE
TO THE GENEVA CONVENTIONS

(a) *Invitations by the International Red Cross*

It has been pointed out above [261] that the *Comité International de la Croix-Rouge* already in 1956, and again in 1960 and 1964, took up with the United Nations the question of the application of the Geneva Conventions by the United Nations Forces in the Middle East, Congo and Cyprus, respectively. The *Comité* suggested, inter alia, that the Organization should declare officially and publicly that it undertook to observe the Geneva Conventions in all circumstances. It was also pointed out that, while the United Nations gave assurances that the Forces would be instructed to observe the *principles and spirit* of the general international conventions concerning the behaviour of military personnel, and while it recognized the importance of the Conventions for the United Nations Forces and agreed to take measures to make these acquainted with their provisions, the Organization did not undertake to comply with their detailed provisions. It was also pointed out that, in

261. ChapterV,2(b)(ii).

these circumstances, when fighting broke out in Katanga in 1961, the *Comité international de la Croix-Rouge* found it necessary to inform all Members of the United Nations that, since the United Nations as such was not a party to the Conventions, each State providing contingents was responsible for their application, a proposition which might prejudice the principle of exclusive United Nations operational control and international responsibility for the Force.

The *Comité* adhered to this position also when in August-September 1963 the International Red Cross held its Centenary Congress in Geneva with the participation of about 400 delegates from the Red Cross, Red Crescent and Red Lion and Sun Societies of 90 States. On this occasion the *Comité* proposed the following draft resolution:

> The Council of Delegates,
> considering that it is necessary that the United Nations Emergency Forces shall observe not only the principles of the Geneva Conventions, but also all the relevant provisions thereof, expresses its appreciation for the efforts already made by the United Nations in this direction and recommends:
> 1. that the Governments of the countries supplying contingents to the United Nations should agree to give orders to their troops, before their departure from the country of origin, to comply with these Conventions;
> 2. that members of these forces should receive, before departure, adequate instruction on Humanitarian Law;
> 3. that the Governments responsible for these contingents should agree to take all the necessary measures to prevent and restrain any infringements of the said Conventions;
> 4. that the United Nations Organisation should continue to give its full support to the application of the resolutions set out above.

During the discussion in the International Humanitarian Law Commission all speakers (Norway, South Africa, United Kingdom, Iraq, Ireland and Australia) supported the draft resolution. However, several of them proposed a stronger text and, in particular, that a greater role should be attributed to the United Nations. Accordingly, a working group was established. This produced a revised text which was unanimously adopted by the Commission and, subsequently, by the Council of Delegates. In its final form the Resolution reads:

> The Council of Delegates,
> considering that the States which are parties to the Geneva Conventions have undertaken to respect and to ensure the respect of these Conventions;
> considering that it is necessary that the United Nations Emergency Forces shall observe and be protected by these Geneva Conventions;
> expresses its appreciation for the efforts already made by the United Nations to that effect and recommends:
> (a) that the United Nations be invited to adopt a solemn declaration accepting that the Geneva Conventions equally apply to their Emergency Forces as they apply to the forces of States parties to the said Conventions;

393

(b) that the Governments of countries providing contingents to the United Nations should as a matter of prime importance give them before departure from their country of origin adequate instructions on the Geneva Conventions as well as orders to comply with them;

(c) that the Authorities responsible for these contingents should agree to take all necessary measures to prevent and repress any infringements of the said Conventions.

The first preambular paragraph, referring to the obligations of *States*, was added at the request of the *Comité international*, after the draft of the working group had come back to the Commission. The paragraph does not specify whether the States providing contingents have any legal responsibility for violations of the Conventions committed by the United Nations Force.

The operative part of the resolution deals, in a clearer fashion, with the two other important legal problems which had arisen, viz. United Nations accession, and prosecution for violations.

The first operative paragraph, inviting the United Nations to accede to the Geneva Conventions, was proposed by the Norwegian Delegation. The declaration which this paragraph invites the United Nations to make would not constitute a formal accession in accordance with the accession clauses of the four Conventions; however, it would probably have the effect of an informal legal acceptance of the Conventions in accordance with their common Article 2.[262] If the Organization makes such a declaration, it will thereby commit itself to apply the Conventions to opposing forces. This would, pursuant to Article 2, automatically commit any contracting party to apply the Conventions to the United Nations Forces, and thus provide these with the protection to which the second preambular paragraph refers.[263] The Resolution appears to envisage *one* declaration covering all the United Nations 'Emergency Forces', rather than an *ad hoc* declaration for each Force.[264] On the other hand, the Resolution speaks only of 'Emergency Forces'. This term may envisage only the peace-keeping Forces, which were the only ones topical at the time of the adoption of the resolution. However, it can hardly be assumed that the International Red Cross would not wish the Convention to apply, *a fortiori*, should the United Nations undertake an enforcement action. Indeed, as submitted above, under 13, it would be better if any formal or informal United Nations accession were to cover enforcement actions, too, both because these are the only actions which call for the application of the laws of war *in any event*, and in order to avoid the political difficulty that a special accession for peace-keeping

262. *Above*, under 12.
263. Cf. also *above*, under 5–8.
264. Cf. *above*, under 12.

Forces might create the false impression that these, too, are *intended* to fight.

The other important legal problem is the repression of infringements of the Conventions. Under the original proposal of the *Comité International* the responsibility for this would have vested in the 'Governments responsible' for the contingents, in recognition of the fact that at present the disciplinary and criminal powers are vested in the States providing contingents. However, the working group replaced this by the term 'Authorities responsible', in order to include also international authorities. This was done, inter alia, in the light of the urgent practical need for the United Nations, too, to take at least some action in this regard, by agreement with the States providing contingents.

The *Comité international* brought the Resolution to the attention of the United Nations and the governments of the States parties to the Geneva Conventions. In reply, a number of governments indicated to the *Comité* that they supported the resolution and the application of the Conventions to United Nations Forces. The United States touched on the legal aspects when, in its reply, it stated that it considered that the forces placed under United Nations command must apply the Geneva Conventions in those cases where these are applicable; the latter may be a reference to the problems discussed in Chapter V,4 above. The United States also added that its troops cannot act independently of the armed forces placed under United Nations command of which they form part. Some governments specifically expressed support for the idea that the Organization should adopt the Conventions and indicated that they would support any initiative in this sense which might be taken in the United Nations. However, at that time the financial crisis of the United Nations became acute and lamed the actions of the General Assembly. Accordingly, the *Comité* reported to the XXth International Red Cross Conference in Vienna in 1965 that 'the whole problem is far from being finally solved'.[265]

That Conference adopted, at the proposal of Monaco, a resolution which was very similar to that adopted by the Centenary Congress. However, the first operative paragraph was worded somewhat differently. The Monaco proposal was 'that the United Nations be invited to adopt an official declaration accepting the application of the Geneva Conventions to their Emergency Forces in the same way as they apply to the armed forces of the States Parties to these Conventions'. This, and particularly the terms 'in the same way', provoked objection from the

---

265. *XXth International Conference of the Red Cross, Vienna, October 1965,* documents Conf. G 2 b/1 (Suites données aux résolutions du Conseil des délégués tenu à Genève en 1963) pp. 5–6, and Conf. D 3/1 (Implementation and Dissemination of the Geneva Conventions, Report submitted by the International Red Cross) p. 8.

United Kingdom delegate, Colonel Draper, who stated that it was controversial whether the United Nations was in a legal position to do this.[266] He proposed that the paragraph be worded as follows: 'that appropriate arrangements be made to ensure that armed forces placed at the disposal of the United Nations observe the provisions of the Geneva Conventions'. This was accepted by the Monaco delegate and adopted by the Conference, together with an amendment adding the words 'and be protected by them'. As has been pointed out above, the latter can only be achieved if the Organization accedes to the Conventions, formally or informally, with or without reservations, unless one is prepared to abandon the principle of United Nations operational command and leave command over and responsibility for the Force in the hands of one or more national States.

(b) *Other proposals*

The *Association médicale mondiale* has also approved and supported the invitation to the United Nations that it should adopt 'une déclaration solennelle acceptant que les Conventions de Genève s'appliquent à leur Forces d'urgence'.[267]

The question was also discussed at the non-governmental conference on United Nations Forces held in Oslo in February 1964. The Conference adopted no resolutions, but a summary of the discussion was published. This contains the following statement on the subject:

> The question was raised of the position of the forces with regard to the laws and customs of war and especially to the Geneva Conventions of 1949 for the protection of the victims of war. UN forces may become engaged in hostilities of a warlike character, as experience in the Congo has shown. The UN position regarding the laws and customs of war has not, however, been clearly defined. It was further stated that these rules and conventions might regulate UN actions,

266. Information supplied by the Norwegian delegate, Mr. Eliassen. As reported *above*, at note 212, Draper himself appears to deny that the Conventions, or even the customary laws of war, can apply to a United Nations Force, because the Organization lacks disciplinary and criminal powers. The French text of the resolution says '*accords*' instead of '*arrangements*'.

267. Guerisse, Jacquemin et Kellens: 'Les forces armées de l'Organisation des Nations Unies face à leur mission sanitaire et humanitaire', *Annales de droit international médical*, No. 11, 1964. The writers refer to this as a 'grave problème' and to the insistence with which the *Comité international de la Croix-Rouge* has drawn the attention of the Secretary-General of the United Nations to the fact that the Organization is not a party to the Conventions. On the basis of a report by three members of the Norwegian Military Medical Unit attached to UNEF they propose the establishment of a medical unit in the proposed military staff element at United Nations Headquarters, whose first duty it should be 'd'obtenir—sans équivoque possible—la garantie que les blessés et les malades seront protégés par les Conventions de Genève. Il s'agit la—est-il besoin de le dire—d'une condition sine qua non de l'activité des Services de Santé de l'ONU'.

and enable UN forces to protect wounded and sick, medical personnel and installations, as well as members of these forces being captured by the adversary. It was felt that the UN should declare more precisely its intention of applying the Geneva Conventions. This could be done by a formal accession to or a solemn declaration or a resolution of the General Assembly or the Security Council; or a clause might be inserted in agreements concluded between states supplying contingents and the Secretary General.[268]

(c) *Steps taken by the United Nations*

As for the latter proposal, it should be noted that the United Nations already in 1963 informed the *Comité international de la Croix-Rouge* that it would propose to insert in any future agreements with States providing contingents a provision under which these States would take those measures which depend upon them to ensure the observation of the laws of war and the Geneva Conventions by the members of their contingents. This was later done in connexion with the Force in Cyprus. In its agreements with the States providing contingents, the United Nations included a provision to the effect that these States would ensure that members of their contingents be fully acquainted with the obligations arising under the Geneva and the 1954 Hague Conventions and that 'appropriate steps be taken to ensure their enforcement'.[269] This may mean that the United Nations accepts the detailed provisions of these five Conventions, although the preceding paragraph of the agree-

---

268. *Frydenberg: Peace-Keeping, Experience and Evaluation – The Oslo Papers* (Oslo 1964) pp. 310–1. Earlier, Evensen, in one of the basic papers, stated, as indicated *above* pp. 387–8, at notes 248 and 252, that the UN Forces must observe the Hague and Geneva Conventions on the treatment of sick, wounded, prisoners and civilians *as a minimum*, but he had hesitations about the Organization acceding to these Conventions, especially in connection with the establishment of peace-keeping forces. Julius Stone, in the other basic study, expressed his 'agreement with Mr. Evensen that technical questions of treaty-making capacity of the UN schould present no obstacle to its accession', and then added:

'I would, however, go further and regard it as eminently desirable that the U.N. should at some suitable early time (not necessarily tied to efforts to establish a permanent security force) seek a suitable mode of declaring itself bound to observe the prevailing rules of war law. Obviously such rules would only apply when its forces were engaged in the kind of operations governed by the conventions; obviously, too, they could not extend beyond the legal control which the U.N. itself is in a position to exercise over each element of its forces, though these should be assembled with due regard to the likelihood of observance of the rules of war law. If, as Mr. Evensen thinks, these prevailing rules should represent minimum requirements for performing U.N. functions, it seems *pessimi exempli* for an organization dedicated to public purposes of the international community to leave the slightest doubt about its intention to be bound by war law in any future situations in which this law is in substance applicable. And we see no reason why this affirmation need be left merely to be made *ad hoc* from case to case as it was, for example, in the Regulations of UNEF'. (*Ibid.*, p. 299)

269. Full text *below*, p. 445, pars. 10–11.

ment quotes par. 40 of the Force Regulations, which merely refers to the 'principles and spirit' of the conventions and which, as pointed out above, p. 190, was not originally intended to cover the detailed provisions.

This action—together with a concomitant United Nations proposal that the Organization might establish an organ in the field which would investigate any violations and transmit any proofs to the State to whose contingent the accused belongs for further action [270]—will probably solve the basic difficulty which arises from the fact that the United Nations, although externally responsible, does not itself have the necessary disciplinary and criminal authority over the members of the Force to enable it to enforce compliance with the Conventions. Such a commitment by the States providing contingents vis-à-vis the United Nations is therefore, together with the fact that the Organization itself has the operational control,[271] a basic measure of great practical importance. However, in order to reach the basic objective of obtaining legal protection under the Conventions for the Force, as the Red Cross and Oslo resolutions clearly intend, one would, for the reasons set forth above, pp. 322 et seq., have to add an undertaking by the United Nations itself to apply the Conventions. Only this would create a legal obligation for the opposing forces. Such an undertaking by the United Nations could also be included in the agreements with the States providing contingents. Indeed, the latter might have to insist upon this, in order to fulfil their obligations under Article 1 common to the Geneva Conventions and if they wish to relieve themselves of any indirect responsibility for the acts of the Force which they might incur by placing troops under the authority of an Organization which is not a party to the Conventions.[272]

270. The basis for this was laid by appropriate additions to the ONUC and UNFICYP Regulations, see *above*, p. 376, and *below*, p. 439, pars. 13–14.

271. See the quotation *above*, p. 362.

272. *Above*, pp. 322–7.

CONCLUSIONS

It will be attempted in the present chapter to survey the main conclusions of the detailed discussion in the eight preceding chapters and to add a few words on recent developments and on steps that may be taken to further develop the law and its application. Although this will be done in a somewhat more complete manner than usual, it must be emphasized that it is still necessary to leave out many of the reservations and modalities which have been made in the course of the full discussion above, and practically all citations. It would therefore be misleading if the views of the present writer were to be reported and evaluated merely on the basis of quotations from the present chapter.

Both the *Covenant* of the League of Nations and the *Charter* of the United Nations contain specific provisions for an international military force to combat an *aggressor*. However, these provisions have never been used, despite the several cases of aggression which have occurred. Only in one case, *Korea,* did the Organization take military action against the aggressor, but then it did so without relying upon the specific provisions on military forces in the Charter.

On the other hand, the League of Nations and the United Nations have on six occasions established so-called *peace-keeping Forces,* similarly without relying upon the specific provisions of the constitution of the Organization, namely in Leticia, the Saar, the Middle East (UNEF), the Congo (ONUC), West New Guinea (Irian Barat, UNSF) and Cyprus (UNFICYP). These Forces were not intended to resist an aggressor, but rather to forestall conflict or recurrence of conflict, by supervising an armistice, by maintaining order in a troubled area, etc. In three cases the Force was established to maintain order in a territory under the Organization's administration (Leticia, the Saar and West New Guinea). In the other three cases the territory where the Force was stationed and operating was under national administration. In none of these six cases was the Force set up for the purpose of defending the territory against aggression; however, it might have been called upon to do so had aggression taken place; in any case it acted, by its mere presence, as a deterrent against external aggression as well as against internal disorders. The Forces were not intended for large-scale fighting. However, they were equipped for fighting on a moderate scale and on one occasion (Congo) the Force became involved in fighting of a war-like nature.

As already pointed out, none of the seven Forces actually established was based upon the *constitutional provisions* for military forces. This was due to a belief on the part of the competent organs at the time that this could not legally be done.

In most cases this belief was well founded. Thus Articles 42 et seq. of the United Nations Charter, according to their location in Chapter VII and after Article 39, can only be applied if the Security Council has determined 'the existence of any threat to the peace, breach of the peace, or act of aggression'. This was not the case, or had not been determined to be the case, in any of the peace-keeping operations referred to above.

Only in respect of Korea had the Security Council determined that 'the armed attack upon the Republic of Korea by forces from North Korea' constituted 'a breach of the peace' (and, subsequently, that the People's Republic of China had 'engaged in aggression'). When the Council nevertheless refrained from basing its action in Korea upon Article 42, it appears to have been because the agreements provided for in Article 43 had not yet been concluded. This derives from the common interpretation of the Charter which is that Article 42 can only be implemented pursuant to the procedure set forth in Articles 43 et seq.

However, there is nothing in Article 42 to indicate that it is so restricted.[1] The article is very broadly formulated. It covers any type of Force, whether composed of individuals recruited directly by the Organization, of national contingents contributed voluntarily (as in Korea) or of contingents contributed in fulfilment of a previous commitment entered into pursuant to Articles 43 et seq. or otherwise, and whether under command of the UN or of one or more participating States. The function of *Article 43* is merely to provide for a method whereby the Organization shall have the right to *order* its Member States to provide contingents.

Article 42 is not even clearly confined to Forces to combat the aggressor. According to its terms it would also comprise a *peace-keeping* Force, if the Security Council has determined 'the existence of any threat to the peace, breach of the peace, or act of aggression' in accordance with Article 39. It is submitted that, on a correct interpretation of the Charter, it was the lack of the latter, and not the terms of Article 42 (and still less Articles 43 et seq.) which initially stood in the way of basing the United Nations action in the Congo upon Article 42. Indeed, it is submitted that once the conditions of Chapter VII (Article 39) are met, any military

---

1. *Above*, Chapter IV,2(b). This view was supported by Stone at the Oslo Conference 1964, see Frydenberg: *Peace-keeping, Experience and Evaluation*—The Oslo Papers (Oslo 1964) p. 294.

action can be based upon Article 42. However, the general view appears to have been to consider the action in the Congo as based upon Article 40 (or other Articles of Chapter VII), after or even before the Security Council on 21 February 1962 had used the terms of Article 39,[2] while Article 42 in the general view was inapplicable.

Although the United Nations action in Korea, and even some of the peace-keeping actions, thus *could* have been based upon Article 42, the fact remains that none of the combat or peace-keeping Forces which the League of Nations and the United Nations actually established in fact was based upon this or the other provisions on military forces, at least not at the time of their establishment.

Instead, a legal basis has been sought subsequently, partly in other Articles of the Charter, such as Articles 1(1),[3] 10-14, 22, 24-25, 29, 39-41 and 97, and partly in the Uniting for Peace Resolution. However, the latter cannot create a new legal basis which was not inherent in the Organization or implied in the Charter in the first place. As for the articles of the Charter that have been referred to, most of them have some legal relevance. Nevertheless, it would be stretching most of them rather far if one were to deduce from them a power which the Organization would not otherwise have possessed, i.e. if one works on assumption that Forces cannot be established unless authorized by the provisions of the Charter, and that Articles 42 et seq. are not applicable. Many of the articles referred to are general enough to mean everything and nothing. Thus the frequently invoked provisions in Articles 22 and 29 that the General Assembly and the Security Council, respectively, 'may establish such subsidiary organs as it deems necessary for the performance of its functions' add nothing to what would apply in any case [4] and cannot legitimately be stretched to provide authority for substantive functions which the Organization otherwise would not be entitled to perform.[5] It is also a fact, although not in itself decisive, that few or none of the Articles referred to were in the mind of the competent organs when they

2. On the question of whether Article 40 could be used even in the absence of a determination under Article 39, see *Repertory of Practice of United Nations Organs*, II, pp. 366–371; cf. also *Franck and Carey: The Legal Aspects of the United Nations Action in the Congo, Background Papers and Proceedings of the Second Hammarskjöld Forum* (Dobbs Ferry, N.Y., 1963) pp. 65–67.

3. This would probably be the best basis if one *has* to be adduced and if Article 42 cannot be used (because of Article 39), see *above*, p. 167, note 155, and Halderman: 'Legal Basis for United Nations Armed Forces' in *AJIL*, LVI (1962) pp. 971–996. As the latter points out (p. 976, note) the present writer considers that Article 1(1) merely states an inherent power in so far as it, in addition to one of the purposes of the Organization, also states the *means* to achieve this purpose, cf. *above*, p. 160.

4. Cf. *Indian Journal of International Law*, IV (1964) p. 72.

5. See also *below*, at note 19.

established the Forces. They have only been thought of later by lawyers who believe that provisions have to be found. The decisive fact, however, is that Forces were established also by the League of Nations, notwithstanding the fact that the Covenant did not contain provisions comparable to most of the Charter Articles referred to above, and certainly not to Articles 1(1), 22 and 29. This confirms that these provisions of the Charter do *not* constitute the legal basis of the Forces. They are merely convenient tools which have been adduced, in those cases where they happen to be available, in order to attempt to reconcile the facts of international life with the common doctrines of delegated and implied powers, under which each power of an intergovernmental organization must be deduced from the express provisions or implied intentions of its particular constitution.

In the view of the present writer, this doctrine is not theoretically founded,[6] nor can it be reconciled with practice without resorting to fictions. The consistent practice of the League of Nations and the United Nations in establishing military forces without basis in the relevant provisions in the Covenant and the Charter is but one example of this. The same is true of other sovereign acts, like the exercise of jurisdiction over organs and territory, and of international acts, like sending and receiving 'diplomatic' representatives enjoying privileges and immunities, convening intergovernmental conferences, membership of other intergovernmental organizations, conclusion of treaties, unilateral acts, presentation and satisfaction of international claims, and settlement of disputes with other subjects of international law by arbitration. All these sovereign and international acts have been performed by the United Nations and/or other intergovernmental organizations—and legitimately so—despite the fact that in most cases there was no provision in their constitution authorizing them to do so, just as there are frequently no provisions authorizing such acts by States in *their* constitutions. If the United Nations has not performed all types of sovereign or international acts which States perform, this is not because it lacks the legal capacity, but because it has not yet been in a practical position to do so. If and when it is, and thus performs a new type of act, its validity cannot be denied as long as it is designed to fulfil the purposes of the Organization. It is not necessary to look in the constitution of (a State or) Organization for provisions authorizing it to employ each particular *means* to achieve its purposes, as long as there is no provision (including a delimitation of the purposes), and no rule of general international law (applicable to States as well) [7] *precluding* the use of such means.

This was the *practical* effect of the well-known statements of the In-

6. *Nordisk Tidsskrift*, XXXIV (1964) pp. 88–93.
7. See for example *above*, VIII,9(a), note 67.

ternational Court of Justice in its advisory opinion of 1949 on *Reparation for Injuries*, that the Organization has those powers which 'are conferred upon it by necessary implication as being essential to the performance of its duties' or which arise 'by necessary intendment out of the Charter', although the theoretical point of departure here still was the Charter. Several writers have subsequently termed these statements of the Court 'judicial legislation'.[8] This criticism is understandable on the part of those who support the common doctrines of delegated and implied powers, because, although the Court in form construed the powers as implied in the Charter, its statements and the conclusions it drew from them went far beyond what it would be natural to read into the Charter. Indeed, the Court's formulation of the implied powers contained no real limitations, because, in actual fact, no court could invalidate an act because it was not 'essential' or 'necessary'. It is submitted that the only real limitations are those referred to in the last sentence of the preceding paragraph. In these circumstances it is a misleading and unduly complicating fiction to start out from the assumption that the capacities exist because they have been *delegated* from the Member States or *implied* in the *constitution* or the intention of its draftsmen. The true position is that the capacities are *inherent ipso facto* in the *Organization* as an intergovernmental organization, in essentially the same manner as the capacities of States follow *ipso facto* from their existence as States and not from their constitutions. It is not necessary to point to any provision of the constitution which by a more or less strained interpretation could offer a legal basis for the act, or to any real or presumed intention of the draftsmen to 'confer' the capacity upon the Organization, as long as the act is not excluded by any such provision. It is not even necessary to demonstrate that the act concerned is 'essential' for the performance of the functions of the Organization, it is enough that the act is designed to serve a purpose within the scope of the constitution. Positive legal basis is necessary only if the Organization wants to impose obligations upon its Member States.[9]

8. Thus McMahon in *BYIL*, XXXVII (1961) p. 340 and Simmonds in *International and Comparative Law Quarterly*, XIII (1964) p. 890.

9. For a full discussion of the inherent powers, with citations, see the present writer's study: 'International Personality of Intergovernmental Organizations' in *Indian Journal of International Law*, IV (1964) pp. 1–74. See also the reviews of his earlier parallel article in *Nordisk Tidsskrift for international Ret og Jus gentium*, XXXIV (1964) pp. 1–112 by Kunz in *AJIL*, LVIII (1964) pp. 1042–4; and by Bothe in *Zeitschrift für ausländisches öffentliches Recht und Völkerrecht*, XXV No. 2 (1965) pp. 394–6; and the discussion by T. S. Rama Rao in *Indian Yearbook of International Affairs*, 1963, at pp. 152–4 (on the basis of the present writer's briefer exposition of his doctrine in *BYIL*, 1961, pp. 447–60). Rao states that the doctrine 'ignores the fact that while states can create new subjects of international law by process of recognition, the extent of their 'subjecthood', or in other words, the quantum of rights and obligations of the

In its subsequent advisory opinion of 20 July 1962 on *Certain Expenses of the United Nations* the International Court of Justice appears to have adopted this view. It did not repeat the restrictive terms ('essential' and 'necessary') which it had used in Reparation for Injuries. Nor did it employ any terms which would indicate that the power of the Organization to perform certain acts was to be deduced from the provisions of the Charter or the express or implied intentions of its framers. On the contrary, the Court stated that 'when the Organization takes action which warrants the assertion that it was appropriate for the fulfilment of one of the stated purposes of the United Nations, the presumption is that such action is not *ultra vires* the Organization'.[10] This statement was the basis of the Court's conclusion that the expenses incurred in connection with the United Nations Forces in the Middle East and the Congo constituted 'expenses of the Organization' within the meaning of Article 17(2) of the Charter (and thus were binding upon the Member States). More specifically, the statement was made in the context of the external validity of the expenses incurred in connection with the Forces and of their resulting effect in relation to Article 17(2) which expressly confers a power of binding assessment upon the Organization. Similarly, in its subsequent discussion *obiter dictum* [11] of the (internal) constitutionality of the establishment of the two Forces, the Court, consistently with the statement quoted above, did not cite any articles of the Charter except in connection with (1) the purposes of the Organization, (2) the internal distribution of powers between the General Assembly, the Security Council and the Secretary-General and (3) the power to *require*

---

candidates for recognition, depends upon the intention of states and is traceable solely to the act and quality of their recognition'. As explained more fully in the *Indian Journal of International Law, loc. cit.*, especially at pp. 59 et seq. and 233 et seq., the present writer does not consider this to be a fact. On the contrary, he has concluded, on the basis of a study of practice and of theoretical considerations, that intergovernmental organizations (and probably other fully sovereign communities and partly sovereign communities as far as their sovereignty goes) are general subjects of international law *ipso facto*, without recognition, even if there is no evidence that the States establishing them had such intention, and even if they did not intend to establish an organization at all *(ibid.,* p. 48). The fact that the present writer 'describes the capacity of intergovernmental organizations as a principle of the *customary law* of international organizations' does not mean (as suggested by Rama Rao, *loc. cit.)* that he 'admits the importance of such intention of States, by implication', because this law is based upon the practice of intergovernmental organizations generally, not upon that of the particular Organization concerned (cf. *Indian Journal of International Law,* IV [1964] p. 60, cf. pp. 51–53). The only *legal* restrictions are those which follow from general international law, as also applicable to States, and from any *limiting* provisions of the constitution of the Organization concerned if and to the extent that such limitations have external effects.

10. *ICJ Reports,* 1962, p. 168
11. *ICJ Reports,* 1962, p. 177 *in initio.*

enforcement by coercive action.[12] Nor did the Court refer to any expressed or implied intentions of the drafters, or to practice subsequent to the adoption of the Charter (except in relation to the interpretation of the provisions on the budgetary aspects).[13]

Accordingly, it is submitted that the United Nations has an *inherent* capacity—i.e. a capacity which need not be deduced from any provision of the Charter or from the intention of its drafters or from the earlier practice of the Organization—to establish, assume command over and employ military forces and to exercise belligerent rights. These capacities, it is submitted, may be exercised within the following limits:

(1) The Force may only be established and used to further the stated purposes of the Organization. However, these cover both the prevention of conflicts and the combat of aggression, and are thus wide enough to cover all needs which have arisen or may arise for combat and peace-keeping Forces.

(2) The Force may not be established or used in violation of any other provision of the Charter. However, the Charter does not contain any provisions which could prevent the establishment and use of a United Nations Force, unless Articles 42 et seq. (cf. Article 39) were to be interpreted *a contrario* in this respect, which would be wrong, cf. below.

(3) The Force must be established and used by the organs which are competent under the Charter, and pursuant to the procedure laid down for their decisions. This is a real limitation of practical significance, because of the provisions which reserve certain of the relevant powers to the Security Council, cf. below.

(4) The Force must be composed on a voluntary basis. It may thus be composed of persons recruited individually or of national contingents contributed voluntarily by Member or non-member States, but no State may be *required* to contribute individuals or contingents.

(5) The Force can only be used within the limits of general international law, i.e. either against an aggressor or with the consent of the State in whose territory the Force operates.

That a Force established within these limits is even internally valid, appears to have been confirmed by the International Court of Justice in its advisory opinion on *Certain Expenses of the United Nations,* when it, as indicated above—after having referred only to the purposes of the Organization, to the distribution of powers between the General As-

---

12. *ICJ Reports,* 1962, p. 163.

13. On the attitude of the International Law Commission, see *above,* Chapter VIII, 9(a), with citations.

sembly and the Security Council [14] and to the fact that UNEF had been established with the consent of the parties contributing units and was stationed in the territory of a given State only with the latter's consent—stated that the Secretary-General had properly exercised the authority given him to incur financial obligations of the Organization in respect of UNEF.[15]

The limitations described under (1)-(3) cannot validly be exceeded, from an *internal* point of view. Nor can the limitations described under (4)-(5) be exceeded without specific legal basis in the Charter or elsewhere. The limitations under (4)-(5) derive from the general principle of international law that no State, Organization or other sovereign community can impose new obligations upon another State, Organization or other sovereign community without basis in a multilateral, bilateral or unilateral act from the latter authorizing the former to impose such new obligations. Therefore, if the United Nations wishes to go beyond the above limits, it needs specific authority therefor, either in the Charter or elsewhere. It is this authority which is conferred upon the Security Council, and upon that only, in Articles 42 et seq., cf. Articles 24-25 and 39 et seq., of the Charter. And it is this authority to impose upon States an obligation to contribute to the Force and to accept its use in their territories, and only this authority, which is limited by the terms and place of these Articles. Thus these Articles cannot be interpreted *a contrario* in respect of the power of the United Nations to establish and operate peace-keeping or combat forces and to exercise belligerent rights, but merely in respect of its power to *require* its Member States to provide contingents or other active assistance therefor and to accept the use of such Forces in their territories even if they have not committed aggression.

As pointed out, the United Nations has an inherent *capacity*, not merely to *establish* military forces and assume command over these, but also to *use* them for military operations and, in this connection, to exercise belligerent rights. However, it has a *right* to engage in hostilities only in the cases provided by the Charter [16] or permitted by general international law. Under the latter, armed force may be used in individual and collective self-defence against aggression, and only then.[17] The United Nations, like States, partakes of this inherent right of individual and collective self-defence. This means that the Organization has,

14. This (and possibly the following) is what really was *obiter dictum*, because the Court had earlier taken the position that the expense incurred might have been an expense of the Organization even if the action was taken by the wrong organ, see the quotation *below*, at note 21.

15. *ICJ Reports*, 1962, pp. 171-2.

16. See *above*, Chapter VI,1.

17. *Above*, Chapter VI,2(a)(i).

not merely the capacity, but also the right to resist aggression against it-self or any Member or non-member State by a Force under its own com-mand or under national command, even if no provision of the Charter authorizes it to do so.

Thus, the inherent power of the United Nations to establish and em-ploy a military Force is not limited to the cases and by the conditions set forth in Articles 42 et seq. However, if the Organization wishes to em-ploy its Force in the territory of any Member or non-meber State which has neither committed aggression nor given its consent, it can only do so on the basis of the relevant Articles of the Charter, including notably Articles 24, 25 and 42, or on the basis of some other instrument or act by which the State concerned has conferred this right upon the Organiza-tion. Similarly, the Organization cannot *require* its Member States to provide contingents for its Force; this it can do only under the proced-ures laid down in Articles 43 et seq., or on the basis of some other pro-vision or act by which the States concerned have conferred this right upon the Organization.

Those provisions of the Charter which authorize the imposition of such obligations upon the Member States all confer the power to do so upon the *Security Council, not upon the General Assembly*. This is true both of the specific provisions in Articles 42 et seq. and of the more ge-neral provisions elsewhere in Chapter VII and in Articles 24-25, if and to the extent that these are considered relevant. The General Assembly has only the competence to require the Member States to contribute to the *costs* of the Forces, on the basis of the specific provision in Article 17(2) of the Charter as interpreted by the International Court of Justice in its advisory opinion of 20 July 1962 on *Certain Expenses of the United Nations*.[18] In this opinion the Court stated that 'it is only the Security Council which can *require* enforcement by coercitive action against an aggressor' or which 'may *order* coercitive action' and that the way in which subsidiary organs of the General Assembly are utilized 'depends on the consent of the State or States concerned'.[19]

However, the Charter also contains other important provisions relat-ing to the distribution of powers between the Security Council and the General Assembly. In particular, Article 11(2) provides that any ques-tion relating to the maintenance of international peace and security 'on which action is necessary shall be referred to the Security Council by the General Assembly either before or after discussion'. In its advisory opin-ion referred to above, the Court found 'that the argument which seeks, by reference to Article 11, paragraph 2, to limit the *budgetary* authority

18. *ICJ Reports*, 1962, pp. 179–80.
19. *ICJ Reports*, 1962, p. 163 (italics added) and p. 165.

of the General Assembly [pursuant to Article 17 (2)] in respect of the maintenance of international peace and security, is unfounded'. In the reasoning leading to this conclusion, the Court stated (*obiter dictum*):

> The kind of action referred to in Article 11, paragraph 2, is coercive or enforcement action. ... The word 'action' must mean such action as is solely within the province of the Security Council. It cannot refer to recommendations which the Security Council might make, as for instance under Article 38, because the General Assembly under Article 11 has a comparable power. The 'action' which is solely within the province of the Security Council is that which is indicated by the title of Chapter VII of the Charter, namely 'Action with respect to threats to the peace, breaches of the peace, and acts of aggression'. .... the last sentence of Article 11, paragraph 2, has no application where the necessary action is not enforcement action.[20]

However, these provisions of the Charter have only effect *within the Organization*. They have no effect *vis-à-vis external parties*. Thus, even a Force established and/or employed by the General Assembly or the Secretary-General in violation of Article 11(2), would externally be a Force of the Organization.

This is quite clear in relation to *non-members* who are not parties to the Charter. These are not entitled to treat a Force under the Organization's command as a coalition army of the States providing contingents, even if the Force were illegal under the Charter (or even if it were to engage in military operations in violation of international law). This they could only do if the United Nations had lacked the *capacity* under *international* law to be a belligerent, which it does not. Nor can non-members treat a United Nations Force as an illegal Force in the sense that it would not be entitled to protection under (and obliged to observe) the laws of war. This is true irrespective of whether the Force is under national or United Nations command and of whether it has been constituted in accordance with or in violation of the provisions of the Charter.

Member States are theoretically in a different position. As parties to the Charter and parts of the Organization they are, in principle, entitled to invoke its provisions. Nevertheless, if they become involved in a conflict with the Organization they must, at least if they have committed aggression, be subject to the same principles as were set forth for non-members in the preceding paragraph. In its advisory opinion of 20 July 1962 on *Certain Expenses of the United Nations* the International Court of Justice even applied the same principle to the internal obligation of the Members to contribute to the expenses of the Organization. The Court stated:

20. *ICJ Reports*, 1962, pp. 164–5, cf. p. 172.

If it is agreed that the action in question is within the scope of the functions of the Organization but it is alleged that it has been initiated or carried out in a manner not in conformity with the division of functions among the several organs which the Charter prescribes, one moves to the internal plane, to the internal structure of the Organization. If the action was taken by the wrong organ, it was irregular as a matter of that internal structure, but this would not necessarily mean that the expense incurred was not an expense of the Organization. Both national and international law contemplate cases in which the body corporate or politic may be bound, as to third parties, by an *ultra vires* act of an agent.[21]

It has been suggested that in view of this pronouncement by the Court exception must be taken to the present writer's comments in *BYIL*, 1961, pp. 459-60 on 'constitutionality, inherent powers and binding obligations'.[22] The suggestion is in fact that the Court did not admit the *limitations* of the inherent powers which the present writer submitted, *loc. cit.*, under (iii) and (iv), as *internal* limitations, and which have been repeated in the text above. However, it is then overlooked that the Court's pronouncement was concerned with the *external* validity and with drawing the necessary internal consequences therefrom.[23] As was pointed out *loc. cit.*, p. 460, and discussed more fully in a subsequent study on the external effects of constitutional limitations,[24] the external validity does not necessarily depend upon the internal limitations. And when the Court assumed that the external validity would produce even internal effects between the Organization and its Members, and when it thereby established an *obligation* for these to contribute, it should be recalled that the Court was at that point interpreting (the term 'expenses of the Organization' in) a constitutional provision which expressly conferred upon the Organization a power to make decisions binding upon Member States[25] (this, in the submission of the present writer, was a necessary condition for such a power [*loc. cit.*, p. 459, (iv)]). Indeed, it is submitted that the Court did not intend to deny that any of the limitations listed above (and in Chapter IV,3(g)) apply *internally* to *inherent* powers. A different matter is that the Court did not pass upon the question of to what extent a procedural irregularity would entail internal *invalidity* and thus affect the 'internal *capacity*' rather than the internal *right.*

If the United Nations establishes a Force by individual enlistment, it has in principle the same exclusive *organic jurisdiction* over this Force and its members as it has over its other organs, and as States and other

21. *ICJ Reports,* 1962, p. 168.

22. *Bowett: United Nations Forces* (London 1964) p. 309, cf. p. 327.

23. Cf. the reference in *ICJ Reports,* 1962, p. 169, to the fact that the Organization has no choice but to pay expenses arising out of obligations already incurred by it.

24. *Indian Journal of International Law,* IV (1964) at pp. 27–35.

25. See *ibid.,* pp. 24 and 66.

subjects of international law have over their armed forces. In particular, the Organization has exclusive operational command. It also has exclusive legislative, executive and judicial powers over the members of the Force in that capacity to the extent that it is in a factual position to exercise them [26] and subject, of course, to the same exceptions as apply to the exclusive organic jurisdiction of States over the members of their armed forces. However, in personal matters the members of a United Nations Force remain subject to the law and authorities of their national State and of the host State, to the extent that the powers of these States are not curtailed by privileges and immunities even in such matters.

However, all the military Forces which the League of Nations and the United Nations so far established or were authorized to establish were composed of national contingents under a central command. The relationship between each contingent and the central command dit not differ much from one Force to another. But the position of the central command itself has been of two different types:

In the majority of cases the command was vested in an officer appointed by (or at the request of) the Organization and responsible to it. This commander then took his orders from the Organization and the Force thereby became an organ of the Organization. However, the States providing contingents retained their powers over the members of their contingents in personnel matters, including the disciplinary powers and the power of criminal jurisdiction. This was the position of all the peace-keeping Forces. It was apparently also the system envisaged for the Forces to combat aggression to be established pursuant to Articles 43 et seq. of the United Nations Charter.

In other cases, however, the commander (or commanders) remained, or was to remain, a national official and to take his orders from his own government or from a group of governments. Thus, in Korea command authority over the entire Force was vested in a United States General. He took his orders from his own government, which in turn consulted with and took advice, but not orders, from the other participating States and from the United Nations. This system, or a system where several or all the participating States would share in the command, was also envisaged under the Uniting for Peace Resolution of 1950 and under Article 16 of the Covenant of the League of Nations, none of which was ever implemented in their military aspects. In all these cases the Force remained, or would remain, an organ of the States concerned.

While both these types of Forces are United Nations (or League of Nations) Forces in a political sense, only Forces under the Organization's command are its Forces in a narrow, legal sense. This is of partic-

---

26. On criminal jurisdiction see *above*, pp. 365–72, and *below*, p. 421.

ular significance in respect of the question of *international responsibility for and representation of the Force.*

In those cases where the Force is an organ of the Organization, under its operational command, the international responsibility for it and its representation internationally must vest in the Organization. The States providing contingents have no such responsibility and representation. They only have (internal) rights and duties vis-à-vis the Organization. These include notably the duty to take such measures as depend upon them to ensure that their contingents obey the operational orders of the Organization and live up to its international obligations.—The international *responsibility* of the United Nations for its Force implies that the Organization alone is the appropriate addressee of claims in respect of the Force and liable to pay reparation for any offences committed by its members *as such.* It is also the bearer of the international duty to take disciplinary and criminal action against such offenders. However it may, and indeed does, have the States providing contingents execute this obligation. While this, for internal political and legal reasons, may be necessary at the present stage in respect of members of national contingents, it is submitted that the United Nations already at the present stage could elaborate its own criminal law and establish its own criminal courts [27] for its own officials and for other personnel enlisted individually by it. Even if it is not expected that there will ever be a need for applying such law and tribunals, their mere existence would offer an external guarantee that the United Nations intends to live up to its international obligations notwithstanding the functional immunity which its officials enjoy. —The international *representation* of the Force by the United Nations implies that it alone concludes agreements and presents international claims on behalf of the Force and its members as such. Practice in respect of claims has not been entirely clear and consistent, because the States providing contingents have also made protests. However, in most cases they may have acted in diplomatic protection of their nationals as persons, rather than in functional protection of the members of the Force as such, or else in support of the claims of the United Nations.[28]

On the other hand, if a Force is under national command, the Organization has no legal responsibility for it and does not represent it internationally. In these cases only the political responsibility vests in the United Nations. Thus, the United Nations Force in Korea was under the international responsibility of the United States and, to a lesser degree, of the other participating States. The responsibility for a Force establish-

27. See further details *above,* Chapter VIII,11.
28. The latter has been submitted by *Bowett: United Nations Forces* (London 1964) p. 243, cf. *above,* p. 115, note 86.

ed under the Uniting for Peace resolution would be divided between the States in command and the other participating States in a similar manner. The States taking part in an action under Article 16 of the League of Nations Covenant would have shared the international responsibility for the Force in a manner even closer to that which applies in a traditional coalition of national armies.

The United Nations has the international responsibility for and representation of a Force under its command also in relation to *non-member States.* The International Court of Justice held already in its advisory opinion on *Reparation for Injuries* that the Organization's international personality is objective, i.e. it is not contingent upon 'recognition'. The criticism of this ruling, on the basis that non-members are not parties to the Charter, is irrelevant, because the international personality of the United Nations, as stated above, does not depend upon the Charter, but follows from the existence of the Organization as such. Therefore neither the fact that a treaty is not binding upon non-parties, nor the many other reasons which have been advanced, can validly restrict the international personality of the United Nations so as not to operate in relation to States which have not 'recognized' the Organization, through membership, treaties, 'diplomatic' relations or other acts. This is true also of the belligerent rights of the Organization in connection with any hostilities in which its Force becomes involved. No recognition of belligerency is required by the opposing State or other community. This is true even if one—in accordance with the general view among writers, but in opposition to practice—refuses to admit belligerent rights for non-recognized *insurgents.* Thus, even if the opposing State or other community has not recognized the United Nations as a general subject of international law or as a belligerent, it must treat the Organization as the party to the conflict if the latter has operational command over its Force. In such cases the opposing State or other community cannot treat for example the States providing contingents as parties to the conflict on the grounds that it does not recognize the Organization as a subject of international law or as a belligerent. Still less does such non-recognition render inapplicable the general laws of war, or those conventions on warfare to which both the United Nations and the other parties to the conflict are contracting parties.

Hostilities calling for *application of the laws of war* have taken place in Korea and Congo. In *Korea* the Geneva Conventions were not applicable as such. They had not been formally ratified or acceded to by the parties on both sides, and most of the declarations that had been made at a time when major hostilities were still on were too vague to constitute informal acceptance *ad hoc* in accordance with Article 2 of the Conventions. The only clear and early informal acceptances, those by the Republic of Korea and the United Nations Command, were confined to Article 3 and to the Prisoners of War Convention, respectively. The legal situation was thus not so good as most or all writers assume. During the hostilities in the *Congo* only the Central Government was a party to the Conventions, and even this was not confirmed until February 1961. Neither the United Nations nor the authorities in Katanga acceded formally, nor did they accept the Conventions in accordance with Article 2.

However, both parties in Korea declared that they would act in accordance with the *principles* of the Conventions. Likewise did the United Nations in respect of the Congo, the Middle East and Cyprus. This, together with the reciprocal accusations of violations in Korea and the Congo, indicates that both parties intended to apply the *general* (customary) laws of war, or even that they considered themselves and the other side bound to do so. However, this practice is not in itself clear and extensive enough to constitute customary law in favour of the applicability of the general laws of war to United Nations actions.

Even if United Nations enforcement actions do not constitute war in a formal sense and should not be referred to as 'war', they display, at the present stage of development, the same factual characteristics as war. They thus constitute war in material sense. The laws of war apply to any armed conflict of an international character and must therefore apply also to a United Nations enforcement action. This is true, not only if the Force is under national command and thus governed in this respect by the international obligations of the participating States, but also if the Force is under the command of the United Nations. Similarly it is true, not only if the action is based upon the right of collective self-defence under general international law, but even if it is based upon the specific provisions of the Charter.

The situation would be different only if a United Nations action were so quick and overwhelming that organized resistance were not possible. At the present stage of development this is hardly thinkable in respect of an enforcement action against an aggressor. However, it is possible, and has indeed proved possible, in most cases of peace-keeping actions, where the Force intervenes *before* large-scale aggression has taken place or after the parties have agreed to an armistice. In such cases the occupation, the occasional hostile incidents, etc., are governed by other legal principles, which, however, will normally stay well within the limits of the general laws of war. On the other hand, if a peace-keeping Force becomes involved in organized hostilities, the general laws of war must apply to these, too. It is submitted that this is true even if the conflict is not with a State, but with a dissident group within a State, unless the 'United Nations Force' has become part of the national forces of the State concerned or is operating against a dissident group in a territory under the Organization's own sovereignty or administration. In the latter cases the conflict will be governed by the general laws of war to the extent that these are applicable to *internal* conflicts, and by the reduced regime of Article 3 of the Geneva Conventions if the State concerned or the Organization, respectively, has acceded to these Conventions, formally or informally. Otherwise, i.e. if the United Nations Force is operating as an independent Force (under the Organization's command) in territory which is not under its administration, the conflict is governed by the regular provisions of the Conventions if both the United Nations and its opponents have acceded formally or informally, or, if they have not, merely by the general laws of war.

When engaged in military action against aggression, the United Nations must benefit from the right of *discrimination against the aggressor* which exists in the modern laws governing war between States.

These imply that the aggressor does not have a 'right' to inflict *any* damage or injury upon the defenders or neutral parties. The aggressor is liable to pay *reparation* and render *restitution* even in respect of acts which all belligerent States were entitled to perform under the traditional laws of war. The United Nations must thus in principle be entitled to restitution and reparation from the aggressor, to the same extent as any State which comes to the assistance of the victim, in respect of loss and damage suffered by the Organization and its Force and of other costs it has incurred. Furthermore, aggression against United Nations troops must entail the same criminal and civil responsibility on the part of the responsible political and military leaders of the aggressor State as an attack upon a State. In both these respects a State victim of aggression already has the maximum rights vis-à-vis the aggressor. And if these are extended to those who come to the victim's assistance, no further extension is possible, even if the national defending forces are turned into, or replaced by, a United Nations Force.

The United Nations must also have the same right as States to prosecute enemy personnel for *war crimes*.[29] (Preferably, war criminals ought to be brought before *international* tribunals composed of neutral[30]

29. On the capacity of the Organization to exercise criminal jurisdiction in this and other respects, see *above*, Chapter VIII,11(a)(ii).

30. It is recalled that, in connection with the Korean war, certain Member States which had not taken an active part in the United Nations military action, were called upon to perform certain neutral functions in connexion with the armistice agreement. See also *above*, Chapter II,4, note 47, and Chapter III,3, at note 54.

judges, rather than before national tribunals of the opposing side of the war criminals; the United Nations is in a better position than States to organize such tribunals.) However, not even in a military conflict with the United Nations can those resisting the United Nations action be prosecuted for war crimes if they have not violated the traditional laws of war. The position in this respect is not appreciably altered by the fact that the United Nations intervenes. Even in these circumstances it would be going too far to prosecute such personnel of the aggressor as are not personally responsible for the decision to attack, for acts which would have been legal in a legal war. And it certainly would not induce them to attempt to observe the traditional laws of war. Criminal sanctions and the stigma of 'war crime' must be reserved for such acts as are serious enough to constitute crimes by whichever side they are committed.

Thus, the principle of discrimination applies with regard to some sanctions, but not with regard to all. The same is true when one considers the main fields of substantive law separately.

The *humanitarian* rules embodied in the traditional laws of war must be fully observed even by a United Nations Force. The overriding need to protect military personnel and civilians on both sides, as well as neutral civilians, from undue suffering applies as fully if the aggressor is resisted by a United Nations Force as if he is resisted by States. The same is true of the need to protect cultural property. This applies to the rules concerning the treatment and protection of the wounded and the sick, prisoners and civilians, and to those parts of the law of military occupation which are designed to protect the population of the occupied territory. It also applies to the rules concerning the actual conduct of hostilities, except that it is not clear whether the outlawry of nuclear weapons declared by the United Nations General Assembly, inter alia on the basis of certain earlier treaties, applies also to the United Nations itself. Similarly the *Geneva Conventions* of 1949 and the Hague Convention of 1954 for the Protection of Cultural Property must apply equally to both sides, both because they are concerned with the humanitarian laws of war and because they were adopted at a time when governments were aware of the illegality of war and should have made any modifications in the texts of the Conventions which this fact might call for if they had considered any discrimination between aggressor and victim justified and expedient. Only the Hague Conventions of 1907 can be considered as having been superseded by the treaties outlawing war, under the principle that recent law supersedes earlier law that is inconsistent therewith.

Should the United Nations on its side violate the traditional laws of war in the humanitarian field or any other laws of war that are binding upon it as upon any other defender, it would be liable to pay reparation, and its personnel would be subject to prosecution as war criminals. It may be questioned whether the aggressor *State* (as opposed to the individual who has suffered the injury, loss or damage) would be entitled to claim such reparation, and in particular whether it might enforce the obligations of the Organization by reprisals, prosecution of the guilty United Nations personnel or other sanctions. Even if the aggressor State is considered to be entitled to do this vis-à-vis a defending *State,* there might in this respect be room for a distinction between the United Nations and other defenders, at least *de lege ferenda.* However, it is doubtful whether or to what extent such a distinction should really be made.

Otherwise there is not even *de lege ferenda* much room for special rules for the United Nations in the military and humanitarian field, since such rules would run counter to over-riding principles of humanity and justice. If discriminatory rules were to be established this would have to be done through the regular procedures of international legislation (treaty, customary law or resolutions which acquire a certain legal effect through estoppel); the Charter does not appear to confer this authority upon the Security Council acting unilaterally.

In the *economic* and other non-military fields, on the other hand, the modern laws of war imply a far-reaching right of discrimination against the aggressor. This must apply in favour of the United Nations as of any other defender. Thus, the United Nations must have the same right as belligerent and neutral States to invalidate the legislation and other measures taken by the illegal occupant, even if these do not violate the traditional laws of war. The same is true in respect of the acquisitions and other economic transactions of the aggressor—including booty, prizes, requisitions and disposal of proceeds of government property— relating to property or rights of the victim State, its allies, the United Nations, neutral States or their nationals, inside or outside occupied territories, if the original owners had not themselves voluntarily (without duress) transferred the property or rights to the aggressor or his nationals, officials or inhabitants. However, in this field there is room for establishing a more rigid and consistent *practice* of invalidation than hitherto. The UN may be in a good practical position to do this, i.e. to utilize the already existing general right of discrimination, through the application of relevant provisions of the Charter and through recommendations and decisions of its organs, pursuant notably to Article 41 of the Charter. These recommendations and decisions could, and indeed should, be prepared in advance by studies and recommendations of the United Nations and private organizations working in the field of international law.

Even if no specific decisions have been made, Member States are under an obligation, pursuant to Article 2(5) of the Charter, not to assist the aggressor State against whom the Organization is taking action. This obligation (and right) is not, any more than the powers arising out of Article 41, limited by the traditional laws of war, except that the provision obviously does not comprise such humanitarian assistance to individuals as does not involve assistance to the aggressor State as well.

However, none of these powers which the Charter confers upon the Security Council is confined to cases where the Organization is taking military action. They apply in all cases where aggression has been determined, even if the military resistance is performed by national forces. Only the automatic obligation not to assist the agressor State would be confined to cases where the United Nations takes *military* action (by a Force under national or international command), if the terms „preventive or enforcement action" in Article 2(5) were interpreted in this sense. However, this would probably be too narrow, quite apart from the fact that this obligation, in so far as aggression is concerned, follows already from the outlawry of war.[31]

The Charter provisions referred to above are of particular importance in the field of *neutrality*. Already as a result of the outlawry of aggressive war by the Briand-Kellog Pact, 'neutral' States are entitled to discriminate against the aggressor. This applies to civilian and military trade and other intercourse with the belligerents, to title to property acquired or transferred by them, to military personnel and escaped prisoners of war who seek refuge in 'neutral' territory, and in other respects where no valid humanitarian considerations are prejudiced. This is true also in respect of a United Nations military action against an agressor. The provisions of the United Nations Charter referred to above imply that States are not only *entitled* to ignore the traditional laws of neutrality, they have even an *obligation* to disregard these laws to the extent that their observance would imply assistance to the aggressor State or would conflict with the decisions of the Security Council. Indeed, the Organization can recommend, or (within the limits of Articles 2(5), 24, 25 and 41 et seq.) order, its Member States to take action against the aggressor and to assist the Organization, the victim State and its allies, in violation of the traditional laws of neutrality, without thereby giving the aggressor the right to attack these Member States or to resort to other in themselves illegal acts as reprisals. However, again, these decisions may be made and are binding even if the United Nations has taken no military action.

The *political* powers conferred upon the United Nations by the Charter may similarly be exercised also in the course of a military action and are then not limited by the traditional laws of war. This may imply, for example, a right to reorganize an occupied territory politically even

31. Cf. *above*, p. 285.

durante bello, even if a defending State would not have such a right under the traditional or modern laws of war.[32] But again, these and other political powers of the United Nations are not in law confined to those cases where the Organization takes military action by a Force of its own.

The conclusion, *de lege lata,* is thus that, with few or no exceptions, a United Nations Force is governed by the same laws of war as are applicable to wars between States. This is true even of a Force established pursuant to the express provisions in Article 42 or Articles 43 et seq. of the Charter, and, at least as far as the substantive law is concerned, also of a Force under the Organization's own command and responsibility.

Even *de lege ferenda* the situation is essentially the same. The reasons which dictate the laws of war in the military and humanitarian field apply with equal force to actions by a United Nations Force. And in the political, economic and related fields of the laws of war and neutrality, the relevant provisions of the Charter, which are not confined to cases where the United Nations itself takes military action, are wide enough as they are. The Security Council has a broad power of decision in respect of Member States, and even in respect of non-member States if these are considered to be bound by the Charter.[33] This obviates the need for establishment of rules of international law by conventional means for military actions decided or recommended by the Security Council. And even in those cases where an action may be undertaken pursuant to a decision or recommendation of the *General Assembly,*[34] the automatic, passive obligation in Article 2(5) goes a long way to meet the need. Any improvements which may be made in those fields of the laws of war which have been discussed above should largely be made applicable to all cases of (aggressive) war, whether or not the resistance is rendered by a United Nations Force.

A different matter is that United Nations actions should be taken into account in the drafting and revision of general conventions on warfare in order to facilitate their application to United Nations action in those respects where the inherent differences between the Organization and States complicate the application of provisions which have been drafted with a view to States only.[35] However, this is a matter of method of application, rather than of any difference in substantive rules.

32. *Above,* p. 281.

33. On this question see *Nordisk Tidsskrift for international Ret og Jus gentium,* XXXIV (1964) pp. 12–14. and *Falk: The authority of the United Nations to Control Non-Members* (Princeton University 1965).

34. On the question of the legality of this, see *above,* Chapter IV,4(d), and *ICJ Reports,* 1962, pp. 164–5 and 170–2. As has been pointed out *above,* pp. 175–7, a United Nations Force is subject to the laws of war irrespective of whether it has been established in a constitutional or a non-constitutional fashion.

35. *Above,* Chapter VIII,11.

Furthermore, there is a need for internal regulations for UN Forces, both to set forth and implement the substantive law applicable to United Nations military action and to secure its enforcement. Such regulations can be enacted by the Security Council, by the General Assembly, by the Secretary-General or by the Commander of the Force.

The question of the applicability of the *conventions on warfare* is of practical importance only in respect of those conventions which provide more than what is already customary law. This is in the first place true of the modern conventions, notably the 1949 Geneva Conventions and the 1954 Hague Convention on the Protection of Cultural Property.

If the United Nations Force is under *national operational command* and responsibility, each contingent is *ipso facto* bound by those conventions to which the State providing it is a party. This creates a number of practical and legal difficulties, some of which arise even if these are all parties to the same conventions. Although already known in respect of regular coalition armies, these difficulties will become more important if the United Nations Force is composed of a great number of contingents and, especially, if these are integrated, unless the contingents were to be integrated under the command of one State to the extent where they would become part of that State's armed forces and subject only to its treaty commitments; however, then the Force would lose its character of a United Nations Force.

On the other hand, if the Force is under *United Nations operational command* and responsibility, the treaty commitments of the States providing contingents are irrelevant, because these States are not even in a limited sense parties to the conflict. The Force is then subject to the conventions only if the United Nations as an Organization has acceded to them. If it has not, the States providing contingents may, if they themselves are parties to the conventions, acquire a certain indirect responsibility for having placed contingents at the disposal of an Organization which is not a contracting party. Whatever protection this may offer the members of the Forces opposing the United Nations and the civilian population against acts of the United Nations Force, it offers no legal protection under the conventions to the members of the United Nations' own Force and to the civilian population against the acts of the opposing forces. Even if the State which the latter forces represent is a party to the conventions, it has no legal obligation to observe their provisions in a conflict with an Organization which is not, except to the extent that the provisions reflect the general laws of war.

It is thus necessary for the Organization itself to be a party to the conventions on warfare in those cases where the United Nations action is conducted under the Organization's own command, but only then.

The following conclusions in respect of the feasibility of United Nations accession to the conventions are therefore confined to these cases.

The United Nations has concluded a great number of agreements with one or several States, without basis in any specific provision of the Charter. There is no legal difference, from the point of view of capacity, between an agreement with a small number of States and one with a large number. Indeed, within the limits set forth *above*, Chapter IV,3(g), the Organization has an inherent legal capacity to conclude international agreements of any type with any number of States. This includes the capacity to become a party to multilateral law-making conventions between States. Intergovernmental organizations have on several occasions been original parties to such conventions in fact, and sometimes even in form. And the distinction between being an original party and becoming a party subsequently is as irrelevant from the point of view of legal capacity as is the number of parties to the agreement. Indeed, the UN has also acceded to such conventions subsequently in fact (i.e. it has assumed the rights and duties thereunder), if not in form. However, the difference between being a party in fact or in form is also submitted to be irrelevant from the point of view of treaty-making capacity. The crucial criterion is *whether*, not *how* the United Nations became a party. On the other hand, there is no provision in the Charter which precludes the United Nations from becoming a party to such conventions in general, or to the conventions on warfare in particular. There can thus be no doubt about the capacity of the United Nations to accede to these conventions.

More difficult is the question whether the conventions are open for accession to the United Nations. Their drafters had only States in mind. However, their purpose is, at least in the case of the Geneva Conventions, to cover all armed conflicts of an international character (and, on a modest scale, even those of an internal character), whatever the status of the conflict and the parties to it. To this end the Geneva Conventions carefully avoid the terms 'State' and 'war'. Instead they talk of 'parties to the conflict' and are open for accession to any 'Power'. These terms cannot be interpreted restrictively, as if they had read 'State'. The same is probably true of the other conventions which use 'Partie' and 'Puissance' and similar more general terms, including notably the 1907 Hague Conventions. These conventions must therefore be open for accession to the United Nations. However, it is hardly possible to extend by analogy the accession clauses of those conventions which refer to 'States'. This is notably true of the formal accession clause of the 1954 Hague Convention on the Protection of Cultural Property. This convention does not necessarily require United Nations accession to achieve its purpose. Moreover, it is the only convention on warfare which was adopted after consideration of the position of the United Nations. Nevertheless, it is probably open for *informal* acceptance in accordance with its Article 18(3), which speaks of 'one of the Powers in conflict'.

The United Nations has an inherent legal capacity to perform any of those sovereign and international acts which are necessary to implement the conventions. These are in fact the same as those which are required to implement the general laws of war, by which the United Nations is bound in any event. Thus the Organization can conclude agreements incidental to warfare, it can administer occupied territory, it can operate ships and aircraft under its own flag, registration and 'territorial' jurisdiction, it can establish prize law and prize courts etc. The Organization also has an inherent capacity to establish criminal law and to exercise *criminal jurisdiction* over its officials and over individually recruited members of its Force in respect of acts they have performed in that capacity, as well as over prisoners of war, over war criminals and over inhabitants of a territory occupied by it, except that if it wishes to establish its courts and carry out their sentences in a territory which is under the jurisdiction of a State, it needs the consent of that State. However, the Organization cannot exercise this inherent capacity over members of national contingents as long as the States providing these contingents have retained for themselves the criminal and disciplinary powers over the members thereof. From many points of view, and in particular in the light of experience in the Congo, it would be a great advantage if these powers, too, could be ceded to the United Nations. However, this is hardly necessary from a legal point of view. The United Nations can also leave it to each State to prosecute those members of its contingents which have violated the laws of war or the conventions on warfare. In the view of the present writer, this does not deprive the Organization of its external responsibility for the Force, if it has operational command. However, in order to live up to its external responsibility the Organization must then make the necessary arrangements with the States providing contingents to ensure that they effectively prosecute any violators.[36] Still less does the retention of criminal powers by these States mean, as has been suggested,[37] that the United Nations is incapable of applying the laws of war and the conventions on warfare and that, consequently, a United Nations Force may not be subject to and not protected by the general laws of war or the conventions on warfare.

The problems discussed in the preceding paragraph are not special to the conventions on warfare; they arise also in connection with the general laws of war. However, in a few respects an accession by the Organization to the Geneva Conventions will give rise to special problems: In the first place these Conventions expressly provide that the contracting

36. The UN has, at the time of writing, taken further steps to this end, see *above*, pp. 376 and 397.
37. By Draper, see *above*, pp. 374-5.

parties shall enact criminal legislation and shall try persons who violate the Conventions. These provisions hardly preclude the Organization from delegating these functions to the States providing contingents, by adopting their criminal law by reference and by turning the offenders over to the competent national authorities for trial.[38] In the second place the Geneva Conventions contain a number of provisions which prescribe the application to protected persons of the *same* law, courts and conditions as apply to the members of the Party's own forces or to his nationals, or which set this law or these conditions as a minimum standard for the treatment of the protected persons. Although the United Nations has the legal competence to establish such law, courts and conditions, it may not always wish, or be in a practical position, to do so, notably if it has no territory. In such cases it will have to resort to the law, courts and conditions of one or more of the States providing contingents. The relevant provisions of the Conventions hardly preclude this, if the selection of the State concerned is made in good faith.

The numerous *practical* questions involved in the implementation of the general laws of war and the conventions on warfare by the United Nations have not been examined here. They require a separate study.

The United Nations can accede to the conventions in two ways: It can either accede formally, pursuant to the accession clause, in those cases where this is not confined to 'States' (as the accession clause of the 1954 Hague Convention is, but not that of the 1907 Hague Conventions and the Geneva Conventions). Or the Organization can accept the conventions informally, pursuant to those provisions of the 1949 Geneva Conventions and the 1954 Hague Convention which provide that the parties to these conventions shall be bound also in relation to any non-contracting Power which declares that it accepts the provisions of the convention and which applies them. Although the provisions for such informal acceptance were included with a view to *ad hoc* acceptance for a particular conflict, their terms do not appear to preclude a general declaration valid for any present or future conflict.—Informal acceptance pursuant to these provisions is only possible if the other party to the conflict is already a formal party to the convention. Thus, if the Organization accedes only informally, it produces no legal effects vis-à-vis an opponent who is not a formal party either. Otherwise there is no difference, from the point of view of capacity to accede, between the two modes of accession; if the Organization is a 'Power' for the purpose of the provision on informal acceptance, it must also be so for the purpose of the formal accession clause. Nor is there any difference as to the substantive legal effects of accession; by either method all the substantive provisions of the conventions become binding upon both parties to

38. *Above*, Chapter III,2(a) and Chapter VIII,11(a)(iii).

the conflict. However, informal acceptance will not make the Organization a contracting party in the *formal* sense, for the purposes of the final clauses.

The conclusion thus is that it is legally possible for the United Nations to accede to most of the conventions on warfare. It has the legal capacity to accede to and to implement all of them. And the majority of them, including the Hague and the Geneva Conventions, are open either for formal or informal accession by the Organization; the Geneva Conventions are open both for formal and for informal accession.

There remains the question of whether the Organization *should* accede.

The main argument *for* accession to the Geneva Conventions is the *humanitarian* consideration that accession is indispensable in order to ensure legal protection under the Conventions for the members of the United Nations Force and for civilians against acts of the opposing side. Accession is also necessary in order to provide a clear and direct legal protection under the Conventions for the members of the opposing forces and for civilians against the acts of the United Nations Force, although this consideration may be less important because it must be presumed that the United Nations, irrespective of any legal obligations, will conduct its operations in a *more* humane manner than required under the laws of war, and because of the indirect responsibility which might arise for the States parties to the Conventions out of the fact that they provide contingents to an Organization which is not a contracting party. The applicability of the *general* laws of war is of course not affected by any non-accession to the Conventions.

Another important argument for United Nations accession to the Conventions is the fact that any indirect responsibility for the States providing contingents which might result from a failure of the Organization to accede, may lead to claims from these States for a corresponding part in the operational decision-making. Indeed, it is difficult to separate operational command and international responsibility. And this difficulty works both ways. This fact could set off a chain reaction which would undermine the exclusive operational command of the United Nations in those cases where the Force has been placed under the Organization's command in order to make sure that the operation is conducted exclusively in the light of United Nations policies and independently of the national policies of particular States. If the United Nations is to have exclusive operational command it must therefore also see to it that it alone has the international responsibility.

The main argument *against* United Nations accession, other than the legal problems discussed above, is that a United Nations action must be distinguished from war between States. From this point both legal and political consequences have been drawn.

Legally it has been maintained that the Organization cannot be governed by the same laws of war as States. This view, as has been demonstrated above, is not justified, if one takes into account the fact that the modern laws of war discriminate between aggressors and defenders. At any event, the view is entirely invalid in respect of the Geneva Conventions, because these contain humanitarian provisions which must apply equally to all parties to an armed conflict, whatever its denomination and legal or political status.

More force is contained by the *political* argument that, even if the United Nations is legally subject to the laws of war, it would blur the political distinction between United Nations actions and wars between States if the Organization were to accede to the conventions on warfare on the same footing as States. This argument has mainly the Hague Conventions in mind, but it has been referred to also in connection with the Geneva Conventions. In the view of the present writer, this argument cannot override the two arguments *for* accession referred to above, as long as there is little or no factual difference between a United Nations action and traditional war. The Geneva Conventions cover, and must cover, all armed conflicts of an international character irrespective of the legal and political status of the parties and the hostilities, and irrespective of the even more fundamental legal and political distinction between aggressor and defender. There is not sufficient reason to make an exception in this respect for United Nations actions. There is even less reason to make an exception merely for United Nations actions under the command of the Organization, as one would have to do because United Nations actions under national command are in any event governed by the Geneva Conventions if the participating States are parties to them.

If it is felt, nevertheless, that a distinction has to be made (in the narrow field of the application of the Geneva Conventions to United Nations actions under the Organization's command) this could be better done by having the United Nations accede in a different *manner*. Thus, it could accede pursuant to the informal acceptance clause in Article 2 common to the four Geneva Conventions, which would produce the same substantive effects, but not the formal effects, of a formal accession.

Whatever form it choses, the United Nations can, if it wishes, attach to its accession such reservations as it may deem fit in order to facilitate the application to the Organization of provisions which were drafted with a view to States, or in order to clarify how it proposes to implement these provisions. This method may be used to remove any legal doubts or practical difficulties arising out of the fact that the United Nations does not have the same means at its disposal as States have.

So far the question of United Nations accession has fallen between two stools. Application of the conventions on warfare is primarily called for in respect of enforcement actions against an aggressor. However, such action has only been undertaken once, and then under national command. The relevant provisions in Articles 43 et seq. of the Charter, which appear to envisage United Nations command, have not been implemented, and as long as this has not been done, an accession specially for this purpose might not command enough support. On the other hand, a number of Forces have been set up for peace-keeping purposes. However, even if these must be prepared to fight, they are not intended to do so, and a United Nations accession specially for the purpose of any such Force might cast doubt upon this intention. It is submitted that the best solution to these two dilemmas is to have the United Nations accede in a general, or absract, fashion (i.e. without linking or confining its accession to either combat forces against aggressors or to peace-keeping forces), for the purpose of any armed conflict in which it may become involved.

Although none of the methods referred to in the three preceding paragraphs is necessary from a legal point of view, it is submitted that it will in fact be easier for the United Nations to accede to the conventions on warfare in the manner indicated there, i.e. by an *informal and abstract acceptance on terms*.

In reply to invitations by the *Comité international de la Croix-Rouge* to accede to the Geneva Conventions, the United Nations has included in its agreements with the States providing contingents to Cyprus specific undertakings by the latter to take the measures necessary to ensure that their contingents will apply the Geneva Conventions and the 1954 Hague Convention. The Organization has also proposed itself to take certain measures to assist these States in their enforcement of these Conventions. These represent important basic steps. However, in order to confer the benefits of the Conventions also upon the members of the United Nations' own Force and to ensure general protection against acts of the forces opposing it, it is necessary, in addition, that the Organization itself undertake an external legal commitment, by acceding to the Conventions; otherwise the opposing force will have no legal obligations under the Conventions vis-à-vis a Force under United Nations command.

Such accession must not be allowed to be prevented by the feeling that the United Nations is more than and above States, and therefore for political reasons could not accede to these Conventions on the same level as States. This would be premature. The world has not reached the stage where the United Nations could effectively exercise supra-national powers. In this situation one must, in respect of those legal questions which have not been answered by the provisions of the Charter, be content to have the United Nations enjoy the *same* rights and duties as

States. If the Organization in these respects does not claim and exercise equal rights with States, it is more likely to fall *below* the level of States than rise above it. Thus, a failure by the United Nations to accede to the Geneva Conventions is not likely to lead to greater rights for the Organization than for States in an armed conflict. It is more likely to result in the United Nations Force enjoying *less* protection than the forces of States do, and in the Organization exercising less control over its Force than it otherwise could.

STATUS AGREEMENT FOR THE UNITED NATIONS
FORCE IN CYPRUS

Letter from the Secretary-General of the United Nations to the Minister for Foreign Affairs of Cyprus

31 March 1964

Sir,

I have the honour to refer to the resolution adopted by the Security Council of the United Nations on 4 March 1964 (S/5575). In paragraph 4 of that resolution the Security Council recommended the creation, with the consent of the Government of the Republic of Cyprus, of a United Nations peace-keeping force in Cyprus. By letter of 4 March 1964, the Minister for Foreign Affairs of Cyprus informed the Secretary-General of the consent of the Government of the Republic of Cyprus to the creation of the Force. The Force was established on 27 March 1964. I have also the honour to refer to Article 105 of the Charter of the United Nations which provides that the Organization shall enjoy in the territory of its Members such privileges and immunities as are necessary for the fulfilment of its purposes, and to the Convention on the Privileges and Immunities of the United Nations to which Cyprus is a party. Having in view the provisions of the Convention on the Privileges and Immunities of the United Nations, I wish to propose that the United Nations and Cyprus should make the following *ad hoc* arrangements defining certain of the conditions necessary for the effective discharge of the functions of the United Nations Force while it remains in Cyprus. These arrangements are set out below under the following headings:

Definitions

1. The 'United Nations Force in Cyprus' (hereinafter referred to as 'the Force') consists of the United Nations Commander appointed by the Secretary-General in accordance with the Security Council resolution of 4 March 1964 (S/5575) and all military personnel placed under his command. For the purpose of these arrangements the term 'member of the Force' refers to any person, belonging to the military service of a State, who is serving under the Commander of the United Nations Force and to any civilian placed under the Commander by the State to which such civilian belongs.

2. 'Cypriot authorities' means all State and local, civil and military authorities of the Government of the Republic of Cyprus called upon to perform functions relating to the Force under the provisions of these arrangements, without prejudice to the ultimate responsibility of the Government of the Republic of Cyprus (hereinafter referred to as 'the Government').

3. 'Participating State' means a Member of the United Nations that contributes military personnel to the Force.

4. 'Area of operations' includes all areas throughout the territory of the Republic of Cyprus (which territory is hereinafter referred to as 'Cyprus') where the Force is deployed in the performance of its functions as defined in operative paragraph 5 of

the Security Council resolution of 4 March 1964 (S/5575); military installations or other premises referred to in paragraph 19 of these arrangements; and lines of communication and supply utilized by the Force pursuant to paragraphs 32 and 33 of these arrangements.

International status of the Force and its members

5. Members of the Force shall respect the laws and regulations of Cyprus and shall refrain from any activity of a political character in Cyprus and from any action incompatible with the international nature of their duties or inconsistent with the spirit of the present arrangements. The Commander shall take all appropriate measures to ensure the observance of these obligations.

6. The Government undertakes to respect the exclusively international character of the Force as established by the Secretary-General in accordance with the Security Council resolution of 4 March 1964 (S/5575) and the international nature of its command and function.

Entry and exit: Identification

7. Members of the Force shall be exempt from passport and visa regulations and immigration inspection and restrictions on entering or departing from Cyprus. They shall also be exempt from any regulations governing the residence of aliens in Cyprus, including registration, but shall not be considered as acquiring any right to permanent residence or domicile in Cyprus. For the purpose of such entry or departure members of the Force will be required to have only (a) an individual or collective movement order issued by the Commander or an appropriate authority of the Participating State; and (b) a personal identity card issued by the Commander under the authority of the Secretary-General, except in the case of first entry, when the personal military identity card issued by the appropriate authorities of the Participating State will be accepted in lieu of the said Force identity card.

8. Members of the Force may be required to present, but not to surrender, their identity cards upon demand of such Cypriot authorities as may be mutually agreed between the Commander and the Government. Except as provided in paragraph 7 of these arrangements the identity card will be the only document required for a member of the Force. If, however, it does not show the full name, date of birth, rank and number (if any), service and photograph of a member of the Force, such member may be required to present likewise the personal military identity card or similar document issued by the appropriate authorities of the Participating State to which he belongs.

9. If a member of the Force leaves the service of the Participating State to which he belongs and is not repatriated, the Commander shall immediately inform the Government, giving such particulars as may be required. The Commander shall similarly inform the Government if any member of the Force has absented himself for more than twenty-one days. If an expulsion order against an ex-member of the Force has been made, the Commander shall be responsible for ensuring that the person concerned shall be received within the territory of the Participating State concerned.

Jurisdiction

10. The following arrangements respecting criminal and civil jurisdiction are made having regard to the special functions of the Force and to be interests of the United Nations, and not for the personal benefit of the members of the Force.

Criminal jurisdiction

11. Members of the Force shall be subject to the exclusive jurisdiction of their respective national States in respect of any criminal offences which may be committed by them in Cyprus.

Civil jurisdiction

12. (a) Members of the Force shall not be subject to the civil jurisdiction of the courts of Cyprus or to other legal process in any matter relating to their official duties. In a case arising from a matter relating to the official duties of a member of the Force and which involves a member of the Force and a Cypriot citizen, and in other disputes as agreed, the procedure provided in paragraph 38 (b) shall apply to the settlement.

(b) In those cases where civil jurisdiction is exercised by the courts of Cyprus with respect to members of the Force, the courts or other Cypriot authorities shall grant members of the Force sufficient opportunity to safeguard their rights. If the Commander certifies that a member of the Force is unable because of official duties or authorized absence to protect his interests in a civil proceeding in which he is a participant the aforesaid court or authority shall at his request suspend the proceeding until the elimination of the disability, but for not more than ninety days. Property of a member of the Force which is certified by the Commander to be needed by him for the fulfilment of his official duties shall be free from seizure for the satisfaction of a judgement, decision or order, together with other property not subject thereto under the law of Cyprus. The personal liberty of a member of the Force shall not be restricted by a court of other Cypriot authority in a civil proceeding, whether to enforce a judgement, decision or order, to compel an oath of disclosure, or for any other reason.

(c) In the cases provided for in sub-paragraph (b) above, the claimant may elect to have his claim dealt with in accordance with the procedure set out in paragraph 38 (b) of these arrangements. Where a claim adjudicated or an award made in favour of the claimant by a court of Cyprus or the Claims Commission under paragraph 38 (b) of these arrangements has not been made satisfied, the Government may, without prejudice to the claimant's rights, seek the good offices of the Secretary-General to obtain satisfaction.

Notification: certification

13. If any civil proceeding is instituted against a member of the Force before any court of Cyprus having jurisdiction, notification shall be given to the Commander. The Commander shall certify to the court whether or not the proceeding is related to the official duties of such member.

Military police: arrest: transfer of custody and mutual assistance

14. The Commander shall take all appropriate measures to ensure maintenance of discipline and good order among members of the Force. To this end military police designated by the Commander shall police the premises referred to in paragraph 19 of these arrangements, such areas where the Force is deployed in the performance of its functions, and such other areas as the Commander deems necessary to maintain discipline and order among members of the Force. For the purpose of this paragraph the military police of the Force shall have the power of arrest over members of the Force.

15. Military police of the Force may take into custody any Cypriot citizen committing an offence or causing a disturbance on the premises referred to in paragraph 19, without subjecting him to the ordinary routine of arrest, in order immediately to deliver him to the nearest appropriate Cypriot authorities for the purpose of dealing with such offence or disturbance.

16. The Cypriot authorities may take into custody a member of the Force, without subjecting him to the ordinary routine of arrest in order immediately to deliver him, together with any weapons or items seized, to the nearest appropriate authorities of the Force: (a) when so requested by the Commander, or (b) in cases in which the military police of the Force are unable to act with the necessary promptness when a

member of the Force is apprehended in the commission or attempted commission of a criminal offence that results or might result in serious injury to persons or property, or serious impairment of other legally protected rights.

17. When a person is taken into custody under paragraph 15 and paragraph 16 (b), the Commander or the Cypriot authorities, as the case may be, may make a preliminary interrogation but may not delay the transfer of custody. Following the transfer of custody, the person concerned shall be made available upon request for further interrogation.

18. The Commander and the Cypriot authorities shall assist each other in the carrying out of all necessary investigations into offences in respect of which either or both have an interest, in the production of witnesses, and in the collection and production of evidence, including the seizure and, in proper cases, the handing over, of things connected with an offence. The handing over of any such things may be made subject to their return within the time specified by the authority delivering them. Each shall notify the other of the disposition of any case in the outcome of which the other may have an interest or in which there has been a transfer of custody under the provisions of paragraphs 15 and 16 of these arrangements. The Government will ensure the prosecution of persons subject to its criminal jurisdiction who are accused of acts in relation to the Force or its members which, if committed in relation to the Cypriot army or its members, would have rendered them liable to prosecution. The Secretary-General will seek assurances from Governments of Participating States that they will be prepared to exercise jurisdiction with respect to crimes or offences which may be committed against Cypriot citizens by members of their national contingents serving with the Force.

Premises of the Force

19. The Government shall provide without cost to the Force and in agreement with the Commander such areas for headquarters, camps, or other premises as may be necessary for the accommodation and the fulfilment of the functions of the Force. Without prejudice to the fact that all such premises remain the territory of Cyprus, they shall be inviolable and subject to the exclusive control and authority of the Commander, who alone may consent to the entry of officials to perform duties on such premises.

United Nations flag

20. The Government recognizes the right of the Force to display within Cyprus the United Nations flag on its headquarters, camps, posts or other premises, vehicles, vessels and otherwise as decided by the Commander. Other flags or pennants may be displayed only in exceptional cases and in accordance with conditions prescribed by the Commander. Sympathetic consideration will be given to observations or requests of the Government concerning this last-mentioned matter.

Uniform: Vehicle, vessel and aircraft markings and registration: Operating permits

21. Members of the Force shall normally wear their national uniform with such identifying United Nations insignia as the Commander may prescribe. The conditions on which the wearing of civilian dress is authorized shall be notified by the Commander to the Government and sympathetic consideration will be given to observations or requests of the Government concerning this matter. Service vehicles, vessels and aircraft shall carry a distinctive United Nations identification mark and licence which shall be notified by the Commander to the Government. Such vehicles, vessels and aircraft shall not be subject to registration and licensing under the laws and regulations of Cyprus. Cypriot authorities shall accept as valid, without a test or fee, a permit or licence for the operation of service vehicles, vessels and aircraft issued by the Commander.

Arms

22. Members of the Force may possess and carry arms in accordance with their orders.

Privileges and Immunities of the Force

23. The Force as a subsidiary organ of the United Nations, enjoys the status, privileges and immunities of the Organization in accordance with the Convention on the Privileges and Immunities of the United Nations. The provisions of article II of the Convention on the Privileges and Immunities of the United Nations shall also apply to the property, funds and assets of Participating States used in Cyprus in connexion with the national contingents serving in the Force. The Government recognizes that the right of the Force to import free of duty equipment for the Force and provisions, supplies and other goods for the exclusive use of members of the Force, members of the United Nations Secretariat detailed by the Secretary-General to serve with the Force, excluding locally recruited personnel, includes the right of the Force to establish, maintain and operate at headquarters, camps and posts, service institutes providing amenities for the persons aforesaid. The amenities that may be provided by service institutes shall be goods of a consumable nature (tobacco and tobacco products, beer, etc.), and other customary articles of small value. To the end that duty-free importation for the Force may be effected with the least possible delay, having regard to the interests of the Government, a mutually satisfactory procedure, including documentation, shall be arranged between the appropriate authorities of the Force and the Government. The Commander shall take all necessary measures to prevent any abuse of the exemption and to prevent the sale or resale of such goods to persons other than those aforesaid. Sympathetic consideration shall be given by the Commander to observations or requests of the Government concerning the operation of service institutes.

Privileges and immunities of officials and members of the Force

24. Members of the United Nations Secretariat detailed by the Secretary-General to serve with the Force remain officials of the United Nations entitled to the privileges and immunities of articles V and VII of the Convention on the Privileges and Immunities of the United Nations. With respect to the locally recruited personnel of the Force, however, who are not members of the Secretariat, the United Nations will assert its right only to the immunities concerning official acts, and exemption from taxation and national service obligations provided in sections 18 (a), (b) and (c) of the Convention on the Privileges and Immunities of the United Nations.

25. The Commander shall be entitled to the privileges, immunities and facilities of sections 19 and 27 of the Convention on the Privileges and Immunities of the United Nations. Officers serving on the Commander's Headquarters Staff and such other senior field officers as he may designate, are entitled to the privileges and immunities of article VI of the Convention on the Privileges and Immunities of the United Nations. Subject to the foregoing, the United Nations will claim with respect to members of the Force only those rights expressly provided in the present or supplemental arrangements.

Members of the Force: taxation, customs and fiscal regulations

26. Members of the Force shall be exempt from taxation on the pay and emoluments received from their national Governments or from the United Nations. They shall also be exempt from all other direct taxes except municipal rates for services enjoyed, and from all registration fees, and charges.

27. Members of the Force shall have the right to import free of duty their personal effects in connexion with their arrival in Cyprus. They shall be subject to the laws

and regulations of Cyprus governing customs and foreign exchange with respect to personal property not required by them by reason of their presence in Cyprus with the Force. Special facilities for entry or exit shall be granted by the Cypriot immigration, customs and fiscal authorities to regularly constituted units of the Force provided that the authorities concerned have been duly notified sufficiently in advance. Members of the Force on departure from Cyprus may, notwithstanding the foreign exchange regulations, take with them such funds as the appropriate pay officer of the Force certifies were received in pay and emoluments from their respective national Governments or from the United Nations and are a reasonable residue thereof. Special arrangements between the Commander and the Government shall be made for the implementation of the foregoing provisions in the mutual interests of the Government and members of the Force.

28. The Commander will co-operate with Cypriot customs and fiscal authorities in ensuring the observance of the customs and fiscal laws and regulations of Cyprus by the members of the Force in accordance with these or any relevant supplemental arrangements.

Communications and postal services

29. The Force enjoys the facilities in respect to communications provided in article III of the Convention on the Privileges and Immunities of the United Nations. The Commander shall have authority to install and operate a radio sending and receiving station or stations to connect at appropriate points and exchange traffic with the United Nations radio network, subject to the provisions of article 47 of the International Telecommunications Convention relating to harmful interference. The frequencies on which any such station may be operated will be duly communicated by the United Nations to the Government and to the International Frequency Registration Board. The right of the Commander is likewise recognized to enjoy the priorities of government telegrams and telephone calls as provided for the United Nations in article 39 and annex 3 of the latter Convention and in article 62 of the telegraph regulations annexed thereto.

30. The Force shall also enjoy, within its area of operations, the right of unrestricted communication by radio, telephone, telegraph or any other means, and of establishing the necessary facilities for maintaining such communications within and between premises of the Force, including the laying of cables and land lines and the establishment of fixed and mobile radio sending and receiving stations. It is understood that the telegraph and telephone cables and lines herein referred to will be situated within or directly between the premises of the Force and the area of operations, and that connexion with the Cypriot system of telegraphs and telephones will be made in accordance with arrangements with the appropriate Cypriot authorities.

31. The Government recognizes the right of the Force to make arrangements through its own facilities for the processing and transport of private mail addressed to or emanating from members of the Force. The Government will be informed of the nature of such arrangements. No interference shall take place with, and no censorship shall be applied to, the mail of the Force by the Government. In the event that postal arrangements applying to private mail of members of the Force are extended to operations involving transfer of currency, or transport of packages or parcels from Cyprus, the conditions under which such operations shall be conducted in Cyprus will be agreed upon between the Government and the Commander.

Freedom of movement

32. The Force and its members together with its service vehicles, vessels, aircraft and equipment shall enjoy freedom of movement throughout Cyprus. Wherever possible the Commander will consult with the Government with respect to large movements of personnel, stores or vehicles on roads used for general traffic. The Government will

432

supply the Force with maps and other information, including locations of dangers and impediments, which may be useful in facilitating its movements.

Use of roads, waterways, port facilities, and airfields

33. The Force shall have the right to the use of roads, bridges, canals and other waters, port facilities and airfields without the payment of dues, tolls or charges either by way of registration or otherwise, throughout Cyprus.

Water, electricity and other public utilities

34. The Force shall have the right to the use of water, electricity and other public utilities at rates not less favourable to the Force than those to comparable consumers. The Government will, upon the request of the Commander, assist the Force in obtaining water, electricity and other utilities required, and in the case of interruption or threatened interruption of service, will give the same priority to the needs of the Force as to essential Government services. The Force shall have the right where necessary to generate, within the premises of the Force either on land or water, electricity for the use of the Force, and to transmit and distribute such electricity as required by the Force.

Cypriot currency

35. The Government will, if requested by the Commander, make available to the Force, against reimbursement in such other mutually acceptable currency, Cypriot currency required for the use of the Force, including the pay of the members of the national contingents, at the rate of exchange most favourable to the Force that is officially recognized by the Government.

Provisions, supplies and services

36. The Government will, upon the request of the Commander, assist the Force in obtaining equipment, provisions, supplies and other goods and services required from local sources for its subsistence and operation. Sympathetic consideration will be given by the Commander in purchases on the local market to requests or observations of the Government in order to avoid any adverse effect on the local economy. Members of the Force and United Nations officials may purchase locally goods necessary for their own consumption, and such services as they need, under conditions not less favourable than for Cypriot citizens. If members of the Force and United Nations officials should require medical or dental facilities beyond those available within the Force, arrangements shall be made with the Government under which such facilities may be made available. The Commander and the Government will co-operate with respect to sanitary services. The Commander and the Government shall extend to each other the fullest co-operation in matters concerning health, particularly with respect to the control of communicable diseases in accordance with international conventions; such co-operation shall extend to the exchange of relevant information and statistics.

Locally recruited personnel

37. The Force may recruit locally such personnel as required. The terms and conditions of employment for locally recruited personnel shall be prescribed by the Commander and shall generally, to the extent practicable, follow the practice prevailing in the locality.

Settlement of disputes or claims

38. Disputes or claims of a private law character shall be settled in accordance with the following provisions:
   (a) The United Nations shall make provisions for the appropriate modes of settle-

433

ment of disputes or claims arising out of contract or other disputes or claims of a private law character to which the United Nations is a party other than those covered in sub-paragraphs (b) and (c) following.

(b) Any claim made by

    (i) a Cypriot citizen in respect of any damages alleged to result from an act or omission of a member of the Force relating to his official duties;

    (ii) the Government against a member of the Force; or

    (iii) the Force or the Government against one another, that is not covered by paragraphs 39 or 40 of these arrangements;

shall be settled by a Claims Commission established for that purpose. One member of the Commission shall be appointed by the Secretary-General, one member by the Government and a chairman jointly by the Secretary-General and the Government. If the Secretary-General and the Government fail to agree on the appointment of a chairman, the President of the International Court of Justice shall be asked by either to make the appointment. An award made by the Claims Commission against the Force or a member thereof or against the Government shall be notified to the Commander or the Government, as the case may be, to make satisfaction thereof.[1]

(c) Disputes concerning the terms of employment and conditions of service of locally recruited personnel shall be settled by administrative procedure to be established by the Commander.

39. All differences between the United Nations and the Government arising out of the interpretation or application of these arrangements which involve a question of principle concerning the Convention on the Privileges and Immunities of the United Nations shall be dealt with in accordance with the procedure of Section 30 of the Convention.

40. All other disputes between the United Nations and the Government concerning the interpretation or application of these arrangements which are not settled by negotiation or other agreed mode of settlement shall be referred for final settlement to a tribunal of three arbitrators, one to be named by the Secretary-General of the United Nations, one by the Government and an umpire to be chosen jointly by the Secretary-General and the Government. If the two parties fail to agree on the appointment of the umpire within one month of the proposal of arbitration by one of the parties, the President of the International Court of Justice shall be asked by either party to appoint the umpire. Should a vacancy occur for any reason, the vacancy shall be filled within thirty days by the method laid down in this paragraph for the original appointment. The Tribunal shall come into existence upon the appointment of the umpire and at least one of the other members of the tribunal. Two members of the tribunal shall constitute a quorum for the performance of its functions, and for all deliberations and decisions of the tribunal a favourable vote of two members shall be sufficient.

---

[1] In this respect attention must be drawn to operative paragraph 6 of the Security Council resolution of 4 March 1964 (S/5575) whereby the Council, *inter alia*, recommends that all costs pertaining to the Force be:

'met, in a manner to be agreed upon by them, by the Governments providing contingents and by the Government of Cyprus. The Secretary-General may also accept voluntary contributions for this purpose'.

It is understood that the obligations of the Commander to make satisfaction as provided for in paragraph 38 (b) of the present arrangements are necessarily limited under the aforementioned paragraph of the Security Council resolution to the extent (a) that funds are available to him for this purpose and/or (b) alternative arrangements are arrived at with the Participating Governments and the Government of Cyprus.

Liaison

41. The Commander and the Government shall take appropriate measures to ensure close and reciprocal liaison in the implementation of the present agreement. Furthermore, arrangements will be made, *inter alia*, for liaison on a State and local level between the Force and the Government security forces to the extent the Commander deems this to be necessary and desirable for the performance of the functions of the Force in accordance with the Security Council resolution of 4 March 1964 (S/5575). In case of requests by the Government security forces for the assistance of the Force, the Commander, in view of the international status and function of the Force, will decide whether, within the framework of the aforesaid resolution, he may meet such requests. The Commander of the Force may make requests for assistance from the Government security forces, at the State or local level, as he may deem necessary in pursuance of the aforesaid resolution, and they will, as far as possible, meet such requests in a spirit of co-operation.

Deceased members: disposition of personal property

42. The Commander shall have the right to take charge of and dispose of the body of a member of the Force who dies in Cyprus and may dispose of his personal property after the debts of the deceased person incurred in Cyprus and owing to Cypriot citizens have been settled.

Supplemental arrangements

43. Supplemental details for the carrying out of these arrangements shall be made as required between the Commander and appropriate Cypriot authorities designated by the Government.

Contacts in the performance of the function of the Force

44. It is understood that the Commander and members of the Force authorized by him may have such contacts as they deem necessary in order to secure the proper performance of the function of the Force, under the Security Council resolution of 4 March 1964 (S/5575).

Effective date and duration

45. Upon acceptance of this proposal by your Government, the present letter and your reply will be considered as constituting an agreement between the United Nations and Cyprus that shall be deemed to have taken effect as from the date of the arrival of the first element of the Force in Cyprus, and shall remain in force until the departure of the Force from Cyprus. The effective date that the departure has occurred shall be defined by the Secretary-General and the Government. The provisions of paragraphs 38, 39 and 40 of these arrangements, relating to the settlement of disputes, however, shall remain in force until all claims arising prior to the date of termination of these arrangements, and submitted prior to or within three months following the date of termination, have been settled.

In conclusion I wish to affirm that the activities of the Force will be guided in good faith by the task established for the Force by the Security Council. Within this context the Force, as established by the Secretary-General and acting on the basis of his directives under the exclusive operational direction of the Commander, will use its best endeavours, in the interest of preserving international peace and security, to prevent a recurrence of fighting and, as necessary, to contribute to the maintenance and restoration of law and order and a return to normal conditions.

Accept, Sir, the assurances of my highest consideration.

U Thant
Secretary-General

Reply from the Minister for Foreign Affairs of Cyprus to the Secretary-General of the United Nations

31 March 1964

Sir,

I have the honour to refer to your letter of 31 March 1964, in which you have proposed that the Republic of Cyprus and the United Nations should make the *ad hoc* arrangements contained therein which define certain of the conditions necessary for the effective discharge of the functions of the United Nations Force in Cyprus while it remains in Cyprus. Recalling that by letter of 4 March 1964, I informed you of the agreement of the Government of the Republic of Cyprus to the establishment of the Force, I now have the pleasure to inform you in the name of the Government of the Republic of Cyprus of its full agreement on, and its acceptance of, the terms of your letter.

The Government of the Republic of Cyprus agrees, furthermore, that subject to ratification by the Republic of Cyprus, your letter and this reply will be considered as constituting an agreement between Cyprus and the United Nations concerning the status of the United Nations Force in Cyprus. Pending such ratification the Government of the Republic of Cyprus undertakes to give provisional application to the arrangements contained in your letter and to use its best efforts to secure the earliest possible ratification of the agreement.

In conclusion, I wish to affirm that the Government of the Republic of Cyprus, recalling the Security Council resolution of 4 March 1964 (S/5575), and in particular, paragraphs 2 and 5 thereof, will be guided in good faith, when exercising its sovereign rights on any matter concerning the presence and functioning of the Force, by its acceptance of the recommendation of the Security Council that a peace-keeping Force be established in Cyprus.

Accept, Sir, the assurances of my highest consideration.

Spyros A. Kyprianou
Minister for Foreign Affairs

REGULATIONS FOR THE UNITED NATIONS FORCE IN CYPRUS (UNFICYP)

Enacted by the Secretary-General on 25 April 1964

Chapter I

General Provisions

1. *Issuance of Regulations.* The Regulations for the United Nations Force in Cyprus (UNFICYP) (hereinafter referred to as the Force) are issued by the Secretary-General and shall be deemed to take effect from the date that the first elements of the Force are placed under the United Nations Commander. The Regulations, and supplemental instructions and orders referred to in Regulations 3 and 4, shall be made available to all units of the Force.

2. *Authority of Regulations.* The present Regulations and supplemental instructions and orders issued pursuant thereto shall be binding upon all members of the Force. Contravention thereof shall constitute an offence subject to disciplinary action in accordance with the military laws and regulations applicable to the national contingent to which the offender belongs.

3. *Amendments and Supplemental Instructions.* These Regulations may be amended or revised by the Secretary-General. Supplemental instructions consistent with the present Regulations may be issued by the Secretary-General as required with respect to matters not delegated to the Commander of the Force (hereinafter referred to as the Commander).

4. *Command Orders.* The Commander may issue Orders not inconsistent with resolutions of the Security Council relating to the Force, these Regulations and amendments thereto, and with supplemental instructions referred to in Regulation 3:
   (a) In the discharge of his duties as Commander of the Force; or
   (b) In implementation or explanation of these Regulations.
Command Orders shall be subject to review by the Secretary-General.

5. *Definitions.* The following definitions shall apply to the terms used in the present Regulations:
   (a) The 'Commander of the United Nations Force in Cyprus' or the 'Commander' is the general officer appointed by the Secretary-General to exercise in the field full command of the Force.
   (b) The 'United Nations Force in Cyprus' or 'Force' is the subsidiary organ of the United Nations described in Regulation 6 below.
   (c) A 'member of the United Nations Force in Cyprus' or a 'member of the Force' is the Commander and any person, belonging to the military services of a State, who is serving under the Commander and any civilian placed under the Commander by the State to which such civilian belongs.
   (d) A 'Participating State' is a Member of the United Nations that contributes military personnel to the Force. A 'Paricipating Government' is the Government of a Participating State.
   (e) The 'authorities of a Participating State' are those authorities who are em-

437

powered by the law of that State to enforce its military or other law with respect to the members of its armed forces.

(f) The 'Host State' is the Republic of Cyprus. The 'Host Government' is the Government of the Host State.

Chapter II
International Character, Uniform, Insignia, and Privileges and Immunities

6. *International Character.* The United Nations Force in Cyprus is a subsidiary organ of the United Nations established pursuant to the resolution of the Security Council of 4 March 1964 (S/5575) and consists of the Commander and all personnel placed under his command by Member States. The members of the Force, although remaining in their national service, are, during the period of their assignment to the Force, international personnel under the authority of the United Nations and subject to the instructions of the Commander, through the chain of command. The functions of the Force are exclusively international and members of the Force shall discharge these functions and regulate their conduct with the interest of the United Nations only in view.

7. *Flag.* The Force is authorized to fly the United Nations Flag in accordance with the United Nations Flag Code and Regulations. The Force shall display the United Nations flag and emblem on its Headquarters and on its posts, vehicles and otherwise as decided by the Commander. Other flags or pennants may be displayed only in exceptional cases and in accordance with conditions prescribed by the Commander.

8. *Uniform and Insignia.* Members of the Force shall wear their national uniform in accordance with their national uniform regulations and with such identifying United Nations insignia as the Commander, in consultation with the Secretary-General, shall prescribe. Civilian dress may be worn at such times and in accordance with such conditions as may be authorized by the Commander.

9. *Markings.* All means of transportation of the Force, including vehicles, vessels and aircraft, and all other equipment when specifically designated by the Commander, shall bear a distinctive United Nations mark and United Nations licence number.

10. *Privileges and Immunities.* The Force, as a subsidiary organ of the United Nations, enjoys the status, privileges and immunities of the Organization provided in Article 105 of the Charter of the United Nations, the Convention on the Privileges and Immunities of the United Nations and the Agreement between the United Nations and the Republic of Cyprus signed on 31 March 1964. The entry without duty or restrictions of equipment and supplies of the Force, and of personal effects required by members of the Force by reason of their presence in the Host State with the Force, shall be effected in accordance with details to be arranged with the Host State. The Provisions of Article II of the Convention on the Privileges and Immunities of the United Nations shall also apply to the property, funds and assets of Participating States used in the Host State in connexion with the national contingents serving in the Force.

Chapter III
Authority and Command in the United Nations Force in Cyprus

11. *Command Authority.* The Secretary-General, pursuant to authority under the resolution of the Security Council of 4 March 1964 (S/5575) shall issue directives to the Commander as appropriate. The Commander exercises in the field full command authority of the Force. He is operationally responsible for the performance of all functions assigned to the Force by the United Nations, and for the deployment and assignment of troops placed at the disposal of the Force.

12. *Chain of Command and Delegation of Authority.* The Commander shall designate the chain of command for the Force, making use of the officers of his Headquarters staff and the commanders of the national contingents made available by

Participating Governments. He may delegate his authority through the chain of command. Changes in commanders of national contingents made available by Participating Governments shall be made in consultation among the Secretary-General, the Commander and the appropriate authorities of the Participating Government concerned. The Commander may make such provisional emergency assignments as may be required. Subject to the provisions of these Regulations, the Commander has full and exclusive authority with respect to all assignments of members of his Headquarters staff and, through the chain of command, of all members of the Force, including the deployment and movement of all contingents in the Force and units thereof. Instructions from the principal organs of the United Nations shall be channelled by the Secretary-General through the Commander and the chain of command designated by him.

13. *Good order and discipline.* The Commander shall have general responsibility for the good order and discipline of the Force. He may make investigations, conduct inquiries and require information, reports and consultations for the purpose of discharging this responsibility. Responsibility for disciplinary action in national contingents provided for the Force rests with the commanders of the national contingents. Reports concerning disciplinary action shall be communicated to the Commander who may consult with the commander of the national contingent and, if necessary, through the Secretary-General with the authorities of the Participating State concerned.

14. *Investigation of incidents and losses.* The Commander shall establish and ensure the effective implementation of procedures for the reporting and investigation of incidents, accidents and losses involving the Force or its members or property used by the Force, making use of the military police, as appropriate, in particular in the following cases: (a) any incident involving (i) death or serious injury to a member of the Force, or (ii) death, injury or property damage to a person or persons not belonging to the Force, wherein a member of the Force or property used by the Force, is involved; (b) the occurence or discovery of any loss of, or damage to equipment, stores or other property used by the Force, whether owned by the Force or by contingents, which exceeds an amount to be determined by the Force Commander and cannot be ascribed to normal wear and tear.

15. *Military police.* The Commander shall provide for military police for any camps, establishments or other premises which are occupied by the Force in the Host State and for such areas where the Force is deployed in the performance of its functions. Elsewhere military police of the Force may be employed, in so far as such employment is necessary to maintain discipline and order among members of the Force or to conduct investigations relating to the Force or its members. For the purpose of this Regulation, the military police of the Force shall have the power to take into custody any member of the Force who thereupon shall be transferred as soon as possible to the custody of his own national contingent commander pending any action taken in accordance with paragraph 13 of the present Regulations. Nothing in this Regulation is in derogation of the authority of arrest conferred upon members of a national contingent vis à vis one another.

Chapter IV
General Administrative, Executive and Financial Arrangements

16. *Authority of the Secretary-General.* The Secretary-General of the United Nations shall have authority for all administrative and executive matters affecting the Force and for all financial matters pertaining to the receipt, custody and disbursement of voluntary contributions in cash or in kind for the maintenance and operation of the Force. He shall be responsible for the negotiation and conclusion of agreements with Governments concerning the Force, the composition and size of the Force being established in consultation with the Governments of Cyprus, Greece, Turkey and the United Kingdom, and the manner of meeting all costs pertaining to the Force being

agreed by the Governments providing contingents and by the Government of Cyprus. Within the limits of available voluntary contributions he shall make provisions for the settlement of any claims arising with respect to the Force that are not settled by the Governments providing contingents or the Government of Cyprus. The Secretary-General shall establish a Special Account for the United Nations Force in Cyprus to which will be credited all voluntary cash contributions for the establishment, operation and maintenance of the Force and against which all payments by the United Nations for the Force shall be charged. The United Nations financial responsibility for the provision of facilities, supplies and auxiliary services for the Force shall be limited to the amount of voluntary contributions received in cash or in kind.

17. *Operation of the Force.* The Commander shall be responsible for the operation of the Force and, subject to the limitation in Regulation 16, for arrangements for the provision of facilities, supplies and auxiliary services. In the exercise of this authority he shall act in consultation with the Secretary-General and in accordance with the administrative and financial principles set forth in Regulations 18–23 following.

18. *Headquarters.* The Commander shall establish the Headquarters for the Force and such other operational centres and liaison offices as may be found necessary.

19. *Finance and accounting.* Financial administration of the Force shall be limited to the voluntary contributions in cash or in kind made available to the United Nations and shall be in accordance with the Financial Rules and Regulations of the United Nations and the procedures prescribed by the Secretary-General.

20. *Personnel.*

(a) The Commander of the Force shall be appointed by the Secretary-General. The Commander shall be entitled to diplomatic privileges, immunities and facilities in accordance with sections 19 and 27 of the Convention on the Privileges and Immunities of the United Nations. The Commander may appoint to his Headquarters staff, officers made available by the Participating States and such other officers as may be recruited in agreement with the Secretary-General. Such officers on his Headquarters staff and such other senior field officers as he may designate shall be entitled to the privileges and immunities of article VI of the Convention on the Privileges and Immunities of the United Nations.

(b) The Commander shall arrange with the Secretary-General for such international recruitment or detailment of staff from the United Nations Secretariat or from the specialized agencies to serve with the Force as may be necessary. Unless otherwise specified in the terms of their contracts such personnel are staff members of the United Nations, subject to the Staff Regulations thereof and entitled to the privileges and immunities of United Nations officials under articles V and VII of the Convention on the Privileges and Immunities of the United Nations.

(c) The Commander may recruit such local personnel as the Force requires. The terms and conditions of employment for locally recruited personnel shall be prescribed by the Commander and shall generally, to the extent practicable, follow the practice prevailing in the locality. They shall not be subject to or entitled to the benefits of the Staff Regulations of the United Nations, but shall be entitled to immunity from legal process in respect of words spoken or written and all acts performed by them in their official capacity as provided in section 18 (a) of the Convention on the Privileges and Immunities of the United Nations and shall be exempt from taxes on their salaries and emoluments received from the Force and from national service obligations as provided in section 18 (b) and (c) of the said Convention. Disputes concerning the terms of employment and conditions of service of locally recruited personnel shall be settled by administrative procedure to be established by the Commander.

21. *Administration.* The Commander with his civilian administrative staff shall, in accordance with procedures prescribed by him within the limits of Regulation 16, and in consultation with the Secretary-General, arrange for:

(a) the billeting and provision of food for any personnel attached to the Force for whom their own Government has not made provision;

(b) the establishment, maintenance and operation of service institutes providing amenities for members of the Force and other United Nations personnel as authorized by the Commander;

(c) the transportation of personnel and equipment;

(d) the procurement, storage and issuance of supplies and equipment required by the Force which are not directly provided by the Participating Governments;

(e) maintenance and other services required for the operation of the Force;

(f) the establishment, operation and maintenance of telecommunication and postal service for the Force;

(g) the provision of medical, dental and sanitary services for personnel in the Force.

22. *Contracts.* The Commander shall, within the limits of Regulation 16, enter into contracts and make commitments for the purpose of carrying out his functions under these Regulations.

23. *Public information.* Public information activities of the Force and relations of the Force with the Press and other information media shall be the responsibility of the Commander acting in accordance with policy defined by the Secretary-General.

Chapter V
Rights and Duties of Members of the Force

24. *Respect for local law and conduct befitting international status.* It is the duty of members of the Force to respect the laws and regulations of the Host State and to refrain from any activity of a political character in the Host State or other action incompatible with the international nature of their duties. They shall conduct themselves at all times in a manner befitting their status as members of the United Nations Force in Cyprus.

25. *United Nations legal protection.* Members of the Force are entitled to the legal protection of the United Nations and shall be regarded as agents of the United Nations for the purpose of such protection.

26. *Instructions.* In the performance of their duties the members of the Force shall receive their instructions only from the Commander and the chain of command designated by him.

27. *Discretion and non-communication of information.* Members of the Force shall exercise the utmost discretion in regard to all matters relating to their duties and functions. They shall not communicate to any person any information known to them by reason of their position with the Force which has not been made public, except in the course of their duties or by authorization of the Commander who shall act in consultation with the Secretary-General in appropriate cases. The obligations of this Regulation do not cease upon the termination of their assignment with the Force.

28. *Honours and remuneration from external sources.* No member of the Force may accept any honour, decoration, favour, gift or remuneration incompatible with the individual's status and functions as a member of the Force.

29. *Jurisdiction.*

(a) Members of the Force shall be subject to the criminal jurisdiction of their respective national States in accordance with the laws and regulations of those States. They shall not be subject to the criminal jurisdiction of the courts of the Host State. Responsibility for the exercise of criminal jurisdiction shall rest with the authorities of the Participating State concerned, including as appropriate the commanders of the national contingents.

(b) Members of the Force shall not be subject to the civil jurisdiction of the courts of the Host State or to other legal process in any matter relating to their official duties.

(c) Members of the Force shall remain subject to the military rules and regulations of their respective national States without derogating from their responsibilities as members of the Force as defined in these Regulations and any rules made pursuant thereto.

(d) Disputes involving the Force or its members shall be settled in accordance with such procedures provided by the Secretary-General as may be required, including the establishment of a claims commission or commissions. Supplemental instructions defining the jurisdiction of such commissions or other bodies as may be established shall be issued by the Secretary-General in accordance with article 3 of these Regulations.

30. *Customs duties and foreign exchange regulations.* Members of the Force shall comply with such arrangements regarding customs and foreign exchange regulations as may be made between the Host State and the United Nations.

31. *Identity cards.* The Commander, under the authority of the Secretary-General, shall provide for the issuance and use of personal identity cards certifying that the bearer is a member of the United Nations Force in Cyprus. Members of the Force may be required to present, but should not surrender, their identity cards upon demand of such authorities of the Host State as may be mutually agreed between the Commander and the Host Government.

32. *Driving.* In driving vehicles members of the Force shall exercise the utmost care at all times. Orders concerning driving of service vehicles and permits or licences for such operation shall be issued by the Commander.

33. *Pay.* Responsibility for pay of members of the Force shall rest with their respective national State. They shall be paid in the field in accordance with arrangements to be made between the appropriate pay officer of their respective national State and the Commander.

34. *Dependants.* Members of the Force may not be accompanied to their duty station by members of their families except where expressly authorized and in accordance with conditions prescribed by the Secretary-General in consultation with the Commander.

35. *Leave.* The Commander shall specify conditions for the granting of passes and leave.

36. *Promotion.* Promotions in rank for members of the Force remain the responsibility of the Participating Governments.

Chapter VI
Relations between the Participating Governments and the United Nations

37. *Channel for communications.* The channel for communications between the United Nations and the Participating Governments concerning their units in the Force, or the Force itself, shall be United Nations Headquarters in New York, through their Permanent Missions to the Organization.

38. *Visits to the Force.* Visits to the Force by officials of the Participating Governments shall be arranged with the Commander through United Nations Headquarters in New York.

39. *Service-incurred death, injury or illness.* In the event of death, injury or illness of a member of the Force attributable to service with the Force, the respective State from whose military services the member has come will be responsible for such benefits or compensation awards as may be payable under the laws and regulations applicable to service in the armed forces of that State. The Commander shall have responsibility for arrangements concerning the body and personal property of a deceased member of the Force.

Chapter VII
Applicability of International Conventions

40. *Observance of Conventions.* The Force shall observe and respect the principles and spirit of the general international Conventions applicable to the conduct of military personnel.

442

AGREEMENT BETWEEN THE UNITED NATIONS AND SWEDEN RELATING TO THE SWEDISH CONTINGENT TO THE UNITED NATIONS FORCE IN CYPRUS

The Permanent Representative of Sweden
to the United Nations
New York, N.Y.

21 February 1966

Sir,

1. I have the honour to refer to the resolution adopted by the Security Council on 4 March 1964 (S/5575) by which it inter alia:

'*Recommends* the creation, with the consent of the Government of Cyprus, of a United Nations peace-keeping force in Cyprus. The composition and size of the force shall be established by the Secretary-General, in consultation with the Governments of Cyprus, Greece, Turkey and the United Kingdom. The commander of the force shall be appointed by the Secretary-General and report to him. The Secretary-General, who shall keep the Governments providing the force fully informed, shall report periodically to the Security Council on its operation;

'*Recommends* that the function of the force should be, in the interest of preserving international peace and security, to use its best efforts to prevent a recurrence of fighting and, as necessary, to contribute to the maintenance and restoration of law and order and a return to normal conditions;

'*Recommends* that the stationing of the force shall be for a period of three months, all costs pertaining to it being met, in a manner to be agreed upon by them, by the Governments providing the contingents and by the Government of Cyprus. The Secretary-General may also accept voluntary contributions for that purpose.'

Subsequent resolutions of the Security Council have extended the mandate of the force for successive three month periods.

2. Pursuant to the resolution of 4 March 1964 the United Nations Force in Cyprus was established operationally on 27 March 1964. By an exchange of letters dated 31 March 1964 an Agreement (S/5634) was concluded with the Republic of Cyprus concerning the Status of the Force. Regulations (ST/SGB/UNFICYP/1) for the Force have been issued on 25 April 1964. Copies of these documents are attached as Annex I and Annex II respectively.[1]

3. I wish to express my appreciaton to your Government for making available a contingent to serve with the United Nations Force in Cyprus. I should like to take this opportunity to bring to your attention the following considerations relating to the Force, and to propose the conclusion herewith of an agreement concerning the services of your national contingent with the Force.

---

[1] See *above*, Annex 1 and 2.

4. The Regulations referred to above affirm the international character of the Force as a subsidiary organ of the United Nations and define the conditions of service for the members of the Force. National contingents provided for the Force serve under these Regulations.

5. The Regulations and the Agreement referred to in paragraph 2 of this letter also secure to the Force and its individual members the privileges and immunities necessary for the independent exercise of its functions. I should like to direct your attention to the provisions of the Regulations and of the Agreement which provide these privileges and immunities and particularly to article 29 of the Regulations and to paragraphs 10, 11 and 12 of my letter to the Minister of Foreign Affairs of Cyprus. It will be noted that paragraph 11 of this letter states that 'Members of the Force shall be subject to the exclusive jurisdiction of their respective national States in respect of any criminal offences which may be committed by them in Cyprus'. This immunity from the jurisdiction of Cyprus is based on the understanding that the authorities of the participating States would exercise such jurisdiction as might be necessary with respect to crimes or offences committed in Cyprus by any members of the Force provided from their own military services. It is assumed that the participating States will act accordingly.

6. I should also like to direct your attention to article 2 of the Regulations concerning their authority and to article 13 of the Regulations concerning 'Good order and discipline'. These articles provide:

'2. *Authority of Regulations.* The present Regulations and supplemental instructions and orders issued pursuant thereto shall be binding upon all members of the Force. Contravention thereof shall constitute an offence subject to disciplinary action in accordance with the military laws and regulations applicable to the national contingent to which the offender belongs.

'...

'13. *Good order and discipline.* The Commander shall have general responsibility for the good order and discipline of the Force. He may make investigations, conduct inquiries and require information, reports and consultations for the purpose of discharging this responsibility. Responsibility for disciplinary action in national contingents provided for the Force rests with the commanders of the national contingents. Reports concerning disciplinary action shall be communicated to the Commander who may consult with the commander of the national contingent and, if necessary, through the Secretary-General with the authorities of the Participating State concerned.'

7. In view of the considerations set out in paragraphs 5 and 6 above. I should appreciate your assurance that the commander of the national contingent provided by your Government will be in a position to exercise the necessary disciplinary authority. I should also appreciate your assurance that your Government will be prepared to exercise firm and effective jurisdiction with respect to any crime or offence which might be committed by a member of such national contingent and to report to the United Nations in each case on the action taken.

8. The effective functioning of the Force requires that some continuity of service of units with the Force be ensured in order that the Commander may be in a position to plan his operations with knowledge of what units will be available. I should, therefore, appreciate your assurance that the national contingent provided by your Government will not be withdrawn without adequate prior notification to the Secretary-General, so as to avoid the impairment of the ability of the Force to discharge its functions. Likewise, should circumstances render the service of your national contingent with the Force no longer necessary, the Secretary-General under-

444

takes to consult with your Government and to give adequate prior notification concerning its withdrawal.

9. Reference is also made to articles 11 and 12 of the Regulations which deal with 'Command authority' and 'Chain of command and delegation of authority'. Article 12 provides, inter alia, that changes in commanders of national contingents which have been made available by participating Governments should be made in consultation among the Secretary-General, the Force Commander, and the appropriate authorities of the participating Government.

10. I should also like to refer to article 40 of the Regulations concerning 'Observance of Conventions' which provides:
'The Force shall observe the principles and spirit of the general international Conventions applicable to the conduct of military personnel'.

11. The international Conventions referred to in this Regulation include, inter alia, the Geneva (Red Cross) Conventions of 12 August 1949 to which your Government is a party and the UNESCO Convention on the Protection of Cultural Property in the event of armed conflict, signed at the Hague on 14 May 1954. In this connexion, and particularly with respect to the humanitarian provisions of these Conventions, it is requested that the Governments of the participating States ensure that the members of their contingents serving with the Force be fully acquainted with the obligations arising under these Conventions and that appropriate steps be taken to ensure their enforcement.

12. (a) Authorities of the participating State will, in accordance with and within their domestic legislation, use their best efforts to bring about settlement of claims and compliance with awards made by a Cypriot court or by the Claims Commission against a member of the contingent of the State with respect to acts committed outside the scope of his official functions.

(b) In addition to the undertaking in subparagraph (a) above, the participating States will, as appropriate, enter into supplementary agreements with the United Nations concerning the settlement of claims arising out of acts committed by a member of their national contingent either within or outside the scope of his official functions.

13. Finally, I suggest that questions involving expenses should be dealt with, in the light of the resolution of the Security Council, in a supplemental agreement. Such other supplementary arrangements concerning the service of your national contingents with the Force may be made as occasion requires.

14. It is the intention that this letter together with your reply accepting the proposals set forth herein shall constitute an agreement between the United Nations and Sweden and shall be deemed to have taken effect from the date that the national contingent provided by your Government departed from its home country to assume duties with the Force. It is also intended that it shall remain in force until such time as your national contingent may be withdrawn from the Force either in accordance with the terms of paragraph 8 above or in the light of developments affecting the functioning of the Force which may render its service no longer necessary. The provisions of paragraph 15 relating to the settlement of disputes should remain in force until all outstanding claims have been settled.

15. It is also proposed that all disputes between the United Nations and your Government concerning the interpretation or application of this agreement which are not settled by negotiation or other agreed mode of settlement shall be referred for final settlement to a tribunal of three arbitrators. One of the arbitrators shall be

appointed by the Secretary-General of the United Nations, one by your Government, and the umpire shall be chosen jointly by the Secretary-General and your Government. If the two parties fail to agree on the appointment of the umpire within one month of the proposal of arbitration by one of the parties, the President of the International Court of Justice shall be asked by either party to appoint the umpire. Should a vacancy occur for any reason, the vacancy shall be filled within thirty days by the method laid down in this paragraph for the original appointment. The tribunal shall come into existence upon the appointment of the umpire and at least one of the other members of the tribunal. Two members of the tribunal shall constitute a quorum for the performance of its functions, and for all deliberations and decisions of the tribunal a favourable vote of two members shall be sufficient.

Accept, Sir, the assurances of my highest consideration.

U THANT
Secretary-General

U Thant,
Secretary-General of the United Nations,
New York.

New York, 21 February 1966

Sir,

I have the honour to refer to your letter of 21 February 1966 concerning the service with the United Nations Force in Cyprus of the national contingent provided by my Government. In this letter you have proposed that my Government and the United Nations should enter into an agreement in accordance with the terms provided therein.

My Government accepts this proposal and agrees that your letter and this reply shall constitute an agreement between Sweden and the United Nations. My Government also gives the assurances requested in paragraphs 7 and 8 of your letter.

Accept, Sir, the assurances of my highest consideration.

(s) SVERKER ÅSTRÖM
*Permanent Representative of Sweden
to the United Nations*

U Thant,
Secretary-General of the United Nations,
New York.

New York, 21 February 1966

Sir,

In signing the present agreement concerning the service with the United Nations Force in Cyprus of the national contingent provided by my Government, I have the honour to declare that the means at the disposal of Swedish authorities to fulfil article 12 (a) of the agreement are the following:

a) In criminal actions brought by Swedish prosecutors before Swedish Courts against members of the Swedish contingent, claims for damages will, upon request by the party having suffered damage, be joined by the prosecutor to the criminal action,

446

where this may be done without inconvenience and the claim does not appear unfounded.

b) In cases where a Cypriot court or the Claims commission has handed down an award against a member of the Swedish contingent, the Swedish Ministry for Foreign Affairs, if need be, may see to it that he will be urged to satisfy the award.

c) In cases where particular circumstances warrant it, the Swedish Government will consider ex gratia payment.

Accept, Sir, the assurances of my highest consideration.

(s) SVERKER ÅSTRÖM
*Permanent Representative of Sweden
to the United Nations*

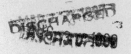